Lecture Notes in Computer Science   9465

Commenced Publication in 1973
Founding and Former Series Editors:
Gerhard Goos, Juris Hartmanis, and Jan van Leeuwen

More information about this series at http://www.springer.com/series/7407

Chiara Bodei · Gian-Luigi Ferrari
Corrado Priami (Eds.)

Programming Languages
with Applications
to Biology and Security

Essays Dedicated to Pierpaolo Degano
on the Occasion of His 65th Birthday

 Springer

Editors
Chiara Bodei
Dipartimento di Informatica
Università di Pisa
Pisa
Italy

Corrado Priami
Dipartimento di Matematica
Università degli Studi di Trento
Povo
Italy

Gian-Luigi Ferrari
Dipartimento di Informatica
Università di Pisa
Pisa
Italy

Cover illustration: "Mondrianized Blackboard" created by Chiara Bodei.
Photograph on p. V: The photograph of the honoree was taken by Massimo Bartoletti.

ISSN 0302-9743   ISSN 1611-3349   (electronic)
Lecture Notes in Computer Science
ISBN 978-3-319-25526-2   ISBN 978-3-319-25527-9   (eBook)
DOI 10.1007/978-3-319-25527-9

Library of Congress Control Number: 2015952034

LNCS Sublibrary: SL1 – Theoretical Computer Science and General Issues

Springer International Publishing AG Switzerland is part of Springer Science+Business Media
(www.springer.com)

Pierpaolo Degano, after 117 pages of proofs

Preface

This Festschrift volume mainly contains 22 refereed research papers and one extended abstract by close collaborators and friends of Pierpaolo Degano to celebrate him on the occasion of his 65th birthday.

The foreword of this volume includes a *laudatio* illustrating the distinguished career and the main scientific contributions by Pierpaolo and a portrait of him made by one of his closest friends. The following sections are dedicated to the scientific papers on the main research topics explored by Pierpaolo and still under his investigation.

Pierpaolo has worked on a large variety of topics including formal program semantics, concurrency theory, systems biology and security, and much more.

Each contribution was carefully reviewed by one or two readers. The editors would like to thank the several anonymous individuals for their assistance.

A preliminary version of this volume has been presented to Pierpaolo on June 19, 2015, during a one-day colloquium held in Pisa at the Department of Computer Science.

Five eminent scientists and also friends of Pierpaolo gave their invited talk on that occasion. We thank Ugo Montanari, Martín Abadi, Luca Cardelli, Joshua Guttman, and Flemming Nielson for having accepted our invitation. Their contributions can be found after the *laudatio* and the portrait of Pierpaolo.

We also would like to thank the Department of Computer Science and the University of Pisa for their logistic support in the organization of the Colloquium.

With this book we want to celebrate Pierpaolo's vision, beside his achievements, and also to witness the great esteem and favor he has in the academic community.

August 2015

Chiara Bodei
Gian-Luigi Ferrari
Corrado Priami

Organization

Reviewers

Flemming Nielson   DTU Compute, Technical University of Denmark,
                              Lyngby, Denmark
Hanne Riis Nielson   DTU Compute, Technical University of Denmark,
                              Lyngby, Denmark
G. Michele Pinna   Dipartimento di Matematica e Informatica,
                              Università degli Studi di Cagliari, Cagliari, Italy
Bent Thomsen   Department of Computer Science, Aalborg University,
                              Aalborg, Denmark
Emilio Tuosto   Department of Computer Science, Leicester University,
                              Leicester, UK
Hugo Torres Vieira   IMT Institute for Advanced Studies Lucca, Lucca, Italy
Roberto Zunino   Dipartimento di Matematica, Università degli Studi di
                              Trento, Trento, Italy

Contents

Pierpaolo Degano

Chiara Bodei[1]([✉]), Gian-Luigi Ferrari[1], and Corrado Priami[2]

[1] Dipartimento di Informatica, Università di Pisa, Pisa, Italy
chiara.bodei@unipi.it
[2] Dipartimento di Matematica, Università di Trento, Trento, Italy

1 The Man

Pierpaolo was born in 1950 in Udine, where he received the Hapsburg imprinting he has always originally combined with his unpredictable nature. In 1969 he came to Pisa to study Computer Science unaware that he would be soon adopted by that little town, where people are generally often suspicious of strangers – but sometimes they could can surprise you – and where so many students coming from any part of Italy met and interact for a handful of years before entering their adult life. The Pisan Laurea curriculum in Computer Science, founded in 1969 by the Faculty of Science, with the substantial boost of the then rector Alessandro Faedo, has been the first in Italy. Most of the people did not believe in this new curriculum, but they were very soon forced to change their mind: at least 600 students attended that course, included Pierpaolo.

Pierpaolo was fascinated by the professors and by their pioneering work. He was in particular mesmerized by professors Antonio Grasselli and Ugo Montanari. Pierpaolo got his Laurea degree in 1973 under the supervision of Ugo Montanari in Computer Science in Italy (till the first one founded in 1983 in Pisa), thus entering and then greatly contributing to one of the most fertile academic family trees of Italian Computer Science.

After his graduation (in Italy there were no PhD program at that time) Pierpaolo got a temporary position at Istituto di Elaborazione dell'Informazione (IEI) of the Italian Research Council (CNR). He moved at the University of Pisa as assistant professor in 1981 and as associate professor in 1989. In 1990 he became full professor at the University of Parma in 1990 and then, back again, in 1993 at the University of Pisa, where he served as head of Department until 1996.

Besides his research activity, which is better illustrated in the next section, it is worth mentioning his passion for teaching and his clear speech. His lectures are careful and at the same time appealing, because Pierpaolo is able to make also a structural operational semantic rule interesting and he is also capable to hold the attention of students with witty remarks coming in the right moment. Someone swears of having seen Pierpaolo somersaulting to reach the teacher's desk on the top of its platform, with students clapping with enthusiasm.

The same passion, along with a huge supply of patience, has been lavished in educating and training the students he has supervised. Hours dedicated to Socratically drive the minds of his students in creating new abstract conceptual

C. Bodei et al. (Eds.): Degano Festschrift, LNCS 9465, pp. 1–6, 2015.
DOI: 10.1007/978-3-319-25527-9_1

frameworks in order to solve problems (the biggest challenge computer scientists have to face) and more hours dedicated to drive the young untrained capacities of his students in putting together reasonable proofs of non trivial statements.

Pierpaolo contributed to found and organize the PhD program in Computer Science that, as we have just mentioned, was the first in Italy. Furthermore, he is member of the Scientific Committee of the Post-Graduate School "Galileo Galilei" since 2001 and its vice-president since 2002. He is the chairman of PhD program in Computer Science since 2006 as well as the national coordinator of the Italian PhD programs since 2007. Pierpaolo has been also president of GRIN (Associazione Nazionale dei Professori di Informatica) from 1999 to 2003, association he contributed to found. He is the chairman of IFIP Working Group 1.7, Theoretical Foundations of Security Analysis and Design.

He has been responsible for several research projects both national and international, scientific coordinator of many PhD schools, among the organizers of various international conferences, as well as member of the editorial board of national and international journals. He is currently a member of the Scientific Council of the Microsoft Research - University of Trento Centre for Computational and Systems Biology. He also did research at leading universities and research institutes, such as the École Normale Supérieure in Paris, the CWI of Amsterdam and the University of Rennes.

2   His Research

It is quite a difficult task to give, in a few words, a complete account of the rich and varied scientific production of Pierpaolo, whose beginning dates back to 1979 and that counts, at the moment, around 200 scientific papers published in refereed journals and in conference proceedings (without considering several edited volumes). His research mainly concerns the semantics of concurrency, the languages for distributed and mobile systems, and the techniques for the verification of programs. He also tackled the application of formal methods to the area of security, biological systems and adaptive systems.

He initially worked on theorem proving [38] and contributed to the unification of logic and functional programming [1,7] but he soon devoted himself to what has been the thread running through his entire scientific production: the foundations of concurrency and distribution. Pierpaolo has made key contributions to this field of research. Among them, only to name a few, we cite the formalization of fairness as convergence in metric spaces [32]; synchronized graph rewriting [33] modeling distributed systems; pioneering work on the partial order and causal semantics of concurrent processes [24–28]. We also recall the introduction of *causal trees* [23] - a concurrent model able to faithfully express causality, although being an interleaving model. After causal trees, *proved trees* [34] were introduced, a parametric model to extract different types of concurrent semantics. In the Nineties Pierpaolo Degano dedicated his investigation to causality and to enriched semantics able to capture causality along with other concurrent properties [15,35,36]. At the end of the decade his research moved to the area of Control Flow Analysis. Pierpaolo is among the researchers who were the forerunners to apply this static technique to process algebras, in order to verify the security properties of models of distributed systems. In this period some of his works [9,13] quickly became relevant in the whole area of security. To security also belong the works in [8,10,11,14,16,31,39,40]. Since the early years of the beginning millennium Pierpaolo Degano joined the new line of research of systems biology, by applying the semantics of concurrency to biological systems [21,22,37], for instance with the aim of detecting the minimal genome of a virtual cell [19,20] or of obtaining the first stochastic and discreet description of synapses [17,18]. Recently his research activities focussed on the foundations of secure service composition [2,3], usage policies [4,5], contract-based design [6] and adaptive and pervasive systems [12,29,30]. The common thread of these research activities is that appropriate security models are mandatory to ensure that secured information is not shared intentionally in a way that compromises the security goals and the concerned systems.

Summary. Pierpaolo Degano is a nice person, a first class scientist and teacher, a discrete, but strong, efficient and reliable scientific leader and organizer, actively supporting the young people and institutions crucial for our work and our area. He is therefore esteemed and respected by colleagues, students, and friends all over the world.

3   His Students

In the following pages, we list those among Pierpaolo's students who have been supervised by Pierpaolo for a PhD or for a *Laurea* (when the Ph.D. programme was not yet well-established in Italy). Many of them are now active in universities or in research centers, in Italy and abroad. And they have descendants as well, still reported in our list. We are very glad that many of the people listed below participated in the Festschrift celebration and also contributed to this volume.

1. Roberto Gorrieri - (with U. Montanari) - Università di Bologna
   (a) Nadia Busi - Università di Bologna
   (b) Riccardo Focardi - Università di Venezia
       i. Matteo Maffei - Saarland University
       ii. Matteo Centenaro - Università di Venezia
       iii. Marco Squarcina - PhD student at Università di Venezia
   (c) Marco Bernardo - Università di Urbino
       i. Edoardo Bontà - Università di Urbino
   (d) Gianluigi Zavattaro - Università di Bologna
   (e) Mario Bravetti - Università di Bologna
   (f) Alessandro Aldini - Università di Urbino
   (g) Roberto Lucchi - Università di Bologna
   (h) Claudio Guidi - Università di Bologna
2. Corrado Priami - Università di Trento; The Microsoft Research - University of Trento Centre for Computational and Systems Biology

(a) Linda Brodo - Università di Sassari
(b) Davide Prandi - Università di Trento
(c) Claudio Eccher - FBK Trento
(d) Radu Mardare - Aalborg University, Denmark
(e) Paola Lecca - University of Trento
(f) Federica Ciocchetta
(g) Debora Schuch da Rosa Machado - Natura, São Paulo, Brazil
(h) Maria Luisa Guerriero - Senior Scientist (physiological modeller) at AstraZeneca
(i) Sean Sedwards - INRIA Rennes
(j) Alessandro Romanel - Università di Trento
(k) Lorenzo Dematté - Servizi ST, Trento
(l) Michele Forlin - Università di Trento
(m) Roberto Larcher - Software Engineer, Trento
(n) Alida Palmisano - National Cancer Institute, Biometric Research Branch
(o) Judit Zamborszky - Hungarian Academy of Sciences
(p) Nerta Gjata
3. Chiara Bodei - Università di Pisa
 (a) Dung Dinh (with G. Ferrari)
4. Stefano Basagni (moved to Milan and Austin) - Northeastern University
 (a) Luke Demoracski
 (b) Rituparna Ghosh
5. Jean-Vincent Loddo (moved to Paris) - Université Paris 7
6. Michele Curti - Project Manager at SM Scientia Machinale
7. Massimo Bartoletti (with G. Ferrari) - Università di Cagliari
 (a) Tiziana Cimoli - Università di Cagliari
 (b) Alceste Scalas - Università di Cagliari
8. Roberto Zunino - Università di Trento
 (a) Thanh Hong Vo - The Microsoft Research - University of Trento Centre for Computational and Systems Biology
9. Davide Chiarugi (with M. Falaschi) - Max-Planck-Institute of Colloids and Interfaces
10. Gabriele Costa - Università di Genova
11. Davide Cangelosi - Ospedale Gaslini (Genova)
12. Letterio Galletta (with G. Ferrari) - Post-Doc Università di Pisa
13. Gianluca Mezzetti (with G. Ferrari) - Post-Doc Aarhus University (DK)
14. Davide Basile (with G. Ferrari) - PhD student at Università di Pisa

References

1. Barbuti, R., Degano, P., Levi, G.: Toward an inductionless technique for proving properties of logic programs. In: Proceedings of International Logic Programming Conference (ICLP 1982), pp. 175–181 (1982)
2. Bartoletti, M., Degano, P., Ferrari, G.: Planning and verifying service composition. J. Comput. Secur. **17**(5), 799–837 (2009)

3. Bartoletti, M., Degano, P., Ferrari, G., Zunino, R.: Semantics-based design for secure web services. IEEE Trans. Softw. Eng. **34**(1), 33–49 (2008)
4. Bartoletti, M., Degano, P., Ferrari, G., Zunino, R.: Local policies for resource usage analysis. ACM Trans. Program. Lang. Syst. **31**(6), 1–43 (2009)
5. Bartoletti, M., Degano, P., Ferrari, G., Zunino, R.: Model checking usage policies. Math. Struct. Comput. Sci. **25**(3), 710–763 (2015)
6. Basile, D., Degano, P., Ferrari, G.: A formal framework for secure and complying services. J. Supercomputing **69**(1), 43–52 (2014)
7. Bellia, M., Dameri, E., Degano, P., Levi, G., Martelli, M.: Applicative communicating processes in first order logic. In: Dezani-Ciancaglini, M., Montanari, U. (eds.) International Symposium on Programming. LNCS, vol. 137, pp. 1–14. Springer, Heidelberg (1982)
8. Bodei, C., Brodo, L., Degano, P., Gao, H.: Detecting and preventing type flaws at static time. J. Comput. Secur. **18**(2), 229–264 (2010)
9. Bodei, C., Buchholtz, M., Degano, P., Nielson, F., Nielson, H.R.: Static validation of security protocols. Inf. Comput. **13**(3), 347–390 (2005)
10. Bodei, C., Degano, P., Focardi, R., Priami, C.: Primitives for authentication in process algebras. Theor. Comput. Sci. **283**(2), 271–304 (2002)
11. Bodei, C., Degano, P., Focardi, R., Priami, C.: Authentication primitives for secure protocol specifications. Future Gener. Comp. Syst. **21**(4), 645–653 (2005)
12. Bodei, C., Degano, P., Galletta, L., Mezzetti, G., Ferrari, G.: Security in pervasive applications: a survey. Eur. J. Law Technol. **4**(2), 15–31 (2013)
13. Bodei, C., Degano, P., Nielson, F., Nielson, H.R.: Static analysis for the π-calculus with applications to security. Inf. Comput. **168**(1), 68–92 (2001)
14. Bodei, C., Degano, P., Nielson, F., Nielson, H.R.: Flow logic for Dolev-Yao secrecy in cryptographic processes. Future Gener. Comp. Syst. **18**(6), 747–756 (2002)
15. Bodei, C., Degano, P., Priami, C.: Names of the Pi-calculus agents handled locally. Theor. Comput. Sci. **253**(2), 155–184 (2001)
16. Bodei, C., Degano, P., Priami, C.: Checking security policies through an enhanced control flow analysis. J. Comput. Secur. **13**(1), 49–85 (2005)
17. Bracciali, A., Brunelli, M., Cataldo, E., Degano, P.: Synapses as stochastic concurrent systems. Theor. Comput. Sci. **408**(1), 66–82 (2008)
18. Bracciali, A., Brunelli, M., Cataldo, E., Degano, P.: Stochastic models for the in silico simulation of synaptic processes. BMC Bioinform. **9**(S–4), 4 (2008)
19. Chiarugi, D., Degano, P., Van Klinken, J.B., Marangoni, R.: Cells *in Silico*: a Holistic approach. In: Zavattaro, G., Bernardo, M., Degano, P. (eds.) SFM 2008. LNCS, vol. 5016, pp. 366–386. Springer, Heidelberg (2008)
20. Chiarugi, D., Degano, P., Marangoni, R.: A computational approach to the functional screening of genomes. PLoS Comput. Biol. **3**(9), e174 (2007)
21. Curti, M., Degano, P., Baldari, C.T.: Causal π-calculus for biochemical modelling. In: Priami, C. (ed.) CMSB 2003. LNCS, vol. 2602, pp. 21–33. Springer, Heidelberg (2003)
22. Curti, M., Degano, P., Priami, C., Baldari, C.T.: Modelling biochemical pathways through enhanced π-calculus. Theor. Comput. Sci. **325**(1), 111–140 (2004)
23. Darondeau, P., Degano, P.: Causal trees. In: Ausiello, G., Dezani-Ciancaglini, M., Rocca, S.R.D. (eds.) Automata, Languages and Programming. LNCS, vol. 372, pp. 234–248. Springer, Heidelberg (1989)
24. Degano, P., De Nicola, R., Montanari, U.: Partial ordering derivations for CCS. In: Budach, L. (ed.) Fundamentals of Computation Theory. LNCS, vol. 199, pp. 520–533. Springer, Heidelberg (1985)

25. Degano, P., De Nicola, R., Montanari, U.: CCS is an (augmented) contact free C/E system. In: Zilli, M.V. (ed.) Mathematical Models for the Semantics of Parallelism. LNCS, vol. 280, pp. 144–165. Springer, Heidelberg (1987)

26. Degano, P., De Nicola, R., Montanari, U.: A distributed operational semantics for CCS based on condition/event systems. Acta Inf. **26**(1/2), 59–91 (1988)

27. Degano, P., De Nicola, R., Montanari, U.: A partial ordering semantics for CCS. Theor. Comput. Sci. **75**(3), 223–262 (1990)

28. Degano, P., De Nicola, R., Montanari, U.: Universal axioms for bisimulations. Theor. Comput. Sci. **114**(1), 63–91 (1993)

29. Degano, P., Ferrari, G.-L., Galletta, L.: A two-phase static analysis for reliable adaptation. In: Giannakopoulou, D., Salaün, G. (eds.) SEFM 2014. LNCS, vol. 8702, pp. 347–362. Springer, Heidelberg (2014)

30. Degano, P., Ferrari, G.-L., Galletta, L., Mezzetti, G.: Types for coordinating secure behavioural variations. In: Sirjani, M. (ed.) COORDINATION 2012. LNCS, vol. 7274, pp. 261–276. Springer, Heidelberg (2012)

31. Degano, P., Levi, F., Bodei, C.: Safe ambients: control flow analysis and security. In: Sato, M., Kleinberg, R.D. (eds.) ASIAN 2000. LNCS, vol. 1961, pp. 199–214. Springer, Heidelberg (2000)

32. Degano, P., Montanari, U.: Liveness properties as convergence in metric spaces. In: Proceedings of the16th Annual ACM Symposium on Theory of Computing (STOC 1984), pp. 31–38. ACM (1984)

33. Degano, P., Montanari, U.: A model for distributed systems based on graph rewriting. J. ACM **34**(2), 411–449 (1987)

34. Degano, P., Priami, C.: Proved trees. In: Kuich, W. (ed.) ICALP 1992. LNCS, vol. 623, pp. 629–640. Springer, Heidelberg (1992)

35. Degano, P., Priami, C.: Enhanced operational semantics. ACM Comput. Surv. **28**(2), 352–354 (1996)

36. Degano, P., Priami, C.: Non-interleaving semantics for mobile processes. Theor. Comput. Sci. **216**(1–2), 237–270 (1999)

37. Degano, P., Priami, C.: Enhanced operational semantics in systems biology. In: Priami, C. (ed.) CMSB 2003. LNCS, vol. 2602, pp. 178–181. Springer, Heidelberg (2003)

38. Degano, P., Sirovich, F.: An evaluation based theorem prover. IEEE Trans. Pattern Anal. Mach. Intell. **7**(1), 70–79 (1985)

39. Gao, H., Bodei, C., Degano, P.: A formal analysis of complex type flaw attacks on security protocols. In: Meseguer, J., Roşu, G. (eds.) AMAST 2008. LNCS, vol. 5140, pp. 167–183. Springer, Heidelberg (2008)

40. Gao, H., Bodei, C., Degano, P., Riis Nielson, H.: A formal analysis for capturing replay attacks in cryptographic protocols. In: Cervesato, I. (ed.) ASIAN 2007. LNCS, vol. 4846, pp. 150–165. Springer, Heidelberg (2007)

Pierpaolo, a Great Friend

Marco Maria Massai$^{(\boxtimes)}$

Dipartimento di Fisica, Università di Pisa, Pisa, Italy
massai@pi.infn.it

> We were young, very young...
> we had many dreams...
> we had a long time, ahead...
> we had no conditioning from the past...
> we had the songs of Bob Dylan...
> we were in the very early seventies.

1 Close Encounters

1.1 Encounter of the First Kind (when I *Saw* him)

It was a cloudy and cold evening in a rainy winter, as unusual in Pisa, where a few days in the year present very low temperature; but, rain and clouds, all the time... During the third year of my course of study in Physics, when I had just found that Physics was not the long list of rules that my Teacher in High School presented to us, poor pupils, I and two colleagues of mine, Mauro and Carla, were performing very strange and difficult experience in Electronics. In my small Group there was a tiny and nice maid from Lucca, one of the more enchanting towns in Tuscany. She had been very careful, up that time, in our measurements and the following data analysis; but, in the last days, something appeared in her behaviour that made us to suspect some problem.

And in that dark evening I discovered the problem, simply giving a look out of the window of our Lab, downstairs, on the road, where I saw a strange, skinny guy, with long hair and bell-bottoms pants: he was waiting for the arrival of our friend, Carla, who stopped her analysis to run down, in the arms of that strange young man.

1.2 Encounter of the Second Kind (when I *Heard* him)

Some days later, I was walking just after the usual lunch at the students "Mensa" (canteen), together with my colleague, Mauro. He was also my companion during the High School studies, in the same small town, Piombino, that lies on the sea cost, just in front of that wonderful paradise called "Arcipelago Toscano", with Elba Island and other seven sisters... We entered a Cafè, the most famous in Pisa, haunted by students, called "Battellino", that prepared the best quality coffee in the town; we sat around a table, where we met two girls, also students in Physics, but one year younger than us, R. and E. We started to discuss

© Springer International Publishing Switzerland 2015
C. Bodei et al. (Eds.): Degano Festschrift, LNCS 9465, pp. 7–9, 2015.
DOI: 10.1007/978-3-319-25527-9_2

about... something, I don't remember what; but, suddenly, I heard very close the voice of Carla that was talking with a guy who had his back to us. So I only succeeded in hearing the voice of this guy, that, because of the long long hair I supposed he was the same of some evenings ago. The place was really small, smoky and noisy, but it was quite easy to distinguish the strange accent of this guy. Perfect italian, also syntactically, and a reach vocabulary; but the accent sounds very foreign! But, also, something sounded ancient and familiar to my ears. Word after word, sentence after sentence, this mystery was explained to me: the accent was the same of my mother, born in the town of Fiume (now Rijeka, in Jugoslavia, at that time), but in Italy, when my grandfather was there and met my grandmother. At this point, I was driven to meet and know that guy, and to try to understand why he was so far from his town. But in a few seconds, Carla and he disappeared in the rainy outdoor.

1.3   Encounter of the Third Kind (when I *Touched* him)

Many days after, may be there was a wonderful weather, as sometimes it happens, also in Pisa, Carla and I were walking towards the Physics Institute, in Piazza Torricelli, a very, very small square in Pisa down-town, hoping to meet others colleagues to discuss some recent social events, very dramatic, that had upset the already troubling political life in Italy, in that time: the early seventies. Just before the entrance, I saw the same strange guy of the previous evenings, and I recognized him at once: hair longer than I supposed, but eyes so bright and so intense a gaze that I stopped to pronounce my jokes, as usually, waiting for his first move. His first move, so, was a very strong handshake, to which, I answered with the same strength, as usual. So, the first simple ordinary words: "How are you?", "What are you studying, here, in Pisa?", "Where are you from?". And so, I discovered that it was really Computer Science that led Pierpaolo to Pisa. And now, he is still here...

2   Lively Discussions

Well, I am sure that there are no subject, no argument, on which Pierpaolo and I didn't spent time, a lot of time, discussing; and, of course, from different positions and opposite points of view, even if we have, substantially,... the same opinions about the most part of arguments! Music, literature, politics, academic life, school of our children, place to spend holidays, the quality of a wine... Therefore: discussion for the only pleasure to discuss, to push our criticism a bit forward, and to know ourselves better and better. So, sometimes, we started to defend opposite positions, independently from our own, deep, opinions. Discussions with Pierpaolo is a creative experience, stimulating my best qualities; in fact, his way to sustain his opinions is strongly rational, and logical, even if with a large amount of emotional ardor. This doesn't avoid to reach, often, a hard contrast between the positions that are, sometimes, rather similar! Very interesting! But, however, at the end, you can be sure to find a glass of good wine.

And his deep, sincere smile; ironic sometimes. Just for example, I can remember a *vexata questio*: was the music of Mozart romantic, or not? How many times we started to discuss, without reaching a common opinion! From music to literature, and back again, with Beethoven, Haydn, Schubert, but also Goethe, as testimonial of our opposite positions!

3   A Great Friend

Pierpaolo (although he is a Colleague of mine!), is one of my best friends, whatever meaning one will give to this wonderful word. Friend since more than 40 years, during the which we spent together many intense experiences, happy the most, but also some dramatic. And after every moment, our friendship appeared stronger and stronger. The friend Pierpaolo and his dear wife Carla, with their fantastic daughter Ila, were very close to me in some dramatic moments of my life. And their help has been really fundamental for my Family. It's easy, and a pleasure, for me remember the period when I was preparing my thesis in Physics, period full of news into my life: the discovery, finally, that Physics, the experimental physics is a very exciting and challenging field where one can find the measure of his own will, and intelligence, of his ability, and a valid objective of the life. Also new friends, in a new country, Switzerland and France, in a new Lab., the most important in world for Physics, i.e. CERN, in Geneva. But when finally, the moment of writing and typing the results of a two years work arrived, again the friend was close to me, with a marvelous, red IBM typewriter (similar to the famous RED IBM...), giving suggestions, helping in writing and correcting the many pages that, one after one, were accumulated on the table; during the night, during the sundays. But the most important contribution I received from Pierpaolo, in that period, was in relation to decision, the hot decision, that I had to take: to present the data already collected, as soon as possible, even though they do not definitively probe the new ideas, or, otherwise, to delay the completion of my thesis until the complete collection of the data that amounted to at least six months. Pierpaolo said to me: "After two years of work, at the beginning of a new academic year, it is better to put the word 'end' to this work. If you want to follow the complete results, you can remain still a few months, but as a Doctor, no more as a Student". And so I did. But, those few months have become 40 years, the data were collected, analysed, and other experiments were done; and now, when I'm approaching the date to retire, I am sure that Pierpaolo's advice was really good! And it is one of the best I ever received. But not the alone advice Pierpaolo gave to me... The second one, unfortunately, cannot be discussed here in details... It must be sufficient hint that if I'm a happy husband and father, well, I have to thank a bit both Pierpaolo and Carla, and this is a big deal.

Distributed Authorization with Distributed Grammars

Martín Abadi$^{(\boxtimes)}$, Mike Burrows, Himabindu Pucha, Adam Sadovsky,
Asim Shankar, and Ankur Taly

Google, Mountain View, CA, USA
distrib-auth-grammar@google.com

Abstract. While groups are generally helpful for the definition of authorization policies, their use in distributed systems is not straightforward. This paper describes a design for authorization in distributed systems that treats groups as formal languages. The design supports forms of delegation and negative clauses in authorization policies. It also considers the wish for privacy and efficiency in group-membership checks, and the possibility that group definitions may not all be available and may contain cycles.

1 Introduction

Groups provide a useful level of indirection for authorization policies, in particular those described by access control lists (ACLs). When ACLs refer to groups, the ACLs can be simple and short. For example, an ACL may permit access to all principals in the group `FriendlyClients`, which itself consists of users in the group `Friends` with devices in the group `Devices` via programs in the group `TrustedApps`. The definitions of these groups can be managed separately from the ACL, and shared by many other ACLs (e.g., [6]).

In distributed systems, the use of groups is not straightforward (e.g., [4,5]). First, it requires a distributed scheme for naming groups. Even with such a scheme, group definitions may not all be available at the time of an ACL check; they may have unintended consequences or circularities that no single participant in the system can detect locally; and the entities that control them may not all be equally trusted. In addition, lookups of group membership may incur the costs of remote communication; and, in general, there is no guarantee of atomicity of lookups across groups. Finally, the lookups need to be secure and provide appropriate privacy guarantees. No universal solution to these difficulties seems likely to emerge because each system faces different trade-offs and constraints.

This paper describes a design for access control with groups in a new set of libraries, tools, and services that aim to simplify the process of building distributed applications. Our design supports forms of delegation, via local names. It also supports negative clauses in ACLs, with a conservative semantics when group definitions are not available or contain cycles. Moreover, it addresses the wish for privacy and efficiency in group-membership checks—at least in the

C. Bodei et al. (Eds.): Degano Festschrift, LNCS 9465, pp. 10–26, 2015.
DOI: 10.1007/978-3-319-25527-9_3

sense that the dissemination of group memberships occurs in response to relevant queries, not promiscuously.

In this setting, each principal is identified with a public key, but it typically has one or more human-readable names, which we call blessings.[1] Concretely, these blessings are granted in public-key certificate chains bound to the principal's public key. For example, a television set owned by a principal with the blessing Alice may have the blessing Alice/TV. Here, TV is a local name, which, much as in previous systems and languages for security (e.g., [2,7]), any principal can generate and apply autonomously. Principals may have multiple blessings, each reflecting the principal that granted it. For example, the same television set may also have the blessing SomeCorp/TV123 from its manufacturer.

Blessings are the basis for authentication and authorization. Specifically, the "Bless" operation allows a principal to extend one of its blessings and create a blessing bound to another principal's public key, thereby delegating the authority associated with the blessing. For example, an ACL may include the clause Allow Alice/TV, so that all principals with a blessing that matches Alice/TV will have access to the object that the ACL protects, and a principal with the blessing Alice may choose to grant the blessing Alice/TV to its television set. In practice, the delegation of authority is seldom unconditional. Caveats [1] can restrict the conditions under which blessings are usable, for instance limiting their validity to a certain time period; we do not discuss these caveats further in this paper, since their generation and validation precedes the access-control checks on which we focus.

Our design supports groups that contain not only atomic names such as Alice and TV, but also longer, compound blessings such as Alice/TV. Furthermore, the definition of a group may refer to other groups at the top level (e.g., "Friends includes OldFriends") and as part of compound blessings (e.g., "FriendlyClients includes Friends/Devices/TrustedApps"). An important theme of the design is to regard groups as formal languages, with group definitions inducing grammar productions. Unlike in traditional formal languages, however, the grammar productions are distributed, so we have to consider concerns such as communication costs, availability, and privacy. The analogy is helpful despite these differences.

By now, many other systems support distributed authorization, in various ways. On the other hand, the combination of local names, groups, and negative clauses is, to our knowledge, rather uncommon and subject to limitations. Beyond the immediate value of our work, we hope that it contributes to shedding light on some of the difficulties and options for systems with these features.

---

[1] Strictly speaking, the term blessing refers to a certificate chain, and the term blessing name refers to the human-readable name specified in the certificate chain. Blessing name is often abbreviated to blessing when there is no risk of confusion, as in the present paper. Below, we use the term blessing rather broadly: we consider that /-separated sequences of names $n_1/\ldots/n_k$ are blessings even when they might never be related to public keys.

The next section introduces the definitions of blessings, groups, ACLs, and related concepts. Section 3 gives a semantics to blessing patterns. Section 4 provides a simple but impractical definition of the semantics of ACLs, as a specification. Section 5 then outlines a distributed implementation of this semantics. Section 6 elaborates on the rationale for one delicate aspect of the semantics of ACLs. Section 7 concludes.

2   Basics: Blessings, Groups, and ACLs

In this section, we define blessings, ACLs, and also blessing patterns, which are generalizations of blessings that allow references to groups.

2.1   Ordinary Names and Group Names

We assume a set of group names, and a disjoint set of other names that we call ordinary names. We let g range over group names, and n over ordinary names.

In our implementation, ordinary names and group names have quite different forms and usages. In particular, each group name suffices for determining an appropriate server who can answer questions about the group and for querying that server. On the other hand, ordinary names are fundamentally local names, simple strings that can be interpreted differently across a system. They may refer to a variety of entities (users, services, programs, program versions, ...). They may however be subject to conventions.

2.2   Blessings and Blessing Patterns

The syntax of blessings and blessing patterns is given by the following grammar:

$$
\begin{aligned}
B ::= \; & n && \text{blessings} \\
| \; & n/B \\
P ::= \; & n && \text{blessing patterns} \\
| \; & g \\
| \; & n/P \\
| \; & g/P
\end{aligned}
$$

Here, B ranges over blessings and P over blessing patterns; / is a binary operator for forming blessings and blessing patterns. Thus, a blessing is a non-empty sequence of ordinary names, separated by /, while a blessing pattern is a non-empty sequence of ordinary names and group names, separated by /. We take / to be associative.

For example, if Alice and Phone are ordinary names and Friends and Devices are group names, then:

- Alice and Alice/Phone are blessings, and they are also blessing patterns;
- so are Alice/Alice, Phone/Phone, and Phone/Alice, though they are not necessarily meaningful—we do not have a type system or other constraints that would prevent such expressions;

- Friends, Friends/Phone, Alice/Devices, and Friends/Devices are all blessing patterns, but not blessings.

We write *AllBlessings* for the set of all blessings. When B and B' are blessings, we write $B \preceq B'$, and say that B is a prefix of B', if the sequence of names in B is a prefix of that in B'. We take this prefix relation to be reflexive, not strict; that is, every blessing is a prefix of itself.

We often have to manipulate lists of blessings and lists of blessing patterns. In particular, below, lists of blessings are an input to ACL checks; lists of blessing patterns appear in group definitions. Therefore, we introduce syntactic categories for them:

$$M ::= \text{empty} \qquad \text{lists of blessings}$$
$$| \quad B, M$$

$$L ::= \text{empty} \qquad \text{lists of blessing patterns}$$
$$| \quad L, P$$

We use the constant empty to represent the empty list, and use comma as a binary operator for forming lists. We often omit empty, and for example may write the list empty, Alice, Bob as Alice, Bob.

2.3   Groups

Group names are of two sorts: those for built-in groups and those for defined groups. In both cases, a group can be thought of as a set of blessings.

Built-In Groups. Some groups are provided by the underlying platform, so do not require extensional definition. The set of all blessings, to which we refer by the name AllBlessings, is an example. Another example—of much narrower interest—might be the set of blessings of the form n_1/n_2 such that n_1 identifies a sports team in a particular league and n_2 identifies one of the players in n_1's roster. We write *BuiltInGroups* for the set of names of these built-in groups.

In general, built-in groups may be implemented by fairly arbitrary pieces of code that answer, in particular, membership queries. Below we discuss the interface that such code should provide.

Formally, we assume a function *Elts* that maps each $g \in BuiltInGroups$ to a set of blessings (intuitively, the elements of g). In this paper, for simplicity, the function *Elts* is fixed—in particular, independent of who computes it and of the definitions of defined groups. For instance, we let *Elts*(AllBlessings) = *AllBlessings*. As in this case, a set *Elts*(g) may be infinite.

Defining Groups. Other group names may be associated with definitions that equate a group name with a list of blessing patterns:

$$g =_{\text{def}} L$$

Given a set *DefSet* of definitions $\{g_1 =_{\text{def}} L_1, \ldots, g_k =_{\text{def}} L_k\}$, we require that the group names g_i be pairwise distinct and distinct from elements in *BuiltInGroups*. As long as each group name is associated with a server, this requirement is easy to enforce in a distributed manner.

On the other hand, we do not require the absence of cycles in the definitions, primarily because we do not count on being able to enforce this requirement in a distributed manner. Secondarily, some simple cycles may occasionally be useful. For example, the definitions

$$\text{Gadgets} =_{\text{def}} \text{TV, Devices}$$
$$\text{Devices} =_{\text{def}} \text{Phone, Gadgets}$$

have the effect of equating `Devices` with `Gadgets` while allowing two different servers to include `TV` and `Phone` in this group. As another example, the definition

$$\text{DeviceChains} =_{\text{def}} \text{Devices, Devices/DeviceChains}$$

lets `DeviceChains` consist of blessings formed by sequences of elements of the group `Devices`. So, we may warn about cycles, and we may discourage their use, but we aspire to provide a clean, helpful semantics at least for simple cycles, and a conservative semantics for all cycles.

We allow the possibility that some group names are neither in *BuiltInGroups* nor have a definition (at least not an available definition). We aim to provide a conservative semantics for those names.

Time. Both the code associated with built-in groups and the definitions associated with other group names may change over time. They may even change during an ACL check. Correctness expectations may have to be relaxed accordingly (for example, so as to allow reordering queries to servers.) Although the definitions and algorithms presented in this paper are mostly silent on this matter, we discuss it briefly in Sect. 5.4.

2.4   ACLs

An ACL is a list of clauses, each of which permits or denies access to principals that present blessings that match a particular blessing pattern:

$$
\begin{aligned}
A ::= \;& \texttt{empty} && \text{ACLs} \\
| \;& A, \texttt{Allow } P \\
| \;& A, \texttt{Deny } P
\end{aligned}
$$

Our present implementation requires that all `Allow` clauses precede all `Deny` clauses, but this paper treats a more general syntax with arbitrary alternations.

Our semantics of ACLs is order-dependent. Basically, later ACL entries will win over earlier ones according to the specification of Sect. 4. For example, when `Alice` is in the group `Friends`, the ACL `Deny Alice, Allow Friends` will permit access with the blessing `Alice` but the ACL `Allow Friends, Deny Alice` will deny it. The default is to deny access, so for example neither the ACL empty nor the ACL Allow Alice will permit access with the blessing Bob. The specification of Sect. 4 also addresses other aspects of the semantics of ACLs, and in particular the rules for matching blessings against the blessing patterns in clauses, which rely on the prefix relation $\preceq$.

We abbreviate ACLs by combining consecutive Allow clauses, for example writing Allow Friends, Alice for Allow Friends, Allow Alice, and similarly for consecutive Deny clauses.

We expect that many ACLs will be of the simple form Allow g, where g is a group name. More generally, many may be of the form Allow $P_1, \ldots, P_k$, or perhaps

$$\text{Allow } P_1, \ldots, P_k, \text{ Deny } P_{k+1}, \ldots, P_{k+k'}$$

where $P_1, \ldots, P_{k+k'}$ are blessing patterns. On the other hand, ACLs with many alternations of Allow and Deny clauses

$$\text{Allow } P_1, \text{ Deny } P_2, \ldots, \text{ Allow } P_{k+k'-1}, \text{ Deny } P_{k+k'}$$

should arise only in advanced cases, as they can be hard to understand.

The current syntax does not allow naming ACLs. This limitation means that sharing happens through named groups.

3 Semantics

Intuitively, each blessing pattern—and, in particular, each group name—denotes a set of blessings. This section defines how we map blessing patterns to sets of blessings.

3.1 The Meaning of Blessing Patterns

Assuming a semantics of group names (a mapping from group names to sets of blessings, given as a parameter ρ), the function Meaning maps blessing patterns and lists of blessing patterns to sets of blessings. It is defined inductively as follows, first for blessing patterns:

$$\text{Meaning}_\rho(n) = \{n\}$$
$$\text{Meaning}_\rho(g) = \rho(g)$$
$$\text{Meaning}_\rho(n/P) = \{n/s \mid s \in \text{Meaning}_\rho(P)\}$$
$$\text{Meaning}_\rho(g/P) = \{s/s' \mid s \in \text{Meaning}_\rho(g), s' \in \text{Meaning}_\rho(P)\}$$

and then for lists of blessing patterns:

$$\text{Meaning}_\rho(\text{empty}) = \emptyset$$
$$\text{Meaning}_\rho(L, P) = \text{Meaning}_\rho(L) \cup \text{Meaning}_\rho(P)$$

3.2   From Group Definitions to Grammars and Languages

A semantics of group names is basically a function ρ that maps each group name to the set of members of the group. However, we have to decide what happens when an expression (for instance, an ACL) refers, directly or indirectly, to a group that has not been defined. In a distributed setting (when the definitions are at different servers), we also have to decide what happens when the group definition may exist but cannot be looked up, for whatever reason. Since we wish to be conservative (fail-safe), our decision may be different in Allow and Deny clauses. For this reason, we define not one function but two functions, called $\rho_\Downarrow$ and $\rho_\Uparrow$. They coincide in the case in which all references to groups can be resolved.

For the construction of $\rho_\Downarrow$, we regard a list of group definitions *DefSet* as inducing formal languages, as follows.

- Ordinary names and / are terminals.
- Group names are non-terminals.
- We associate productions with the group definitions, for example turning a definition

$$g_1 =_{\text{def}} \text{Alice/Phone}, \ g_2/\text{Phone}$$

  into the two productions

$$g_1 \rightarrow \text{Alice/Phone}$$
$$g_1 \rightarrow g_2/\text{Phone}$$

- We also associate productions with each built-in-group name g: $g \rightarrow B$ for each $B \in \textit{Elts}(g)$.
- Finally, we do not associate productions with any remaining group names (those that are neither defined in *DefSet* nor built-in-group names).

For each group name g, we let $\rho_\Downarrow(g)$ be the set of blessings generated from g by these productions. Thus, the question of group membership can be reduced to that of formal-language membership.

When $\textit{Elts}(g)$ is finite for each $g \in \textit{BuiltInGroups}$, the productions above constitute a context-free grammar. Otherwise, we still obtain a formal language $\rho_\Downarrow(g)$ for each group name g, though these need not be context-free languages. More precisely, much as in formal-language theory, $\rho_\Downarrow$ is the least fixed-point of the function F such that, for every g,

- $F(\rho)(g) = \text{Meaning}_\rho(L)$ if g is defined by $g =_{\text{def}} L$;
- $F(\rho)(g) = \textit{Elts}(g)$ for $g \in \textit{BuiltInGroups}$; and
- $F(\rho)(g) = \emptyset$ otherwise.

The existence of this least fixed-point follows from the facts that Meaning_ρ is monotone as a function of ρ and that *Elts* does not depend on ρ.

The construction of $\rho_\Uparrow$ is analogous, except that in the last case we let $F(\rho)(g) = \textit{AllBlessings}$. In particular, we still take a least fixed-point (not a greatest fixed-point).

In practice, we need not always compute least fixed-points: we may allow ourselves to treat some group definitions as being unavailable whenever we wish—for instance, when the corresponding server has failed, or when we have exhausted our computational budget. The result will be a conservative approximation. Section 5 follows this approach.

Regular expressions are fairly common in access control, for example in defining firewall rules. The Singularity security model used them for defining groups, without negation, via a file-system name-space [8]. With the definitions above, we go beyond regular languages, not because we expect to need the full power of context-free languages (and perhaps more), but in order to avoid cumbersome syntactic conditions in group definitions. Still, it is conceivable that restricting attention to regular languages would have advantages.

4   Specifying Authorization Checks

A principal that has collected multiple blessings may present a subset for the purposes of an authorization decision. It may decide not to present all its blessings, perhaps because of concerns about performance or confidentiality. However, it should not gain additional rights by virtue of withholding some blessings.

Accordingly, the function that performs authorization checks, IsAuthorized, is applied to a list of blessings M and an ACL A. It decides whether access should be granted according to A when the blessings in M are presented. It is defined in terms of an auxiliary function $\text{IsAuthorized}_1(B, A)$ that is applied to a single blessing B and an ACL A. This auxiliary function works by cases on the three possible forms of A, namely (1) empty, (2) A', Allow P for some A' and P, and (3) A', Deny P for some A' and P. In the first case, it returns false; in the second and the third, it checks B against P and against A', then returns an appropriate boolean combination of the results. If B happens to match both Allow and Deny clauses in A, later clauses win over earlier ones. Since each blessing B is treated separately, $\text{IsAuthorized}(\cdot, A)$ is monotonic in its first argument, as desired.

$$\text{IsAuthorized}(M, A) = \exists B \in M.\text{IsAuthorized}_1(B, A)$$

$\text{IsAuthorized}_1(B, A) =$
    case A of
      empty : false
    | A', Allow P : $(\exists B' \in \text{Meaning}_{\rho_\Downarrow}(P).B' \preceq B) \vee \text{IsAuthorized}_1(B, A')$
    | A', Deny P : $(\neg \exists B' \in \text{Meaning}_{\rho_\Uparrow}(P).B' \preceq B) \wedge \text{IsAuthorized}_1(B, A')$

This definition relies on the mappings $\rho_\Downarrow$, $\rho_\Uparrow$, and Meaning, described in Sect. 3. It is intended as a specification, without a directly evident concrete implementation.

ACL clauses that refer (directly or indirectly) to undefined groups are treated conservatively by relying on $\rho_\Downarrow$ and $\rho_\Uparrow$ depending on the type of clause. This conservative treatment is done "one entry at a time". In some cases, this approach might yield slightly surprising (but safe) results. Let us consider, for example, the unusual ACL

Allow Alice, Deny Friends, Allow Friends

where `Friends` is a group name but it has no corresponding definition, or its definition is unavailable, and `Friends` is not in *BuiltInGroups*. Suppose that we wish to know whether this ACL allows access to a request with the blessing `Alice`. We start from the end. The clause `Allow Friends` does not permit access, because we make the conservative assumption that `Friends` is empty. The clause `Deny Friends` denies access, because we make the conservative assumption that `Friends` contains all blessings. So we never look at `Allow Alice`, and deny access! Although this outcome may be counterintuitive, it is conservative, and seems adequate because we do not expect to give pleasing results when groups are undefined or their definitions are unavailable. One may certainly imagine more elaborate approaches, perhaps with some form of symbolic constraint-solving.

The definition uses the prefix relation $\preceq$ (instead of requiring exact equality) for checking both `Allow` and `Deny` clauses. While this consistency is certainly attractive, the choice of $\preceq$ has different significance in the two cases:

- For `Allow` clauses, the use of the relation $\preceq$ is a matter of convenience. For example, when one writes the ACL `Allow Alice` for an object that one wishes to share with a principal with the blessing `Alice`, it is typically expedient that this principal gain access even when this access may happen via a phone with the blessing `Alice/Phone`. Thus, lengthening a blessing does not reduce authority with respect to the `Allow` clauses in ACL checks.
  The longer blessing is however not equivalent to the shorter one in other respects: the longer blessing may trigger a `Deny` clause, and a principal that holds the blessing `Alice/Phone` cannot in general obtain other extensions of `Alice`, such as `Alice/TV`.
  This semantics is definable from a semantics that requires exact equality. For example, under the latter semantics, one could write the ACL

  `Allow Alice, Alice/AllBlessings`

  rather than `Allow Alice`. Conversely, even with the semantics that uses $\preceq$ it is possible to define ACLs that insist on exact equality. For example, one can write

  `Allow Alice, Deny Alice/AllBlessings`

  Alternatively,[2] assuming that `eob` is a reserved name that appears in blessings only at the end, one can write

  `Allow Alice/eob`

- For `Deny` clauses, it generally does not make sense to forbid access with the blessing B but to permit it with a longer blessing, from a security perspective. Whoever has B would be able to extend it in order to circumvent the `Deny` check.

---

[2] In general, these two approaches do not always yield equivalent results. Suppose that the group g is defined to contain `Alice` and `Alice/Phone`. The ACL `Allow` g, `Deny` g`/AllBlessings` denies access with `Alice/Phone`, while the ACL `Allow` g`/eob` allows access with `Alice/Phone/eob`. Both ACLs deny access with `Alice/Phone/FunnyApp` and `Alice/Phone/FunnyApp/eob`.

One may be tempted by an even weaker criterion for matching in `Allow` clauses, which we call "prefix matching". For example, with this criterion, the ACL `Allow Alice/Phone` would permit access with the blessing `Alice`. The main motivation for this decision is that denying this access has no clear security benefit: whoever holds `Alice` could form `Alice/Phone` in order to gain access. Section 6 discusses prefix matching in more detail and explains why we have not adopted it.

5   An Implementation of Authorization Checks

The function `IsAuthorized`, as defined above, might be implemented by calculating the functions $\rho_\Downarrow$, $\rho_\Uparrow$, and `Meaning` at the relying party, then applying the definitions blindly. However, these calculations generally require knowledge of the group definitions, which we may not want to disseminate for reasons of efficiency and privacy. The relevant groups might even be infinite, so we cannot enumerate them in general. Moreover, a full computation of `Meaning` is sometimes not required for determining if some particular blessing is or is not a member of the corresponding set of blessings. Therefore, we consider distributed, query-driven implementations of `IsAuthorized`. We first reduce `IsAuthorized` to a basic function R, then we discuss how to implement the required invocations of R. Basically, we rely on a form of top-down parsing.

Other algorithmic approaches may perhaps be derived from work on formal languages. More speculatively, the connection with formal languages suggests problems in secure multiparty computation (e.g., [3]): if several parties hold parts of a context-free grammar, can they cooperate to establish membership of a string in the corresponding language while not revealing any other information? General results on secure multiparty computation indicate that they can, but an efficient solution does not seem straightforward.

5.1   An Auxiliary Function: R

Suppose that we wish to know whether a particular blessing is in $\text{Meaning}_\rho(P)$. When the blessing is an ordinary name n, we may proceed as follows:

- If $P = m$ or $P = m/P_1$ or $P = n/P_1$ or $P = g/P_1$ then fail, for every $m \neq n$ and every group name g.
- If $P = n$ then succeed.
- If $P = g$ then ask a server responsible for g whether n is an element of g and return the result.

When the blessing is a compound blessing n/B_1, we may instead proceed as follows:

- If $P = m$ or $P = m/P_1$ then fail, for every $m \neq n$.
- If $P = n$ then fail.
- If $P = n/P_1$ then recurse with B_1 and P_1.

- If $P = g$ then ask a server responsible for g whether n/B_1 is an element of g and return the result.
- If $P = g/P_1$ then ask a server responsible for g whether there exist B_2, B_3 such that $n/B_1 = B_2/B_3$, and B_2 is an element of g, and if so recurse with B_3 and P_1 (for each suitable B_3, for completeness).

Thus, a server responsible for g needs to answer questions of the following forms:

- whether a blessing B is in $\text{Meaning}_\rho(g)$,
- whether a blessing B can be written in the form B_2/B_3 where B_2 is an element of $\text{Meaning}_\rho(g)$.

While each question of the latter kind can be reduced to several questions of the former kind (one per prefix B_2 of B), providing an interface for asking questions of the latter kind allows a more direct, efficient interaction.

Therefore, we assume a function R with the following specification: R is such that, given a blessing B and a set of blessings S, $\text{R}(B, S)$ returns the set that consists of

- ϵ if $B \in S$, and
- every blessing B'' such that for some B' we have $B = B'/B''$ and $B' \in S$.

Note that $\text{R}(B, S)$ may, in general, contain both blessings and ϵ. For example, if $S = \{n_1, n_1/n_2, n_1/n_2/n_3\}$ then $\text{R}(n_1/n_2, S) = \{\epsilon, n_3\}$. The name R stands for "rest", "remainder", or "residue".

Below we consider how to implement R.

5.2   Reducing IsAuthorized to R

Using R, we can reformulate the definition of IsAuthorized:

$$\text{IsAuthorized}(M, A) = \exists B \in M.\text{IsAuthorized}_1(B, A)$$

$$\text{IsAuthorized}_1(B, A) =$$
$$\quad \text{case } A \text{ of}$$
$$\quad\quad \text{empty} : \text{false}$$
$$\quad\quad | \ A', \text{Allow } P : \text{R}(B, \text{Meaning}_{\rho_\Downarrow}(P)) \neq \emptyset \vee \text{IsAuthorized}_1(B, A')$$
$$\quad\quad | \ A', \text{Deny } P : \text{R}(B, \text{Meaning}_{\rho_\Uparrow}(P)) = \emptyset \wedge \text{IsAuthorized}_1(B, A')$$

This formulation is equivalent to our original one, but closer to our implementation.

5.3   Implementing the Calls to R

Next we consider how to compute and how to approximate $\text{R}(B, \text{Meaning}_{\rho_\Downarrow}(P))$ and $\text{R}(B, \text{Meaning}_{\rho_\Uparrow}(P))$ without fully expanding the definitions of $\rho_\Downarrow$, $\rho_\Uparrow$, and Meaning. We present basic algorithms first, then elaborate on distributed implementations.

We assume that we have $R(B, Elts(g))$ for each $g \in BuiltInGroups$. In practice, this assumption means that the code that implements a built-in group g should offer an interface for asking queries of the form $R(B, Elts(g))$. Note that $R(B, Elts(g))$ is always finite, even when $Elts(g)$ is infinite. In the case of `AllBlessings`, this set consists of ϵ and the proper suffixes of B. We write $S(B)$ for this set.

Basic Algorithms. Suppose that we want functions $R_{\Downarrow}$ and $R_{\Uparrow}$ such that:

$$R_{\Downarrow}(B, P) = R(B, \text{Meaning}_{\rho_{\Downarrow}}(P))$$
$$R_{\Uparrow}(B, P) = R(B, \text{Meaning}_{\rho_{\Uparrow}}(P))$$

where $R_{\Downarrow}$ and $R_{\Uparrow}$ have, as implicit parameter, the group definitions $DefSet$. For brevity, we write R_X when we wish to refer to both $R_{\Downarrow}$ and $R_{\Uparrow}$ (but, in an equation such as $R_X(\ldots) = \ldots R_X(\ldots) \ldots$ we mean the same R_X on both sides). Given a list of blessing patterns $L = P_1, \ldots, P_k$, we let $R_X(B, L) = \cup_{i=1..k} R_X(B, P_i)$.

The desired functions $R_{\Downarrow}$ and $R_{\Uparrow}$ satisfy the equations:

$$
\begin{aligned}
R_X(n, n) \quad &= \{\epsilon\} \\
R_X(n, m) \quad &= \emptyset \quad \text{if } m \neq n \\
R_X(n/B, n) \quad &= \{B\} \\
R_X(n/B, m) \quad &= \emptyset \quad \text{if } m \neq n \\
R_X(n, m/P) \quad &= \emptyset \\
R_X(n/B, n/P) &= R_X(B, P) \\
R_X(n/B, m/P) &= \emptyset \quad \text{if } m \neq n \\
R_X(B, g) \quad &= \begin{cases} R_X(B, L) \text{ if } g =_{\text{def}} L \in DefSet, \text{ or else} \\ R(B, Elts(g)) \text{ if } g \in BuiltInGroups, \text{ or else} \\ \emptyset \text{ if } X \text{ is } \Downarrow, \text{ or else} \\ S(B) \text{ if } X \text{ is } \Uparrow \end{cases} \\
R_X(B, g/P) \quad &= \{s \mid \exists s' \neq \epsilon.s' \in R_X(B, g), s \in R_X(s', P)\}
\end{aligned}
$$

When oriented from left to right, these equations immediately suggest an algorithm for computing $R_X(B, P)$. This algorithm proceeds by cases on the form of P. When P is not a group name and does not start with a group name, the algorithm then proceeds by cases on the form of B. When P is a group name g with a definition $g =_{\text{def}} L$ in $DefSet$, the algorithm unfolds this definition. When P is a group name $g \in BuiltInGroups$, the algorithm simply returns $R(B, Elts(g))$, which we have according to our assumptions. Finally, if P is any other group name g (so, a group name for which no definition or implementation is available), the algorithm returns $\emptyset$ (for $R_{\Downarrow}$) or $S(B)$ (for $R_{\Uparrow}$).

The computation of $R_X(B, P)$ basically amounts to parsing B, top-down, as an element of the formal language associated with P. It is common for top-down parsing not to work, or not to work well, when any grammar productions are left-recursive (of the form $g \rightarrow g \ldots$ where g is a non-terminal). Here, left-recursion could cause the algorithm to fall into an infinite loop. In theory, left-recursive productions can always be avoided (in particular, by using Greibach normal form). In our setting, however, we do not wish to restrict or to rewrite group definitions in order to prevent left-recursion.

Therefore, we prefer weakenings of the definition of $R_\Downarrow$ and $R_\Uparrow$ that work without the assumption. For a conservative implementation, we require only:

$$R_\Downarrow(B, P) \subseteq R(B, \mathtt{Meaning}_{\rho_\Downarrow}(P))$$
$$R_\Uparrow(B, P) \supseteq R(B, \mathtt{Meaning}_{\rho_\Uparrow}(P))$$

Fortunately, it is not hard to adapt our algorithm to achieve these properties while improving its efficiency and guaranteeing its termination. In particular, we can allow calculations to terminate—with a conservative decision—whenever a given computational budget has been exhausted. As a special case, we can allow queries on servers to time out. Furthermore, by passing an additional argument to $R_\Downarrow$ and $R_\Uparrow$, we can keep track of the set of groups that we have examined, and terminate—again, with a conservative decision—when we detect a loop. We have studied variants that detect all loops or only those loops that arise as a result of left-recursion. Only the latter loops cause divergence, but the former variant is a little simpler and, we expect, adequate for our purposes. (We omit lengthy details on this point.)

Writing $R_\Downarrow(B, P)$ and $R_\Uparrow(B, P)$, respectively, for these approximations of $R(B, \mathtt{Meaning}_{\rho_\Downarrow}(P))$ and $R(B, \mathtt{Meaning}_{\rho_\Uparrow}(P))$, we obtain a conservative implementation of $\mathtt{IsAuthorized}$:

$$\mathtt{IsAuthorized}^{\mathrm{imp}}(M, A) = \exists B \in M.\mathtt{IsAuthorized}_1^{\mathrm{imp}}(B, A)$$

$$\mathtt{IsAuthorized}_1^{\mathrm{imp}}(B, A) =$$
$$\quad \mathbf{case}\ A\ \mathbf{of}$$
$$\quad\quad \mathbf{empty} : \mathbf{false}$$
$$\quad\quad |\ A', \mathbf{Allow}\ P : R_\Downarrow(B, P) \neq \emptyset \vee \mathtt{IsAuthorized}_1^{\mathrm{imp}}(B, A')$$
$$\quad\quad |\ A', \mathbf{Deny}\ P : R_\Uparrow(B, P) = \emptyset \wedge \mathtt{IsAuthorized}_1^{\mathrm{imp}}(B, A')$$

Thus, we replace occurrences of R with $R_\Downarrow$ for $\mathbf{Allow}$ checks and with $R_\Uparrow$ for $\mathbf{Deny}$ checks.

5.4   Distribution

When ACLs and groups are defined in terms of other groups, it remains to spell out how the corresponding servers contribute to an ACL check. This process may be orchestrated by the client that requests access or by the entity that holds the ACL. For example, if the ACL refers to a group g_1 which is itself defined in terms of a group g_2, the client may obtain and present evidence about g_1 and g_2, or the entity that holds the ACL may do the lookups for both groups. Alternatively, this entity may contact a server responsible for g_1, which in turn may contact a server responsible for g_2.

It is this alternative scheme that we adopt as our primary one:

– the evaluation of $\mathtt{IsAuthorized}^{\mathrm{imp}}(M, A)$ happens locally at the entity that holds A, with calls to others for evaluating R_X;

– the evaluation of $R_X(B, P)$ uses local recursive calls in all cases indicated by the definition of R_X, except in the case of $R_X(B, g)$, for which a server responsible for g should be consulted (unless, as indicated above, this would cause looping).

In practice, this scheme can be subject to many optimizations, such as caching, batching of queries, and "pushing" of credentials by clients (e.g., [5]).

With this scheme, ACLs and the group memberships are partly revealed only in response to queries (IsAuthorized^{imp} queries for the ACLs, R_X queries for the groups). An observer who can see enough message flows may also infer dependencies, namely that particular ACLs or groups depend on certain other groups. However, the full contents of ACLs and groups are not disclosed wholesale.

Without atomicity assumptions, it is possible that group definitions are changing during the evaluation of IsAuthorized$^{\text{imp}}(M, A)$. For example, let A be the ACL Allow Friends, Deny Friends, and suppose that a member Alice is being added to the group Friends. If the addition to the group happens between the processing of the two clauses of the ACL, IsAuthorized^{imp}(Alice, A) will return true, a behavior that could happen neither before nor after the addition. We have considered techniques that prevent this behavior. One of them consists in asking the servers responsible for the relevant groups to provide information current as of the time of the ACL check of interest, via an extra "time" parameter for R_X. Assuming that the servers keep a log of recent group changes, this technique would help for ACL checks that complete reasonably fast, subject to the limitations of clock synchronization. Whether such techniques are in fact necessary remains open to debate.

6   On Prefix Matching

In this section we elaborate on prefix matching, described in Sect. 4, and explain why we do not adopt it. Our reasons have to do with Deny clauses and groups; they are weaker if either of those features is absent. Since we believe that prefix matching is not essential for expressiveness or usability, we opted to omit it in order to give a better treatment of those features.

The rationale for prefix matching is as follows. Suppose that a blessing B' matches an ACL and that $B \preceq B'$. Whoever holds B can extend it to B', thus passing the ACL check; therefore, not letting B match the ACL may cause inconvenience and has no immediate benefit if B behaves maliciously. (It may however protect against accidental misbehavior.)

Adopting prefix matching would mean, for example, that the ACL

$$\text{Allow } n_1/n_2$$

grants access when the blessing n_1 is presented. Beyond this trivial example, it is less clear what to do in other situations.

Let us consider the ACL

$$\text{Allow } n_1/g$$

and imagine that g is defined to be empty. Should access be granted when the blessing n_1 is presented? A positive answer would seem rather surprising, and is not justified by the proposed rationale for prefix matching: there is no way to extend n_1 so that it matches n_1/g exactly. Prefix matching for a blessing pattern P (n_1/g in this example) is about the prefixes of the blessings that match P, not the blessings that match the prefixes of P. In other words, it is about the prefixes of the meaning of P, not the meaning of the prefixes of P.

Next let us consider the ACL

$$\text{Allow } n_1/n_2, \text{ Deny } n_1/n_2$$

Should access be granted when the blessing n_1 is presented?

- We could answer this question positively by computing the meaning of the Allow clause (which, with prefix matching, implies authorizing n_1), the meaning of the Deny clause (which does not imply rejecting n_1), and then taking the difference. This behavior seems odd, and is not justified by the proposed rationale for prefix matching: there is no way to extend n_1 so that it matches n_1/n_2 but does not match n_1/n_2.
- An alternative approach consists in computing all the blessings allowed by the entire ACL (subtracting for Deny clauses, but without prefixing for Allow clauses), and then adding all their prefixes. As the example illustrates, subtracting for Deny clauses does not commute with adding prefixes. This alternative approach does conform to the rationale for prefix matching.

Unfortunately, the alternative approach appears difficult at best. Let us consider the ACL

$$\text{Allow } n_1/g_1/\text{eob}, \text{ Deny } n_1/g_2/\text{eob}$$

where g_1 and g_2 are group names and eob is our special terminator name. According to the alternative approach, access should be granted when the blessing n_1 is presented if and only if there is some element of g_1 that is not in g_2. In the general case where group definitions may contain cycles, we face the inclusion problem for context-free languages, which is undecidable! Even without cycles, we do not have a satisfactory solution. Straightforward algorithms that require enumerating the members of g_1 or the non-members of g_2 seem unattractive from efficiency and privacy perspectives.

7   Conclusion

As noted in the Introduction, many systems support distributed authorization. Generally, their features include groups; sometimes, they also include forms of negation, and more rarely compound names and local names. There is no canonical solution to problems such as missing, unavailable, and circular group definitions, which are made more delicate by negation and compound names. The pioneering article on Digital's DSSA noted that "it is impractical, in a distributed environment where group nonmembership cannot be certified, to implement denial to arbitrary groups" [4]. Years later, SDSI allowed an operator NOT on groups, requiring certificates of non-membership. In SDSI, the fundamental algorithm for checking group membership worked entirely locally, by computing on credentials; in contrast, we describe a distributed algorithm.

A salient aspect of our design, which mitigates those difficulties, is that ACLs contain negative clauses but groups do not, and that ACLs cannot be reused for defining groups or other ACLs. This choice also enables us to provide a liberal semantics for ACLs (in which, for example, the ACL Allow Alice permits access with Alice/Phone) distinct from that of groups (according to which a group that contains Alice need not contain Alice/Phone). The semantics of ACLs contrasts with the treatment of compound principals in previous work (e.g., [5,7,8]). There, an ACL that would grant access to Alice would generally not automatically grant access to a compound principal of the form Alice op Phone, where op is a binary operator, unless this operator happens to be conjunction ($\wedge$). Conjunction hardly resembles /, for example because it is commutative; other operators previously considered seem closer to /. Beyond these differences, the fact that we have only one operator (/) and that it is associative allows us to sharpen the helpful connection with formal languages.

The realization of our design is under way. While the design addresses expressiveness and semantic questions with some consideration for implementation strategies, its realization may rely on a number of optimizations, such as caching. It may also lead to the development of auxiliary tools and idioms; in particular, further work on conventions and on grouping objects could be helpful in writing and managing policies.

Acknowledgments. We are grateful to Cosmos Nicolaou and to Jiří Šimša for helpful comments on drafts of this paper.

References

1. Birgisson, A., Politz, J.G., Erlingsson, Ú., Taly, A., Vrable, M., Lentczner, M.: Macaroons: cookies with contextual caveats for decentralized authorization in the cloud. In: 21st Annual Network and Distributed System Security Symposium (2014)
2. Bodei, C., Degano, P., Focardi, R., Priami, C.: Authentication via localized names. In: Proceedings of the 12th IEEE Computer Security Foundations Workshop, CSFW, pp. 98–110 (1999)
3. Cramer, R., Damgård, I.: Multiparty computation, an introduction. In: Contemporary Cryptology. Advanced Courses in Mathematics - CRM Barcelona, pp. 41–87. Birkhäuser, Basel (2005)
4. Gasser, M., Goldstein, A., Kaufman, C., Lampson, B.: The Digital Distributed System Security Architecture. In: Proceedings of the 1989 National Computer Security Conference, pp. 305–319 (1989)
5. Lampson, B., Abadi, M., Burrows, M., Wobber, E.: Authentication in distributed systems: theory and practice. ACM Trans. Comput. Syst. **10**(4), 265–310 (1992)
6. Lampson, B.W.: Computer security in the real world. IEEE Comput. **37**(6), 37–46 (2004)

7. Rivest, R.L., Lampson, B.: SDSI – A Simple Distributed Security Infrastructure, version 1.1, 2 October 1996. http://theory.lcs.mit.edu/rivest/sdsi11.html
8. Wobber, T., Yumerefendi, A., Abadi, M., Birrell, A., Simon, D.R.: Authorizing applications in Singularity. In: EuroSys 2007: Proceedings of the 2007 Eurosys Conference, pp. 355–368 (2007)

Causal Trees, Finally

Roberto Bruni[1]([⊠]), Ugo Montanari[1],
and Matteo Sammartino[2]

[1] Dipartimento di Informatica, Università di Pisa, Pisa, Italy
bruni@di.unipi.it
[2] ICIS, Radboud University, Nijmegen, The Netherlands

Abstract. Causal trees are one of the earliest pioneering contributions of Pierpaolo Degano, in joint work with Philippe Darondeau. The idea is to record causality dependencies in processes and in their actions. As such, causal trees sit between interleaving models and truly concurrent ones and they originate an abstract, event-based bisimulation semantics for causal processes, where, intuitively, minimal causal trees represent the semantic domain. In the paper we substantiate this feeling, by first defining a nominal, compositional operational semantics based on History-Dependent automata and then we apply categorical techniques, based on named-sets, showing that causal trees form the final coalgebra semantics of a suitable coalgebraic representation of causal behaviour.

1 Introduction

Causal trees [7, 8] are one of the key pioneering contributions of Pierpaolo Degano, in joint work with Philippe Darondeau, to the field of concurrency. The idea is to enrich Milner's synchronisation trees, the classical model for interleaving semantics, with causality information between the currently performed action and previous ones. As such, causal trees sit between interleaving models and truly concurrent ones. They differ from the non-sequential processes/event structures of Petri nets (see [2, 11] for a comparison between causal trees and event structures). In fact, the causal tree semantics does not offer an operational setting, where a concurrent computation is seen as the equivalence class of all sequential computations with concurrent events executed in any order. Rather, it suggests an abstract, event-based bisimulation semantics, where minimal causal trees represent the semantic domain. We will see in this paper that our categorical developments confirm this conclusion, since it turns out that causal trees form the final coalgebra semantics of a suitable coalgebraic representation of causal behaviour (see [16] for details about coalgebras).

At the syntax level, the basic idea is to have *causal processes*, i.e., processes in which each sequential agent comes with the set of its past events, called *causes*. When one agent performs an action, or two agents synchronise, a new event

Research supported by MIUR PRIN Project CINA Prot. 2010LHT4KM and by NWO Project 612.001.113 Practical Coinduction.

C. Bodei et al. (Eds.): Degano Festschrift, LNCS 9465, pp. 27–43, 2015.
DOI: 10.1007/978-3-319-25527-9_4

is generated and the causes of the involved agents are recorded in the label, together with the action. These causes, updated with the new event, are then assigned to the continuations of the agents. Correspondingly, the usual notion of bisimulation becomes history preserving [10], because causes must be matched.

The main issue with causal semantics is that the state-space is usually infinite, because the causes of causal processes grow after each transition. A solution was proposed in [13] by Montanari and Pistore. They introduced a class of operational models, namely *causal automata*, for the causal semantics of Petri nets[1]. Causal automata have no direct minimal realisations, but they can be mapped (possibly provoking a state explosion) to equivalent ordinary automata, which can in turn be minimised. Later, it was observed by the same authors that event generation mechanisms of causal automata can be generalised to handle name generation in nominal calculi. This led to *History Dependent (HD-)Automata* [15]. They are automata featuring name allocation and deallocation, and were initially intended for the π-calculus. Unlike causal automata and causal trees, each state of an HD-automaton is equipped with a *symmetry group*, telling under which permutation of names the state is invariant. This is essential to have minimal representatives.

HD-automata admit a categorical representation as *coalgebras over named sets* [6], because states and transitions are indexed by sets of names. This perspective led to several results and generalisations. In [6,12], a connection between HD-automata and the categorical operational semantics of the π-calculus [9] has been established. More precisely, the former can be *automatically* derived from the latter through a categorical equivalence. In [5] it is shown that this equivalence is much more general: if the presheaf category on which coalgebras are based has certain properties, then we have equivalent notions of named sets and coalgebras over them.

Our original contribution is two-fold, as explained next.

History-Dependent Semantics for Causal Processes. In the first part of our contribution we derive compact operational models for causal processes. In Theorem 1 we show full abstraction w.r.t. Darondeau-Degano causal semantics (DD-semantics for short). The state-space of our models is usually significantly smaller, often finite instead than infinite, than the one produced by the corresponding DD-semantics.

In order to do this, we represent events as names, and event generation as name generation. States are special causal processes, called P-processes, with the following features:

- they include a *poset*, describing the causal relations among the process' events;
- they only keep track of *immediate causes*, that are the most recent events, according to the poset, for each agent;
- they are *canonical representatives* of isomorphic processes.

---

[1] An analogous concept of *location automata* was introduced in [14] for modelling the *location* semantics of CCS.

Transitions have *history maps* that record the correspondence between event names along transitions. The semantics is *history-dependent* (HD-semantics in short), in the sense that events may have different meanings depending on past transitions.

The poset plays a crucial role in bisimilarity: two states can be compared for bisimilarity only if their posets can be related via a suitable (partial) isomorphism. This ensures that bisimilar states have the same history of events, which is essential for the correspondence with causal trees and, equivalently, with history dependent bisimilarity.

Our work is based on [4], where an analogous semantics for causal processes was first introduced. It was rather indirect and cumbersome, because it was gradually built on top of the whole (possibly infinite) DD-semantics of a causal process. Here HD-semantics is computed directly and more efficiently, via a compositional, inductive procedure that starts from transitions of individual agents in the basic, non-causal LTS.

Final Semantics. The second part of our work is concerned with representing our semantics of causal processes as coalgebras over named sets, i.e., HD-automata. This construction enables us to use results from the well-established theory of coalgebras. In particular, we have a final semantics and corresponding minimal models. This construction crucially depends on states being equipped with symmetry groups, formed by isomorphisms over the state's poset under which the state is invariant. This way, all bisimilar states have a unique representative as a state with symmetries. A simple counterexample shows that this cannot be achieved if symmetries are not considered.

We base our technical development on [5], where a general notion of named set is introduced: symmetry groups are defined over a category **C**, and then named sets are defined as families of such groups. To instantiate **C**, we introduce a category **P** of posets, where symmetry groups are formed by poset automorphisms. Then we define HD-automata as coalgebras for a suitable behavioural endofunctor on named sets, which captures causal information and event generation in transitions.

We provide a direct translation of causal HD-semantics into HD-automata. Behavioural equivalence is preserved by the translation, and in Theorem 2 we prove that it is indeed induced by causal trees. Thus we can conclude that causal trees, even if infinite, are the right abstract notion to represent causal semantics. The finite case, represented by a finite minimal HD automaton, corresponds to a causal tree with a finite number, up to isomorphism, of subtrees.[2]

---

[2] As it is common in final semantics, the final coalgebra is typically an infinite object that accounts for all possible behaviours, but the minimal representative of an HD-automaton needs to account just for the behaviours of that automaton: it decomposes uniquely the map from the HD-automaton to the final object into a surjective mapping from the HD-automaton to the representative and an embedding of the latter into the final object.

Structure of the Paper. In Sect. 2 we fix some notation on posets, recall the basic ideas around causal processes and their semantics and introduce a very simple running example, which is expressive enough to show all the key features of our approach. In Sect. 3 we introduce P-processes, our main ingredient for addressing causal semantics with nominal techniques, together with the basic operations to combine them. In Sect. 4 we define a causal semantics for P-processes, called HDC-bisimilarity and show that it agrees with the classical Darondeau and Degano's semantics (Theorem 1). Finally, in Sect. 5, we address the issue of finding minimal models up-to HDC-bisimilarity, exploiting symmetries to the purpose (Theorem 2). Due to space limitation, the reader must have some familiarity with categories and coalgebras to appreciate the technical development in Sect. 5, although this is not needed to understand the construction of the operational model and to follow its application to the running example.

2   Background and Running Example

A *poset* over a set S is a pair $O = (|O|, \preccurlyeq_O)$, where $|O| \subseteq S$ and $\preccurlyeq_O$ is a reflexive, transitive and antisymmetric (binary) relation on $|O|$. We will sometimes write posets as sets of elements and pairs, omitting reflexive and transitive pairs, for instance $\{e_1, e_2 \preccurlyeq_O e_3\}$ is the poset with elements e_1, e_2, e_3 such that $e_1 \preccurlyeq_O e_1$, $e_2 \preccurlyeq_O e_2 \preccurlyeq_O e_3 \preccurlyeq_O e_3$. A morphism of posets $O \to O'$ is a function $\sigma: |O| \to |O'|$ that preserves order, namely $x \preccurlyeq_O y$ implies $\sigma(x) \preccurlyeq_{O'} \sigma(y)$. We say that σ *reflects order* whenever $\sigma(x) \preccurlyeq_{O'} \sigma(y)$ implies $x \preccurlyeq_O y$; σ is an *order-embedding* whenever it both preserves and reflects order. A set $K \subseteq |O|$ is *down-closed* w.r.t. O whenever $y \in K$ and $x \preccurlyeq_O y$ implies $x \in K$.

Throughout the paper we assume that posets are over a countable set of *event names* $\mathcal{E}$. We will model event generation via the following *event allocation operator*, which takes a poset O and adds a new element $e \notin |O|$ to it, with a given set of causes $K \subseteq |O|$:

$$\delta(O, K, e) = (O \cup (K \times \{e\}))^* .$$

For example, $\delta(\{e_1, e_2 \preccurlyeq_O e_3\}, \{e_1\}, e) = \{e_1 \preccurlyeq_O e, e_2 \preccurlyeq_O e_3\}$

2.1   Abstract Posets

We assume a choice of isomorphism representatives for posets. We call such representatives *abstract posets*. We write $[O]$ for the canonical representative of O and we assume a choice of an *abstraction map* $\alpha_O: O \to [O]$, to be exploited in the definition of synchronised product of causal processes (see Fig. 2, where we omit the subscript because it is clear from the context).

For abstract posets, the event allocation operator is simpler: we do not need to specify e, as we can add a(ny) new event, up to isomorphism. Therefore the *abstract* allocation operator $\delta(O, K)$ gives $[\delta(O, K, e)]$, for any e. We assume the following operations:

- the (injective) morphism $old(O, K)$ embeds O into $\delta(O, K)$;
- $new(O, K) \in \delta(O, K) \smallsetminus old(O, K)(O)$ gives the unique new event in $\delta(O, K)$.

For example, letting $O = \{e_1, e_2 \lessdot_O e_3\}$, if $\delta(O, \{e_1\}) = \{e_2 \lessdot_O e_1, e_3 \lessdot_O e_4\}$ we can have $new(O, \{e_1\}) = e_1$ and $old(O, \{e_1\})(e_i) = e_{i+1}$ for $i = 1, 2, 3$.

These operations can be used to define the *extension* of $\sigma: O \to O'$ to a morphism $\sigma^+_K: \delta(O, K) \to \delta(O', \sigma(K))$ given by

$$\sigma^+_K(x) = \begin{cases} new(O', \sigma(K)) & \text{if } x = new(O, K) \\ old(O', \sigma(K))(\sigma(y)) & \text{if } x = old(O, K)(y) \end{cases}$$

The intuition is that σ^+_K does not mix up old and new events: it acts "as" σ (modulo suitable embeddings) on events that were already in O, and maps the new event in $\delta(O, K)$ to the new one in $\delta(O', \sigma(K))$. To ease notation, we will just write σ^+ when K is clear from the context.

2.2 Darondeau-Degano Causal Semantics

Let $p, q, \ldots$ denote sequential agents. Processes are generated by the following grammar

$$t ::= \mathbf{0} \mid p \mid t_1 \parallel t_2$$

where $\mathbf{0}$ is a distinguished *inactive agent* and the operator $\parallel$ is the *parallel composition* of processes, which is associative and has unit $\mathbf{0}$.

Let Act be a set of actions such that, for each $a \in Act$, there is also $\bar{a} \in Act$ (we let $\bar{\bar{a}} = a$). We assume a set of basic transitions for non-ϵ agents

$$\Delta = \{p \xrightarrow{a} t \mid a \in Act\}$$

such that the subset $\Delta_p = \{p \xrightarrow{a} t \in \Delta\}$ is finite, for all p. Notice that continuations from an agent can be parallel compositions of agents.

Causal processes are process terms whose agents are decorated with finite subsets of positive natural numbers, representing their causes. They are written[3]

$$K_1 \vdash p_1 \parallel \cdots \parallel K_n \vdash p_n$$

where $K_1, \ldots, K_n \subseteq \mathbb{N}^+$ are finite. Intuitively, the cause 1 represents a dependency with the last executed event, 2 with the one but last, and so on. The Darondeau-Degano causal semantics (DD-semantics hereafter) is a labelled transition system computed from basic transitions of agents. We illustrate it later via our running example.

Bisimilarity for the DD-semantics is the standard LTS bisimilarity. We call it DD-bisimilarity, denoted $\sim_{dd}$. It has been shown (see, e.g., [1]) that DD-bisimilarity is fully abstract w.r.t. causal trees.

---

[3] Note that inactive agents of the form $K \vdash \mathbf{0}$ are just disregarded.

Example 1 (Running example). Consider two agents p_1 and p_2, with basic transitions

$$p_1 \xrightarrow{a_1} p_1 \qquad p_2 \xrightarrow{a_2} p_2 \ .$$

The DD-semantics of corresponding causal agents, for each set of causes K, is the following

$$K \vdash p_i \xrightarrow{K \vdash a_i} \delta(K) \cup \{1\} \vdash p_i \qquad (i = 1, 2).$$

The label shows the action a_i and the set K of causes of the moving agent. A new event is generated, canonically denoted 1, and is added to the causes of the continuation agent. The old causes are incremented by one, written $\delta(K)$, to avoid a clash between the new event and the old ones.

The DD-semantics of parallel composition is computed from that of single agents. For instance

$$\{2\} \vdash p_1 \parallel \{1\} \vdash p_2 \xrightarrow{\{1\} \vdash a_2} \{3\} \vdash p_1 \parallel \{1, 2\} \vdash p_2$$

Here only the right component (p_2) moved, its label (a_2 with cause $\{1\}$) became the overall one and its set of causes became $\{1, 2\}$. Note that despite the same symbol, the cause 1 in the source and label of the transition refer to a different event than the one associated with the cause 1 in the target of the conclusion. The left component is idle, but its event 2 needs to be incremented to avoid clashes with the continuation of the moving agent. In general, δ needs to be applied to causes of idle agents. If we have more than one moving agent, i.e., two agents can do complementary actions $K_1 \vdash a$ and $K_2 \vdash \bar{a}$, their parallel composition can do $K_1 \cup K_2 \vdash \tau$, and causes $\delta(K_1 \cup K_2)$ are assigned to both continuations of synchronised agents.

In Fig. 1 we show a finite part of the DD-semantics of $\varnothing \vdash p_1 \parallel \varnothing \vdash p_2$: the state-space is actually infinite. States are tagged with marks (1) to (4) that will be used later to establish a correspondence with the named semantics (see Example 2 and Fig. 4): for the moment they can be ignored.

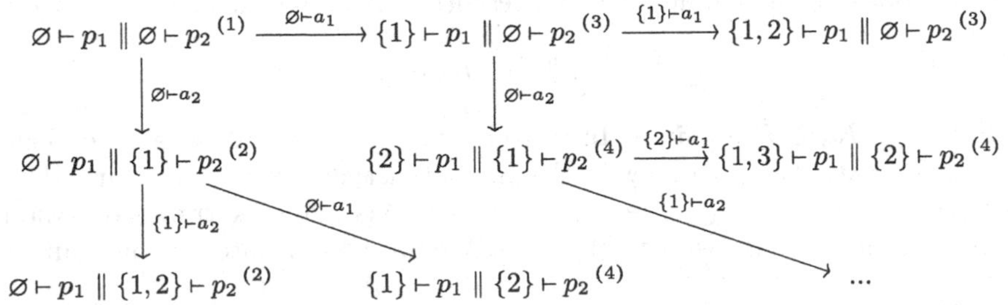

Fig. 1. Part of the infinite LTS in the running example.

3   P-processes

Since we want to apply nominal techniques to model causal semantics, we introduce an abstraction of causal processes, where events are drawn from a set $\mathcal{E}$ instead of $\mathbb{N}^+$.

Definition 1 (Nominal causal process). *A nominal causal process (n-process in short) is an expression of the form*

$$K_1 \vdash p_1 \parallel \cdots \parallel K_n \vdash p_n$$

where $p_1, \ldots, p_n$ are agents and $K_1, \ldots, K_n$ are finite subsets of $\mathcal{E}$. We will use $k, k', \ldots$ to denote these processes.

We use finite posets over $\mathcal{E}$ to keep track of causal dependencies among events in n-processes. We say that a n-process k is *consistent* with a poset O whenever, for all agents $K \vdash p$ in k, K is down-closed w.r.t. O. Intuitively, agents in k contain the whole history of their events, as described by O.

   The history of events in a n-process can be augmented via the following *closure operator.*

Definition 2 (Closure operator). *Given $K \subseteq |O|$ and O' such that O is a subposet of O', the* closure *of K w.r.t. O' is given by*

$$K{\downarrow}_{O'} = \bigcup_{x \in K} \{y \in |O'| \mid y \leqslant_{O'} x\}$$

Its extension to n-processes is $(K \vdash p){\downarrow}_{O'} = (K{\downarrow}_{O'}) \vdash p$ and distributes over parallel composition.

Given k consistent with O and $O' \supseteq O$, $k{\downarrow}_{O'}$ is clearly consistent with O'.

Definition 3 (Causes, immediate causes). *The sets of* causes $\mathcal{K}(k)$ *and* immediate causes $ic_O(k)$ *of a n-process k w.r.t. a poset O are recursively defined by letting:*

$$\mathcal{K}(K \vdash p) = K \qquad\qquad \mathcal{K}(k_1 \parallel k_2) = \mathcal{K}(k_1) \cup \mathcal{K}(k_2)$$
$$ic_O(K \vdash p) = max_O(K) \qquad ic_O(k_1 \parallel k_2) = ic_O(k_1) \cup ic_O(k_2)$$

where $max_O(K)$ is the set of maximal elements in K w.r.t. O.

The immediate causes of a n-process are events that are maximal with respect to at least one of its agents.

   We assume that we have canonical representatives of n-processes. Let $Aut(O)$ be the set of automorphisms on O, we pick a representative from $\{k\phi \mid \phi \in Aut(O)\}$, for any k consistent with O. We introduce an *abstraction operator* $[k]_O$ that, given k consistent with O, returns a canonical representative of k that is consistent with $[O]$ and a map that allows us to recover k from its representative.

Definition 4 (Process abstraction operator). *Given a process k consistent with O, the* process abstraction operator $[k]_O$ *gives a pair* $(\hat{k}, \hat{\varphi})$ *of a n-process $\hat{k}$ consistent with $[O]$ and the isomorphism $\hat{\varphi}: O \to [O]$ such that $k\hat{\varphi} = \hat{k}$.*

We now introduce the states of our causal semantics, namely P-processes.

Definition 5 (P-process). *A P-process is a pair $O \triangleright k$ where O is an abstract poset and k is a n-process, such that:*

1. $|O| = \mathscr{K}(k)$;
2. k *is consistent with O;*
3. *for all agents $K \vdash p$ in k, $K \subseteq ic_O(k)$;*
4. $[k]_O = (k, \varphi)$, *for some φ;*

Condition 1 says that the causes recorded in O are all and only the ones mentioned in k; condition 2 guarantees that the causes of each component in k are down-closed according to the order in O; condition 3 enforces only the most recent causes to be recorded in agents; finally, condition 4, establishes that k is a canonical representative. This makes event names *local*, i.e., there is no obvious relation among events in different P-processes.

3.1   Operations on P-processes

We introduce some operations on P-processes. The first one computes the "minimal" P-process that can be formed from a given poset and n-process.

Definition 6 (Immediate causes reduction operator). *Given a poset O and a n-process k consistent with O, let O_I be O restricted to $ic_O(k)$ and define $norm_O(K \vdash p) = K \cap |O_I| \vdash p$, distributing over parallel composition. Then the immediate causes reduction operator is*

$$ic(O, k) = [O_I] \triangleright \hat{k}$$

where $[norm_O(k)]_{O_I} = (\hat{k}, \hat{\varphi})$, and we denote by $\langle O, k \rangle$ the map $[O_I] \to O$ given by $(O_I \hookrightarrow O) \circ \hat{\varphi}^{-1}$.

Here the map $[O_I] \to O$ records the original identity of events of the reduced P-process.

We define an operation of *amalgamated parallel composition*, that allows us to form the parallel composition of two P-processes $O_1 \triangleright k_1$ and $O_2 \triangleright k_2$. Since events are local to P-processes, we need to specify how those in O_1 and O_2 are related. We do this through *amalgamations*, that are cospans

$$O_1 \xrightarrow{\epsilon_1} O \xleftarrow{\epsilon_2} O_2$$

of order-embeddings such that $|O| = img(\epsilon_1) \cup img(\epsilon_2)$. We denote by $am(O_1, O_2)$ the set of all amalgamations of O_1 and O_2.

Definition 7 (Amalgamated parallel composition). *Given two n-processes* k_1, k_2, *consistent respectively with* O_1 *and* O_2, *and an amalgamation* $\epsilon = O_1 \xrightarrow{\epsilon_1} O \xleftarrow{\epsilon_2} O_2 \in am(O_1, O_2)$, *we can form their* amalgamated parallel composition

$$k_1 \underset{\epsilon}{\|\|} k_2 = (k_1 \epsilon_1) \!\downarrow_O \| (k_2 \epsilon_2) \!\downarrow_O .$$

We extend the operator to P-processes $O_1 \triangleright k_1$ *and* $O_2 \triangleright k_2$ *as follows:*

$$O_1 \triangleright k_1 \underset{\epsilon}{\|\|} O_2 \triangleright k_2 = O \triangleright k_1 \underset{\epsilon}{\|\|} k_2 .$$

4   HD Causal Semantics

Our causal semantics for P-processes is inductively computed from basic transitions of their agents. Transitions are of the following form

$$O \triangleright k \underset{h}{\overset{K \vdash \mu}{\Longrightarrow}} O' \triangleright k'$$

Here $O \triangleright k$ is performing an action $\mu \in Act \cup \{\tau\}$ with causes $K \subseteq max(O)$. Unlike the DD-semantics, K only contains the *most recent* events among the causes of moving agents. This choice is sound, because down-closed sets, such as causes of agents, are fully determined by their maxima. The poset O' is $\delta(O, K)$ reduced to immediate causes. The *history map* $h{:}O' \to \delta(O, K)$ keeps track of the original identity of events. The presence of history maps makes the semantics *history dependent*, in the sense that the identity of events depend on the past transitions.

4.1   Interleaved and Synchronised Product

Our SOS rules will use two operations of *left/right interleaved product* and *synchronised product* to compute interleaving and synchronisation of two P-processes. They are defined in Fig. 2. The definitions are complicated by the need to deal with several embeddings, amalgamations, and removal of non-maximal causes, but are otherwise straightforward.

Suppose we want to compute the interleaving behaviour of a P-process that can be decomposed as an amalgamated parallel composition with amalgamation $O_1 \xrightarrow{\epsilon_1} O \xleftarrow{\epsilon_2} O_2$. In defining the left interleaved product $O_1' \triangleright k_1 \ltimes O_2 \triangleright k_2$, we assume that the left component has a transition to $O_1' \triangleright k_1$, with causes $K_1 \subseteq max(O_1)$ and history map $h_1{:}O_1' \to \delta(O_1, K_1)$, while the right component is $O_2 \triangleright k_2$ and is idle. We want to compute action causes, history map and continuation of the interleaved transition. Action causes $K_1^\ltimes$ are those K_1 of the moving P-process, embedded in O via ϵ_1 (the superscript $\ltimes$ is just an annotation to make clear that we are considering the left interleaved product). Some of them may become non-maximal, so they must be removed. To compute continuation and history map, we form a new amalgamation $O_1' \xrightarrow{\nu_1} \delta(O, K_1^\ltimes) \xleftarrow{\omega_1} O_2$. Here

Given $O_1 \xrightarrow{\epsilon_1} O \xleftarrow{\epsilon_2} O_2 \in am(O_1, O_2)$, $K_i \subseteq max(O_i)$ and $h_i : O_i' \to \delta(O_i, K_i)$ $(i = 1, 2)$:

Interleaved products:

Left:

$$O_1' \rhd k_1 \ltimes O_2 \rhd k_2 = ic(O_\delta^1, k_1 \parallel\!\parallel k_2) \quad K_1^\ltimes = max_O(\epsilon_1(K_1)) \quad h^\ltimes = \langle O_\delta^1, k_1 \parallel\!\parallel k_2 \rangle$$
$$\underset{(\nu_1, \omega_1)}{} \qquad\qquad\qquad\qquad\qquad\qquad\qquad\qquad\qquad \underset{(\nu_1, \omega_1)}{}$$

Right:

$$O_1 \rhd k_1 \rtimes O_2' \rhd k_2 = ic(O_\delta^2, k_1 \parallel\!\parallel k_2) \quad K_2^\rtimes = max_O(\epsilon_2(K_2)) \quad h^\rtimes = \langle O_\delta^2, k_1 \parallel\!\parallel k_2 \rangle$$
$$\underset{(\omega_2, \nu_2)}{} \qquad\qquad\qquad\qquad\qquad\qquad\qquad\qquad\qquad \underset{(\omega_2, \nu_2)}{}$$

where $O_\delta^1 = \delta(O, K_1^\ltimes)$, $O_\delta^2 = \delta(O, K_2^\rtimes)$ and, for $i, j = 1, 2, i \ne j$:

$$\nu_i = O_i' \xrightarrow{h} \delta(O_i, K_i) \xrightarrow{\epsilon_i^\dagger} O_\delta^i \qquad \omega_i = O_j \xrightarrow{\epsilon_j} O \xrightarrow{old(O, K_i^{\ltimes/\rtimes})} O_\delta^i$$

Synchronised product:

$$O_1' \rhd k_1 \Join O_2' \rhd k_2 = ic(O_\delta, k_1 \parallel\!\parallel k_2)$$
$$\underset{(\theta_1, \theta_2)}{}$$

$$K_1 \Join K_2 = max_O(\epsilon_1(K_1) \cup \epsilon_2(K_2)) \qquad h^\Join = \langle O_\delta, k_1 \parallel\!\parallel k_2 \rangle$$
$$\underset{(\theta_1, \theta_2)}{}$$

where $O_\delta = \delta(O, K_1 \Join K_2)$ and, for $i, j = 1, 2, i \ne j$:

$$\gamma_i = O_\delta^i \xrightarrow{\alpha^{-1}} \delta(O, \epsilon_i(K_i), new(O, \epsilon_i(K_i)) \xrightarrow{\subseteq} \delta(O, K_1 \Join K_2, new(O, \epsilon_i(K_i))) \xrightarrow{\alpha} O_\delta$$

$$\theta_i = \gamma_i \circ \nu_i$$

Fig. 2. Operations to compute continuations of parallel P-processes in the HDC-semantics.

the vertex poset models event allocation for the overall transition. We use this amalgamation to compute parallel composition of k_1 and k_2. The resulting n-process may contain non-immediate causes, so we use ic to discard them and to compute a suitable history map $h^\ltimes$, because we want to get a P-process. The right interleaved product $O_1 \rhd k_1 \rtimes O_2' \rhd k_2$ is defined analogously.

The synchronised product is also similar. Now we assume that both components move, and we know their action causes, history maps and continuations. The action causes $K_1 \Join K_2$ of the synchronisation are simply the union of all action causes, embedded into O, namely $\epsilon_1(K_1) \cup \epsilon_2(K_2)$. Again, non-maximal causes are removed. Overall continuation and history map are computed as in the interleaved product, via a new amalgamation $O_1' \xrightarrow{\gamma_1 \circ \nu_1} \delta(O, K_1 \Join K_2) \xleftarrow{\gamma_2 \circ \nu_2} O_2'$.

4.2 HDC-semantics and Bisimulation

The *History Dependent causal semantics* (HDC-semantics) is the smallest LTS generated by the rules in Fig. 3.

Remark 1. Note that, given the particular nature of n-processes and P-processes, each agent p will have at most one immediate cause to expose in a transition. If a synchronisation is performed, at most two causes are recorded in the label and only one event is added to the target.

(Agent)
$$\frac{p \xrightarrow{a} t \in \Delta \qquad O \in \{\varnothing, \{e\}\} \qquad h : e \mapsto new(O, |O|)}{O \rhd |O| \vdash p \xRightarrow[h]{|O| \vdash a} \{e\} \rhd \{e\} \vdash t}$$

(Par-Left)
$$\frac{O_1 \rhd k_1 \xRightarrow[h_1]{K_1 \vdash \mu} O_1' \rhd k_1' \qquad O_2 \rhd k_2 \qquad \epsilon \in am(O_1, O_2)}{O_1 \rhd k_1 \underset{\epsilon}{\|} O_2 \rhd k_2 \xRightarrow[h^\ltimes]{K_1^\ltimes \vdash \mu} O_1' \rhd k_1' \ltimes O_2 \rhd k_2}$$

(Sync)
$$\frac{O_1 \rhd k_1 \xRightarrow[h_1]{K_1 \vdash a} O_1' \rhd k_1' \qquad O_2 \rhd k_2 \xRightarrow[h_2]{K_2 \vdash \overline{a}} O_2' \rhd k_2' \qquad \epsilon \in am(O_1, O_2)}{O_1 \rhd k_1 \underset{\epsilon}{\|} O_2 \rhd k_2 \xRightarrow[h^\bowtie]{K_1 \bowtie K_2 \vdash \tau} O_1' \rhd k_1' \bowtie O_2' \rhd k_2'}$$

Fig. 3. SOS rules for the HDC-semantics. The rule (Par-Left) has a symmetric one (Par-Right), which is omitted.

The rule (Agent) says that an agent p can become a P-process with either empty or singleton poset O. Any transition exhibits $|O|$ as action causes, and goes to a P-process where each agent has a single cause e. The history map takes e to the maximal element of $\delta(O, |O|)$. For instance, if $O = \{e\}$, $\delta(O, \{e\}) = \{e_1 \preccurlyeq e_2\}$, and $h(e) = e_2$.

The rules (Par-Left) ((Par-Right) is analogous, so it is omitted) and (Sync) handle the (amalgamated) parallel composition of two P-processes. The first two rules derive interleaving behaviour, and the latter derives a synchronisation between P-processes performing complementary actions. We use appropriate product operations to compute the derived transition.

We now introduce bisimilarity for P-processes, called *HDC-bisimilarity*. It is quite involved: when comparing two P-processes, we need to establish an explicit correspondence between their events. This correspondence can be a partial function, because some events may not be observable. Then a P-process is allowed to simulate a transition with a different transition, provided that this transition can be mapped to the original one via the partial function.

Definition 8 (HDC-bisimilarity). *A HDC-bisimulation R is a ternary relation such that, whenever $(O_1 \triangleright k_1, \sigma, O_2 \triangleright k_2) \in R$:*

- *σ is a partial isomorphism (i.e., an isomorphism between subposets) from O_1 to O_2;*
- *if $O_1 \triangleright k_1 \xADBELL{K \vdash a}{h_1} O_1' \triangleright k_1'$ then σ is defined on K, and there are a transition $O_2 \triangleright k_2 \xADBELL{\sigma(K) \vdash a}{h_2} O_2' \triangleright k_2'$ and σ' such that $(O_1' \triangleright k_1', \sigma', O_2' \triangleright k_2') \in R$ and the following diagram commutes*

$$
\begin{array}{ccc}
O_1' & \xrightarrow{\;h_1\;} & \delta(O_1, K) \\
{\scriptstyle\sigma'}\Big\downarrow & & \Big\downarrow{\scriptstyle\sigma^+} \\
O_2' & \xrightarrow[\;h_2\;]{} & \delta(O_2, \sigma(K))
\end{array}
$$

- *if $O_2 \triangleright k_2 \xADBELL{K \vdash a}{h_2} O_2' \triangleright k_2'$ then σ is defined on K, and there are a transition $O_1 \triangleright k_1 \xADBELL{\sigma^{-1}(K) \vdash a}{h_1} O_1' \triangleright k_1'$ and σ' analogous to the previous item.*

The greatest such bisimulation is denoted $\sim_{hdc}$. We write $O_1 \triangleright k_1 \sim_{hdc}^{\sigma} O_2 \triangleright k_2$ to mean $(O_1 \triangleright k_1, \sigma, O_2 \triangleright k_2) \in \sim_{hdc}$.

The commuting diagram essentially says that σ' should act as σ on "old" events, and preserve freshness of events. The identity of new and old events is specified by the history maps.

Now we show how we can derive a HDC-semantics for (Darondeau-Degano) causal processes that is fully abstract w.r.t. DD-bisimilarity.

Theorem 1. *Consider the following implementation of event names and event generation: $\mathcal{E} = \mathbb{N}^+$ and $\delta(O, K)$ is the reflexive and transitive closure of*

$$
\{(n+1, m+1) \mid (n, m) \in |O|\} \cup \{n + 1 \mid n \in K\} \times \{1\}
$$

with $new(O, K) = 1$ and $old(O, K)(n) = n + 1$. Then $k_1 \sim_{dd} k_2$ implies $ic(O_1, k_1) \sim_{hdc} ic(O_2, k_2)$, for any O_i consistent with k_i (i = 1, 2).

Example 2 (HDC-semantics for the running example). In order to derive the HDC-semantics of $\varnothing \triangleright \varnothing \vdash p_1 \parallel \varnothing \vdash p_2$, we start from the HDC-semantics of agents

$$
\varnothing \triangleright \varnothing \vdash p_i \xADBELL{\varnothing \vdash a_i}{id_{\{1\}}} \{1\} \triangleright \{1\} \vdash p_i \qquad \{1\} \triangleright \{1\} \vdash p_i \xADBELL{\varnothing \vdash a_i}{h_1} \{1\} \triangleright \{1\} \vdash p_i.
$$

where $h_1 \colon \{1\} \to \delta(\{1\}) = \{2 \leqslant 1\}$ maps 1 to itself. Then we derive other P-processes using (Par-Left) and (Par-Right). The resulting HDC-semantics is in Fig. 4, where states tagged with numbers (1) to (4) are "representations" of states in Fig. 1 with the same mark, in the sense that they are obtained from the latter by immediate causes reduction. Remarkably, this gives a finite state-space.

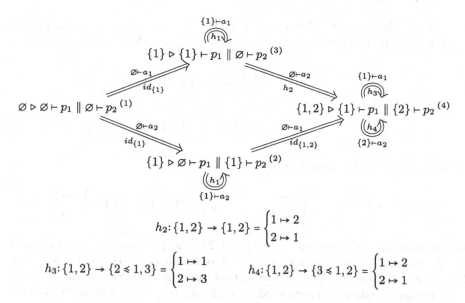

$$h_2 : \{1,2\} \to \{1,2\} = \begin{cases} 1 \mapsto 2 \\ 2 \mapsto 1 \end{cases}$$

$$h_3 : \{1,2\} \to \{2 \lessdot 1, 3\} = \begin{cases} 1 \mapsto 1 \\ 2 \mapsto 3 \end{cases} \qquad h_4 : \{1,2\} \to \{3 \lessdot 1, 2\} = \begin{cases} 1 \mapsto 2 \\ 2 \mapsto 1 \end{cases}$$

Fig. 4. The finite LTS for the HDC operational semantics of our running example

5   Causal History-Dependent Automata with Symmetries

We now consider minimal models for our HDC-semantics, up to HDC-bisimilarity. We do this by characterising HDC-semantics as *History Dependent (HD-)automata*, that are coalgebras over a suitable category of *named sets*. We call these coalgebras causal HD-automata (HDC-automata) because they will be defined in such a way that their transition relation matches our HDC-semantics. HDC-bisimilarity is then characterised as behavioural equivalence induced by the final HDC-automaton.

One important feature of HDC-automata is the presence of *symmetries* over states. Given an abstract poset O, a *symmetry over O* is a set $\Phi \subseteq Aut(O)$ (called just *permutations* hereafter) such that $id \in \Phi$ and it is closed under composition. States are of the form $O \triangleright_\Phi s$, where Φ is a symmetry over O.

Symmetries are essential for a correct notion of minimal model. In the case of ordinary labelled transition systems (LTSs), one can compute minimal versions w.r.t. bisimilarity, where all bisimilar states have been identified. Bisimilar LTSs have isomorphic minimal versions, so we may use any of them as canonical representative of the class of bisimilar LTSs. For HDC-automata, if we remove symmetries this fails: we may have minimal HDC-automata that are bisimilar but not isomorphic. We provide an example that explains this phenomenon.

Example 3. Consider the P-process $\{1,2\} \vartriangleright \{1\} \vdash p_1 \parallel \{2\} \vdash p_2$ of Example 2, together with its two looping transitions. Consider the following HD-automaton

$$\{1\}\vdash a_1$$
$$\mathbb{(h_3')}$$
$$\{1,2\} \vartriangleright s$$
$$\mathbb{(h_4')}$$
$$\{2\}\vdash a_2$$

$$h_3' \colon \{1,2\} \to \{2 \preccurlyeq 1,3\} = \begin{cases} 1 \mapsto 1 \\ 2 \mapsto 3 \end{cases}$$

$$h_4' \colon \{1,2\} \to \{3 \preccurlyeq 1,2\} = \begin{cases} 1 \mapsto 1 \\ 2 \mapsto 2 \end{cases}$$

Reminding that in Example 2 we had

$$h_3 \colon \{1,2\} \to \{2 \preccurlyeq 1,3\} = \begin{cases} 1 \mapsto 1 \\ 2 \mapsto 3 \end{cases} \qquad h_4 \colon \{1,2\} \to \{3 \preccurlyeq 1,2\} = \begin{cases} 1 \mapsto 2 \\ 2 \mapsto 1 \end{cases}$$

we can note that $h_3' = h_3$ and $h_4' = h_4 \circ (1\ 2)$ (the permutation $(1\ 2)$ swaps 1 and 2). Suppose we want to find a minimal realisation of these HDC-automata. They are not isomorphic, in the sense that there is no permutation on $\{1,2\}$ that, applied to labels and composed with history maps, turns transitions of the former into transitions of the latter. However, we have

$$\{1,2\} \vartriangleright \{1\} \vdash p_1 \parallel \{2\} \vdash p_2 \sim_{hdc}^{(1\ 2)} \{1,2\} \vartriangleright s$$

so these states should be identified in some way. This way is provided by symmetries: minimal behaviour, according to $\sim_{hdc}$, is invariant under $(1\ 2)$, so we can identify those states, provided that the resulting state is annotated with the permutation $(1\ 2)$.

In [5] a *symmetry group over a category* **C** is defined to be a collection of morphisms in $\mathbf{C}[c,c]$, for any $c \in |\mathbf{C}|$, which is a group w.r.t. composition of morphisms. Then generalised named sets are defined to be families of such groups. Since our symmetries are over abstract posets, we instantiate **C** to the following category.

Definition 9 (Category P). *The category* **P** *has abstract posets as objects and order-embeddings as morphisms.*

We give an equivalent presentation of our named sets, closer to the original one in [6]. Given a set S of morphisms and a morphism σ in **P**, we write $S \circ \sigma$ for the set $\{\tau \circ \sigma \mid \tau \in S\}$ (analogously for $\sigma \circ S$).

Definition 10 (Category Sym(P)). *Let* **Sym(P)** *be the category defined as follows:*

- *objects Φ are subsets of $\mathbf{P}[O,O]$ that are groups w.r.t. composition in* **P***;*
- *morphisms $\Phi_1 \to \Phi_2$ are sets of morphisms $\sigma \circ \Phi_1$ such that $\sigma \colon dom(\Phi_1) \to dom(\Phi_2)$ and $\Phi_2 \circ \sigma \subseteq \sigma \circ \Phi_1$.*

Definition 11 (Category NSet(P)). *The category* **NSet(P)** *is defined as follows:*

– *objects are* **P**-*named sets, that are pairs* $N = (Q_N, \mathsf{G}_N)$ *of a set* Q_N *and a function* $\mathsf{G}_N\colon Q_N \to |Sym(\mathbf{P})|$. *The* local poset *of* $q \in Q_N$, *denoted* $\|q\|$, *is* $dom(\sigma)$, *for any* $\sigma \in \mathsf{G}_N(q)$.
– *morphisms* $f\colon N \to M$ *are* **P**-*named functions, that are pairs* (h, Σ) *of a function* $h\colon Q_N \to Q_M$ *and a function* Σ *mapping each* $q \in Q_N$ *to a morphism* $\mathsf{G}_M(h(q)) \to \mathsf{G}_N(q)$ *in* $Sym(\mathbf{P})$.

Then we can define the category of HDC-automata as coalgebras over a suitable endofunctor on **NSet(P)**. Formally, this endofunctor is yielded by a categorical equivalence between pullback-preserving presheaves on **P** and **NSet(P)** (cf. [3, 4]). We give an informal description below.

Definition 12 (Category of HDC-automata). *Let* $B\colon \mathbf{NSet(P)} \to \mathbf{NSet(P)}$ *be the following endofunctor*

$$BN = \mathcal{P}_f(L \times \Delta N)$$

where:

– $\mathcal{P}_f\colon \mathbf{NSet(P)} \to \mathbf{NSet(P)}$ *is the finite powerset on* **NSet(P)**, *mapping* N *to its finite subsets that satisfy some requirements (see [6] for the corresponding functor on named sets), equipped with a compatible symmetry group;*
– L *is a* **P**-*named set of labels whose elements are pairs* (K, μ), *where* $a \in Act \cup \{\tau\}$ *and* K *represents the causes of* a;
– $\Delta\colon \mathbf{NSet(P)} \to \mathbf{NSet(P)}$ *is the* event generation functor, *mapping* N *to a* **P**-*named set made of pairs* (q, e), *with* $q \in Q_N$ *and* $e \in \|q\|$ *is an event marked as fresh; the symmetry group is the subgroup of* $\mathsf{G}_N(q)$ *that fixes* e.

5.1   HDC-automata for P-processes

We now show how we can derive HDC-automata from the HDC-semantics. The **P**-named set of states for these automata is defined as follows.

Definition 13 (P-named set of P-processes). *The* **P**-*named set of P-processes is* (Q_P, G_P), *where:*

– Q_P *is the set of n-processes* k *such that* $O \triangleright k$ *is a P-process and* $\|k\| = O$;
– $\mathsf{G}_P(k) = \{\phi \subseteq Aut(\|k\|) \mid k\phi = k\}$;

We write $O \triangleright_\Phi k$ *for* $k \in Q_P$ *such that* $\|k\| = O$ *and* $\mathsf{G}_P(k) = \Phi$.

Intuitively, in $O \triangleright_\Phi k$, Φ is a set of permutations that do not affect the state. Typically, when states are syntactic entities, we have $\Phi = \{id\}$.

Transitions from $O \triangleright_\Phi k$ to $O' \triangleright_{\Phi'} k'$ are derived from those between the underlying P-processes. The idea is that we only keep one transition among the set of transitions that can be computed from each other using permutations in Φ and Φ'. Formally, we say that two transitions $O \triangleright k \xrightarrow[h_i]{K_i \vdash a} O' \triangleright k'$, $i = 1, 2$, are *symmetric* whenever there are $\phi \in \Phi$ and $\phi' \in \Phi'$ such that $K_2 = \phi(K_1)$ and the following diagram commutes

$$
\begin{array}{ccc}
O' & \xrightarrow{\;h_1\;} & \delta(O, K_1) \\
\phi' \downarrow & & \downarrow \phi^+ \\
O' & \xrightarrow[\;h_2\;]{} & \delta(O, K_2)
\end{array}
$$

The derivation is done by taking a canonical representative among symmetric transitions. Clearly all other transitions can be reconstructed.

Bisimilarity for HDC-automata induced by the HDC-semantics can be characterised as a slight variant of Definition 8, where permutations are taken into account. It is a set of triples $(O_1 \triangleright_{\Phi_1} k_1, \sigma, O_2 \triangleright_{\Phi_2} k_2)$ such that, for all $\phi_1 \in \Phi_1$ and every transition of $O_1 \triangleright_{\Phi_1} k_1$, there is a transition of $O_2 \triangleright_{\Phi_2} k_2$ obtained by applying $\phi_2^{-1} \circ \sigma \circ \phi_1$ to the former transition, for some $\phi_2 \in \Phi_2$. The commuting diagram for the new map σ', relating the continuations, now involves $\phi_2^{-1} \circ \sigma \circ \phi_1$.

It can be proved that this new notion of bisimilarity is fully abstract w.r.t HDC-bisimilarity. Under the assumptions of Theorem 1, this is equivalent to DD-bisimilarity. Therefore we have our final theorem.

Theorem 2 (Causal trees, finally). *Under the assumptions of Theorem 1, the final semantics of a P-process is a HDC-automaton that represents the causal tree of the underlying causal process.*

As mentioned, symmetries allow computing minimal realisations, where all bisimilar P-markings are identified. More precisely, we can identify two states $O_1 \triangleright_{\Phi_1} k_1$ and $O_2 \triangleright_{\Phi_2} k_2$ that are related by $\sim_{hdc}^{\sigma}$, for some σ. Then σ becomes part of the state symmetry. Actually, σ is a permutation between subposets of O_1 and O_2, but it can be shown that all HDC-bisimilar states have the same poset of observable events on which σ is defined. This means that σ is indeed a permutation on that poset.

Example 4 (HDC-automaton for the running example). The HDC-automaton for the running example can be derived by taking $O \triangleright_{\{id\}} k$, for each P-process $O \triangleright k$ in Example 2. Its minimal realisation has the same shape and the same transitions, but the state $\{1, 2\} \triangleright \{1\} \vdash p_1 \parallel \{2\} \vdash p_2$ is equipped with symmetry $\{id, (1\ 2)\}$.

6   Conclusion

In this paper we have revisited causal tree semantics under the new light offered by nominal techniques, not available when causal trees were first introduced by Pierpaolo Degano and Philippe Darondeau. While doing so, we have outlined a general methodology for providing minimal realisation up to causal semantics. The methodology is based on a nominal framework, here enriched with poset information. While the work in this paper builds on the work in [3,4], Sect. 4

provides causal processes with a direct, compositional definition of operational semantics and of the associated bisimilarity. Moreover, the minimal realisation is shown to provide a, possibly finite, causal tree semantics.

References

1. Basagni, S.: A note on causal trees and their applications to CCS. Int. J. Comput. Math. **71**(2), 137–159 (1999)
2. Bodei, C.: Some concurrency models in a categorical framework. In: ICTCS (1998)
3. Bruni, R., Montanari, U., Sammartino, M.: A coalgebraic semantics for causality in Petri nets. J. Logic Algebr. Meth. Progr. (2015, in press). http://cs.ru.nl/M. Sammartino/publications/JLAMP15.pdf
4. Bruni, R., Montanari, U., Sammartino, M.: Revisiting causality, coalgebraically. Acta Inf. **52**(1), 5–33 (2015). http://www.cs.ru.nl/M.Sammartino/publications/ ACTA2014.pdf
5. Ciancia, V., Kurz, A., Montanari, U.: Families of symmetries as efficient models of resource binding. Electr. Notes Theor. Comput. Sci. **264**(2), 63–81 (2010)
6. Ciancia, V., Montanari, U.: Symmetries, local names and dynamic (de)-allocation of names. Inf. Comput. **208**(12), 1349–1367 (2010)
7. Darondeau, P., Degano, P.: Causal trees. In: Dezani-Ciancaglini, M., Ronchi Della Rocca, S., Ausiello, G. (eds.) ICALP 1989. LNCS, vol. 372, pp. 234–248. Springer, Heidelberg (1989)
8. Darondeau, P., Degano, P.: Causal trees interleaving + causality. In: Guessarian, I. (ed.) LITP 1990. LNCS, vol. 469, pp. 239–255. Springer, Heidelberg (1990)
9. Fiore, M.P., Turi, D.: Semantics of name and value passing. In: LICS, pp. 93–104 (2001)
10. Fröschle, S.B., Hildebrandt, T.T.: On plain and hereditary history-preserving bisimulation. In: Kutyłowski, M., Wierzbicki, T.M., Pacholski, L. (eds.) MFCS 1999. LNCS, vol. 1672, pp. 354–365. Springer, Heidelberg (1999)
11. Fröschle, S.B., Lasota, S.: Causality versus true concurrency. Theor. Comput. Sci. **386**(3), 169–187 (2007)
12. Gadducci, F., Miculan, M., Montanari, U.: About permutation algebras, (pre)sheaves and named sets. Higher-Order Symbolic Comput. **19**(2–3), 283–304 (2006)
13. Montanari, U., Pistore, M.: Minimal transition systems for history-preserving bisimulation. In: Morvan, M., Reischuk, R. (eds.) STACS 1997. LNCS, vol. 1200, pp. 413–425. Springer, Heidelberg (1997)
14. Montanari, U., Pistore, M., Yankelevich, D.: Efficient minimization up to location equivalence. In: Riis Nielson, H. (ed.) ESOP 1996. LNCS, vol. 1058, pp. 265–279. Springer, Heidelberg (1996)
15. Pistore, M.: History dependent automata. Ph.D. thesis, University of Pisa (1999)
16. Rutten, J.J.M.M.: Universal coalgebra: a theory of systems. Theor. Comput. Sci. **249**(1), 3–80 (2000)

Limited Disclosure and Locality in Graphs

Joshua D. Guttman$^{(\boxtimes)}$

Worcester Polytechnic Institute, Worcester, USA
guttman@wpi.edu

Incremental Design with Information Flow Goals. Designers of secure systems would like to be able to work incrementally. Having designed a fragment of a system—and checked that it establishes some security goal—they would like to be able to design additional portions and combine them. It is, however, very difficult to ensure that the resulting composite system still establishes the security goals that the initial fragment was found to have. Particularly when the security goals are expressed as information flow properties, i.e. as limitations on what a hostile observer can know about the behavior of a fragment.

Because this problem is so challenging, we focus only on a part of it. We use a system model in which a set of processing elements ("nodes") interact by synchronous messages passing over a fixed set of unidirectional channels. Execution never creates channels, or moves their endpoints, in this model. Thus, we are emphasizing the part of the security composition problem that is about message passing in fixed communication patterns.

Frames, Executions, and Local Runs. An instance of our model (a "frame") consists of a directed graph, together with an assignment of a set of permissible traces to each node. In each event in a trace, a message is sent or received through a channel attached to the node. Each *execution* is a partially ordered set of events. The partially ordered set $(E, \preceq)$ is an execution if, for every node ℓ, the subset of E consisting of events on channels attached to ℓ forms a trace of ℓ, under the given ordering $\preceq$.

We understand the observations of the adversary as *local runs*. Let C be a subset of the set of channels $\mathcal{CH}$. Consider a partially ordered set of events $(E_C, \preceq_C)$ where every event $e \in E_C$ occurs on some channel $c \in C$. $(E_C, \preceq_C)$ is a *local C-run* if, for some execution $(E, \preceq)$, E_C contains exactly the events of E that occur on channels in C, and $\preceq_C$ is the restriction of $\preceq$ to this subset. That is, a local C-run is the part of some execution that happens on C. If $\mathcal{A}$ is an execution, we write $\mathcal{A} \upharpoonright C$ for its restriction to the channels C.

We regard any observation the adversary makes as a local run on some set of channels obs $\subseteq \mathcal{CH}$. Thus, observing a particular local obs-run $\mathcal{B}_o$ tells the observer that the global execution is a member of $\{\mathcal{A} \colon \mathcal{A} \upharpoonright \text{obs} = \mathcal{B}_o\}$. Any other global execution is incompatible with what he actually observed.

We also assume that the goal of the adversary is to learn about what local runs may have happened on some set of channels src $\subseteq \mathcal{CH}$ that he does not

---

This abstract, which summarizes the motivation and results of [1], is dedicated in warm friendship to Pierpaolo Degano.

© Springer International Publishing Switzerland 2015
C. Bodei et al. (Eds.): Degano Festschrift, LNCS 9465, pp. 44–46, 2015.
DOI: 10.1007/978-3-319-25527-9_5

immediately observe. The channels src are the source of the information; the security designer may want to limit the flow of information from this source to the channels obs. What the observer learns about the behavior at src when he observes a particular local obs-run $\mathcal{B}_o$? He learns that whatever local src-run has occurred, it must be the restriction of some global execution compatible with $\mathcal{B}_o$. Thus, what he has learned is summarized in the set

$$\{\mathcal{A} \restriction \mathsf{src} \colon \mathcal{A} \restriction \mathsf{obs} = \mathcal{B}_o\}.$$

We call this set $J_{\mathsf{src} \triangleleft \mathsf{obs}}(\mathcal{B}_o)$. The subscripts give typing information: it is a set of local src-runs, namely all those *jointly compatible with* the local obs-run $\mathcal{B}_o$.

Non-disclosure and Limited Disclosure. The observer learns more when this set $J_{\mathsf{src} \triangleleft \mathsf{obs}}(\mathcal{B}_o)$ is smaller: his knowledge is a tighter approximation to what has happened. He learns nothing at all about the behavior at src when it is as large as possible, namely when it equals the set of all local src-runs. We call this *non-disclosure*, and it adapts the non-deducibility [2] approach to our framework.

Unfortunately, few systems need to achieve non-disclosure. When there is no causal connection between src and obs, there is no reason to include them within the same system. What is more common is that we would like to limit the disclosure from src to obs, so that some information is disclosed and some is not. Consider for example a voting system. Figure 1 shows the voters $v_1, \ldots, v_k$ of a precinct, their ballot box BB_1, a channel delivering the results to the election commission EC, and then a public bulletin board Pub that reports the results.

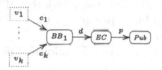

Fig. 1. A precinct with a single ballot box

The ballot box BB_1 must disclose the numbers of voters in this precinct that have voted for each of the candidates. But it should provide voter anonymity: neither EC nor anyone observing the results Pub should be able to associate any particular vote with any particular voter v_i.

This is effectively a closure operator on $J_{\mathsf{src} \triangleleft \mathsf{obs}}(\mathcal{B}_o)$, the set of local runs on the source channels $\mathsf{src} = \{c_1, \ldots, c_k\}$ that are compatible with any observations on the channels $\mathsf{obs} = \{d, p\}$. The closure operator requires that if a local run $\mathcal{B}_s$ can occur on the c_i, then any run obtained from $\mathcal{B}_s$ by permuting which vote was received from which voter should be equally possible.

This operation of closing under permutations actually obeys a slightly stronger property than being a closure operator. It satisfies the three properties:

Inclusion: For all sets S, $S \subseteq f(S)$;
Idempotence: f is idempotent, i.e. for all sets S, $f(f(S)) = f(S)$; and
Union: f commutes with unions: If $S_{a \in I}$ is a family indexed by the set I, then

$$f(\bigcup_{a\in I} S_a) = \bigcup_{a\in I} f(S_a). \tag{1}$$

We will call any operator f that satisfies these three properties a *blur operator*. They are slightly stronger than closure operators, which satisfy Inclusion, Idempotence, and Monotonicity. Monotonicity is equivalent to $f(\bigcup_{a\in I} S_a) \supseteq \bigcup_{a\in I} f(S_a)$, i.e. only half of the equation in (1). We say that a set S is f-*blurred* iff f is a blur operator and $S = f(S)$.

We argue that any notion of limited disclosure from src to obs determines a blur operator on the sets of local src-runs $J_{\text{src} \triangleleft \text{obs}}(\mathcal{B}_o)$ (see [1, Lemma 22]).

The Cut-Blur Principle. It remains now to connect limited disclosure to the graph structure of a frame. In our execution model, causal influence is propagated locally along channels. Knowledge is determined by this causal influence, although—in a synchronous model—knowledge is propagated in both directions. If I receive a message on channel c, I know that my peer holding the other end of the channel has sent it. But also conversely, if I transmit a message on c, I know that my peer on the other end of c has (synchronously) received it. All knowledge must be the consequence of some set of local inferences of these two kinds. Therefore, consequences that are inferred by a remote observer must also be available to a suitable intermediate observer.

We say that a set of channels cut is a *cut set* between src and obs if every path in the *undirected* graph from an edge in one set to an edge in the other set must include an edge in cut. We can now prove that if information flow from src to cut is limited to within a blur operator f, then information flow from src to obs is also limited to within f.

We call this the *cut-blur* principle. It follows almost directly from the blur properties.

It justifies relying exclusively on a portion of a system—such as the ballot box BB_1 in Fig. 1—to blur the behaviors of the voters. If an observer at $\{d\}$ cannot determine the correct permutation of votes, then observers at $\{p\}$ etc. cannot do so either. We have justified relying on an information flow property in a larger system in terms of the flow limitation achieved by the portion involving only the voters and BB_1.

Acknowledgments. I am grateful to Paul Rowe, my joint author in the underlying work [1] on cuts and flow. See [1] for definitions and proofs, and for extensive discussion of related work.

References

1. Guttman, J.D., Rowe, P.D.: A cut principle for information flow? In: Computer Security Foundations Symposium. IEEE CS Press, July 2015
2. Sutherland, D.: A model of information. In: 9th National Computer Security Conference. National Institute of Standards and Technology (1986)

Hoare Logic for Disjunctive Information Flow

Hanne Riis Nielson, Flemming Nielson[(✉)], and Ximeng Li

DTU Compute, Technical University of Denmark, Kongens Lyngby, Denmark
{hrni,fnie,ximl}@dtu.dk

Abstract. Information flow control extends access control by not only regulating who is allowed to access what data but also the subsequent use of the data accessed. Applications within communication networks require such information flow control to depend on the actual data. For a concurrent language with synchronous communication and separate data domains we develop a Hoare logic for enforcing disjunctive information flow policies. We establish the soundness of the Hoare logic with respect to an operational semantics and illustrate the development on a running example.

1 Introduction

Access control is a standard technique for guarding the confidentiality and integrity of data. It may take the flavour of a *discretionary* policy where for each file and user it is determined whether or not there is read-access (regarding confidentiality) or write-access (regarding integrity). Alternatively, it may take the flavour of a *mandatory* policy where files and users are characterised according to some security lattice and where flows are only permitted as allowed by the partial order. Examples include Bell and LaPadula [5] (for confidentiality) and Biba [6] (for integrity). Typically, access control is implemented dynamically by a reference monitor that halts execution when a policy is violated.

Information flow control goes one step further in attempting to ensure that subsequent use of the data adheres to the intended policy. It may take the flavour of a *mandatory* policy expressed using security lattices embodying confidentiality considerations (motivated by Bell and LaPadula) or integrity considerations (motivated by Biba). Typically, information flow control is implemented statically by a type system that ensures that policies cannot be violated, and the semantic guarantees are expressed using non-interference results [12,24]. Alternatively, it may take the flavour of a *discretionary* policy where data variables are marked with security labels indicating which users may read (for confidentiality) or write (for integrity) the data variables. A prominent example is the Decentralized Label Model (DLM) [17,18], which is also implemented statically by a type system enforcing the policies. Since the security labels can be seen as elements of a lattice one might employ non-interference ideas for the semantic characterisation.

Information Flow Control in Avionics: The increased use of wireless communication within avionics gives rise to new security challenges that cannot be

© Springer International Publishing Switzerland 2015
C. Bodei et al. (Eds.): Degano Festschrift, LNCS 9465, pp. 47–65, 2015.
DOI: 10.1007/978-3-319-25527-9_6

fully mitigated by current practices. In particular, there is a growing demand for techniques for controlling the information flow between different security and safety domains on-board and off-board the aircraft. Such techniques have to be integrated with the existing software architectures, in particular the MILS (Multiple Independent Levels of Security) architecture [21]. The MILS architecture is based on a strict separation of processes into partitions with isolated resources and a (certifiable) separation kernel controlling (and limiting) the interprocess communication (IPC) between the partitions [16]. This architecture provides a compositional approach for validating the security of the system – however, the constrained flow of information between the partitions being enforced by the separation kernel is now being challenged.

The ARINC-811 report [10] explicitly addresses the security issues in avionics and calls for separating the software in a number of security domains. This is illustrated by a "closed domain" for highly critical applications controlling the aircraft, a "private domain" for the less critical application operating the airline and for informing and entertaining the passengers and a "public domain" for the passenger owned devices. These domains will exchange information with one another and with external domains as for example ground control. The Bell and LaPadula approach and the Biba approach go some way towards controlling the information flow but a more fine-grained control is needed to handle the flexibility required in future avionics architectures.

An emerging challenge [16] is to let policies depend on the actual data. This is illustrated for an avionics gateway where the possible interactions between security domains depend not only on the security domains themselves but also on the content of messages exchanged between them. The essence of the scenario can be illustrated by a simple example: *A multiplexer that merges data from several sources, transport them over a joint channel, and then split them to reach different targets.* The different sources and targets belong to different security domains and hence they are likely to have different security policies; the merged data will include information about the intended source and destination. It then becomes challenging to express the policy for the merged data, as it is dependent on the data values specifying the intended source and destination.

Our Contribution: We extend discretionary information flow policies to deal with content-dependent security policies in a setting inspired by the MILS architecture and adhering to the separation of the software into security domains as advocated by the ARINC-811 report. We illustrate our approach on the multiplexer example mentioned above (and further elaborated in Sect. 2) and we prove the correctness of our approach with respect to a co-inductive correctness predicate defined by means of a formal semantics.

A language of *concurrent processes* each with their own memory and with synchronous communication as the only means for exchange of data is introduced in Sect. 3. It is equipped with a Structural Operational Semantics [20] that is instrumented to record the use of data in the form of a *flow relation*; for dealing with the implicit uses of data [12,24] we use the technique of "local environments" of [20]. The flow relation captures the duality between readers and influencers that also will be present in the policies in the sense that *forward* flows are appropriate for the constraints on influencers, whereas *backward* flows are appropriate for the constraints on readers.

Our basic and disjunctive policies are introduced in Sect. 4. *Basic policies* are concerned with channels as well as variables and are based on policies for readers (confidentiality) and influencers (integrity) defined using ideas from DLM [17,18]. We extend on DLM by including also content-based policies characterising the permissible value ranges of data. The policies are equipped with a partial ordering capturing the duality between confidentiality and integrity – as known from other studies of access control and information flow control [14,15,17,18]. We define what it means for a flow relation (from the semantics) to satisfy a set of basic policies. *Disjunctive policies* are sets of basic policies and allow to shift between policies as required by the value-range information; they are essential for dealing with the motivating multiplexer example. We conclude by providing a *co-inductively defined* notion of *self-similarity* for expressing what it means for a system to satisfy a disjunctive security policy.

A *combined Hoare logic and type system* for verifying whether a system adheres to the specified disjunctive policies is developed in Sect. 5. While type systems have been used extensively for formulating information flow policies, the need to consider the actual data values leads us to combining it with a Hoare logic in order to determine the appropriateness of the basic security policies contained in the overall disjunctive policy. The preconditions of the Hoare formulae allow us to select the relevant basic security policies and to perform the relevant check on the readers and influencers on just these policies; analogously, the postconditions may restrict which security policies that are enforced for the continuation of the process. Another advantage of using a Hoare logic is that this allows to cleanly incorporate also the results of prior static analyses into the information flow type system; this is needed in order to interact with the approach of industrial users and is a need also discussed in [1]. Although we are studying a concurrent language, the underlying Hoare logic is fairly standard because we are modelling a MILS architecture and therefore the individual processes have no shared variables. The semantic correctness takes the form of proving that *typability is a self-simulation*.

Related Work: The approach of [7] shares some of our aims of discretionary information flow, but we deal with both confidentiality and integrity as well as value ranges, we provide a clear explanation of the opposite directions of flow that are appropriate for their formalisation, we deal with a concurrent language rather than a purely sequential (functional) language, and we admit disjunctive policies; although we do not consider the relationship to non-interference our self-simulation based approach points in that direction. Our use of "local environments" may be compared with the use of stacks in the monitoring rules of [22] for achieving mandatory information flow for confidentiality.

The use of locks [8] would appear to have some relationship to value ranges (whether or not a lock is taken) but the main purpose is that of modelling stateful policies. An interesting Hoare logic for dealing with mandatory information

flow for confidentiality is considered for a rich concurrent language with procedures in [2]; the Hoare logic permits dealing with data in the spirit of our value
ranges, but there is no consideration of integrity nor of any semantic notion of
correctness. The approach of [1] considers a Hoare logic directly relating pairs
of states thereby being able to express non-interference properties in a natural
manner. The development of [1] is proved sound, and while it deals with our
value ranges in a rather advanced manner, there is no consideration of neither
readers nor influencers nor of the difficulties of dealing with concurrency; indeed,
one of the strong points of our work is that we are able to use security policies
explicitly just as in the classical approaches and to do so in a concurrent setting.
Focusing instead on strongest postconditions (in the form of a dynamic logic)
the approach of [11] is able to directly formulate non-interference properties for
a notion of mandatory information flow policies for confidentiality — but again
without taking concurrency into account.

Many other papers deal with the Decentralized Label Model and information flow policies with aims that differ from ours. As an example, [26] aims
at extending policies to give information about the availability of data (supple-
menting confidentiality and integrity of information), and [9] aims to connect the
confidentiality and integrity dimensions by ensuring that data of low integrity
cannot be used for deciding whether or not to declassify with respect to confidentiality. Considering a synchronous data flow language, [25] considers trace-based
formulations of influencers and relates it to a non-interference property, and [13]
considers the application of mandatory policies to avionics.

2   Motivating Example

Our development is motivated by the example illustrated in Fig. 1: two producers
p_1 and p_2 send data to a multiplexer m over the channels in_1 and in_2, respectively.
The multiplexer wraps the data up and forwards it over the channel ch to a
demultiplexer d. The demultiplexer will then unwrap the data and forward it to
the consumers c_1 and c_2 while adhering to the policy that data from p_1 is only
allowed to reach c_1 and similarly data from p_2 is only allowed to reach c_2.

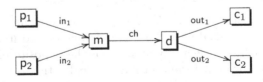

Fig. 1. The principals and channels of the multiplexer example.

We shall mainly be interested in the multiplexer and demultiplexer; we may
write their code as follows:

```
m : while true do              d : while true do
      ( in₁?x₁; ch!(1, x₁)          ( ch?(y, z);
      ⊕ in₂?x₂; ch!(2, x₂) )          if y = 1 then out₁!z else out₂!z )
```

Here the channel ch is dyadic while the other channels are monadic. The multiplexer iterates through a loop, where it non-deterministically chooses to read from one of the channels in_1 or in_2 (as indicated by the operator $\oplus$), and then sends the data on the channel ch tagged with the constant 1 or 2 to record the source of the data. The demultiplexer also iterates through a loop; it will read a message from the channel ch and decides from the tag of the message whether the data itself has to be sent on the channel out_1 or out_2.

In the setting of the avionics gateway the principals may belong to the same security domain or they may belong to different security domains.

The Policies: We now associate policies with the channels; there will be a *confidentiality* part describing who is allowed to read the data sent on the channel, and there will be an *integrity* part describing who is allowed to have influenced the data sent on the channel.

Let us write P^i for the policy catering for data flowing from p_i to c_i (for $i = 1, 2$). The data will first be sent over the channel in_i and the integrity part of our policy will express that only p_i is allowed to influence the data sent on this channel. The confidentiality part of the policy is more complex: clearly m should be allowed to read the data, but we shall also allow d and c_i to read, since the data is to be passed from m to d and further on to c_i. We formalise this by specifying

$$P_i^i(in_i) = \{p_i\} \qquad P_r^i(in_i) = \{m, d, c_i\}$$

where we use the subscript i for the integrity part of the policy and the subscript r for the confidentiality part.

Let us next consider the policy for the channel out_i. Clearly d influences the data but since the data originates from p_i and has passed through m, we shall include all three as influencers. However, there is only one reader, namely c_i, so we specify

$$P_i^i(out_i) = \{p_i, m, d\} \qquad P_r^i(out_i) = \{c_i\}$$

We are now left with the challenging task of specifying the policy for the (dyadic) channel ch. We have policies for the tag field (ch.1) as well as the payload (ch.2) of the messages and we may want to record this as follows (for $i = 1, 2$):

$$\begin{aligned} P_i^i(ch.1) &= \{m\} & P_r^i(ch.1) &= \{d, c_i\} \\ P_i^i(ch.2) &= \{p_i, m\} & P_r^i(ch.2) &= \{d, c_i\} \end{aligned} \qquad (1)$$

In the case of the payload we state that p_i and m may be influencers of the data, whereas d and c_i will be the permitted readers of the data. For the tag field we can omit p_i from the set of influencers but otherwise the policy equals that of the payload.

Unfortunately, information flow policies that are *not* content-based (like DLM) do *not* allow us to have two distinct policies for the channel ch. This means that we would need to settle for a policy merging the policies P^1 and P^2. In particular, we would be forced to include both p_1 and p_2 as influencers of both out_1 and out_2. This means that the policy would be *unable* to provide the required guarantees for the system.

Our Contribution: This motivates providing the desired security guarantees by introducing *disjunctive* policies into a concurrent language with synchronous communication. In this approach we allow the channel ch to have the disjunctive policy $\{P^1, P^2\}$. To reduce the uncertainty as to which of the policies P^1 and P^2 that actually applies we next incorporate a *value-range* component in our policies. We will extend the policies of (1) with a record of the value of the tag component of the messages (for $i = 1, 2$):

$$P_v^i(\text{ch.1}) = \{i\}$$

Our subsequent analysis is based on a combined type system and Hoare logic that allows us to reason about the values of variables and hence the value of the tag field of the messages. In this way our analysis allows us to guarantee that data from p_1 only reaches c_1 and data from p_2 only reaches c_2.

3   Syntax and Instrumented Semantics

Preparing for the formal development we define the concurrent imperative language used and we develop its instrumented operational semantics.

Syntax of Processes and Systems: A system consists of a fixed number of *principals* running in parallel; each principal runs a process with its own local state and exchanges messages with other principals by synchronous communication over channels. The syntax of processes (or statements) S, arithmetic expressions a, boolean expressions b and systems Sys is:

$$S ::= \text{skip} \mid x := a \mid S_1; S_2 \mid \text{if } b \text{ then } S_1 \text{ else } S_2 \mid \text{while } b \text{ do } S$$
$$\mid ch?x_1..x_k \mid ch!a_1..a_k \mid S_1 \oplus S_2 \mid \{X\} S$$
$$a ::= n \mid x \mid a_1 \ op \ a_2$$
$$b ::= \text{true} \mid a_1 \ rel \ a_2$$
$$Sys ::= p_1 : S_1 \parallel \cdots \parallel p_n : S_n$$

We write $x, y, z \in \mathbf{Var}$ for variables, $X \subseteq \mathbf{Var}$ for sets of variables, and $p \in \mathbf{Pr}$ for principals. We use ch for a polyadic channel name, n for unspecified constants, op for unspecified arithmetic operators, rel for unspecified relational operators, true for the boolean constant denoting truth, and we let u range over $\mathbf{Var} \cup \mathbf{Ch}$. We assume that $\mathbf{Pr} = \{p_1, \cdots, p_n\}$ is the set of principals, $\mathbf{Var} = \biguplus_{p \in \mathbf{Pr}} \mathbf{Var}_p$ is the union of mutually disjoint sets $\mathbf{Var}_p$ of variables, where each principal p is only allowed to use variables from $\mathbf{Var}_p$, and $\mathbf{Ch} = \{ch.1, \cdots, ch.k \mid ch \text{ is a polyadic channel name with arity } k\}$ is the set of *channel positions*. Arithmetic and boolean expressions may contain variables but neither channels nor principals. We denote by $\mathsf{fv}(\cdot)$ the free variables occurring inside arithmetic and boolean expressions.

The statements are mostly self-explanatory; $ch?x_1..x_k$ denotes the input of a k-tuple of variables over the channel ch and the assignment of the components to $x_1..x_k$, $ch!a_1..a_k$ denotes the output of a k-tuple of values over the channel ch, and $S_1 \oplus S_2$ denotes the "external" non-deterministic choice between S_1 and S_2. The statement $\{X\}\,S$ will be explained below; it will arise only during execution in the manner of Structural Operational Semantics [20].

Instrumented Semantics for Processes: The semantics is based on a standard Structural Operational Semantics [20] where the states are mappings from variables to values, i.e. $\sigma \in \mathbf{Var} \to \mathbf{Val}$. The instrumentation amounts to adding *flows* to the transitions; a flow F is a subset of pairs of variables, channels and principals

$$F \subseteq (\mathbf{Var} \cup \mathbf{Ch} \cup \mathbf{Pr}) \times (\mathbf{Var} \cup \mathbf{Ch} \cup \mathbf{Pr})$$

and it provides a *precise* record of the *explicit* and *implicit* information flow. The intuitive idea is that the value of the first component of a pair may influence the value of the second component; in case the component is a channel position $ch.i$ we refer to the value being communicated in the i'th position of the channel and in the case the component is a principal p it is instructive to think of it as the program counter for the process p.

In order to handle communication, the transitions are also annotated with the *action* taking place; an action α takes one of three forms:

$$\alpha ::= ch!v_1..v_k \mid ch?v_1..v_k \mid \tau$$

where the first two are for output and input over the channel ch and τ is an internal action; here $v_1..v_k$ denotes the sequence of values (from $\mathbf{Val}$) being communicated over the channel. We tacitly assume that arities match without having explicitly to require this in the semantics.

The general form of the transitions for processes is

$$\vdash_p \langle S; \sigma \rangle \xrightarrow[\alpha]{F} \langle S'; \sigma' \rangle$$

where the subscript p indicates the principal in which the process resides; here configurations of the form $\langle \mathsf{skip}; \sigma \rangle$ serve as terminal configurations. The definition is given in Fig. 2 (ignoring the two last rules concerned with systems) and the most interesting clauses are explained below.

First, in the clause for assignment the flow clearly should include $\mathsf{fv}(a) \times \{x\}$ as the values of the free variables of a are used to compute the value of x. Additionally we include (p, x) as the program counter of p also influences the value of x. Furthermore, the program counter is also influenced by the assignment so we also record the flow $(\mathsf{fv}(a) \cup \{p\}) \times \{p\}$. The clause for skip can be viewed as a special case only recording the flow $\{(p,p)\}$ to express that a process owned by principal p was active.

In the clause for conditionals and iteration we construct a block construct of the form $\{\mathsf{fv}(b)\}\,S$ for recording the implicit flow that result from passing the boolean condition b before embarking on the process S. This is in line with the

$$\vdash_p \langle \mathsf{skip}; \sigma \rangle \xrightarrow[\tau]{F} \langle \mathsf{skip}; \sigma \rangle \quad \text{if } F = \{p\} \times \{p\}$$

$$\vdash_p \langle x := a; \sigma \rangle \xrightarrow[\tau]{F} \langle \mathsf{skip}; \sigma[x \mapsto \mathcal{A}[\![a]\!]\sigma] \rangle \quad \text{if } F = (\mathsf{fv}(a) \cup \{p\}) \times \{x, p\}$$

$$\frac{\vdash_p \langle S_1; \sigma \rangle \xrightarrow[\alpha]{F} \langle S_1'; \sigma' \rangle}{\vdash_p \langle S_1; S_2; \sigma \rangle \xrightarrow[\alpha]{F} \langle S_1'; S_2; \sigma' \rangle} \text{ if } S_1' \neq \mathsf{skip} \qquad \frac{\vdash_p \langle S_1; \sigma \rangle \xrightarrow[\alpha]{F} \langle \mathsf{skip}; \sigma' \rangle}{\vdash_p \langle S_1; S_2; \sigma \rangle \xrightarrow[\alpha]{F} \langle S_2; \sigma' \rangle}$$

$$\vdash_p \langle \mathsf{if}\ b\ \mathsf{then}\ S_1\ \mathsf{else}\ S_2; \sigma \rangle \xrightarrow[\tau]{F} \langle \{\mathsf{fv}(b)\}\, S_1; \sigma \rangle \quad \text{if } \begin{array}{l} \mathcal{B}[\![b]\!]\sigma = \mathsf{true} \text{ and} \\ F = (\mathsf{fv}(b) \cup \{p\}) \times \{p\} \end{array}$$

$$\vdash_p \langle \mathsf{if}\ b\ \mathsf{then}\ S_1\ \mathsf{else}\ S_2; \sigma \rangle \xrightarrow[\tau]{F} \langle \{\mathsf{fv}(b)\}\, S_2; \sigma \rangle \quad \text{if } \begin{array}{l} \mathcal{B}[\![b]\!]\sigma = \mathsf{false} \text{ and} \\ F = (\mathsf{fv}(b) \cup \{p\}) \times \{p\} \end{array}$$

$$\vdash_p \langle \mathsf{while}\ b\ \mathsf{do}\ S; \sigma \rangle \xrightarrow[\tau]{F} \langle (\{\mathsf{fv}(b)\}\, S); \mathsf{while}\ b\ \mathsf{do}\ S; \sigma \rangle \quad \text{if } \begin{array}{l} \mathcal{B}[\![b]\!]\sigma = \mathsf{true} \text{ and} \\ F = (\mathsf{fv}(b) \cup \{p\}) \times \{p\} \end{array}$$

$$\vdash_p \langle \mathsf{while}\ b\ \mathsf{do}\ S; \sigma \rangle \xrightarrow[\tau]{F} \langle \mathsf{skip}; \sigma \rangle \quad \text{if } \mathcal{B}[\![b]\!]\sigma = \mathsf{false} \text{ and } F = (\mathsf{fv}(b) \cup \{p\}) \times \{p\}$$

$$\vdash_p \langle ch!a_1..a_k; \sigma \rangle \xrightarrow[ch!v_1..v_k]{F} \langle \mathsf{skip}; \sigma \rangle \quad \text{if } \begin{array}{l} v_i = \mathcal{A}[\![a_i]\!]\sigma \text{ (for all } i) \text{ and} \\ F = \bigcup_{i \leq k}(\mathsf{fv}(a_i) \cup \{p\}) \times \{ch.i, p\} \end{array}$$

$$\vdash_p \langle ch?x_1..x_k; \sigma \rangle \xrightarrow[ch?v_1..v_k]{F} \langle \mathsf{skip}; \sigma[(x_i \mapsto v_i)_{i \leq k}] \rangle \quad \text{if } F = \bigcup_{i \leq k}\{ch.i, p\} \times \{x_i, p\}$$

$$\frac{\vdash_p \langle S_i; \sigma \rangle \xrightarrow[\alpha]{F} \langle S_i'; \sigma' \rangle}{\vdash_p \langle S_1 \oplus S_2; \sigma \rangle \xrightarrow[\alpha]{F} \langle S_i'; \sigma' \rangle} \quad \text{for } i = 1, 2$$

$$\frac{\vdash_p \langle S; \sigma \rangle \xrightarrow[\alpha]{F} \langle S'; \sigma' \rangle}{\vdash_p \langle \{X\}\, S; \sigma \rangle \xrightarrow[\alpha]{\{X\}\, F} \langle \{X\}\, S'; \sigma' \rangle} \text{ if } S' \neq \mathsf{skip} \qquad \frac{\vdash_p \langle S; \sigma \rangle \xrightarrow[\alpha]{F} \langle \mathsf{skip}; \sigma' \rangle}{\vdash_p \langle \{X\}\, S; \sigma \rangle \xrightarrow[\alpha]{\{X\}\, F} \langle \mathsf{skip}; \sigma' \rangle}$$

$$\frac{\vdash_{\mathsf{p}_i} \langle S_i; \sigma \rangle \xrightarrow[\tau]{F} \langle S_i'; \sigma' \rangle}{\langle \mathsf{p}_1 : S_1 \parallel \cdots \parallel \mathsf{p}_i : S_i \parallel \cdots \parallel \mathsf{p}_n : S_n; \sigma \rangle \xRightarrow{F} \langle \mathsf{p}_1 : S_1 \parallel \cdots \parallel \mathsf{p}_i : S_i' \parallel \cdots \parallel \mathsf{p}_n : S_n; \sigma' \rangle}$$

$$\frac{\vdash_{\mathsf{p}_i} \langle S_i; \sigma \rangle \xrightarrow[ch!v_1..v_k]{F_i} \langle S_i'; \sigma' \rangle \qquad \vdash_{\mathsf{p}_j} \langle S_j; \sigma' \rangle \xrightarrow[ch?v_1..v_k]{F_j} \langle S_j'; \sigma'' \rangle}{\langle \cdots \parallel \mathsf{p}_i : S_i \parallel \cdots \parallel \mathsf{p}_j : S_j \parallel \cdots ; \sigma \rangle \xRightarrow{\mathcal{F}} \langle \cdots \parallel \mathsf{p}_i : S_i' \parallel \cdots \parallel \mathsf{p}_j : S_j' \parallel \cdots ; \sigma'' \rangle}$$
$$\text{if } \mathcal{F} = (F_i \circ \mathbb{I}_{\mathbf{Ch}} \circ F_j) \cup (F_i \circ \mathbb{I}_{\mathbf{Var} \cup \mathbf{Pr}}) \cup (\mathbb{I}_{\mathbf{Var} \cup \mathbf{Pr}} \circ F_j) \quad (\text{and } i \neq j)$$

Fig. 2. Instrumented semantics of processes and systems.

treatment of implicit flows using block labels [12,17,18] and technically uses the technique of "local environments" developed in Structural Operational Semantics [20].

This then requires us to define the semantics of the block construct just created and in the clause for $\{X\}\,S$ we use the operation $\{X\}\,F$ defined by

$$\{X\}\,F = F \cup (X \times \mathsf{snd}(F))$$

where $\mathsf{snd}(F)$ is the projection on the second components of the pairs in F. In this way the implicit dependence on the variables of X is incorporated in the flow of the statement.

The flows constructed for input and output are easiest to understand if $ch!a$ is thought of as $ch := a$ and $ch?x$ is thought of as $x := ch$ with the obvious extensions to polyadic output and input. Note that these clauses introduce the channels in the flows and that this only happens when the action α is different from τ.

Example 1. *Consider the process* d *of Sect. 2 and assume that it performs the action* $\mathsf{out}_1!z$. *This will give rise to the flow*

$$F = \{(z, \mathsf{out}_1), (z, \mathsf{d}), (\mathsf{d}, \mathsf{out}_1), (\mathsf{d}, \mathsf{d})\}$$

However there is an implicit dependence on the variable y *of the test of the conditional so the resulting flow will be* $\{y\}F$ *which will add the two pairs* (y, out_1) *and* (y, d) *to* F.

Instrumented Semantics for Systems: The configurations now take the form $\langle \mathsf{p}_1 : S_1 \mid\mid \cdots \mid\mid \mathsf{p}_n : S_n; \sigma \rangle$. Since we assumed that the n processes have mutually disjoint sets of variables no confusion arises by using $\sigma : \mathbf{Var} \to \mathbf{Val}$ to denote the state of the combined system. The transitions have the form

$$\langle \mathsf{p}_1 : S_1 \mid\mid \cdots \mid\mid \mathsf{p}_n : S_n; \sigma \rangle \overset{\mathcal{F}}{\Longrightarrow} \langle \mathsf{p}_1 : S_1' \mid\mid \cdots \mid\mid \mathsf{p}_n : S_n'; \sigma' \rangle$$

where $\mathcal{F}$ is a *system flow* meaning that it is a flow that does not mention any channels and hence

$$\mathcal{F} \subseteq (\mathbf{Var} \cup \mathbf{Pr}) \times (\mathbf{Var} \cup \mathbf{Pr})$$

The semantics is defined by the last two rules in Fig. 2. The first rule embeds a process action not involving communication (as indicated by the τ annotation on the arrow) in the system level; since no communication takes place there will be no mentioning of channels in F so indeed $F \subseteq (\mathbf{Var} \cup \mathbf{Pr}) \times (\mathbf{Var} \cup \mathbf{Pr})$. The second rule takes care of communication between processes; here we need to combine the flows from the two processes taking part in the communication. First we have the flow resulting from the communication over the channel (written $F_i \circ \mathbb{I}_{\mathbf{Ch}} \circ F_j$), then we have the remaining flows from the two processes (written $F_i \circ \mathbb{I}_{\mathbf{Var}\cup\mathbf{Pr}}$ and $\mathbb{I}_{\mathbf{Var}\cup\mathbf{Pr}} \circ F_j$); here we write $\mathbb{I}_Y$ for the identity relation on the set Y (for Y being $\mathbf{Var} \cup \mathbf{Pr}$ or $\mathbf{Ch}$) and use this relation to select the relevant part of the flows F_i and F_j. Note that the resulting flow $\mathcal{F}$ is indeed a subset of $(\mathbf{Var} \cup \mathbf{Pr}) \times (\mathbf{Var} \cup \mathbf{Pr})$.

Example 2. *Returning to Sect. 2, suppose that* p_1 *performs the operation* $in_1!v$ *for some value* v *and that* m *is ready to perform the operation* $in_1?x_1$. *The flow constructed for one step of execution of* p_1 *and* m *will then be*

$$F_1 = \{(p_1, in_1), (p_1, p_1)\}$$
$$F_2 = \{(in_1, x_1), (in_1, m), (m, x_1), (m, m)\}$$

These two flows are then combined into a flow for the overall communication:

$$\mathcal{F} = \{(p_1, x_1), (p_1, m), (p_1, p_1), (m, x_1), (m, m)\}$$

Here the first two pairs come from the flow through the channel, the third pair comes from F_1 *and the last two pairs come from* F_2.

4 Security Policies

We now introduce our security policies. We start with so-called *basic policies* for influencers and readers, where we borrow ideas from [17,18]. We extend on DLM in that the basic policies are content-based thanks to a component for value ranges. We next introduce so-called *disjunctive policies* that are sets of basic policies; they are needed to deal with the challenges illustrated in the multiplexer example in Sect. 2.

Basic Policies: Our basic policies provide information for each variable and channel about the principals that might have *influenced* their values, about the principals that might be allowed to *read* their values, and about their actual *value range*. Formally, a basic policy P is given by three component mappings

$$P_i : \textbf{Pol}_i = (\textbf{Var} \cup \textbf{Ch}) \rightarrow \textbf{Lab}_i \text{ influencers}$$
$$P_r : \textbf{Pol}_r = (\textbf{Var} \cup \textbf{Ch}) \rightarrow \textbf{Lab}_r \text{ readers}$$
$$P_v : \textbf{Pol}_v = (\textbf{Var} \cup \textbf{Ch}) \rightarrow \textbf{Lab}_v \text{ value range}$$

where $\textbf{Lab}_i = \wp(\textbf{Pr})$, $\textbf{Lab}_r = \wp(\textbf{Pr})^{op}$, and $\textbf{Lab}_v = \wp(\textbf{Val})$.

The orderings $\sqsubseteq$ on $\textbf{Lab}_i$, $\textbf{Lab}_r$ and $\textbf{Lab}_v$ are obtained from those of the powersets: for $\textbf{Lab}_i$ it is the subset ordering $\subseteq$ on the powerset $\wp(\textbf{Pr})$ of principals, for $\textbf{Lab}_r$ it is the superset ordering $\supseteq$ on $\wp(\textbf{Pr})$ (because the notation $\wp(\textbf{Pr})^{op}$ indicates that the natural ordering is the *opposite*, or *dual*, of the one for powersets), and for $\textbf{Lab}_v$ it is the subset ordering $\subseteq$ on $\wp(\textbf{Val})$. The orderings are lifted to policy components and basic policies in a pointwise manner.

Flows Adhering to Basic Policies: We shall now define a predicate $sec(P, F, P')$ that specifies when a flow F adheres to the basic policies P and P'; here P will be the policy that is relevant before the flow F whereas P' is the policy that is relevant after the flow F. As we shall see P will primarily be used to provide information about the permitted readers whereas P' will primarily be used to provide information about the permitted influencers.

We define the predicate $\mathsf{sec}(P, F, P')$ by

$$\forall (p, u') \in F : p \in P'_i(u') \wedge$$
$$\forall (u, u') \in F : (P_i(u) \sqsubseteq P'_i(u') \wedge P_r(u) \sqsubseteq P'_r(u')) \wedge$$
$$\forall (u, p') \in F : p' \in P_r(u) \wedge$$
$$\forall y \in \mathbf{Var} \setminus (\mathsf{snd}(F)) : (P_i(y) \sqsubseteq P'_i(y) \wedge P_r(y) \sqsubseteq P'_r(y))$$

The first line of the definition of $\mathsf{sec}(P, F, P')$ ensures that the principals p recorded as an influencer of the variable or channel u' is indeed permitted to be an influencer according to the resulting policy P'. The third line is analogous and ensures that the principal p' recorded as a reader of the variable or channel u is indeed permitted to be a reader according to the initial security policy P. The second line extends these considerations to the flow recorded between variables and channels. Note that the definition considers the constraints on influencers and readers to go in *opposite directions*: the partial order $\sqsubseteq$ amounts to $\subseteq$ in the case of influencers and to $\supseteq$ in the case of readers. This observation is central for the *duality* between the treatment of influencers and readers in our information flow type system; it expresses that it is always secure to remove readers and to add influencers. The fourth line merely ensures that we only make secure changes to the policies for variables *not* recorded in the flow: we may include more influencers and we may remove some readers for these variables.

The definition of $\mathsf{sec}(P, F, P')$ simplifies a bit when F is a system flow $\mathcal{F}$ in that u and u' now only need to range over variables rather than variables and channels.

Disjunctive Policies: We shall introduce *disjunctive policies* $\mathcal{P}$ to be finite sets $\{P^1, \cdots, P^m\}$ of basic policies each having the three components $P^i_i \in \mathbf{Pol}_i$, $P^i_r \in \mathbf{Pol}_r$, and $P^i_v \in \mathbf{Pol}_v$ as explained above. Intuitively, this corresponds to a disjunctive formula of basic policies where each basic policy only uses conjunction.

The state σ of a configuration in the semantics will determine whether or not a policy P of $\mathcal{P}$ applies in that configuration. We write $\sigma \models \overline{P_v}$ to mean $\forall x \in \mathbf{Var} : \sigma(x) \in P_v(x)$ and use $\overline{P_v}$ for the logical formula $\bigwedge_{x \in \mathbf{Var}} x \in P_v(x)$.

We do *not* require that for each σ there exists $P \in \mathcal{P}$ such that $\sigma \models \overline{P_v}$ because there may be states that do not conform to the desired policy. Also we do *not* require that for each σ there exists at most one $P \in \mathcal{P}$ such that $\sigma \models \overline{P_v}$ although this may be a natural property to arrange in many cases and may make the subsequent development more intuitive. In fact, the notation would come close to what could be expressed using a notion of dependent types which would constitute a more intuitive interface for the industrial programmer.

Example 3. *Returning to the motivating example we consider the disjunctive policy* $\{\mathsf{P}^1, \mathsf{P}^2\}$ *consisting of just two basic policies. For the channels the specification is given already in Sect. 2 and for the variables it is given by the following table (for $i, j \in \{1, 2\}$):*

	x_j	y	z
P_r^i	$\{c_j, m, d\}$	$\{c_1, c_2, d\}$	$\{c_i, d\}$
P_i^i	$\{p_j, m\}$	$\{m, d\}$	$\{p_i, m, d\}$
P_v^i	$\mathbb{Z}$	$\{i\}$	$\mathbb{Z}$

When no explicit specification is given, the policy is the least restrictive, allowing no influencers, all readers and all values. Note that the policy for y (and indeed also ch.1) allows c_1 as well as c_2 to learn the outcome of the test on the first component of the message exchanged over ch.

Systems Adhering to Disjunctive Policies: We are now ready to explain when a system adheres to a disjunctive policy. We shall take a co-inductive approach and formulate a self-simulation condition in the manner of bi-simulation.

It will be useful to consider systems together with their preconditions. We shall write

$$\{\phi_1 \wedge \cdots \wedge \phi_n\}\mathsf{p}_1 : S_1 \mid\mid \cdots \mid\mid \mathsf{p}_n : S_n$$

for a system $\mathsf{p}_1 : S_1 \mid\mid \cdots \mid\mid \mathsf{p}_n : S_n$ that is intended only to be started in a state σ satisfying the logical formula $\phi_1 \wedge \cdots \wedge \phi_n$. We shall require that the free variables of the formula ϕ_i are contained in $\mathbf{Var}_{\mathsf{p}_i}$ (the variables belonging to the process p_i) thereby ensuring that ϕ_i only applies to S_i. The simplest choice of $\phi_1 \wedge \cdots \wedge \phi_n$ would be $\mathsf{true} \wedge \cdots \wedge \mathsf{true}$ and we sometimes abbreviate it to true; the usefulness of considering other choices of $\phi_1 \wedge \cdots \wedge \phi_n$ will emerge in the next section.

Definition 1. *A predicate $\mathcal{R}$ on systems with preconditions is a self-simulation with respect to $\mathcal{P}$ whenever*

$$\mathcal{R}(\{\phi_1 \wedge \cdots \wedge \phi_n\}\mathsf{p}_1 : S_1 \mid\mid \cdots \mid\mid \mathsf{p}_n : S_n)$$

implies that

$$\forall \sigma, \sigma', S_1' \cdots S_n', \mathcal{F} :$$
$$\langle \mathsf{p}_1 : S_1 \mid\mid \cdots \mid\mid \mathsf{p}_n : S_n; \sigma \rangle \overset{\mathcal{F}}{\Longrightarrow} \langle \mathsf{p}_1 : S_1' \mid\mid \cdots \mid\mid \mathsf{p}_n : S_n'; \sigma' \rangle$$
$$\Downarrow$$
$$\exists \phi_1', \cdots, \phi_n' :$$
$$\mathcal{R}(\{\phi_1' \wedge \cdots \wedge \phi_n'\}\mathsf{p}_1 : S_1' \mid\mid \cdots \mid\mid \mathsf{p}_n : S_n') \wedge$$
$$\forall P \in \mathcal{P} : \sigma \models (\phi_1 \wedge \cdots \wedge \phi_n \wedge \overline{P_\mathsf{v}})$$
$$\Downarrow$$
$$\exists P' \in \mathcal{P} : \sigma' \models (\phi_1' \wedge \cdots \wedge \phi_n' \wedge \overline{P_\mathsf{v}'}) \wedge \mathsf{sec}(P, \mathcal{F}, P')$$

The self-simulation part of the definition expresses that for all states, whenever one system configuration evolves into another system configuration and the first system is in the relation $\mathcal{R}$ for a certain precondition, then there is an updated precondition for the resulting system ensuring that it also is in the relation $\mathcal{R}$. The last three lines of the definition put extra requirements on the relationship between the states, preconditions, policies and flows: whenever the initial state satisfies the preconditions and some policy from $\mathcal{P}$ applies, then there must be some policy in $\mathcal{P}$ such that the next configuration satisfies the updated preconditions and the latter policy applies; furthermore, the observed flow $\mathcal{F}$ has to be acceptable with respect to the two policies. These requirements may be easiest to appreciate in the case where the policy set $\mathcal{P}$ satisfies that for each σ there is at most one (or perhaps exactly one) $P \in \mathcal{P}$ such that $\sigma \models \overline{P_v}$.

As in the case of bi-simulation it is immediate to show that any union of self-simulations is itself a self-simulation. This allows us to define self-similarity in the same co-inductive manner as used for bi-similarity:

Definition 2. Self-similarity *(with respect to $\mathcal{P}$) is the largest self-simulation (with respect to $\mathcal{P}$) and it is denoted* $\models^{\mathcal{P}}$ *(or simply $\models$).*

A system $p_1 : S_1 \parallel \cdots \parallel p_n : S_n$ respects the disjunctive policy $\mathcal{P}$ whenever it is self-similar:

$$\models^{\mathcal{P}} \{\mathsf{true} \wedge \cdots \wedge \mathsf{true}\} p_1 : S_1 \parallel \cdots \parallel p_n : S_n$$

5 Type System and Correctness

Given a disjunctive policy we now specify a type system for ensuring that processes and systems obey the policy and we prove that a well-typed system respects the disjunctive policy. To deal with the value-range components of policies, the type system is combined with a Hoare logic for reasoning about the values of variables [3,4]. We already mentioned that using a Hoare logic allows to cleanly incorporate also the results of prior static analyses into the information flow type system.

Type System: The Hoare logic part of the type system is fairly simple because we use local variables and synchronous communication (in the manner of MILS [21] and ARINC-811 [10]) rather than shared variables between processes [23]. The judgement of the type system for processes has the form

$$X \vdash_p \{\phi\} S \{\phi'\}$$

where X is a set of implicitly used variables, p is the name of the principal in which the process S executes, and ϕ and ϕ' are the pre- and post-conditions of S in the form of logical formulae over program variables in $\mathbf{Var}_p$. (We shall assume that each $\mathbf{Var}_p$ is sufficiently big to account for all logical variables needed in the Hoare logic.)

The definition is given in Fig. 3 and requires some auxiliary notation. Given a set $X \subseteq \mathbf{Var}$ we then define the mappings $P_i[X]$ and $P_r[X]$ in $\mathbf{Lab}_i$ and $\mathbf{Lab}_r$, respectively, by taking least upper bounds over the variables in X; to be specific:

$$P_i[X] = \bigcup_{x \in X} P_i(x) \qquad P_r[X] = \bigcap_{x \in X} P_r(x)$$

In Fig. 3 we shall use $P_r[a; X]$ as a shorthand for $P_r[\mathsf{fv}(a) \cup X]$ and $P_i[a; X]$ as a shorthand for $P_i[\mathsf{fv}(a) \cup X]$ and similarly for boolean expressions b instead of arithmetic expressions a. This notation is often used in an expression of the form

$$X \vdash_p \{\phi\}\mathsf{skip}\{\phi'\} \quad \text{if } \forall P \in \mathcal{P} : \phi \wedge \overline{P_{\mathsf{v}}} \;\Rightarrow\; \phi' \wedge p \in P_{\mathsf{r}}[X]$$

$$X \vdash_p \{\phi\}x := a\{\phi'\} \quad \text{if } \forall P \in \mathcal{P} : \phi \wedge \overline{P_{\mathsf{v}}} \;\Rightarrow\; \exists P' \in \mathcal{P} : \left(\begin{array}{l} \phi'[a/x] \wedge \overline{P'_{\mathsf{v}}}[a/x] \wedge \\ P_{\mathsf{i}}[x \mapsto P_{\mathsf{i}}[a;X]] \sqsubseteq P'_{\mathsf{i}} \;\wedge\; p \in P'_{\mathsf{i}}(x) \wedge \\ P_{\mathsf{r}}[x \mapsto P_{\mathsf{r}}[a;X]] \sqsubseteq P'_{\mathsf{r}} \;\wedge\; p \in P_{\mathsf{r}}[a;X] \end{array}\right)$$

$$\frac{X \vdash_p \{\phi\}S_1\{\phi''\} \qquad X \vdash_p \{\phi''\}S_2\{\phi'\}}{X \vdash_p \{\phi\}S_1; S_2\{\phi'\}}$$

$$\frac{\begin{array}{c} X \cup \mathsf{fv}(b) \vdash_p \{\phi \wedge b\}S_1\{\phi'\} \\ X \cup \mathsf{fv}(b) \vdash_p \{\phi \wedge \neg b\}S_2\{\phi'\} \end{array}}{X \vdash_p \{\phi\}\mathsf{if}\ b\ \mathsf{then}\ S_1\ \mathsf{else}\ S_2\{\phi'\}} \quad \text{if } \forall P \in \mathcal{P} : \phi \wedge \overline{P_{\mathsf{v}}} \;\Rightarrow\; p \in P_{\mathsf{r}}[b;X]$$

$$\frac{X \cup \mathsf{fv}(b) \vdash_p \{\phi \wedge b\}S\{\phi\}}{X \vdash_p \{\phi\}\mathsf{while}\ b\ \mathsf{do}\ S\{\phi \wedge \neg b\}} \quad \text{if } \forall P \in \mathcal{P} : \phi \wedge \overline{P_{\mathsf{v}}} \;\Rightarrow\; p \in P_{\mathsf{r}}[b;X]$$

$$\frac{X \cup X_0 \vdash_p \{\phi\}S\{\phi'\}}{X \vdash_p \{\phi\}\{X_0\}\ S\{\phi'\}}$$

$$X \vdash_p \{\phi\}ch!a_1..a_k\{\phi'\} \quad \text{if } \forall P \in \mathcal{P} : \phi \wedge \overline{P_{\mathsf{v}}} \;\Rightarrow\; \exists P' \in \mathcal{P} : \left(\begin{array}{l} \phi' \wedge \overline{P'_{\mathsf{v}}} \wedge \bigwedge_{i \le k} a_i \in P'_{\mathsf{v}}(ch.i) \wedge \\ P_{\mathsf{i}}[(ch.i \mapsto P_{\mathsf{i}}[a_i;X])_{i \le k}] \sqsubseteq P'_{\mathsf{i}} \wedge \bigwedge_{i \le k} p \in P'_{\mathsf{i}}(ch.i) \\ P_{\mathsf{r}}[(ch.i \mapsto P_{\mathsf{r}}[a_i;X])_{i \le k}] \sqsubseteq P'_{\mathsf{r}} \wedge \bigwedge_{i \le k} p \in P_{\mathsf{r}}[a_i;X] \end{array}\right)$$

$$X \vdash_p \{\phi\}ch?x_1..x_k\{\phi'\} \quad \text{if } \forall P \in \mathcal{P} : \left(\begin{array}{l} (\exists x_1..x_k.\phi \wedge \overline{P_{\mathsf{v}}}) \;\wedge \\ \bigwedge_{i \le k} x_i \in P_{\mathsf{v}}(ch.i) \end{array}\right) \Rightarrow \exists P' \in \mathcal{P} : \left(\begin{array}{l} \phi' \wedge \overline{P'_{\mathsf{v}}} \wedge \\ P_{\mathsf{i}}[(x_i \mapsto P_{\mathsf{i}}[ch.i;X])_{i \le k}] \sqsubseteq P'_{\mathsf{i}} \wedge \bigwedge_{i \le k} p \in P'_{\mathsf{i}}(x_i) \\ P_{\mathsf{r}}[(x_i \mapsto P_{\mathsf{r}}[ch.i;X])_{i \le k}] \sqsubseteq P'_{\mathsf{r}} \wedge \bigwedge_{i \le k} p \in P_{\mathsf{r}}[ch.i;X] \end{array}\right)$$

$$\frac{X \vdash_p \{\phi\}S_1\{\phi'\} \qquad X \vdash_p \{\phi\}S_2\{\phi'\}}{X \vdash_p \{\phi\}S_1 \oplus S_2\{\phi'\}} \quad \text{if } \forall P \in \mathcal{P} : \phi \wedge \overline{P_{\mathsf{v}}} \;\Rightarrow\; p \in P_{\mathsf{r}}[X]$$

$$\frac{X \vdash_p \{\psi\}S\{\psi'\}}{X \vdash_p \{\phi\}S\{\phi'\}} \quad \text{if } (\phi \Rightarrow \psi) \wedge (\psi' \Rightarrow \phi')$$

Fig. 3. Type system for processes.

$P_r[x \mapsto P_r[a; X]]$ that denotes P_r' defined by $P_r'(u) = P_r(u)$ whenever $u \neq x$ and $P_r'(x) = P_r[a; X]$ and similarly for $P_i[x \mapsto P_i[a; X]]$.

Most axiom schemes and rules in Fig. 3 strengthen a precondition of the form ϕ to the formula $\phi \wedge \overline{P_v}$ that allows us to use the value-range information from the appropriate basic policy in $\mathcal{P}$. With the exception of assignment, input and output, most axiom schemes and rules demand that the strengthened precondition ensures that the principal p is correctly recorded as a reader of the variables whose values are either used implicitly (typically by being a member of the set X) or explicitly (typically $\mathsf{fv}(b)$). As an example, the axiom scheme for skip illustrates both points.

The axiom scheme for assignment is more complex because the state of the system changes. It therefore considers all basic policies P whose value-range component is consistent with the (strengthened) precondition and demands that there is a basic policy P' that appropriately records the state change. The pattern $\forall P \in \mathcal{P} : (\cdots) \Rightarrow \exists P' \in \mathcal{P} : (\cdots)$ takes care of this and is in line with the definition of self-simulation. The first line of requirements ensures that the strengthened precondition establishes the formulae obtained from the strengthened postcondition by mimicking the effect of the assignment; the use of a substitution $[a/x]$ on a logical formula is classical for Hoare logic (when using the weakest precondition approach). To be explicit, the notation $\overline{P_v}[a/x]$ means $a \in P_v(x) \wedge \bigwedge_{y \in \mathbf{Var} \setminus \{x\}} y \in P_v(y)$. The second line of requirements ensures that the new policy P' records all the influencers of the variable assigned due to both implicit use of variables in X and explicit use of variables in a; additionally it ensures that the influence on the principal p is recorded in the new policy P'. The third line of requirements ensures that the new policy P' records all the readers of the variable assigned due to both implicit use of variables in X and explicit use of variables in a; additionally it ensures that the reading within p of X and a is recorded in the original policy P.

Once again note that the partial order for influencers is such that it is always secure to add influencers, that the partial order for readers is such that it is always secure to remove readers, and that the *semantic underpinning* of these statement is expressed by $\mathsf{sec}(P, F, P')$ (and Theorem 1 below).

The axiom schemes for output and input are easiest to understand if $ch!a$ is thought of as $ch := a$ and $ch?x$ is thought of as $x := ch$. The rule for input differs from assignment in that the pure Hoare logic component takes a strongest postcondition approach (as opposed to the weakest precondition approach used for assignment). The remaining axioms are rather standard from a Hoare logic point of view.

The type system is lifted to systems as follows:

$$\frac{\emptyset \vdash_{\mathsf{p}_1} \{\phi_1\} S_1 \{\mathsf{true}\} \quad \cdots \quad \emptyset \vdash_{\mathsf{p}_n} \{\phi_n\} S_n \{\mathsf{true}\}}{\vdash^{\mathcal{P}} \{\phi_1 \wedge \cdots \wedge \phi_n\} \mathsf{p}_1 : S_1 \parallel \cdots \parallel \mathsf{p}_n : S_n}$$

where we once more require that the free variables of the formula ϕ_i are contained in $\mathbf{Var}_{\mathsf{p}_i}$ (the variables belonging to the process p_i) thereby ensuring that ϕ_i only applies to S_i.

Example 4. *Returning to the motivating example we shall now highlight some of the steps in proving that the overall system guarantees the disjunctive security policy* $\mathcal{P} = \{\mathsf{P}^1, \mathsf{P}^2\}$. *To establish the judgement*

$$\emptyset \vdash_m \{\mathsf{true}\}\ \mathsf{ch}!(1, x_1)\ \{\mathsf{true}\}$$

we will choose P' *to be* P^1 *independently of whether* P *is* P^1 *or* P^2. *To establish the judgement*

$$\emptyset \vdash_d \{\mathsf{true}\}\ \mathsf{ch}?(y, z)\ \{\mathsf{true}\}$$

we will choose P' *to be equal to* P. *Finally, to establish the judgement*

$$\{y\} \vdash_d \{y = 1\}\ \mathsf{out}_1!z\ \{y = 1\}$$

we use the precondition $y = 1$ *together with* $y \in P_v(y)$ *to conclude that, even though we only seem to know that* $P \in \{\mathsf{P}^1, \mathsf{P}^2\}$ *it must be the case* $P = \mathsf{P}^1$, *and we can therefore choose* $P' = \mathsf{P}^1$ *and complete the proof.*

Correctness Results: Our overall correctness result shows that well-typed programs satisfy self-similarity:

Theorem 1. *If* $\vdash^{\mathcal{P}} \{\mathsf{true}\}Sys$ *then* $\models^{\mathcal{P}} \{\mathsf{true}\}Sys$.

The proof is by directly showing that typability is a self-simulation:

Proposition 1. $\vdash^{\mathcal{P}}$ *is a self-simulation with respect to* $\mathcal{P}$.

Among other things this establishes a *subject reduction* result (saying that typing is preserved under evaluation).

6   Conclusion and Future Work

We have extended basic *discretionary* information flow policies for readers (confidentiality) and influencers (integrity) to be dependent on *content* (values) and have introduced *disjunctive* information flow policies to facilitate the content-dependent shift between basic policies.

Our approach has been motivated by the challenges of the avionics gateway (as illustrated by the multiplexer example in Sect. 2) suggested by the avionics partners in the European Artemis Project SESAMO. Prior attempts at using DLM uncovered a number of weaknesses of information flow policies that are not able to incorporate content; however, the explicit use of security labels denoting readers and influencers were considered extremely relevant. This motivated our combination of Hoare logic assertions with classical security labels (unlike approaches like [1] that do not admit classical security labels) and our introduction of disjunctive policies. We are currently working on developing annotations for avionics software in C using dependent types and restricted logical formulae as an interface to the underlying disjunctive information flow policies.

We developed a *combined Hoare logic and type system* (Sect. 5) for verifying whether a system adheres to the specified disjunctive policies. Apart from the technical convenience of using a Hoare logic as the basis of a type system it also facilitates incorporating the results of prior static analyses into the information flow type system; this is needed in order to interact with the approach of industrial users. To obtain a stronger type system it would be useful to strengthen the rule of consequence to admit analysis by cases

$$\frac{X \vdash_p \{\phi_1\} S \{\psi_1\} \qquad X \vdash_p \{\phi_2\} S \{\psi_2\}}{X \vdash_p \{\phi\} S \{\psi\}}$$

$$\text{if } (\phi \Rightarrow \phi_1 \vee \phi_2) \wedge (\psi_1 \Rightarrow \psi) \wedge (\psi_2 \Rightarrow \psi)$$

although we are not going to claim any (relative) completeness results for the combined Hoare logic and type system. For practical use one would need to limit the logical assertions to a restricted format so as to support efficient type inference.

The development has been performed for *concurrent systems* with synchronous communication and local memory as required by MILS [21] and ARINC-811 [10]. In addition to extensions with bypassing security policies it would be feasible to add polymorphism of annotations, add a principal hierarchy, incorporate procedures and methods, borrowing from DLM and other information flow policies.

Our semantic justification was based on an instrumented operational semantics in the manner used in static program analysis (Sect. 3). It provided a semantic interpretation that makes it clear that *opposite directions of flow* are appropriate for confidentiality and integrity, and hence agrees with the intuition about the *duality* of readers (always safe to remove some) and influencers (always safe to add some) in information flow type systems. Based on this we took a *co-inductive* approach to defining *self-similarity* (Sect. 4) borrowing from the development of bi-simulations. Our main correctness results showed that typability suffices for self-similarity (Sect. 5). Technically the proof amounted to showing that typability is itself a self-simulation.

This approach should not be seen as a dismissal of the value of a non-interference result (meaning that the system is contained in the reflexive part of a notion of bi-simulation). However, non-interference results are not easy to "get right" as is discussed at length in [7] and adding concurrency only adds to the complexities [14]: should non-interference be termination-sensitive, should it be timing-sensitive, etc. In particular, the approaches of [1,11] do not directly carry over because they do not deal with concurrent systems. While a non-interference result would be a welcome additional development, we would like to follow [7] in letting the non-interference result provide a stronger basis for the instrumented semantics rather than being the primary mechanism for ensuring the correctness of the type systems. This approach is in line with the research in programming languages where the vast majority of program analyses are formulated with respect to an understanding of program behaviour comparable to our instrumented semantics; looking for further justification is possible and considerations similar to those of non-interference are appropriate [19].

The exposition provided in this paper is a simplification of our formal development that has been checked using the Coq proof assistant (including the motivating multiplexer example of Sect. 2).

Acknowledgement. We are supported by IDEA4CPS (DNRF 86-10) and benefitted from discussions with Michael Paulitsch and Kevin Müller from Airbus.

References

1. Amtoft, T., Dodds, J., Zhang, Z., Appel, A., Beringer, L., Hatcliff, J., Ou, X., Cousino, A.: A certificate infrastructure for machine-checked proofs of conditional information flow. In: Degano, P., Guttman, J.D. (eds.) Principles of Security and Trust. LNCS, vol. 7215, pp. 369–389. Springer, Heidelberg (2012)
2. Andrews, G.R., Reitman, R.P.: An axiomatic approach to information flow in programs. ACM Trans. Program. Lang. Syst. **2**(1), 56–76 (1980)
3. Apt, K.R.: Ten years of Hoare's logic: A survey - part I. ACM Trans. Program. Lang. Syst. **3**(4), 431–483 (1981)
4. Apt, K.R.: Ten years of Hoare's logic: a survey part II: nondeterminism. Theoret. Comput. Sci. **28**, 83–109 (1984)
5. Bell, D.E., LaPadula, L.J.: Secure computer systems: a mathematical model. Technical report, MITRE Corporation (1973)
6. Biba, K.J.: Integrity considerations for secure computer systems. Technical report, MITRE Corporation (1977)
7. Boudol, G.: Secure information flow as a safety property. In: Guttman, J., Degano, P., Martinelli, F. (eds.) FAST 2008. LNCS, vol. 5491, pp. 20–34. Springer, Heidelberg (2009)
8. Broberg, N., Sands, D.: Paralocks: role-based information flow control and beyond. In: 37 th POPL, pp. 431–444. ACM (2010)
9. Chong, S., Myers, A.C.: Decentralized robustness. In: 19'th CSFW, pp. 242–256. IEEE Computer Society (2006)
10. Airlines Electronic Engineering Committee. ARINC 811: Commercial aircraft information security concepts of operation and process framework. Technical report (2005)
11. Darvas, Á., Hähnle, R., Sands, D.: A theorem proving approach to analysis of secure information flow. In: Hutter, D., Ullmann, M. (eds.) SPC 2005. LNCS, vol. 3450, pp. 193–209. Springer, Heidelberg (2005)
12. Denning, D.E., Denning, P.J.: Certification of programs for secure information flow. CACM **20**(7), 504–513 (1977)
13. Greve, D.: Data flow logic: Analyzing Information Flow Properties of C Programs. Rockwell Collins (2011)
14. Hedin, D., Sabelfeld, A.: A Perspective on Information-Flow Control. Marktoberdorf Summerschool (2011)
15. Montagu, B., Pierce, B.C., Pollack, R.: A theory of information-flow labels. In: 26th CSF, pp. 3–17. IEEE Computer Society (2013)
16. Müller, K., Paulitsch, M., Tverdyshev, S., Blasum, H.: MILS-related information flow control in the avionic domain: a view on security-enhancing software architectures. In: IEEE/IFIP International Conference on Dependable Systems and Networks Workshops, DSN 2012, pp. 1–6. IEEE (2012)

17. Myers, A.C., Liskov, B.: A decentralized model for information flow control. In: 16th ACM Symposium on Operating Systems Principles, pp. 129–142 (1997)
18. Myers, A.C., Liskov, B.: Protecting privacy using the decentralized label model. ACM Trans. Softw. Eng. Methodol. 9(4), 410–442 (2000)
19. Nielson, F.: Program transformations in a denotational setting. ACM Trans. Program. Lang. Syst. 7(3), 359–379 (1985)
20. Plotkin, G.D.: A structural approach to operational semantics. J. Logic Algebraic Program. 60–61, 17–139 (2004)
21. Rushby, J.: Separation and Integration in MILS (The MILS Constitution). Technical report SRI-CSL-08-XX, SRI International, February 2008
22. Sabelfeld, A., Russo, A.: From dynamic to static and back: riding the roller coaster of information-flow control research. In: Virbitskaite, I., Voronkov, A., Pnueli, A. (eds.) PSI 2009. LNCS, vol. 5947, pp. 352–365. Springer, Heidelberg (2010)
23. Stirling, C.: A generalization of Owicki-Gries's Hoare logic for a concurrent while language. Theoret. Comput. Sci. 58, 347–359 (1988)
24. Volpano, D.M., Irvine, C.E., Smith, G.: A sound type system for secure flow analysis. J. Comput. Secur. 4(2/3), 167–188 (1996)
25. Whalen, M.W., Greve, D.A., Wagner, L.G.: Model checking information flow. In: Hardin, D.S. (ed.) Design and Verification of Microprocessor Systems for High-Assurance Applications, pp. 381–428. Springer, New York (2010)
26. Zheng, L., Myers, A.C.: End-to-end availability policies and noninterference. In: 18'th CSFW, pp. 272–286. IEEE Computer Society (2005)

Alice and Bob: Reconciling Formal Models and Implementation

Omar Almousa[1], Sebastian Mödersheim[1], and Luca Viganò[2]([⊠])

[1] DTU Compute, Lyngby, Denmark
[2] Department of Informatics, King's College London, London, UK
luca.vigano@kcl.ac.uk

Abstract. This paper defines the "ultimate" formal semantics for Alice and Bob notation, i.e., what actions the honest agents have to perform, in the presence of an arbitrary set of cryptographic operators and their algebraic theory. Despite its generality, this semantics is mathematically simpler than any previous attempt. For practical applicability, we introduce the language SPS and an automatic translation to robust real-world implementations and corresponding formal models, and we prove this translation correct with respect to the semantics.

1 Introduction

Alice-and-Bob notation is a simple and succinct way to specify security protocols: one only needs to describe what messages are exchanged between the protocol agents in an unattacked protocol run. However, it has turned out to be surprisingly subtle to define a formal semantics for such a notation, i.e., defining an inference system for how agents should compose, decompose and check the messages they send and receive. Such a semantics is necessary in order to automatically generate formal models and implementations from Alice-and-Bob specifications. However, even modeling messages in the free algebra, defining the semantics has proved far from trivial [11–13,20,22,23]. To make matters worse, many modern protocols rely, for instance, on the Diffie-Hellman key agreement where the algebraic properties of modular exponentiation are necessarily part of the operational semantics, since the key exchange would be non-executable in the free algebra. For practical purposes, one can augment the semantics with support for just this special example like [27], but a general and mathematically succinct and rigorous theory is desirable.

We give in this work a semantics for an arbitrary set of operators and their algebraic properties. Despite this generality, the semantics is a much more succinct and mathematically simple definition than all the previous works (it fits on half a page) because it is based on a few general and uniform principles to

This work was partially supported by the EU FP7 Projects no. 318424, "FutureID: Shaping the Future of Electronic Identity" (futureid.eu), and by the PRIN 2010–2011 Project "Security Horizons".

© Springer International Publishing Switzerland 2015
C. Bodei et al. (Eds.): Degano Festschrift, LNCS 9465, pp. 66–85, 2015.
DOI: 10.1007/978-3-319-25527-9_7

define the behavior of the participants. This semantics was inspired by the similar works of [14,24], which we further simplify considerably. Our semantics is also subsuming the previous works in the free algebra and limited algebraic reasoning, as they are instances of our semantics for a particular choice of operators and algebraic properties (although this is not easy to show as explained below). We thus see our semantics as one of our main contributions since, from a mathematical point of view, a simple general principle that subsumes the complex definitions of many special cases is the most desirable property of a definition[1].

This simple mathematical semantics, however, cannot be directly used as a translator from Alice-and-Bob notation to formal models or implementations since it entails an infinite representation and several of the underlying algebraic problems are in fact not recursive in general. We thus consider a particular set of operators and their algebraic properties that supports a large class of protocols, including modular exponentiation and multiplication. This theory not only subsumes the theories of previous papers, but also clarifies subtle details of the behavior of operators that were left implicit previously. For this theory, we define a *low-level* semantics that is much more complex than the mathematical *high-level* one but it is computable, and we formally prove that the low-level semantics is a correct implementation of the high-level one. The division into a simple mathematical high-level semantics as a "gold standard" and a low-level "implementable" semantics not only allows for a reasonable correctness criterion of the low-level semantics, but is in our opinion a major advantage over previous works that are a blending between mathematical and technical aspects.

To make our work applicable in practice, we have designed the *Security Protocol Specification language SPS* as a variant of existing Alice-and-Bob languages that contains many novel features valuable in practice. In particular, our notion of *formats* allows us to integrate the particular way of structuring messages of real-world protocols like TLS, rather than academic toy implementations; at the same time, we can use a sound abstraction of these formats in the formal verification. We have implemented the low-level semantics in a translator that can generate both formal models in the input languages of popular security protocol analysis tools (e.g., Applied π calculus in the syntax of ProVerif [10] or ASLAN for AVANTSSAR [5]) and implementations in JavaScript for the execution environment of the FutureID project (www.futureid.eu). We have demonstrated practical feasibility with a number of major and minor case studies, including TLS and the EAC/PACE protocols used in the German eID card.

We proceed as follows: we give the syntax of SPS in Sect. 2 and an extension of strands in Sect. 3. We define the semantics of SPS in Sect. 4 and discuss the connections from SPS to implementations and formal models in Sect. 5. In Sect. 6, we discuss related and future work, and conclude the paper.

---

[1] We have learned that from Pierpaolo Degano, who is renowned for his ability to explain complex things in a simple way.

2   SPS Syntax

In this section, we briefly introduce the syntax of SPS, which we will illustrate by referring to the example protocol specification in SPS given in Listing 1.1, in which two agents A and B use a symmetric key shk(A,B) to establish a fresh Diffie-Hellman key and securely exchange a Payload message.

```
Protocol: example
Types:
    Agent A,B;
    Number g, Payload, X, Y;
Mappings:
    shk: Agent,Agent-> SymmetricKey;
Knowledge:
    A: A, B, shk(A,B), g;
    B: A, B, shk(A,B), g;
Actions:
    A : Number X
    A -> B   : scrypt(shk(A,B), f1(A,B,exp(g,X)))
    B : Number Y
    B -> A   : scrypt(shk(A,B), f1(B,A,exp(g,Y)))
    A : Number Payload
    A -> B   : scrypt(exp(exp(g,Y),X), f2(Payload))
Goals:
    Payload secret of A,B
```

Listing 1.1. Example Protocol in APS

We give the syntax of SPS in EBNF, where we set all meta-symbols in blue and write Xs (for a non-terminal symbol X) to denote a comma-separated list X(, X)* of X elements; CONST and FUNC are alphanumeric strings starting with a lower-case letter (e.g., g and scrypt in the example) and VAR is an alphanumeric string starting with an upper-case letter (e.g., X in the example).

$$
\begin{aligned}
\text{SPS} ::= \ &\textbf{Types :}\ (\text{TYPE IDENT}s;)^* \\
&\textbf{Mappings :}\ (\text{FUNC} : \text{TYPE}s \to \text{TYPE};)^* \\
&\textbf{Formats :}\ (\text{FUNC}(\text{TYPE}s);)^* \\
&\textbf{Knowledge :}\ (\text{ROLE} : \text{MSG}s;)^* [\textbf{where}\ \text{ROLE} \neq \text{ROLE}\ (\ \&\ \text{ROLE} \neq \text{ROLE}\ )^*] \\
&\textbf{Actions :}\ (\ \text{ROLE CHANNEL ROLE} : \text{MSG}\ |\ \text{ROLE} :\ \textbf{TYPE VAR})^* \\
&\textbf{Goals :}\ (\ \text{ROLE}\ \textbf{authenticates}\ \text{ROLE}\ \textbf{on}\ \text{MSG}\ |\ \text{MSG}\ \textbf{secret of}\ \text{ROLE}s\ )^* \\
\\
\text{MSG} ::= \ &\text{CONST}\ |\ \text{VAR}\ |\ \text{FUNC}(\text{MSG}s) \\
\text{IDENT} ::= \ &\text{CONST}\ |\ \text{VAR}\ |\ \text{FUNC} \\
\text{ROLE} ::= \ &\text{CONST}\ |\ \text{VAR} \\
\text{TYPE} ::= \ &\textbf{Agent}\ |\ \textbf{Number}\ |\ \textbf{PublicKey}\ |\ \textbf{PrivateKey}\ |\ \textbf{SymmetricKey}\ |\ \textbf{Bool}\ |\ \textbf{Msg} \\
\text{CHANNEL} ::= \ &[\ \bullet\ ] \to [\ \bullet\ ]
\end{aligned}
$$

We begin our explanation with the atomic elements: constants (CONST) and variables (VAR). One may think of the variables as parameters of a protocol description that must be instantiated for a concrete execution of the protocol; in our example, the variables A and B shall be instantiated with concrete agent names such as a, b or the intruder p[2], whereas X and Y should be instantiated with random numbers that are freshly chosen by A and B, respectively.

In the Types section, all constants and variables are declared with one of the pre-defined types, where the type Msg subsumes all types. By default, the

---

[2] We use p instead of i in honor of our "favorite intruder" Pierpaolo.

interpretation of SPS is *untyped*, i.e., types are used only by the SPS translator to check that the user did not specify any ill-typed terms. The types can however be used to generate a more restrictive typed model and under certain conditions this restriction is without loss of attacks [3]. The type Agent has a special relevance: constants and variables of this type we call *roles*, and the symbol ROLE in the above grammar must only be used for identifiers of type Agent (This is an additional check we cannot directly express in a context-free grammar.).

While the semantics of Alice-and-Bob style languages that we give in the next section is generic for an arbitrary set of function symbols and their algebraic properties, the concrete implementation of SPS is for a set of fixed cryptographic function symbols. These are asymmetric and symmetric encryption (crypt and scrypt), digital signatures (sign), hash and keyed-hash functions (hash and mac), and modular exponentiation (exp) and multiplication (mult). There are of course corresponding operations for decryption and verification, but these are not part of an SPS specification; instead, their use is *derived* by the SPS translator according to the semantics in the next section.

In the Mappings section, one can specify a special kind of function symbols. These do not represent any actual operation that honest agents or the intruder can perform, but are used to describe the pre-existing setup of long-term keys. In our example, the mapping shk assigns to every pair of agents a unique value of type symmetric key; this is the easiest way to define shared keys for agents— including the intruder who will then share keys $shk(p, A)$ and $shk(A, p)$ with every other agent A. Public key infrastructures can be modeled in a similar way.

In the Formats section, one can specify a third kind of function symbols called *formats*. They abstractly represent how the concrete implementation structures the clear-text part of a message, such as XML-tags or explicit message-length fields. A format thus basically represents a concatenation of information, but in contrast to a plain concatenation operator as in other formal languages, the abstract format function symbols allow us to generate implementations with real-world formats such as TLS (see below). In the example, we have two formats: f1 is used to exchange the Diffie-Hellman half-keys together with the agent names, and f2 indicates the transmission of the Payload message. For simplicity, we model a payload message using a fresh random number Payload, representing a placeholder for an arbitrary message (depending on the concrete application); alternatively, this could be modeled using a mapping (e.g., $payload(A, B)$) that A knows initially and sends to B after the key establishment.

The three kinds of function symbols are thus: the cryptographic function symbols, the mappings and the formats. Except for the mappings, these are all *public*: all agents, including the intruder, can apply them to messages they know. Additionally, formats are *transparent*: every agent can extract the fields of a format. We can now build composed messages with these function symbols, where we assume the additional check that all SPS messages are well-typed (and are used with the proper arity). As typing is not essential for this paper, we do not discuss the details of the type expressions.

In the Knowledge section, we specify the *initial knowledge* of each of the protocol roles. This is essential as it determines how (and if) honest agents can execute the protocol. For instance, if in the example we were to omit the item shk(A, B) in the knowledge of role B, then B could not decrypt the first message from A and thus not obtain A's half key. Moreover, in the next step B would be unable to build the response message for A. Also, as we will define below, this specification indirectly determines the initial knowledge of the intruder: if a role is instantiated with p, then the intruder obtains the corresponding knowledge (in our case, all shared keys shk(A, B) where A = p or B = p). We require that all variables in the knowledge section be of type Agent. Finally, one can optionally forbid some instantiations of the roles, e.g., by the side condition A ≠ p or A ≠ B.

The Actions section is the core of the specification: it specifies the messages that are exchanged between the roles. Additionally, we specify here explicitly when agents freshly create new values. In our example, A first creates the secret exponent X for the Diffie-Hellman exchange, computes the half-key exp(g, X), inserts it into format f1 and encrypts the message with the shared key shk(A, B). To send this message, A uses the standard *insecure channel* (denoted with →) on which the intruder can read, intercept, and insert messages arbitrarily. SPS also supports a notion of authentic, confidential, and secure channels as in [24], denoted with •→, →• and •→•, respectively. For instance, one may have specified the exchange of the half-keys without the encryption but using authentic channels where the intruder can see messages, but not insert messages except under his real name. This represents the *assumption* that the messages between A and B cannot be manipulated by an intruder, e.g., in device pairing of mobile devices, when A and B meet physically in a public place. The assumptions are reflected only in the formal model (by restricting the intruder behavior on such channels), while in the implementation it is the duty of the surrounding software module to connect a properly secured channel to the protocol module. One last point about the Actions section is that it shows the simplicity of an SPS specification, i.e., this section is very similar to the way one would informally describe a protocol in Alice and Bob notation.

In the final Goals section, we specify the *goals* the protocol aims to achieve. SPS provides built-in macros for the standard secrecy and authentication goals. In general, we instrument the description with events that reflect what is happening in the protocol execution, e.g., the event secret(A, B, Payload) reflects that Payload is supposed to be a secret between A and B. We then define attack states as predicates over these events. The events allow us to formulate security goals in a protocol-independent way rather than referring to the messages of the protocol.

3   Operational Strands

As a preparation for defining the SPS semantics, we first clarify the target language, i.e., we define an extension of the popular *strands* [28] that we call *operational strands*. For space reasons (and since strands are very intuitive), we only summarize the five extensions we make and point to [4] for details. A concrete example is shown in Fig. 1 and explained below.

First, send and receive steps can be annotated with a channel. Recall that SPS supports default insecure channels as well as authentic, confidential and secure ones. For the SPS semantics, this is only a label on the channels that is left unchanged in the translation; for the semantics of operational strands, the channels mean a restriction on the operations that the intruder can perform on the channel as explained in [4]. In textual representation, we write send(ch, t) and receive(ch, t) for sending and receiving message t over channel ch.

Second, we annotate each strand with the initial knowledge of the role it represents, denoted by a box above the strand (we define knowledge formally in Definition 2). The annotation has no meaning for the behavior of strands and is only needed during the translation process. In textual representation, we write the annotation with the knowledge M as M : *steps* at the beginning of the strand.

Third, recall that the original strand spaces are used to characterize sets of protocol executions and contain only ground terms. In contrast, we use them like a "light-weight" process calculus: terms may contain variables (representing values that are instantiated during the concrete execution). Also, we have the construct fresh X where the variable X will be bound to a fresh value. An important requirement is that operational strands are *closed* in the following sense: every variable must be *bound* by first occurring in the initial knowledge, in a fresh operation, in a macro (that we introduce shortly), or in a receive step. A bound variable must not occur subsequently in a fresh operation (i.e., it cannot be "re-bound"). In contrast, a bound variable may occur in a subsequent receive step, meaning simply that the agent expects the same value that the variable was bound to before.

Fourth, we extend strands with *events* (predicates over terms) to formulate security goals in a protocol-independent way. For instance, as we already remarked above, we may use the event secret(A, B, Payload) to express that message Payload is regarded as a secret between protocol roles A and B. Then we can define (independent of the concrete protocol) a violation of secrecy as a state where the intruder has learned Payload but is neither A nor B. We do not give here more details on goals, because from a semantical point of view we just treat the events as if they were messages on a special channel to a "referee" who decides if the present state is an attack; the handling of these events is uniform for a wide class of goals [3] and only limited by the abilities of current verification tools. In textual representation, we will simply write event(t) where t is a term characterizing the event.

Fifth, we add *checks* of the form $s \doteq t$. The meaning is that the agent can only continue if the terms s and t are equal and aborts otherwise. Also, we have *macros* of the form $\mathcal{X}_i := t$, which mean that we consider the same strand with all occurrences of $\mathcal{X}_i$ replaced by t. This is helpful for generating protocol implementations, because the result of a computation t is stored in a variable $\mathcal{X}_i$ and does not need to be computed again later.

A formal definition of operational strands can be given as a process (interacting with a given environment). In the extended version [4], we define a semantics as state-transition systems similar to [15], where a state $(S; K; E)$ consists of a set S of strands, a set K of messages that the intruder currently knows and a set E of events that have occurred. For instance, if S contains the strand send(insec, t).rest, where insec represents an insecure channel, then we can make the transition to a successor state where t is added to K and the send step is removed from the given strand.

4   SPS Semantics

Above we described the SPS syntax for a fixed set of cryptographic operators (for which we later give a fixed set of algebraic equations). In this section, we give a semantics that is parametrized over an *arbitrary* set of operators and algebraic properties, inspired by [14,24]. One of the main contributions of our work is to give this general definition of a semantics for Alice-and-Bob style languages in a concise, mathematical way that is based on a few simple, general principles. The semantics is a function from SPS to (operational) strands; this function is in general not recursive because many of the underlying algebraic reasoning problems are not. The value of this general definition is its simplicity and uniformity: this is in fact the best mathematical argument why to define a concept in a particular way and not differently. In the next section, we then show that we can actually implement this semantics for the operators of SPS; in fact, we define a "low-level" semantics that is a computable function from SPS to strands (that is however so complicated that we give only an overview in this paper) and prove that it coincides with the general "high-level" semantics.

4.1   Message Model

We define messages as algebraic terms and use the words *message* and *term* interchangeably. We distinguish two kinds of messages: (1) the *protocol messages* that appear in an SPS specification and (2) *labels* (or *recipes*) that are the messages in the strands the semantics translates to. It is necessary to make this distinction as the SPS specification reflects the ideal protocol run, while the semantics reflects the actual actions and checks that an honest agent performs in the run of the protocol. For the same reason, we will also distinguish between two kinds of variables: *protocol variables* and *label variables*.

Definition 1. A *message model* is a four-tuple $(\Sigma, V, \mathcal{L}, \approx)$. Σ is a countable set of *function symbols*, all denoted by lower-case letters, where: $\Sigma_0 \subseteq \Sigma$ is a countable set of *constants*, $\Sigma_p \subseteq \Sigma$ is a finite set of *public operators* such as public-key encryption, and $\Sigma_m \subseteq \Sigma$ is a finite set of *mappings* (or *private operators*), disjoint from Σ_p. We assume a global public constant $\top \in \Sigma_p \cap \Sigma_0$. V is a countable set of *protocol variables*. $\mathcal{L} = \{\mathcal{X}_1, \mathcal{X}_2, \mathcal{X}_3 \ldots\}$ is a countable set of *label variables* disjoint from Σ and V. $\approx$ is a congruence relation over *ground* *terms* over Σ (i.e., terms without variables), which are denoted by $\mathcal{T}_\Sigma$. A *term* is thus a constant, a variable, or an application of a function (of Σ) on a term, and we write $\mathcal{T}_S(A)$ for the set of terms over signature S and variables from set A.

As we define in a deduction relation below, the public operators in Σ_p are those functions that every agent and the intruder can apply to messages they know, i.e., the cryptographic operators (including operators for decryption that do not occur in the SPS specification) and the non-cryptographic formats. In contrast, the mappings in Σ_m are private, like shk in our example protocol that maps from two agents to their shared secret key, or inv that maps from public to private keys.

Table 1. Example of an equational theory $\approx$

(1)	$\mathtt{dscrypt}(k,\ \mathtt{scrypt}(k,m)) \approx m$	(2)	$\mathtt{vscrypt}(k,\ \mathtt{scrypt}(k,m)) \approx \top$
(3)	$\mathtt{dcrypt}(\mathtt{inv}(k),\ \mathtt{crypt}(k,m)) \approx m$	(4)	$\mathtt{vcrypt}(\mathtt{inv}(k),\ \mathtt{crypt}(k,m)) \approx \top$
(5)	$\mathtt{open}(\mathtt{sign}(k,m)) \approx m$	(6)	$\mathtt{vsign}(k,\mathtt{sign}(\mathtt{inv}(k),m)) \approx \top$
For every $\mathtt{f} \in \Sigma_f$ with arity n and for every $i \in \{1,\dots,n\}$			
(7)	$\mathtt{get}_{i,\mathtt{f}}(\mathtt{f}(t_1,\dots,t_n)) \approx t_i$	(8)	$\mathtt{verify}_\mathtt{f}(\mathtt{f}(t_1,\dots,t_n)) \approx \top$
(9)	$\mathtt{exp}(\mathtt{exp}(t_1,t_2),t_3)) \approx \mathtt{exp}(t_1,\mathtt{mult}(t_2,t_3))$	(10)	$\mathtt{mult}(t_1,t_2) \approx \mathtt{mult}(t_2,t_1)$
(11)	$\mathtt{mult}(t_1,\mathtt{mult}(t_2,t_3)) \approx \mathtt{mult}(\mathtt{mult}(t_1,t_2),t_3)$		

Example 1. As a concrete example of a message model that is representative for a large class of security protocols, let Σ_p contain all operators of the equations in Table 1, where $\approx$ is the least congruence relation satisfying the equations. For instance, scrypt represents symmetric encryption, dscrypt is the corresponding decryption operator and vscrypt is a *verifier*: given a term t and a key k, it tells us whether t is a valid symmetric encryption with key k. This models the fact that most symmetric ciphers include measures to detect when the decryption fails (e.g., when it is actually not an encrypted message or the given key is not correct) and in concrete implementations this verification will be part of the call to dscrypt. We emphasize that our message model explicitly describes such fine details that most security protocol analysis tools silently assume; we could similarly define a set of primitives that do not allow verification and the semantics will accordingly define which verifications honest agents can and cannot do.

Similarly, the operators crypt, dcrypt and vcrypt formalize asymmetric encryption, and sign, open and vsign formalize digital signatures.

Let $\Sigma_f \subseteq \Sigma_p$ be a set of formats declared in an SPS specification. Then, for each format $f \in \Sigma_f$ of arity n, $\mathtt{get}_{i,\mathtt{f}} \in \Sigma_p$ is an *extraction function* for the i-th field of the format (for all $1 \leq i \leq n$) and $\mathtt{verify}_\mathtt{f} \in \Sigma_p$ is a verifier to check that a given message has format $\mathtt{f}$.

Moreover, we have exp and mult for modular exponentiation and multiplication as needed in many Diffie-Hellman-based protocols. As is often done, we omit the modulus for ease of notation. Σ_p also contains hash and mac representing hash and keyed hash functions, respectively (hash and mac do not appear in

Table 1 since they have no algebraic properties). Finally, a typical set of mappings could be: shk : Agent × Agent → SymmetricKey to denote a shared key of two agents, pk : Agent → PublicKey for the public key of an agent, and inv : PublicKey → PrivateKey for the private key corresponding to a given public key. Although pk is typically publicly available, it should not be a public operator as it does not correspond to a computation that honest agents or the intruder can perform (rather the initial distribution of keys should be specified in the knowledge section of SPS).   □

Definition 2. A *labeled message* t^l consists of a *protocol message* $t \in \mathcal{T}_\Sigma(V)$ and a *label* $l \in \mathcal{T}_{\Sigma_p}(\mathcal{L})$. A *knowledge* is a substitution of the form $M = [\mathcal{X}_1 \mapsto t_1, \ldots, \mathcal{X}_n \mapsto t_n]$, where $\mathcal{X}_i \in \mathcal{L}$ and $t_i \in \mathcal{T}_\Sigma(V)$. We call the set $\{\mathcal{X}_1, \ldots, \mathcal{X}_n\}$ the *domain* of M and write $|M| = n$ for the *length* of M. We may also refer to M as a set of entries and write, e.g., $M \cup \{\mathcal{X}_j \mapsto t_j\}$ to add a new entry (where $\mathcal{X}_j$ is not in the domain of M).

Intuitively, the label variables represent *memory locations* of an honest agent. A label l is composed from label variables and public operators, and reflects what actions an honest agent has performed on elements of its knowledge. A labeled message t^l expresses that an honest agent performed the actions of l to obtain what the SPS specification represents by the term t. For instance, we represent the initial knowledge of A in Listing 1.1 by $[\mathcal{X}_1 \mapsto A, \mathcal{X}_2 \mapsto B, \mathcal{X}_3 \mapsto \text{shk}(A, B), \mathcal{X}_4 \mapsto g]$ to express that A stores her name and B's name in her memory locations $\mathcal{X}_1$ and $\mathcal{X}_2$, a key shared with B in $\mathcal{X}_3$, and the group g in $\mathcal{X}_4$.

4.2   Message Derivation and Checking

We now define how *honest* agents can derive terms from their knowledge. This is in the style of Dolev-Yao deduction relations, but extended to labeled messages to keep track of the operations that have been applied. The relation has the form $M \vdash t^l$ where M is a knowledge and t^l a labeled term.[3]

Definition 3. $\vdash$ *is the least relation that satisfies the following rules:*

$$\frac{}{M \vdash t^{\mathcal{X}_i}} \; Ax, \quad \frac{M \vdash t^l}{M \vdash s^m} \; Eq, \quad \frac{M \vdash t_1^{l_1} \; \ldots \; M \vdash t_n^{l_n}}{M \vdash f(t_1, \ldots, t_n)^{f(l_1, \ldots, l_n)}} \; Cmp,$$

$[\mathcal{X}_i \mapsto t] \in M \qquad s \approx t, l \approx m \qquad f \in \Sigma_p$

The rule Ax expresses that an agent can deduce any message that it has in its knowledge, Eq expresses that deduction is closed under equivalence in $\approx$ (on terms and their labels), and Cmp allows agents to apply any public operator to deducible terms.

---

[3] One may employ an entirely different model for the intruder (e.g., a cryptographic one); using a Dolev-Yao style deduction for honest agents is simply the semantic decision that they perform only standard public operations (that would be part of a crypto API), but no operations that would amount to cryptographic attacks.

Example 2. As an example, consider again the algebraic theory of Table 1 and the knowledge $M = [\mathcal{X}_1 \mapsto \mathtt{k}, \mathcal{X}_2 \mapsto \mathtt{X}, \mathcal{X}_3 \mapsto \mathtt{scrypt}(\mathtt{k}, \mathtt{exp}(\mathtt{g}, \mathtt{Y}))]$. M contains three messages (or "memory locations") $\mathcal{X}_1, \ldots, \mathcal{X}_3$ that we associate with the corresponding messages of the SPS specification. We explain later how to reach a particular memory state, but for the intuition let us just consider an example scenario that would produce M for an agent A: the constant $\mathtt{k}$ could be part of the initial knowledge of A, $\mathtt{X}$ could be her secret Diffie-Hellman exponent, and the message stored in $\mathcal{X}_3$ could be what she received from another agent— *supposedly* the Diffie-Hellman half-key $\mathtt{exp}(\mathtt{g}, \mathtt{Y})$ encrypted with the key $\mathtt{k}$. The tricky part here is that in general A will be unable to check that the received message has the correct form (i.e., that she did not receive just some garbage); it is part of the semantics to describe what A can check and what messages she will construct on the basis of the labels $\mathcal{X}_1, \ldots, \mathcal{X}_3$. Let us for instance consider the case that A should now—according to the SPS specification—generate the Diffie-Hellman full-key $t = \mathtt{exp}(\mathtt{exp}(\mathtt{g}, \mathtt{X}), \mathtt{Y})$. That amounts to finding a label l such that $M \vdash t^l$, i.e., that *would* produce the Diffie-Hellman key, if the received message has the required form. Indeed, there is such a label as the following proof tree shows:

$$
\cfrac{
  \cfrac{M \vdash \mathtt{X}^{\mathcal{X}_2} \; Ax \qquad \cfrac{\cfrac{M \vdash \mathtt{k}^{\mathcal{X}_1} \; Ax \qquad M \vdash \mathtt{scrypt}(\mathtt{k}, \mathtt{exp}(\mathtt{g}, \mathtt{Y}))^{\mathcal{X}_3} \; Ax}{M \vdash \mathtt{dscrypt}(\mathtt{k}, \mathtt{scrypt}(\mathtt{k}, \mathtt{exp}(\mathtt{g}, \mathtt{Y})))^{\mathtt{dscrypt}(\mathcal{X}_1, \mathcal{X}_3)}} \; Cmp}{M \vdash \mathtt{exp}(\mathtt{g}, \mathtt{Y})^{\mathtt{dscrypt}(\mathcal{X}_1, \mathcal{X}_3)}} \; Eq
  }{M \vdash \mathtt{exp}(\mathtt{exp}(\mathtt{g}, \mathtt{Y}), \mathtt{X})^{\mathtt{exp}(\mathtt{dscrypt}(\mathcal{X}_1, \mathcal{X}_3), \mathcal{X}_2)}} \; Cmp
}{M \vdash \mathtt{exp}(\mathtt{exp}(\mathtt{g}, \mathtt{X}), \mathtt{Y})^{\mathtt{exp}(\mathtt{dscrypt}(\mathcal{X}_1, \mathcal{X}_3), \mathcal{X}_2)}} \; Eq
$$

In fact, we see the "recipe" to generate the term $\mathtt{exp}(\mathtt{exp}(\mathtt{g}, \mathtt{X}), \mathtt{Y})$ in the label $\mathtt{exp}(\mathtt{dscrypt}(\mathcal{X}_1, \mathcal{X}_3), \mathcal{X}_2)$, i.e., A has to first apply decryption to term $\mathcal{X}_3$ using the term $\mathcal{X}_1$ as decryption key; if the received $\mathcal{X}_3$ message was indeed of the right form, this gives the other agent's half-key ($\mathtt{exp}(\mathtt{g}, \mathtt{Y})$ in SPS), and this is further exponentiated with $\mathcal{X}_2$ to supposedly yield the full key ($\mathtt{exp}(\mathtt{exp}(\mathtt{g}, \mathtt{Y}), \mathtt{X})$ in SPS). Note that the semantics also tells us what happens if A in the actual execution receives some improper term for $\mathcal{X}_3$: she will simply apply the operations to it as prescribed and that may lead for instance to the protocol getting stuck (if nobody else can generate the key) or to an attack (if the intruder manages to find a term that breaks some security goals), or the garbage term may actually be detected by the checks on messages that we describe next, which in this example amounts to checking that the given term is indeed an encryption with the right key.   □

The definition of the checks that honest agents can make on their knowledge is in fact based on the deduction relation $\vdash$. The checks will be written as equations between terms. To that end, we introduce the symbol $\doteq$ and define $\doteq$-*equations* as follows: an *interpretation* $\mathcal{I}$ is a total mapping from $\mathcal{L}$ to $\mathcal{T}_\Sigma(V)$ that we extend to a function from $\mathcal{T}_\Sigma(V \cup \mathcal{L})$ to $\mathcal{T}_\Sigma(V)$ as expected; then we define $\mathcal{I} \models s \doteq t$ iff $\mathcal{I}(s) \approx \mathcal{I}(t)$, and extend this to (finite or infinite) conjunctions of equations

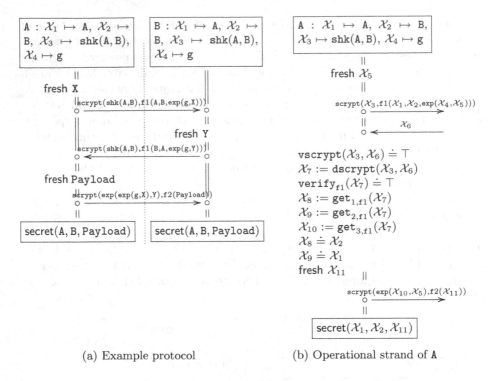

(a) Example protocol   (b) Operational strand of A

Fig. 1. (a) Example protocol, (b) Operational strand of A

as expected. We define $\phi \models \psi$ iff $\mathcal{I} \models \phi$ implies $\mathcal{I} \models \psi$ for every interpretation $\mathcal{I}$; and $\phi \equiv \psi$ iff both $\phi \models \psi$ and $\psi \models \phi$.

Definition 4. We define a *complete set of checks* $ccs(M)$ for a knowledge M as follows: $ccs(M) = \bigwedge\{l_1 \doteq l_2 \mid \exists\, m \in \mathcal{T}_\Sigma(V). M \vdash m^{l_1} \wedge M \vdash m^{l_2}\}$.

$ccs(M)$ yields an infinite conjunction of checks that an agent can perform on his knowledge. Intuitively, $M \vdash m^{l_1}$ and $M \vdash m^{l_2}$ expresses that, according to the SPS specification, computing l_1 and l_2 *should* yield the same result m, and the agent can thus check that they actually do. For instance, consider $M = [\mathcal{X}_1 \mapsto k, \mathcal{X}_2 \mapsto \mathsf{hash}(m), \mathcal{X}_3 \mapsto \mathsf{scrypt}(k,m)]$. Amongst others, $ccs(M)$ then entails the checks $\phi = \mathsf{vscrypt}(\mathcal{X}_1, \mathcal{X}_3) \doteq \top \wedge \mathsf{hash}(\mathsf{dscrypt}(\mathcal{X}_1, \mathcal{X}_3)) \doteq \mathcal{X}_2$, i.e., the agent A can verify that $\mathcal{X}_3$ is an encryption and that $\mathcal{X}_2$ is the hash of the content of the encrypted message $\mathcal{X}_3$. Note that there are many more equations (e.g., $\mathcal{X}_1 \doteq \mathcal{X}_1$) and for every equation $s \doteq t$, we also have $h(s) \doteq h(t)$ for every unary public operator h. However, it holds that $ccs(M) \equiv \phi$, i.e., $ccs(M)$ is logically equivalent to ϕ and thus all other checks are redundant.

4.3 High-Level Semantics

Now we can put everything together to define the semantics of SPS specifications by translation to operational strands. Figure 1(a) shows our example protocol in the style of message sequence charts. The first step towards an operational semantics is to split the protocol into different strands, one for each role, as indicated in Fig. 1(a) by the dotted line. We refer to the resulting strands as *plain strands*. Each plain strand shows how the protocol looks like from the point of view of that role in an ideal protocol run: what messages it is supposed to send and what messages it receives. The second step towards the operational semantics is to identify the precise set of actions, i.e., how messages are composed or decomposed, and what checks need to be performed on received messages. Figure 1(b) shows how this operational description looks like for role A of the example (role B is very similar). Now we define the *high-level semantics* as a function $\llbracket \cdot \rrbracket_H$ (with initial case $\llbracket \cdot \rrbracket_{H_0}$) that maps from plain strands like (a) to the operational strands like (b).

In a nutshell, we use the labeled deduction $M \vdash t^l$ to define how an agent composes an outgoing message (or event), and we use the *ccs* function whenever an agent receives a new message, formalizing the set of checks that the agent can perform at this point. Note that this is an infinite conjunction and we later show how to obtain an equivalent finite conjunction for the example theory.

Definition 5. $\llbracket \cdot \rrbracket_H$ *translates from plain to operational strands as follows:*

$$\llbracket M : strand \rrbracket_{H_0} = M : ccs(M).\llbracket strand \rrbracket_H(M)$$
$$\llbracket receive(ch, t).rest \rrbracket_H(M) = receive(ch, \mathcal{X}_{|M|+1}).ccs(M \cup [\mathcal{X}_{|M|+1} \mapsto t]).$$
$$\llbracket rest \rrbracket_H(M \cup [\mathcal{X}_{|M|+1} \mapsto t])$$
$$\llbracket send(ch, t).rest \rrbracket_H(M) = send(ch, l).\llbracket rest \rrbracket_H(M) \text{ where } M \vdash t^l \text{ for some label } l$$
$$\llbracket event(t).rest \rrbracket_H(M) = event(l).\llbracket rest \rrbracket_H(M) \text{ where } M \vdash t^l \text{ for some label } l$$
$$\llbracket fresh \ X.rest \rrbracket_H(M) = fresh \ \mathcal{X}_{|M|+1}.\llbracket rest \rrbracket_H(M \cup \{\mathcal{X}_{|M|+1} \mapsto X\})$$
$$\llbracket 0 \rrbracket_H(M) = 0$$

The first rule initializes the translation, by computing the checks that can be made on the initial knowledge of the strands. The second rule says that each received message is associated with a new label variable $\mathcal{X}_{|M|+1}$ in the agent's knowledge and afterwards we use *ccs* to generate all checks that the agent can perform on the augmented knowledge. The third rule is for sending the SPS protocol message t. Here we use the relation $M \vdash t^l$ to require that the agent can generate the required term t from the current knowledge M using the concrete sequence of actions l; this is explained in more detail below. The event rule is very similar to sending. The fifth rule translates the construct fresh X: we simply pick a new label variable $\mathcal{X}_{|M|+1}$ that will store the fresh value in the translated strand, and bind it in the knowledge to the protocol variable X. The final rule is straightforward.

Let us continue Example 2, where we considered an agent with knowledge $M = [\mathcal{X}_1 \mapsto k, \mathcal{X}_2 \mapsto X, \mathcal{X}_3 \mapsto scrypt(k, exp(g, Y))]$. (As explained above, this may result from a strand that initially knows a key in $\mathcal{X}_1$, has freshly generated an exponent $\mathcal{X}_2$, and has received the message $\mathcal{X}_3$.) Suppose that the next step is $send(insec, exp(exp(g, X), Y))$ (in fact, in a more realistic example, it would be a message encrypted with this term as a key). The semantics tells us to determine any label l such that $M \vdash exp(exp(g, X), Y)^l$, which is possible for the label $l = exp(dscrypt(\mathcal{X}_1, \mathcal{X}_3), \mathcal{X}_2)$ as shown in the example previously. Thus, the translation can be in this case send(insec, $\exp(\mathrm{dscrypt}(\mathcal{X}_1, \mathcal{X}_3), \mathcal{X}_2)$). Note that we said *"can"* here, because there are other labels, e.g., any label l' such that $l \approx l'$.

More generally, given M and t, there is in general not a unique l such that $M \vdash t^l$. First, consider the case that there is no such l. In this case, the agent has no means (within the deduction relation) to obtain the term t from its current knowledge. We thus say the protocol is *non-executable* and its semantics is undefined. This executability check is an important sanity check on SPS specifications, ensuring that all steps of the protocol can actually be performed at least when no intruder is interfering and the network does not loose messages. Other formal specification language like Applied π that specify the different roles separately as processes cannot have such an executability check, because unlike SPS, there is no formal relationship between the messages that one role is sending and another is receiving. Thus, if a modeler accidentally specifies messages slightly differently in two processes, they may be unable to communicate and get stuck in their execution; then a flawed protocol may be trivially verified as secure because of the specification mistake. The executability check in SPS drastically reduces the chance of such mistakes.

Second, if there is a label l, then there will typically be infinitely many of them (trivially by performing redundant encryptions and decryptions). Our semantics does not prescribe which of the labels has to be taken (and the implementation below will take in some sense the simplest one). A key insight is that this does not make the semantics ambiguous: if $M \vdash t^{l_1}$ and $M \vdash t^{l_2}$ then $ccs(M) \models l_1 \doteq l_2$. Thus, since we always perform the checks on the knowledge after each received message, we know that the choice of labels does not make a difference.

As an example, observe that the operational strand we have given in Fig. 1(b) for our example protocol is correct according to this semantics (when resolving the $\mathcal{X} := t$ macros): all outgoing messages have an appropriate label (for which $M \vdash t^l$ holds), and all checks $s \doteq t$ do indeed logically follow from $ccs(M)$ for the respective M. In fact, we claim that the checks are logically equivalent to $ccs(M)$, i.e., all other checks are redundant; it is part of the results of the next section to prove that and derive the given checks automatically.

We emphasize the succinctness of the definitions: Definitions 2–5 together fit on half a page and yet we define the semantics for an arbitrary set of cryptographic operators and algebraic properties. We believe that this is the best argument that the semantics of Alice-and-Bob notation should be defined this way—deriving from simple, general, uniform principles. However, this simple semantics cannot be directly used as a translator from Alice-and-Bob notation to formal models or implementations as it entails an infinite representation and several of the underlying algebraic problems are in fact not recursive in general.

Theorem 1. *For a given strand S, the problem to compute a finite representation of $[\![S]\!]_H$, if it exists, is not recursive.*

Proof Sketch. It is immediate that $\vdash$ is in general an undecidable relation (take an undecidable $\approx$). Similarly, the relation $\{(M, s, t) \mid ccs(M) \models s \doteq t\}$ is undecidable. It follows that for given a knowledge M, the problem to compute a finite conjunction ϕ, such that $\phi \equiv ccs(M)$, if one exists, is not recursive.   □

4.4 Implementing the Semantics

Despite this general undecidability result, for a special theory we can give a more low-level, procedural semantics that is actually computable and prove that it correctly implements the high-level semantics. More specifically, we now sketch how to actually compute the semantics for the example theory in Table 1 and where we additionally require that the SPS specification (and thus the plain strands) does not contain any destructors or verifiers.

Theorem 2. *For our example theory in Table 1, for every strand S in which no destructors or verifiers occur, $[\![S]\!]_H$ can be finitely represented and it is recursive.*

Implementation/Constructive Proof. First we split the problem into a *constructor* and a *destructor/verifier* part (note they are not independent, e.g., in order to decrypt a message one may need to first compose a key). We also split the example theory into (i) equations C that describe destructors and verifiers (the first 8 equations in the Table 1) and (ii) equations F that just "rearrange" terms (the remaining equations). We then use equations C as rewrite rules and apply them modulo F (working on F-equivalence classes); the resulting rewrite relation $\rightarrow_{C/F}$ is convergent and we consider only normalized terms.

For our example theory (Table 1), we define two functions, $compose_M(t)$ and $analyze(M, \varphi)$. First, $compose_M(t)$ implements the "constructor" part of the $\vdash$ relation: find all labels l such that $M \vdash t^l$ when using only constructors of Σ_p (no destructors and verifiers) and using only equations from F. Note that the set of such labels l is always finite. Second, $analyze(M, \varphi)$ starts with a knowledge M and a set of checks φ that have already been performed (so they do not need to be checked again). It computes a pair (M', φ'). Here, M' is an *analyzed* extension by all subterms that can be obtained by applying destructors and normalizing the result; for this purpose, *analyze* calls the *compose* function to compose decryption keys when necessary. Also, for each decryption, the analysis will produce as part of φ' a new macro $\mathcal{X}_i := l$, where $\mathcal{X}_i$ is the label variable in the augmented knowledge that holds the result of the decryption and l is the recipe for obtaining it. Similarly, for each such decomposition step, we have a check from the respective verifier that is also added to φ'. Further, *analyze* will check for every term whether there is a different way to compose it (using again the *compose* function) and, if so, generate the according checks. Finally, for all pairs of terms where the root operator is mult (and analogously for exp), we must check if the least common multiple can be generated from each of them. For instance, knowing $[\mathcal{X}_1 \mapsto ab, \mathcal{X}_2 \mapsto ac, \mathcal{X}_3 \mapsto b, \mathcal{X}_4 \mapsto c]$, we can derive the check $\mathcal{X}_1 \mathcal{X}_4 \doteq \mathcal{X}_2 \mathcal{X}_3$.

We then show that for an analyzed knowledge, every derivable term can be derived using only *compose* and the checks resulting from *analyze* are equivalent to those of *ccs* modulo resolving the macros that *analyze* generates. Based on this, we obtain the following computable low-level semantics that translates from plain strands to operational strands and mirrors the structure of the high-level semantics:

$$
\begin{aligned}
[\![M:strand]\!]_{L_0}(\emptyset, \top) &= M : \varphi.[\![strand]\!]_L(M', \varphi) \text{ where } (M', \varphi) = analyze(M, \top) \\
[\![receive(ch, t).rest]\!]_L(M, \varphi) &= receive(ch, \mathcal{X}_{|M|+1}).\varphi'.[\![rest]\!]_L(M', (\varphi \wedge \varphi')) \\
&\quad \text{where } (M', \varphi \wedge \varphi') = analyze(M \cup [\mathcal{X}_{|M|+1} \mapsto t], \varphi) \\
[\![send(ch, t).rest]\!]_L(M, \varphi) &= send(ch, l).[\![rest]\!]_L(M, \varphi) \text{ where } l \in compose_M(t) \\
[\![event(t).rest]\!]_L(M, \varphi) &= event(l).[\![rest]\!]_L(M, \varphi) \text{ where } l \in compose_M(t) \\
[\![fresh\ X.rest]\!]_L(M, \varphi) &= fresh\ \mathcal{X}_{|M|+1}.[\![rest]\!]_L(M \cup \{\mathcal{X}_{|M|+1} \mapsto X\}, \varphi) \\
[\![0]\!]_L(M, \varphi) &= 0
\end{aligned}
$$

The full details of *compose* and *analyze* and the proofs of their correctness can be found in [4]. Based on this, we also prove that the two levels of our semantics ($[\![\cdot]\!]_H$ and $[\![\cdot]\!]_L$) coincide, i.e., given the same plain strand as input, they produce equivalent operational strands.   □

5   Translations from Operational Strands

We now come to the "last mile" of the translation: to translate operational strands into an actual implementation and into a formal model for automated verification. Figure 2 shows this translation for the role A of our example in Fig. 1(b); as target languages we have here JavaScript for protocol implementations and Applied π for the formal model[4].

One can easily see a very close correspondence between the two translations: roughly, they both use the same operators in the same way, only in the formal model they are function symbols in an "abstract" term algebra, whereas in the implementation they are *corresponding* API calls. It is one of the contributions of this work to achieve such a close correspondence. While the use of crypto-APIs is of course standard, our notion of formats extends this API idea also to the non-cryptographic operations: all the technical details of parsing and pretty-printing are hidden in the classes for the given formats. Of course, just like the crypto-API, also the "non-crypto-APIs" require a robust implementation (that does not suffer from buffer overflows, for instance), but we want to argue that our setup with APIs is a suitable way to "cut the cake".

The close correspondence allow us to argue that there is no systematic discrepancy between formal model and implementation, if the function symbols have the corresponding meaning—but that is indeed subtle. Comparing the translation with the input strand of Fig. 1(b), there are only two significant differences: all the explicit verifiers of the strands are removed and the implementation does not contain events; besides that, the translation is mainly adapting to the syntax of the target language. For this reason, we do not give here a

---

[4] One may argue that JavaScript is not suitable for implementing security protocols, but in fact, using systematic mechanisms such as our formats, we can produce robust implementations that do not suffer from type flaw attacks, for instance. It is relatively easy to adapt to other languages like Java or the AVANTSSAR Platform [5], e.g., for using the tool OFMC, for which we have implemented a connector.

formal definition of the translation functions to JavaScript and Applied π (that can be found in [4]), but only discuss a few interesting aspects.

5.1 Experimental Results

The translator has been implemented as part of the FutureID project and is available at [4]. In the project, we have considered several real-world case studies such as the TLS handshake [16] as one of the most widely used protocols, the protocols EAC and PACE [19] that are used by the German eID card, and 30 smaller protocols. In particular, for our main case studies TLS, EAC and PACE, we did implement the precise message formats of the standards [18]. As part of FutureID, an execution environment has been defined that invokes the JavaScript code with suitable values for the parameters [17]. For the formal verification, we have used our case studies to check that ProVerif finds the known attacks in the small examples and verifies all other protocols. The entire test suite runs in less that 11 s on a 2.67 GHz machine.

5.2 JavaScript Translation

Crypto API. We of course rely on the execution environment to have suitable implementations of the cryptographic primitives, e.g., the exp operator will in fact be mapped to elliptic curve cryptography. We assume that the call dscrypt(k, m) will fail (aborting execution) if m is not a message encrypted with key k. This is why we do not include verifier checks in this translation. For simplicity, we omitted the optional annotation of primitives with the precise algorithm and key length (that is only necessary when using different ones in the same protocol).

Formats. The notion of formats allows us to integrate the actual message formats of real-world protocols like TLS. Similar to the cryptographic operators, we also rely on an API and implementation of non-cryptographic operators: for each format declared in the specification, we require a Java class that basically contains a parser and a pretty printer for that format (a.k.a. serialization/deserialization). For the example format f1 the class f1 must have three member variables of type byte string to represent the three fields of the form (as raw data). It must have two constructors: the first takes three strings as input and just stores them in the member variables (cf. the first new f1 in the example), the second takes a single string and tries to parse it as format f1, and this may fail (cf. the second new f1 in the example). Further, we have the get$i$() functions to obtain the i-th field and encode() to output a string. For a more detailed discussion of formats and TLS see [26].

5.3 Applied π Translation

Algebraic Properties. Let us start with the most subtle problem: the algebraic properties of the cryptographic and non-cryptographic operators. We can express

```
function proc_A(X1,X2,X3,X4,ch){    let proc_A(x1,x2,x3,x4:bitstring,ch:Chann)=
  Number   X5 = genNumber();          new x5:bitstring;
  ch.send(scrypt(X3,new f1(X1,X2,      out(ch,scrypt(x3,f1(x1,x2,
    exp(X4,X5))).encode()));             exp(x4,x5))));
  var X6 = ch.receive();              in(ch,x6:bitstring);
  var X7 = dscrypt(X3, X6);           let x7:bitstring = dscrypt(x3,x6) in
  f1 X7a = new f1(X7);
  var X8 = X7a.get1();                let x8:bitstring = f1get1(x7) in
  var X9 = X7a.get2();                let x9:bitstring = f1get2(x7) in
  var X10 = X7a.get3();               let x10:bitstring = f1get3(x7) in
  if(X8 != X2) error();              if(x8 = x2) then
  if(X9 != X1) error();              if(x9 = x1) then
  Number   X11 = genNumber();         new x11:bitstring;
  ch.send(scrypt(exp(X10,X5),         out(ch,scrypt(exp(x10,x5),
    new f2(X11).encode()));             f2(x11)));
                                      event secret(x1,x2,x11);
}                                     0.  .
```

Fig. 2. Translation to JavaScript and Applied π Calculus of role A of the example

cancelation, e.g., reduc forall m, k : bitstring; $\mathrm{dscrypt}(k, \mathrm{scrypt}(k, m)) = m$. (and the translator will automatically generate corresponding rules for the get-functions of the declared formats). However, during the verification process of ProVerif, where processes get translated into Horn clauses, these destructors get encoded into pattern matching—in the Horn clauses occur no destructors or verifiers. This transformation corresponds to an implicit verifier: in our example, the let x7 clause will fail if the message x6 is not of the form $\mathrm{scrypt}(x3, \cdot)$. Thus, also the ProVerif translation does not have verifiers. While this is expressing the algebraic theory we want at this point, directly formulating the equations for exp and mult, ProVerif will not terminate. For standard Diffie-Hellman, it is sound to restrict ourselves to the following equation that works with ProVerif [21, 25]:

$$\mathtt{equation\ forall\ x, y : bitstring;}\ \exp(\exp(g, x), y) = \exp(\exp(g, y), x).$$

The translator can only give a warning when the SPS specification is outside the fragment for which the soundness result holds.

Process Instantiation. We formulate all possible instantiations of the protocol: every role can be played by any agent, including the intruder, and we want to allow for any number of sessions of the protocol in parallel. It is not trivial to specify this manually, but the SPS compiler offers a systematic way to generate the instantiation. Recall that the initial knowledge of each role in the SPS specification can only contain variables of type Agent and long-term keys have to be specified using functions like shk. This allows us to instantiate the knowledge for any value of the role variables. For our example, we have the following specification (where the free name pub represents an insecure channel):

```
process
!new x:bitstring;out(pub,x)|
  !in(pub,(b:bitstring));proc_A(x,b,shk(x,b),g,pub)|
    out(pub,(p,b,shk(p,b),g))|
  !in(ch,(a:bitstring));proc_B(a,x,shk(a,x),g,pub)|
    out(pub,(a,p,shk(a,p),g))
```

The first replication operator generates an unbounded number of honest agent names (in variable x) that are broadcast on pub. Then we generate an unbounded number of instances of proc_A for each x and each name b that we receive from the public channel (thus, the intruder can choose who will play role B). We also output on pub the initial knowledge that the intruder needs for playing role A under his real name p. The last two lines are similar for role B.

6   Conclusions and Related Work

The formal definition of languages based on the Alice-and-Bob notation requires one to identify the concrete set of actions that honest agents have to perform, which is relevant both for a formal model for verification and for generating implementations. Previous works have proposed fairly involved deduction systems for this purpose and there is no (even informal) justification why these systems would be suitable definitions. Our high-level semantics $[\![\cdot]\!]_H$, inspired by [14,24], gives a mathematically succinct and uniform definition of Alice-and-Bob notation following a few general principles, and at the same time it supports an arbitrary set of operators and algebraic properties. The succinctness and generality is, in our opinion, a strong argument for this semantics as a standard. As $[\![\cdot]\!]_H$ entails problems that are not recursively computable in general, we defined the low-level semantics $[\![\cdot]\!]_L$ for a particular theory and proved its correctness with respect to $[\![\cdot]\!]_H$. While $[\![\cdot]\!]_L$ is similar (and similarly involved) as previous definitions of semantics for the Alice-and-Bob notation [7,12,13,20,22,23], we are the first to give a complete formal treatment of the key algebraic properties for destructors, verifies, exponentiation and multiplication[5].

With respect to other implementation generators like [27,29], our key improvements are as follows. First, we give a uniform way to generate both formal models and implementation from the operational strands, ensuring a one-to-one correspondence between them. Second, replacing the abstract concatenation operator from formal models with formats allows us to generate code for any real-world structuring mechanism like XML formats or TLS-style messages. The only work that provides similar features is [6], which however starts at the π calculus level, comparable to the output of our low-level semantics. In reference to works that consider the verification of the actual implementation source code like [8], we agree with [9] that the converse problem, i.e., turning formal models into code like in this paper, is harder. However, in the case of SPS this extra effort takes a large part of the burden off the user, i.e., SPS carries the task of formally verifiable implementations to a higher level of abstraction without suffering from flaws that are abstracted away in the formal model.

Finally, we point out a strong similarity between our notion of knowledge and the notion of *frames* in Applied π calculus [2]. We allow ourselves minor

---

[5] Interestingly also the Festschrift for José Meseguer this year received a treatment of Alice and Bob notation [7] that is very similar to our low-level semantics $[\![\cdot]\!]_L$, however cannot handle exponentiation and multiplication. Thus, we can conclude that Pierpaolo received a strictly stronger Festschrift.

deviations from the frame concept, in particular not using *name restrictions*; instead, constants are by default not public in our setting. This makes the treatment in this paper easier but does not fundamentally change the concept (or its expressive power). For what concerns existing decision results for frames, the deduction relation $\vdash$ has been studied, e.g., in [1]. It is known that deduction is decidable for convergent subterm theories (like our equations (1)–(8)) and that disjoint associate-commutative operators as in (9)–(11) can easily be combined with it. Many results consider the static equivalence of frames which is interesting for privacy properties, namely whether the intruder is able to distinguish two frames ("knowledges"). In the SPS semantics, we have a substantially different problem to solve: we have only one knowledge M (and it is the knowledge of an honest agent) and we need to finitely characterize $ccs(M)$, i.e., what checks the agent can make on M to ensure that all received messages have the required shape. This indeed has some similar traits to static equivalence: also here one has to check pairs of recipes (albeit with respect to two frames). Despite this similarity, the problems are so different that it seems not directly possible to re-use decision procedures for static equivalence for computing $ccs(M)$. Moreover, our exp/mult theory is not yet supported in static equivalence results. A further investigation and generalization, namely with inverses for mult, is part of our ongoing research.

References

1. Abadi, M., Cortier, V.: Deciding knowledge in security protocols under equational theories. Theoret. Comput. Sci. **367**(1–2), 2–32 (2006)
2. Abadi, M., Fournet, C.: Mobile values, new names, and secure communication. In: POPL, pp. 104–115. ACM (2001)
3. Almousa, O., Mödersheim, S., Modesti, P., Viganò, L.: Typing and Compositionality for Security Protocols: A Generalization to the Geometric Fragment. In: ESORICS 2015, 2015, to appear, http://compute.dtu.dk/~samo
4. Almousa, O., Mödersheim, S., Viganò, L.: Alice and Bob: reconciling formal models and implementation (Extended Version). Technical report 2014-10, DTU Compute (2015). http://www.imm.dtu.dk/~samo/
5. Armando, A., et al.: The AVANTSSAR platform for the automated validation of trust and security of service-oriented architectures. In: Flanagan, C., König, B. (eds.) TACAS 2012. LNCS, vol. 7214, pp. 267–282. Springer, Heidelberg (2012)
6. Hrițcu, C., Busenius, A., Backes, M.: On the development and formalization of an extensible code generator for real life security protocols. In: Goodloe, A.E., Person, S. (eds.) NFM 2012. LNCS, vol. 7226, pp. 371–387. Springer, Heidelberg (2012)
7. Basin, D., Keller, M., Radomirović, S., Sasse, R.: Alice and Bob meet equational theories. In: Festschrift for José Meseguer on his 65th Birthday (2015)
8. Bhargavan, K., Fournet, C., Corin, R., Zălinescu, E.: Verified cryptographic implementations for TLS. ACM Trans. Inf. Syst. Secur. **15**, 1 (2012). Article 3
9. Bhargavan, K., Fournet, C., Gordon, A.D., Tse, S.: Verified interoperable implementations of security protocols. In: CSF 19, pp. 139–152. IEEE (2006)
10. Blanchet, B.: An efficient cryptographic protocol verifier based on Prolog rules. In: CSF, pp. 82–96. IEEE (2001)

11. Bodei, C., Buchholtz, M., Degano, P., Nielson, F., Riis Nielson, H.: Static validation of security protocols. J. Comput. Secur. **13**(3), 347–390 (2005)
12. Briais, S., Nestmann, U.: A formal semantics for protocol narrations. Theoret. Comput. Sci. **389**(3), 484–511 (2007)
13. Caleiro, C., Viganò, L., Basin, D.: On the semantics of Alice&Bob specifications of security protocols. Theoret. Comput. Sci. **367**(1), 88–122 (2006)
14. Chevalier, Y., Rusinowitch, M.: Compiling and securing cryptographic protocols. Inf. Process. Lett. **110**(3), 116–122 (2010)
15. Cremers, C.J.F., Mauw, S.: Operational semantics of security protocols. In: Leue, S., Systä, T.J. (eds.) Scenarios: Models, Transformations and Tools. LNCS, vol. 3466, pp. 66–89. Springer, Heidelberg (2005)
16. Dierks, T., Rescorla, E.: RFC 5246: The Transport Layer Security (TLS) Protocol, Version 1.2 (2008)
17. FutureID Project: Deliverable D42.6: Specification of execution environment (2014). www.futureid.eu
18. FutureID Project: Deliverable D42.8: APS Files for Selected Authentication Protocols (2015). www.futureid.eu
19. German Federal Office for Information Security (BSI): Advanced Security Mechanism for Machine Readable Travel Documents (2008). www.bsi.bund.de/EN/Publications/TechnicalGuidelines/TR03110/BSITR03110
20. Jacquemard, F., Rusinowitch, M., Vigneron, L.: Compiling and verifying security protocols. In: Parigot, M., Voronkov, A. (eds.) LPAR 2000. LNCS (LNAI), vol. 1955, pp. 131–160. Springer, Heidelberg (2000)
21. Küsters, R., Truderung, T.: Using ProVerif to analyze protocols with Diffie-Hellman exponentiation. In: CSF, pp. 157–171. IEEE (2009)
22. Lowe, G.: Casper: a compiler for the analysis of security protocols. In: CSFW, pp. 18–30. IEEE (1997)
23. Millen, J.: CAPSL: common authentication protocol specification language. Technical report, Technical Report MP 97B48, The MITRE Corporation (1997)
24. Mödersheim, S.: Algebraic properties in Alice and Bob notation. In: ARES 2009, pp. 433–440. IEEE (2009)
25. Mödersheim, S.: Diffie-Hellman without difficulty. In: Barthe, G., Datta, A., Etalle, S. (eds.) FAST 2011. LNCS, vol. 7140, pp. 214–229. Springer, Heidelberg (2012)
26. Mödersheim, S., Katsoris, G.: A sound abstraction of the parsing problem. In: CSF, pp. 259–273. IEEE (2014)
27. Modesti, P.: Efficient Java code generation of security protocols specified in AnB/AnBx. In: STM (2014)
28. Thayer, F.J., Herzog, J.C., Guttman, J.D.: Strand spaces: proving security protocols correct. J. Comput. Secur. **7**(1), 191–230 (1999)
29. Tobler, B., Hutchison, A.C.: Generating network security protocol implementations from formal specifications. In: Nardelli, E., Talamo, M. (eds.) Certification and Security in Inter-Organizational E-Service. IFIP, vol. 177, pp. 33–54. Springer, Heidelberg (2005)

Asynchronous Traces and Open Petri Nets

Paolo Baldan[1], Filippo Bonchi[2], Fabio Gadducci[3](✉),
and Giacoma V. Monreale[3]

[1] Dipartimento di Matematica, Università di Padova, Padova, Italy
[2] ENS Lyon, Université de Lyon, LIP (UMR 5668 CNRS ENS Lyon
UCBL INRIA), Lyon, France
[3] Dipartimento di Informatica, Università di Pisa, Pisa, Italy
gadducci@di.unipi.its

Abstract. The relation between process calculi and Petri nets, two fundamental models of concurrency, has been widely investigated. Many proposals exist for encoding process calculi into Petri nets while preserving some behavioural features of interest. We recently introduced a framework where a net encoding can be defined uniformly for calculi with different communication patterns, including synchronous two-party, multiparty, and asynchronous communication. The encoding preserves and reflects several behavioural semantics, notably bisimulation equivalence. The situation is less immediate for asynchronous calculi and trace semantics: considering traces that arise when viewing asynchronous calculi as a fragment of the synchronous ones, trace equivalence is not reflected by the encoding. Focusing on CCS, we argue that this phenomenon is related to the imperfect match between trace inclusion and may testing preorder. We consider an alternative labelled transition systems where the latter issue is solved, and we show that, indeed, the corresponding trace semantics is preserved and reflected by the net encoding.

Keywords: Asynchronous CCS · (Open) Petri nets · Modular
encoding · May testing · Trace semantics

"Ci sono più reti di Petri in terra di quanti baci abbia dato Catullo."
"There are more Petri nets in earth than kisses given by Catullo"

PD, circa 1989

1 Introduction

The theory of concurrency and distribution contains several studies on the relation between two fundamental models, process calculi and Petri nets. In particular, Petri nets have been used as the target for the encoding of many process

Research partly supported by the MIUR PRIN 2010LHT4KM CINA, the ANR
121S02001 PACE and the University of Padua ANCORE.

C. Bodei et al. (Eds.): Degano Festschrift, LNCS 9465, pp. 86–102, 2015.
DOI: 10.1007/978-3-319-25527-9_8

calculi (and other textual formalisms). On the one hand, thanks to the simple and immediate visual presentation of nets, a suitable encoding can clarify the nature of concurrency and distribution in the formalism at hand. At the same time, it can highlight if and how the different synchronisation mechanisms can be represented in the net setting. On the other hand, the availability of many tools and techniques for the analysis of net behavioural properties, like reachability, boundedness, and deadlock-freedom, suggests that suitable encodings might offer the possibility of a fruitful technology transfer. Indeed, there has been since a long time an interest for the net encoding of calculi. Special attention has been devoted to CCS. There are several papers which show how the handshaking communication pattern of CCS (and π-calculus) can be implemented in the Petri net setting in such a way that the operational behaviour of a process is (at least) preserved by the encoding [15–17, 26]. Pierpaolo was one of the initiators of this line of research [12, 13], also devoting some attention [14] to a less explored paradigm, the multi-party communication pattern of e.g. CSP [18].

Most of those works exploit C/E systems, and are wired towards synchronous communication patterns. In recent works [2, 3] we showed how resorting to the P/T paradigm, these ideas can be generalised in order to include asynchronous communication. This has been exemplified in the asynchronous CCS (ACCS) [7]. The encodings rely on *open nets* [4, 8, 22, 24], a reactive extensions of the ordinary net model equipped with *open places* and *visible transitions*, i.e., distinguished sets of places and transitions which are accessible to the environment: a net may then interact with its environment either asynchronously, by exchanging tokens on open places, or by synchronising on visible transitions. We identified fragments of CSP and ACCS, hereafter referred to as *bound*, which can be mapped *in a modular way* into Petri nets via encodings that preserve as well as reflect the standard operational semantics of the two calculi. Modularity here means that we identify suitable operators on nets which exactly correspond to operators on processes, such that the encoding is built inductively from a set of basic net constants, and at the same time it preserves structural congruence. The term bound refers to limitations that are imposed to the use of recursion/replication which will be made precise later. The fragments are not Turing powerful (e.g., reachability is decidable), but expressive enough to model infinite state systems where standard behavioural equivalences (barbed bisimilarity for ACCS and trace equivalence for CSP) are undecidable.

Since most behavioural semantics for process calculi are based on their transition system, this correspondence at the operational level translates to a correspondence between virtually any observational equivalence.

The situation is less clearly cut with trace semantics for ACCS, which is in fact paradigmatic of a general problem of labelled operational semantics for asynchronous calculi. This is witnessed by the relationship of may testing with trace semantics, as explored in [7, 11]: differently from the synchronous case, trace inclusion does not correspond directly to the may preorder, but some adjustment (working modulo some preorder on traces) is needed in order to take into account the unobservability of message reception. This fact also causes a mismatch with the notion of trace for open Petri nets, which instead directly describes all the possible interactions of a system with its environment. Indeed, it can be easily observed that labelled transitions, and thus trace inclusion, are only preserved but not reflected by our net encoding of ACCS processes. The problem can be solved by resorting to a different LTS, that we call saturated LTS, proposed in [11] (in turn inspired by [19]). The saturated LTS induces a notion of trace that directly captures all the possible interactions with the environment and has an immediate correspondence with the may preorder, namely the may preorder and trace inclusion coincide. For these reasons it fits nicely with the aforementioned encoding into open nets: the operational semantics via the saturated LTS is now preserved and reflected, and thus also trace semantics.

Among other technology transfers, our work opens the way to the study of testing semantics for Petri nets, so far scarcely investigated in the literature [20].

Synopsis. The paper is structured as follows. In Sect. 2 we recall the syntax, operational semantics and may testing theory of ACCS. In Sect. 3 we present the saturated LTS for ACCS, and we show that the corresponding notion of trace semantics exactly corresponds to may preorder. In Sect. 4 we describe open Petri nets with interfaces, and we define the modular encoding of (bound) ACCS processes into open nets. Finally, in Sect. 5 we prove that the net encoding of ACCS preserves and reflects saturated trace semantics. In Sect. 6 we then draw some conclusions and provide pointers to future works.

2   Asynchronous CCS

Asynchronous process calculi are characterised by the fact that message sending and reception are not synchronised. Rather, messages are sent and travel through some media until they reach destination. Thus sending is non-blocking (i.e., a process may send even if the receiver is not ready to receive), while receiving is (processes must wait until a message becomes available). One can think that output messages are buffered [25] or stored in some shared workspace [9].

Asynchronous π-calculus was originally introduced in [1,19]. Here we consider a restriction – not featuring name passing – called asynchronous CCS (ACCS) [7, 11]. Besides the absence of name passing, the main difference with respect to the syntax of the calculus in [1] is the presence of a guarded input replication $!_a.P$, instead of the pure replication of a summation. Indeed, unguarded replication can have (unrealistic) infinitely branching behaviour, especially when considering a concurrent semantics. Just think of process $!\tau.\bar{a}$, which can concurrently generate an unbounded number of messages on channel a.

Definition 1 (ACCS processes). *Let $\mathcal{N}$ be a set of* names, *ranged over by $a, b, c, \ldots$ and let $\tau \notin \mathcal{N}$ be the silent action. We let $\gamma, \gamma_1, \ldots$ range over the set of* guards *$\mathcal{N} \cup \{\tau\}$, $v, v_1, \ldots$ over the set of* visible actions *$\mathcal{V} = \mathcal{N} \cup \overline{\mathcal{N}}$, and $\mu, \mu_1, \ldots$ over the set of all actions $\mathcal{A} = \mathcal{V} \cup \{\tau\}$. A process is a term generated by the syntax in Fig. 1. We let $P, Q, R, \ldots$ range over the set of processes $\mathcal{P}$.*

$$
\begin{array}{llll}
P & ::= & 0 & \text{inactive process} \\
& & \oplus_{i=1}^{n}\gamma_i.P_i & \text{summation} \\
& & \bar{a} & \text{output} \\
& & P \mid Q & \text{parallel} \\
& & (\nu a)P & \text{restriction} \\
& & !_a.P & \text{replication}
\end{array}
$$

Fig. 1. ACCS processes.

The main difference with standard CCS is the absence of output prefixes. The occurrence of an unguarded $\bar{a}$ indicates a message that is available on some communication media named a. It will disappear whenever it is received.

We assume the standard definition for the set of free names of a process P, which is denoted by $\mathtt{fn}(P)$. Similarly, we assume that α-convertibility holds with respect to the *restriction* operators $(\nu a)P$: the name a is restricted in P, and thus it can be freely α-converted.

$$(\text{Alt})\ \frac{\rho\ \text{permutation}}{\oplus_{i=1}^{n}\gamma_i.P_i = \oplus_{i=1}^{n}\gamma_{\rho(i)}.P_{\rho(i)}}$$

$$(\text{Par}_1)\frac{}{P \mid Q = Q \mid P} \qquad (\text{Par}_2)\frac{}{P \mid (Q \mid R) = (P \mid Q) \mid R}$$

$$(\text{Res}_1)\frac{X \cap \mathtt{fn}(P) = \emptyset}{(\nu X)P = P} \qquad (\text{Res}_2)\frac{X \cap \mathtt{fn}(C[0]) = \emptyset}{C[(\nu X)P] = (\nu X)C[P]}$$

Fig. 2. ACCS structural axioms: $C[-]$ is a process context with no occurrence of $!_a.-$.

Structural equivalence ($\equiv$) is the smallest congruence induced by the axioms in Fig. 2, where $C[-]$ denotes a process context such that the "hole" $-$ does not occur inside the scope of a replication $!_a$. With respect to [1] we added an axiom schema for distributing the restriction under each operator different from replication, thus also under the sum and the prefix.

The operational rules in Fig. 3, taken from [7], arise as a direct rephrasing of the rules of synchronous CCS restricted to the asynchronous fragment (whence the subscript "s"). The behaviour of a process P is then described as a relation over processes up to $\equiv$, obtained by closing the rules under structural congruence.

Definition 2 (Labeled semantics). *The* labelled transition system *for ACCS processes is the relation* $S \subseteq \mathcal{P} \times \mathcal{A} \times \mathcal{P}$ *inductively defined by the set of rules in Fig. 3, where* $P \xrightarrow{\mu}_s Q$ *means that* $\langle P, \mu, Q\rangle \in S$. *Weak transitions* $P \overset{w}{\Rightarrow}_s Q$ *are defined by the following rules, where* $w \in \mathcal{V}^*$ *and* ϵ *denotes the empty trace.*

$$\frac{P(\xrightarrow{\tau}_s)^*Q}{P\overset{\epsilon}{\Rightarrow}_s Q} \qquad \frac{P\xrightarrow{v}_s Q}{P\overset{v}{\Rightarrow}_s Q} \qquad \frac{P\overset{w_1}{\Rightarrow}_s Q\overset{w_2}{\Rightarrow}_s R}{P\overset{w_1 w_2}{\Rightarrow}_s R}$$

We write $P\overset{w}{\Rightarrow}_s$ if there exists some Q such that $P\overset{w}{\Rightarrow}_sQ$ and we define the set of traces of a process P as $traces_s(P) = \{w \mid P\overset{w}{\Rightarrow}_s\}$.

$$(\text{Act}) \ \frac{j \in \{1,\ldots,n\}}{\oplus_{i=1}^n \gamma_i.P_i \ \overset{\gamma_j}{\longrightarrow}_s P_j} \qquad (\text{Repl})\frac{}{!_a.P \ \overset{a}{\longrightarrow}_s \ !_a.P \mid P}$$

$$(\text{Par}) \ \frac{P \overset{\mu}{\longrightarrow}_s P'}{P \mid Q \overset{\mu}{\longrightarrow}_s P' \mid Q} \qquad (\text{Syn}) \frac{P \overset{a}{\longrightarrow}_s P', Q \overset{\bar{a}}{\longrightarrow}_s Q'}{P \mid Q \overset{\tau}{\longrightarrow}_s P' \mid Q'}$$

$$(\text{Res}) \ \frac{P \overset{\mu}{\longrightarrow}_s P' \quad \mu \notin \{a, \bar{a}\}}{(\nu a)P \overset{\mu}{\longrightarrow}_s (\nu a)P'} \qquad (\text{Out}) \frac{}{\bar{a} \mid P \overset{a}{\longrightarrow}_s P}$$

$$(\text{Con})\frac{P \equiv P', \ P' \overset{\mu}{\longrightarrow}_s Q', \ Q' \equiv Q}{P \overset{\mu}{\longrightarrow}_s Q}$$

Fig. 3. ACCS labelled semantics.

Testing semantics equates processes that cannot be taken apart by the interaction with external observers. This is formalised via a notion of test.

Definition 3 (May testing preorder). *An observer is an ACCS process that can perform a distinguished output action $\sqrt{}$ (the success action), with $\sqrt{} \notin \mathcal{N}$. For process P and observer O, P may O if there exists a successful computation of $P \mid O$, namely $P \mid O\overset{\sqrt{}}{\Rightarrow}_s$. For processes P and Q, we write $P \sqsubseteq_m Q$ $(P \equiv_m Q)$ if P may O implies Q may O (and vice versa) for all observers O.*

The above definition can be (and usually is) hard to verify, since it requires to take into account all possible observers. For synchronous languages like CCS and π-calculus, this problem can be easily avoided by observing that $\sqsubseteq_m$ coincides with the standard trace inclusion. Unfortunately, this is no longer true for asynchronous calculi. For instance, it is easy to see that $a.b.P \sqsubseteq_m b.a.P$ and $a.\bar{a} \sqsubseteq_m 0$, but clearly neither in the former nor in the latter case the traces of the first process are included in those of the second one.

A solution is devised in [7], by relying on the following order on traces.

Definition 4 (Trace order). *The trace order for processes is the reflexive and transitive relation $\leq_A \subseteq \mathcal{V}^\star \times \mathcal{V}^\star$ inductively defined by the set of rules in Fig. 4 and closed under pre- and post-composition.*

For processes P and Q, we write $P \leq_m Q$ if whenever $w \in traces_s(P)$ then $w' \in traces_s(Q)$ for some $w' \leq_A w$.

The trace order takes into account the asynchronous nature of communications. The intuition is that, given a process P and a trace s, if P may offer $\bar{s}$ (for a trace s, its dual $\bar{s}$ is defined in the obvious way), then it may also offer $\bar{t}$ for all

$t \leq_A s$. The inequality $\epsilon \leq_A a$ is motivated by the fact that whenever a process can exhibit a trace including an output message $\bar{a}$, it can offer the same trace where $\bar{a}$ has been removed, since output is non-blocking, hence any transition that follows can be performed independently of the output. For a quite similar reason, an output can be deferred as much as desired, whence the inequality $va \leq_A av$. Finally, if a process can emit an output on a and later input on the same channel, then it can input its own message, leading to an internal move. This motivates the last inequality $\epsilon \leq_A a\bar{a}$.

$$\epsilon \leq_A a \qquad va \leq_A av \qquad \epsilon \leq_A a\bar{a}$$

Fig. 4. Trace ordering laws.

As shown in [7], the relevant fact concerning the relation $\leq_m$ is that t coincides with the may preorder.

Theorem 1 (Alternative may testing). *Let P, Q be ACCS processes. Then $P \sqsubseteq_m Q$ iff $P \leq_m Q$.*

Example 1. Consider the processes $P = (\nu d)(!_d.\bar{e} \mid (a.(\bar{a} \mid \bar{d} \mid d.\bar{c}) \oplus \tau.(\bar{d} \mid d.\bar{c})))$ and $Q = (\nu d)(\tau.(d.\bar{c} \mid d.\bar{e} \mid \bar{d}))$. It is not difficult to see that $P \equiv_m Q$. For instance, consider the trace $\bar{e}$, which can be obtained in P via the sequence $P \xrightarrow{\tau}_s (\nu d)(!_d.\bar{e} \mid \bar{d} \mid d.\bar{c}) \xrightarrow{\tau}_s (\nu d)(!_d.\bar{e} \mid \bar{e} \mid d.\bar{c}) \xrightarrow{\bar{e}}_s (\nu d)(!_d.\bar{e} \mid d.\bar{c})$, and the trace is terminated as the replication is stuck. For Q we have the same trace via $Q \xrightarrow{\tau} (\nu d)(d.\bar{c} \mid d.\bar{e} \mid \bar{d}) \xrightarrow{\tau}_s (\nu d)(d.\bar{c} \mid \bar{e}) \xrightarrow{\bar{e}}_s (\nu d)(d.\bar{c})$.

A different execution is $P \xrightarrow{a}_s (\nu d)(!_d.\bar{e} \mid \bar{a} \mid \bar{d} \mid d.\bar{c}) \xrightarrow{\bar{a}}_s (\nu d)(!_d.\bar{e} \mid \bar{d} \mid d.\bar{c}) \xrightarrow{\tau}_s (\nu d)(!_d.\bar{e} \mid \bar{e} \mid d.\bar{c}) \xrightarrow{\bar{e}}_s (\nu d)(!_d.\bar{e} \mid d.\bar{c})$. The corresponding traces a, $a\bar{a}$ and $a\bar{a}\bar{e}$, can be matched in Q by $\epsilon \leq_m a$, $\epsilon \leq_m a\bar{a}$ and $\bar{e} \leq_m a\bar{a}\bar{e}$.

Similar considerations lead to show that process $a.\bar{a} \equiv_m 0$, one of the idiosyncratic features of asynchronous communication.

3 May Testing via Saturated Traces

In this section we show that the may preorder can be characterised in terms of trace inclusion by resorting to traces defined on a different LTS for ACCS processes, which originates from [11], in turn similar to [19]. We will see later, in Sect. 4, that with this notion of trace there is a perfect match between trace semantics for ACCS processes and for their net encodings.

Definition 5 (Saturated LTS). *The saturated LTS for ACCS processes is the relation $R \subseteq \mathcal{P} \times \mathcal{A} \times \mathcal{P}$ inductively defined by the set of rules in Fig. 5, where $P \xrightarrow{\mu} Q$ means that $\langle P, \mu, Q \rangle \in R$. For a process P, weak transitions (denoted by $P \overset{w}{\Rightarrow}$) and the set of traces (denoted traces(P)) are defined as before.*

$$(\text{Syn}) \frac{\gamma_1 = a}{\oplus_{i=1}^n \gamma_i.P_i \mid \bar{a} \xrightarrow{\tau} P_1} \qquad (\text{Tau}) \frac{\gamma_1 = \tau}{\oplus_{i=1}^n \gamma_i.P_i \xrightarrow{\tau} P_1}$$

$$(\text{Repl}) \frac{}{!_a.P \mid \bar{a} \xrightarrow{\tau} !_a.P \mid P} \qquad (\text{Par}) \frac{P \xrightarrow{\mu} P'}{P \mid Q \xrightarrow{\mu} P' \mid Q}$$

$$(\text{Res}) \frac{P \xrightarrow{\mu} P' \quad \mu \notin \{a, \bar{a}\}}{(\nu a)P \xrightarrow{\mu} (\nu a)P'} \qquad (\text{Con}) \frac{P \equiv P' \quad P' \xrightarrow{\mu} Q' \quad Q' \equiv Q}{P \xrightarrow{\mu} Q}$$

$$(\text{Out}) \frac{}{\bar{a} \mid P \xrightarrow{\bar{a}} P} \qquad (\text{In}) \frac{}{P \xrightarrow{a} \bar{a} \mid P}$$

Fig. 5. Saturated labelled semantics.

The main novelty with respect to the previous set of rules is the presence of rule (In), stating that the environment can freely provide output messages. Dually, rule (Out) can be interpreted as the environment receiving (and thus consuming) a message. Rules (Syn) and (Repl) now model internal reductions. It is easy to see (indeed, this is the definition proposed in [11]) that $\rightarrow$ can be alternatively defined as the least relation on $\mathcal{P} \times \mathcal{A} \times \mathcal{P}$ such that

- $\xrightarrow{\mu}_s \subseteq \xrightarrow{\mu}$ and
- for all $a \in \mathcal{N}$, $P \xrightarrow{a} P \mid \bar{a}$.

The relation between the two LTSs is summarized by the following lemma.

Lemma 1 (Non-saturated vs saturated). *Let P, Q be ACCS processes. Then*

1. *$P \xrightarrow{\tau}_s Q$ iff $P \xrightarrow{\tau} Q$;*
2. *$P \xrightarrow{\bar{a}}_s Q$ iff $P \xrightarrow{\bar{a}} Q$;*
3. *if $P \xrightarrow{a}_s Q$ then $P \xrightarrow{a} \xrightarrow{\tau} Q$.*

Proof. It is easy to show that for any name $a \in \mathcal{N}$, process P performs an input $P \xrightarrow{a}_s Q$ iff $P \equiv (\nu a_1)\ldots(\nu a_m)(\oplus_{i=1}^n \gamma_i.P_i \mid P')$, with $\gamma_1 = a \neq a_k$ for $k \in \{1, \ldots, m\}$ and $Q \equiv (\nu a_1)\ldots(\nu a_m)(P_1 \mid P')$. Dually, process P performs an output $P \xrightarrow{\bar{a}}_s Q$ iff $P \equiv P' \mid \bar{a}$. From these facts items (1)-(3) follow. □

Example 2. Consider again the processes $P = (\nu d)(!_d.\bar{e} \mid (a.(\bar{a} \mid \bar{d} \mid d.\bar{c}) \oplus \tau.(\bar{d} \mid d.\bar{c})))$ and $Q = (\nu d)(\tau.(d.\bar{c} \mid d.\bar{e} \mid \bar{d}))$ from Example 1. It can be seen that $P \approx_T Q$. For instance, consider the execution $P \xrightarrow{a} (\nu d)(!_d.\bar{e} \mid (a.(\bar{a} \mid \bar{d} \mid d.\bar{c}) \oplus \tau.(\bar{d} \mid d.\bar{c}))) \mid \bar{a} \xrightarrow{\tau} (\nu d)(!_d.\bar{e} \mid \bar{a} \mid \bar{d} \mid d.\bar{c}) \xrightarrow{\bar{a}} \bar{a}(\nu d)(!_d.\bar{e} \mid \bar{d} \mid d.\bar{c}) \xrightarrow{\tau} \tau(\nu d)(!_d.\bar{e} \mid \bar{e} \mid d.\bar{c}) \xrightarrow{\tau} \bar{e}(\nu d)(!_d.\bar{e} \mid \bar{e} \mid d.\bar{c})$ that generates the trace $a\bar{a}\bar{e}$, which in the previous LTS could only be simulated up to $\leq_m$.

In the saturated LTS we have that $Q \xrightarrow{a} (\nu d)(\tau.(d.\bar{c} \mid d.\bar{e} \mid \bar{d})) \mid \bar{a} \xrightarrow{\bar{a}} (\nu d)(\tau.(d.\bar{c} \mid d.\bar{e} \mid \bar{d})) \xrightarrow{\tau} (\nu d)(d.\bar{c} \mid d.\bar{e} \mid \bar{d}) \xrightarrow{\tau} (\nu d)(d.\bar{c} \mid \bar{e}) \xrightarrow{\bar{e}} (\nu d)(d.\bar{c} \mid \bar{e})$, which gives exactly the same trace.

We can now prove that trace inclusion in the saturated LTS is a further characterisation of the may preorder. In order to show this fact, we prove that trace inclusion in the saturated LTS coincide with $\leq_m$ in the LTS of Definition 2.

Proposition 1 (Soundness). *Let P be an ACCS process and $w \in traces(P)$. If $w' \geq_A w$ then $w' \in traces(P)$.*

Proof. The proof proceeds by induction on $\leq_A$, but we need to strengthen the inductive hypothesis. For a set of ACCS processes S, we define its closure $\mathcal{C}(S)$ as the least set of processes such that

$$\mathcal{C}(S) = S \cup \{P \mid \overline{a} : P \in \mathcal{C}(S) \wedge a \in \mathcal{N}\}.$$

Observe that (†) $\mathcal{C}(\mathcal{C}(S)) = \mathcal{C}(S)$ and (‡) if $P \overset{w}{\Rightarrow} Q$ and $P' \in \mathcal{C}(\{P\})$, then $P' \overset{w}{\Rightarrow} Q'$ with $Q' \in \mathcal{C}(\{Q\})$. Now, the proof that

$$\text{if } P \overset{w}{\Rightarrow} Q \text{ and } w \leq_A w', \text{ then } P \overset{w'}{\Rightarrow} Q' \text{ and } Q' \in \mathcal{C}(\{Q\})$$

is easily carried out and it immediately implies our statement. □

Proposition 2 (Completeness). *Let P be an ACCS process and $w \in traces(P)$. Then there exists $w' \leq_A w$ such that $w' \in traces_s(P)$.*

Proof. The statement is proved by induction on w. For the base case, if $w = \epsilon$, then by Lemma 1(1) $P \overset{\epsilon}{\Rightarrow} Q$ iff $P \overset{\epsilon}{\Rightarrow}_s Q$. For the inductive case, we distinguish two sub-cases according to the first action in the trace.

- If $w = \overline{a} w'$, then $P \overset{\overline{a}}{\Rightarrow} Q$ and $w' \in traces(Q)$. By Lemma 1(1–2), $P \overset{\overline{a}}{\Rightarrow}_s Q$. By induction hypothesis, there exists $w'' \leq_A w'$ such that $Q \overset{w''}{\Rightarrow}_s$. Therefore $P \overset{\overline{a}w''}{\Rightarrow}_s$ and $\overline{a}w'' \leq_A w$.
- If $w = aw'$, then $P \overset{\epsilon}{\Rightarrow} P' \overset{a}{\rightarrow} Q$ and $w' \in traces(Q)$. By definition of $\overset{a}{\rightarrow}$ we have that $Q = P' \mid \overline{a}$. Relying on the fact that the set of traces of $P \mid \overline{a}$ can be characterised as

$$traces(P) \cup \{w_1 w_2 \mid w_1 a w_2 \in traces(P)\} \cup \{w_1 \overline{a} w_2 \mid w_1 w_2 \in traces(P)\}$$

  from $w' \in traces(P' \mid \overline{a})$ we have that
  - If $w' \in traces(P')$, $w = aw' \geq_A w'$. By induction hypothesis, there exists $w'' \leq_A w'$ such that $P' \overset{w''}{\Rightarrow}_s$. Therefore $P \overset{w''}{\Rightarrow}_s$ and $w'' \leq_A w$.
  - If $w' \in \{w_1 w_2 \mid w_1 a w_2 \in traces(P)\}$, $w = aw' = aw_1 w_2 \geq w_1 a w_2 \in traces(P')$. By induction hypothesis, there exists $w'' \leq_A w_1 a w_2$ such that $P' \overset{w''}{\Rightarrow}_s$. Therefore $P \overset{w''}{\Rightarrow}_s$ and $w'' \leq_A w$.
  - If $w' \in \{w_1 \overline{a} w_2 \mid w_1 w_2 \in traces(P)\}$, $w = aw' = aw_1 \overline{a} w_2 \geq_A w_1 a \overline{a} w_2 \geq_A w_1 w_2 \in traces(P')$. By induction hypothesis, there exists $w'' \leq_A w_1 w_2$ such that $P' \overset{w''}{\Rightarrow}_s$. Therefore $P \overset{w''}{\Rightarrow}_s$ and $w'' \leq_A w$. □

Now, the desired result immediately follows.

Theorem 2 (May testing via traces inclusion). *Let P, Q be ACCS processes. Then $traces(P) \subseteq traces(Q)$ iff $P \leq_m Q$.*

The result above is similar to [11, Theorem 1], which states that $traces_s(P) \subseteq traces(Q)$ iff $P \sqsubseteq_m Q$. However, it is worth remarking that the latter theorem does not imply ours.

Indeed, we believe that our work provides some interesting, despite preliminary, insights: soundness and completeness (Propositions 1 and 2) state exactly that $traces(P)$ is the upward closure of $traces_s(P)$ with respect to the ordering $\leq_A$. The preorder $\leq_m$ is one of the standard ways to lift an ordering to its powerset, and it is well-known that such a lifting coincides with the inclusion of upward closure.

4   Open Petri Nets

Let $X^\oplus$ be the free commutative monoid over a set X and let 2^X be the powerset of X. An element $m \in X^\oplus$ is referred to as a *multisets* over X, since it can be viewed as a function $m : X \rightarrow \mathbb{N}$ (the set of natural numbers) associating a multiplicity with each $x \in X$. A subset $Y \subseteq X$ is often confused with the multiset $\bigoplus_{y \in Y} y$. We write $m_1 \subseteq m_2$ if $\forall x \in X$, $m_1(x) \leq m_2(x)$. If $m_1 \subseteq m_2$, the multiset $m_2 \ominus m_1$ is defined as $\forall x \in X$ $m_2 \ominus m_1(x) = m_2(x) - m_1(x)$. The symbol 0 denotes the empty multiset. Given $f : X \rightarrow Y$ we denote its extension to multisets by $f^\oplus : X^\oplus \rightarrow Y^\oplus$.

Definition 6 (Petri nets). *A Petri net is a tuple $N = (S, T, {}^\bullet(.), (.)^\bullet)$ where S is the set of places, T is the set of transitions, ${}^\bullet(.), (.)^\bullet : T \rightarrow 2^S$ are functions mapping each transition to its pre- and post-set.*

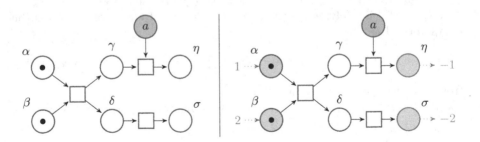

Fig. 6. Graphical representation of open Petri nets, on the right with interfaces.

In order to encode a process calculus into Petri nets we consider a reactive generalisation of Petri nets, in the line of [4,8,22,24]. More precisely, nets are endowed with distinguished sets of *open* places. They represent the places through which the environment interacts with the net, by putting and removing tokens visible from the environment. Open places carry a label, and hereafter we let $\mathcal{N}$ be the corresponding set of labels. The choice is driven by our need of encoding ACCS channels: messages on channels would correspond to tokens in places.

Definition 7 (Open Petri net). *An* open net *is a triple* $ON = \langle N, O, \lambda \rangle$, *where N is a net, $O \subseteq S$ is a set of* open *places, and* $\lambda : O \to \mathcal{N}$ *is an injective* labelling *function.*

A marked open net **N** *is a pair* $\langle ON, m_0 \rangle$, *where ON is an open net and $m_0 \in S^{\oplus}$ is the* initial *marking.*

The operational semantics of open nets is presented in Fig. 7. Rule (Step) is the standard rule of P/T nets (seen as multiset rewriting), represented as a silent action τ. The remaining rules model interaction with the environment. They state that in an open place at any moment the environment can generate (In) or remove a token (Out). Note that interactions based on exchanging tokens is naturally asynchronous. For a word $w \in \mathcal{V}^{\star}$, weak transitions $m \overset{w}{\Rightarrow} m'$ are defined as in ACCS. Similarly, for the traces $traces(\mathbf{N})$ of a marked open net **N**.

$$\text{(Step)} \ \frac{m = {}^{\bullet}t \oplus m' \quad t \in T}{m \xrightarrow{\tau} t^{\bullet} \oplus m'} \qquad \text{(In)} \ \frac{s \in O}{m \xrightarrow{\lambda(s)} m \oplus s} \qquad \text{(Out)} \ \frac{s \in O}{m \xrightarrow{\overline{\lambda(s)}} m \ominus s}$$

Fig. 7. Operational semantics of open nets.

Example 3. A marked open net is shown in Fig. 6 (left). As usual, circles represent places and rectangles transitions. Arrows represent pre- and post-sets of transitions. Bullets in places, referred to as tokens, represent the initial marking m_0 of the net. For the sake of readability, places are often provided with an identifier, yet positioned outside of the corresponding item.

Any open place has a name which is placed inside the corresponding circle. In particular, there is one open place, the green one, which is labelled by a. Finally, in the initial marking m_0 of the net, the places α and β are marked. For example, by applying the (Step) rule in Fig. 7, we obtain the firing $m_0 \xrightarrow{\tau} m_1 = \{\gamma, \delta\}$. By applying again the same rule $m_1 \xrightarrow{\tau} m_2 = \{\gamma, \sigma\}$, while by the (In) rule $m_1 \xrightarrow{a} m_3 = \{\gamma, \delta, a\}$. Moreover, by applying twice the (Step) rule, $m_3 \xrightarrow{\tau} m_4 = \{\eta, \delta\}$ and $m_4 \xrightarrow{\tau} m_5 = \{\eta, \sigma\}$.

It is easy to see that the set of traces of this net consists of all and only the traces $w \in \mathcal{V}^{\star}$ such that (1) only a and $\overline{a}$ occur in w; and (2) in every prefix of w, the number of occurrences of a is larger than the number of occurrences of $\overline{a}$.

4.1 Open Petri Nets with Interfaces

In order to allow for an inductive construction of open Petri nets from a set of basic components, we enrich open nets with interfaces and suitable operators for net composition along the interfaces.

In the following, for each $n \in \mathbb{N}$ we denote by n^+ the set $\{1, \ldots, n\}$, by n^- the set $\{-1, \ldots, -n\}$ and by 0 the empty set $\emptyset$. Also, for $f : n^+ \to S$ and $g : m^+ \to S$, we denote $f + g : (n + m)^+ \to S$ the function $(f + g)(x) = f(x)$ if $x \leq n$ and $g(x - n)$ otherwise (and similarly for n^- and m^-).

Definition 8 (Open nets with interfaces). *Let $l, r \in \mathbb{N}$. An open net with left interface l and right interface r is a triple $IN = \langle li, ON, ri \rangle$, where ON is an open net, $li : l^+ \to S$ and $ri : r^- \to S$ are the left and right interface functions, respectively.*

We denote by $l^+ \xrightarrow{li} ON \xleftarrow{ri} r^-$ a net with left interface l^+ and right interface r^-. With an abuse of notation, in the following we refer to the places belonging to the image of the left interface function as left places, and similarly for the places in the image of the right one. From now on we will denote the components of an open net with interfaces by l^+, li, ON, ri, and r^-, possibly with subscript.

Graphically, a net with interfaces is represented as an open net, with the left interface on the left and the right interface on the right, marked with incoming and outgoing dotted arrows, respectively. Arrows of the left places are blue while those of right places are red (grey when in b & w).

Example 4. A net with interfaces is shown in Fig. 6 (right). The left interface consists of the places α, and β, while the right one contains η and σ. The places labelled γ and δ are internal, i.e., they do not belong to the interfaces.

Relying on the notion of interface, we can define two suitable composition operators on nets. Here we just provide an informal description: The reader is referred to [2,3] for a detailed definition.

Definition 9 (Composition operations). *Let $IN_1 = l_1^+ \xrightarrow{li_1} ON_1 \xleftarrow{ri_1} r_1^-$ and $IN_2 = l_2^+ \xrightarrow{li_2} ON_2 \xleftarrow{ri_2} r_2^-$ be (point-wise disjoint) nets with interfaces.*

- *When $r_1 = l_2$, their sequential composition $IN_1 \circ IN_2$ is the net with interfaces l_1^+ and r_2^- obtained by taking the disjoint union of the nets N_1 and N_2 and merging the open (right) places of N_1 with the corresponding open (left) places of N_2.*
- *Their parallel composition $IN_1 \otimes IN_2$ is the net with interfaces $(l_1 + l_2)^+$ and $(r_1 + r_2)^-$ obtained by taking the disjoint union of the nets N_1 and N_2, and merging the open places of N_1 with the corresponding open places of N_2.*
- *The restriction $(\nu a) IN_1$ of IN_1 with respect to $a \in \mathcal{N}$ is the net with interfaces l_1^+ and r_1^- obtained by closing the open places labelled by a. We often generalise the operator to any $X \subseteq \mathcal{N}$.*

After building the encoding of a process, we also need to fix its initial state. This is accomplished by marking the the left places of the resulting open net. To this end, the following operation will then be used.

Definition 10 (Marking). *Let IN be a net with interfaces. The marking of IN is the marked open net $init(IN) = \langle ON, m_0 \rangle$, where $m_0 = \biguplus_{n=1}^{l^+} li(n)$.*

4.2   From ACCS Processes to Nets

Exploiting the algebra of open nets outlined in the previous section, we introduce an encoding for ACCS processes into open nets that preserves and reflects the behaviour. The encoding will be restricted to *bound* processes, i.e., processes where restrictions never occurs under replications.

Definition 11 (Bound ACCS processes). *An ACCS process is called* bound *if no restriction* $(\nu a)-$ *occurs under replication.*

Intuitively, by restricting to bound processes we avoid the generation of an unbounded number of restricted (and thus conceptually different) names. This will be essential to guarantee the finiteness of the Petri net encoding.

The encoding of a process is defined inductively starting from a set of constant nets, those depicted in Fig. 8, which are then combined using the composition operators on nets in Sect. 4.1. The net *nil* in Fig. 8(a), which is later used to represent the inactive process, consists of a single unmarked place. The net out_a in Fig. 8(b) models the output action on a channel name a and it consists of a single left place, which is also open. The net a in Fig. 8(c), where $a \in \mathcal{N}$, is very similar to the previous but it has an empty left interface. It is going to be used to model additional free names in the encoding of a process. The net $dupl_i$ in Fig. 8(d) is a combinator for the summation of prefixes (input and τ actions) where i, the cardinality of the right interface, matches the number of prefixes involved in the sum. The net $repl_i^a$ in Fig. 8(e), where $a \in \mathcal{N}$, is going to be used as a combinator for replication. It allows for a new "parallel activation" of the net which follows, each time a token is inserted in the open place a. Once more, i is the cardinality of the right interface which will match that of the left interface of the encoding of the process under the replication operator. The net act_i^a in Fig. 8(f), where $a \in \mathcal{N}$, provides a combinator for the input action on a channel a. It consists of a transition with two places in the pre-set, a left place for the flow of control and the open place a modelling the channel on which the input is required. Again, i is the cardinality of the right interface matching the left interface of the encoding of the continuation of a. Finally, the net act_i^τ in Fig. 8(g) models a τ prefix: the only difference with respect to act_i^a is the absence of an open place modelling the channel.

The definition below introduces the net encoding of bound ACCS processes.

Definition 12 (Encoding for processes). *Let P be an ACCS bound process. The encoding of P, denoted by $[\![P]\!]$, is defined as $[\![P]\!] = init(|P|)$, where $|.|$ is given by the inductive rules in Fig. 9, where $l_{|P|}$ and $l_{|P_j|}$ denote the left interfaces of the corresponding encodings.*

The encoding of an ACCS process P is built inductively by composing those of its sub-processes, and by marking the places in the left interface of the resulting net. The encoding contains one place for each operator $!_a$, $\oplus$ and process $\mathbf{0}$ of P and a place for each name of P, which are open just for free names. Transitions mimic the control flow of a process, passing the token between its sequential

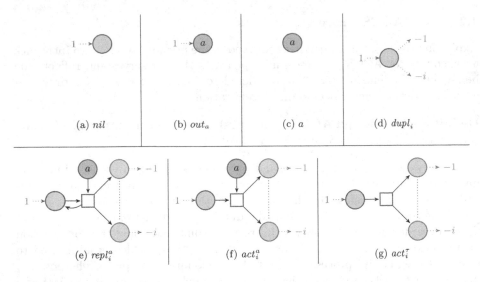

(a) *nil*   (b) *out_a*   (c) *a*   (d) *dupl_i*

(e) *repl_i^a*   (f) *act_i^a*   (g) *act_i^τ*

Fig. 8. The constant nets *stop*, $repl_i^a$, out_a, act_i^a, $dupl_i$ and act_i^τ.

$$
\begin{aligned}
|0| &= nil \\
|\bar{a}| &= out_a \\
\left|\bigoplus_{j=1}^n \gamma_j.P_j\right| &= dupl_n \circ \{\otimes_{j=1}^n (act_{l_{|P_j|}}^{\gamma_j} \circ |P_j|)\} \\
|!_a.P| &= repl_{l_{|P|}}^a \circ |P| \\
|(\nu a)P| &= (\nu a)\,|P| \\
|P \mid Q| &= |P| \otimes |Q|
\end{aligned}
$$

Fig. 9. Encoding for ACCS processes.

components. It can be shown that the encoding respects structural congruence: structurally equivalent processes are mapped into isomorphic nets and vice versa.

Example 5. ([Restricted and parallel processes]) Consider again the process $Q = (\nu d)Q_1$, with $Q_1 = \tau.(d.\bar{c} \mid d.\bar{e} \mid \bar{d})$, which was introduced in Example 1. The encoding $|Q|$ is shown in Fig. 10. It is obtained by applying the $init(\cdot)$ operation to the net $(\nu d)\,|Q_1|$. In particular, $|Q|_1$ is the result of the sequential composition between $dupl_1$ and $act_1^\tau \circ |Q_2|$, where $Q_2 = d.\bar{c} \mid d.\bar{e} \mid \bar{d}$. In turn, the net $|Q_2|$ is obtained by the parallel composition between $d.\bar{c} \mid d.\bar{e}$ and $\bar{d}$, where the former is obtained via the parallel and sequential compositions of constant nets. The places labelled by c, d, and e correspond to the output actions $\bar{c}$, $\bar{d}$, and $\bar{e}$ of Q_2. They are all open in $|Q_2|$, meaning that they represent free names of Q_2. The sub-net rooted at α is the encoding of the sub-process $d.\bar{c}$, while the one rooted at β encodes the sub-process $d.\bar{e}$. The place d is open in $|Q_1|$, but since d is restricted in Q, it is removed from the set of open places of $|Q_1|$ by applying the restriction operation of nets.

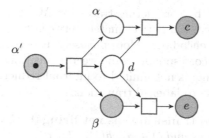

Fig. 10. Net encoding the process $(\nu d)(\tau.(d.\bar{c} \mid d.\bar{e} \mid \bar{d}))$.

We denote by $[\![P]\!]_\Gamma$, the encoding of a bound process P with respect to a set of names Γ, that is, $[\![P]\!]_\Gamma = init(|P| \otimes (\otimes_{a \in \Gamma} a))$. The addition of the component $\otimes_{a \in \Gamma} a$ determines the presence in the encoding of a place for each channel in Γ (which could possibly not occur free in P). One can establish a correspondence between the ACCS processes reachable from P, hereafter denoted by the set $reach(P) = \{Q : \exists w \in \mathcal{V}^*, P \overset{w}{\Rightarrow}_s Q\}$, and the markings of $[\![P]\!]_\Gamma$, through which we can relate internal reductions in ACCS processes and their encodings.

Theorem 3 (Process reductions as net firings). *Let P be an ACCS bound process and Γ a set of names. Then there is a function $\mathbf{m}_\Gamma^P : reach(P) \to S_{[\![P]\!]_\Gamma}^\oplus$, mapping any process $Q \in reach(P)$ into a marking of $[\![P]\!]_\Gamma$, such that*

1. *if $Q \overset{\tau}{\to}_s R$ then $\mathbf{m}_\Gamma^P(Q) \overset{\tau}{\to} \mathbf{m}_\Gamma^P(R)$ in $[\![P]\!]_\Gamma$;*
2. *if $\mathbf{m}_\Gamma^P(Q) \overset{\tau}{\to} m$ in $[\![P]\!]_\Gamma$ then $Q \overset{\tau}{\to}_s R$ with $m = \mathbf{m}_\Gamma^P(R)$.*

Proof. Since by Lemma 1(1) silent transitions in $\to$ and $\to_s$ are exactly the same, the result follows from a straightforward adaption of [2, Theorem1]. □

5 Traces in ACCS and in Open Nets

The correspondence between the reduction-based operational semantics of ACCS processes and their net encodings immediately lifts to a preservation and reflection of various behavioural equivalence, notably weak and strong barbed bisimilarity (see [2,3]). In this section we show that the correspondence holds also for trace equivalence, as it is easily proved if the saturated LTS is considered.

We first observe a mismatch between the notion of trace for ACCS processes in Sect. 2, which captures the interactive behaviour of a process only up to the $\leq_m$ preorder on traces, and that for Petri nets, which instead fully describe all the possible interactions of a system with its environment. Indeed, for such notion of trace, trace inclusion is not reflected by the net encoding of processes.

Example 6. Consider again the processes $P = (\nu d)(!_d.\bar{e} \mid (a.(\bar{a} \mid \bar{d} \mid d.\bar{c}) \oplus \tau.(\bar{d} \mid d.\bar{c})))$ and $Q = (\nu d)(\tau.(d.\bar{c} \mid d.\bar{e} \mid \bar{d}))$ as introduced in Example 1. We already observed there that $a\bar{a}\bar{e} \in traces_s(P)$, while $a\bar{a}\bar{e} \notin traces_s(Q)$. On the contrary, the encodings of P and Q have exactly the same traces: indeed, this also happens in the saturated LTS, as shown in Example 2.

We next prove that by considering traces for ACCS processes on the saturated LTS of Sect. 3 there is a perfect match between trace semantics for ACCS processes and for their encodings. More precisely, it is possible to prove that in the saturated LTS the correspondence between transitions of an ACCS process and those of its encoding, is not limited to internal reductions (as expressed by Theorem 3) but extends to labelled transitions.

Theorem 4 (Labelled transitions as net firings). *Let P be a bound ACCS process, Γ a set of names and $Q \in reach(P)$. Then*

1. *if $Q \xrightarrow{v} R$ and $v \in \Gamma \cup \overline{\Gamma}$ then $\mathbf{m}_\Gamma^P(Q) \xrightarrow{v} \mathbf{m}_\Gamma^P(R)$ in $[\![P]\!]_\Gamma$;*
2. *if $\mathbf{m}_\Gamma^P(Q) \xrightarrow{v} m$ in $[\![P]\!]_\Gamma$ then $Q \xrightarrow{v} R$ with $m = \mathbf{m}_\Gamma^P(R)$.*

Proof. 1. Assume that $Q \xrightarrow{v} R$ and $v \in \Gamma \cup \overline{\Gamma}$. We distinguish two cases. If $v = a \in \Gamma$ then by definition of the saturated semantics $R = Q \mid \bar{a}$. By definition of the encoding a is an open place in $[\![P]\!]_\Gamma$, hence $\mathbf{m}_\Gamma^P(Q) \xrightarrow{a} \mathbf{m}_\Gamma^P(Q) \oplus a = \mathbf{m}_\Gamma^P(R)$.

If instead, $v = \bar{a} \in \overline{\Gamma}$, then by definition of the saturated semantics it must be $Q \equiv R \mid \bar{a}$. By definition of the encoding a is an open place in $[\![P]\!]_\Gamma$, hence $\mathbf{m}_\Gamma^P(Q) \xrightarrow{\bar{a}} \mathbf{m}_\Gamma^P(Q) \ominus a = \mathbf{m}_\Gamma^P(R)$.

2. Analogous.   □

Finally, by using the above result and by recalling that, by Lemma 1(1), silent transitions in $\rightarrow$ and $\rightarrow_s$ coincide, we can conclude the following.

Corollary 1 (Preservation and reflection of trace semantics). *Let P, Q be ACCS bound processes and Γ a set of names such that $fn((P)) \cup fn((Q)) \subseteq \Gamma$. Then $traces(P) \subseteq traces(Q)$ iff $traces(\mathbf{m}_\Gamma^P(P)) \subseteq traces(\mathbf{m}_\Gamma^Q(Q))$.*

6   Conclusions and Further Works

In this paper we investigated trace semantics and its may testing characterisation for asynchronous calculi, focusing on asynchronous CCS, and their encodings based on open Petri nets. By considering the LTS of [11,19], we proved that the trace semantics is preserved and reflected by the encoding.

It has to be noted that Theorems 3 and 4 are reminiscent of the similar results in [2,3], and they are actually made easier by the simpler net encoding for ACCS, with respect to CSP, which is presented here. Also noteworthy is the possible connection between the testing semantics and the minimal context semantics, as originally proposed in [21]. We already explored the connection with weak and strong barbed bisimilarities for ACCS in [6], and we do hope that the present work will help cast further lights on other observational equivalences.

Indeed, observe that the results in the paper naturally suggests also a notion of (may) testing semantics for Petri nets, where an observer is any other net including some success transition. Few studies exist in the literature (see, e.g., [20]) and it seems non-trivial to understand whether may testing for nets would coincide with trace equivalence. Differently from processes, the notion of context for nets, intended as a expression built out of constants and sequential and parallel composition, seems too powerful, since it allows for reusing the same transition several times and to merge open places.

In [12], Pierpaolo and coauthors pointed out that a good encoding of a (synchronous) calculus into nets should also preserve the intended degree of concurrency. Our proposal seems to move away from this requirement in the encoding of the replication $!_a.P$ (see Fig. 8(e)). Each unfolding step causes not only its continuation P but also the following occurrences of $a.P$ while, intuitively, these should be considered independent as $!_a.P$ is a finite shorthand for $a.P \mid a.P \mid \ldots$. A solution to this problem – as suggested in a different context in [10, Section 7.2] – could be found by using contextual nets [23] and replacing the feedback edges in Fig. 8(e) with a single read arc. We did not adopt this solution in order to keep our model as simple as possible, and because we decided to leave out of the scope of this paper any analysis of concurrency. The validity of our choice is motivated by a general analysis concerning the concurrent features of systems communicating by means of asynchronous interactions: as we showed in [5], concurrency cannot be observed in such systems, and they include those specified by ACCS and open Petri nets.

Acknowledgements. We are indebted in many ways to Pierpaolo Degano. Indeed, the earliest exposure of the third author to Petri nets was in a remote cycle of seminars, whose initial lesson was introduced by the quotation in the first page. A scary moment, if there ever was one. Along the years, we all –either as Ph.D. students or later on as co-authors/colleagues/partners in projects– benefited from the insights and availability of Pierpaolo. More technically, we already mentioned his early contributions on net encoding for calculi. In general terms, the insistence on the proof structure of a computation in order to distill a suitable (concurrent) semantics for a calculus, which is typical of the work of Pierpaolo since the early Eighties, has been a fixed star: the modularity of our net encoding spills out of this "commandment".

We are most grateful to the anonymous reviewers whose suggestions and remarks helped us to improve the paper.

References

1. Amadio, R., Castellani, I., Sangiorgi, D.: On bisimulations for the asynchronous π-calculus. Theoret. Comput. Sci. **195**(2), 291–324 (1998)
2. Baldan, P., Bonchi, F., Gadducci, F., Monreale, G.: Modular encoding of synchronous and asynchronous interactions using open Petri nets. Sci. Comput. Program. **109**, 96–124 (2015)
3. Baldan, P., Bonchi, F., Gadducci, F., Monreale, G.V.: Encoding synchronous interactions using labelled Petri nets. In: Kühn, E., Pugliese, R. (eds.) COORDINATION 2014. LNCS, vol. 8459, pp. 1–16. Springer, Heidelberg (2014)
4. Baldan, P., Corradini, A., Ehrig, H., Heckel, R.: Compositional semantics for open Petri nets based on deterministic processes. Math. Struct. Comput. Sci. **15**(1), 1–35 (2004)

5. Baldan, P., Bonchi, F., Gadducci, F., Monreale, G.V.: Concurrency cannot be observed, asynchronously. Math. Struct. Comput. Sci. **25**(4), 978–1004 (2015)
6. Bonchi, F., Gadducci, F., Monreale, G.V.: A general theory of barbs, contexts, and labels. ACM Trans. Comput. Logic **15**(4), 35:1–35:27 (2014)
7. Boreale, M., De Nicola, R., Pugliese, R.: Trace and testing equivalence on asynchronous processes. Inf. Comput. **172**(2), 139–164 (2002)
8. Bruni, R., Melgratti, H.C., Montanari, U., Sobocinski, P.: Connector algebras for C/E and P/T nets' interactions. Log. Methods Comput. Sci. **9**(3), 1–65 (2013)
9. Busi, N., Gorrieri, R., Zavattaro, G.: Comparing three semantics for Linda-like languages. Theoret. Comput. Sci. **240**(1), 49–90 (2000)
10. Busi, N., Gorrieri, R.: Distributed semantics for the π-calculus based on Petri nets with inhibitor arcs. Logic Algebraic Program. **78**(3), 138–162 (2009)
11. Castellani, I., Hennessy, M.: Testing theories for asynchronous languages. In: Sarukkai, S., Arvind, V. (eds.) FST TCS 1998. LNCS, vol. 1530, pp. 90–102. Springer, Heidelberg (1998)
12. Degano, P., De Nicola, R., Montanari, U.: CCS is an (augmented) contact free C/E system. In: Zilli, M.V. (ed.) Mathematical Models for the Semantics of Parallelism. LNCS, vol. 280, pp. 144–165. Springer, Heidelberg (1986)
13. Degano, P., De Nicola, R., Montanari, U.: A distributed operational semantics for CCS based on condition/event systems. Acta Informatica **26**(1/2), 59–91 (1988)
14. Degano, P., Gorrieri, R., Marchetti, S.: An exercise in concurrency: a CSP process as a condition/event system. In: Rozenberg, G. (ed.) APN 1998. LNCS, vol. 340, pp. 85–105. Springer, Heidelberg (1987)
15. Devillers, R., Klaudel, H., Koutny, M.: A compositional Petri net translation of general π-calculus terms. Formal Aspects Comput. **20**(4–5), 429–450 (2008)
16. Goltz, U.: CCS and Petri nets. In: Guessarian, I. (ed.) Semantics of Systems of Concurrent Processes. LNCS, vol. 469, pp. 334–357. Springer, Heidelberg (1990)
17. Gorrieri, G., Montanari, U.: SCONE: A simple calculus of nets. In: Baeten, J.C.M., Klop, J.W. (eds.) CONCUR 1990. LNCS, vol. 458, pp. 2–31. Springer, Heidelberg (1990)
18. Hoare, C.A.R.: Communicating Sequential Processes. Prentice Hall, Upper Saddle River (1985)
19. Honda, K., Tokoro, M.: An object calculus for asynchronous communication. In: Tokoro, M., Nierstrasz, O., Wegner, P. (eds.) ECOOP 1991. LNCS, vol. 612, pp. 21–51. Springer, Heidelberg (1991)
20. Jenner, L., Vogler, W.: Fast asynchronous systems in dense time. Theoret. Comput. Sci. **254**(1–2), 379–422 (2001)
21. Leifer, J.J., Milner, R.: Deriving bisimulation congruences for reactive systems. In: Palamidessi, C. (ed.) CONCUR 2000. LNCS, vol. 1877, p. 243. Springer, Heidelberg (2000)
22. Milner, R.: Bigraphs for Petri nets. In: Reisig, W., Desel, J., Rozenberg, G. (eds.) Lectures on Concurrency and Petri Nets. LNCS, vol. 3098, pp. 686–701. Springer, Heidelberg (2004)
23. Montanari, U., Rossi, F.: Contextual nets. Acta Informatica **32**(6), 545–596 (1995)
24. Sassone, V., Sobociński, P.: A congruence for Petri nets. In: Mens, T., Schürr, A., Taentzer, G. (eds.) PNGT 2004. ENTCS, vol. 127, pp. 107–120. Elsevier (2005)
25. Selinger, P.: Categorical structure of asynchrony. In: Brookes, S., Jung, A., Mislove, M., Scedrov, A. (eds.) MFPS 1999. ENTCS, vol. 20. Elsevier (1999)
26. Winskel, G.: A new definition of morphism on Petri nets. In: Fontet, M., Mehlhorn, K. (eds.) STACS 1984. LNCS, vol. 166, pp. 140–150. Springer, Heidelberg (1984)

Compliance in Behavioural Contracts: A Brief Survey

Massimo Bartoletti[1(✉)], Tiziana Cimoli[1], and Roberto Zunino[2]

[1] Università Degli Studi di Cagliari, Cagliari, Italy
bart@unica.it
[2] Università Degli Studi di Trento, Trento, Italy

Abstract. Behavioural contracts are formal specifications of interaction protocols between two or more distributed services. Despite the heterogeneous nature of the formalisms for behavioural contracts that have appeared in the literature, most of them feature a notion of *compliance*, which characterises when two or more contracts lead to correct interactions between services respecting them. We discuss and compare a selection of these notions in four different models of contracts: τ-less CCS, session types, interface automata, and contract automata.

1 Introduction

Several recent works study *behavioural contracts* as a tool to formalise and discipline correct interactions between distributed services [46]. Many of these works define, or build upon, some notion of *compliance* (also called *duality*, *conformance*, or *agreement*) between two or more contracts. Intuitively, compliance between contracts guarantees that services respecting them will interact "correctly", according to some notion of correctness which varies from approach to approach. This notion is exploited e.g., to type-check whether the specification of a service respects its contracts [33,42–45], or to dynamically compose services with compliant ones [15,16,18].

To choose the most suitable notion of "correct behaviour" for a given distributed application, it would be desirable to have a clear understanding of the actual properties enjoyed by various notions of compliance, and of the relations among them. This is not an easy task, because the ecosystem of notions proposed in the literature is wide and heterogeneous. Indeed, many different compliance relations have been considered in the literature, and they have been defined on, or applied to, a variety of different languages and formalisms, among which session-types [17,22,23], Petri nets [8,56], process algebras [26–28,34,47] and various automata-based models [20,21,37,51], among others.

In this paper we start a systematic investigation of compliance relations between behavioural contracts. We aim for a semantic, language-independent analysis, which abstracts from the actual formalism wherein contracts are given meaning. Along the lines of the treatment of behavioural equivalences and preorders in concurrency theory, we model contracts as states in Labelled Transition

© Springer International Publishing Switzerland 2015
C. Bodei et al. (Eds.): Degano Festschrift, LNCS 9465, pp. 103–121, 2015.
DOI: 10.1007/978-3-319-25527-9_9

Systems (LTSs), with labels ranging over input, output, and internal actions. This interpretation is straightforward for some models of contracts (e.g., interface automata [37] are just finite-state LTSs), while others can be dealt with by relating them to LTSs (e.g., session types and τ-less CCS processes induce an LTS through their operational semantics). By exploiting this common ground, we formalise different notions of compliance as relations between LTS states, and we compare them in four classes of contracts: τ-less CCS [39], session types [43], interface automata [37], and contract automata [20]. The results of our investigation are reported in Sect. 4, and an overview of other related approaches, not yet included in our formal comparison, is given in Sect. 5.

2   Contracts

In this Sect. 2 we provide a unifying ground for behavioural contracts. They will be formalised as states of a Labelled Transition System (LTS) where labels are partitioned into *internal*, *input*, and *output* actions. We will show that contracts expressed in other formalisms (e.g., τ-less CCS and session types) can be interpreted as states of this LTS. All the compliance relations defined later on in Sect. 3. will be formalised as binary relations between states.

2.1   Basics

Our treatment is developed within the LTS $\left(\mathbb{U}, \mathsf{A}_\tau, \{\xrightarrow{\ell_\tau} \mid \ell_\tau \in \mathsf{A}_\tau\} \right)$, where:

- $\mathbb{U}$ is the universe of *states* (ranged over by $p, q, \ldots$), also called *contracts*;
- A_τ (ranged over by $\ell_\tau, \ell'_\tau, \ldots$) is the set of *labels*, partitioned into *input actions* $?\mathsf{a}, ?\mathsf{b}, \ldots \in \mathsf{A}^?$, *output actions* $!\mathsf{a}, !\mathsf{b}, \ldots \in \mathsf{A}^!$, and the *internal action* τ;
- $\xrightarrow{\ell_\tau} \subseteq \mathbb{U} \times \mathbb{U}$ is a *transition relation*, for all ℓ_τ.

We let $\ell, \ell', \ldots$ range over $\mathsf{A} = \mathsf{A}^? \cup \mathsf{A}^!$. We postulate an involution $\mathrm{co}(\cdot)$ on A, such that $\mathrm{co}(?\mathsf{a}) = \,!\mathsf{a}$ and $\mathrm{co}(!\mathsf{a}) = \,?\mathsf{a}$. The *reducts of* p are the states reachable from p with an arbitrary sequence of transitions; we say that p is *finite-state* when the set of its reducts is finite. A *trace* is a (possibly infinite) sequence $p_0 \xrightarrow{\ell_\tau{}^{(1)}} p_1 \xrightarrow{\ell_\tau{}^{(2)}} \cdots$. A τ-trace is a trace where $\ell_\tau{}^{(i)} = \tau$, for all i (similarly for τ-reduct). We denote with $\mathbf{0}$ a state with no outgoing transitions, and we will interpret $\mathbf{0}$ as the *success* state. We show some (finite-state) contracts in Fig. 1.

Notation 1. *We adopt the following notation:*

- $\mathcal{R}^*$ *for the reflexive and transitive closure of a relation* $\mathcal{R}$
- $p \xrightarrow{\ell_\tau}$ *when* $\exists p'. p \xrightarrow{\ell_\tau} p'$. *Further, we write* $p \to$ *when* $\exists \ell_\tau. p \xrightarrow{\ell_\tau}$
- *for a set* $L \subseteq \mathsf{A}$, *we define* $L^? = L \cap \mathsf{A}^?$ *and* $L^! = L \cap \mathsf{A}^!$
- $\Rightarrow \; = (\xrightarrow{\tau})^*$ *is the* weak transition relation. *We define* $\overset{\ell_\tau}{\Rightarrow}$ *as* $\Rightarrow \xrightarrow{\ell_\tau} \Rightarrow$
- $p\!\downarrow \; = \{\ell \mid p \xrightarrow{\ell}\}$ *are the* barbs *of* p, *and* $p\!\Downarrow \; = \{\ell \mid p \overset{\ell}{\Rightarrow}\}$ *are its* weak barbs
- $p\!\uparrow$ *is true when* p *has an infinite internal computation* $p \xrightarrow{\tau} p_1 \xrightarrow{\tau} p_2 \xrightarrow{\tau} \cdots$

The above notation for $\rightarrow$ is extended to $\Rightarrow$ as expected.

Two contracts can be composed with the operator $\parallel$, which formalises the standard synchronisation à la CCS [52].

Definition 1 (Parallel composition). *For all $p, q \in \mathbb{U}$, we define the parallel composition $p \parallel q$ as the state in $\mathbb{U}$ whose transitions are given by the rules:*

$$\frac{p \xrightarrow{\ell_\tau} p'}{p \parallel q \xrightarrow{\ell_\tau} p' \parallel q} \qquad \frac{q \xrightarrow{\ell_\tau} q'}{p \parallel q \xrightarrow{\ell_\tau} p \parallel q'} \qquad \frac{p \xrightarrow{\ell} p' \quad q \xrightarrow{co(\ell)} q'}{p \parallel q \xrightarrow{\tau} p' \parallel q'}$$

We describe in the following subsections some classes of contracts which have been considered in the literature.

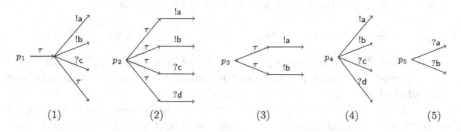

(1)   (2)   (3)   (4)   (5)

Fig. 1. Some contracts.

2.2 Interface Automata

As a first subclass of the set $\mathbb{U}$, we consider *interface automata* [37]. These are finite-state automata, which can communicate through the synchronization of input and output actions, and they can perform internal actions (possibly of different kinds). Synchronization of input and output actions is obtained in [37] by constructing the cartesian product of interface automata, with the restriction that matching input and output actions must fire simultaneously.

To adapt interface automata to our framework, we collapse the different internal actions to τ. Once this is done, interface automata simply correspond to finite-state contracts. Note that in our framework we do not need to explicitly construct the cartesian product, since we obtain a contract with the same behaviour through Definition 1. We then denote with IA the set of finite-state contracts (so, IA $\subset \mathbb{U}$). For instance, all the contracts in Fig. 1 belong to IA.

2.3 τ-less CCS

The contracts used in [32, 34, 47] are terms of the process calculus CCS without τs [39]. Differently from Milners CCS [52], these have two kinds of choice. In an *internal choice* $C \oplus D$ the process decides which one of the two branches to follow, whereas in an *external choice* $C \And D$, the decision is taken by the environment.

To have a simple embedding of τ-less CCS into our framework, we restrict our study to the fragment where choices are prefix-guarded.

Definition 2 (τ-less CCS). τ-less CCS processes *are terms with the syntax:*

$$C ::= \bigwedge_{i \in I} \ell_i.C_i \ \big| \ \bigoplus_{i \in I} \ell_i.C_i \ \big| \ \mathrm{rec}_X \, C \ \big| \ X$$

where (i) the set I is finite, (ii) the actions ℓ_i in internal/external choices are pairwise distinct, and (iii) recursion is prefix-guarded.

We write 0 for the empty (internal/external) choice, and omit trailing occurrences of 0. We adopt the equi-recursive approach, by considering terms up-to unfolding of recursion. The semantics of τ-less CCS is given below.

Definition 3. *We denote with τC the set of contracts of the form C or $[!a]\,C$, with C closed, and transitions given by the following rules:*

$$\bigwedge_{i \in I} \ell_i.C_i \xrightarrow{\ell_k} C_k \ (k \in I) \qquad \bigoplus_{i \in I} \ell_i.C_i \xrightarrow{\tau} [\ell_k]\,C_k \ (k \in I) \qquad [\ell]\,C \xrightarrow{\ell} C$$

An external choice can always perform each of its actions. An internal choice $\bigoplus_{i \in I} \ell_i.C_i$ must first commit to one of the branches $\ell_k.C_k$, and this produces a *committed choice* $[\ell_k]\,C_k$, which can only perform the action ℓ_k. As a consequence, a contract in τC may have several outgoing transitions (either input or output), but internal transitions cannot be mixed with input/output ones. There cannot be two internal transitions in a row, and after an internal transition, the target state will have exactly one outgoing transition. Contracts in τC are finite-state, so τC $\subseteq$ IA.

Example 1. The process $C = \, !a \oplus !b \oplus ?c \oplus ?d$ is denoted by the contract p_2 in Fig. 1, while the contract p_4 denotes the process $!a \& !b \& ?c \& ?d$: indeed, since the latter is an external choice, all the labels are enabled at the same time. Instead, the contract p_1 in Fig. 1 does not belong to τC, for two different reasons. First, it has an internal transition at the same level of a non-internal one; second, there are two consecutive internal transitions.

Note that, if we allowed internal actions in external choices, we would essentially turn the choice into an internal one. Indeed, the abstraction operator of [31] makes internal choices emerge from external ones. However, such abstraction produces contracts which go beyond τC, and are instead contained in IA.

2.4 Session Types

Session types [43,44] are terms of a process algebra featuring a *selection* construct (i.e., an internal choice among a set of branches, each one performing some output), and a *branching* construct (i.e., an external choice among a set of inputs offered to the environment). With the restriction given in Sect. 2.3 (i.e., choices are prefix-guarded), and further assuming no channel passing, session types are just a special case of τ-less CCS contracts, where the actions in internal choices are all outputs, and the actions in external choices are all inputs.

Definition 4 (Session types). Session types *are τ-less CCS processes respecting the following syntax:*

$$T \quad ::= \quad \&_{i \in I} ?\mathsf{a}_i . T_i \mid \bigoplus_{i \in I} !\mathsf{a}_i . T_i \mid \mathrm{rec}_X T \mid X$$

We denote with ST the set of contracts of the form T or $[!\mathsf{a}]\, T$, with T closed and transitions given as in Definition 3. Note that all the outgoing transitions from a state must have the same (internal/input/output) kind. It is easy to check that $\mathrm{ST} \subset \tau\mathrm{C}$.

Example 2. The contract p_4 in Fig. 1 represents the session type $!\mathsf{a} \oplus !\mathsf{b}$. Since it is an internal choice, according with Definition 3, there is a commit on the chosen branch before actually firing the output action. The contract p_4 does not belong to ST because it has two output transitions on the same level, and they are also mixed with input ones. The contract p_2 does not belong to ST, because it has a internal transition before an input transition.

While ST is a strict subset of $\tau\mathrm{C}$, note that it is possible to encode the latter in the former, as shown in [48].

2.5 Contract Automata

Contract automata [19,20] are similar to interface automata, from which they differ in the interpretation of labels. Labels are either *requests*, modelling resources/interactions expected from the environment, or *offers*, modelling resources/interactions produced in exchange. Internal actions are not allowed. The interaction between contract automata is obtained through a composition operation, similar to that of interface automata. An interaction is considered *successful* if all the requested actions are met, while the offered actions may be ignored. Offered actions are considered to be available to the counterpart, which can either choose to use or ignore them. This is similar to the intuition of external choices in session types, so we model offers as actions in $\mathsf{A}^?$; symmetrically, we model requests as actions in $\mathsf{A}^!$. The contracts obtained from contract automata are finite-state and they have no internal actions. We denote them with CA.

Lemma 1. $\mathrm{CA} \subset \tau\mathrm{C}$, *and* $\mathrm{ST} \cap \mathrm{CA} \neq \emptyset$.

Proof. Since a contract automaton is finite-state, one can regard it as a set of recursive equations of the form $X_i = \&_j \ell_j . C_j$, where C_j are τ-less CCS processes. These can be turned into a $\tau\mathrm{C}$ contract applying Bekič's lemma.

To show that $\mathrm{ST} \cap \mathrm{CA} \neq \emptyset$, it suffices to pick p_5 in Fig. 1. $\qquad\square$

Example 3. The contract p_4 in Fig. 1 belongs to CA: it fires input and output actions at the same level and no τ is present. On the contrary, the contracts p_1, p_2 and p_3 do not belong to CA, because of the presence of internal transactions.

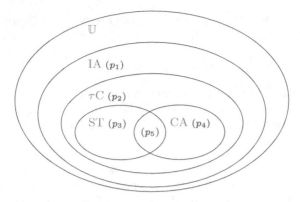

Fig. 2. Relations between some classes of contracts (all the inclusions are strict).

2.6 Relations Between Classes of Contracts

Figure 2 relates the classes of contracts considered in the previous subsections, and the derived class $\tau C^- = \tau C \setminus (ST \cup CA)$. To show that all the inclusions are strict, consider the contracts in Fig. 1. We have that $p_1 \in IA \setminus \tau C$; $p_2 \in \tau C \setminus \{ST \cup CA\}$; $p_3 \in ST \setminus CA$; $p_4 \in CA \setminus ST$; $p_5 \in ST \cap CA$. To show $IA \subset U$, it suffices to take an infinite-state contract.

3   Compliance Relations

In this section we survey some notions of compliance that have appeared in the literature, and we formalise them as relations between contracts in the LTS of Sect. 2. Since many of the original definitions apply to specific models, in order to unify the study of these notions we had to adapt some of them. For instance, some works focus on symmetric relations, while some others on *asymmetric* ones, where one of the two contracts (e.g., playing the role of a client), may be allowed to terminate interaction or to skip messages despite of the state of the other one (e.g., playing the role of a server). For uniformity, in this paper we only consider asymmetric relations. In most cases, a symmetric compliance relation $\bowtie$ can be obtained by intersecting asymmetric compliance $\lhd$ with its inverse relation (a notable exception is $\lhd_{may}$ in Definition 6). Further, although some notions of compliance in the literature are naturally multi-party (e.g., compatibility in IA [37]), for uniformity we restrict them to the *binary* case, where only two participants are involved.

Progress. We start by considering the notion of *progress*, where compliance is interpreted as the absence of deadlock (on the client-side, since we are considering the asymmetric relation). Formally, in Definition 5 we say that a contract p has progress with q (in symbols, $p \lhd_{pg} q$) iff, whenever a τ-reduct of $p \parallel q$ cannot take internal transitions, then p has reached the success state.

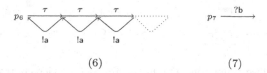

(6)   (7)

Fig. 3. Two session types with an asynchronous semantics.

Definition 5 (Progress). *We write* $p \lhd_{pg} q$ *iff:*

$$p \parallel q \Rightarrow p' \parallel q' \not\xrightarrow{\tau} \quad \text{implies} \quad p' = \mathbf{0}$$

Example 4. Consider the pair of contracts (10) in Fig. 6. When composed together, p_{10} and q_{10} can synchronise on label a, after which they both reach success. Hence, $p_{10} \bowtie_{pg} q_{10}$. The two contracts in (12) can synchronise forever, so $p_{12} \bowtie_{pg} q_{12}$. Consider now the pair (13): when composed together, we have $p_{13} \parallel q_{13} \xrightarrow{\tau} \xrightarrow{\tau} p' \parallel \mathbf{0} \not\xrightarrow{\tau}$, with $p' \neq \mathbf{0}$. Therefore, $p_{13} \not\bowtie_{pg} q_{13}$, while $q_{13} \lhd_{pg} p_{13}$.

This notion has been used e.g. in τ-less CCS [34], in session types (both untimed [3] and timed [7]), and in types for CaSPiS [1]. Note that in *asynchronous* session types [36] the progress-based compliance of Definition 5 can relate contracts which arguably admit correct interactions. For instance, consider the session types $C_6 = \text{rec}_X\, !\text{a}.X$ and $C_7 = ?\text{b}$, and let p_6 and p_7 (displayed in Fig. 3) denote their asynchronous semantics. In p_6, internal actions are used to enqueue outputs in a FIFO buffer; queued outputs can then be fired. The asynchronous semantics of C_7 (denoted by p_7) is identical to the synchronous one. Clearly, $C_6 \not\bowtie_{pg} C_7$, because $C_6 \parallel C_7$ is stuck. Instead, we have that $p_6 \bowtie_{pg} p_7$, because the interaction of the two contracts produces an infinite τ-trace, even if no synchronisation ever happens. Stricter notions of compliance, like e.g. those in Definition 8 to 10, manage to avoid such "vacuous" progress, where two contracts merely advance via internal τ-transitions (without ever synchronising).

May-testing compliance. The following three notions of compliance (Definitions 6 to 8) are inspired by the theory of testing in concurrent systems [38]. In Definition 6, a contract p is said *may-testing compliant* with q (in symbols, $p \lhd_{may} q$) if there exists a finite τ-trace of $p \parallel q$ which leads p to the success state.

Definition 6 (May-testing compliance). *We write* $p \lhd_{may} q$ *iff*

$$\exists q' . \ p \parallel q \Rightarrow \mathbf{0} \parallel q'$$

Example 5 The pair of contracts (15) in Fig. 6 can synchronise on a and then succeed (on both sides); hence, $p_{15} \bowtie_{may} q_{15}$. In (12), both contracts can fire actions in a loop but they cannot terminate, so $p_{12} \not\bowtie_{may} q_{12}$ and $q_{12} \not\bowtie_{may} p_{12}$.

May-testing compliance assumes a *cooperative* scenario, where all the participants collaborate to achieve a common goal: if there is a way for the interaction

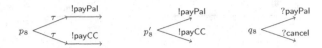

Fig. 4. Two client contracts p_8, p_8' and one service contract q_8.

to succeed, it is enough, disregarding all the possible unsuccessful interactions. This requires participants to pre-agree on their internal choices, and the scheduler to only permit the synchronisations leading to success. For instance, in (15) the scheduler must not allow p_{15} and q_{15} to synchronise on b, since this would prevent p_{15} from reaching the success state. The $\lhd_{may}$ relation is similar to the *agreement* relation used in CA [19], under the assumption that there are only two contracts, and there exists a unique success state.

Example 6. Figure 4 shows two different ways to represent choices. The contracts p_8 and p_8' model two clients of an online store, which want to pay by PayPal (payPal) or by credit card (payCC). Instead, the contract q_8 models an online store which accepts payments with PayPal, or it allows clients to cancel the transaction. Using progress-based compliance, we have $p_8 \not\lhd_{pg} q_8$ and $p_8' \lhd_{pg} q_8$. Instead, using may-testing compliance, we have that $p_8 \lhd_{may} q_8$ and $p_8' \lhd_{may} q_8$. From this we may observe two facts. First, under progress-based compliance, p_8 and p_8' represent two different kinds of choice. The τ actions in p_8 force Definition 5 to consider *both* paths; instead, in p_8' the transition !payCC can be ignored when testing compliance with q_8, because no synchronisation on payCC can happen. So, in a sense the choice in p_8 is made by the client, while that in p_8' is made by the scheduler (or by the server). Second, note that may-testing compliance cannot discriminate between the two kinds of choice: indeed, Definition 6 assumes that all the choices are performed by an oracle, which always follows the path (if any) leading to success.

Must-testing compliance. The notion of compliance in [2] is inspired to must-testing [38]. This relation is stricter than may-testing, because it requires a contract to reach success in *all* (sufficiently long) traces. Formally, we say that a τ-trace $r_0 \to r_1 \to \cdots$ is *maximal* if it is infinite, or if it ends in a state r_n such that $r_n \not\to$. A contract p is must-testing compliant with q (in symbols, $p \lhd_{mst} q$) if, in all the maximal τ-traces of $p \parallel q$, the contract p reaches the success state.

Definition 7 (Must-testing compliance). *We write* $p_0 \lhd_{mst} q_0$ *iff*

$$\text{for all maximal } \tau\text{-traces } p_0 \parallel q_0 \xrightarrow{\tau} p_1 \parallel q_1 \xrightarrow{\tau} \cdots \ : \ \exists i \geq 0 \,.\, p_i = \mathbf{0}$$

Example 7. Consider the pair of contracts (16) in Fig. 6. We have $p_{16} \bowtie_{mst} q_{16}$: indeed, there are two finite maximal τ-traces, and they lead both contracts to success. For the pair (20), there are two infinite maximal τ-traces. In the first trace, there is a finite number of synchronisations on a, then one synchronisation on b, and finally the contract q_{20} loops forever with internal moves. Here, the contract p_{20} reaches success after the synchronisation on b. In the other maximal τ-trace, the two contracts synchronise on a forever, but p_{20} never reaches success. Hence, we have that $p_{20} \not\lhd_{mst} q_{20}$ and $q_{20} \not\lhd_{mst} p_{20}$.

Compared to may-testing compliance, in must-testing compliance we are no longer assuming that participants are cooperative: indeed, p must succeed, whatever internal choices q takes, and whatever synchronisations the scheduler enables. In a sense, all the choices (of q, of the scheduler, and also of p) are considered *demonic*, while in may-testing compliance they are all *angelic*.

Fig. 5. The contract of an online store (q_9) and of a client (p_9).

Example 8. Consider the contract q_9 of an online store, and the contract p_9 of one of its clients. The client can iteratively add items to the shopping cart, or eventually choose to check out (and succeed). On the other side, the online store acknowledges the chosen items, and it succeeds when the client checks out. These contracts can be described in ST as $p_9 = \text{rec}_X\ !\text{addItem}.X \oplus !\text{checkOut}$, and $q_9 = \text{rec}_X\ ?\text{addItem}.X\ \&\ ?\text{checkOut}$. Note that there exists a maximal (infinite) trace where the client always chooses to add a new item, hence by Definition 7 it follows that $p_9 \not\lessdot_{mst} q_9$ and $q_9 \not\lessdot_{mst} p_9$. The fact that $p_9 \not\lessdot_{mst} q_9$ is somehow arguable. Actually, Definition 7 is considering the choice between !addItem and !checkOut as a *demonic* non-deterministic choice, and not as a proper internal choice of the client. In the second interpretation of the choice, it would be reasonable to say that p_9 is compliant with q_9, because the client always has the opportunity to terminate. Instead, it is intuitively correct to say q_9 is *not* compliant with p_9, because the store cannot internally choose to terminate the loop and succeed.

Should-testing compliance. We now present a notion of compliance inspired by the theory of should-testing [29,53]. A contract p is *should-testing compliant* with q (in symbols, $p \lessdot_{shd} q$) if, after every possible *finite* τ-trace of $p \parallel q$, there exists a subsequent (finite) τ-trace which leads p to the success state.

Definition 8 (Should-testing compliance). *We write $p \lessdot_{shd} q$ iff*

$$p \parallel q \Rightarrow p' \parallel q' \quad implies \quad \exists q'' \ . \ p' \parallel q' \Rightarrow 0 \parallel q''$$

A notion similar to the one in Definition 8 has been used in [26] (under the name of *correct contract composition*), and in [9,56] (where it is named *weak termination*). A stricter notion, called *strong compliance* in [28], also requires that each output is matched by a corresponding input (similarly to *interface automata compatibility* in Definition 11).

Example 9. Consider the pair of contracts (21) in Fig. 6. After each (finite) sequence of internal actions of q_{21}, the two contracts can synchronise and reach success. Therefore, $p_{21} \bowtie_{shd} q_{21}$. In the pair (11), even though the two contracts enjoy progress, they can never reach the success state. Hence, we have that $p_{11} \not\lessdot_{shd} q_{11}$ and $q_{11} \not\lessdot_{shd} p_{11}$.

The previous example shows that, unlike progress, to be should-testing compliant it is not enough that two contracts have infinite interactions, but at any moment, it must be possible for them to succeed.

Example 10. Recall the contracts p_9 and q_9 from Example 8. We have that $p_9 \bowtie_{shd} q_9$, because at each point of the interaction it is possible to make both the client and the online store succeed. As remarked in Example 8, $q_9 \lhd_{shd} p_9$ may be counter-intuitive, because the success of the store relies on the assumption that the client will eventually choose to check out.

The previous example highlights the difference among the three notions of testing-based compliance in Definition 6 to 8. While in may-testing compliance all choices are angelic and in must-testing compliance they are all demonic, in should-testing compliance there are two kinds of choices. In the first part of the computation, $p \parallel q \Rightarrow p' \parallel q'$ in Definition 8, all the choices are demonic, while in the second part, $p' \parallel q' \Rightarrow \mathbf{0} \parallel q''$, they are all angelic.

None of the notions of compliance studied in this section considers the case where the choices of participant p are angelic, while those of its counterpart q are demonic. The works [10,11] explore this research direction, by interpreting contracts as multi-player concurrent games. However, since the setting is quite different from ours (i.e., the contracts in [10,11] are event structures, while in Sect. 2 we model them as states of an LTS), we do not include these game-theoretic notions of compliance in this survey.

Behavioural compliance. Definition 9 below formalises in our setting the relation called *behavioural compliance* in [47,49]. A contract p is compliant with q (in symbols, $p \lhd_{beh} q$), if, in every possible τ-reduct $p' \parallel q'$ of $p \parallel q$, two conditions are satisfied: if the reduct is stuck, then p' has reached success; otherwise, if q' alone can produce an infinite τ-trace, then p' must be able to reach success without further synchronisations.

Definition 9 (Behavioural compliance). *We write $p \lhd_{beh} q$ iff:*

$$p \parallel q \Rightarrow p' \parallel q' \quad implies \quad (p' \parallel q' \not\rightarrow implies \, p' = \mathbf{0}) \wedge (q' \uparrow implies \, p' \Rightarrow \mathbf{0})$$

Example 11. The pair of contracts (18) in Fig. 6. can loop forever with internal actions, but since neither p_{18} nor q_{18} can reach success, we have $p_{18} \not\lhd_{beh} q_{18}$ and $q_{18} \not\lhd_{beh} p_{18}$. For the pair (21), we have that q_{21} can prevent p_{21} from reaching the success state, by following an infinite internal computation: hence, $p_{21} \not\lhd_{beh} q_{21}$. However, $q_{21} \lhd_{beh} p_{21}$, because $q_{21} \parallel p_{21}$ never gets stuck (so, the first condition in Definition 9 holds), and p_{21} cannot perform internal actions (thus satisfying also the second condition).

Compared to must- and should-testing compliance, behavioural compliance allows two contracts to synchronise forever, without ever reaching success: for instance, in the pair (12) of Fig. 6, we have $p_{12} \lhd_{beh} q_{12}$, while $p_{12} \not\lhd_{mst} q_{12}$ and $p_{12} \not\lhd_{shd} q_{12}$. Unlike the notion of progress, behavioural compliance does not allow q (i.e., the participant playing the role of server) to produce infinite vacuous interactions: for instance, we have that $p_{21} \lhd_{pg} q_{21}$, but $p_{21} \not\lhd_{beh} q_{21}$.

I/O compliance. In [17], a contract p is considered compliant with q (in symbols, $p \lhd_{io} q$), if, in every possible τ-reduct $p' \parallel q'$ of $p \parallel q$, the weak outputs of p' are included in the weak inputs of q'; further, if p' has no weak outputs but still some weak inputs, then they include the weak outputs of q'.

Definition 10 (I/O compliance). *We write $p \lhd_{io} q$ iff $p \parallel q \Rightarrow p' \parallel q'$ implies:*

$$p'\Downarrow^! \subseteq \mathrm{co}(q'\Downarrow^?) \;\wedge\; ((p'\Downarrow^! = \emptyset \wedge p'\Downarrow^? \neq \emptyset) \implies \emptyset \neq q'\Downarrow^! \subseteq \mathrm{co}(p'\Downarrow^?))$$

Example 12. Consider the pair of contracts (19) in Fig. 6. We have that $p_{19}\Downarrow^! = \{!a\} \subseteq \mathrm{co}(q_{19}\Downarrow^?) = \mathrm{co}(\{?a, ?b\})$. After the synchronisation on a, p_{19} has no more output actions, and one of its input actions (?c) is matched by a weak output of q_{19}. Hence, $p_{19} \lhd_{io} q_{19}$. With similar arguments, we can show that $q_{19} \lhd_{io} p_{19}$. Consider now the pair (16). After the synchronisation on a, and after that q_{16} commits to the ?b branch, we have that one of the weak outputs of p_{16} (i.e., !c) is not matched by any of the inputs of the reduct of q_{16}, and so $p_{16} \not\lhd_{io} q_{16}$. Further, the inputs of the reduct of q_{16} (i.e., ?c) do not include the weak co-outputs of the reduct of p_{16}, and so $q_{16} \not\lhd_{io} p_{16}$.

Note that, unlike the other notions of compliance seen so far, in I/O compliance output actions are interpreted differently from input actions. This difference can be understood by interpreting Definition 10 as a game between the two players p and q, similarly to the bisimulation game [54]. The first condition in Definition 10 requires that, if p' wants to do some output (possibly after some τ-moves), then q' must match it with its inputs; the second condition requires that, if p' is *not* going to do any outputs, but she wants to do some input, then q' must be ready (possibly after some τ-moves) to do some output, and q' cannot have outputs other than those accepted by p'. I/O compliance coincides with progress on synchronous session types (see Theorem 1 to 2). Instead, when considering *asynchronous* session types, where the interaction between participants is mediated by two unbounded FIFO buffers, I/O compliance is equivalent to a notion of compliance based on progress, orphan messages and unspecified receptions [55]. Note that I/O compliance does not completely rule out vacuous infinite interactions, as witnessed by the pair of contracts (21) in Fig. 6.

Interface automata compatibility. Definition 11 below formalises in our setting the notion of *compatibility* between interface automata proposed in [37]. A contract p is compliant with q (in symbols, $p \lhd_{ia} q$), if, in every possible τ-reduct $p' \parallel q'$ of $p \parallel q$, the outputs of p' are included in the *immediate* inputs of q'. The symmetric version of this relation (i.e., $\lhd_{ia} \cap \lhd_{ia}^{-1}$) is equivalent to the notion of compatibility in [37], under the assumptions that there are only two automata, and that all non-internal variables are shared.

Definition 11 (Interface Automata compatibility). *We write $p \lhd_{ia} q$ iff:*

$$p \parallel q \Rightarrow p' \parallel q' \;\; and \;\; p' \xrightarrow{!a} \;\; implies \;\; q' \xrightarrow{?a}$$

Example 13. Consider the pair of contracts (13) in Fig. 6. After the synchronisation on a, the reduct of p_{13} has no more outputs, so $p_{13} \lhd_{ia} q_{13}$ — even though success has not been reached. The contract q_{13} has no outputs, and so $q_{13} \lhd_{ia} p$, for all p. Consider now the pair (17). Even though in all reachable τ-reducts $p' \parallel q'$ of $p_{17} \parallel q_{17}$, the outputs of p' are included in the *weak* inputs of q', in the reduct where p' and q' have synchronised on a but q' has *not* yet performed its internal action, we have that the outputs p' are not matched by the *immediate* inputs of q' (which are empty). Therefore, $p_{17} \not\lhd_{ia} q_{17}$. We also have that $q_{17} \not\lhd_{ia} p_{17}$, because the output !a in q_{17} is not immediately matched by the input ?a in p_{17}, which is preceeded by an internal action.

The relation in Definition 11 differs from the others seen so far in several aspects. First, output actions are interpreted differently from input actions (this features is shared only with I/O compliance). Second, $\lhd_{ia}$ is more sensitive to internal actions: if an input action ?a is preceded by an internal action, then it is not considered to match the output action !a. For instance, the contracts p_{17} and q_{17} in Fig. 6 are compliant according to all the relations considered in this Sect. 3, except $\lhd_{ia}$. Finally, unlike the other compliance relations (except $\lhd_{may}$), $\lhd_{ia}$ does not guarantee progress, as established by Theorem 1. Indeed, since input actions can be neglected, they can be left waiting forever, as in the contracts in (13)–(15) in Fig. 6.

4   Comparing Compliance Relations

The main results of the paper are summarised in Table 1, which establishes relations between the notions of compliance presented in Sect. 3. The table may be interpreted as follows. Let the metavariable $\mathbb{P}$ range over *sets* of contracts. If $\mathbb{P}$ occurs in row with label $\lhd_i$ and column with label $\lhd_j$ of Table 1, then:

$$\forall p, q \in \mathbb{P} : p \lhd_i q \implies p \lhd_j q \tag{1}$$

Table 1. Comparison of compliance relations.

	$\lhd_{pg}$	$\lhd_{shd}$	$\lhd_{io}$	$\lhd_{ia}$	$\lhd_{may}$	$\lhd_{mst}$	$\lhd_{beh}$
$\lhd_{pg}$		¬ST(11) ¬CA(12)	ST (th. 2) ¬CA(10)	ST (th. 3) ¬τC⁻(16) ¬CA(10)	¬ST(11) ¬CA(12)	¬ST(11) ¬CA(12)	τC (th. 5) ¬IA (18)
$\lhd_{shd}$	U (th. 1)		ST (th. 1 and 2) ¬CA(10)	ST (th. 1 and 3) ¬CA(10)	U (th. 1)	¬ST (20)	τC (th. 1 and 5) ¬IA (21)
$\lhd_{io}$	U (th. 1)	¬ST(11) ¬CA(12)		¬τC⁻(17) ST CA (th. 4)	¬ST(11) ¬CA(12)	¬ST(11) ¬CA(12)	τC (th. 1 and 5) ¬IA (18)
$\lhd_{ia}$	¬ST(13) ¬CA(14)	¬ST(13) ¬CA(14)	¬ST(13) ¬CA(14)		¬ST(11) ¬CA(12)	¬ST(11) ¬CA(12)	¬ST(13) ¬CA(14)
$\lhd_{may}$	¬CA(15)	¬CA(15)	¬CA(15)	¬CA(10)		¬CA(15)	¬CA(15)
$\lhd_{mst}$	U (th. 1)	U (th. 1)	¬CA(10)	¬CA(10)	U (th. 1)		U (th. 1)
$\lhd_{beh}$	U (th. 1)	¬ST(11) ¬CA(12)	¬CA(10)	¬CA(10)	¬ST(11) ¬CA(12)	¬ST(11,20) ¬CA(12)	

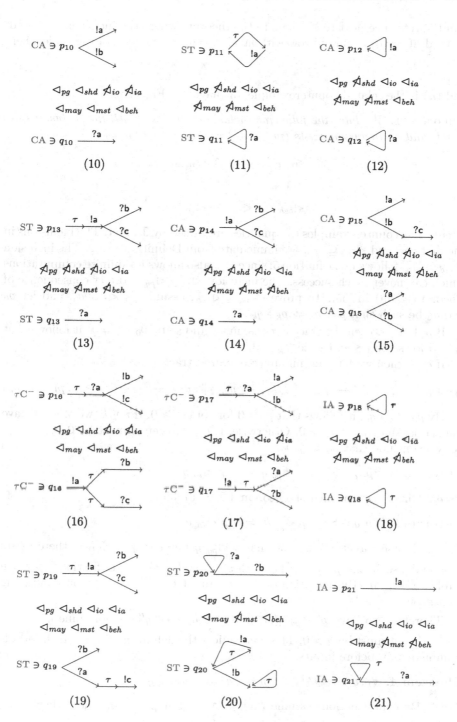

Fig. 6. Some pairs of contracts.

and the reference next to $\mathbb{P}$ points to the theorem where the inclusion is proved. Instead, if $\neg\mathbb{P}(n)$ occurs in row with label $\lhd_i$ and column $\lhd_j$ of the table, then:

$$\exists p, q \in \mathbb{P} \;:\; p \lhd_i q \,\wedge\, p \not\lhd_j q \tag{2}$$

and (n) is the related counterexample, displayed in Fig. 6.

Theorem 1. *We have the following inclusions in* $\mathbb{U} \times \mathbb{U}$. *All the inclusions are strict, and no inclusion exists (in* $\mathbb{U} \times \mathbb{U}$*) where none is shown.*

$$\lhd_{mst} \subset \lhd_{shd} \subset \lhd_{may}$$
$$\cap \qquad\quad \cap$$
$$\lhd_{beh} \subset \lhd_{pg} \supset \lhd_{io}$$

Proof. The counterexamples to equalities are linked by Table 1. The inclusions in the first row and $\lhd_{beh} \subseteq \lhd_{pg}$ are immediate from Definition 5 to 9. The inclusion $\lhd_{shd} \subseteq \lhd_{pg}$ follows by Definition 5, since $\lhd_{pg}$ also allows for infinite computations which can never reach success. The inclusion $\lhd_{io} \subseteq \lhd_{pg}$ is direct consequence of Theorem 4.9(a) in [55]. To prove $\lhd_{mst} \subseteq \lhd_{beh}$, assume $p_0 \lhd_{mst} q_0$, and let p_k and q_k be such that $p_0 \parallel q_0 \Rightarrow p_k \parallel q_k$.

If $p_k \parallel q_k \not\rightarrow$, then the trace is τ-maximal, and so by $p_0 \lhd_{mst} q_0$ it follows that $p_i = \mathbf{0}$ for some $i \leq k$. Hence, $p_k = \mathbf{0}$.

If $q_k \uparrow$, then we have an infinite τ-maximal trace:

$$p_0 \parallel q_0 \;\Rightarrow\; p_k \parallel q_k \xrightarrow{\tau} p_{k+1} \parallel q_{k+1} \xrightarrow{\tau} p_{k+2} \parallel q_{k+2} \xrightarrow{\tau} \cdots \quad (\forall j \geq 0 \,.\, p_{k+j} = p_k)$$

By $p_0 \lhd_{mst} q_0$, it follows that $p_i = \mathbf{0}$ for some $i \geq 0$. If $i \leq k$, we already have the thesis, since $p_i = p_k = \mathbf{0}$. Otherwise, if $i > k$, then it must be $\mathbf{0} = p_i = p_k$. So, we conclude that $p_0 \lhd_{beh} q_0$. $\qquad\square$

Theorem 2. $\forall p, q \in \mathrm{ST} \;:\; p \lhd_{pg} q \implies p \lhd_{io} q$

Proof. Direct consequence of Theorem 4.9(b) in [55]. $\qquad\square$

Theorem 3. $\forall p, q \in \mathrm{ST} \;:\; p \lhd_{pg} q \implies p \lhd_{ia} q$

Proof. By contradiction, assume that $p \lhd_{pg} q$ but $p \not\lhd_{ia} q$. Hence, there exists p', q' and a such that $p \parallel q \Rightarrow p' \parallel q'$ with $p' \xrightarrow{!a}$ and $q' \not\xrightarrow{?a}$. By Definition 5, $p \lhd_{pg} q$ implies $p' \lhd_{pg} q'$. By definition of ST, it cannot be $q' \uparrow$, and the only outgoing transition of p' is $!a$.

Therefore, to have $p' \lhd_{pg} q'$ it must be $q' (\xrightarrow{\tau})^n q'' \xrightarrow{?a}$, for some q''. Since $q' \not\xrightarrow{?a}$, then it must be $n > 0$. This contradicts the definition of ST, which forbids τ immediately before inputs. $\qquad\square$

Theorem 4. $\forall p, q \in \mathrm{ST} \cup \mathrm{CA} \;:\; p \lhd_{io} q \implies p \lhd_{ia} q$

Proof. By contradiction, assume that $p \lhd_{io} q$ but $p \not\lhd_{ia} q$. Then, there exist p', q' and a such that $p \parallel q \Rightarrow p' \parallel q'$, with $p' \xrightarrow{!a}$ and $q' \not\xrightarrow{?a}$. However, by definition of $\lhd_{io}$, we have $!a \in \mathrm{co}(q'\Downarrow^?)$, i.e. $?a \in q'\Downarrow^?$. Since $q \in \mathrm{ST} \cup \mathrm{CA}$, this implies that $?a \in q' \downarrow$, and so $q' \xrightarrow{?a}$ — contradiction. $\qquad\square$

Theorem 5. $\forall p, q \in \tau C : p \lhd_{pg} q \implies p \lhd_{beh} q$

Proof. Since $q \in \tau C$, then by Definition 3 it is not possible that $q \uparrow$, hence the thesis follows by Definitions 5 and 9.   □

5 Related Work and Conclusions

We have given a unifying overview of some notions of compliance found in the literature. Although our analysis is still preliminary and partial, as far as we know ours is the first study which systematically organizes compliance relations between behavioural contracts, specified in a general model as arbitrary LTSs.

Previous works survey compliance relations in restricted classes of contracts. The work [24] proposes three notions of compliance for Web services, which are modelled as deterministic contract automata (i.e., there are no internal transitions, and a state cannot have two outgoing transitions with the same label). Two of the proposed notions correspond to $\bowtie_{ia}$ and $\bowtie_{may}$, while the other one requires that, for all reachable states $p' \parallel q'$, it holds $p' \downarrow = \mathrm{co}(q' \downarrow)$; hence, this relation is stricter than $\bowtie_{io}$. The work [30] surveys some compliance relations for τ-less CCS contracts, while [22] considers *higher-order* session types (i.e., also featuring session delegation). The latter work also studies how the choice of the compliance relation impacts the type systems. Our investigation focuses instead on compliance relations among *arbitrary* LTSs, of which τ-less CCS contracts and (first-order) session types are a special case.

Much work remains to do: besides including other notions of compliance and of contract, we also aim at classifying them according to some relevant criteria: e.g., decidability, computational complexity, *etc.* Another property is whether a compliance relation is preserved when passing from synchronous to asynchronous semantics. For instance, in [17] it is shown that if two session types are I/O compliant, then they will be such also in the presence of asynchrony, i.e. when the communication is mediated by unbounded buffers. This is a relevant property, because it allows to safely approximate an undecidable notion (e.g., compliance between *asynchronous* session types) with a decidable one (e.g., compliance between *synchronous* session types).

The starting point of our investigation about compliance dates back to [12], where the idea of defining a function invocation mechanism based on abidance by behavioural contracts was first developed. In this setting, functions are specified in a λ-calculus enriched with side effects (called *events*), and contracts are automata denoting sets of permitted sequences of events. Calling a function consists in advertising a contract; any function with a behaviour conforming to the contract can be dynamically bound to the callee. This *call-by-contract* mechanism is further studied in [13,14], where techniques are developed to compose untrusted services while guaranteeing to always respect contracts at run-time.

The notion of agreement introduced in [11] is built on an interpretation of contracts as multi-player concurrent games on event structures. A participant (with a given contract) agrees with another participant's contract if she has a *strategy* to interact with the other so that in each interaction she either wins, or it is possible to blame the other participant for not honouring his obligations. A relation between this notion of agreement and progress in session types is shown in [10]: two session types are compliant according to Definition 5 whenever, in their encoding as event structures, *all* innocent strategies of the first participant are winning. We expect that this game-theoretic interpretation of compliance can lead to further correspondence results: for instance, we conjecture that compliance between retractable contracts [5] (which is like progress, but in a semantics which allows some internal choices to be rolled back), corresponds to the existence of a winning *cooperative* strategy in their encodings at event structures. Other notions of compliance which are coarser than progress allow clients to skip some of the messages sent by the server [4], to asynchronously match requests after the corresponding offers have been delivered [19], or they use an external orchestrator with buffering capabilities to suitably rearrange messages [6,34].

In asynchronous models, like e.g. communicating finite-state machines [25] (CFSMs), asynchronous session types [45], and in the choreographies in [27], one has to take into account for vacuous progress due to iterated output and buffering of messages which are never read. Therefore, besides progress, in these asynchronous models compliance usually requires that certain unsafe configurations, like e.g. *orphan messages* and *unspecified receptions*, are not reachable [40]. Compliance in these models is undecidable in general, e.g. the halting problem in Turing machines can be reduced to reachability in CFSMs [25] (decidability only holds under strong restrictions on the general model, e.g. by considering two CFSMs with half-duplex buffers [35]). Algorithmic techniques to safely over-approximate compliance have then been studied, e.g. in [21,41,50,51]. For instance, the results in [50] guarantee that a set of asynchronous session types are compliant whenever it is possible to synthesise a choreography from them. To set asynchronous notions of compliance in our framework, one has to interpret CFSMs / asynchronous session types as contracts in the LTS of Sect. 2. Some first results in this direction are presented in [55], which shows that for *binary* asynchronous session types, I/O compliance is equivalent to a notion of compliance based on progress, orphan messages and unspecified receptions.

Acknowledgment. We warmly thank Emilio Tuosto and the anonymous reviewers for their insightful comments. This work has been partially supported by Aut. Reg. of Sardinia grants L.R.7/2007 CRP-17285 (TRICS) and P.I.A. 2010 ("Social Glue"), by MIUR PRIN 2010-11 project "Security Horizons", and by EU COST Action IC1201 "Behavioural Types for Reliable Large-Scale Software Systems" (BETTY).

References

1. Acciai, L., Boreale, M.: A type system for client progress in a service-oriented Calculus. In: Degano, P., De Nicola, R., Meseguer, J. (eds.) Concurrency, Graphs and Models. LNCS, vol. 5065, pp. 642–658. Springer, Heidelberg (2008)
2. Acciai, L., Boreale, M., Zavattaro, G.: Behavioural contracts with request-response operations. In: Clarke, D., Agha, G. (eds.) COORDINATION 2010. LNCS, vol. 6116, pp. 16–30. Springer, Heidelberg (2010)

3. Barbanera, F., de'Liguoro, U.: Two notions of sub-behaviour for session-based client/server systems. In: Proceedings of PPDP, pp. 155–164 (2010)
4. Barbanera, F., de'Liguoro, U.: Loosening the notions of compliance and sub-behaviour in client/server systems. In: Proceedings of ICE. EPTCS, vol. 166, pp. 94–110 (2014)
5. Barbanera, F., Dezani-Ciancaglini, M., Lanese, I., de'Liguoro, U.: Retractable contracts. In: Proceedings of PLACES. EPTCS (2015) (to appear)
6. Barbanera, F., van Bakel, S., de'Liguoro, U.: Orchestrated compliance for session-based client/server interactions. In: Proceedings of ICE. EPTCS (2015) (to appear)
7. Bartoletti, M., Cimoli, T., Murgia, M., Podda, A.S., Pompianu, L.: Compliance and subtyping in timed session types. In: Proceedings of FORTE, pp. 161–177 (2015)
8. Bartoletti, M., Cimoli, T., Pinna, G.M.: Lending Petri Nets and contracts. In: Arbab, F., Sirjani, M. (eds.) FSEN 2013. LNCS, vol. 8161, pp. 66–82. Springer, Heidelberg (2013)
9. Bartoletti, M., Cimoli, T., Pinna, G.M.: Lending Petri nets. Science of Computer Programming (2015) (to appear)
10. Bartoletti, M., Cimoli, T., Pinna, G.M., Zunino, R.: Contracts as games on event structures. JLAMP (2015) (to appear)
11. Bartoletti, M., Cimoli, T., Zunino, R.: A theory of agreements and protection. In: Basin, D., Mitchell, J.C. (eds.) POST 2013 (ETAPS 2013). LNCS, vol. 7796, pp. 186–205. Springer, Heidelberg (2013)
12. Bartoletti, M., Degano, P., Ferrari, G.L.: Types and effects for secure service orchestration, pp. 57–69. In: Proceedings of IEEE Computer Security Foundations Workshop (2006)
13. Bartoletti, M., Degano, P., Ferrari, G.L.: Planning and verifying service composition. J. Comput. Secur. 17(5), 799–837 (2009)
14. Bartoletti, M., Degano, P., Ferrari, G.L., Zunino, R.: Semantics-based design for secure Web services. IEEE Trans. Software Eng. 34(1), 33–49 (2008)
15. Bartoletti, M., Lange, J., Scalas, A., Zunino, R.: Choreographies in the wild. Science of Computer Programming (2015)
16. Bartoletti, M., Scalas, A., Tuosto, E., Zunino, R.: Honesty by typing. In: Boreale, M., Beyer, D. (eds.) FORTE 2013 and FMOODS 2013. LNCS, vol. 7892, pp. 305–320. Springer, Heidelberg (2013)
17. Bartoletti, M., Scalas, A., Zunino, R.: A semantic deconstruction of session types. In: Baldan, P., Gorla, D. (eds.) CONCUR 2014. LNCS, vol. 8704, pp. 402–418. Springer, Heidelberg (2014)
18. Bartoletti, M., Tuosto, E., Zunino, R.: On the realizability of contracts in dishonest systems. In: Sirjani, M. (ed.) COORDINATION 2012. LNCS, vol. 7274, pp. 245–260. Springer, Heidelberg (2012)
19. Basile, D., Degano, P., Ferrari, G.-L.: Automata for analysing service contracts. In: Maffei, M., Tuosto, E. (eds.) TGC 2014. LNCS, vol. 8902, pp. 34–50. Springer, Heidelberg (2014)
20. Basile, D., Degano, P., Ferrari, G.L., Tuosto, E.: From orchestration to choreography through contract automata. In: Proceedings of ICE, pp. 67–85 (2014)
21. Basu, S., Bultan, T., Ouederni, M.: Deciding choreography realizability. In: Proceedings of POPL, pp. 191–202 (2012)
22. Bernardi, G., Dardha, O., Gay, S.J., Kouzapas, D.: On duality relations for session types. In: Maffei, M., Tuosto, E. (eds.) TGC 2014. LNCS, vol. 8902, pp. 51–66. Springer, Heidelberg (2014)

23. Bernardi, G., Hennessy, M.: Compliance and testing preorders differ. In: Counsell, S., Núñez, M. (eds.) SEFM 2013. LNCS, vol. 8368, pp. 69–81. Springer, Heidelberg (2014)
24. Bordeaux, L., Salaün, G., Berardi, D., Mecella, M.: When are two web services compatible? In: Shan, M.-C., Dayal, U., Hsu, M. (eds.) TES 2004. LNCS, vol. 3324, pp. 15–28. Springer, Heidelberg (2005)
25. Brand, D., Zafiropulo, P.: On communicating finite-state machines. J. ACM **30**(2), 323–342 (1983)
26. Bravetti, M., Zavattaro, G.: Contract based multi-party service composition. In: Arbab, F., Sirjani, M. (eds.) FSEN 2007. LNCS, vol. 4767, pp. 207–222. Springer, Heidelberg (2007)
27. Bravetti, M., Zavattaro, G.: Contract compliance and choreography conformance in the presence of message queues. In: Proceedings of WS-FM, pp. 37–54 (2008)
28. Bravetti, M., Zavattaro, G.: A theory of contracts for strong service compliance. Math. Struct. Comput. Sci. **19**(3), 601–638 (2009)
29. E. Brinksma, A. Rensink, and W. Vogler. Fair testing. In Proc. CONCUR, pages 313–327, 1995
30. Bugliesi, M., Macedonio, D., Pino, L., Rossi, S.: Compliance preorders for Web services. In: Proceedings of WS-FM, pp. 76–91 (2009)
31. Buscemi, M.G., Melgratti, H.C.: Contracts for abstract processes in service composition. In: Proceedings of FIT, pp. 9–27 (2010)
32. Carpineti, S., Castagna, G., Laneve, C., Padovani, L.: A formal account of contracts for Web services. In: Proceedings of WS-FM, pp. 148–162 (2006)
33. Castagna, G., Dezani-Ciancaglini, M., Giachino, E., Padovani, L.: Foundations of session types. In: Proceedings of PPDP (2009)
34. Castagna, G., Gesbert, N., Padovani, L.: A theory of contracts for Web services. ACM TOPLAS **31**(5), 19:1–19:61 (2009)
35. Cécé, G., Finkel, A.: Verification of programs with half-duplex communication. Inf. Comput. **202**(2), 166–190 (2005)
36. Coppo, M., Dezani-Ciancaglini, M., Yoshida, N.: Asynchronous session types and progress for object oriented languages. In: Bonsangue, M.M., Johnsen, E.B. (eds.) FMOODS 2007. LNCS, vol. 4468, pp. 1–31. Springer, Heidelberg (2007)
37. de Alfaro, L., Henzinger, T.A.: Interface automata. In: Proceedings of ACM SIG-SOFT, pp. 109–120 (2001)
38. De Nicola, R., Hennessy, M.: Testing equivalences for processes. Theor. Comput. Sci. **34**, 83–133 (1984)
39. De Nicola, R., Hennessy, M.: CCS without tau's. In: Proceedings of TAPSOFT, pp. 138–152 (1987)
40. Deniélou, P.-M., Yoshida, N.: Multiparty session types meet communicating automata. In: Seidl, H. (ed.) Programming Languages and Systems. LNCS, vol. 7211, pp. 194–213. Springer, Heidelberg (2012)
41. Deniélou, P.-M., Yoshida, N.: Multiparty compatibility in communicating automata: characterisation and synthesis of global session types. In: Fomin, F.V., Freivalds, R., Kwiatkowska, M., Peleg, D. (eds.) ICALP 2013, Part II. LNCS, vol. 7966, pp. 174–186. Springer, Heidelberg (2013)
42. Gay, S., Hole, M.: Subtyping for session types in the Pi calculus. Acta Inf. **42**(2), 191–225 (2005)
43. Honda, K.: Types for dyadic interaction. In: Best, E. (ed.) CONCUR 1993. LNCS, vol. 715. Springer, Heidelberg (1993)

44. Honda, K., Vasconcelos, V.T., Kubo, M.: Language primitives and type discipline for structured communication-based programming. In: Hankin, C. (ed.) ESOP 1998. LNCS, vol. 1381, pp. 122–138. Springer, Heidelberg (1998)
45. Honda, K., Yoshida, N., Carbone, M.: Multiparty asynchronous session types. In: Proceedings of POPL, pp. 273–284 (2008)
46. Hüttel, H. et al.: Foundations of behavioural types (2015). (Submitted) www.behavioural-types.eu/publications/WG1-State-of-the-Art.pdf
47. Laneve, C., Laneve, C., Padovani, L., Padovani, L.: The *Must* preorder revisited. In: Caires, L., Caires, L., Vasconcelos, V.T., Vasconcelos, V.T. (eds.) CONCUR 2007. LNCS, vol. 4703, pp. 212–225. Springer, Heidelberg (2007)
48. Laneve, C., Padovani, L.: The pairing of contracts and session types. In: Degano, P., De Nicola, R., Meseguer, J. (eds.) Concurrency, Graphs and Models. LNCS, vol. 5065, pp. 681–700. Springer, Heidelberg (2008)
49. Laneve, C., Padovani, L.: An algebraic theory for Web service contracts. Formal Aspects of Computing, pp. 1–28 (2015)
50. Lange, J., Tuosto, E.: Synthesising Choreographies from local session types. In: Koutny, M., Ulidowski, I. (eds.) CONCUR 2012. LNCS, vol. 7454, pp. 225–239. Springer, Heidelberg (2012)
51. Lange, J., Tuosto, E., Yoshida, N.: From communicating machines to graphical choreographies. In: Proceedings of POPL, pp. 221–232 (2015)
52. Milner, R.: Communication and concurrency. Prentice-Hall Inc. (1989)
53. Rensink, A., Vogler, W.: Fair testing. Inf. Comput. **205**(2), 125–198 (2007)
54. Sangiorgi, D.: An introduction to bisimulation and coinduction. Cambridge University Press, Cambridge (2012)
55. Scalas, A.: A semantic deconstruction of session types. PhD thesis, University of Cagliari (2015)
56. van der Aalst, W.M.P., Lohmann, N., Massuthe, P., Stahl, C., Wolf, K.: Multiparty contracts: Agreeing and implementing interorganizational processes. Comput. J. **53**(1), 90–106 (2010)

Safe Adaptation Through Implicit Effect Coercion

Davide Basile[1,2], Letterio Galletta[3], and Gianluca Mezzetti[4](✉)

[1] Department of Computer Science, University of Pisa, Pisa, Italy
[2] Institute of Science and Technologies of Information "A.Faedo",
Consiglio Nazionale Delle Ricerche, ISTI-CNR, Pisa, Italy
davide.basile@isti.cnr.it
[3] Department of Computer Science, University of Pisa, Pisa, Italy
galletta@di.unipi.it
[4] Department of Computer Science, Aarhus University, Aarhus, Denmark
mezzetti@cs.au.dk

Abstract. Context-Oriented programming languages provide us with primitive constructs to adapt programs behaviour depending on the evolution of their operational environment. In this paradigm developers must provide behaviour for any context a program may find in. A missing behaviour causes a new kind of runtime error: an *adaptation error*. We propose a novel mechanism, based on *implicit function*, that allows the execution environment to supply such behaviour when the program is not able to adapt. We assess our proposal extending a core functional language designed for adaptivity. We integrate the mechanism in a type and effect system, in the form of *implicit coercions*, showing that our type discipline guarantees that no adaptation errors occur.

1 Introduction

The now longstanding trend towards mobility and ubiquity of computing platforms is calling for the development of adaptive software components, that are capable of dynamically modifying their behaviour depending on changes in their execution environment and in response to the interactions with other components. Current development practices take advantage of recent proposals in control theory, artificial intelligence and programming languages to tackle this challenge. We refer to [8,9,25] for a more comprehensive discussion.

Context-Oriented Programming (COP) [17] is a paradigm providing language level support for adaptation, which is advocated to enhance the design and development of ubiquitous and autonomic systems [26]. Standard programming languages are extended in COP with suitable constructs to express context-dependent behaviour in a modular fashion.

In [17] the fundamental constructs of COP are listed. The main concept is the one of *behavioural variation*. A behavioural variation is a chunk of behaviour that can be activated depending on the current working environment so to dynamically modify the execution. The current working environment is represented by

© Springer International Publishing Switzerland 2015
C. Bodei et al. (Eds.): Degano Festschrift, LNCS 9465, pp. 122–141, 2015.
DOI: 10.1007/978-3-319-25527-9_10

the notion of *context*. The context is a stack of layers, i.e. properties identifying the actual structure of the environment. In this setting a programmer can (de)activate layers to represent changes in the environment. This (de)activation mechanism is the engine of context evolution. Usually, behavioural variations are bound to layers: the (de)activation of a layer correspond to the (de)activation of a behavioural variation.

Degano et al. contributed to the foundations of the COP paradigm [14,15] by giving a precise semantics to the key COP constructs in a typed core functional language. A type and effect system is shown effective to guarantee that the program will always be able to adapt during the execution, known the initial context, and in reaction to any further context modification. The initial context is the one at deployment, i.e. is the one immediately provided by the environment where the application is installed. In the case of a mobile app, the deployment context may contain all the features and peripherals offered by the device.

Typically, in the COP paradigm a programmer is supposed to detect and to provide a behavioural variation for any context the application may find in. If we only account for the deployment contexts, this is already a challenge. In the mobile setting, this is known as fragmentation problem, e.g. more than 18000 different device models[1] have Android installed. One way to tackle this problem is to provide wrappers and abstractions, which allows uniform patterns to access the resources.

In this work we envision a novel way of specifying and providing such wrappers and abstractions at programming language level, in a way which is compatible within the COP paradigm. We propose to extend COP paradigm with a mechanism based on *implicit functions*, that are applied in order to provide a disciplined recover when (it is the case that) a program is not able to successfully adapt to the deployment context. In particular, implicit functions allow a fine-grained control of any failing adaptation attempt of the app and can be specified in the deployment context by the hardware vendor, or provided seamlessly by third-party software modules.

In the formal setting of [14], unsuccessfully adaptations are detected earlier by the type and effect system. We aim at extending conservatively [14], in order to deal with implicit functions retaining all guarantees of a strict type discipline. Hence, the adaptation recovery provided by an implicit function need to be casted into a seamless recovery of type safety. We will show how, at the level of the type system, this mechanism can be expressed by *implicit effect coercions*, a novel typing paradigm inspired by implicit type coercions (see [4,23,24]).

If implicit type coercions are programmable (as in their instantiation in e.g. `Scala` and `Haskell`), they are an effective way to enhance existing libraries and programs, while preserving type safety and modularisation. In `Scala` the type system is allowed to rewrite any program expression by applying the set of *implicit* functions in the scope, provided by the programmer, whenever that expression is not able to type-check. When performing type coercion, implicit functions change the type of an expressions so satisfying the type system.

---

[1] http://opensignal.com/reports/2014/android-fragmentation/.

In `Haskell`, implicit type conversions applies to typeclasses, which can be derived by the programmer.

A novelty of our approach is that implicit functions are triggered by the (missing) adaptation behaviour of a program, in order to generate a different safe behaviour. In this sense we talk about effects coercions rather than type coercions. Moreover, in our approach, the scope of the implicit functions follows the one of a standard contextual information. Other proposals either use a global scoping rule such that an implicit function can be applied extensively by the type system (e.g. `Haskell` and [4]), or follow the program syntactical scoping rules (e.g. `Scala`).

Now we discuss the stages required in order to extend [15] (not in the order in which are presented in the paper). First, we extend the `ContextML` [15] language with constructs for specifying implicit functions (Sect. 3). Next, we design a type and effect system for `ContextML` (Sect. 5) with implicit effect coercions. We exploit it for ensuring that programs adequately react to context changes and for computing an abstract as effect representation of the overall behaviour. This representation, in the form of *History Expressions* (Sect. 4), describes the sequences of resource manipulation and communication with external parties in a succinct form.

In the following we intuitively present our proposal through a motivating example (Sect. 2), showing the way implicit functions allow for easily specifying complex adaptive behaviour. This is also instrumental in displaying our methodology at a glance.

2   Motivating Example

In this Section we focus on some paradigmatic challenges that may arise when developing a mobile app. We will walk-through some idiomatic `ContextML` snippets, which demonstrate how the `ContextML` constructs allow to overcome these challenges.

Our scenarios are inspired by the *ShopSavvy 2*[2] app. This app allows users to share information about price, quality, and other features of a particular commercial product. A user can publish the price of a product she found in a shop close to her current location, together with a rating and options on its quality. The product is identified by the app using its bar code. After the price is published, the app suggests other stores where the same product can be obtained at lower price, using the knowledge obtained by other users.

One of the main challenges that the developers of *ShopSavvy 2* have to deal with, is to make it adaptable. Adaptation mechanisms affect the program at different stages in the development cycle: at design time all possible situations that may occur at runtime have to be considered; at deploy time all the possible kind of host devices need to be supported (each device offers a different set of functionalities); at runtime the behaviour of the application depends on the

---

[2] http://shopsavvy.mobi/.

current location, on the signal strength, on the lighting conditions, etc., as well on the interaction with the user.

Consider the simple feature that allows to identify a product by the picture of its bar-code. In our example, at design time the developer has considered the following situation: if the smartphone turns out to be a lower-end one, so that the camera is not equipped with the focus function, an external service is invoked through the Internet to recover the bar-code scan functionality.

We will now describe three different scenarios, which show how the adaptation mechanism offered by the developers deals with a device that offers no focus functionality, and in particular we will show how the context can provide the program with additional adaptation mechanisms which can be activated at deployment time.

1. the connectivity is available, so the focus of the image can be recovered through the external service;
2. the connectivity is not available, but the context provides the program with a local function to compute an approximation of the image focus. The image has a lower quality and there could be an increased probability the image is not recognised as bar code;
3. the focus service is available, but the vendor of the smartphone is interested in constraining the resource usage. In particular, the vendor wants to record every time an app accesses to an online service. In this case, the code that calls the online service is substituted at runtime by a module which stores the information regarding the access before calling the online service.

ContextML naturally implements the adaptive behaviour described above through the *layered expressions*. This construct is similar to standard pattern matching where layers replace patterns. Indeed, an expression Layer. *e* represents a chunk of behaviour **e** to be executed only if the layer Layer is active in the current context.

For example, the layer CameraFocus in the context may represent the fact that the camera has the focus function available. Similarly, the layer RemoteFocus may represent that the app can use a remote service for manipulating the image.

The layered expression *e* that implements the functionality described above is displayed in Fig. 1. First the event α_{click} is issued, which represents the action of taking a picture by clicking on the cellphone. This event will be recorded in the history of relevant events executed by the application. If the layer CameraFocus is active in the context, then the function *FocusImage* is applied to the picture img. Otherwise, the app performs a remote call procedure to the service, namely *CallService*, sending the picture img if the RemoteFocus service is available in the context.

We now discuss how the snippet of code *e* displayed in Fig. 1 manifests the three behaviours described above. The Scenario (1) is equivalent to run the expression *e* in a context where the layer CameraFocus is active, i.e. [CameraFocus] ⊢ *e*. The current context is on the left-hand side of ⊢, the program to run is on the right-hand side. Note that in this section we use a sugared

---

Program expression e

$$e = \begin{array}{l} \alpha_{\text{click}} \,; \\ \textsf{CameraFocus}\,.\,\textsf{FocusImage(img)}\,; \\ \textsf{RemoteFocus}\,.\,\textsf{CallService(img)}\,; \end{array}$$

Scenario 1

$\textsf{CameraFocus} \vdash e$

Scenario 2

$\vdash \textbf{implicit}(f \leftarrow (\alpha_{\text{click}}, \textsf{CameraFocus})\,,e)$

where

$$f = \lambda_f\, x \;\Rightarrow\; \textsf{FocusApprox(img)}$$

Scenario 3

$\textsf{RemoteFocus} \vdash \textbf{without}(\textsf{RemoteFocus})$
$$\{$$
$$\quad \textbf{implicit}(f \leftarrow (\alpha_{\text{click}}, \textsf{RemoteFocus})\,,e)$$
$$\}$$

where

$$f = \lambda_f\, x \;\Rightarrow\; \alpha_{\text{access}}, \textbf{with}(\textsf{RemoteFocus})\{x\}$$

Fig. 1. The `ContextML` snippets implementing the scenarios

notation, that we will make more precise later on. Since in the context the layer `CameraFocus` is active, the execution of e results in `FocusImage(img)`.

If we run the expression e under the assumptions of the Scenario (2), the execution would fail because no required layer is active in the context. However, the context can handle this failure by exploiting the implicit construct, which allows an application to run in scenarios not considered at design time. In the case we consider the `FocusApprox(img)` routine is implicitly provided by the context, so that an approximation of the focus of img can be computed.

This is shown in the Scenario 2 of Fig. 1 where the expression e, embedded inside the implicit construct, runs in an empty context. The construct

$$\textbf{implicit}(f \leftarrow (\alpha_{\text{click}}, \textsf{CameraFocus})\,,e)$$

defines a function f which is invoked when the following conditions are met:

1. no layers defined in the layered expression of e are available in the current context, i.e. the dispatch mechanism fails;
2. the layer `CameraFocus` is one of the layers which caused the dispatching failure;
3. the last action executed by the program is α_{click}.

In the Scenario 3 the implicit construct is used to modify the behaviour of e, by providing a wrapper which manages the access to contextual resources. This time the layer `RemoteFocus` is available in the context, and the dispatch mechanism would succeed. However, the vendor wants to modify the behaviour variation of e when it comes to handle the case `RemoteFocus`. This is achieved by removing the relevant layer from the context using the construct **without**, so that the remote service can only be used through the implicitly provided function.

Scenario 3 of Fig. 1 shows the embedding of e inside an **implicit** and **without** constructs which achieve the explained behaviour.

When the dispatching mechanism fails, the **implicit** f is executed, namely:

$$\lambda_f \, x \; \Rightarrow \alpha_{\text{access}}, \textbf{with}(\texttt{RemoteFocus})\{x\}$$

In the body of this function we first record the remote access by issuing the event α_{access} and then the layer `RemoteFocus` is re-activated. The layered expression of e (bound to the parameter x) can now run successfully in the modified context.

We note that also in Scenario 2 the layered expression of e is passed as argument to f. However in that case, the layered expression is discarded (indeed the parameter x is never used), as the vendor has no interest in recovering the original behaviour of e.

3   ContextML: A Context-Oriented ML Core

`ContextML` [15] is a fragment of ML designed to deal with adaptation, providing mechanisms to change the context and to define behavioural variations in a functional style. In [14] we extended the language by introducing resources manipulation, enforcement of security properties and communication.

We recall here the syntax of `ContextML`, omitting those constructs that are not relevant for the purpose of this paper. In particular we do not detail the **without** construct, but it can be easily derived from [14]. We propose a conservative extension that includes the implicit effect coercions as a further adaptation mechanism.

The resources of the systems are represented by identifiers, moreover they can be made available in the context and manipulated by a fixed set of actions.

The syntax and the structural operational semantics of `ContextML` follow.

3.1   Syntax

Let $\mathbb{N}$ be the naturals, Ide a set of identifiers, LayerNames a finite set of layer names, Res a finite set of resources identifiers and Act a finite set of actions for manipulating resources. The syntax of `ContextML` is defined by the following grammar:

$$n \in \mathbb{N} \qquad x, f \in \textsf{Ide} \qquad L \in \textsf{LayerNames}$$
$$r \in \textsf{Res} \qquad \alpha, \beta \in \textsf{Act}$$

$$v, v_1, v' :: = n \mid L \mid () \mid \lambda_f \, \mathbf{x} \Rightarrow \mathbf{e}$$
$$e, e_1, e' :: = v \mid x \mid e_1 e_2 \mid \mathbf{let} \; x = e_1 \; \mathbf{in} \; e_2 \mid e_1 \; \mathbf{op} \; e_2 \mid$$
$$\mathbf{if} \; e_0 \; \mathbf{then} \; e_1 \; \mathbf{else} \; e_2 \mid \mathbf{with}(e_1) \; \mathbf{in} \; e_2 \mid lexp$$
$$\mathbf{implicit}(v \leftarrow (\alpha, L), e) \mid eaux$$
$$lexp :: = L.e \mid L.e, lexp$$
$$eaux :: = \mathbf{with}(\bar{L}) \; \mathbf{in} \; e_2$$

The novelties of ContextML with respect to ML are the primitives for handling resources, communication and some features borrowed from COP languages (for their description we refer the reader to the seminal paper [17]). Usually, COP paradigm has layers as expressible values; the **with** construct for manipulating the context by activating layers (**with**($\bar{L}$) **in** e_2 denotes an auxiliary expression not used by the programmer but exploited in the dynamic semantics for intermediate configurations); layered expressions *lexp*, defined by cases each specifying a context-dependent behaviour. The expression $\alpha(r)$ indicates that we access the resource r through the action α, possibly causing side effects. In the lambda abstraction $\lambda_f x \Rightarrow e$, the identifier f represents the abstraction itself within the expression e. The **implicit**($v \leftarrow (\alpha, L), e$) construct declares an implicit effect coercion. Note that the value v appearing in the **implicit** is assumed to be a lambda $\lambda_f x \Rightarrow e$ for some identifier f. In the following, by abuse of notation we will refer to that lambda by f, i.e. **implicit**($f \leftarrow (\alpha, L), e$). The **implicit** adds the function f to the context, thus allowing it to be applied whenever the dispatching is about to fail, if L is one of the candidate for the dispatching and the last action performed is α.

A few additional constructs, not present in the syntax, are used: $e_1; e_2$ which is an abbreviation for $(\lambda_f x \Rightarrow e_2) e_1$ where x and f are not free in e_2, and $\lambda.e$ which is a shorthand for $\lambda_f().e$, for some f.

3.2 Dynamic Semantics

In [14] we endowed ContextML with a history dependent small-operational semantics, only defined for closed expressions. Here we review and extend the semantics to introduce rules for the new construct.

As usual we call histories the sequences of events occurring during program execution. Events ev indicate activation layers, selection of behavioural variations and resource accesses. The syntax of events ev and programs histories η is the following:

$$ev ::= (\!|_L \mid)\!|_L \mid \mathsf{Disp}(L) \mid \alpha(r) \tag{1}$$
$$\eta ::= \epsilon \mid ev \mid \eta \, \eta \tag{2}$$

The event $(\!|_L$ signals that the evaluation of a **with** body is started in a context where the layer L is activated; the event $\mathsf{Disp}(L)$ signals that layer L has been selected by the dispatch mechanism; the event $\alpha(r)$ marks that the action α has been performed over the resource r.

A context is a pair $K = (C, I)$ where C is a stack of active layers like in [14] and I is a stack recording the active implicit functions which could be applied when a layered expression is about to fail. In the following, we denote an active implicit by $\iota = f \leftarrow (\alpha, L)$, an empty stack by $[]$ and stack with n elements $a_1, \ldots, a_n$, where a_1 is the top by $[a_1 \ldots, a_n]$.

Let a_0 be a layer L or an active implicit ι, the notation $a_0 :: K$ means the pushing of a_0 on the corresponding element of K, i.e. C for layers and I for implicits. If the element we are pushing is in the stack it is moved at the top. Formally, we have the following

Definition 1 (Context extension). *Let $K = (C, I)$ be a context where $C = [L_1, \ldots, L_n]$ is a stack of layers and $I = [\iota_1, \ldots, \iota_m]$ is a stack of implicits, then*

$$L :: K = \begin{cases} ([L_i, L_1, \ldots, L_{i-1}, L_{i+1}, \ldots, L_n], I) & \text{if } L = L_i \text{ for some } i \\ ([L, L_1, \ldots, L_n], I) & \text{if } L \neq L_i \text{ for all } i \end{cases}$$

$$\iota :: K = \begin{cases} (C, [\iota_j, \iota_1, \ldots, \iota_{j-1}, \iota_{j+1}, \ldots, \iota_m]) & \text{if } \iota = \iota_j \text{ for some } j \\ (C, [\iota, \iota_1, \ldots, \iota_m]) & \text{if } \iota \neq \iota_j \text{ for all } j \end{cases}$$

The transitions have the form $K \vdash \eta, e \rightarrow \eta', e'$, meaning that in the context K, starting from a program history η, the expression e may evolve to e' and the history η to η' in one evaluation step.

Figure 2 shows some semantics rules (most of them are inherited from ML). We briefly comment on the ones for the relevant constructs.

The rules for **with**(e_1) **in** e_2 first evaluate e_1 in order to obtain a layer L; then, the body of the **with** construct, i.e. e_2, is evaluated in a context extended with L.

The rule ACTION performs an action α over a resource r, yielding the unit value $()$ and extending η with $\alpha(r)$.

When a layered expression $e = L_1.e_1, \ldots, L_n.e_n$ has to be evaluated, the stack of layers in the current context is inspected top-down to select the expression to which e reduces. This mechanism is called *dispatching* and it is implemented by the function Dsp which takes as input a stack of layers and a set of layers A:

$$\mathsf{Dsp}(L' :: K, A) = \begin{cases} L' & \text{if } L' \in A \\ \mathsf{Dsp}(K, A) & \text{otherwise} \end{cases}$$

Note that to simplify the notation above we use the operator :: to perform a sort of pattern matching. The function returns the first layer in the stack of the context which matches one of the layers in the set A. If such a layer L_i exists than the premises of rule LEXP$_\checkmark$ are satisfied, so that the layered expression e reduces to the subexpression e_i labelled by L_i. If no layer matches, the dispatching mechanism fails. This failure is represented in our semantics by the fact that the function Dsp is undefined (denoted by $\bot$). In case of dispatching failure, the computation can continue if there exists an implicit in the context that can be applied. The rule LEXP$_\times$ handles this case. To select an appropriate implicit from the context we use the partial function lmdsp:

$$\boxed{K \vdash \eta, e \rightarrow \eta', e'}$$

IF$_1$
$$\frac{K \vdash \eta, e_0 \rightarrow \eta', e_0'}{K \vdash \eta, \textbf{if } e_0 \textbf{ then } e_1 \textbf{ else } e_2 \rightarrow \eta', \textbf{if } e_0' \textbf{ then } e_1 \textbf{ else } e_2}$$

IF$_2$
$$\frac{}{K \vdash \eta, \textbf{if } 0 \textbf{ then } e_1 \textbf{ else } e_2 \rightarrow \eta, e_2}$$

IF$_3$
$$\frac{v \neq 0}{K \vdash \eta, \textbf{if } v \textbf{ then } e_1 \textbf{ else } e_2 \rightarrow \eta, e_1}$$

APP$_1$
$$\frac{K \vdash \eta, e_2 \rightarrow \eta', e_2'}{K \vdash \eta, e_1 \, e_2 \rightarrow \eta', e_1 \, e_2'}$$

APP$_2$
$$\frac{K \vdash \eta, e_1 \rightarrow \eta', e_1'}{K \vdash \eta, e_1 \, v \rightarrow \eta', e_1' \, v}$$

APP$_3$
$$\frac{}{K \vdash \eta, (\lambda_f \, x \Rightarrow e)v \rightarrow \eta, e\{\lambda_f \, x \Rightarrow e/f, v/x\}}$$

LET$_1$
$$\frac{K \vdash \eta, e_1 \rightarrow \eta', e_1'}{K \vdash \eta, \textbf{let } x = e_1 \textbf{ in } e_2 \rightarrow \eta', \textbf{let } x = e_1' \textbf{ in } e_2}$$

LET$_2$
$$\frac{}{K \vdash \eta, \textbf{let } x = v \textbf{ in } e_2 \rightarrow \eta, e_2\{v/x\}}$$

WITH$_1$
$$\frac{K \vdash \eta, e_1 \rightarrow \eta', e_1'}{K \vdash \eta, \textbf{with}(e_1) \textbf{ in } e_2 \rightarrow \eta', \textbf{with}(e_1') \textbf{ in } e_2}$$

WITH$_2$
$$\frac{}{K \vdash \eta, \textbf{with}(L) \textbf{ in } e \rightarrow \eta \langle\!|_L, \textbf{with}(\bar{L}) \textbf{ in } e}$$

WITH$_3$
$$\frac{L :: K \vdash \eta, e \rightarrow \eta', e'}{K \vdash \eta, \textbf{with}(\bar{L}) \textbf{ in } e \rightarrow \eta', \textbf{with}(\bar{L}) \textbf{ in } e'}$$

WITH$_4$
$$\frac{}{K \vdash \eta, \textbf{with}(\bar{L}) \textbf{ in } v \rightarrow \eta |\!\rangle_L, v}$$

ACTION
$$\frac{}{K \vdash \eta, \alpha(r) \rightarrow \eta \, \alpha(r), ()}$$

LEXP$_{\checkmark}$
$$\frac{\mathsf{Dsp}(K, \{L_1, \ldots, L_n\}) = L_i}{K \vdash \eta, L_1.e_1, \ldots, L_n.e_n \rightarrow \eta \, \mathsf{Disp}(L_i), e_i}$$

LEXP$_{\times}$
$$\frac{\mathsf{Dsp}(K, \{L_1, \ldots, L_n\}) = \bot \quad \mathsf{Imdsp}(K, \alpha, \{L_1, \ldots, L_n\}) = f}{K \vdash \eta\alpha, L_1.e_1, \ldots, L_n.e_n \rightarrow \eta\alpha, f(\lambda.L_1.e_1, \ldots, L_n.e_n)}$$

IMPL$_1$
$$\frac{f \leftarrow (\alpha, L) :: K \vdash \eta, e \rightarrow \eta', e'}{K \vdash \eta, \textbf{implicit}(f \leftarrow (\alpha, L), e) \rightarrow \eta', \textbf{implicit}(f \leftarrow (\alpha, L), e')}$$

IMPL$_2$
$$\frac{v \neq \lambda_g \Rightarrow e}{K \vdash \eta, \textbf{implicit}(f \leftarrow (\alpha, L), v) \rightarrow \eta, v}$$

Fig. 2. A glimpse of ContextML semantic rules

$$\mathsf{Imdsp}(f_1 \leftarrow (\alpha_1, L_1) :: K, \alpha, A) = \begin{cases} f_1 & \text{if } L_1 \in A \text{ and } \alpha_1 = \alpha \\ \mathsf{Imdsp}(K, \alpha, A) & \text{otherwise} \end{cases}$$

This function takes as argument a context K, an action α and a set of layers A. Intuitively, it inspects the stack of implicits top-down in order to find a function f recorded with the same action α and with a layer L which is in A. In the premises of the rule LEXP$_\times$ the function Imdsp is invoked with the current context, the last action stored in the history and with the layers of $e = L_1.e_1, \ldots, L_n.e_n$. If such a function f exists, the layered expression e reduces to the application of f to $\lambda.e$. Otherwise, the program gets stuck signalling the occurrence of an adaptation error, since both the rules LEXP$_\times$ and LEXP$_\checkmark$ cannot be applied.

The rules for $\mathbf{implicit}(f \leftarrow (\alpha, L), e)$ evaluate the body e until it reduces to a value v in a context where the stack of implicits is extended by the implicit function $f \leftarrow (\alpha, L)$. In the rule IMPL$_2$ we require that the value v is not a function, indeed, the body e may rely on the implicit function f, which could be no longer available on the application site of g.

Example 1. We show the running example using the code in Fig. 1, the rules of Fig. 2, and a slightly modified version of scenario 3 in Fig. 1 showed below:

$$\vdash \mathbf{implicit}(f \leftarrow (\alpha_{\text{click}}, \texttt{RemoteFocus}), e) \quad \text{where}$$
$$f = \lambda_{\mathbf{f}}\, x \implies \alpha_{\text{access}}; \mathbf{with}(\texttt{RemoteFocus})\{x\}$$

We provide now the rules applied to reduce the expression. The first rule applied is IMPL$_1$, where in the premise we apply the rule `action`:

$$\text{IMPL}_1 \ \frac{\text{ACTION} \ \dfrac{}{(\emptyset, f \leftarrow (\alpha_{\text{click}}, RemoteFocus)) \vdash \varepsilon, e \rightarrow \alpha_{\text{click}}, e'}}{\begin{array}{l} \vdash \varepsilon, \mathbf{implicit}(f \leftarrow (\alpha_{\text{click}}, \texttt{RemoteFocus}), e) \rightarrow \\ \quad \alpha_{\text{click}}, \mathbf{implicit}(f \leftarrow (\alpha_{\text{click}}, \texttt{RemoteFocus}), e') \end{array}}$$

where $e' = \texttt{CameraFocus.FocusImage(img)}, \texttt{RemoteFocus.CallService(img)}$

Note that at every step we need to apply the rule IMPL$_1$ until e evaluates to a value v. For brevity we omit to write the derivations from this rule and we describe only the reductions for its premises. In $(\emptyset, f \leftarrow (\alpha_{\text{click}}, \texttt{RemoteFocus})) \vdash \alpha_{\text{click}}, e'$ the standard dispatching mechanism for the layered expression e' fails because the stack of layers is empty. However the implicit allows the dispatching to succeeds through the application of the rule LEXP$_\times$:

$$(\emptyset, f \leftarrow (\alpha_{\text{click}}, \texttt{RemoteFocus})) \vdash \alpha_{\text{click}}, e' \rightarrow \alpha_{\text{click}}, f(\lambda.e')$$

By applying rules APP$_3$, ACTION and WITH$_2$ we obtain:

$$(\emptyset, f \leftarrow (\alpha_{\text{click}}, \texttt{RemoteFocus})) \vdash \alpha_{\text{click}}\alpha_{\text{access}}(\overline{\texttt{RemoteFocus}}, \mathbf{with}(\overline{\texttt{RemoteFocus}})\{e\}$$

Now it is possible to apply rule WITH3, where in the premises we apply the rule:

$$\text{ACTION} \quad \frac{(\texttt{RemoteFocus}, f \leftarrow (\alpha_{\text{click}}, \texttt{RemoteFocus})) \vdash \eta, e \rightarrow \eta\alpha_{\text{click}}, e'}{(\emptyset, f \leftarrow (\alpha_{\text{click}}, \texttt{RemoteFocus})) \vdash \eta, \textbf{with}(\overline{\texttt{RemoteFocus}})\{e\} \rightarrow \\ \eta\alpha_{\text{click}}, \textbf{with}(\overline{\texttt{RemoteFocus}})\{e'\}}$$

where $\eta = \alpha_{\text{click}}\alpha_{\text{access}} (\!|_{\texttt{RemoteFocus}}$

As done before, for brevity we discuss only the premise of the next rule which is again WITH3. This time the expression e' is evaluated in a context where the layer RemoteFocus occurs, hence the standard dispatching mechanism succeeds and it possible to apply rule LEXP$_\checkmark$:

$$(\texttt{RemoteFocus}, f \leftarrow (\alpha_{\text{click}}, \texttt{RemoteFocus})) \vdash \eta\alpha_{\text{click}}, e' \rightarrow \eta', \mathsf{CallService(img)}$$
$$where \; \eta' = \eta\alpha_{\text{click}}\mathsf{Disp}(\texttt{RemoteFocus})$$

Finally, assuming that after some reductions $\mathsf{CallService(img)}$ evaluates to a value v, by applying rules WITH4 and IMPL2 we obtain the final configuration

$$\vdash \alpha_{\text{click}}\alpha_{\text{access}} (\!|_{\texttt{RemoteFocus}}\alpha_{\text{click}}\mathsf{Disp}(\texttt{RemoteFocus}))\!)_{\texttt{RemoteFocus}}, \; v$$

4   History Expressions

History Expressions [5,6,28] are a simple process algebra providing an abstraction over the set of histories that a program may generate. We recall here the definitions and the properties in [5] but we consider histories with a different set of events ev, also endowing layer activation and dispatching.

Definition 2 (History Expressions). *History Expressions are defined as follows:*

$H, H_1 ::=$	ϵ	*empty*	$H_1 + H_2$	*sum*
	ev	*events in (1)*	$H_1 \cdot H_2$	*sequence*
	h	*recursion variable*	$\mu h.H$	*recursion*

The signature defines sequentialization, sum and recursion operations over sets of histories containing events; μh is a binder for the recursion variable h.

The following definition exploits the labelled transition system in Fig. 3.

Definition 3 (Semantics of History Expressions). *Given a closed H (i.e. without free variables), we define its semantics $[\![H]\!] \subseteq (ev \cup \{\downarrow\})^*$ to be the set of histories*

$$[\![H]\!] = \{w_1 \ldots w_n \mid \exists H'. \; H \xrightarrow{w_1} \cdots \xrightarrow{w_n} H'\} \cup \{w_1 \ldots w_n \downarrow | \; H \xrightarrow{w_1} \cdots \xrightarrow{w_n} \varepsilon\}$$

We remark that the semantics of a history expression is a prefix closed set of histories, where a history terminated by the symbol $\downarrow$ represents a terminated computation. Closed history expressions are partially ordered: $H \sqsubseteq H'$ means

$$\overline{\varepsilon \cdot H \xrightarrow{\varepsilon} H} \qquad\qquad \overline{\alpha(r) \xrightarrow{\alpha(r)} \varepsilon} \qquad\qquad \overline{\mu h.H \xrightarrow{\varepsilon} H\{\mu h.H/h\}}$$

$$\frac{H_1 \xrightarrow{ev} H_1'}{H_1 \cdot H_2 \xrightarrow{ev} H_1' \cdot H_2} \qquad\qquad \frac{H_1 \xrightarrow{ev} H_1'}{H_1 + H_2 \xrightarrow{ev} H_1'} \qquad\qquad \frac{H_2 \xrightarrow{ev} H_2'}{H_1 + H_2 \xrightarrow{ev} H_2'}$$

Fig. 3. Transition system of History Expressions.

that the abstraction represented by H' is less precise than the one by H. The structural ordering $\sqsubseteq$ is defined over the quotient induced by the (semantic preserving) equational theory presented in [6] as the least relation such that $H \sqsubseteq H$ and $H \sqsubseteq H + H'$. Clearly, $H \sqsubseteq H'$ implies $[\![H]\!] \subseteq [\![H']\!]$.

Back to the example in Sect. 2, assume that the function FocusImage uses no resource and that the function CallService creates a remote connection through the action α_{conn}. Then, assume that the history expression over-approximating the behaviour of expression e is $H = \alpha_{\text{click}} \cdot (\text{CameraFocus} + \text{RemoteFocus} \cdot \alpha_{\text{conn}})$. According to Definition 3 the semantics of H is the set

$$[\![H]\!] = \{\epsilon, \ \alpha_{\text{click}}, \ \alpha_{\text{click}} \ \text{CameraFocus}, \ \alpha_{\text{click}} \ \text{CameraFocus} \downarrow, \ \alpha_{\text{click}} \ \text{RemoteFocus},$$
$$\alpha_{\text{click}} \ \text{RemoteFocus} \ \alpha_{\text{conn}}, \ \alpha_{\text{click}} \ \text{RemoteFocus} \ \alpha_{\text{conn}} \downarrow\}$$

5   ContextML Types

We extend here the ContextML type and effect system defined in [14] with implicit effect coercion to deal with implicit functions. As usual, our type and effect system computes an over-approximation of program behaviour in the form of a history expression and ensures that the dispatching mechanism always succeeds at runtime, by applying the required implicit functions. Here, we only give a logical presentation of our type and effect system, and we are confident that an inference algorithm can be developed, along the lines of [28].

Our typing judgements have the form $\langle \Gamma; K; \overline{H} \rangle \vdash e : \tau \triangleright H$: in the type environment Γ, context K and accumulated history $\overline{H}$, the expression e has type τ and effect H. The accumulated history expression abstracts the histories from which the evaluation of the relevant expression e starts.

Types are the same of [14], i.e. integers, unit, layers and functions:

$$\sigma \in \wp(\text{LayerNames}) \qquad \mathbb{P} \in \wp((\wp(\text{LayerNames}), \mathbb{I}))$$

$$\tau, \tau_1, \tau' ::= \text{int} \mid \text{unit} \mid ly_\sigma \mid \tau_1 \xrightarrow{\mathbb{P}|H} \tau_2$$

We denote by $\mathbb{I}$ the set of all possible stack of implicit functions. We annotate types with sets of layer names for analysis reason. In layer types ly_σ, the set σ over-approximates the layers that an expression can be reduced to at runtime. In function types $\tau_1 \xrightarrow{\mathbb{P}|H} \tau_2$, $\mathbb{P}$ is a set of *preconditions*, i.e. (v, I) where I is a stack of implicits. Each $v \in \mathbb{P}$ over-approximates the set of layers that must occur in the context in order to apply the function, and I predicts the stack of implicits

$$\text{S}\textsc{ref} \quad \frac{}{\tau \le \tau}$$

$$\text{S}\textsc{fun} \quad \frac{\tau_1' \le \tau_1 \qquad \tau_2 \le \tau_2' \qquad \mathbb{P} \sqsubseteq \mathbb{P}' \qquad H \sqsubseteq H'}{\tau_1 \xrightarrow{\;\mathbb{P}|H\;} \tau_2 \le \tau_1' \xrightarrow{\;\mathbb{P}'|H'\;} \tau_2'}$$

$$\text{S}\textsc{ly} \quad \frac{\sigma \subseteq \sigma'}{ly_\sigma \le ly_{\sigma'}}$$

$$\text{T}\textsc{sub} \quad \frac{\langle \Gamma; K; \overline{H} \rangle \vdash e : \tau' \triangleright H' \qquad \tau' \le \tau \qquad H' \sqsubseteq H}{\langle \Gamma; K; \overline{H} \rangle \vdash e : \tau \triangleright H}$$

Fig. 4. Subtyping rules

in the context of the application. The history expression H is the latent effect, i.e. the sequence of events generated while evaluating the function.

The rules for subeffecting ($H \sqsubseteq H'$) and for subtyping ($\tau_1 \le \tau_2$) are in Fig. 4. Through the rule S\textsc{ref} the subtyping relation is reflexive. The rule S\textsc{ly} says that if an annotation σ is a subset of σ', then a layer type ly_σ is a subtype of $ly_{\sigma'}$. As usual, a functional type is contravariant in τ_1 but covariant in $\mathbb{P}, \tau_2$ and H (rule S\textsc{fun}). The ordering on the set of preconditions is defined as follows $\mathbb{P} \sqsubseteq \mathbb{P}'$ iff $\forall(v, I) \in \mathbb{P} . \exists(v', I) \in \mathbb{P}' . v' \subseteq v$, where $\subseteq$ is the usual subset relation. By the T\textsc{sub} rule, we can always enlarge types and effects.

Figure 5 shows the rules of our type and effect system. Most of them are inherited from that of ML, so we only comment in detail on the rules for the new constructs. The rule T\textsc{alpha} gives expression $\alpha(r)$ type **unit** and effect $\alpha(r)$. The rule T\textsc{ly} asserts that the type of a layer L is ly annotated with the singleton set $\{L\}$ and its effect is empty. In the rule T\textsc{fun} we guess a set of preconditions $\mathbb{P}$, a type for the bound variable x and for the function f. For all precondition $(v, I) \in \mathbb{P}$ we also guess a context K'. We require that preconditions (v, I) contain all the layers of K', in symbols $|C| \subseteq v$, where $|C|$ is the set of layers active in the context K'. Moreover, the context K' is composed by the stack of implicits I predicted by the preconditions.

We determine the type of the body e under these additional assumptions. Implicitly, we require that the guessed type for f, as well as its latent effect H, fit with the ones of the body e. Additionally, we require that the resulting type is annotated with $\mathbb{P}$.

The rule T\textsc{app} is almost standard and reveals the mechanism of function precondition. The application gets a type if there exists a precondition $(v, I) \in \mathbb{P}$ such that it is satisfied in the current context K. The effect is obtained by concatenating the ones of e_2 and e_1 and the latent effect H. For example, the function $\lambda_f \, x \Rightarrow L_1.0$ is has type $\text{int} \xrightarrow{\;\{L_1\}|\cdots\;} \text{int}$, this means that L_1 must be in the context in order to apply the function. The complete derivation tree for such typing can be found in [14].

The rule T\textsc{with} establishes that the expression **with**(e_1) **in** e_2 has type τ, provided that the type for e_1 is ly_σ (recall that σ is a set of layers) and e_2 has type τ in the context K extended by each of the layers in σ. The effect is the union of the possible effects resulting from evaluating the body. This evaluation is carried

$$\boxed{\langle \Gamma; K; \overline{H} \rangle \vdash e : \tau \triangleright H}$$

TVAR
$$\frac{\Gamma(x) = \tau}{\langle \Gamma; K; \overline{H} \rangle \vdash x : \tau \triangleright \varepsilon}$$

TINT
$$\langle \Gamma; K; \overline{H} \rangle \vdash n : \mathbf{int} \triangleright \varepsilon$$

TUNIT
$$\langle \Gamma; K; \overline{H} \rangle \vdash () : \mathbf{unit} \triangleright \varepsilon$$

TLY
$$\langle \Gamma; K; \overline{H} \rangle \vdash L : ly_{\{L\}} \triangleright \varepsilon$$

TALPHA
$$\langle \Gamma; K; \overline{H} \rangle \vdash \alpha(a) : \mathbf{unit} \triangleright \alpha(a)$$

TFUN
$$\frac{\forall (v, I) \in \mathbb{P}. \quad \langle \Gamma, x : \tau_1, f : \tau_1 \xrightarrow{\mathbb{P}|H} \tau_2; K'; \overline{H} \rangle \vdash e : \tau_2 \triangleright H \quad K' = (C, I) \quad |C| \subseteq v}{\langle \Gamma; K; \overline{H} \rangle \vdash \lambda_f \, x \Rightarrow e : \tau_1 \xrightarrow{\mathbb{P}|H} \tau_2 \triangleright \varepsilon}$$

TLET
$$\frac{\langle \Gamma; K; \overline{H} \rangle \vdash e_1 : \tau_1 \triangleright H \quad \langle \Gamma, x : \tau_1; K; \overline{H} \cdot H \rangle \vdash e_2 : \tau_2 \triangleright H'}{\langle \Gamma; K; \overline{H} \rangle \vdash \mathbf{let} \, x = e_1 \, \mathbf{in} \, e_2 : \tau_2 \triangleright H \cdot H'}$$

TIF
$$\frac{\langle \Gamma; K; \overline{H} \rangle \vdash e_0 : \mathbf{int} \triangleright H \quad \langle \Gamma; K; \overline{H} \cdot H \rangle \vdash e_1 : \tau \triangleright H' \quad \langle \Gamma; K; \overline{H} \cdot H \rangle \vdash e_2 : \tau \triangleright H'}{\langle \Gamma; K; \overline{H} \rangle \vdash \mathbf{if} \, e_0 \, \mathbf{then} \, e_1 \, \mathbf{else} \, e_2 : \tau \triangleright H \cdot H'}$$

TWITH
$$\frac{\langle \Gamma; K; \overline{H} \rangle \vdash e_1 : ly_{\{L_1, \dots, L_n\}} \triangleright H' \quad \forall L_i \in \{L_1, \dots, L_n\}. \langle \Gamma; L_i :: K; \overline{H} \cdot H' \cdot (\!| L_i |\!) \rangle \vdash e_2 : \tau \triangleright H_i}{\langle \Gamma; K; \overline{H} \rangle \vdash \mathbf{with}(e_1) \, \mathbf{in} \, e_2 : \tau \triangleright H' \cdot \sum_{L_i} (\!| L_i \cdot H_i |\!)_{L_i}}$$

TAPP
$$\frac{\langle \Gamma; K; \overline{H} \cdot H_2 \rangle \vdash e_1 : \tau_1 \xrightarrow{\mathbb{P}|H} \tau_2 \triangleright H_1 \quad \langle \Gamma; K; \overline{H} \rangle \vdash e_2 : \tau_1 \triangleright H_2 \\ \exists (v, I) \in \mathbb{P}. v \subseteq |C| \wedge K = (C, I)}{\langle \Gamma; K; \overline{H} \rangle \vdash e_1 e_2 : \tau_2 \triangleright H_2 \cdot H_1 \cdot H}$$

TLEXP✓
$$\frac{\{L_1, \dots, L_n\} \cap |K| = J \neq \emptyset \quad \forall i \, (1 \leq i \leq n). \langle \Gamma; K; \overline{H} \cdot \mathsf{Disp}(L_i) \rangle \vdash e_i : \tau \triangleright H_i}{\langle \Gamma; K; \overline{H} \rangle \vdash L_1.e_1, \dots, L_n.e_n : \tau \triangleright \sum_{\forall i \, (1 \leq i \leq n)} \mathsf{Disp}(L_i) \cdot H_i}$$

TLEXP✗
$$\frac{\begin{array}{c} \{L_1, \dots, L_n\} \cap |K| = \emptyset \\ B = \{f \leftarrow (\alpha, L) \in |K| \mid L \in \{L_1, \dots, L_n\} \wedge \{\alpha \downarrow\} = \mathsf{Suffix}(\llbracket \overline{H} \rrbracket) \cap \{\beta \downarrow | \beta \in ev \cup \{\varepsilon\}\}\} \\ \forall f \leftarrow (\alpha, L) \in B. \langle \Gamma; K - f \leftarrow (\alpha, L); \overline{H} \rangle \vdash f(\lambda. L_1.e_1, \dots, L_n.e_n) : \tau \triangleright H \\ \forall i \, (1 \leq i \leq n). \langle \Gamma; K; \overline{H} \cdot \mathsf{Disp}(L_i) \rangle \vdash e_i : \tau \triangleright H_i \end{array}}{\langle \Gamma; K; \overline{H} \rangle \vdash L_1.e_1, \dots, L_n.e_n : \tau \triangleright H + \sum_{\forall i \, (1 \leq i \leq n)} \mathsf{Disp}(L_i) \cdot H_i}$$

TIMPL
$$\frac{\langle \Gamma; f \leftarrow (L, \alpha) :: K; \overline{H} \rangle \vdash e : \tau \triangleright H \quad \tau \neq \tau' \xrightarrow{\mathbb{P}|H'} \tau''}{\langle \Gamma; K; \overline{H} \rangle \vdash \mathbf{implicit}(f \leftarrow (L, \alpha), e) : \tau \triangleright H}$$

Fig. 5. Typing rules

on the different contexts obtained by extending K with one of the layers in σ. The special events $(_L$ and $)_L$ express the scope of this layer activation.

By TLEXP$_\checkmark$ the type of a layered expression e is τ, provided that each subexpression e_i has type τ and that at least one among the layers $L_1, \ldots L_n$ occurs in K. Since J is not empty, when evaluating a layered expression one of the mentioned layers will be active in the current context so guaranteeing that the layered expressions will correctly evaluate. The whole effect is the sum of the effects H_j of those sub-expressions that can be evaluated at runtime, preceded by $\mathsf{Disp}(L_j)$. When there is no guarantee that at least one of the layers $L_1, \ldots L_n$ occurs in K, the expression e could still evaluate to a value if an implicit was defined to handle this situation. The rule TLEXP$_\times$ collects in B all the implicit functions $f \leftarrow (L, \alpha)$ in the context K such that α is the last action of $\overline{H}$ and L is equal to some L_i we are trying to dispatch. If the application of all the implicits f in B to e type-check with type τ and effect H the overall expression inherits those type and effect. In the definition of B we denote by $\mathsf{Suffix}(A)$ the set of all suffixes of the language A, the condition $\mathsf{Suffix}(\llbracket \overline{H} \rrbracket) \cap \{\beta \downarrow \mid \beta \in ev \cup \{\varepsilon\}\}$ verifies that the suffixes of length at most two of the histories in $\llbracket \overline{H} \rrbracket$ are the singleton set $\{\alpha \downarrow\}$.

Note that such condition is decidable, because $\llbracket \overline{H} \rrbracket$ is a context-free language, the suffixes of a context-free language are context-free, the intersection with a finite set gives a finite language (decidable) and finite language equivalence is decidable. The rule TIMPL establishes that an expression $\mathbf{implicit}(f \leftarrow (L, \alpha), e)$ has the same type τ and effect H computed for the expression e in a context extended with the implicit $f \leftarrow (L, \alpha)$. Of course, as required by the semantic rule IMPL$_2$, the typing rule rejects any expression e which is a functional value.

For technical reasons, we also need the rules to handle the auxiliary syntactic construct $\mathbf{with}(\overline{L})$ in e_2, we omit it being a trivial extension of [14] where the typing environment is extended with the implicits stack.

Some typing examples can be found in the same source. Here we provide an example involving the new constructs, using the rules in Fig. 5.

Example 2. Consider the following typing judgment:

$$\vdash \mathbf{implicit}(f \leftarrow (\alpha_{\mathrm{click}}, \mathtt{RemoteFocus}), \alpha_{\mathrm{click}}; e')$$

where

$$f = \lambda_f \; x \; \Rightarrow \alpha_{\mathrm{access}}; \mathbf{with}(\mathtt{RemoteFocus})\{x\,()\}$$
$$e' = \mathtt{CameraFocus.FocusImage(img)}, \mathtt{RemoteFocus.CallService(img)}$$

In Fig. 6 the derivation tree of such judgment is shown. For typografica reasons we only detail the application of the typing rules for implicit coercions, layered expression and the **with** construct, omitting the others (replaced by dots). For typographical reasons, we also shorten the $\mathtt{RemoteFocus}$ layer identifier with $\mathtt{RF}$. The first rule applied, that is the root of the derivation tree, is the one that declares the implicit function IMPL, where $\eta = \alpha_{\mathrm{click}}\alpha_{\mathrm{access}}$ and the implicits stack I is $[f \leftarrow (\mathtt{RF}, \alpha_{\mathrm{click}})]$. In order to type the premises we need to

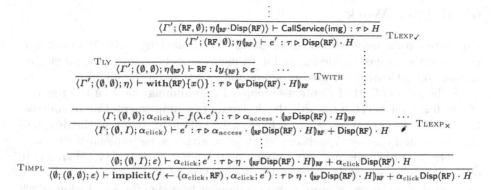

Fig. 6. A fragment of derivation tree

apply the rule for the layered expression. The standard one $\text{TLEXP}_\checkmark$ fails because there are no layers in the context, so we use $\text{TLEXP}_\times$, that applies the implicit coercion. In the implicit function f, the construct **with** is used for modifying the context, the typing rule applied is TWITH. The application $x()$ requires the premises of the function bound with x (i.e. $\lambda.e'$) to be satisfied. The type of $\lambda.e'$ is $\text{unit} \xrightarrow{\{(\{\text{RF}\},\emptyset)\}|\text{Disp}(\text{RF})\cdot H} \tau$, the precondition $(\{\text{RF}\}, \emptyset)$ is obtained because in the rule $\text{TLEXP}_\checkmark$ at the top, the context with only RF suffices to type-check. Such precondition is then satisfied in the premises of TWITH, since $x()$ will be typed in the context $(\{\text{RF}\}, \emptyset)$.

Our type system enjoys the following soundness results.

Theorem 1 (Subject reduction). *Let e be a closed expression,*
if $\langle \Gamma; K; \overline{H} \rangle \vdash e ; \tau \triangleright H$ and $K \vdash \eta, e \rightarrow \eta\eta', e'$ and $\eta \in [\![\overline{H}]\!]$ then

$$\langle \Gamma; K; \overline{H}\eta' \rangle \vdash e' : \tau \triangleright H' \text{ with } \eta H \sqsupseteq \eta\eta' H'$$

As a corollary we get that the history expression obtained as effect of an expression e over-approximates the set of histories that may actually be generated during the execution of e.

Corollary 1 (Over-approximation). *Let e be a closed expression, if $\langle \Gamma; K; \epsilon \rangle \vdash e : \tau \triangleright H$ and $K \vdash \epsilon, e \rightarrow^* \eta, e'$ then $\eta \in [\![H]\!]$.*

We also have the following result, where $K \vdash \eta, e \not\rightarrow$ means that e is stuck.

Theorem 2 (Progress). *Let e be a closed expression, if*

$$\forall \Gamma, K, \overline{H}.\langle \Gamma; K; \overline{H} \rangle \vdash e : \tau \triangleright H \text{ and } \forall \eta \downarrow \in [\![\overline{H}]\!]. \ K \vdash \eta, e \not\rightarrow$$

then e is a value.

Subject reduction and progress prove the soundness of our type system.

Theorem 3 (Type safety). *Let e be a closed expression, if*

$$\langle \emptyset; K; \epsilon \rangle \vdash e : \tau \triangleright H \text{ and } K \vdash \epsilon, e \rightarrow^* \eta', e' \text{ and } K \vdash \eta', e' \not\rightarrow$$

then e' is a value.

6   Related Work

Numerous works have addressed the problem of adaptivity [8,9,25] and in particular at the level of the design and implementation of programming languages, among which Context-oriented programming is a seminal paradigm.

So far, in the field of Context-Oriented Programming, most of the research efforts has been directed towards the design and the implementation of concrete languages. The survey by Salvaneschi et al. [27] discusses in detail the design of languages, and that by Appeltauer et al. [3] analyses some implementations.

Here, we briefly discuss only foundational studies. Besides [14,15] there are other contributions of Degano to the foundation of COP languages. In [13] Degano et al. proposed ML_{CoDa} a two component language for adaptation which inherits many features from [14,15]: the first constituent is Datalog with negation to logically describe the context; the second one is a core ML, extended with powerful primitives for context management and for expressing adaptation. In [12] Degano et al. equipped ML_{CoDa} with a two-step static analysis to prevent adaptation failures: a type and effect system (at compile time) and a control flow analysis (at load-time). During the type-checking of a program a history expression is computed, over-approximating the capabilities that the application needs at runtime. When entering a new context, before running the program, the history expression is exploited to check that the application adapts to the actual context, and those resulting from its evolution. In [7] Degano et al. extend ML_{CoDa} with primitives to enforce security policies on the code execution. The results of the static analysis are used to instrument programs by inserting further checks guaranteeing that no violation of the required security policies occurs at runtime.

Another functional language is Contextλ [10] proposed by Clarke and Sergey which extends the λ-calculus with layer definition, activation/deactivation and a dispatching mechanism. Contextλ has no type system to ensure adaptation because is designed to study the issues deriving from the combination of closures and the special **proceed** construct, a sort of **super** invocation in object oriented languages [17]. The problem arises when a **proceed** appears within a closure that escapes the context where it was defined. This opens interesting semantic issues because by escaping from a context the required layers could not be active any longer. In [10] several ways to deal with this semantically relevant problem have been proposed, yet to the best of our knowledge, the question is still open.

The majority of COP literature targeted object oriented languages. Indeed, there are different papers extending **Featherweight Java** [19] with COP features. Some of them focus on ensuring adaptation through a static type system. In [11] **ContextFJ** is proposed including layers, scoped layers activation and deactivation. Since layers may introduce methods not appearing in classes, a type system ensures that there exists a binding for each dispatched method call.

A different model, based on Featherweight Java, called **ContextFJ** as well, is introduced in [16]. Also in this case, a type system has been specified to statically prevent erroneous invocations at runtime, but it prohibits layers from introducing new methods that do not exist in the class and it has no construct for deactivating a layer. This means that every method defined in a layer has to override a method with the same name in the class. The first restriction is addressed in [18], the second one in [21]. Furthermore, ContextFJ was further extended to include more complex features, e.g. first-class layers, inheritance and subtyping between layers, and event-driven adaptation [1,2,20,22].

We now discuss some related works concerning implicits coercions, a useful tool to simplify the life of programmers. Basic coercions are widespread in all programming languages. For example the C language endows an automatic type cast from int to double when only one of the operands of a primitive operation is a double; in JavaScript type coercions rules allow to convert numbers to string if specific conditions are met. Type system which deal with such mechanisms only need to take into account a fixed set of coercion rules, specified by the language designer. This is the same settings of early type-level investigations [4], where the set of coercions was fixed once and for all.

Recent proposals extend implicit coercions allowing them to be programmable. In Scala [23] implicit functions can be defined in objects, the type system is allowed to use them whenever they are visible in the scope, the import directive makes them visible in the lexical scope. In Haskell the implicit type coercions are tied together with the creation of typeclasses. The typing mechanisms behind these implementations have inspired the extension in [24], where a type system with programmable implicit is formalised.

To the best of our knowledge no previous work has shown the benefits of implicits in COP. The closest to our approach is probably [29], where a core calculus is developed and type coercions are shown effective to enhance the behaviour of an existing program to track various kind of security relevant events.

7 Conclusions

In this paper we extended the previous COP proposal of Degano et al. [14] with implicit effect coercion. We have shown that this new mechanism is an effective tool for programming adaptivity, retaining the type safety guarantees of previous approaches by Degano et al. [14,15].

In particular, we have introduced in the ContextML language the implicit function construct, through which one can program a disciplined recover from adaptation failures. Indeed, in our approach an implicit is triggered when the dispatching mechanism is about to fail in order to generate a different safe behaviour.

The original type and effect system by Degano et al. [14] was designed to prevent adaptation failures to happen; this was achieved by computing an over-approximation of the contexts that may arise at runtime and by ensuring that the dispatching mechanism never fails. We extend the type and effect system with implicit effect coercion: when a possible failure is detected the type system searches whether there exists an implicit function to apply. If this search succeeds the program type-checks and its effect stores information about the new behaviour.

For simplicity, we have not introduced history based security policies in the language. We have left this as future work, which can be accomplished by integrating the approach of [14] with the implicit effect coercion. We believe implicit effect coercion could be an useful tool for security, as highlighted in [29]: programs that are about to violate a security policy could be implicitly deviated towards more safe behaviour.

References

1. Aotani, T., Kamina, T., Masuhara, H.: Featherweight EventCJ: a core calculus for a context-oriented language with event-based per-instance layer transition. In: Proceedings of the 3rd International Workshop on Context-Oriented Programming, pp. 1:1–1:7. ACM (2011)
2. Aotani, T., Kamina, T., Masuhara, H.: Unifying multiple layer activation mechanisms using one event sequence. In: Proceedings of 6th International Workshop on Context-Oriented Programming. ACM, NY (2014)
3. Appeltauer, M., Hirschfeld, R., Haupt, M., Lincke, J., Perscheid, M.: A comparison of context-oriented programming languages. In: International Workshop on Context-Oriented Programming. ACM, NY (2009)
4. Barthe, G.: Implicit coercions in type systems. In: Coppo, M., Berardi, S. (eds.) TYPES 1995. LNCS, vol. 1158, pp. 1–15. Springer, Heidelberg (1996)
5. Bartoletti, M., Degano, P., Ferrari, G.L.: Planning and verifying service composition. J. Comput. Secur. 17(5), 799–837 (2009)
6. Bartoletti, M., Degano, P., Ferrari, G.L., Zunino, R.: Local policies for resource usage analysis. ACM Trans. Program. Lang. Syst. 31(6), 1–43 (2009)
7. Bodei, C., Degano, P., Galletta, L., Salvatori, F.: Linguistic mechanisms for context-aware security. In: Ciobanu, G., Méry, D. (eds.) ICTAC 2014. LNCS, vol. 8687, pp. 61–79. Springer, Heidelberg (2014)
8. Bruni, R., Corradini, A., Gadducci, F., Lluch Lafuente, A., Vandin, A.: A conceptual framework for adaptation. In: de Lara, J., Zisman, A. (eds.) Fundamental Approaches to Software Engineering. LNCS, vol. 7212, pp. 240–254. Springer, Heidelberg (2012)
9. Cheng, B.H.C., et al.: Software engineering for self-adaptive systems: a research roadmap. In: Cheng, B.H.C., de Lemos, R., Giese, H., Inverardi, P., Magee, J. (eds.) Software Engineering for Self-Adaptive Systems. LNCS, vol. 5525, pp. 1–26. Springer, Heidelberg (2009)
10. Clarke, D., Costanza, P., Tanter, E.: How should context-escaping closures proceed? In: International Workshop on Context-Oriented Programming. ACM (2009)
11. Clarke, D., Sergey, I.: A semantics for context-oriented programming with layers. In: International Workshop on Context-Oriented Programming. ACM, NY (2009)
12. Degano, P., Ferrari, G.-L., Galletta, L.: A two-phase static analysis for reliable adaptation. In: Giannakopoulou, D., Salaün, G. (eds.) SEFM 2014. LNCS, vol. 8702, pp. 347–362. Springer, Heidelberg (2014)
13. Degano, P., Ferrari, G.L., Galletta, L.: A two-component language for COP. In: 6th International Workshop on Context-Oriented Programming (2014)
14. Degano, P., Ferrari, G.-L., Galletta, L., Mezzetti, G.: Types for coordinating secure behavioural variations. In: Sirjani, M. (ed.) COORDINATION 2012. LNCS, vol. 7274, pp. 261–276. Springer, Heidelberg (2012)

15. Degano, P., Ferrari, G.L., Galletta, L., Mezzetti, G.: Typing context-dependent behavioural variation. In: Gay, S.J., Kelly, P. (eds.) Proceedings of Fifth Workshop on Programming Language Approaches to Concurrency- and Communication-cEntric Software, PLACES 2012. EPTCS, vol. 109, pp. 28–33 (2012)
16. Hirschfeld, R., Igarashi, A., Masuhara, H.: ContextFJ: a minimal core calculus for context-oriented programming. In: Proceedings of the 10th International Workshop on Foundations of Aspect-Oriented Languages, pp. 19–23. ACM (2011)
17. Hirschfeld, R., Costanza, P., Nierstrasz, O.: Context-oriented programming. J. Object Technol. **7**(3), 125–151 (2008). March–April 2008, ETH Zurich
18. Igarashi, A., Hirschfeld, R., Masuhara, H.: A type system for dynamic layer composition. In: FOOL 2012, p. 13 (2012)
19. Igarashi, A., Pierce, B.C., Wadler, P.: Featherweight Java: a minimal core calculus for Java and GJ. ACM Trans. Program. Lang. Syst. **23**(3), 396–450 (2001)
20. Inoue, H., Igarashi, A., Appeltauer, M., Hirschfeld, R.: Towards type-safe JCop: a type system for layer inheritance and first-class layers. In: International Workshop on Context-Oriented Programming. ACM (2014)
21. Kamina, T., Aotani, T., Igarashi, A.: On-demand layer activation for type-safe deactivation. In: Proceedings of 6th International Workshop on Context-Oriented Programming, pp. 4:1–4:7. ACM (2014)
22. Kamina, T., Aotani, T., Masuhara, H.: A core calculus of composite layers. In: Proceedings of the 12th Workshop on Foundations of Aspect-Oriented Languages, pp. 7–12. ACM (2013)
23. Oliveira, B., Moors, A., Odersky, M.: Type classes as objects and implicits. In: Proceedings of the ACM International Conference on Object Oriented Programming Systems Languages and Applications, OOPSLA 2010, pp. 341–360. ACM (2010)
24. Oliveira, B., Schrijvers, T., Choi, W., Lee, W., Yi, K.: The implicit calculus: a new foundation for generic programming. In: ACM SIGPLAN Conference on Programming Language Design and Implementation, PLDI 2012, pp. 35–44 (2012)
25. Salehie, M., Tahvildari, L.: Self-adaptive software: landscape and research challenges. TAAS **4**(2), 1–42 (2009)
26. Salvaneschi, G., Ghezzi, C., Pradella, M.: Context-oriented programming: a programming paradigm for autonomic systems. CoRR abs/1105.0069 (2011)
27. Salvaneschi, G., Ghezzi, C., Pradella, M.: An analysis of language-level support for self-adaptive software. ACM Trans. Auton. Adapt. Syst. **8**(2), 7:1–7:29 (2013)
28. Skalka, C., Smith, S., Horn, D.V.: Types and trace effects of higher order programs. J. Funct. Program. **18**(2), 179–249 (2008)
29. Swamy, N., Hicks, M.W., Bierman, G.M.: A theory of typed coercions and its applications. In: Proceedings of the 14th ACM SIGPLAN International Conference on Functional Programming, ICFP 2009, Edinburgh, Scotland, UK, 2 August 31–September 2009, pp. 329–340 (2009)

Validation of Decentralised Smart Contracts Through Game Theory and Formal Methods

Giancarlo Bigi[1], Andrea Bracciali[2](✉), Giovanni Meacci[3,4], and Emilio Tuosto[5]

[1] Università di Pisa, Pisa, Italy
giancarlo.bigi@unipi.it
[2] Stirling University, Stirling, UK
abb@cs.stir.ac.uk
[3] BitHalo, Los Angeles, CA 90024, USA
[4] Coin Cube LLC, New York, NY 11213, USA
giovannimeacci@gmail.com
http://www.BitHalo.org
[5] Leicester University, Leicester, UK
et52@leicester.ac.uk

Abstract. *Decentralised smart contracts* represent the next step in the development of protocols that support the interaction of independent players without the presence of a coercing authority. Based on protocols à la BITCOIN for digital currencies, smart contracts are believed to be a potentially enabling technology for a wealth of future applications. The validation of such an early developing technology is as necessary as it is complex. In this paper we combine game theory and formal models to tackle the new challenges posed by the validation of such systems.

1 Introduction

The introduction of the BITCOIN protocol in 2008 has strongly pushed forward the development of *decentralised distributed systems*. BITCOIN is decentralised since it is not controlled by any central coercing authority. Rather, a computationally expensive distributed consensus over the internet certifies its transitions, for instance preventing the double expenditure of immaterial money. Due to the computational costs involved, the consensus of the whole BITCOIN network over the internet cannot realistically be overturned. Although BITCOIN has been highly volatile and associated to illegal activities, institutional players, including governments and banks, as well as the general public, have shown interest in it. BITCOIN has started to appear as a potentially reliable and enabling technology.

Currently, the next step builds on top of BITCOIN, aiming to introduce decentralised distributed technologies on a larger scale. One example of this are *decentralised smart contracts*, i.e. protocols designed to define self-enforcing contracts

Authors would like to thank David Zimbeck for useful discussions and for sharing information about BITHALO.

amongst untrusted and independent players. BITHALO is a paradigmatic, very recent and innovative example of a decentralised smart contract.

The validation of such protocols is clearly highly desirable and, as usual, very complex. Interestingly, the distributed and decentralised aspects of smart contracts add to complexity since free choices and gaming strategies come into play. Protocols are run by autonomous players, possibly mixing physical actions, e.g. the shipment of goods, and computer-mediated ones, e.g. an electronic payment, without any possibility of a coercing central authority. Differently from more traditional protocols, a sort of socio-economical aspect becomes relevant for the validation of smart contracts.

In this paper, we analyse and validate DSCP, an idealised smart contract inspired by BITHALO. A distinguished feature of our approach is the combination of *game theory* and *formal methods* to suitably address the mentioned complexity of the analysis and validation of smart contracts. Game theory has been widely exploited to analyse how contracts are settled through bargaining procedures (see, for instance, [21]) but the analysis of protocols that enforce contracts is a novel area of application. Formal methods have been extensively used for protocol validation, from security protocols to the more recent behavioural contracts of application level protocols. However, it is worth remarking that such kind of contracts and the contracts supported by BITHALO exist in different contexts and for different purposes. Indeed, in behavioural contracts the main focus is to ensure that the parallel composition of distributed participants does not yield communication problems such as deadlocks (see, for instance, [3,5,6]) or to analyse communication misbehaviours in untrusted settings (see, for instance, [4]). Noticeably, BITHALO also embeds steps that depend upon decisions made by human players, which do not appear in application level protocols.

In our framework game theory and formal methods complement each other: the former caters for the study of the gaming strategy aspects, while the latter provide the grounds for a precise definition of the protocol and related working hypotheses. Furthermore, the probabilistic framework we adopted allows us to properly model uncertainty and non-determinism in players' behaviour, and to exploit effective automated techniques, like statistical model checking, to validate the properties of the smart contract. To the best of our knowledge, the proposed combined approach is here firstly applied to the validation of smart contracts.

A detailed analysis of DSCP is carried out both analytically from the viewpoint of game theory, and computationally, via the definition of a model, the properties of interest, and their validation through probabilistic model checking. Sensitivity of various parameters is studied, including monetary values and fraudulence profiles of the players. Our combined analysis formally and quantitatively clarifies the intended behaviour of the protocol, which relies on a deposit scheme to enforce trust. Sometimes, assumptions on the deposit scheme may result in being unrealistic. Our analysis explores the details of the system under the uncertainty introduced when the deposit enforcing trust assumption is weakened.

2   Bitcoin-Based Smart Contracts

Smart contracts [26,27] are protocols defining self-enforcing, digital contracts. The main aim of such contracts is to guarantee fair exchanges between untrusted and independent entities. The recent introduction of the BITCOIN protocol [1] by Satoshi Nakamoto[1] in 2008 [22] allowed for decentralised smart contracts. BITCOIN provides decentralised virtual monetary instruments that can support contracts which do not require intermediaries, central repositories or single administrators. The huge potential of these contracts calls for a formal analysis and validation of their properties.

BITHALO [7,29] is a recently developed smart contract based on BITCOIN. It is supported by a freely available software platform and, to the best of our knowledge, is the first off-blockchain, decentralized smart contract. A short introduction to BITCOIN and BITHALO follows.

2.1   BITCOIN: A Protocol for Decentralised Applications

The first application of the BITCOIN protocol has been the digital, decentralised, partially anonymous currency called *bitcoin* (BTC), which is not redeemable for gold, and not backed by any government or legal entity.

BTC total market capitalization ranges between three and four billion USD, depending on the BTC/USD exchange rate (June 2015). There are nearly nine million of BTC wallets (April 2015), reaching 100,000 transactions per day (February 2015). The New York State Department of Financial Services has released a regulatory framework for digital currencies [18] (June 2015). California and UK government are considering similar options. BITCOIN venture capitalist investments are expected to reach 1 billion USD by the end of 2015 [28].

Digital currency predecessors of BITCOIN used centralised clearinghouse systems in order to address the problem of fraudulent transactions, exactly like traditional banking systems. However, these centralised structures provided them with a potential single point of attack and failure, and they became easy targets of governments, hackers, and criminal entities, and eventually failed.

BITCOIN combined previous inventions such as b-money [13] and HashCash [2], and introduced four critical innovations that eliminated the main weakness of its predecessors [1]: (1) a decentralised peer-to-peer network that allows users to transfer BTCs; (2) a trusted public ledger (called blockchain) with the list of all transactions that took place within the system; (3) a process called *mining* that let the BITCOIN protocol act as decentralised clearinghouse and allows new BTCs to be created through the solution (called *proof-of-work*, POW) of a mathematical problem based on a cryptographic hash algorithm; (4) a decentralised transaction verification system.

These additions addressed the problem of double spending, where a coin is spent twice, and other fraudulent transactions. Let consider a simple practical example. Using (1) user A transfers to user B the money that he received in a

---

[1] This name is believed to be a pseudonym.

previous transaction T. Because of (2) each user in the BITCOIN network can check the blockchain and verify whether money from transaction T has been already spent by A or not. Correctness of the blockchain information is given in terms of consensus by the vast majority of the nodes in the network. This is achieved with the points (3) and (4), which rely on distributed computational resources and can be informally summarised as follows.

Each BITCOIN node keeps a record of the blockchain, which literally is a chain of blocks. Once mined and validated, blocks are assembled one after the other to form the blockchain. The difficulty to find the POW, i.e. mine a new block, is periodically adjusted to the current computing power of the participants in such a way that a single block validation happens on average each 10 min [12]. The system contains an incentive for *miners* to validate transaction and finding POWs in terms of BTCs and transaction fees.

Originally, the blockchain was just a long single chain of blocks, but more recently it has a more complex topology with bifurcations and even "orphan" isolated blocks. The longest chain, i.e. the chain which has the most POWs, is independently selected by every node as the main chain, i.e. the blockchain. In practice, if the block containing T is deep in the blockchain, the amount of computational power needed to force a fork and rebuild an alternative, longest chain with a modified T, makes invalidating T unfeasible.

Nakamoto's idea of POW-based consensus makes unnecessary any central trusted authority in charge of issuing currency and validating fast, secure, borderless, and commission-fees free, financial transactions. The approach is applicable to a variety of different fields, such as the registry of property (see, e.g., "The Property Rights Project" [25]), fairness of elections, lotteries, digital notarisation, storage of personal and sensitive data, smart contracts and more.

2.2 BITHALO: Decentralised Smart Contracts

We consider here BITHALO as a paradigmatic example of smart contract. The term "smart contract", together with the idea of "smart property" [11], was introduced by computer scientist Nick Szabo, during the early 1990's [26].

The BITCOIN scripting system already had a variety of script hashes aimed at supporting different kinds of smart contracts [10]. However, BITHALO doesn't rely on those hashes because of known drawbacks in the BITCOIN smart contract protocol [10], as well as in some proposal based on it [9,20].

The purpose of BITHALO is to create unbreakable trade contracts without the need of arbiters or escrow agents, lowering significantly the costs for the two parties involved in the contract. Since it does not require trust, nothing in the BITHALO system is centralised. It does not require a server, just the Internet. Its peer-to-peer communication system allows the two parties to use email, Bitmessage, IRC, or other methods to exchange messages and data. BITHALO is off-blockchain in the sense that the record of BITHALO contracts is not kept in the blockchain, and therefore the use of BITHALO will not bloat the blockchain.

BITHALO can be used for bartering, self-insuring, backing commodities, performing derivatives, making good-faith employment contracts, performing two-party escrow, and more general business contracts.

Transactions are insured by a *deposit* in one of the supported digital currencies (including BTC) on a joint account, double-deposit escrow. The BITHALO protocol forces each party to uphold the contract in order to achieve the most economically optimal outcome. In a typical contract exchanging a payment for goods or services, the payment can be sent either separately, using checks, money transfer, crypto-currencies, etc., or paid directly with the deposit. The deposit will only be refunded to both parties on *shared consent*, which has to be expressed by both parties. In the lack of expression of shared consent, the joint account will self-destruct after a time-out. Time limits and deposit amounts are all flexible and agreed upon by both parties. Dissatisfaction about the outcome of the transaction by one of the parties, for instance because of theft or deception, will lead to the destruction of the deposit due to the lack of shared consensus. When the deposit exceeds the amount being transacted, the loss typically results larger than the benefits possibly obtainable by a fraudulent behaviour. However, deposits exceeding the transacted amount may be in some cases unfeasible. In some situations, smaller deposits may incentivate one or both parties to break the contract.

2.3 DSCP, a Decentralised Smart Contract Protocol

While the BITHALO platform enables users to interact through several variations of a core smart contract protocol, for the purposes of our analysis we fix here the details of DSCP, an idealised distributed and decentralised contracting protocol that mimics one of the possible interaction modalities of BITHALO. The results of the analysis of DSCP, carried out by means of the contribution of both game theory and formal verification, will be presented in the rest of the paper.

As standard, DSCP allows two parties, i.e. the two players of the protocol, to autonomously exchange money against goods without the need of a centralised arbiter. It is worth remarking that the two players are completely independent, not subject to any third party authority in the execution of the exchange protocol, and can, for instance, decide to leave the protocol at any time.

DSCP is based on the mentioned notion of "enforced trust" in the fact that none of the two parties will ever be in a position in which breaking the protocol is for them advantageous. We will see that this, as expected, will be properly enforced only when the deposit, whose payment is a pre-requisite for the execution of the protocol, exceeds the value of the goods.

DSCP allows payments to be made disjointly from the trust-enforcing deposit. This adds flexibility, e.g. users may want to pay in fiat currencies and use BTCs only for the deposit (which can only be in crypto-currencies), and makes the set of possible interactions richer and therefore more interesting to be analysed.

In our interpretation, we distinguish between the *money* m and the *value* v belonging to a player of the protocol. The former being the cash availability and the latter the asset value of the player. When a buyer (analogously a seller) successfully buys an item, their money will decrease, while the value of the goods they possess will increase of the same quantity, assuming fair prices. We assume that both price and value coincide, and the buyer and the seller give the same value to a given item (other choices are possible, see Footnote 2). In an ideal world with "robust" contracting protocols, the sum of money and value of each player and therefore the overall value and money in the system should stay constant in time. We will show that such a "wealth preservation property" holds when the deposit exceeds the value/price[2] (and players do not behave against their interests). Autonomous players can decide to break the protocol because either it is advantageous for them or because of contingencies and free human behaviour, even if not necessarily advantageous. Examples are, respectively, breaking the protocol when the consequent loss of the deposit is less than the advantage obtained, and abandoning a transaction due to a too long response time of the other party and, perhaps, a not too constraining deposit. Players' free choices may clearly break the conservation of wealth in the system. A player may gain money while another may loose asset, or both may loose money because breaking the protocol leads to the loss of deposits.

We will not model time explicitly. Consequences of time-outs like a too long response are understood as the possibility for players to leave the protocol, and negate consent, at any time.

Furthermore, we will consider probabilities, together with parameters like money and value, to model players' behaviour and their choice capabilities. This will allow us to account for diverse player profiles.

These assumptions lead to a quite reach model where different aspects have to be accommodated in order to fully describe the protocol and its implications at various levels. These aspects range from the precise description of the possible interplay of the two autonomous players, to the psycho-economical forces that may drive their choices.

3   Game Theoretic Analysis of DSCP

Once the terms of the contract are agreed, the two players - the buyer and the seller - act independently of each other in the actual transaction, but the choices of the former affect the result and the behaviour of the latter and vice versa. Therefore, concepts and ideas from noncooperative game theory can be exploited to analyse the transaction protocol and, as a consequence, the quality of the agreement as well.

The agreement requires setting a price p for the item and the value of the safety deposits of the buyer and seller, namely d_b and d_s. Clearly, the buyer has to consider the item worth paying p: turning the utility of the item for the buyer into a (monetary) value v_b, it must be greater than p. Similarly, the value v_s that

---

[2] We stick to a quite simple vision of trading. An interesting alternative would be assuming that $v < p$ for the seller and $p < v$ for the buyer. In this case both would have an incentive to come to the shared consent, both increasing their wealth. The wealth preservation property would not hold. This is scope for future work.

the seller assigns to the item has to be at most p. The determination of prices is a central topic of economics that goes far beyond the aim of this paper, so we will simply consider p as given and any pair of values $v_b \geq p$ and $v_s \leq p$.

Table 1. "One shot" strategic game.

Seller → / Buyer ↓	S/C	S/D	L_s
P/C	$p - v_s$ / $v_b - p$	$p - v_s - d_s$ / $v_b - p - d_b$	$p - d_s$ / $-p - d_b$
P/D	$p - v_s - d_s$ / $v_b - p - d_b$	$p - v_s - d_s$ / $v_b - p - d_b$	$p - d_s$ / $-p - d_b$
L_b	$-v_s - d_s$ / $v_b - d_b$	$-v_s - d_s$ / $v_b - d_b$	$-d_s$ / $-d_b$

The role of the deposits is more relevant for our analysis: they are meant to guarantee that the players will actually perform the transaction. The choice of their value requires some kind of pre-transaction analysis of the transaction itself by both sides. Imagining that both decide their full strategies at the very beginning of the transaction in one shot, each player can analyse all the possible outcomes as the result of the behaviour of both. Relying on game theory, this analysis can be carried out modelling the transaction as a *strategic or normal game* of two players (see, for instance, Sect. 2.1 in [24]).

A priori, once that the agreement is settled and the deposits paid, the buyer can behave in the following ways: pay the item and confirm a satisfactory transaction, namely *strategy* $[P/C]$, pay and leave the system denying a satisfactory transaction $[P/D]$, leave the system without paying $[L_b]$. Similarly, the seller can ship the item and confirm a satisfactory transaction $[S/C]$, ship and leave the system denying a satisfactory transaction $[S/D]$, leave the system without shipping $[L_s]$. Each pair of strategies leads to an outcome given by a pair of *pay-offs*, one for each player. The nine possible outcomes of the transaction are given in Table 1 through a bimatrix where the top entry in each cell is the pay-off for the seller and the bottom entry for the buyer.

Comparing the strategies of the buyer, $[L_b]$ *dominates* $[P/D]$ since the former provides a better pay-off than the latter for any possible strategy of the seller: the buyer would never select $[P/D]$. Notice that $[P/C]$ *dominates* $[P/D]$ *weakly*, that is some payoffs are equal while none is better for the latter strategy. If $p > d_b$, then $[L_b]$ dominates $[P/C]$ as well and the buyer would select the strategy $[L_b]$: as a consequence, the seller shouldn't have agreed such a price and deposit. The comparison of the strategies of the seller is analogous: $[L_s]$ dominates $[S/D]$,

$[S/C]$ dominates $[S/D]$ weakly; if $p > d_s$, then $[L_s]$ dominates $[S/C]$ as well and the seller would select the strategy $[L_s]$.

Indeed, the technique of iterated elimination of dominated strategies shows that, whenever $p > d_b$ or $p > d_s$, the strategy profile $([L_b], [L_s])$ is the unique Nash equilibrium of the game, that is the unique profile such that no player can improve their own pay-off changing strategy while the other does not.

This basic analysis suggests that the players should agree deposits $d_b \geq p$ and $d_p \geq p$. Indeed, in this case the successful transaction $([P/C],[S/C])$ is a Nash equilibrium as well.

Though the above formulation as a strategic game can be useful for a preliminary analysis, it does not fully catch the nature of the actual transaction: the choices are not taken altogether at the very beginning but somehow sequentially. As the players are perfectly aware of the state of the system, this knowledge may and actually does influence their next choices.

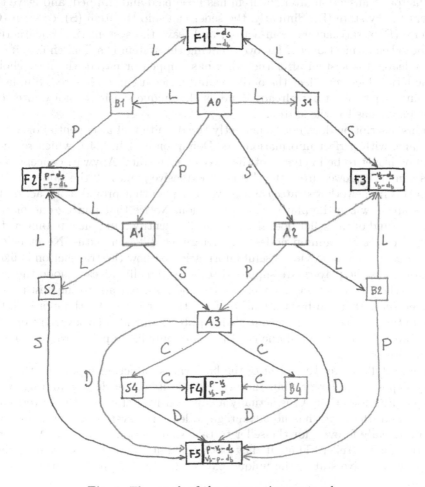

Fig. 1. The graph of the transaction protocol.

The transaction can be described through the directed graph of Fig. 1. Each node represents one possible state of the system, while each arc represents one action that can be taken by one of the players in the state at the tail node leading to the state at the head node. Node A0 represents the initial state (agreement settled), while the nodes labelled with F represent the end of the transaction with a specific outcome. Notice that there are five end (F) nodes and they match the five different outcomes given in Table 1. The remaining nodes are labelled with the player or the players that may take an action. Notice that the same state/node may allow actions by both players: there is no player exclusively in charge of the next move and they could also act simultaneously. In this latter case no problem arises as considering arbitrarily one action before the other leads eventually to the same state. A node is labelled with A if both players can act, with B or S if only the buyer or the seller can act. The buyer can take the following actions: pay the item (arc label P), confirm (C) or deny (D) a satisfactory transaction after the item has been paid and shipped, and leave the system at any state (L). Similarly, the seller can ship the item (S), confirm (C) or deny (D) a satisfactory transaction, and leave the system (L). Each action can be taken at most once. Moreover, leaving the system is a final choice: if one player leaves the system after the other has shipped or payed, the next choice of the latter does not affect the outcome and hence it can be ignored. Similarly, shipping or paying, if not already done, is the unique sensitive choice after the other player has left the system.

This description does not fit perfectly the definition of a sequential or extensive game with perfect information (see Definition 89.1 in [24]), which requires a unique player to be in charge of the next at each state. Anyway, concepts and ideas can be borrowed from the theory of extensive games all the same.

In this framework a *strategy* of a player is a plan that provides one action for each state at which the player can take action. Notice that pairing one plan of the buyer and of the seller does not necessarily identify a unique outcome as the order of moves at common nodes may determine different paths. Nevertheless, *backwards induction* provides useful information on how the transaction is likely to happen: as the players are supposed to act rationally, at each node they are going to choose one action, if any exists, that necessarily leads to the best pay-off between those that can be still reached from the current state; therefore, all the "non-optimal" actions can be cancelled. Applying this idea backwards from the final states (F) to the initial one (A0) provides only likely paths from the latter to the former.

Figure 2 illustrates the result of the backwards induction supposing that the safety deposits are larger than the price of the item, i.e. $d_b > p$ and $d_s > p$. The picture shows that A1 is actually a time sensitive state for the buyer: after having paid, the buyer has no advantage to leave the system rather than waiting, potentially forever, for the seller to take some action. Similarly, A2 is time sensitive for the seller. Thus, if they both rule out leaving the system at their own time sensitive states, the unique paths left describe the ideal transaction:

the buyer pays, the seller ships and both confirm a satisfactory transaction (no matter in which order).

If the safety deposits are equal to the price, i.e. $d_b = p$ and $d_s = p$, the same kind of analysis does not exclude any possible final state except F5 coming out as the result of the following unreasonable behaviour: the buyer pays, the seller ships and one of them denies a satisfactory transaction. Finally, if the deposits are smaller than the price, the backwards induction provides only the final state in which both leave the system without paying and shipping, as it was already suggested by the strategic game given in Table 1.

In conclusion, the above analysis based on game theory suggests that the players are likely to perform DSCP satisfactorily if the deposits are larger than the price, no matter how much bigger. It is worth stressing that the whole analysis is based on the assumption that the seller, if not leaving earlier, ships the right item and in turn the buyer, if not leaving earlier, pays exactly the agreed price. The analysis of this kind of unfair behaviours is beyond the aim of this paper.

4   Formal Verification of DSCP

Players' strategies under the hypotheses of a perfectly rational, utilitaristic and deterministic behaviour have been analysed by means of game theory. It has also been proved that a deposit exceeding the value of the traded goods guarantees the fair execution of DSCP under the mentioned hypotheses.

However, as observed, the requirement on the deposit might be unrealistic, especially for expensive goods. It is therefore worth studying the protocol behaviour with smaller deposits, when players adopt a less strict and more realistic behaviour, and also when considering the impact of different players' profiles on the protocol, e.g. honest and fraudulent ones.

This is done by defining a probabilistic formal model of DSCP and exploiting the PRISM probabilistic model checker [17] to validate the properties of interest.

4.1   Protocols, Contracts and Formal Verification

Communication and interaction protocols are not simple to design, verify, and implement. A paradigmatic case is that of the well studied security protocols, which can typically be described in terms of very few steps describing the participants involved in the communication, the sharing of secrets among them, and the information they generate and exchange during the protocol execution. Their simplicity is however only apparent; designing a provably correct protocol is very hard and there are several examples of security protocols found flawed after having been considered correct for a few years, the paradigmatic example being the Needham-Shroeder [23] protocol and the Lowe's attack to it [19], discovered by means of formal verification. Among the reasons behind such a complexity, is the difficulty in formally identify an "attacker model" (and often a precise definition of the security properties to guarantee/check).

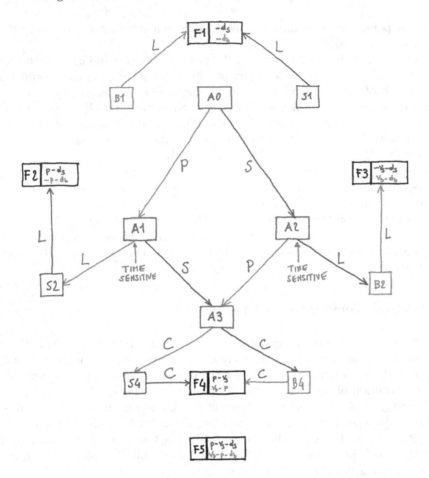

Fig. 2. The graph reduced by backwards induction (for $d_b, d_s > p$).

Formal methods have been advocated as suitable tools for the rigorous specification and verification of security protocols and their attacker models and several formal approaches to the verification of security protocols have been successful. For instance, the precise definition of the attacker model of Dolev-Yao [14] allows the execution of protocols to be clearly described.

Various kind of contract protocols are being verified by means of formal techniques. A key difference between security protocols and smart contracts like DSCP is the fact that the properties of interest of the latter escape the usual domain of the properties of security protocols, hence providing new interesting research directions. Intuitively, DSCP aims to guarantee that one of the two parties involved in a financial transaction cannot "cheat without a penalty". Although intuitively simple, such property alone is not satisfactory; in fact, the penalty which one of the parties incurs in has to be compared to the advantage to cheat. Therefore, a crucial phase of DSCP is the determination of the penalties the two parties are agreeable with.

4.2   Markov Decision Processes

In the execution of DSCP under the mentioned hypotheses, players can synchronise their actions, exhibit probabilistic behaviour typically depending on the state in which they are, and make non-deterministic and probabilistic choices. A *Markov Decision Process (MDP)* conveniently describes decision making processes that may depend on non-deterministic and random choices (see [15] for an introduction to MDPs, associated temporal logics and their use in PRISM).

Informally speaking, an MDP can be understood a state-based automata which first resolves the nondeterministic choice of the next action to be performed, and then resolves the probabilistic choice amongst the possible next states the chosen action may lead to.

PRISM supports MDPs and their analysis and simulation in process algebra like settings. For instance, PRISM caters for synchronisation, i.e. different automata synchronise on the execution of certain actions, which belong to some specified synchronisation set. By "unfolding" the effects that non-deterministic choices may have on probabilistic ones, non-determinism may be resolved and the MDP reduced to a Discrete Time Markov Chain (DTMC).

PRISM also supports Temporal Logics for expressing properties of an MDP, which can then be validated. For our purposes, validation will consist in an approximated statistical approach: a suitable number of system evolutions are explored in order to approximate the probability that a property of interest holds. Probabilistic properties have been expressed in the PCTL logic [8,16], whose temporal operators include, amongst others, $X\phi$, i.e. property ϕ holds in the next state with a given probability, and $F\phi$, eventually a state satisfying ϕ will be reached with a given probability.

4.3   A Probabilistic Model of DSCP

The automaton in Fig. 3(a) formalises the assumptions about the functioning of DSCP outlined in Sect. 2.3, and makes other details unambiguous, such as the choice that price and value coincide and are the same for both players. Furthermore, we do not distinguish here between leaving (L) and denying (D) a protocol. While such a distinction may be useful for more complete game theory analyses, the two actions have in the current settings the same effect.

The automaton describes the behaviour of the buyer. The whole model of DSCP, an MDP, consists of this automaton and a symmetrical one for the seller, which only swaps paying for shipping, highlighting the high symmetry of the two roles under the assumptions made.

From the initial state 0 only the transition to state 1 is enabled and used to reset the initial conditions of a protocol execution. Therefore it is not relevant to the player behaviour. From state 1 only the *deposit* transition to state

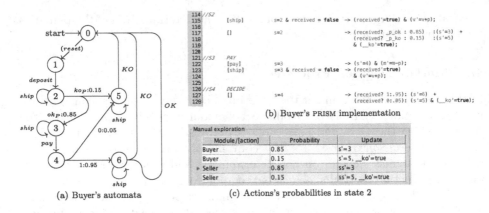

(a) Buyer's automata

(b) Buyer's PRISM implementation

(c) Actions's probabilities in state 2

Fig. 3. Model and implementation of the Buyer's player.

2 is enabled. This models the agreement and payment of the deposit and the actual start of the protocol. Here *deposit* is a synchronisation action that the two automata can only perform together. It is worth noting another synchronisation action, i.e. *ship*, that appears in several states in a loop transition. This represents the seller sending goods and has been modelled as a synchronisation, as the buyer must be aware of the shipment, too. In order to avoid deadlocks, the buyer is (almost) always ready to synch on *ship*. Symmetrically, the seller is (almost) always ready to accept payments by synching on *pay* (this avoids both being deadlocked on *ship/pay*, the other not being ready to synch).

State 2 is actually one of the two nodes where players can make a decision (double arrow): either leave, and hence break the protocol, by moving to state 5 with loss of the deposit, or play their own part by moving to state 3, which in this case leads to the payment of the agreed price. There is not synchronisation here as this is a personal (a.k.a. internal) choice. The two branches of the arrow are labeled with $n : m$. These are the two probabilities associated with each branch for the case in which the buyer (seller, resp.) has (n) or has not (m) received the goods (payment, resp.).

The modelling of such a probabilistic choice is key. If the buyer has received, but not yet paid at this stage, the probabilities ok_P to follow the protocol and ko_P to abandon it (both players loose the deposit) take into account the ratio of the paid deposit over the price still to be paid (symmetrically, the deposit over the value of the goods to be sent):

$$ok_P = min(1, \left(\frac{d}{p}\right)^r) \qquad ko_P = 1 - ok_P$$

As expected, if $p \le d$ the protocol is followed with probability 1 because there is no gain in stealing the goods and loosing the deposit. Otherwise, the probability decreases as much as the deposit is irrelevant with respect to the price/value. Furthermore, we have added the exponential r to model the player's attitude. With $r = 1/2$, say, the value d/p is amplified towards 1, i.e. reducing the attitude to steal, as an honest player would typically do. With $r \geq 1$ the effect is the opposite, increasing the probability to steal.

If goods have not yet been received (m value on the arrow), it is assumed that the buyer (seller) will proceed to payment (shipment) with $P = 0.85$, hence following the protocol most of the times. This choice is worth some consideration. As detected by game theory, this is a critical choice: players can abandon now the protocol and loose the deposit, or proceed and be possibly driven to an even larger loss (see the pay-offs of Sect. 3 when $v_s = v_b = p$). In the game theory interpretation, then, abandoning now, after having paid the deposit, is a plausible choice. This has informed our choice to retain a minimal probability of abandoning. A possible alternative and indecisive $P = 0.5$, or any probability leaning towards abandoning, would invalidate the spirit of the protocol, neglecting the interest of the players to trade (see Footnote 2). Moreover, it should also be considered that, although we do not model *time* explicitly, players may decide to abandon the protocol and loose the deposit after a too long wait for the counterpart to act, possibly not wanting to make the first move (it is worth remarking here that in our idealised DSCP, participants do not communicate directly). This can be accounted for by the non-null 0.15 probability of abandoning the protocol at this stage. Such probability could be tailored on empirical data about protocol usage.

It is worth remarking how aspects such as the utility and attitude of players and some form of time-dependent events can be easily and clearly embedded in the model, as done in the transition described above.

Finally, the co-existence of non-determinism and probabilistic choices in state 2 has to be noted. Informally speaking, according to MDP theory, this is dealt with by first resolving the non-determinism between *ship* and the action regarding the probabilistic choice about abandoning or continuing the protocol. Several possibilities may arise, e.g. the seller might not be ready to synch on *ship*, making the choice deterministic, or the buyer might follow a specific policy to resolve non-determinism (the theory defines the concept of possible *adversaries*). A probabilistic choice will be made only if the probabilistic action has been selected when resolving non-determinism.

From state 3 only the *pay* action is enabled leading to the next choice state 4, with analogous conditions to state 2, the difference being that the player has paid/shipped. If the player has already received they are happy, $P = 1$, to express consent, i.e. move to state 6, otherwise, they are however more incentivised to reach consent, $P = 0.95$. The 0.05 probability of abandoning the protocol accounts for timeouts and other contingencies.

In state 5 the choice has been made and, although *ship* is still enabled, the only synchronising exit action is KO, abandoning the protocol with the mutual loss of deposits. Analogously for state 6, where it is still possible to synch on KO if the counterpart abandons, otherwise the preferred choice (carried out by a specific implementation of non-determinism) will be OK, back to state 0. Variables representing players' wealth are updated in the transitions from states 5 and 6.

Figure 3(b) shows a snapshot of the PRISM code that illustrates how the model is implemented. Each transition is labeled with the action name, if any, variable s represents the current state and some tests are performed in the selection of the next transition, e.g. the test received = false. Probabilistic choices are represented by the + operator and preceded by the associated probabilities, e.g. the expression (received? _p_ok : 0.85) in state 2.

Figure 3(c) shows the enabled actions in state 2 for both players. Here the choice is probabilistic for both. The action leading the seller to state 3 has been selected. Updates, including the state change, are shown for each action.

5 Validating DSCP

5.1 Model Validation

A simple sanity check is presented in Fig. 4 to provide validation of the defined model. This is based on the idea of wealth preservation within the system under the assumptions made and ideal players' behaviour (Sect. 2.3) and shows the expected fair execution of the protocol: all buyer's money is transformed into value and correspondingly seller's value is transformed into money with no loss.

5.2 Deposits, Prices and Players' Profiles

Following the results of the game theory analysis and further considerations about adding realism to the model, the case of a deposit smaller than the price/value of goods is considered here. In this case, DSCP may loose some of its expected "enforced trust" effect on players. Under these assumptions it is also of interest to explore how players with different attitudes towards behaving fraudulently can perturbe the protocol.

Six profiles have been considered, for $r = 0.5$, inching towards honesty and trust, $r = 1$ simply depending on the ratio between d and p, and r assuming values in $\{1.5, 2, 2.5, 3\}$, a progressively more fraudulent attitude. The deposit assumes values in $\{0, 2, 4, 6, 8, 10\}$, against a price of 10.

Validation has been carried out using $PCTL$ logic to express the properties of interest and exploiting the statistical model checking facilities provided by PRISM, [17]. Starting again from the idea of wealth preservation, we have investigated the probability of one of the two symmetric players, both with the same profile, reporting a loss of a certain percentage after a given amount of time. Specifically, the tested property was

$$Pmax = ?\ [F < 700\ SellerLossX]$$

which, informally, reads as "What is the probability that the seller will loose about X% of their initial wealth within 700 time units?" The predicate $SellerLossX$ identifies all the states where seller wealth has been reduced by $(X \pm 5)\%$. The operator F, finally, requires that the property $SellerLossX$ will eventually be

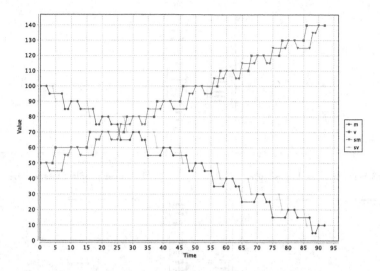

Fig. 4. Wealth preservation. The figure shows a sample of protocol executions, with
$m = 1000$ and $v = 500$, and $sm = 500$ and $sv = 1000$, the money and the value of
the buyer and the seller, respectively. Both cannot run up a debt i.e. transactions
would stop when one of the two runs out of money. The protocol is executed in "ideal"
conditions: the ratio between the deposit and the price of objects does not make it
convenient to break the protocol ($p = sp = 10$ and $d = sd = 10$), each player makes
fully rational and protocol compliant choices all the time (e.g. there are no minimal
probabilities to abandon the protocol as in the general model illustrated in Sect. 4.3).
The graph shows the results of a series of about 100 transactions between a typical
seller and a typical buyer, after which the sum of money and value is preserved for
both players and therefore for the whole system.

satisfied in the states reached by the repeated execution of the protocol. This
has to happen within 700 time units.

PRISM automatically validates such a formula by a statistical approach: a
sufficiently large number of simulations is run in order to asses the desired probability, as required by the $Pmax = ?$ operator (10,000 simulations in our case
for each possible combination of profiles and deposits. Each simulation runs for
at most 1500 time units).

Figure 5(a) and (b) report probabilities of loosing 40 % of the initial wealth,
while Fig. 5(c) and (d) report probabilities of loosing 30 % of the initial wealth
for the seller and buyer, respectively. These results are about protocols run by
players with the same profile. Seller and buyer results are symmetric in all the
cases, as expected. The figures show a quite consistent probability of a 30 % loss,
up to about 0.3, and a tenfold lower probability for a 40 % loss.

Quite interestingly, a very low deposit, e.g. from 0 to 2 in the 30 % case, may
incentivate fraudulent behaviour due to "lack of risk", however not much wealth
is lost, because of the scarce impact of the loss of a minimal deposit. Analogously,
a deposit close or equal to the price, 10 in this case, causes a phase switch as

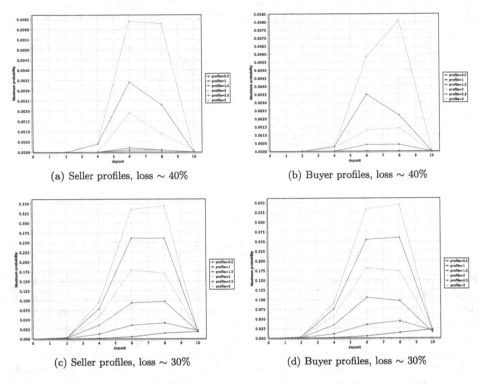

(a) Seller profiles, loss ~ 40%   (b) Buyer profiles, loss ~ 40%

(c) Seller profiles, loss ~ 30%   (d) Buyer profiles, loss ~ 30%

Fig. 5. Deposit and profiles sensitivity. Loss probability for different player profiles within 700 time units. Different curves represent different profiles. Profiles less than 1 tend to be honest, those bigger fraudulent.

stealing becomes non-convenient (note the *min* operator in the definition of the probability choices of players). A deposit close to the price, 3/4 of it say, results in being the most harmful situation, combining the probability of fraudulent behaviour with relevant loss following deposit loss.

Not surprisingly, profiles behave as expected. The honest one has a physiological minimal loss due to those minimal probabilities of abandoning the protocol even in potentially rewarding cases. Protocol executions in the presence of fraudulent players report larger losses, proportional to the r parameter.

These results, beyond explicating the details of the functioning of the protocol, can be used to determine preferred player behaviour when operating in untrustable environments. In those cases where a deposit equal to the price is unfeasible, some sort of trade-off analysis between deposit, profiles and levels of risk can be carried out through graphics like Fig. 5. For instance one might wonder: *which is the maximum deposit within a range that allows keeping the risk of an X% loss below a given threshold? which is the minimum risk of such a loss for a range of deposits? which fraudulence profiles can be tolerated when one wants to keep the loss below a given threshold for a given deposit?*

5.3   Being Fraudulent Pays Off

As a final step, the different profiles are compared. This is done by letting an honest buyer ($r = 0.5$) interact with a quite fraudulent ($r = 1$) seller (symmetrical cases are analogous due to the symmetry of players). Results are reported in Fig. 6 obtained by validating again the property of loosing about 30 % of wealth within 700 time units.

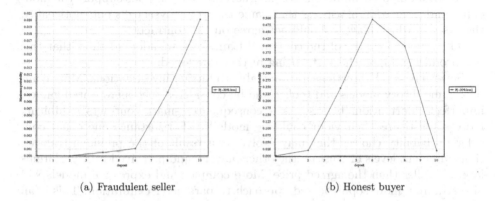

(a) Fraudulent seller   (b) Honest buyer

Fig. 6. A fraudulent seller and an honest buyer. Figures shows the probability of loosing about 30 % for a fraudulent seller (a), who will leave the protocol whenever convenient with an high probability, and an honest buyer (b) who tend to follow the protocol. The curve is drawn for different deposits in $[0, 10]$ with 10 the price/value.

The fraudulent seller, Fig. 6(a), has an almost negligible probability of incurring in a 30 % loss,%[3] i.e. 0.02 in the worst case when $d = 10$ (which is when the "enforced trust" by the deposit forces players to behave fairly and loss are only due to the minimal probabilities of abandoning the protocol - Sect. 4.3).

For the honest buyer instead, Fig. 6(b), the risk is consistently higher, with a peak half-way in the deposit scale, as expected. In the worst case the probability of incurring in a 30 % loss is 0.5.

6   Conclusions

We analysed and validated DSCP, an idealised protocol for decentralised smart contracts, inspired by BITHALO. Several works can be found in literature on the security of virtual currencies such as BITCOIN. Our focus is on the validation of players' behaviour while carrying out a smart contract. Our methodological

---

[3] It must be recalled that larger probabilities could hold for lesser-percentage losses, e.g. the seller could have a 0.1 probability of a 20 %. Probabilities for different losses can be determined, if of interest.

approach to the validation of DSCP combines game theory and formal verification. Beyond the validation results, this kind of joint analysis applied to smart contracts is, to the best of our knowledge, an innovative aspect of the paper.

Game theoretic models provide an analysis of the behaviour of the players in the game/protocol under the assumption of perfect rationality and return maximization. Such models also suggest conditions for agreeing on the contract. The results are exploited to shape the actual behaviour of the system in a formal model for automated validation. Furthermore, formal methods support the modelling and simulation of aspects that game theory analysis calls out, noticeably, the cases in which players should not agree on the contract.

The reported results of the combined framework we adopted show that this is a promising approach, worth being further developed.

Several research directions are amenable to further investigations. More complex game theory models and tools could be considered such as repeated games, imperfect information, beliefs. As a consequence, smart contracts exhibiting more sophisticated behaviour could be modelled. For instance one could consider probability choices that may evolve as a result of the previous transactions, different levels of trust on the other players, and perceived utility of items larger/smaller than the agreed price. More complex and expressive models will also require a more sophisticated approach to parameter calibration. This is an interesting and open aspect of our approach, to be addressed in future work when larger datasets about the usage and performances of smart contracts will be available and hence usable to identify critical parameters.

Finally, smart contracts with multiple parties could be analysed through similar techniques as well.

References

1. Antonopoulos, A.: Mastering Bitcoin. O'Relly, San Francisco (2015)
2. Back, A.: Hashcash a denial of service counter-measure (2002). http://www.hashcash.org/papers/hashcash.pdf
3. Bartoletti, M., Cimoli, T., Zunino, R.: Compliance in behavioural contracts: a brief survey. In: Bodei, C., Ferrari, G.-L., Priami, C. (eds.) Programming Languages with Applications to Biology and Security - Colloquium in Honour of Pierpaolo Degano for his 65th Birthday. LNCS. Springer (2015) (to appear)
4. Bartoletti, M., Scalas, A., Tuosto, E., Zunino, R.: Honesty by typing. In: Beyer, D., Boreale, M. (eds.) FORTE 2013 and FMOODS 2013. LNCS, vol. 7892, pp. 305–320. Springer, Heidelberg (2013)
5. Basile, D., Degano, P., Ferrari, G.-L.: Automata for analysing service contracts. In: Maffei, M., Tuosto, E. (eds.) TGC 2014. LNCS, vol. 8902, pp. 34–50. Springer, Heidelberg (2014). http://dx.doi.org/10.1007/978-3-662-45917-1_3
6. Basile, D., Degano, P., Ferrari, G.L.: A formal framework for secure and complying services. J. Supercomput. **69**(1), 43–52 (2014). http://dx.doi.org/10.1007/s11227-014-1211-0
7. BITHALO: https://bithalo.org/
8. Bianco, A., de Alfaro, L.: Model checking of probabilistic and nondeterministic systems. In: Thiagarajan, P.S. (ed.) FSTTCS 1995. LNCS, vol. 1026, pp. 499–513. Springer, Heidelberg (1995)

9. BitcoinWiki: Atomic   trading.   https://en.bitcoin.it/wiki/atomic_cross-chain_trading
10. BitcoinWiki: Script. https://en.bitcoin.it/wiki/script
11. BitcoinWiki: Smart property. https://en.bitcoin.it/wiki/Smart_Property
12. Blockchain.info: Average transaction confirmation time. https://blockchain.info/charts/avg-confirmation-time
13. Dai, W.: b-money (1998). http://www.weidai.com/bmoney.txt
14. Dolev, D., Yao, A.: On the security of public key protocols. IEEE Trans. Inf. Theory **29**(2), 198–208 (1983)
15. Forejt, V., Kwiatkowska, M., Norman, G., Parker, D.: Automated verification techniques for probabilistic systems. In: Bernardo, M., Issarny, V. (eds.) SFM 2011. LNCS, vol. 6659, pp. 53–113. Springer, Heidelberg (2011)
16. Hansson, H., Jonsson, B.: A logic for reasoning about time and reliability. Formal Aspects Comput. **6**(5), 512–535 (1994)
17. Kwiatkowska, M., Norman, G., Parker, D.: PRISM 4.0: verification of probabilistic real-time systems. In: Gopalakrishnan, G., Qadeer, S. (eds.) CAV 2011. LNCS, vol. 6806, pp. 585–591. Springer, Heidelberg (2011)
18. Lawsky, B.M.: Bitlicense. http://www.dfs.ny.gov/legal/regulations/adoptions/dfsp200t.pdf
19. Lowe, G.: An attack on the Needham-Schroeder public-key authentication protocol. Inf. Process. Lett. **56**(3), 131–133 (1995)
20. Malinowski, D., Mazurek, L., Andrychowicz, M., Dziembowski, S.: Secure multi-party computations on bitcoin. IACR Cryptology ePrint Archive, p. 784 (2013)
21. Muthoo, A.: Bargaining Theory with Applications. Cambridge University Press, Cambridge (1999)
22. Nakamoto, S.: Bitcoin: A peer-to-peer electronic cash system (2008). https://bitcoin.org/bitcoin.pdf
23. Needham, R., Schroeder, M.: Using encryption for authentication in large networks of computers. Commun. ACM **21**(12), 993–999 (1978)
24. Osborne, M.J., Rubinstein, A.: A Course in Game Theory. MIT Press, Cambridge (1994)
25. de Soto, H.P.: The property rights project. http://www.ild.org.pe
26. Szabo, N.: Formalizing and securing relationships on public networks. First Monday (1997). http://firstmonday.org/ojs/index.php/fm/article/view/548/469
27. Szabo, N.: The idea of smart contracts (1997). http://szabo.best.vwh.net/smart_contracts_idea.html
28. VV.AA: Special report bitcoin. Bloomberg Briefs (2015). http://www.bloombergbriefs.com/
29. Zimbeck, D.: Two party double deposit trustless escrow in cryptographic networks and bitcoin (2014). https://bithalo.org/

Static Evidences for Attack Reconstruction

Chiara Bodei[1]([✉]), Linda Brodo[2], and Riccardo Focardi[3]

[1] Dip. di Informatica, Università di Pisa, Pisa, Italy
chiara.bodei@unipi.it
[2] Dip. di Sci. Pol., Sci. della Com. e Ing. dell'Inform.,
Università di Sassari, Sassari, Italy
[3] Dip. di Scienze Ambientali, Informatica e Statistica,
Università di Venezia, Venezia, Italy

Abstract. Control Flow Analysis (CFA) has been proven successful for the analysis of cryptographic protocols. Due to its over-approximative nature, the absence of detected flaws implies their absence also at run time, while their presence only says that there is the possibility for flaws to occur. Nevertheless, the static detection of a flaw can be considered as a warning bell that alerts against a possible attack, of which the flaw is the result. Reconstructing the possible attack leading to the detected flaw is not trivial, though. We propose a CFA enriched with *causal* information that accounts for attacker activity. In case a flaw is predicted, the causal information provides a sort of climbing holds that can be *escalated* to reconstruct the attack sequence leading to the flaw.

1 Introduction

A security protocol description is a list of messages exchanged by principals that usually includes recurring terms, resembling *rhymes* in poem verses. The entities involved in a cryptographic protocol do not indeed *see* each other and necessarily base their respective trust on the presence of expected and known terms in the received messages. Protocol messages are not merely a way to transmit information, e.g. new session keys: they also ensure that the entities really are who they declare they are, that their content is fresh, that a message is the response to a previous challenge and so on. Nevertheless, the terms used to confirm that messages are as expected sometimes do not suffice to guarantee that a protocol will provide the desired security guarantees. Due to weaknesses in the protocol design, attackers can forge messages that are unfortunately accepted by legitimate parties, breaking the intended *rhymes* and leading to security attacks.

In the last decades, many formal techniques have been applied to cryptographic protocols to detect possible flaws and attacks. In this work, we focus on the Control Flow Analysis (CFA) presented in [5], which soundly over-approximates the behaviour of protocols described in the process algebra LySA. The analysis addresses message authenticity, in the presence of a Dolev-Yao [11] attacker. This

This work has been partially supported by the MIUR PRIN project *Security Horizons*.

is achieved by tracking the origin and the destination of encrypted messages, and verifying that a message encrypted by principal A and intended for B does indeed come from A and reaches B only. This approach has been successfully applied to many classical cryptographic protocols. Due to the over-approximative nature of static analysis, if no violation of the message authentication property is detected, then no violation will ever arise at run time. Instead, the existence of violations at static time does not necessarily imply their existence at run time, but possible violations should be considered such as warnings bells and should be further investigated. The CFA in [5] detects static violations, but it does not give many hints on what could have gone wrong, because a violation is just the result or a side effect of a possible attack. Determining the attacks sequences possibly leading to the predicted violations is not straightforward.

In this paper, we begin to tackle this problem, by enriching the analysis in [5] with additional information of *causal* nature that facilitates the reconstruction of attack sequences in the presence of violations. In particular, we use LySA+, a dialect of LySA where decryptions are performed on-the-fly inside inputs, when receiving a message. This allows us to focus on the message tuples, in particular the ones the attacker can forge, that can be correctly decrypted and accepted by an input. The extended CFA still predicts the behaviour of protocols, as in [5], by tracking the set of message tuples that are communicated over the network and by recording the potential values of variables and possible violations. Our extension consists of: (*i*) locally recording the output message tuples that can be accepted for each input; (*ii*) annotating tuples with information somewhat reminiscent of Sewell's "colours" [17]. Information on annotated tuples can include the name of the principal that has composed the tuple, the number of the step of the protocol corresponding to the output, an identification code for the tuple and whatever can be helpful for the investigation of a specific security property. The tuples that are forged by the attacker come with a special annotation relating the tuple to the attacker. This information is exploited to decorate the potential values for the variables with *causal* information on their *history*.

Intuitively, our analysis enriches [5] with a sort of *climbing holds* that can be *escalated* to reconstruct the attack leading to a detected potential flaw. When the CFA reports a mismatch in the intended origin or destination of an encrypted message, we can now discover the association to a specific tuple and in which input the tuple has been accepted. At this point, we can try to reconstruct the message exchange chain leading to this one, by observing the causal relationships between this message and the previous ones, typically based on the use of terms (nonces or keys) received before. Due to the information on the values received, it is possible to further climb up and to look for possible routes of message sequences. Our running example, a flawed variant of the Wide Mouthed Frog (WMF) protocol, is a lucky one, because we are able to uniquely reconstruct the attack sequences related to the detected violations. This is good to illustrate the approach but in general it is not guaranteed that a static violation corresponds to one or more attacks. Since the static analysis provides an over-approximation of the possible violations, false positives can arise. In this case the reconstruction can lead to spurious attacks. However, even in these cases, our CFA gives hints for advancing educated guesses on the possible attack sequences, if any. Furthermore, besides this backward reconstruction, the analysis can be exploited forward, by determining, at each point, which tuples the attacker is able to inject in the protocol, and how they can percolate in the rest of the messages and impact on the protocol.

Our extension does not meaningfully increase the computational cost of the analysis and therefore allows us to provide useful ingredients for the reconstruction of possible attack sequences while keeping the efficiency of [5].

Related Work. CFA has been extensively applied to protocol analysis, in particular on protocols expressed in LYSA. Several kinds of annotations for this calculus have been developed for validating various security properties. Besides message authentication [5], freshness is addressed in [13] and violations due to type flaw attacks are addressed in [4,12].

In the literature we also find various models based on causal information. Strand Spaces [18] explicitly represent the causal interaction among protocol events in a way that helps writing simple and informative security proofs. Security Protocol Language [9] is equipped with a semantics based on Petri nets and event structures that, again, make explicit the causal correlation among events. Causal graphs have been specifically introduced in [3] to abstract away from protocol sessions, still capturing causality. Even in this case, the model explicitly represents the causal interaction among protocol events.

In the spirit of the above models, we introduce causality to make the analysis more informative. However, our approach is different: instead of equipping the calculus with a causal semantics (e.g. along the lines of the one for π-calculus in [10]), we enrich the standard one with causal information that helps understanding what might go wrong in a protocol. We collect causal information about the interaction of events in order to enable more sophisticated reasoning on the analysis result: causal information is only used when the protocol cannot be validated by the analysis and does not have any semantic impact on the execution.

In [2] it is studied how to reconstruct attacks in the setting of ProVerif tool. As in our framework, finding attack sequences when the analysis fails is not trivial due to the approximations in the protocol model. The technique proposed in [2] is based on the information provided by Horn clauses resolution algorithm and does not involve causal information.

Structure of the Paper. The paper is organised as follows. In Sect. 2, we present the LYSA+ calculus. In Sect. 3, we recall the CFA of [5], we adapt it to LYSA+, and we introduce the annotations necessary for the extension. In Sect. 4, we show how our approach works on a variant of the WMF protocol [8] that is subject to attacks. We conclude in Sect. 5.

2   The LYSA+ Calculus

LYSA+ is a dialect of LYSA [5], a process algebra, in the line of the π-calculus [14], with cryptographic primitives as in the Spi calculus [1]. In LYSA there are no channels: communication is on a single global network. Furthermore, in LYSA, pattern matching is incorporated into inputs and into decryptions, i.e. into those language constructs where values can be bound to variables. In LYSA+, decryptions are directly embedded inside inputs and are performed on the fly when receiving the corresponding outputs. This is not a completely novel feature, see e.g. [3,7,15]. More precisely, our primitive for input tests the components of the received message. If the received tuple matches the input pattern tuple, including the encryptions, then the variables occurring in the input pattern tuple are bound to the corresponding terms in the output tuple. Otherwise, the received tuple is not accepted. Suppose e.g. to have a server S waiting a message that S knows to include the name of the principal A, a nonce (which S still do not know), and an encryption that S knows to include the name of the principal B together with a key (which S still do not know). The input pattern tuple would be: $(A, x_N, \{B, x_K\}_{K_{AS}})$. If S receives the matching tuple $\langle A, N_A, \{B, K_{AB}\}_{K_{AS}}\rangle$, the variables x_N and x_K are bound to N_A and to K_{AB}, respectively.

The use of pattern matching directly embedded inside the input primitive makes the control flow analysis simpler than having a separate matching construct (e.g. as in π-calculus). In particular, all the tuples that do not match either at the level of terms or at the level of encryptions are directly filtered out, instead of being first accepted and then filtered out.

LYSA+ consists of terms and processes, as presented in Table 1. Values, which correspond to *closed* (i.e. without free variables) terms, are used to code keys, nonces, messages and so on. Terms may be either *terms E* or *pattern terms M*. Terms are used for modelling outputs including encryptions. Instead, for modelling inputs including decryptions we use pattern terms. In particular, pattern terms may contain variables that can receive their values, provided that the pattern matching succeeds. We call these variables *definition (or binding) variables*, while the others are called *use variables*. A definition occurrence is when a variable gets its binding value, while a use occurrence is an appearance of a declared variable where its binding value is used. As in [4], we syntactically obtain the use/definition distinction: the definition occurrence of a variable x is denoted by $\natural x$, while in the scope of the declaration, the variable appears as x.

In the syntax of terms E and the one of pattern terms M, $\mathcal{N}$ denotes the set of names and $\mathcal{X}$ denotes the set of variables. Encryption terms are tuples of terms $E_1, \cdots, E_k$ encrypted under a term E_0 representing a shared key, while pattern encryption terms are tuples of terms $M_1, \cdots, M_k$ encrypted under a term E_0 (keys used to decrypt cannot be definition variables). Here, we only model symmetric key protocols. Asymmetric ones can be similarly dealt (see [5]). We assume perfect cryptography.

Another difference w.r.t. LYSA consists in labelling each input in the syntax of processes P. Labels $X \in \mathbf{X}$ (in blue in the pdf) are exploited to support the analysis and do not affect the dynamic semantics. Our pattern terms,

Table 1. Syntax of LySA+.

$E ::=$ *terms*		$M ::=$ *pattern terms*	
$n \in \mathcal{N}$	name	E	term
$x \in \mathcal{X}$	use variable	$\natural x \ (x \in \mathcal{X})$	defining variable
$\{E_1, \cdots, E_k\}_{E_0}$ symm. encryption		$\{M_1, \cdots, M_k\}_{E_0}$ symm. encryption	

$P ::=$ *processes*	
0	nil
$\langle E_1, \cdots, E_k \rangle.P$	output
$(M_1, \cdots, M_k)^X.P$	input (with matching)
$P_1 \mid P_2$	parallel composition
$(\nu n)P$	restriction
$!P$	replication

in the form $(M_1, .., M_k)^X$, are matched against tuples of terms $(E_1, .., E_k)$. In the above example, the input should be $(A, \natural x_N, \{B, \natural x_K\}_{K_{AS}})^X$ and a possible matching tuple $\langle A, N_A, \{B, K_{AB}\}_{K_{AS}} \rangle$. Note that, at run time, each E_i only includes closed terms, i.e. each variable composing each one of the E_i has been bound in the previous computations. Instead, matching terms M_i may include closed terms, variables to be bound or encryption pattern terms including, in turn, closed terms and variables to be bound. Intuitively, the matching succeeds when the closed terms, inside each M_i, pairwise match to the corresponding terms inside E_i, and its effect is to bind the definition variables inside each M_i to the corresponding closed terms inside each E_i. In the example, the definition variables x_N and x_K are bound to the corresponding terms N_A and K_{AB}.

As in [5], we now extend the encryption terms and pattern terms in order to deal with the property of message authentication studied there. To do this, we decorate encryption terms and pattern terms with fixed labels, called *crypto-points* $\ell \in \mathcal{C}$ (where $\mathcal{C}$ is a denumerable set disjoint from $\mathcal{N}$ and $\mathcal{X}$), and with *assertions* specifying the origin and destination of encrypted messages. Crypto-points are mechanically attached to program points where encryptions and decryptions occur. Encryption terms and pattern terms are rendered as

$$\{E_1, \cdots, E_k\}^{\ell}_{E_0}[\text{dest } \mathcal{L}] \quad \text{and as} \quad \{M_1, \cdots, M_k\}^{\ell}_{E_0'}[\text{orig } \mathcal{L}]$$

where the assertions [dest $\mathcal{L}$] and [orig $\mathcal{L}$] specify the intended crypto-points $\mathcal{L} \subseteq \mathcal{C}$ for decryption and for encryption. We shall write $\lfloor \cdot \rfloor$ for a term with all annotations removed.

To simplify the definition of the control flow analysis in the next section, we discipline the α-renaming of bound names. We stipulate that for each name n there is a canonical representative $\lfloor n \rfloor$, and we demand that two names are α-convertible only when they have the same canonical name. A similar assumption applies to variables. The function $\lfloor \cdot \rfloor$ is then extended homomorphically to terms (we will write E for $\lfloor E \rfloor$ when unambiguous). Finally, we assume that the bound names of a process are renamed apart and that they do not clash with the free names; much in the same way variables are assumed to be all distinct.

Table 2. Predicate $Match$ and operational semantics, $P \rightarrow_{\mathcal{R}} P'$, parameterised on $\mathcal{R}$.

$$\frac{\lfloor n \rfloor = \lfloor n' \rfloor}{Match(\lfloor n \rfloor, \lfloor n' \rfloor) \qquad Match(\lfloor n \rfloor, \lfloor \natural x \rfloor)}$$

$$\frac{\wedge_{i=0}^{k} Match(\lfloor E_i \rfloor, \lfloor M_i \rfloor) \quad \wedge \quad \mathcal{R}(\ell, \mathcal{L}', \ell', \mathcal{L})}{Match(\{E_1, \cdots, E_k\}_{E_0}^{\ell}[\text{dest } \mathcal{L}], \{M_1, \cdots, M_k\}_{M_0}^{\ell'}[\text{orig } \mathcal{L}'])}$$

(Com)
$$\frac{\wedge_{i=1}^{j} Match(\lfloor E_i \rfloor, \lfloor M_i \rfloor)}{\langle E_1, \cdots, E_k \rangle.P \ | \ (M_1, \cdots, M_k)^X.Q \rightarrow_{\mathcal{R}} P \ | \ Q[E_1/M_1, \cdots, E_k/M_k]}$$

(Par)	(Res)	(Congr)
$\dfrac{P \rightarrow_{\mathcal{R}} P'}{P \ | \ Q \rightarrow_{\mathcal{R}} P' \ | \ Q}$	$\dfrac{P \rightarrow_{\mathcal{R}} P'}{(\nu\, n)P \rightarrow_{\mathcal{R}} (\nu\, n)P'}$	$\dfrac{P \equiv Q \ \wedge \ Q \rightarrow_{\mathcal{R}} Q' \ \wedge \ Q' \equiv P'}{P \rightarrow_{\mathcal{R}} P'}$

The semantics of LySA+ is given by the reduction rules in Table 2, modulo the structural congruence rules, here omitted because standard (see [5]), and where we use a slightly modified notion of substitution applied to a process $P[E/x]$, which extracts and replaces the definition variables with the corresponding terms, and leaves the other terms unchanged.

$$P[E/M] = \begin{cases} P[x \mapsto E] & \text{if } M = \natural x \wedge E \in \mathcal{N} \\ P[E_1/M_1, \cdots, E_k/M_k] & \text{if } M = \{M_1, \cdots, M_k\}_{E_0'}^{\ell}[\text{dest } \mathcal{L}] \wedge \\ & E = \{E_1, \cdots, E_k\}_{E_0}^{\ell'}[\text{orig } \mathcal{L}'] \\ P & \text{otherwise} \end{cases}$$

Moreover, we resort to the predicate $Match$, defined in Table 2, testing terms for pattern matching. As expected, the pattern matching between two names in the same equivalence class returns true, as well as the pattern matching between two composite terms, whose subterms pointwise match. Matching a name against a definition variable always succeeds.

To capture the message authentication property we are interested in, we consider two variants of *reduction relation* $\rightarrow_{\mathcal{R}}$, graphically identified by a different instantiation of the relation $\mathcal{R}$, which decorates the transition relation. One variant ($\rightarrow_{\mathsf{RM}}$) checks annotations, the other one ($\rightarrow$) discards them. In both cases, the reduction relation is the least relation on closed processes, i.e. processes with no free variables, that satisfies the rules in Table 2, where we assume to apply our disciplined α-conversion whenever needed. More precisely,

- the *reference monitor semantics*, written $P \rightarrow_{\mathsf{RM}} Q$, takes $\mathsf{RM}(\ell, \mathcal{L}', \ell', \mathcal{L}) = (\ell \in \mathcal{L}' \wedge \ell' \in \mathcal{L})$; thus, decryptions may only occur at crypto-points designated when the corresponding encryptions were made, and vice-versa, otherwise the execution is stopped;
- the *standard semantics*, written $P \rightarrow Q$, takes, by construction, $\mathcal{R}(\ell, \mathcal{L}', \ell', \mathcal{L})$ to be universally true and thus can be ignored.

The rule (Com) expresses that an output prefix in $\langle E_1, \cdots, E_k \rangle.P$ is matched by an input $(M_1, \cdots, M_k).Q$ in case the *Match* predicate returns true for each comparison (E_i, M_i), including the ones on the encryption subterms in E_i and M_i. In case all comparisons are successful each E_i causes the substitution $[E_i/M_i]$ on the corresponding pattern term M_i. Moreover, when comparing an encryption term with the corresponding encryption pattern term, in the *reference monitor semantics*, we ensure that the crypto-point of the encrypted value is acceptable at the decryption (i.e. $\ell \in \mathcal{L}'$) and that the one of the decryption is acceptable for the encryption (i.e. $\ell' \in \mathcal{L}$). The rules (Par), (Res) and (Congr) are standard.

Example 1. Consider the Wide Mouthed Frog protocol [8], aiming at establishing a secret (symmetric) session key K between the two principals A and B sharing master keys K_A and K_B, resp., with a trusted server S, in one of its *flawed* variants (abbreviated hereafter WMF_1), where the responder's name is not encrypted.

$$1.\ A \to S : A, B, \{K\}_{K_A}$$
$$2.\ S \to B : \{A, K\}_{K_B}$$
$$3.\ A \to B : \{m_1, ..., m_k\}_K$$

We now revisit in LYSA+ the specification of the protocol in [5], where only the *legitimate* part of the system is explicitly described. Since each principal may play many different roles and many principals may use the protocol at the same time, we assume to have $n + 2$ principals I_i ($i \in \{-1, 0, 1, \cdots, n\}$). Each of the "legitimate" principals ($i \in \{1, \cdots, n\}$) may play the initiator role of A, (I_i, A), as well as the responder role of B, (I_j, B). We assume there is *a single* server S, modelled as (I_{-1}, S). Instead, any principals *outside* the legitimate part (i.e. potential attackers) are given the name I_0 and may take on any role. Each principal can participate in an unlimited number of concurrent runs.

$$0.\ (\nu_{i=1}^n K_i^A)(\nu_{j=1}^n K_j^B)$$

$$1.\ |_{i=1}^n\ |_{\substack{j=1 \\ j \neq i}}^n\ !(\nu\,K_{ij})$$
$$\langle I_i, A, I_{-1}, S, I_i, A, I_j, B, \{K_{ij}\}_{K_i^A}^{A_i}[\mathsf{dest}\ S]\rangle.$$

$$3.\qquad (\nu\,m_{1ij}) \cdots (\nu\,m_{kij})$$
$$\langle I_i, A, I_j, B, \{m_{1ij}, \cdots, m_{kij}\}_{K_{ij}}^{A_i}[\mathsf{dest}\ B_j]\rangle$$

$$1'.\ |\ |_{i=0}^n\ |_{j=0}^n\ !(I_i, A, I_{-1}, S, I_i, A, I_j, B, \{\natural x_{ij}^K\}_{K_i^A}^S[\mathsf{orig}\ A]).^{X_{ij}}$$
$$2.\qquad \langle I_{-1}, S, I_j, B, \{I_i, A, x_{ij}^K\}_{K_j^B}^S[\mathsf{dest}\ B_j]\rangle.0$$

$$2'.\ |\ |_{j=1}^n\ |_{i=-1}^n\ !(I_{-1}, S, I_j, B, \{I_i, A, \natural y_{ij}\}_{K_{ij}}^{B_j}[\mathsf{orig}\ S]).^{Y_{ij}}$$
$$3'.\qquad (I_i, A, I_j, B, \{\natural z_{ij}^{m_1}, \cdots, \natural z_{ij}^{m_k}\}_{y_{ij}^K}^{B_j}[\mathsf{orig}\ A_i]).^{Z_{ij}}$$

- Master keys (line 0) between the legitimate principals (in each of their roles) and the server are unknown to outsiders, as well as session keys (line 1).
- The next three lines model the "legitimate" principals I_i ($1 \leq i \leq n$) in their initiator roles. Each initiator wants to engage in a communication with any of

the other "legitimate" principals I_j in their responder roles apart from itself ($1 \leq j \leq n$ and $j \neq i$). An encrypted message sent from the principal I_i in the initiator role is labelled with the crypto-point A_i and annotated with the intended crypto-point for decryption such as S (line 1). Similarly, the principal I_j in responder role uses the crypto-point B_j, while the server uses S.

- The next two lines model the server. It is ready to handle requests from principles inside as well as outside the legitimate part of the system ($0 \leq i, j \leq n$), but not from itself. Note that also agents outside the legitimate part of the system share master keys K_0^A and K_0^B with the server that are not restricted, and therefore available to the attacker.

- The last two lines model the legitimate principals I_j in their responder roles. The match of the first decryption (line 2') reveals the identity of the sender and here we are prepared to receive input from *any* agent ($-1 \leq i \leq n$). Indeed, whenever we do an input, we *never* restrict our attention to the legitimate part of the system; semantically our encoding is indistinguishable from writing one input, which matches the name of any principal.

3 Control Flow Analysis

The aim of the CFA in [5] was to statically verify a message authentication property, by checking for each exchanged encryption, whether a messages encrypted by a principal A and intended for principal B does indeed come from A and reaches B only. More precisely, if the analysis does not predict any violation of this message authentication property, then the reference monitor does not need to abort the computation of a process P. Indeed, because of over-approximations, the absence of static violations guarantees their absence also at run time, while their existence does not imply their existence at run time. Nevertheless, possible violations deserve to be investigated, because they can be the result of possible attacks. In these cases, reconstructing attacks is not a trivial activity. To move a step forward in this direction, we enrich the analysis in [5] with *causal* information, whose usage can help in the reconstruction of possible attacks, when the analysis predicts possible violations. We start by adapting the previous analysis to LYSA+ and then we extend it with the new features. In particular, the labels used to decorate inputs are used to track the tuples coming from the network that can be accepted in each input. The new pattern matching on inputs and on included decryptions allows us to focus on the output tuples, included the ones produced by the attacker, that can be accepted by an input in the analysed protocol. There are other tuples that the attacker can send on the network, but they are not interesting if they cannot be accepted by any principal in an input.

We recall that, being a context-insensitive CFA (see [16] for a comprehensive overview of static analysis), each time in which more than a tuple can be accepted by a particular input, the analysis records in each definition variable all the possible values that can be bound there (one for each accepted tuple), therefore losing precision. This mechanism mixes indeed the outcome of the possible computations and also breaks the possible association among bindings in

Table 3. Analysis of terms, $\rho \models E : \vartheta$, $SMatch$ predicate, and analysis of processes, $(\rho, \kappa) \models_{\mathsf{RM}} P : \psi$.

$$\frac{\lfloor n \rfloor \in \vartheta}{\rho \models n : \vartheta} \qquad \frac{\rho(\lfloor x \rfloor) \subseteq \vartheta}{\rho \models x : \vartheta}$$

$$\frac{\wedge_{i=0}^{k} \rho \models E_i : \vartheta_i \ \wedge}{\forall V_0, V_1, \cdots, V_k : \wedge_{i=0}^{k} V_i \in \vartheta_i \ \Rightarrow \ \{V_1, \cdots, V_k\}_{V_0}^{\ell} [\text{dest } \mathcal{L}] \in \vartheta}{\rho \models \{E_1, \cdots, E_k\}_{E_0}^{\ell} [\text{dest } \mathcal{L}] : \vartheta}$$

$$\frac{\lfloor n \rfloor = \lfloor n' \rfloor}{SMatch(\lfloor n \rfloor, \lfloor n' \rfloor, \rho, X, \psi)} \quad \frac{}{SMatch(\lfloor n \rfloor, \lfloor \natural x \rfloor, \rho, X, \psi)} \quad \frac{\rho \models x : \vartheta \wedge \lfloor n \rfloor \in \vartheta}{SMatch(\lfloor n \rfloor, \lfloor x \rfloor, \rho, X, \psi)}$$

$$\frac{\rho \models E : \vartheta \ \wedge \ \forall \{V_1, \cdots, V_k\}_{V_0}^{\ell}[\text{dest } \mathcal{L}] \in \vartheta :}{\wedge_{i=0}^{j} SMatch(V_i, M_i, \rho, X) \ \Rightarrow \ (\neg\mathsf{RM}(\ell, \mathcal{L}', \ell', \mathcal{L}) \Rightarrow ((\ell, \ell'), X) \in \psi)}{SMatch(E, \{M_1, \cdots, M_k\}_{M_0}^{\ell'}[\text{orig } \mathcal{L}'], \rho, X, \psi)}$$

$$\frac{\wedge_{i=1}^{k} \rho \models E_i : \vartheta_i \ \wedge}{\forall V_1, \cdots, V_k : \wedge_{i=1}^{k} V_i \in \vartheta_i \ \Rightarrow \ \langle V_1, \cdots, V_k \rangle \in \kappa \ \wedge}{(\rho, \kappa) \models_{\mathsf{RM}} P : \psi}{(\rho, \kappa) \models_{\mathsf{RM}} \langle E_1, \cdots, E_k \rangle . P : \psi}$$

$$\frac{\forall \langle V_1, \cdots, V_k \rangle \in \kappa : \wedge_{i=1}^{k} SMatch(V_i, M_i, \rho, X, \psi) \Rightarrow \langle V_1, \cdots, V_k \rangle \in \rho(X) \ \wedge}{\wedge_{i=1}^{k} Bind[V_i, M_i, \rho] \ \wedge}{(\rho, \kappa) \models_{\mathsf{RM}} P : \psi}{(\rho, \kappa) \models_{\mathsf{RM}} (M_1, \cdots, M_k)^{X} . P : \psi}$$

$$(\rho, \kappa) \models_{\mathsf{RM}} 0 : \psi \qquad \frac{(\rho, \kappa) \models_{\mathsf{RM}} P : \psi}{(\rho, \kappa) \models_{\mathsf{RM}} (\nu\, n) P : \psi} \qquad \frac{(\rho, \kappa) \models_{\mathsf{RM}} P : \psi}{(\rho, \kappa) \models_{\mathsf{RM}} \,! P : \psi}$$

$$\frac{(\rho, \kappa) \models_{\mathsf{RM}} P_1 : \psi \ \wedge \ (\rho, \kappa) \models_{\mathsf{RM}} P_2 : \psi}{(\rho, \kappa) \models_{\mathsf{RM}} P_1 | P_2 : \psi}$$

the same tuple. Consider, e.g., the following process P, receiving a tuple binding two variables to be sent in the next output

$$P = (A, x, y)^{X} . \langle B, x, y \rangle$$

and in the presence of two possible matching tuples, i.e. $\langle A, a, b \rangle$ from the process B and $\langle A, c, d \rangle$ from the process C. According to our analysis, both a and c can be bound to x, and similarly b and d can be bound to y. As a consequence,

Table 4. Dolev-Yao condition.

$$(1); \{n_\bullet\} \cup \lfloor \mathcal{N}_f \rfloor \subseteq \rho(z_\bullet)$$

$$(2) \wedge_{k \in \mathcal{A}_\kappa} \forall \langle V_1, \cdots, V_k \rangle \in \kappa : \wedge_{i=1}^k V_i \in \rho(z_\bullet)$$

$$(3) \wedge_{k \in \mathcal{A}_{\mathsf{Enc}}^+} \forall \{V_1, \cdots, V_k\}_{V_0}^\ell [\mathsf{dest}\ \mathcal{L}] \in \rho(z_\bullet):$$
$$\qquad V_0 \in \rho(z_\bullet) \Rightarrow (\wedge_{i=1}^k V_i \in \rho(z_\bullet) \wedge (\neg \mathsf{RM}(\ell, \mathcal{C}, \ell_\bullet, \mathcal{L}) \Rightarrow ((\ell, \ell_\bullet), Z_\bullet) \in \psi))$$

$$(4) \wedge_{k \in \mathcal{A}_{\mathsf{Enc}}^+} \forall V_0, \cdots, V_k : \wedge_{i=0}^k V_i \in \rho(z_\bullet) \Rightarrow \{V_1, \cdots, V_k\}_{V_0}^{\ell_\bullet} [\mathsf{dest}\ \mathcal{C}] \in \rho(z_\bullet)$$

$$(5) \wedge_{k \in \mathcal{A}_\kappa} \forall V_1, \cdots, V_k : \wedge_{i=1}^k V_i \in \rho(z_\bullet) \Rightarrow \langle V_1, \cdots, V_k \rangle \in \kappa$$

still according to the analysis of the continuation of P, there are at least four possible tuples for the next output: $\langle B, a, b \rangle$, $\langle B, c, d \rangle$, $\langle B, a, d \rangle$ and $\langle B, c, b \rangle$, where only the first two can be produced at run time. This choice of decoupling the values belonging to the same received tuple makes the analysis simple and not expensive. Refining the analysis to gain precision is possible, but can easily lead to an exponential computational complexity. Here, we propose instead to *locally* bind information on tuples in the places they are received, without letting this information flow on the analysis, thus not increasing the computational cost of the original analysis [5]. The CFA will record indeed that both $\langle A, a, b \rangle$ and $\langle A, c, d \rangle$ can be accepted in the input labelled X. This information can be useful, when trying to understand what can have gone wrong in a protocol. This technique is reasonable when dealing with protocols, where there are few degrees of freedom, because communication must follow the scheduled steps.

The static approximation is represented by a triple (ρ, κ, ψ) (resp. a pair (ρ, ϑ) when analysing a term E), called *estimate* for P (resp. for E), that satisfies the judgements defined by the axioms and rules of Table 3, whose components are:

- ρ is the *abstract environment* that maps (i) the canonical variables to the sets of closed canonical values that they may be bound to, and (ii) the input variables X to the sets of output tuples that they may be accepted by the input they are associated with.
- κ is the *abstract network environment* that includes all the message sequences that may flow on the network.
- ψ is the *error* component, including the possibly empty set of "error messages" of the form $((\ell, \ell'), X)$ indicating that something encrypted at ℓ was unexpectedly decrypted at ℓ' in the input labelled X.

For each term E, the analysis determines a *superset* of the possible canonical values that it may evaluate to. The judgement for terms (defined in the upper part of Table 3) is

$$\rho \models E : \vartheta$$

and expresses that $\vartheta \subseteq \mathcal{V}$ is an acceptable estimate of the set of values that E may evaluate to in the abstract environment ρ. Basically, the rules amount to demanding that ϑ contains all the canonical values associated with the components of a term; indeed, when $\mathsf{fv}(E) = \emptyset$ we have $\rho \models E : \{\lfloor E \rfloor\}$. In the sequel, we will use the *faithful* test $V \in \vartheta$ that holds if there is a value V' in ϑ that equals V when ignoring the annotations.

A name n evaluates to the set ϑ, if its canonical representative $\lfloor n \rfloor$ belongs to ϑ. Similarly for a variable x, provided that ϑ includes the set of values to which its canonical representative $\lfloor x \rfloor$ is associated with. To produce the set ϑ, the rule for k-ary *encryption* (i) finds the sets ϑ_i for each term E_i, (ii) collects all k-tuples of values $(V_0, \cdots, V_k)$ taken from $\vartheta_0 \times \cdots \times \vartheta_k$ into values of the form $\{V_1, \cdots, V_k\}_{V_0}^{\ell}[\mathsf{dest}\ \mathcal{L}]$ (iii) requires these values to belong to ϑ.

In the analysis of processes we focus on which values can flow on the network. The judgement (defined in the lower part of Table 3) for processes is

$$(\rho, \kappa) \models_{\mathsf{RM}} P : \psi$$

We need two auxiliary predicates in the analysis rules. The first is a binding predicate that checks whether the bindings for variables are correctly predicted.

$$Bind[V, M, \rho] = \begin{cases} V \in \rho(x) & \text{if } M = \natural x \wedge V \in \mathcal{N} \\ \wedge_{i=0}^{k} Bind[V_i, M_i, \rho] & \text{if } M = \{M_1, \cdots, M_k\}_{M_0}^{\ell}[\mathsf{dest}\ \mathcal{L}] \wedge \\ & V = \{V_1, \cdots, V_k\}_{V_0}^{\ell'}[\mathsf{orig}\ \mathcal{L}'] \\ true & \text{otherwise} \end{cases}$$

Furthermore, we have a predicate $SMatch$ to check whether the values match with the values associated with the corresponding terms in the pattern. The predicate $SMatch$ is defined in the central part of Table 3. The checks used by $SMatch$ are actually expressed using the faithful membership predicate, i.e. as $V_i \in \vartheta_i$, because annotations are ignored for matching just as in the semantics. For each encrypted value $\{V_1, \cdots, V_k\}_{V_0}^{\ell'}[\mathsf{dest}\ \mathcal{L}']$ in ϑ the analysis checks whether the values $V_0, \ldots . V_k$ match (still ignoring annotations) with the values associated with the corresponding terms in the pattern. If the check is successful then the values predicted for the variables x_i should point-wise contain the corresponding values in V_i.

The rule for k-ary *output* (i) finds the sets ϑ_i for each term E_i, (ii) requires that all k-tuples of values $\langle V_1, \cdots, V_k \rangle$ taken from $\vartheta_1 \times \cdots \times \vartheta_k$ are in κ (i.e. they can flow on the network), and (iii) requires that (ρ, κ, ψ) are also valid analysis estimates of process P.

In the rule for *input* the terms $M_1, \cdots, M_k$ are used for matching values sent on the network. Thus, this rule, by exploiting the $SMatch$ predicate, checks whether these terms can match with the values of any message $\langle V_1, \cdots, V_k \rangle$ in κ. If the check is successful then the definition variables in the terms M_i in the pattern input tuple can be bound to the corresponding terms included in the values V_i. These checks are performed also at the level of encryptions, still with the predicate $SMatch$, which also checks whether the destination or origin assertions may be violated, i.e. if $(\ell \notin \mathcal{L}')$ or $(\ell' \notin \mathcal{L})$ resulting in the entry $((\ell, \ell'), X)$ in ψ. The predicate $SMatch$ has indeed a parameter X, to recall the input in which the pattern matching is tested and to associate it to the entries of the error component ψ (we will use $Z_{\bullet}$ for the attacker, as clarified in the next paragraph). This allows us to localise the possible violation.

Note that in the case of input, we analyse the continuation process P only when the pattern matching succeeds on its terms and subterms (encryptions). This increases the precision of the analysis that is shown to rarely report errors (false positives) on correct protocols.

The rule for the *inactive process* does not restrict the analysis result while the rules for *parallel composition, restriction,* and *replication* ensure that the analysis also holds for the immediate subprocesses.

Example 2. We now present the analysis of the WMF_1 protocol, introduced in Sect. 2. An estimate (ρ, κ, ψ) satisfying $(\rho, \kappa) \models_{\mathsf{RM}} \mathsf{WMF}_1 : \psi$ is given by $\psi = \emptyset$ (attackers are not yet considered) and by the following non-empty ρ entries (for $1 \leq i, j \leq n$, $i \neq j$, and $1 \leq l \leq k$) for

$$
\begin{aligned}
\rho : X_{ij} &\mapsto \{\langle I_i, A, I_{-1}, S, I_i, A, I_j, B, \{K_{ij}\}_{K_i^A}^{A_i} [\mathsf{dest}\ S]\rangle\} \\
x_{ij}^K &\mapsto \{K_{ij}\} \\
Y_{ij} &\mapsto \{\langle I_{-1}, S, I_j, B, \{I_i, A, K_{ij}\}_{K_j^B}^{S} [\mathsf{dest}\ B_j]\rangle\} \\
y_{ij}^K &\mapsto \{K_{ij}\} \\
Z_{ij} &\mapsto \{\langle I_i, A, I_j, B, \{m_{1ij}, \cdots, m_{kij}\}_{K_{ij}}^{A_i} [\mathsf{dest}\ B_j]\rangle\} \\
z_{ij}^{m_l} &\mapsto \{m_{lij}\}
\end{aligned}
$$

whereas κ includes all the tuples listed in $\rho(X_{ij})$, $\rho(Y_{ij})$ and $\rho(Z_{ij})$. Moreover, observe that x_{ij}^K and y_{ij}^K are bound to the session key K_{ij}, and that $z_{ij}^{m_l}$ is bound to m_{lij}, that indicates the communication of m_{lij} from principal I_i to I_j.

Modelling the Attacker. We assume an active Dolev-Yao attacker [11], i.e. it can eavesdrop, replay, encrypt, decrypt, and generate messages providing that the necessary information is within his/her knowledge, which increases while interacting with the network. We shall briefly recall how the CFA is used to analyse protocols running in an insecure environment.

This scenario can be modelled as a process running in parallel with the protocol process. Formally, we shall have $P_{sys} \mid P_\bullet$, where P_{sys} represents the protocol process and $P_\bullet$ is some *arbitrary* attacker. To get an account of the infinitely many possible attackers, we find a formula $\mathcal{F}_{DY}$ that characterises all attackers $P_\bullet$: this means that whenever an estimate $\rho, \kappa, \Gamma, \psi$ satisfies $\mathcal{F}_{DY}$, then $\rho, \kappa, \Gamma \models P_\bullet : \psi$ for all attackers $P_\bullet$ (for a similar treatment see [5]). Intuitively, the formula has to mimic how all the $P_\bullet$ are analysed. As in [5], it is possible to establish the correctness of the formula for LySA+.

The attacker process is parameterised on some attributes of P_{sys}, e.g. the length of all the encryptions occurred and of all the messages sent over the network. Since we have no control over the canonical names and variables used of attackers, we postulate a new canonical name $n_\bullet$, a new canonical variable $z_\bullet$ and a new input label $Z_\bullet$, not used in P_{sys}, where all the canonical names and variables of the attacker are coalesced into. Similarly, annotations at encryption and decryption points are added and are the trivial ones [$\mathsf{dest}\ \mathcal{C}$] and [$\mathsf{orig}\ \mathcal{C}$], and that all crypto-points are replaced by the crypto-point $\ell_\bullet$ not occurring in P_{sys}.

We are now ready to define the formula $\mathcal{F}_{RM}^{DY}$ for expressing the Dolev-Yao condition for LySA+ as the conjunction of the five components in Table 4, illustrating that: the attacker has some initial knowledge (1), that it may learn more by eavesdropping (2) or by decrypting messages with keys already known (3), that it may construct new encryptions using the keys the attacker knows (4) and that it may actively forge new communications (5).

Extension of the Analysis. To statically add causal information useful in the reconstruction of attacks, we annotate tuples with labels $C \in \mathbf{C}$ (in blue in the pdf) corresponding to causal information, whose idea is somewhat reminiscent of that of "colours" a là Sewell [17]. The more basic one is information that records the principal that composes the tuple, but it can also include the number of the step of the protocol corresponding to the output, an identification code for the tuple and/or whatever can help in the investigation. Suppose we record the name of the sender and the number of message. Then, back to our previous example, we will have that $\mathtt{B}^{\mathtt{msg1}}::\langle A, a, b \rangle, \mathtt{C}^{\mathtt{msg1}}::\langle A, c, d \rangle \in \rho(X)$. Of course, this information should be also present in the syntax of processes and in the semantics, where output prefixes the (Com), respectively, are now in the form

$$\mathtt{A}^{\mathtt{msg}}::\langle E_1, \cdots, E_k \rangle.P$$

(Com)

$$\frac{\wedge_{i=1}^{j} Match(\lfloor E_i \rfloor, \lfloor M_i \rfloor)}{\mathtt{A}^{\mathtt{msg}}::\langle E_1, \cdots, E_k \rangle.P \mid (M_1, \cdots, M_k)^X.Q \to_{\mathcal{R}} P \mid Q[E_1/M_1, \cdots, E_k/M_k]}$$

Also the treatment of the attacker should be adapted: the tuples that the attacker can send on the network are recorded by the analysis with $\mathtt{M}_\bullet$ in front of (without any message information, since the tuple can be used in every message step). This is very important to track the "penetrability" of attacker tuples inside protocols. The additional information on tuples recorded by the analysis can be exploited to determine in which points the attacker is able to make principals accept his/her messages in place of the "legitimate" ones.

The same information can be further exploited to decorate bindings. Each definition variable could be associated with the value together with $C \in \mathbf{C}$ (in violet in the pdf, to distinguish this use from the one of tuples) that represents the recent *history* of the association, in this case, the "author" of the tuple that causes that binding and the message step. In the example, we would have $\{\mathtt{B}^{\mathtt{msg1}} \triangleright a, \mathtt{C}^{\mathtt{msg1}} \triangleright c\} \subseteq \rho(x)$ (where ρ is suitably extended).

Again, this information does not flow into the analysis, e.g., we still have in κ the four tuples where the values come without history annotations on values: $\mathtt{P}^{\mathtt{msg2}}::\langle B, a, b \rangle, \mathtt{P}^{\mathtt{msg2}}::\langle B, c, d \rangle, \langle B, a, b \rangle, \mathtt{P}^{\mathtt{msg2}}::\langle B, a, d \rangle$ and $\mathtt{P}^{\mathtt{msg2}}::\langle B, c, b \rangle$. Nevertheless, what this information preserves can offer useful hints to reconstruct what happens in message exchanges, especially when an attacker is present in the scenario. The adapted rules for output and input are as follows.

$$\wedge_{i=1}^k \rho \models E_i : \vartheta_i \wedge$$
$$\forall \lceil V_1 \rceil, \cdots, \lceil V_k \rceil : \wedge_{i=1}^k V_i \ \mathsf{E} \ \vartheta_i \ \Rightarrow \ \mathtt{A^{msg}} :: \langle \lceil V_1 \rceil, \cdots, \lceil V_k \rceil \rangle \in \kappa \wedge$$
$$\frac{(\rho, \kappa) \models_{\mathsf{RM}} P : \psi}{(\rho, \kappa) \models_{\mathsf{RM}} \mathtt{A^{msg}} :: \langle E_1, \cdots, E_k \rangle.P : \psi}$$

$$\forall \mathtt{A^{msg}} :: \langle V_1, \cdots, V_k \rangle \in \kappa : \wedge_{i=1}^k SMatch(V_i, M_i, \rho, X, \psi) \Rightarrow \mathtt{A^{msg}} :: \langle V_1, \cdots, V_k \rangle \in \rho(X) \wedge$$
$$\wedge_{i=1}^k Bind[\mathtt{A^{msg}}, V_i, M_i, \rho] \wedge$$
$$\frac{(\rho, \kappa) \models_{\mathsf{RM}} P : \psi}{(\rho, \kappa) \models_{\mathsf{RM}} (M_1, \cdots, M_k)^X.P : \psi}$$

where the predicate *Bind* becomes

$$Bind[\mathtt{A^{msg}}, V, M, \rho] = \begin{cases} \mathtt{A^{msg}} \triangleright V \in \rho(x) & \text{if } M = \natural x \wedge V \in \mathcal{N} \\ \wedge_{i=0}^k Bind[\mathtt{A^{msg}}, V_i, M_i, \rho] & \text{if } M = \{M_1, \cdots, M_k\}_{M_0}^{\ell} [\text{dest } \mathcal{L}] \\ \qquad \wedge V = \{V_1, \cdots, V_k\}_{V_0}^{\ell'} [\text{orig } \mathcal{L}'] \\ true & \text{otherwise} \end{cases}$$

Moreover, not to propagate the history information, we use a new function $\lceil \rceil$ to denote terms with history annotations removed and we force the predicate *SMatch* to ignore history annotations in the ρ component, by overloading the function $\lfloor \rfloor$. Back to our example, suppose that the output of the process P is received and accepted by the process

$$Q = (B, x', y')^X$$

In this case, we have that $\{\mathtt{P^{msg2}} \triangleright a, \mathtt{P^{msg2}} \triangleright c\} \subseteq \rho(x')$ and $\{\mathtt{P^{msg2}} \triangleright b, \mathtt{P^{msg2}} \triangleright d\} \subseteq \rho(y')$, i.e. the present analysis does not record the whole path of bindings, or overall *history*, but just the last step. Of course, it is possible to further extend the analysis in this direction. Finally, note that the information on the history of bindings could be easily added to semantics, as well. We avoid it to keep the presentation simple.

As in [5], it is possible to prove (the proofs are very similar) that our analysis respects the operational semantics of LySA $+$, in both its versions, and that, when the ψ component is empty, we can safely dispense with the reference monitor.

Theorem 1 (Subject reduction)
   If $P \to_\mathcal{R} Q$ *and* $(\rho, \kappa) \models_{\mathsf{RM}} P : \psi$ *then* $(\rho, \kappa) \models_{\mathsf{RM}} Q : \psi$.

Theorem 2 (Static check for reference monitor)
   If $(\rho, \kappa) \models_{\mathsf{RM}} P : \emptyset$ *then* RM *cannot abort* P.[1]

---

[1] i.e. whenever there exist no Q, Q' such that $P \to^* Q \to Q'$ and $P \to_{\mathsf{RM}}^* Q \not\to_{\mathsf{RM}}$, where $*$ stands for the transitive and reflexive closure of the relation, and $Q \not\to_{\mathsf{RM}}$ stands for $\neg \exists Q' : Q \to_{\mathsf{RM}} Q'$.

4   Wide Mouthed Frog Variant 1: Study

We now extend the analysis of the WMF_1 protocol of Sect. 3. In the presence of an attacker, the ψ error component is no longer empty. In particular, an estimate (ρ, κ, ψ) satisfying $(\rho, \kappa) \models_{\text{RM}} \text{WMF}_1 : \psi$ is given by

$$\psi = \frac{\{((A_i, B_j), Z_{ij}) \mid 1 \leq i, j \leq n \wedge i \neq j\} \cup \{((A_i, \ell_\bullet), Z_\bullet) \mid 1 \leq i \leq n\} \cup}{\{((\ell_\bullet, B_j), Z_{ij}) \mid 1 \leq j \leq n\},}$$

by the following entries[2] (for $1 \leq i, j \leq n$, $i \neq j$, and $1 \leq l \leq k$) for

$$\rho : X_{ij} \mapsto \{\mathsf{A}_{ij}^{\mathtt{msg1}} :: \langle I_i, A, I_{-1}, S, I_i, A, I_j, B, \{K_{ij}\}_{K_i^A}^{A_i} [\mathsf{dest}\ S] \rangle,$$
$$\mathsf{M}_\bullet :: \langle I_i, A, I_{-1}, S, I_i, A, I_j, B, \{K_{ij}\}_{K_i^A}^{A_i} [\mathsf{dest}\ S] \rangle,$$
$$\mathsf{M}_\bullet :: \langle I_i, A, I_{-1}, S, I_i, A, I_j, B, \{K_{il}\}_{K_i^A}^{A_i} [\mathsf{dest}\ S] \rangle \text{ with } l \neq j \text{ and } j \in [0, n]\}$$
$$x_{ij}^K \mapsto \{\mathsf{A}_{ij}^{\mathtt{msg1}} \triangleright K_{ij}, \mathsf{M}_\bullet \triangleright K_{il} \text{ with } l \neq j \text{ and } j \in [0, n]\}$$
$$Y_{ij} \mapsto \{\mathsf{S}_{ij}^{\mathtt{msg2}} :: \langle I_{-1}, S, I_j, B, \{I_i, A, K_{ij}\}_{K_j^B}^{S} [\mathsf{dest}\ B_j] \rangle,$$
$$\mathsf{M}_\bullet :: \langle I_{-1}, S, I_j, B, \{I_i, A, K_{ij}\}_{K_j^B}^{S} [\mathsf{dest}\ B_j] \rangle,$$
$$\mathsf{S}_{ij}^{\mathtt{msg2}} :: \langle I_{-1}, S, I_j, B, \{I_i, A, K_{il}\}_{K_j^B}^{S} [\mathsf{dest}\ B_j] \rangle,$$
$$\mathsf{M}_\bullet :: \langle I_{-1}, S, I_j, B, \{I_i, A, K_{il}\}_{K_j^B}^{S} [\mathsf{dest}\ B_j] \rangle\}$$
$$y_{ij}^K \mapsto \{\mathsf{S}_{ij}^{\mathtt{msg2}} \triangleright K_{ij}, \mathsf{S}_{ij}^{\mathtt{msg2}} \triangleright K_{il}\}$$
$$Z_{ij} \mapsto \{\mathsf{A}_{ij}^{\mathtt{msg3}} :: \langle I_i, A, I_j, B, \{m_{1ij}, \cdots, m_{kij}\}_{K_{ij}}^{A_i} [\mathsf{dest}\ B_j] \rangle,$$
$$\mathsf{M}_\bullet :: \langle I_i, A, I_j, B, \{m_{1ij}, \cdots, m_{kij}\}_{K_{ij}}^{A_i} [\mathsf{dest}\ B_j] \rangle,$$
$$\mathsf{M}_\bullet :: \langle I_i, A, I_j, B, \{m_{1il}, \cdots, m_{kil}\}_{K_{il}}^{A_i} [\mathsf{dest}\ B_l] \rangle\}$$
$$z_{ij}^{m_l} \mapsto \{\mathsf{A}_{ij}^{\mathtt{msg3}} \triangleright m_{lij}, \mathsf{M}_\bullet \triangleright m_{lil}\}$$

and by κ, which includes all the entries of $\rho(X_{ij})$, $\rho(Y_{ij})$ and $\rho(Z_{ij})$ that are listed above. Note that, besides the "legitimate" tuples produced by the principals, we find all the tuples (prefixed by $\mathsf{M}_\bullet$ ::) produced by the attacker and accepted by principals. Some of them (the one in black in the pdf) include exactly the same terms of the tuples immediately above. They correspond to the "legitimate" tuples of the protocol that the attacker can always intercept and send again. These tuples cannot cause any harm if used in the same session, while they can be exploited to mount parallel session attacks (see next paragraph). As a consequence, for simplicity in this paragraph, we ignore the bindings they induce.

The ψ component entries, as established in [5], show that static authentication fails. The pairs (A_i, B_j) show that a value encrypted at A_i has wrongfully been decrypted at B_j in the input labelled Z_{ij} (with $i \neq j$); the pairs $(A_i, \ell_\bullet)$ show that a value created by A_i has been decrypted by the attacker (in the attacker input $Z_\bullet$), while the pairs $(\ell_\bullet, B_j)$ show that a value created by the attacker has been decrypted at B_j in the input labelled Z_{ij}.

To check whether there really is a corresponding dynamic violation, it is necessary to find an execution leading to the determined violation, possibly

---

[2] Where the tuples produced by the attacker or due to its messages and the histories of interest are indigo in the pdf.

corresponding to an attack. This is not straightforward. Our aim here is to show that our extended CFA can help us in systematically reconstructing the attacks, corresponding to the violations predicted in ψ, and find again the attacks reconstructed in [5] (reported here in Table 5), with the help of climbing holds.

Table 5. Attacks on WMF variation, where M_X denotes the attacker pretending to be the principal X.

$A \to M_S$: $A, B, \{K\}_{K_A}$	$A \to M_S$: $A, B, \{K\}_{K_A}$	$A \to M_S$: $A, B, \{K\}_{K_A}$
$M_A \to S$: $A, B', \{K\}_{K_A}$	$M_S \to S$: $A, M, \{K\}_{K_A}$	$M_S \to S$: $A, M, \{K\}_{K_A}$
$S \to B'$: $\{A, K\}_{K_{B'}}$	$S \to M$: $\{A, K\}_{K_M}$	$S \to M$: $\{A, K\}_{K_M}$
$A \to M_B$: $\{m_1 \cdots m_k\}_K$	$A \to M_B$: $\{m_1 \cdots m_k\}_K$	$M_A \to S$: $A, B, \{K\}_{K_A}$
$M_A \to B'$: $\{m_1 \cdots m_k\}_K$		$S \to B$: $\{A, K\}_{K_B}$
		$M \to B$: $\{m_1 \cdots m_k\}_K$
Attack 1	Attack 2	Attack 3

We now try to backtrack in order to reconstruct the attack, whose side effect is the violation corresponding to the entry $((A_i, B_j), Z_{ij})$ in ψ. To simplify, we consider $i = 1$ and $j = 2, 3$ ($i \neq j$) and we investigate the instance $((A_1, B_2), Z_{12})$ of the first entry of ψ. In the same way, we can investigate the instance $((A_1, B_3), Z_{13})$.

- The presence of $((A_1, B_2), Z_{12})$ is tested, when analysing the input/decryption in B_2, labelled Z_{12}: $(I_1, A, I_2, B, \{\natural z_{12}^{m_1}, \cdots, \natural z_{12}^{m_k}\}_{y_{12}^K}^{B_2} [\text{orig } A_1])$. Z_{12} For reader's convenience, in the table below, we place the input side by side with the tuples that the analysis predicts as associated to its label Z_{12}.

$\mathtt{A}_{12}^{\mathtt{msg3}} :: \langle I_1, A, I_2, B, \{m_{112}, ..., m_{k12}\}_{K_{12}}^{A_1} [\text{dest } B_2] \rangle$	
$\mathtt{M_\bullet} :: \langle I_1, A, I_2, B, \{m_{112}, ..., m_{k12}\}_{K_{12}}^{A_1} [\text{dest } B_2] \rangle$	$(I_1, A, I_2, B, \{\natural z_{12}^{m_1}, ..., \natural z_{12}^{m_k}\}_{y_{12}^K}^{B_2} [\text{orig } A_1])^{Z_{12}}$
$\mathtt{M_\bullet} :: \langle I_1, A, I_2, B, \{m_{113}, ..., m_{k13}\}_{K_{13}}^{A_1} [\text{dest } B_3] \rangle$	

The pair (A_1, B_2) is in ψ because $B_2 \notin \{B_3\}$ and thus $\neg RM(A_1, \{A_1\}, B_2, \{B_3\})$ in the successful matching of the third tuple in the table

$$\mathtt{M_\bullet} :: \langle I_1, A, I_2, B, \{m_{113}, \cdots, m_{k13}\}_{K_{13}}^{A_1} [\text{dest } B_3] \rangle$$

that leads to the binding for Z_{12} and for $z_{12}^{m_s}$, recorded by the analysis in $\rho(Z_{12}) \ni \mathtt{M_\bullet} :: \langle I_1, A, I_2, B, \{m_{113}, \cdots, m_{k13}\}_{K_{13}}^{A_1} [\text{dest } B_3] \rangle$ and $\rho(z_{12}^{m_s}) \ni \mathtt{M_\bullet} \triangleright m_{s13}$ where $\mathtt{M_\bullet} \triangleright m_{s13}$ stands for m_{s13} with *history* $\mathtt{M_\bullet} \triangleright$. Note that the attacker can produce this message by intercepting the message

$$\mathtt{A}_{13}^{\mathtt{msg3}} :: \langle I_1, A, I_3, B, \{m_{113}, \cdots, m_{k13}\}_{K_{13}}^{A_1} [\text{dest } B_3] \rangle$$

and by modifying the name of the receiver from B_3 to B_2.

Statically speaking, interception can be detected by observing that the output tuple $\mathtt{A}_{13}^{\mathtt{msg3}} :: \langle I_1, A, I_3, B, \{m_{113}, \cdots, m_{k13}\}_{K_{13}}^{A_1} [\text{dest } B_3] \rangle \in \kappa$ and that therefore each of its terms is in $\rho(z_\bullet)$ (see rule (2) in Table 4).

The third tuple statically matches with the input pattern, because $\rho(y_{12}^K) \ni K_{13}$, with *history* $S_{13}^{\text{msg2}}\triangleright$. This information points at the possible forged message of the attacker that is acceptable by B_2 in the input labelled Z_{12}, where for reader's convenience, we add the destination assertion:

$$3'.M_{A_1} \to B_2 : A_1, B_2, \{m_1, \cdots, m_k\}_{K_{13}}^{A_1} [\text{dest } B_3]$$

that replaces the "legitimate" message expected by B_2 from A_1:

$$3.A_1 \to B_2 : A_1, B_2, \{m_1, \cdots, m_k\}_{K_{12}}^{A_1} [\text{dest } B_2]$$

corresponding to the tuple in $\rho(Z_{12})$, (the first in the above table):

$$A_{12}^{\text{msg3}} :: \langle I_1, A, I_2, B, \{m_{112}, \cdots, m_{k12}\}_{K_{12}}^{A_1} [\text{dest } B_2] \rangle$$

As a consequence, accepting the tuple, coming from the attacker instead of the one from A_1, suggests that the attacker could have intercepted the "legitimate" message from A_1 to B_3 and could have injected its forged one. In other words, it suggests the following message exchange.

$$3.A_1 \to M_{B_3} : A_1, B_3, \{m_1, \cdots, m_k\}_{K_{13}} [\text{dest } B_3]$$
$$3'.M_{A_1} \to B_2 : A_1, B_2, \{m_1, \cdots, m_k\}_{K_{13}} [\text{dest } B_2]$$

- To *statically* backtrack, we have to observe the *causal* relationship between the third message and the second one. This consists in the use, in the third message, of the key received by B_2, in the second message, that binds the variable y_{12}^K. This relationship simply descends from the fact that in the input $(I_1, A, I_2, B, \{\natural z_{12}^{m_1}, \cdots, \natural z_{12}^{m_k}\}_{y_{12}^K}^{B_2} [\text{orig } A_1])^{Z_{12}}$, y_{12}^K is a use occurrence of the definition variable bound in the previous input. We recall in the table below the tuples that the analysis predicts as associated to Y_{12}.

$S_{12}^{\text{msg2}} :: \langle I_{-1}, S, I_2, B, \{I_1, A, K_{12}\}_{K_2^B}^{S} [\text{dest } B_2] \rangle,$ $M_\bullet :: \langle I_{-1}, S, I_2, B, \{I_1, A, K_{12}\}_{K_2^B}^{S} [\text{dest } B_2] \rangle,$ $S_{12}^{\text{msg2}} :: \langle I_{-1}, S, I_2, B, \{I_1, A, K_{13}\}_{K_2^B}^{S} [\text{dest } B_2] \rangle$ $M_\bullet :: \langle I_{-1}, S, I_2, B, \{I_1, A, K_{13}\}_{K_j^B}^{S} [\text{dest } B_2] \rangle$	$(I_{-1}, S, I_2, B, \{I_1, A, \natural y_{12}\}_{K_2^B}^{B_2} [\text{orig } S])^{Y_{12}}$

Now, the possible value K_{13}, with *history* $S_{13}^{\text{msg2}}\triangleright$, is instantiated in the second step of the protocol, when accepting the third tuple in the table above, leading to the required binding for y_{12}^K. This suggests the following message:

$$2'.S \to B_2 : S, B_2, \{A_1, K_{13}\}_{K_2^B}^{S} [\text{dest } B_2]$$

- Again, the only binding with the previous steps is the use of the variable x_{12}^K instantiated in the input $(I_1, A, I_{-1}, S, I_1, A, I_2, B, \{x_{12}^K\}_{K_1^A}^{S} [\text{orig } A]^{X_{12}})$ in S as K_{13} with *history* $M_\bullet\triangleright$. We recall in the table below the tuples that the analysis predicts as associated to X_{12}.

$A_{12}^{\text{msg1}} :: \langle I_1, A, I_{-1}, S, I_1, A, I_2, B, \{K_{12}\}_{K_1^A}^{A_1} [\text{dest } S] \rangle$ $M_\bullet :: \langle I_1, A, I_{-1}, S, I_1, A, I_2, B, \{K_{12}\}_{K_1^A}^{A_1} [\text{dest } S] \rangle$ $M_\bullet :: \langle I_1, A, I_{-1}, S, I_1, A, I_2, B, \{K_{13}\}_{K_1^A}^{A_1} [\text{dest } S] \rangle$	$(I_1, A, I_{-1}, S, I_1, A, I_2, B, \{\natural x_{12}^K\}_{K_1^A}^{S} [\text{orig } A])^{X_{12}}$

The tuple responsible for the investigated binding is the third in the table above. This suggests the corresponding output message:

$$1'.M_{A_1} \to S : A_1, S, A_1, B_2, \{K_{13}\}_{K_1^A}^{A_1}[\text{dest } S]$$

This tuple competes with the "legitimate" tuple:

$$A_{12}^{\text{msg1}} :: \langle I_1, A, I_{-1}, S, I_1, A, I_2, B, \{K_{12}\}_{K_1^A}^{A_1}[\text{dest } S]\rangle$$

that corresponds to the message step

$$1.A_1 \to S : A_1, S, A_1, B_2, \{K_{12}\}_{K_1^A}^{A_1}[\text{dest } S]$$

By summarising, we have exploited the climbing holds provided by the CFA, intuitively illustrated by the following schema

They have helped us in the reconstruction of the following attack, that can be concisely represented by the first attack in Table 5.

$$
\begin{aligned}
&1.A_1 \to M_S : \quad A_1, S, A_1, B_3, \{K_{13}\}_{K_1^A}^{A_1}[\text{dest } S] \\
&1'.M_{A_1} \to S : \quad A_1, S, A_1, B_2, \{K_{13}\}_{K_1^A}^{A_1}[\text{dest } S] \\
&2'.S \to B_2 : \quad S, B_2, \{A_1, K_{13}\}_{K_B^B}^{S}[\text{dest } B_2] \\
&3.A_1 \to M_{B_3} : \quad A_1, B_3, \{m_1, \cdots, m_k\}_{K_{13}}[\text{dest } B_3] \\
&3'.M_{A_1} \to B_2 : \quad A_1, B_2, \{m_1, \cdots, m_k\}_{K_{13}}[\text{dest } B_3]
\end{aligned}
$$

Similarly, we can reconstruct the attack leading to the inclusion of $((A_1, \ell_\bullet), Z_\bullet)$ in ψ, corresponding to the second attack in Table 5. Succinctly, this violation is due to the decryption the attacker can perform of the intercepted tuple

$$A_{12}^{\text{msg3}} :: \langle I_1, A, I_1, B, \{m_{112}, \cdots, m_{k12}\}_{K_{12}}^{A_1}[\text{dest } B_2]\rangle$$

because the attacker knows the key, i.e. $K_{12} \in \rho(z_\bullet)$, and this is because, in the second step, the server can send the tuple:

$$S_{ij}^{\text{msg2}} :: \langle I_{-1}, S, I_0, B, \{I_1, A, x_{10}^K\}_{K_0^B}^{S}[\text{dest } B_0]\rangle$$

where $x_{10}^K \ni M_\bullet \triangleright K_{12}$, because the tuple, forged by the attacker,

$$M_\bullet :: \langle I_1, A, I_{-1}, S, I_1, A, I_0, B, \{K_{12}\}_{K_1^A}^{A_1}[\text{dest } S]\rangle$$

can be accepted by S, in place of the "legitimate" one:

$$A_{12}^{ms1} ::\langle I_1, A, I_{-1}, S, I_1, A, I_2, B, \{K_{12}\}_{K_1^A}^{A_1}[\text{dest } S]\rangle$$

Further Extensions. The attack 3 in Table 5, corresponding to the inclusion of $((\ell_\bullet, B_j), Z_{ij})$ in ψ, is a *parallel session* attack, because the attack is performed in two runs. In this setting, indeed, the attacker can just intercept tuples in a run of the protocol and send them in other runs, as they are or forged *ad hoc*. To facilitate the reconstruction of the attack, the analysis should be further refined. For lack of space, we just give the idea of how we can proceed. Information on the run (in some way reminiscent of the treatment in [6]) can be appended to the tuples and to the annotations in encryptions and decryptions, e.g.:

$$S_{ij}^{msg2}, \text{run } k ::\langle I_{-1}, S, I_0, B, \{I_1, A, x_{10}^K\}_{K_0^B}^{S \; run \; k}[\text{dest } B_0]\rangle$$

Also input variables, e.g. $X_{ij}^{run \; s}$, should come with indication of the run. We can also suppose not to consider the matching of the run labels when decrypting. Of course, it is possible to do it and also to make it checkable at run time, by suitably extending the relation RM. For similar annotations on runs, we can follow [13].

To keep it simple, we just distinguish between two runs 1 and 2. The attacker can e.g. replay the above message, stolen from *run 1*, in *run 2* and make it acceptable for S. The attacker could have attacked the previous run as in Attack 2 of Table 5 and therefore it could have learned the key A_1 created for B_2. As a consequence, the replay allows the attacker to cheat on B_2, by sending messages encrypted with the key that B_2 knows coming from A_1.

In more detail, choosing $i = 1$ and $j = 2$, the violation arises in the input labelled $Z_{12}^{run \; 2}$ in *run 2*, where B_2 is waiting for the message of A_1.

$$(I_1, A, I_2, B, \{\natural z_{12}^{m_1}, \cdots, \natural z_{12}^{m_k}\}_{y_{12}^K}^{B_2^{run \; 2}}[\text{orig } A_1]^{Z_{12}^{run \; 2}})$$

matching with the attacker's tuple (note that attackers's tuples come without any *run* annotation, as well as the encryptions they can produce and send):

$$M_\bullet ::\langle I_1, A, I_2, B, \{m_{1_\bullet}, \cdots, m_{k_\bullet}\}_{K_{12}}^{\ell_\bullet}[\text{dest } C]\rangle$$

In this case, the message tuple produced by the attacker points at the fact that the key K_{12}, created by A_1 for B_2, is in its knowledge $\rho(z_\bullet)$. This is due to an attack sequence similar to the one seen for the second attack. Now, B_2 knows the key because S sends it in the previous message. The analysis indeed associates the session key K_{12} with history $S_{ij}^{msg2}\triangleright$ to the variable y_{12}^K. The direction to follow for our investigation focusses on the way S is triggered to send K_{12}. Actually, besides the "legitimate" flow of the protocol, this can be due to the replay of the initial message of A_1 in the first run, i.e. in the input S in the second run

$$(I_1, A, I_{-1}, S, I_1, A, I_2, B, \{\natural x_{12}^K\}_{K_1^A}^{S \; run \; 2}[\text{orig } A]^{X_{12}})$$

the following attacker's tuple can be accepted

$$\mathsf{M}_\bullet :: \langle I_1, A, I_{-1}, S, I_1, A, I_2, B, \{K_{12}\}_{K_1^A}^{A_1}\,^{run\ 1}[\mathsf{dest}\ S]\rangle$$

Looking at the *run* annotations, we can reconstruct that the message of the attacker is the replay of the same message, between the same principals, but belonging to the previous run:

$$\mathsf{A}_{ij}^{msg1},\ \mathbf{run}\ 1 :: \langle I_1, A, I_{-1}, S, I_1, A, I_2, B, \{K_{12}\}_{K_1^A}^{A_1}\,^{run\ 1}[\mathsf{dest}\ S]\rangle$$

In all the above cases, we are lucky because each entry of the ψ component corresponds to a violation that can arise at run time and that is bound to a particular attack sequence of WMF_1. In general, this is not guaranteed. Nevertheless, our CFA annotations should however help, by determining which tuples the attacker is able to inject with impunity in the protocol, how they can percolate in the rest of the messages, and by giving hints for advancing educated guesses of the attack sequences.

5   Conclusions

Attack reconstruction is a sort of *crime reconstruction* in which one tries to determine the sequence of actions that led to a violation. It is inherently hard: different pieces must be put together without knowing in advance how the resulting picture should be. When a protocol cannot be validated by CFA, and this is not due to over-approximation, it is interesting to look for the attacks that made the analysis fail. To achieve this goal, we have enhanced the CFA in [5] with static *causal* evidences that add details to the *crime scene* and that help establishing the attack sequence. We have shown that the obtained analysis is effective and we have given an articulated example of attack reconstruction.

Our approach is different from existing proposals in the literature as it mixes the power and efficiency of CFA with the clarifying nature of causal information, without resorting to a causal semantics. This work constitutes a proof-of-concept that the approach is viable but there are still many aspects that need to be inspected. We intend (*i*) to formalise the reconstruction method and prove its correctness: in particular, we would like to provide an algorithm to perform reconstruction; (*ii*) to apply the technique to other kinds of protocols to check how our approach scales; (*iii*) to explore more elaborated causal information, e.g. by including many steps of history, to see to which extent this improves the precision of the reconstruction method.

Acknowledgements. We would like to thank Mikael Bucholtz, Hanne Riis Nielson, Flemming Nielson and, in particular, Pierpaolo Degano for the many valuable discussions on CFA, on LySa, and on other issues. Some of the ideas developed here have their roots in those discussions. Furthermore, we thank our anonymous referees for their useful comments.

References

1. Abadi, M., Gordon, A.D.: A calculus for cryptographic protocols - the Spi Calculus. Inf. Comput. **148**(1), 1–70 (1999)
2. Allamigeon, X., Blanchet, B.: Reconstruction of attacks against cryptographic protocols. In: 18th IEEE Computer Security Foundations Workshop, (CSFW-18 2005), pp. 140–154 (2005)
3. Backes, M., Cortesi, A., Maffei, M.: Causality-based abstraction of multiplicity in security protocols. In: IEEE Computer Security Foundations Symposium (CSF'07), pp. 355–369 (2007)
4. Bodei, C., Brodo, L., Degano, P., Gao, H.: Detecting and preventing type flaws at static time. J. Comput. Secur. **18**(2), 229–264 (2010)
5. Bodei, C., Buchholtz, M., Degano, P., Nielson, F., Nielson, H.R.: Static validation of security protocols. Inf. Comput. **13**(3), 347–390 (2005)
6. Buchholtz, M., Maidl, M., Bodei, C., Degano, P., Priami, C.: Deliverable D14, Final Report on Static Techniques. Technical report, Project DEGAS IST-2001-32072 (2004)
7. Buchholtz, M., Nielson, F., Nielson, H.R.: A calculus for control flow analysis of security protocols. Int. J. Inf. Secur. **2**(3–4), 157–167 (2004)
8. Burrows, M., Abadi, M., Needham, R.: A logic of authentication. ACM Trans. Comput. Syst. **8**, 18–36 (1990)
9. Crazzolara, F., Winskel, G.: Events in security protocols. In: Proceedings of the 8th ACM Conference on Computer and Communications Security (CCS 2001), pp. 96–105 (2001)
10. Degano, P., Priami, C.: Non-interleaving semantics for mobile processes. Theor. Comput. Sci. **216**(1–2), 237–270 (1999)
11. Dolev, D., Yao, A.C.: On the security of public key protocols. IEEE Trans. Inf. Theor. **IT–29**(12), 198–208 (1983)
12. Gao, H., Bodei, C., Degano, P.: A formal analysis of complex type flaw attacks on security protocols. In: Meseguer, J., Roşu, G. (eds.) AMAST 2008. LNCS, vol. 5140, pp. 167–183. Springer, Heidelberg (2008)
13. Gao, H., Bodei, C., Degano, P., Nielson, H.R.: A formal analysis for capturing replay attacks in cryptographic protocols. In: Cervesato, I. (ed.) ASIAN 2007. LNCS, vol. 4846, pp. 150–165. Springer, Heidelberg (2007)
14. Milner, R., Parrow, J., Walker, D.: A calculus of mobile processes (I and II). Inf. Comput. **100**(1), 1–77 (1992)
15. Nielsen, C.R., Nielson, F., Nielson, H.R.: Cryptographic pattern matching. Electr. Notes Theor. Comput. Sci. **168**, 91–107 (2007)
16. Nielson, F., Nielson, H.R., Hankin, C.: Principles of Program Analysis. Springer, Heidelberg (1999)
17. Sewell, P., Vitek, J.: Secure composition of untrusted code: box pi, wrappers, and causality. J. Comput. Secur. **11**(2), 135–188 (2003)
18. Thayer, F.J., Herzog, J.C., Guttman, J.D.: Strand spaces: proving security protocols correct. J. Comput. Secur. **7**(1), 191–230 (1999)

A Declarative View of Signaling Pathways

Davide Chiarugi[1], Moreno Falaschi[2]([✉]), Carlos Olarte[3],
and Catuscia Palamidessi[4]

[1] Department of Theory and Bio-Systems,
Max Planck Institute for Colloids and Interfaces, Potsdam, Germany
davide.chiarugi@gmail.com
[2] Dipartimento di Ingegneria dell'Informazione e Scienze Matematiche,
Università di Siena, Siena, Italy
moreno.falaschi@unisi.it
[3] ECT, Universidade do Rio Grande do Norte, Natal, Brazil
carlos.olarte@gmail.com
[4] INRIA and LIX, École Polytechnique, Paris, France
catuscia@lix.polytechnique.fr

Abstract. Due to the inherent limitations of wet-lab techniques, the experimental data regarding cellular signaling pathways often consider single pathways or a small subset of them. We propose a methodology for composing signaling pathways data in a coherent framework. Our method consists in specifying the signaling pathway as a computationally executable model. We rely on the timed concurrent constraint language ntcc to represent the system in hand as a set of stoichiometric-like equations resembling the essential features of molecular interactions. The main advantages of our approach stem from the use of constraints (formulas in logic) and from modeling of discrete time clocks in ntcc. We can deal with partial information, representing the fact that several features of the biological system may be undetermined. We can explicitly represent the time needed for a reaction to occur. We model and simulate some well known cross-talking networks, such as the TNFα, the EGF and the insulin signaling pathways as well as their interactions.

1 Introduction

Experimental techniques in biology are facing an impressive improvement in the last few years. However, an exhaustive characterization of the whole set of cellular biochemical processes is a task which is still far from being accomplished. In this paper, we report on a computational method designed for integrating biological data in a coherent framework thus fostering a system-level understanding of the studied phenomenon. Even though our method can be useful in more general contexts, here we focus on its application to cellular signaling pathways.

Cellular signaling pathways consist in groups of interacting proteins belonging to various functional classes, e.g., receptors, adaptor proteins and kinases [14]. Each pathway is specialized in sensing and transducing particular environmental signals such as growth factors, hormones, cytokines, light and nutrients.

© Springer International Publishing Switzerland 2015
C. Bodei et al. (Eds.): Degano Festschrift, LNCS 9465, pp. 183–201, 2015.
DOI: 10.1007/978-3-319-25527-9_13

Typically they are composed by a receptor molecule which senses the environmental stimuli and a set of transductor molecules. These molecules are functionally coupled with the receptor and have the role of amplifying and transducing the signal. The activation of a signaling pathway may trigger events such as gene transcription, cell movement and secretion of particular molecules. Moreover, misfunctioning or defects in signaling pathways are often associated with important diseases such as diabetes, immune disorders and cancer [14,18].

In living cells, individual signaling pathways do not act in isolation. Rather, they cross talk, i.e. they either share one or more components or they interact through long or short range feedback loops. Thus, the overall behavior of a cell embedded in a given environment should be seen as the integrated response to a variety of sensed signals coming from the outside [3,14]. The overall picture that emerges from this description is that of a complex interaction network. This complexity makes it hard to obtain the complete knowledge of the dynamics underlying the functioning of whole cellular signaling pathways. In principle it might be possible to study the complexity of signaling pathways relying on experimental techniques. This approach could be used for observing and measuring the evolution in time and space of the whole cellular network at all the possible hierarchical levels, i.e. from the molecular dynamics to the whole-cell level. This strategy is, in fact, hard to conceive even theoretically. In addition, also the technical limitations inherent to the currently available experimental methods makes it difficult to cope with this kind of "systemic" investigation. What is possible to achieve experimentally are partial views of the complete scenario, e.g. the behavior of a subset of the cellular signaling pathways or the biochemical properties of their components. The information contained in these frames need to be recomposed *a posteriori* for obtaining, at least, some sketches of the complete picture.

Organizing the available information in a coherent framework is an hard task, especially for taking into account the dynamics of the interactions. Computational models and, in particular, *executable models* [19] can provide some help for tackling this issue. Executable models are descriptions of the studied system that are specified through formalisms typical of computer science. We can thus rely on well established techniques for studying the formal properties of the model in hand that can be meaningful from a biological point of view, as shown, e.g., in [5,6,10]. Thus it becomes possible to use the same framework for both simulating the dynamics of the phenomena of interest and for assessing formally their properties, with a clear advantage over modeling strategies grounding only on simulation algorithms. Even though this approach might be of little help in providing solutions to the biological complexity, it represents a useful way for gaining insights on studied systems on the base of the existing information. In this context a number of proposals relying on different formalisms and modeling techniques, have been presented in the last ten years and some of them are reviewed in Sect. 6.

In this paper we present a computational methodology for describing molecular interaction networks, which allows the organization of the existing knowledge in a compositional fashion. We specify a biological system as a set of stoichiometric-like equations resembling the essential features of molecular inter-actions. These equations are automatically parsed, translated and computed by an interpreter written in the timed concurrent constraint programming (ntcc) language [28,34].

The ntcc language is a model of concurrency based on the concurrent con-straint programming [35] model where processes interact by posting and querying constraints on a store of partial information. Constraints can be seen as formulas in logic that assert some information about the system variables. For instance, the process tell($x > 42$) increases the information accumulated on the store and states that the concentration of a given component x is greater than 42. A process when $y < 20$ do tell($x < 70$) ask whether the information $y < 20$ can be deduced (i.e., entailed via logical rules) from the current store. In that case, it executes tell($x < 70$) and increases the information we know about x. The ask construct in ntcc then offers a declarative way (via logic) of synchronizing concurrent processes.

Processes in ntcc are also subject to timed constraints. This feature makes it an ideal language to specify reactive systems, i.e., those that constantly interact with the environment as in the case of signaling pathways. For instance, the (timed) process when c do next P queries whether c can be entailed from the store in the current time-unit and then, executes P in the next time-unit. Hence, the context where P is executed may be different from the current one due to different signals/stimuli sensed from the next interaction with the environment.

The advantages of the methodology we propose here root in the above men-tioned features of ntcc. In particular, this language allows us to represent partial information, thus taking into account the fact that several features of the biolog-ical system may be undetermined or affected by experimental errors [15]. Hence, even in the absence of detailed information, our method makes it straightforward building runnable models which can help in gaining insights on the behavior of the studied system. When new knowledge becomes available, models can be eas-ily refined with the new information. Moreover, differently from other methods similar to ours that also rely on declarative languages (see, e.g., [17]), ntcc allows us to model explicitly the time which is necessary for a reaction to occur. We exploit our methodology for modeling and simulating some well known signaling pathways, namely the TNFα, EGF, and insulin signaling pathways. For that, we use BioWayS [9], a software tool implementing the methodology that allows users to perform in silico experiments.

The rest of the paper is structured as follows. Section 2 describes the tem-poral concurrent constraint programming model and the syntax of the ntcc calculus. The model in ntcc is presented in Sect. 3 as well as a brief description of its implementation in the tool BioWayS [9]. Section 4 presents the modeling and simulation of the TNFα, EGFR and insulin systems. We then describe the related works in Sect. 5, and conclude the paper in Sect. 6.

A preliminary short version of this paper was published in [11]. Here we give many more details and explanations. We also present at length the models of the TNFα, EGFR and insulin systems.

2   Concurrent Constraint Process Calculi

Concurrent systems, i.e. systems whose components act simultaneously and potentially interacting with each other, are ubiquitous in several domains and applications. They pervade different areas in science (e.g., as in biological, physical and chemical systems) and engineering (e.g., as in security protocols and mobile systems).

Due to their complex forms of interaction, concurrent systems are difficult to specify and reason on. In computer science, process calculi like the π-calculus [27] and CCS [26], among sever others, have been proposed to investigate such systems. Process calculi provide a mathematical language where concurrent systems can be modeled. They also offer a set of reasoning techniques to formally describe and predict the behavior of the modeled system.

Concurrent Constraint Programming (CCP) [33] (see a survey in [30]) has emerged as a simple and powerful declarative model for concurrency tied to logic. A fundamental issue in CCP is the specification of concurrent systems by means of constraints. A constraint, e.g., $x > 42$, represents partial information about some variables: the value of x is unknown (or not precisely determined) but its value is greater than 42. Constraints represent then a piece of information (or partial information) upon which processes may act.

The type of constraints in CCP is not fixed but parametric on a constraint system. A constraint system provides a signature from which constraints can be constructed and an entailment relation $\models$ specifying inter-dependencies between these constraints.

Usually the notion of constraint system is set up as first-order theory over a given signature (i.e., a set of predicate and function symbols). The inter-dependency $c \models d$ expresses that the information specified by d follows from the information specified by c, e.g., $(x > 42) \models (x > 0)$. For a formal definition of a constraint system we refer the reader to [33,35,36].

Processes in CCP can change the state of the system by telling information to the store (i.e., adding constraints), and synchronize by asking information to the store (i.e., determining whether a given constraint can be entailed from the store). Processes are then built from constraints and the following constructs:

Definition 1 (Syntax of CCP). *Processes $P, Q, \ldots$ in CCP are built from constraints $c, d, \ldots$ by the following syntax:*

$$P, Q := \mathbf{skip} \mid \mathbf{tell}(c) \mid \mathbf{when}\ c\ \mathbf{do}\ P \mid P \parallel Q \mid (\mathbf{local}\, x)\, P \mid p(x)$$

The process **skip** does nothing thus representing <u>inaction</u>. The process **tell**(c) adds c to the store, thus making it available to the other processes. The process **when** c **do** P <u>asks</u> if c can be deduced from the store. If so, it behaves as P. In other case, it remains blocked until the store contains at least as much information as c.

The process $P \parallel Q$ denotes P and Q running concurrently possibly communicating via the common store. The process $(\mathbf{local}\, x)\, P$ behaves like P, except that all the information on x produced by P can only be seen by P (i.e., x is a local variable in P). Finally, consider a (recursive) definition of the form $p(y) \overset{\text{def}}{=} Q$. The process $p(x)$ triggers the execution of the body of the definition and evolves into $Q[x/y]$.

Timed CCP. The ntcc calculus [28] extends CCP to consider the execution of CCP processes along time-units. In ntcc, time is conceptually divided into time intervals (or time-units). In a particular time interval, a CCP process P gets an input (constraint) c from the environment, it executes with this input as the initial store, and when it reaches its resting point (i.e., no further evolution is possible), it outputs the resulting store d to the environment. The resting point determines also a residual process Q which is then executed in the next time interval.

This view of reactive computation is particularly appropriate for programming reactive systems in the sense of Synchronous Languages [2], i.e., systems that react continuously with the environment at a rate controlled by the environment.

Definition 2 (Syntax of ntcc). *Processes $P, Q, \ldots$ in ntcc are built from constraints $c, d, \ldots$ by the following syntax:*

$$P, Q := \textbf{skip} \mid \textbf{tell}(c) \mid \sum_{i \in I} \textbf{when } c_i \textbf{ do } P_i \mid P \parallel Q \mid$$

$$(\textbf{local } x)\, P \mid p(x) \mid \textbf{next } P \mid \textbf{unless } c \textbf{ next } P \mid \star P \mid \,!\, P$$

The processes **skip**, **tell**(c), $P \parallel Q$, (**local** x) P and $p(x)$ are similar to those in CCP.

Assume a finite set of indexes $I = \{i_1, i_2, \ldots, i_n\}$. The process $\sum_{i \in I} \textbf{when } c_i \textbf{ do } P_i$ represents a process that, in the current time interval, must non-deterministically choose one of the P_i whose corresponding guard (constraint) c_i is entailed by the store. The chosen alternative, if any, precludes the others. If no choice is possible then the summation remains blocked until more information is added to the store. If I is a singleton, then we recover the ask process **when** c **do** P in CCP.

The process **next** P delays the execution of P to the next time-unit. The negative ask **unless** c **next** P is also a unit-delay but P is executed in the next time unit when c is not entailed by the final store at the current time interval. This can be viewed as a (weak) time-out: It waits one time unit for a piece of information or stimulus c to be present and if it is not, it triggers activity in the next time interval.

The process $\star P$ corresponds to the unbounded but finite delay of the execution of P. It allows us to express asynchronous behavior through the time intervals. Intuitively, $\star P$ means $P + \textbf{next } P + \textbf{next }^2 P \cdots$

The replication $!\, P$ means $P \parallel \textbf{next } P \parallel \textbf{next }^2 P \parallel \cdots$, i.e. unboundedly many copies of P but one at a time. We note that some forms of recursive definitions can be encoded into ntcc by using the $!$ operator [28], in particular,

D. Chiarugi et al.

parameterless recursive definitions used in the models proposed here. For this reason, the syntax of ntcc processes usually omits the process $p(x)$. However, for the sake of presentation, we shall continue using this kind of constructs.

3 Biochemical Interactions as Concurrent Processes

A biochemical pathway can be represented as a group of interconnected biochemical reaction, having the form:

$$A + B \dashrightarrow C \qquad C + D \dashrightarrow E \qquad E + F \dashrightarrow G \qquad \cdots$$

in which the product of a reaction is the reactant of another one. A signaling pathway is a biochemical pathway supporting the transduction of signals in a biological cell: molecules present in the external environment can affect cellular behavior linked to a specific receptor on the cell membrane and triggering the biochemical reactions of the receptor-dependent signaling pathways.

Let us consider the following reaction scheme:

$$\text{Insulin} + \text{Insulin\_Receptor} \dashrightarrow \text{Insulin\_Receptor\_P} \qquad (1)$$

This equation represents the interaction between insulin and its receptor. We abstracted away various details regarding chemical features, such as reaction rate dependence from the temperature. These approximations are consistent with the in-vitro experiments, where the temperature is kept constant. The reaction rate will be considered at simulation time, embedded in stochastic parameters. This equation represents the occurrence of the reaction of one insulin molecule and its receptor (IR). This reaction causes the (auto)phosphorilation of the receptor molecule, and triggers the following events of the signal transduction pathway.

The Mathematical Model. We shall represent the signaling pathway by a finite set of equations of the form

$$
\begin{aligned}
r_1 &: \sum_{i \in I} a_i^1 A_i \dashrightarrow \sum_{i \in I} b_i^1 A_i \\
&\cdots \\
r_m &: \sum_{i \in I} a_i^m A_i \dashrightarrow \sum_{i \in I} b_i^m A_i
\end{aligned}
\qquad (2)
$$

In the sequel, we shall use $n = |I|$ to denote the number of components involved in the signaling pathway and m to denote the number of equations (reactions) considered. The constants $a_1^j, ..., a_n^j$ and $b_1^j, ..., b_n^j$ are the stoichiometric coefficients. Therefore, $a_1^j A_1, a_2^j A_2, ..., a_3^j A_n$ are reactants, while $b_1^j A_1, b_2^j A_2, ..., b_3^j A_n$ are products. We also assume that each equation r_j has associated a duration $dur(r_j)$ defining the number of time-units required for that reaction to produce the components on the right-hand side.

In the equation r_j, a_1^j molecules of reactant A_1 interacts with a_2^j molecules of reactant A_2, ... and with a_n^j molecules of reactant A_n and are thus consumed, yielding b_1^j molecules of product A_1, ... and b_n^j molecules of product A_n.

Our idea is to represent sets of reaction schemes as ntcc processes. Before given the technical details, let us elaborate on the advantages of having such a (formal) model of the system. First at all, the ntcc model can be seen as a declarative and runnable specification. With declarative we mean that interactions and synchronization patterns can be neatly characterized by logical entailment. Moreover, parallel composition (roughly speaking, conjunction in logic) allows us to refine the model by adding new processes posting more precise information when available. On the other side, with runnable we mean that the operational semantics of the calculus [28] can be used to simulate the system as we show in Sect. 3.2. Then, in silico experiments can be directly implemented from the model.

Another interesting feature of the proposed ntcc model is its constraint-based nature and the ability to deal with partial information. This shall allow us to specify systems where we do not have a complete description of it. For instance, we can observe the behavior of the system even if we only have a partial information about the concentration of the reactants involved. Moreover, the timed nature of ntcc allows us to precisely capture the time dependencies between interactions.

Finally, another advantage of using CCP-based languages, is that they can be endowed with logical semantics (see e.g., [1,25,28,31]). This provides a valuable tool for the verification of the modeled system.

3.1   The Model in ntcc

The model we propose consists of three different components: a process to choose the rule to be applied in each time-unit; the processes modeling the equations and the processes changing the state of the concentrations of each reactant/product according to the equation applied. In the following, we show some excerpts of the model.

We assume a set of equations as in Eq. (2). Recall that n denotes the number of components and m the number of equations. Our model involves the following variables:

– eq: with domain $1, \ldots m$. If $eq = j$, then the equation r_j is applied in the current time-unit.
– $x_1, \ldots, x_n$: representing the current concentrations of the components $A_1, \ldots, A_n$ respectively.

Choosing the Rule Scheme. This component of the model chooses non-deterministically one of the equations to be applied by binding the variable eq. This is done by means of the non-deterministic choice operator as follows:

$$\text{choose} \stackrel{\text{def}}{=} \begin{array}{l} \textbf{when } x_1^1 \geq a_1^1 \wedge \ldots \wedge x_n^1 \geq a_n^1 \textbf{ do tell}(eq = 1) \\ +\textbf{when } x_1^2 \geq a_1^2 \wedge \ldots \wedge x_n^2 \geq a_n^2 \textbf{ do tell}(eq = 2) \\ +\ldots \\ +\textbf{when } x_1^m \geq a_1^m \wedge \ldots \wedge x_n^m \geq a_n^m \textbf{ do tell}(eq = m) \end{array}$$

Intuitively, the process **choose** selects non-deterministically one of the equations such that the current concentration of each component is higher than the reactant necessaries for the equation to take place (e.g., $x_j^i \geq a_j^i$). This process binds eq to the number of the equation chosen.

Improvements here can be done by adding the stochastic information about the reaction rate of each equation (if it is known). In this case, the non-deterministic operator is replaced by a probabilistic choice to take into account such rates (see e.g., [23]).

Representation of the Reaction. A reaction r_j is modeled by a process binding the variables x_{i+}^j and x_{i-}^j to a_i^j and b_i^j respectively. This variables determine how the concentration of the component A_i must be affected due to the application of the reaction: a_i^j units are consumed and b_i^j units are produced.

$$\text{equation}_j \overset{\text{def}}{=} \textbf{when } eq = j \textbf{ do}$$
$$\textbf{next tell}(x_{1-}^j = a_1^j \wedge ... \wedge x_{n-}^j = a_n^j) \parallel$$
$$\textbf{next }^{dur(r_j)}\textbf{tell}(x_{1+}^j = b_1^j \wedge ... \wedge x_{n+}^j = b_n^j)$$

The process equation_j checks if the selected equation is r_j (i.e., $eq = j$). Then, in the next time-unit, the concentration of the reactants is reduced. Recall that $dur(r_j)$ stands for the duration of the reaction r_j to take place. Then, $dur(r_j)$ time-units later, the concentration of the right hand components are incremented.

State of the System. Finally, we have a process that computes the current concentration of the components according to the concentration of them in the previous time-unit and the above mentioned variables x_{i+}^j and x_{i-}^j.

$$\textbf{init } \overset{\text{def}}{=} \textbf{tell}(x_1 \in in_1..in_1') \parallel ... \parallel \textbf{tell}(x_n \in in_n..in_n')$$
$$\textbf{state} \overset{\text{def}}{=} \textbf{next}!\,(\textbf{tell}(x_1 = x_1.prev + \sum_{j=1}^{m} x_{1+}^j - \sum_{j=1}^{m} x_{1-}^j) \parallel$$
$$...$$
$$\textbf{tell}(x_n = x_n.prev + \sum_{j=1}^{m} x_{n+}^j - \sum_{j=1}^{m} x_{n-}^j))$$

As a parameter of the simulation, the user must provide the range of the initial concentration of each component $(in_i, in_i'$ above). The process **init** imposes the needed constraints to assert that the initial concentration of a component A_i should be a value between in_i and in_i'. On the other side, the process **state** updates the concentration of the components. As we explained before, the concentration of A_i in the current time-unit (i.e., x_i) is calculated by taking the value of x_i in the previous time-unit (i.e., $x_i.prev$) and: (1) adding the variables $x_{i+}^1, ..., x_{i+}^m$ which are the components produced when a rule is applied, and (2) subtracting $x_{i-}^1, ..., x_{i-}^m$ which are the required reactants to apply a rule.

Finally, the whole system looks like this:

$$\text{system} \overset{\text{def}}{=} \textbf{init} \parallel \textbf{state} \parallel \textbf{choose} \parallel \text{equation}_1 \parallel ... \parallel \text{equation}_n$$

Besides encoding reaction schemes, we can also introduce in the model specific processes to describe behaviors that we are interested in studying. For instance, a process of the form $\star!\,\text{tell}(x = 0)$ models the fact that eventually, in the future, the concentration of x will drop to zero. This process, running in parallel with system, may be used to study the behavior of the system when a disease suppresses certain component from the environment.

3.2 A Simulation Tool: BioWayS

We have implemented a simulation tool based on our model, which we have called *BioWayS* and which is freely available on author's web sites. This tool is based on a interpreter of the ntcc calculus written in the Oz Languages (http://www.mozart-oz.org/).

BioWayS takes as input a text file containing the initial parameters of the simulation as well as the description of the equations. Then, it computes the final stores of each time-unit and outputs the number of equation applied and the concentration of each component. In the following sections we shall show some examples of simulations executed in this tool.

4 In Silico Experimentation

We used our modeling technique to study some interconnected cellular signaling pathways related to three receptors: Tumor Necrosis Factor Receptor I (TNFR1 - a transmembrane protein specialized in binding a ligand molecule called Tumor Necrosis factor α), Insulin Receptor (IR - a transmembrane protein specialized in binding insulin), and the Epidermal Growth Factor Receptor (EGFR - a transmembrane protein specialized in binding the epidermal growth factor). This choice is motivated by the fact that both structural and experimental data regarding these pathways are relatively abundant. These data can be used to verify the viability of the model comparing them with the output of the simulation. A schematic representation of the considered network is depicted in Fig. 1. Note that, for the sake of readability, the depicted graph does not represent all the reactions actually occurring in the real cell.

4.1 The Biological Data

As reported in [20] some aspects of the dynamics of this network have been characterized through wet-lab techniques typical of proteomics. Roughly speaking, these techniques allow to measure the quantity (concentration or activity) of a group of cellular proteins over a period of time. The amount of a given protein may remain constant or may vary during the considered time interval depending on the experimental conditions. As an example, Fig. 2 reports a plot of the time course of the concentration of the protein Akt measured in different experiments in which the initial amount of Insulin, TNF and EGF was varied. Figure 3 reports the so-called "heat map" (see figure caption for details) corresponding to the plot of Fig. 2.

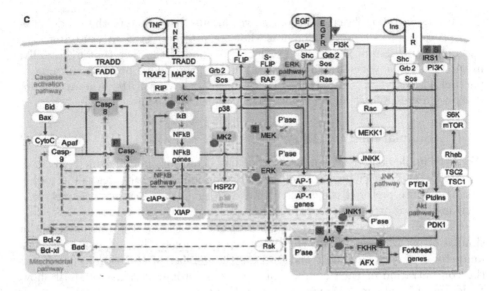

Fig. 1. Schematic representation of the considered signaling network. The colored arrows describe different kinds of interaction: green = activation, blue = slow activation, red = inhibition. Taken from [20] (Color figure online).

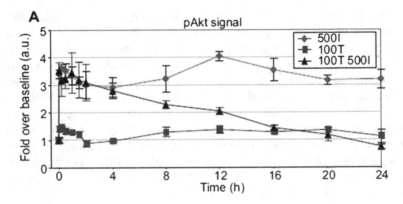

Fig. 2. Time course of the amount of phosphorylated Akt protein (pAkt) measured through proteomic techniques in different experimental conditions: 500I = 500 μM of insulin; 100T = 100 μM of TNFα; 100T 500I = 100 μM of TNFα <u>and</u> 500I = 500 μM of insulin. Taken from [20].

4.2   The Model

We consider now the set of signaling pathways composing the network outlined in Fig. 1. Using a system-level approach, our aim is to build a model based on the information available in the literature, adequate for describing the measured data and, eventually, to make predictions regarding the modeled system. Our model network is composed by 37 different kind of molecules (nodes) and 48 equations

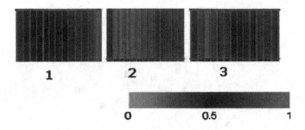

Fig. 3. Heat map for pAkt. Each vertical colored bar corresponds to a measurement of pAkt concentration at a given time. Reading the bars from left to right it is possible to obtain the time course of akt concentration plotted in Fig. 2: 1 corresponds to 100T, 2 to 500I and 3 to 100T 500I. The "color code" must be interpreted as: green indicates low concentrations, black indicates intermediate concentrations, red indicates high concentrations. Note that, for better comparing the obtained results, the concentration values expressed through the color code <u>are not absolute values</u> as they are normalized to the maximum value obtained in <u>all</u> the measurements concerning the considered protein performed in [20] (Color figure online).

(interactions). Each interaction is rendered by a "reaction rule" resembling the corresponding chemical equation. Each rule is written in the format accepted by BioWayS. The input for a simulation run is composed by the list of rules (i.e. the model of the network), a set of parameters specifying the number of copies for each involved molecule (i.e. the amount of reacting molecules) and the length of the computation (i.e. the time length of the experiment). Noteworthy, for each rule, it is possible to specify a parameter indicating the amount of time needed for the corresponding reaction to occur. More precisely, this parameter corresponds to the <u>first passage time</u> and is evaluated according to [29].

Note that, for estimating the first passage time for an enzymatically catalyzed reaction, it is not necessary to know the details regarding the reaction's mechanism and, thus, the kinetic constants (namely the <u>elementary</u> or <u>microscopic</u> kinetic constants) related to each elementary step. Instead, the needed data are the enzyme and substrate(s) concentrations, the enzyme-substrate(s) "affinity constant(s)" and the overall (<u>macroscopic</u> or <u>apparent</u>) rate constant. The first two parameters were taken from the literature or determined heuristically letting their initial amounts ranging on reasonably realistic intervals estimated by comparison with similar cases. The last parameter was estimated using Kinfer (http://www.cosbi.eu/index.php/research/prototypes/kinfer) and literature data.

It is worth noticing that the choice of the above mentioned approach reflects the need of building a "biochemically consistent" model using correctly the available data. This allows us to avoid common misconceptions such as the use of apparent rate constants instead of the microscopic rate constants. This mistake is often done in works relying on the Gillespie's Stochastic Simulation Algorithm (SSA) [21] for the (stochastic) simulation of biochemical pathways. This Monte Carlo Based SSA, needs the knowledge of the microscopic rate constants,

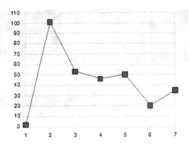

Fig. 4. Plot of the amount of tyrosine-phosphorylated IRS1 present at the end of simulations in presence of EGF (arbitrary units). The plot should be compared with that in Fig. 5. Taken from [20].

which are often impossible to measure and evaluate in biochemistry. To circumvent this problem, apparent rate constants are typically used. This introduces a heavy approximation with unpredictable effects on the results of simulations.

According the underlying model, in each step of the computation, BioWay chooses non deterministically one rule and simulates the occurrence of a chemical reaction. Hence, what we observe is that reactant molecules are "consumed" and new copies of other molecules are "produced" according to the reaction scheme[1].

4.3   Experiments and Results

The in silico experiments were performed by simulating the model described in Sect. 4.2 through BioWayS. In the first experimental session, we tuned the model and tested its viability by comparing the simulations outputs with the corresponding wet-lab data reported in [20]. In particular, the in silico experiments were performed under different initial conditions mimicking the presence of different combinations of insulin, TNFα and EGF in the extracellular environment. For each combination of these three molecules, simulations differing in time length were performed so to obtain time courses of the measured values, namely, the amount of the various kind of molecules at the end of each computation. To measure the goodness of fit, we compared the "real" and "virtual" time series through the X^2 test ($p > 0.05$). In all the tested cases, the X^2 test showed that our results are consistent with wet-lab data. Some examples of these results can be seen in Figs. 4 and 6. The reader may wish to compare these figures with Figs. 5 and 2 respectively, representing the "real" counterparts.

For further validate our proposal, we studied particular cases of cross talk among the considered signaling pathways. In particular, it is known by the literature [13] that the pathways regulated by TNFR1 and IR interact influencing their signaling dynamics. Indeed, when TNFR1 receptor is active (i.e. when

---

[1] This is the more general case. It may happen that the consumption of a reactant does not lead to the production of other molecules or that, as in the case of enzymes, a molecule takes part to a reaction but is not consumed by it.

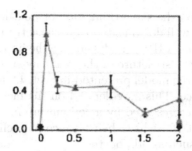

Fig. 5. Plot representing the time course of tyrosine-phosphorylated IRS1 as measured in [20] in presence of 100 ng/ml of EGF. The plot should be compared with that in Fig. 4.

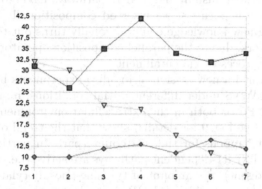

Fig. 6. Plot representing the amount of phosphorylated Akt protein (pAkt) present at the end of simulations in different experimental conditions corresponding to that presented in Fig. 2. The plot should be compared with that in Fig. 2.

TNFα is bound) IR-dependent pathways are inhibited. In other words, TNFα negatively interferes with insulin signaling. The effects of this cross-talk interaction can be observed through proteomic techniques monitoring the amount of phosphorylated Insulin Receptor Substrate 1 (IRS1). This protein is specifically phosphorylated in different points, namely on tyrosine and serine residues[2]. Phosphorylation on tyrosine enhances the activity (i.e. the catalytic capabilities) of IRS1 and is typically performed by IR when is bound to insulin. Thus, tyrosine phosphorylation of IRS1 characterizes the <u>activation</u> of IR-dependent signaling pathways. Phosphorylation on serine residues decreases the activity of IRS1 and prevents tyrosine phosphorilation. This typically occurs when certain signaling pathways, such as TNFR dependent pathways, are active and leads to the inactivation of IR-dependent signaling pathways. As it can be noticed in Fig. 1, while the relationship between IR and IRS1 is structurally well characterized (IRS1

---

[2] Proteins are composed by chains of aminoacyds. For biochemical reasons, aminoacyds are often called residues.

directly interacts with IR) the same thing cannot be said for TNFR and IRS1. Indeed, even though it is well documented that the activation of TNFR1 leads to the serine phosphorylation of IRS1 (and, thus, to the inhibition of tyrosine phosphorilation (see Fig. 8)) the structure of the pathway sustaining this interaction is still unclear. Actually, the model presented in Sect. 4.2 is not able to reproduce insulin/TNFα interference. This may depend on the fact that the experimental substrate used in [20] is represented by a cell culture line (namely human colon adenocarcinoma cells, ATCC) which, being cancerous cells, may not function as the non-cancerous ones such as adipocytes.

Our hypothesis was that our model, being shaped on the findings reported in [20], does not mimic "correctly" the insulin-TNF interactions. Some experimental evidences have lead to the characterization of a possible pathway responsible of the cross-talk between insulin and TNFR pathways having this function [13] (Fig. 7). To test our hypothesis, we inserted compositionally this pathway in our model. Adding new knowledge compositionally turns out to be particularly easy in our framework, due to the parallel composition operator in ntcc and the synchronization of processes via entailment.

We then performed a new session of in silico experiments by simulating the model through BioWayS under different initial conditions, mimicking the presence of insulin, TNFα or both in the extracellular environment. The results of these experiments (see Fig. 9 for details) show that the trend of in silico behavior resembles what happens for the real counterpart. In particular when both IR-dependent and TNFR1-dependent pathways are active (i.e., when TNFα and insulin are both present), the amount of tyrosine-phosphorylated IRS1 is lower with respect to the case in which only IR-dependent pathways are active.

Summing up, our approach allows us to integrate different pieces of information into a coherent framework, thus obtaining a model in which the experimental results reported in [20] and [13] can be composed in a common picture. Even though the model we propose is consistent with the available data, we are aware that tailored experimental studies are needed for validating exhaustively our results.

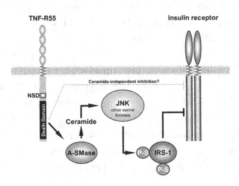

Fig. 7. Synoptical representation of the pathway linking activation of TNFR1 with IRS1 serine phosphorylation reconstructed on the base of experimental evidences

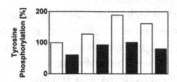

Fig. 8. Measured amount of phosphorylated IRS1 (pIRS1) in presence of only insulin (−) or TNFα and insulin (+) measured at different time intervals (0,1,3,5 min). Note that pIRS1 is lower when also TNFα is present in the extracellular medium

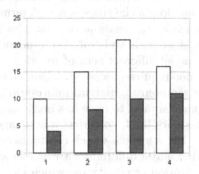

Fig. 9. Amount of tyrosine-phosphorylated IRS1 present at the end of the simulation in different experiments, mimicking those reported in Fig. 8. The white columns represents the final amount of tyrosine-phosphorylated IRS1 (arbitrary units) when only insulin is present in the environment. The colored columns represent the final amount of tyrosine-phosphorylated IRS1 (arbitrary units) when both insulin and TNFα are initially present. The histogram should be compared with those in Fig. 8.

5   Related Work

In this work we have presented the theoretical framework, while the work [9] focuses on the implementation made by the tool BioWayS.

Many works in the literature describe computational models for biological systems. They use many different formalisms, depending on the aspects to focus on. Here we cite some examples of those approaches in the literature which are closer to our methodology without the aim of being exhaustive.

In [8] the authors report on the specification and analysis of a VIrtual CEll (VICE) modelling a hypothetical cell with a genome as basic as possible. They use an enhanced version of the π-calculus and have implemented a prototype for studying the behavior of VICE.

Petri Nets (PN), both in their classical version [22] and in their stochastic ones [32] are one of the first approaches which has been used for modeling living systems. Pathway Logic (PL) [37] is a symbolic approach to the modeling and analysis of biological systems which is based on rewriting logic [24]. Rewriting logic is a logical framework which allows one to easily formalize systems. The states of a system are represented as elements of an algebraic data type, specified by an equational theory. The applications of rewrite rules allow to describe local transitions between states. A sequence of states corresponds to a computation, and —in the case of biological systems—to pathways. Our methodology should have the advantage of modeling the time of reactions and treat in a natural way partial information.

The language Biocham was introduced in [16], and was designed for being be very close to the classical rules biologists use to describe biochemical reactions. For example, the formation of a complex composed by two proteins, A and B, is governed by the rule $A, B \longrightarrow A+B$, where A, B models the presence of two separated proteins. The application of the rules is non-deterministic. Reaction rules for kinetic expressions, such as the mass action law, for the Michaelis-Menten kinetics and for the Hills kinetics, have been also implemented in Biocham [16]. We believe that we can model different sets of reaction rules by exploiting the fact that our models do not require precise stoichiometric data. This is due to the use of constraints for representing partial information.

A programming language similar to ours has been used for representing Biological systems in [4]. The work in [4] considers a language which is suitable for modeling hybrid systems, i.e., a system which combines continuous and discrete time evolutions. Some other major differences are as follows. We mainly focus on deriving a simple representation of equations, which can be easily used by non expert users. We model time duration of reactions as well as partial information, like [4], but we present a new methodology which allows us to compose several pathways and find results which normally requires the availability of more refined data. We also refer the reader to [7] where a stochastic extension of CCP is considered for the modeling of biological systems.

We note that there exist other formalisms which can exploit compositionality. For instance the formalisms which have an algebraic semantics, e.g. [4]. Another formalism which allows for a compositional development is possible in the framework BioPepa [12], in which they define a new language for biological modeling, while we want to show the suitability of an existing general purpose language.

6   Concluding Remarks

We have described a methodology for representing biochemical systems in a compositional fashion. In our framework, a biological system is specified by a set of stoichiometric-like equations which capture the essential features of molecular interactions. These equations are then evaluated and computed by an interpreter written in a Timed Concurrent Constraint Programming language. Our approach allows us to model partial information as set of constraints, thus dealing with the possible lack of precise information about some components of the system. Differently from other approaches similar to ours, we are able also to model the fact that a (bio)chemical reaction can occur within a certain time. We have also implemented a software tool used here to study the system involving TNFα, EGFR and insulin signaling pathways. In this context, we have shown how our approach makes it possible to compose different pieces of information coming from experimental studies, thus giving rise to a model which integrates the available knowledge.

Acknowledgements. We thank the anonymous referees for their helpful comments.

References

1. Arias, J., Guzman, M., Olarte, C.: A symbolic model for timed concurrent constraint programming. Electr. Notes Theor. Comput. Sci. **312**, 161–177 (2015)
2. Berry, G.: The foundations of esterel. In: Plotkin, D., Stirling, C., Tofte, M. (eds.) Proof, Language, and Interaction, Essays in Honour of Robin Milner, pp. 425–454. The MIT Press, Cambridge (2000)
3. Blinov, M.L., Ruebenacker, O., Moraru, I.I.: Complexity and modularity of intracellular networks: a systematic approach for modelling and simulation. IET Syst. Biol. **2**(5), 363–368 (2008)
4. Bockmayr, A., Courtois, A.: Using hybrid concurrent constraint programming to model dynamic biological systems. In: Stuckey, P.J. (ed.) ICLP 2002. LNCS, vol. 2401, p. 85. Springer, Heidelberg (2002)
5. Bodei, C., Bracciali, A., Chiarugi, D.: On deducing causalities in metabolic networks. BMC Bioinform. **9**, S8 (2008)
6. Bodei, C., Bracciali, A., Chiarugi, D., Gori, R.: A taxonomy of causality-based biological properties. Electron. Notes Theoret. Comput. Sci. **9**, 116–133 (2008)
7. Bortolussi, L., Policriti, A.: Modeling biological systems in stochastic concurrent constraint programming. Constraints **13**(1–2), 66–90 (2008)
8. Chiarugi, D., Curti, M., Degano, P., Marangoni, R.: VICE: a virtual cell. In: Schachter, V., Danos, V. (eds.) CMSB 2004. LNCS (LNBI), vol. 3082, pp. 207–220. Springer, Heidelberg (2005)
9. Chiarugi, D., Falaschi, M., Hermith, D., Guzman, M., Olarte, C.: Simulating signalling pathways with bioways. Electr. Notes Theor. Comput. Sci. **293**, 17–34 (2013)
10. Chiarugi, D., Falaschi, M., Hermith, D., Olarte, C.: Verification of spatial and temporal modalities in biochemical systems. In: Electronic Notes in Theoretical Computer Science, page In press (2015)
11. Chiarugi, D., Falaschi, M., Olarte, C., Palamidessi, C.: Compositional modelling of signalling pathways in timed concurrent constraint programming. In: Proceedings of the First ACM International Conference on Bioinformatics and Computational Biology, BCB 2010, pp. 414–417. ACM (2010)
12. Ciocchetta, F., Hillston, J.: Bio-pepa: a framework for the modelling and analysis of biological systems. Theor. Comput. Sci. **410**(33–34), 3065–3084 (2009)
13. Csehi, S., Mathieu, S., Seifert, U., Lange, A., Zweyer, M., Wernig, A., Adam, D.: Tumor necrosis factor (TNF) interferes with insulin signaling through the p55 TNF receptor death domain. Biochem. Biophys. Res. Commun. **329**, 397–405 (2005)

14. Devlin, T.M.: Textbook of Biochemistry with Clinical Correlations. Wiley-Liss, New York (2002)
15. Gaudet, S., et al.: A compendium of signals and responses triggered by prodeath and prosurvival cytokines. Mol. Cell. Proteomics **4**, 1569–1590 (2008)
16. Fages, F., Soliman, S., Chabrier-Rivier, N.: Modeling and querying interaction networks in the biochemical abstract machine biocham. J. Biol. Phys. Chem. **4**(2), 64–73 (2004)
17. Fayruzov, T., Janssen, J., Vermeir, D., Cornelis, C., De Cock, M.: Modelling gene and protein regulatory networks with answer set programming. IJDMB **5**(2), 209–229 (2011)
18. Finkel, T., Gutkind, J.S.: Signal Transduction and Human Disease. Wiley-Liss, Hoboken (2003)
19. Fisher, J., Henzinger, T.A.: Executable cell biology. Nat. Biotechnol. **25**, 1239–1249 (2007)
20. Gaudet, S., Janes, K.A., Albeck, J.G., Pace, E.A., Lauffenburger, D.A., Sorger, P.K.: A compendium of signals and responses triggered by prodeath and prosurvival cytokines. Mol. Cell. Proteomics **4**(10), 1569–1590 (2005)
21. Gillespie, D.T.: Stochastic simulation of chemical kinetics. Annu. Rev. Phys. Chem **58**, 35–55 (2007)
22. Goss, P., Peccoud, J.: Quantitative modeling of stochastic systems in molecular biology by using stochastic petri nets. Biochemistry **95**, 6750–6754 (1998)
23. Gupta, V., Jagadeesan, R., Saraswat, V.A.: Probabilistic concurrent constraint programming. In: Mazurkiewicz, A., Winkowski, J. (eds.) CONCUR 1997. LNCS, vol. 1243, pp. 243–257. Springer, Heidelberg (1997)
24. Martí-Oliet, N., Meseguer, J.: Rewriting logic: roadmap and bibliography. Theoret. Comput. Sci. **285**(2), 121–154 (2002)
25. Mendler, N.P., Panangaden, P., Scott, P.J., Seely, R.A.G.: A logical view of concurrent constraint programming. Nord. J. Comput. **2**(2), 181–220 (1995)
26. Milner, R.: Communication and Concurrency. International Series in Computer Science. Prentice Hall, Upper Saddle River (1989)
27. Milner, R.: Communicating and Mobile Systems: The π-Calculus. Cambridge University Press, Cambridge (1999)
28. Nielsen, M., Palamidessi, C., Valencia, F.: Temporal concurrent constraint programming: denotation, logic and applications. Nord. J. Comput. **9**(1), 145–188 (2002)
29. Ninio, J.: Alternative to the steady-state method: derivation of reaction rates from first-passage times and pathway probabilities. Proc. Natl. Acad. Sci. USA **84**, 663–667 (1987)
30. Olarte, C., Rueda, C., Valencia, F.D.: Models and emerging trends of concurrent constraint programming. Constraints **18**(4), 535–578 (2013)
31. Olarte, C., Valencia, F.D.: Universal concurrent constraint programing: symbolic semantics and applications to security. In: Wainwright, R.L., Haddad, H. (eds.) Proceedings of the 2008 ACM Symposium on Applied Computing (SAC), Fortaleza, Ceara, Brazil, March 16–20, 2008, pp. 145–150. ACM (2008)
32. Reddy, V.N., Liebman, M.N., Mavrovouniotis, M.L.: Qualitative analysis of biochemical reaction systems. Comput. Biol. Med. **26**(1), 9–24 (1996)
33. Saraswat, V.: Concurrent Constraint Programming. The MIT Press, Cambridge (1993)
34. Saraswat, V.A., Jagadeesan, R., Gupta, V.: Timed default concurrent constraint programming. J. Symb. Comput. **22**(5/6), 475–520 (1996)

35. Saraswat, V.A., Rinard, M.C., Panangaden, P.: Semantic foundations of concurrent constraint programming. In: Wise, D.S. (ed.) Conference Record of the Eighteenth Annual ACM Symposium on Principles of Programming Languages, Orlando, Florida, USA, January 21–23, 1991, pages 333–352. ACM Press (1991)
36. Smolka, G.: A foundation for higher-order concurrent constraint programming. In: Jouannaud, J.-P. (ed.) Constraints in Computational Logics. LNCS, vol. 845, pp. 50–72. Springer, Heidelberg (1994)
37. Talcott, C.: Pathway Logic. In: Degano, P., Bernardo, M., Zavattaro, G. (eds.) SFM 2008. LNCS, vol. 5016, pp. 21–53. Springer, Heidelberg (2008)

Securing Android with Local Policies

Gabriele Costa[✉]

DIBRIS, Università di Genova, Genova, Italy
gabriele.costa@unige.it

Abstract. Local policies have been proposed in [6] as a formalism for efficient and effective policy verification and enforcement. The basic approach consists of an enriched syntax of a programming language with a scope operator that the developer uses to apply a local policy to a specific portion of her code. Due to their fair expressiveness and modularity, they have been successfully applied also to object-orienter languages and web services. In this paper we apply the existing approach to the Android application framework. To this aim, we present a novel programming language, namely λ , which includes both the Android IPC logic and local policies.

1 Introduction

The Android security framework aims to both "reduce the frequency and impact of application security issues" and "avoid difficult decisions about security"[1]. Oversimplifying, it consists of a permissions system and a monitor which dynamically checks whether access operations have appropriate privileges. Permissions are labels, e.g., `a.p.INTERNET` and `a.p.CAMERA`[2], which precisely identify a set of privileged operations. Such operations can be performed, typically by an application, only after exhibiting the appropriate permission. Developers declare the list of permissions requested by their applications and users inspect them before installing the code. If a user agrees on the requested permissions, she confirms the installation and the application obtains all the permissions in the list.

The main limitations of the permission system are the coarse-grained protection and the lack of a formal semantics. These drawbacks have been highlighted by several authors. For instance, in [17,18] the authors show how the dynamic permission checking of Android is ineffective when applications interact, i.e., they are not compositional. Moreover, after a systematic study of more than thousand Android applications, Enck et al. [16] confirm that "many developers fail to take necessary security precautions".

Local policies [7,9] have been proposed by Bartoletti et al. as a formalism for defining safety and liveness policies which admit both static verification and runtime enforcement. Application developers attach one or more policies to a piece of source code they want to secure through a language operator. A type

---

[1] http://developer.android.com/training/articles/security-tips.html.
[2] For brevity, we write `a.p` instead of `android.permission`.

© Springer International Publishing Switzerland 2015
C. Bodei et al. (Eds.): Degano Festschrift, LNCS 9465, pp. 202–218, 2015.
DOI: 10.1007/978-3-319-25527-9_14

and effect system is responsible for inferring behavioural models of the applications, namely *history expressions*. Then, the policies and history expressions are automatically verified, through model checking. All the policies that pass the verification are simply removed as they cannot be violated at runtime. The others are dynamically enforced. Due to their modular nature, local policies have been also successfully exploited for defining security policies of web services [8].

In this paper we present an extension of the Android security framework with local policies. We show that the existing theory for web services can be adopted for the Android applications. Since the theoretical framework is unchanged, our proposal preserves all the existing formal guarantees, e.g., well-typed programs cannot cause wrong executions. Interestingly, the application of local policies to the Android application framework is even more natural than for web services (see Sect. 7).

Structure of the Paper. In Sect. 2 we briefly present some preliminary notions about the Android OS and applications. In Sect. 3 we present a case study with the twofold objective of clarifying the Android framework and serving as a working example. Section 4 introduces our programming model based on an enriched version of the λ-calculus, while Sect. 5 describes the type and effect system. Then, in Sect. 7 we briefly discuss few relevant aspects and open issues. Finally, Sect. 8 concludes the paper.

2   Background

Below we briefly recall the Android OS structure and, in particular, its application level. Moreover, we present the relevant aspects of the Android Security Framework.

Android Application Framework. The Android Application Framework (AAF) is mainly based on Java with few, still substantial, differences. The first one is that Android does not mount a standard Java virtual machine. Instead, it adopts a customized/optimized one called Art VM (which recently replaced the Dalvik VM). Although using a different VM has noticeable effects (mostly the usage of a distinct intermediate language), it does not impact on the semantics of programs, as the Art VM is just another implementation of the interpreter of the high level language[3]. Hence, we can neglect this aspect in the rest of the paper.

The second and more interesting difference is the presence of Android-specific APIs. These APIs provide high level abstractions of the underling system operations. Among them, *inter-process communication* (IPC) and *application components* are of paramount importance. As a matter of fact, Android applications use IPC to perform application-to-application invocations. Invocations activate a component that the callee has published to the system (at install time).

---

[3] More precisely, it is the interpreter of the intermediate language obtained from the compilation of the high level one. As far as the compilation process is semantic-preserving, the argument holds.

Four types of components exist in Android, i.e., *Activity*, *ContentProvider*, *Service* and *BroadcastReceiver*, and we briefly introduce them below. An Activity implements a graphic element of the application, i.e., a user interface and its controls. ContentProviders mediate the access to data sources, e.g., databases. Instead, a Service represents an asynchronous, background computation often providing a binding between events and handlers, e.g., for geolocalization. Finally, a BroadcastReceiver is an IPC dedicated component which handles intents, i.e., IPC-specific objects carrying invocation data, coming from other applications.

Components are contractually defined through a xml file, called *manifest*, included in each application package. At installation time, Android retrieves the list of application components from the manifest file. The list is registered and made publicly visible among the existing applications to permit IPC invocations.

Android Security Framework. The Android Security Framework (ASF) consists of a collection of security mechanisms residing at different levels of the OS structure. For instance, the original Android/Linux kernel implements DAC mechanisms while, from OS version 4.4., SEAndroid supports MAC policies. Also, the Art VM carries the same security mechanisms as a standard JVM, e.g., stack inspection and application sandboxing.

Instead, at application level, Android exploits a *permissions system* for regulating the access to resources and components. Briefly, applications wanting to access security critical resources, e.g., the storage card or the internet, must be authorized by the user. The request is carried by the Android manifest which includes a list of the permissions requested by the application, e.g., `a.p.READ_SD` and `a.p.INTERNET`. At installation time, the user is prompted with such list and, if she confirms, the application is installed and receives all the requested permissions. Since a manifest can also declare its own permissions, the mechanism can be extended to application-specific resources.

Moreover, application can apply *filters* to their components. Filters are declared in the manifest for restricting the access to the components. Briefly, a filter consists of a list of permissions that an application must exhibit when invoking the watched component.

At runtime, IPC calls are labeled with the permissions owned by the source of the invocation. Then, IPC invocations are compared with the existing filters and components declaring unsatisfied constraints, i.e., requiring at least one permission that the caller does not own, are not triggered. If two or more compatible receivers exist, the user must pick one.

3   Case Study

In order to present our methodology we propose the following case study. *Smart-Town* is a mobile application allowing citizens to organize their urban life. The application takes advantage of an existing ecosystem of components for planning city travels and booking events. Users select among several events located in the urban area and schedule their visit through an interactive map. Then, the Smart-Town triggers the existing applications dedicated to public transportation, event booking and e-payment. We briefly introduce each application in the ecosystem.

WebPay is an application for electronic payments over the internet. It consists of two components, *WebPayReceiver* (**wpr**) and *WebPayActivity* (**wpa**). Applications can trigger a payment by sending a pair $p = (a, t)$. Then the application displays WPA to ask the user whether she confirm the payment of $a\$$ to t. If so, the application performs the payment.

TubeRider provides a subway connection between the current position and a final destination d. In consists of a *TubeRiderReceiver* (**trr**), which receives requests carrying d, and a *TubeRiderActivity* (**tra**), which shows the subway map.

CabWhistle is a single-component taxi reservation application. External components can invoke *CabWhistleReceiver* (**cwr**) by submitting a destination d for requesting a taxi at the current location.

TableBooking allows for checking a list of restaurants and make reservations. The *TableBookingReceiver* (**tbr**) can be invoked by submitting a date w. The application uses w to search the restaurants having free tables and make a reservation. The component *TableBookingActivity* (**tba**) is used to display the list of restaurants.

MovieMania works in a similar way: *MovieManiaReceiver* (**mmr**) requires a date w for reserving a seat and *MovieManiaActivity* (**mma**) displays the list of cinemas.

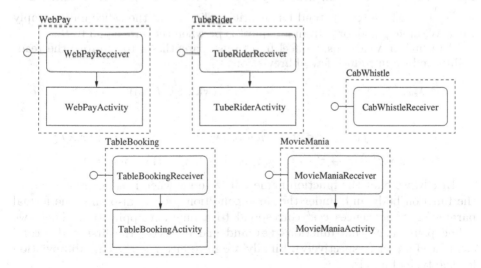

Fig. 1. Applications and components participating in the SmartTown case study.

Figure 1 depicts the applications and components described above. We use rectangular boxes for the activities and rounded ones for receivers. Moreover, we mark the publicly visible, interface receivers with the symbol ○.

4 Programming Model

In this section we present the programming language λ (lamdba-droid), which is an adaptation of λ^{req} to the Android application framework.

Syntax. Briefly, that of λ amounts to the syntax of the λ-calculus enriched with special operators for defining the scope of security policies and for declaring invocations of Android components. The syntax of λ is the following.

$$e, e' ::= * \mid x \mid \alpha \mid \text{if } b \text{ then } e \text{ else } e' \mid \lambda_z x.e \mid ee' \mid \varphi[e] \mid \psi\langle e \rangle \mid \text{ipc}_r \tau$$

The atomic expressions of λ are the empty term $*$, the variables $x, y \in \mathsf{Var}$ and the access events $\alpha, \beta \in \mathsf{Act}$. Intuitively, access events denote all and only the security relevant operations that a program can perform. Other expressions are the conditional branches (where b stands for a boolean condition being immaterial for the current dissertation), function abstractions (where z denotes the function itself in its body e) and function applications. The main differences with the standard λ−calculus are *policy framings* and *inter-process communications* (IPC). Framings enclose an expression e to denote that it lays in the scope of a security policy. Policies can be either *safety* ($\varphi[e]$) or *liveness* ($\psi\langle e \rangle$) ones. A detailed presentation of the used policy language can be found in [10]. Instead, an IPC term $\text{ipc}_r \tau$ represents a request for an Android component having type τ. Each request is uniquely identified by a label r. Request types can be either $\mathbf{1}$ or $\tau \xrightarrow{(\varphi, \psi)} \tau'$, where (φ, ψ) stand for security policies that the callee must comply with. We omit φ and/or ψ from a request type when they are equal to tt.

As usual in λ-calculus, we feel free to use parentheses to improve the readability and we introduce few abbreviations.

$$\lambda x.e \triangleq \lambda_z x.e \text{ (with } z \notin fv(e)) \qquad \lambda.e \triangleq \lambda x.e \text{ (with } x \notin fv(e)) \qquad e; e' \triangleq (\lambda.e')e$$

$$\langle v, v' \rangle \triangleq \lambda f.(fv)v' \qquad \text{fst} \triangleq \lambda p.p(\lambda x.\lambda y.x) \qquad \text{snd} \triangleq \lambda p.p(\lambda x.\lambda y.y)$$

$$\tau \times \tau' \triangleq \tau \to \tau' \to (\tau \to \tau' \to \tau'') \to \tau'' \quad \text{(for some } \tau'')$$

Briefly, we omit the function name z in λ terms when it is not referenced in the function body and, under the same condition, we can also omit the formal parameter x. Sequences $e; e'$ correspond to a function application. Then, we define pairs $\langle v, v' \rangle$ and functions fst and snd to access the first and second element of a pair (respectively). Finally, we introduce $\tau \times \tau'$ as an abbreviation for the type of a pair.

Table 1. Implementation of the components defined in Sect. 3.

Component	Implementation
WebPayReceiver	$e_{\text{wpr}} = \lambda p.\text{if } ok \text{ then } \alpha_{idn}; \alpha_{net}; \text{ else } *$
TubeRiderReceiver	$e_{\text{trr}} = \lambda d.\alpha_{cgl}; (\text{rec}_{r1}\, \mathcal{C} \times \mathcal{A})\langle 2, ticket@csc.com\rangle$
CabWhistleReceiver	$e_{\text{cwr}} = \lambda d.\alpha_{fgl}; (\text{rec}_{r2}\, \mathcal{C} \times \mathcal{A})\langle 10, whistle@trs.net\rangle; \alpha_{sms}; \alpha_{cap}$
TableBookingReceiver	$e_{\text{tbr}} = \lambda w.\alpha_{net}; (\text{rec}_{r3}\, \mathcal{C} \times \mathcal{A})\langle 50, booking@res.com\rangle$
MovieManiaReceiver	$e_{\text{mmr}} = \lambda w.(\text{rec}_{r4}\, \mathcal{C} \times \mathcal{A})\langle 15, buy@cinema.tv\rangle; \alpha_{net}$

Moreover we define the following abbreviations which are specific for the four kinds of Android components.

$$\text{act}_r^{(\varphi,\psi)} \triangleq \text{ipc}_r 1 \xrightarrow{(\varphi,\psi)} 1 \qquad \text{srv}_r^{(\varphi,\psi)}\tau \triangleq \text{ipc}_r(1 \to 1) \xrightarrow{(\varphi,\psi)} \tau$$

$$\text{rec}_r^{(\varphi,\psi)}\tau \triangleq \text{ipc}_r\tau \xrightarrow{(\varphi,\psi)} 1 \qquad \text{prv}_r^{(\varphi,\psi)}\tau \to \tau' \triangleq \text{ipc}_r 1 \xrightarrow{(\varphi,\psi)} (\tau \to \tau')$$

Example 1. Consider again the components of Sect. 3. In Table 1 e provide an implementation for all the components our case study.

Intuitively, WebPayReceiver (e_{wpr}) receives payment coordinates p and, if the user confirms (constant ok), accesses the user identity (α_{idn}) and connects to the payment service (α_{net}). Otherwise, no operation is carried out. TubeRider-Receiver (e_{trr}) gets a destination d, accesses the course-grained location of the device (α_{cgl}) and, finally, requests a payment of 2\$ to the city subway company ($ticket@csc.com$). Also notice that here we introduce the types for currency, i.e., $\mathcal{C}$, and email addressed, i.e., $\mathcal{A}$. Instead, CabWhistleReceiver (e_{cwr}) uses the fine-grained location of the device (α_{fgl}), triggers a component for paying 10\$ to the taxi request service ($whistle@trs.net$), sends an SMS carrying the taxi request (α_{sms}) and captures the answer message (α_{cap}). TableBookingReceiver (e_{tbr}) receives a date w, accesses the network (α_{net}) and requests a payment of 50\$ for booking the restaurant ($booking@res.com$). Finally, MovieManiaReceiver (e_{mmr}) requests a payment of 15\$ for the cinema reservation system ($buy@cinema.tv$) and uses the network to confirm the operation (α_{net}).

Example 2. We propose the following implementation for the SmartTown application.

$$\lambda.(\text{rec}_r\, \mathcal{D})tdy; (\text{rec}_{r'}\, \mathcal{L})loc$$

Briefly, the application consists of an activity which requests a reservation to some event for today (tdy) and then requests a connection to the event location (loc). Here we introduce types $\mathcal{D}$ and $\mathcal{L}$ for dates and locations, respectively.

Operational Semantics. The computation performed by a program, i.e., a term of λ, consists of a sequence of steps. Each step is a transition from a source configuration to a resulting one. Configurations are pairs $\langle \eta, e \rangle$ where η is the current execution trace, i.e., the sequence of events generated so far by the execution, and e the expression under evaluation. Transitions are denoted by $\to_\pi$

where π is a finite mapping, called *simple plan* (hereafter just plan), between IPC requests and a component id, defined as follows.

$$\pi, \pi' \quad ::= \quad \emptyset \quad | \quad r[\ell] \quad | \quad \pi \circ \pi'$$

The symbol $\emptyset$ stands for the empty mapping, $r[\ell]$ maps the request r to the component labeled with ℓ (we assume labels to be unique) and $\pi \circ \pi'$ is the composition of two plans. For brevity, we write $\pi(r) = \ell$ whenever the plan π maps r to ℓ.

Rules are mostly inherited from [8]. Below we recall them, also highlighting the differences. In words, function application $e_1 e_2$ proceeds by reducing the first expression until a value is reached (rule (E-App$_1$)), then e_2 is also reduced to a value (rule (E-App$_2$)). Eventually (rule (E-App$_3$)), the application reduces to the function body where the formal parameter x and the function name

Table 2. Operational semantics

NAME	RULE
(E-App$_1$)	$\dfrac{\langle \eta, e_1 \rangle \to_\pi \langle \eta', e_1' \rangle}{\langle \eta, e_1 e_2 \rangle \to_\pi \langle \eta', e_1' e_2 \rangle}$
(E-App$_2$)	$\dfrac{\langle \eta, e_2 \rangle \to_\pi \langle \eta', e_2' \rangle}{\langle \eta, v e_2 \rangle \to_\pi \langle \eta', v e_2' \rangle}$
(E-App$_3$)	$\dfrac{\quad}{\langle \eta, (\lambda_z x.e)v \rangle \to_\pi \langle \eta, e\{v \setminus x, \lambda_z x.e \setminus z\} \rangle}$
(E-Ev)	$\dfrac{\quad}{\langle \eta, \alpha \rangle \to_\pi \langle \eta\alpha, * \rangle}$
(E-If$_1$)	$\dfrac{\mathcal{B}(b) = tt}{\langle \eta, \text{if } b \text{ then } e_1 \text{ else } e_2 \rangle \to_\pi \langle \eta, e_1 \rangle}$
(E-If$_2$)	$\dfrac{\mathcal{B}(b) = ff}{\langle \eta, \text{if } b \text{ then } e_1 \text{ else } e_2 \rangle \to_\pi \langle \eta, e_2 \rangle}$
(E-SF$_1$)	$\dfrac{\langle \eta, e \rangle \to_\pi \langle \eta', e' \rangle \qquad \eta' \models \varphi}{\langle \eta, \varphi[e] \rangle \to_\pi \langle \eta', \varphi[e'] \rangle}$
(E-SF$_2$)	$\dfrac{\eta \models \varphi}{\langle \eta, \varphi[v] \rangle \to_\pi \langle \eta, v \rangle}$
(E-LF$_1$)	$\dfrac{\langle \eta, e \rangle \to_\pi \langle \eta', e' \rangle \qquad \eta' \not\models \psi}{\langle \eta, \psi\langle e \rangle \rangle \to_\pi \langle \eta', \psi\langle e \rangle \rangle}$
(E-LF$_2$)	$\dfrac{\eta \models \psi}{\langle \eta, \psi\langle e \rangle \rangle \to_\pi \langle \eta, e \rangle}$
(E-IPC$_1$)	$\dfrac{e_\ell : \tau \in \mathsf{Cmp} \qquad \pi(r) = \ell}{\langle \eta, (\mathtt{ipc}_r \tau)v \rangle \to_\pi \langle \eta, e_\ell v \rangle}$

z are replaced with the actual value v and the function itself (respectively). An event α extends the current trace η and reduces to $*$ (rule (E-Ev)). The evaluation of conditionals branches is driven by two rules (rules (E-IF$_1$) and (E-IF$_2$)). Depending on whether the guard b evaluates to tt or ff^4, they reduce to either the first or the second branch. Safety framing admits reduction of the target expression e as the obtained trace complies with the policy φ (in symbols $\eta' \models \varphi$ — rule (E-SF$_1$)). When the expressions reduces to a value, the framing operator can be removed if the current trace does not violate φ (rule (E-SF$_2$)). Dually, liveness framings permit reductions of their target till the current trace does not satisfy the property ψ (rule (E-LF$_1$)). Instead, when the trace satisfies ψ the frame is removed (rule (E-LF$_2$)). Clearly, liveness properties cannot be effectively enforced at runtime. Thus, their verification is demanded to the static analysis procedure (see Sect. 5). IPC invocations require more attention. An implicit invocation (rule (E-IPC$_1$)) is resolved by retrieving the function $e_\ell \in \mathsf{Cmp}$ provided by the current plan π. Also, its type τ must comply with the requested one. Notice that, unlike previous proposals for web service composition [8], here we force an exact matching between the type of the request and that of the callee. The motivation is that available web services are typically unknown to the caller and they are retrieved through a discovery phase. Instead, the Android application framework uses types to establish predefined connections between components. By design, application developers must know the type of the component they want to invoke when writing their code[5]. Nevertheless, this restriction does not affect the existing programming framework (i.e., it has no effect on the rules of Table 2).

Example 3. We show the execution of the term $(e_{\mathsf{wpr}})v$ (for some value v) from execution trace ε, under plan $\emptyset$. Also we assume $\mathcal{B}(ok) = true$.

$$(\text{E-App}_3) \; \frac{\qquad\qquad}{\langle \varepsilon, (e_{\mathsf{wpr}})v \rangle \to_\emptyset \langle \varepsilon, \text{if } ok \text{ then } \alpha_{idn}; \alpha_{net}; \text{ else } * \rangle}$$

$$(\text{E-If}_1) \; \frac{\mathcal{B}(ok) = tt}{\langle \varepsilon, \text{if } ok \text{ then } \alpha_{idn}; \alpha_{net}; \text{ else } * \rangle \to_\emptyset \langle \varepsilon, \alpha_{idn}; \alpha_{net} \rangle}$$

$$(\text{E-App}_2) \; \frac{(\text{E-Ev}) \; \dfrac{\qquad}{\langle \varepsilon, \alpha_{idn} \rangle \to_\emptyset \langle \alpha_{idn}, * \rangle}}{\langle \varepsilon, (\lambda.\alpha_{net})\alpha_{idn} \rangle \to_\emptyset \langle \alpha_{idn}, (\lambda.\alpha_{net})* \rangle}$$

$$(\text{E-App}_3) \; \frac{\qquad\qquad}{\langle \alpha_{idn}, (\lambda.\alpha_{net})* \rangle \to_\emptyset \langle \alpha_{idn}, \alpha_{net} \rangle}$$

$$(\text{E-Ev}) \; \frac{\qquad\qquad}{\langle \alpha_{idn}, \alpha_{net} \rangle \to_\emptyset \langle \alpha_{idn}\alpha_{net}, * \rangle}$$

From top to bottom, we start by applying rule (E-App$_3$) since both (e_{wpr}) and v admit no reductions. Then, we apply rule (E-IF$_1$) to the conditional statement.

---

[4] We assume an evaluation function $\mathcal{B}$ to be defined.

[5] http://developer.android.com/guide/components/intents-filters.html.

Since, we assume the guard to evaluate to *true*, we reduce to the first branch. The sequence $\alpha_{idn}; \alpha_{idn}$ stands for $(\lambda.\alpha_{net})\alpha_{idn}$. Thus, we follow rule (E-APP₂) to reduce the actual parameter of the function application. Such reduction requires to apply rule (E-Ev). The computation terminates by applying rules (E-APP₃) and (E-Ev) to the remaining terms.

5   Type and Effect

A type and effect system infers a behavioural model from each λ term. Models are represented through *history expressions* which statically denote the execution traces that the term generates at runtime. In this section we recall the type and effect system for λ^{req} and adapt to λ. For further details we refer the interested reader to [8].

5.1   History Expressions

History expressions are all and only the terms respecting the following abstract syntax.

$$H, H' ::= \varepsilon \mid h \mid \alpha \mid H \cdot H' \mid H + H' \mid \varphi[H] \mid \psi\langle H \rangle \mid \mu h.H \mid \{\pi_i \triangleright H_i\}$$

An history expression can be the empty one ε, a variable h, a single access event α, a sequence $H \cdot H'$, a non-deterministic choice $H + H'$, safety (liveness) framing $\varphi[H]$ ($\psi\langle H \rangle$, resp.), a recursion $\mu h.H$ or a planned selection $\{\pi_1 \triangleright H_1 \ldots \pi_n \triangleright H_n\}$. Most of the terms are straightforward and resemble their analogous in λ. Given the plan π, a planned selection $\{\pi_1 \triangleright H_1 \ldots \pi_n \triangleright H_n\}$ describes a computation which behaves as H_i if π includes π_i.

Denotational Semantics. The denotational semantics is a function $[\![H]\!]_\rho^\pi$ mapping a history expression H to a set of execution traces $\mathcal{H}$. Also, the denotational semantics requires a plan π and a variable environment ρ. The denotational semantics is defined by the following rules.

$$[\![\varepsilon]\!]_\rho^\pi = \{\varepsilon\} \qquad [\![\alpha]\!]_\rho^\pi = \{\alpha\} \qquad [\![h]\!]_\rho^\pi = \rho(h) \qquad [\![H \cdot H']\!]_\rho^\pi = [\![H]\!]_\rho^\pi [\![H']\!]_\rho^\pi$$

$$[\![H + H']\!]_\rho^\pi = [\![H]\!]_\rho^\pi \cup [\![H']\!]_\rho^\pi \qquad [\![\varphi[H]]\!]_\rho^\pi = {}_\varphi[[\![H]\!]_\rho^\pi]_\varphi \qquad [\![\psi\langle H\rangle]\!]_\rho^\pi = {}_\psi\langle[\![H]\!]_\rho^\pi\rangle_\psi$$

$$[\![\mu h.H]\!]_\rho^\pi = \bigcup_{n>0} f^n(!) \quad \text{where } f(X) = [\![H]\!]_{\rho\{X/h\}}^\pi$$

$$[\![\{\pi_1 \triangleright H_1 \ldots \pi_n \triangleright H_n\}]\!]_\rho^\pi = \bigcup_{i\in[1,n]} [\![\{\pi_i \triangleright H_i\}]\!]_\rho^\pi \qquad [\![\{\emptyset \triangleright H\}]\!]_\rho^\pi = [\![H]\!]_\rho^\pi$$

$$[\![\{\pi_0 \circ \pi_1 \triangleright H\}]\!]_\rho^\pi = [\![\{\pi_0 \triangleright H\}]\!]_\rho^\pi \cup [\![\{\pi_1 \triangleright H\}]\!]_\rho^\pi$$

$$[\![\{r[\ell] \triangleright H\}]\!]_\rho^\pi = \begin{cases} [\![H]\!]_\rho^\pi & \text{if } \pi(r) = \ell \\ \bot & \text{otherwise} \end{cases}$$

Briefly, a history expression ε denotes the set only containing the empty trace, similarly α denotes the singleton set $\{\alpha\}$ and the set denoted by a variable h

is provided by the environment ρ. Sequences denote the set of traces obtained through concatenation and choices correspond to sets union. Policy framings result in sets of traces wrapped between two special events, i.e., $[_\varphi$ and $]_\varphi$ (safety) or $\langle_\psi$ and $\rangle_\psi$ (liveness). Instead, a recursion corresponds to the least fixed point of a function f (the symbol ! stands for trace truncation). A planned selection denotes the finite union of the sets denoted by each selection, individually, and similarly, composed plans results in set union. Finally, a selection denotes the same set as the history expression H if the left-hand side $r[\ell]$ is compatible with the current plan π.

Example 4. Consider the history expression $H = \{r_1[\ell_1] \triangleright \alpha, r_2[\ell_2] \triangleright \mu h.\beta \cdot h + \varepsilon\}$ and the plan $\pi = r_1[\ell_1] \circ r_2[\ell_2]$. We compute $[\![H]\!]_\emptyset^\pi$ as follows.

$$
\begin{aligned}
[\![H]\!]_\emptyset^\pi &= [\![\{r_1[\ell_1] \triangleright \alpha, r_2[\ell_2] \triangleright \mu h.\beta \cdot h + \varepsilon\}]\!]_\emptyset^\pi \\
&= [\![\{r_1[\ell_1] \triangleright \alpha\}]\!]_\emptyset^\pi \cup [\![\{r_2[\ell_2] \triangleright \mu h.\beta \cdot h + \varepsilon\}]\!]_\emptyset^\pi \\
&= [\![\alpha]\!]_\emptyset^\pi \cup [\![\mu h.\beta \cdot h + \varepsilon]\!]_\emptyset^\pi \\
&= \{\alpha\} \cup [\![\mu h.\beta \cdot h + \varepsilon]\!]_\emptyset^\pi \\
&= \{\alpha\} \cup \{\varepsilon, \beta\} \cup \{\varepsilon, \beta, \beta\beta\} \cup \{\varepsilon, \beta, \beta\beta, \beta\beta\beta\} \cup \cdots
\end{aligned}
$$

Validity. Valid history expressions are those denoting traces that never violate the security policies they are subject to. Checking the validity of a history expression can be reduced to a language inclusion problem. Intuitively, a special class of finite state automata, namely *Usage Automata*, model the security policies appearing in a history expression. A usage automaton accepts a trace if and only if it violates the corresponding security policy. Then, the set of traces generated by a history expression is compared with those accepted by the usage automata (for the local policies) appearing in it. If an intersection exists, the history expression denotes at least an illegal trace. For a detailed presentation of the problem of model checking usage automata see [10, 11].

5.2   Type and Effect System

The type and effect system is defined by the rules of Table 3. A typing judgement has the form $\Gamma \vdash_{\mathsf{Cmp}} e : \tau \triangleright H$ with the meaning that the expression e, under environment Γ, has type τ and side effect H. Type environments are finite mapping between variables and types (we write $\emptyset$ for the empty mapping and $\Gamma; x : \tau$ for the environment mapping x to τ and behaving like Γ in the other cases). A type can be the unit one 1 or a functional type $\tau \xrightarrow{H} \tau'$ where H stands for the latent effect generated by the function upon invocation.

A term $*$ has type 1 and effect ε, while an access event α has type 1 and effect α. Instead, the type for a variable x is provided by the environment Γ. Functional abstraction requires more attention. We type a function $\lambda_z x.e$ to $\tau \xrightarrow{H} \tau'$ with effect ε if we can type the function body e to τ' and effect H under the environment where proper bindings the function z and its parameter x have

Table 3. Typing relation

NAME	RULE
(T-UNIT)	$$\Gamma \vdash_{\mathsf{Cmp}} * : \mathbf{1} \triangleright \varepsilon$$
(T-EV)	$$\Gamma \vdash_{\mathsf{Cmp}} \alpha : \mathbf{1} \triangleright \alpha$$
(T-VAR)	$$\dfrac{\Gamma(x) = \tau}{\Gamma \vdash_{\mathsf{Cmp}} x : \tau \triangleright \varepsilon}$$
(T-ABS)	$$\dfrac{\Gamma; z : \tau \xrightarrow{H} \tau'; x : \tau \vdash_{\mathsf{Cmp}} e : \tau' \triangleright H}{\Gamma \vdash_{\mathsf{Cmp}} \lambda_z x.e : \tau \xrightarrow{H} \tau' \triangleright \varepsilon}$$
(T-APP)	$$\dfrac{\Gamma \vdash_{\mathsf{Cmp}} e : \tau \xrightarrow{H''} \tau' \triangleright H \qquad \Gamma \vdash_{\mathsf{Cmp}} e' : \tau \triangleright H'}{\Gamma \vdash_{\mathsf{Cmp}} ee' : \tau' \triangleright H \cdot H' \cdot H''}$$
(T-IF)	$$\dfrac{\Gamma \vdash_{\mathsf{Cmp}} e_1 : \tau \triangleright H \qquad \Gamma \vdash_{\mathsf{Cmp}} e_2 : \tau \triangleright H}{\Gamma \vdash_{\mathsf{Cmp}} \mathbf{if}\ b\ \mathbf{then}\ e_1\ \mathbf{else}\ e_2 : \tau \triangleright H}$$
(T-SF)	$$\dfrac{\Gamma \vdash_{\mathsf{Cmp}} e : \tau \triangleright H}{\Gamma \vdash_{\mathsf{Cmp}} \varphi[e] : \tau \triangleright \varphi[H]}$$
(T-LF)	$$\dfrac{\Gamma \vdash_{\mathsf{Cmp}} e : \tau \triangleright H}{\Gamma \vdash_{\mathsf{Cmp}} \psi\langle e \rangle : \tau \triangleright \psi\langle H \rangle}$$
(T-WKN)	$$\dfrac{\Gamma \vdash_{\mathsf{Cmp}} e : \tau \triangleright H}{\Gamma \vdash_{\mathsf{Cmp}} e : \tau \triangleright H + H'}$$
(T-IPC)	$$\dfrac{\tau' = \bigcup\{\tau \oplus_{r[\ell]} \tau_\ell \mid e_\ell : \tau_\ell \in \mathsf{Cmp} \wedge \tau_\ell \approx \tau\}}{\Gamma \vdash_{\mathsf{Cmp}} \mathbf{ipc}_r \tau : \tau' \triangleright \varepsilon}$$

been defined. The type of an application is the right-hand side of the function type and its effect is the concatenation of those generated by the functional term, by its argument and the latent one. A conditional statement has type τ and effect H if the same holds for its two branches. Policy framings have the same type as their target e and a wrapped effect. Also, the weakening rule (T-WKN) allows for passing from an effect H to a more general one $H + H'$. Finally, the rule for planned selection requires to define three auxiliary operators, i.e., $\oplus, \approx$ and $\bigcup$. We say that $\tau \approx \tau'$ iff $\tau = \tau' = \mathbf{1}$ or

$$\tau = \tau_1 \xrightarrow{\cdot} \tau_2 \qquad \tau' = \tau'_1 \xrightarrow{\cdot} \tau'_2 \quad \text{and} \quad \tau_1 \approx \tau'_1 \text{ and } \tau_2 \approx \tau'_2$$

Instead the operator $\oplus_{r[\ell]}$ combines a request type $\tau_0 \xrightarrow{(\varphi, \psi)} \tau_1$ with a component type $\tau'_0 \xrightarrow{H} \tau'_1$ to obtain

$$\tau_0 \oplus_{r[\ell]} \tau'_0 \xrightarrow{\{r[\ell] \triangleright \varphi[\psi\langle H \rangle]\}} \tau_1 \oplus_{r[\ell]} \tau'_1$$

The last operator combines component types so that $\tau \xrightarrow{H} \tau' \uplus \tau \xrightarrow{H'} \tau' = \tau \xrightarrow{H+H'} \tau'.$[6]

Example 5. We type e_{wpr} from Example 1 and we obtain the following derivation.

$$\cfrac{\cfrac{\Gamma; p : \tau \vdash_{\mathsf{Cmp}} * : \mathbf{1} \triangleright \varepsilon}{\textcircled{a} \quad \cfrac{\Gamma; p : \tau \vdash_{\mathsf{Cmp}} * : \mathbf{1} \triangleright \alpha_{idn}\alpha_{net} + \varepsilon}{\cfrac{\Gamma; p : \tau \vdash_{\mathsf{Cmp}} \text{if } ok \text{ then } \alpha_{idn}; \alpha_{net} \text{ else } * : \mathbf{1} \triangleright \alpha_{idn}\alpha_{net} + \varepsilon}{\Gamma \vdash_{\mathsf{Cmp}} \lambda p.\text{if } ok \text{ then } \alpha_{idn}; \alpha_{net} \text{ else } * : \tau \xrightarrow{\alpha_{idn}\alpha_{net}+\varepsilon} \mathbf{1} \triangleright \varepsilon}}}}{}$$

where $\textcircled{a}$ stands for the derivation below.

$$\cfrac{\cfrac{\cfrac{\Gamma; p : \tau \vdash_{\mathsf{Cmp}} \alpha_{net} : \mathbf{1} \triangleright \alpha_{net}}{\Gamma; p : \tau \vdash_{\mathsf{Cmp}} \lambda.\alpha_{net} : \tau' \xrightarrow{\alpha_{net}} \mathbf{1} \triangleright \varepsilon} \quad \Gamma; p : \tau \vdash_{\mathsf{Cmp}} \alpha_{idn} : \mathbf{1} \triangleright \alpha_{idn}}{\Gamma; p : \tau \vdash_{\mathsf{Cmp}} (\lambda.\alpha_{net})\alpha_{idn} : \mathbf{1} \triangleright \alpha_{idn}\alpha_{net}}}{\Gamma; p : \tau \vdash_{\mathsf{Cmp}} (\lambda.\alpha_{net})\alpha_{idn} : \mathbf{1} \triangleright \alpha_{idn}\alpha_{net} + \varepsilon}$$

6 Policy Language

In this section we recall the policy language used for defining local policies and we compare it with some existing proposals, as well as with the Android policy framework.

Usage Automata. In [10] *Usage Automata* (UA) are used to specify local policies. Intuitively, a UA resembles a a Büchi automaton. The main aspect to be noticed is that whenever a trace η is accepted by a UA A_φ, it means that η violates the corresponding policy φ.[7]

Formally, a *Usage Automaton* A_φ is a tuple $\langle \mathsf{Act}, Q, q_0, F, \delta \rangle$ where:

- Act is the input alphabet,
- Q is a finite set of states,
- $q_0 \in Q \setminus F$ is the initial state,
- $F \subset Q$ is the set of final states,
- $\delta \subseteq Q \times \mathsf{Act} \times Q$ is a finite set of transitions.

We use $q \xrightarrow{\alpha} q$ as a shorthand for $(q, \alpha, q') \in \delta$.

Given a trace η, we write $\eta \models \varphi$ whenever $\eta \notin \mathcal{L}(A_\varphi)$, where $\mathcal{L}(A_\varphi)$ is the language accepted by the UA A_φ. Conversely, we write $\eta \not\models \varphi$ whenever $\eta \in \mathcal{L}(A_\varphi)$.[8]

---

[6] Notice that here we use a simplified version of the $\uplus$ operator. For the detailed version see [8].

[7] In this section we generally refer to local policies without distinguishing between safety and liveness.

[8] Notice that, although acceptance is only defined for ω-traces, we can extend finite traces with τ^ω where $\tau \in \mathsf{Act}$ is a special event denoting the termination.

Example 6. Consider the policy φ saying "never connect to the internet after reading the user's identity". The corresponding UA is

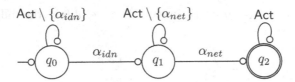

Adequacy of the Policy Language. Since version 2.2 the Android framework has been enriched with Device Administration APIs.[9] These APIs can be used to define advanced security policies over certain aspects of the application behaviour. The available security policies include password format and usage, encrypted data storage, screen lock time and camera disabling. Each of these features can be encoded as local policies by mapping the corresponding behaviour to the system API triggering it. For instance, the following UA prevents its target from accessing the camera.[10]

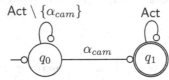

Several authors investigated the Android policy framework and possible alternatives. Among them, few formalizations exist. For instance, in [2] the authors use Hennessy-Milner logic (HML) for expressing security properties over execution and invocation traces. HML in possibly the least expressive logic of interest for specifying security properties as it only permits to reason about finite traces [19]. Hence, it is not clear whether HML actually surpasses the Android policy framework.

A more precise characterization is presented in [1]. There, the authors propose a different implementation of the Android permission system and policy language which substantially extend the existing one (being a proper subset). Their policy language includes propositional logic, using Android permissions as atomic propositions, and three modalities for declaring policies over the invocation of Android components. The modalities include

- *direct* $\triangledown$ rules, i.e., formulae that a caller must (individually) fulfil to perform an invocation;
- *local* $\diamondsuit$ rules, i.e., formulae that a component enforces over its ancestors and descendants in the invocation stack, and;
- *global* $\square$ rules, i.e., formulae that must be evaluated against all the running components as a whole.

---

[9] http://developer.android.com/guide/topics/admin/device-admin.html.
[10] Here α_{cam} stands for the Android API CameraManager.openCamera(...).

Moreover, a rule can be *sticky*, i.e., it is attached to the components interacting with the policy owner.

Android permissions are labels used to identify finite, disjoint sets of security-relevant operations/actions. For instance, several methods of the class Socket are associated to the permission $INTERNET$. Called $\mathbb{P}$ the set of all the permissions p and $\Lambda(p)$ the set of actions associated to p, we can assume $\mathsf{Act} = \bigcup_{p \in \mathbb{P}} \Lambda_p$. Under this assumption, UA are at least as powerful as the local rules of [1]. To exemplify, consider a component C declaring the policy $\Diamond \neg INTERNET$ which means that none of the components in the same stack of C can have the $INTERNET$ permission. The same behaviour can be obtained by defining $C = \varphi[e]$ where e is the implementation of the component and A_φ is

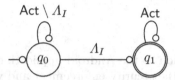

where Λ_I is a shorthand for $\Lambda_{INTERNET}$. Intuitively, a component can invoke C only if its trace contains no actions of Λ_I and, similarly, these actions cannot be performed by the components possibly invoked by C itself.

Since a UA can deal with (i) individual actions (rather than sets of indistinguishable elements) and (ii) ω-regular languages, they can express a wider class of policies than the local rules of [1]. Instead, global rules cannot be encoded as local policies without assuming a unique entry point for all the application executions, i.e., a root term/component invoking all the others. Summing up, we claim that the local policies defined through UA are strictly more expressive than the local rules of [1], but they cannot encode the global ones (under reasonable assumptions).

7   Discussion

Below we discuss some open aspect which are relevant for motivating the feasibility of the proposed approach and identifying possible limitations.

Applicability. There are typically two main objections to the application of local policies for web services: (i) the source code of web services is not available for the typing process (i.e., services are black boxes) and (ii) services appear/disappear continuously as the network is an extremely dynamic environment (i.e., it is very unlikely that a service is typed and executed under the same service repository). Interestingly, these two limitations do not affect the Android environment. As a matter of fact, Android applications consist of software packages containing the application bytecode. The bytecode contains all the instructions that an application executes. The type and effect system can be applied at install time, i.e., when an application is installed and its components registered in the system. Then, the verification process can be carried out whenever a new application is installed (which we can expect to happen not very frequently).

Implementation. Since the Android application framework is based on Java, we can follow the approach already used in [4,5]. Briefly, the Android developers attach their policies to the instructions contained in a Java block. Then, the compiler applies the type and effect system and attaches the generated history expressions to the Android package. History expressions can be added to the application manifest through dedicated XML tags. The code receiver, i.e., the mobile device, checks the history expressions by re-executing the typing rules or with other techniques, e.g., proof carrying code [21]. Finally, the model checker is executed to find possible policy violations. If no liveness policies are violated, (reference monitors controlling) the unverified safety policies are injected through instrumentation, e.g., as done in [15].

8   Conclusion

We presented an adaptation to the Android application framework of the approach proposed in [8] for the security enforcement and verification of local policies. Android IPC interaction resembles the invocation of web services in a closed environments (where services are known). Indeed, invocations carry a functional interface for specifying what components can answer the request. For this reason, the existing theory can be applied with minor adjustments also preserving the theoretical guarantees. We claim that local policies can support a compositional and fine-grained security framework for the Android OS.

Related work. In the last years, several authors targeted the Android security framework. Most of the existing proposals focus on (i) extending the native security policy, (ii) enhancing the Android Security Framework (ASF) with new tools for specific security-related checks, or (iii) detecting vulnerabilities and security threats. For instance, in [24] the (informal) Android security policy is analysed in terms of effectiveness and some extensions are proposed. Besides, in [20] the authors propose an extension to the basic Android permission systems and some new policies built on top of the extended permission system. Moreover, in [26] new privacy-related security policies are proposed for addressing security problems related to users' personal data. The authors of [22] propose a method for monitoring the Android permissions system by properly customizing the Android stack. Regarding detection, XManDroid [12] and Crowdroid [13] are currently the most effective malware detection approaches. Instead, [3] reported a vulnerability of the Android OS enabling a DoS attack, and [23] described some exploitable covert channels.

Some works also present formalizations of the Android application and security frameworks. In [25] the authors formalize the permission scheme of Android. Briefly, their formalization consists of a state-based model representing entities, relations and constraints over them. Also, they show how their formalism can be used to automatically verify that the permissions are respected. Another formalization of the Android permission system is presented in [1]. Intuitively, the authors describe the runtime composition of Android components and encode it as a satisfiability problem. Finally, a SAT solver automatically verifies whether an invocation can lead to policy violations. A language-based approach to infer security properties from Android applications is proposed by Chaudhuri [14]. The paper also proposes a type system that guarantees that well-typed programs respect user data access permissions. A type and effect system for generating history expressions from Android applications is proposed in [2]. There the authors also propose an alternative application market for the static verification of the mobile applications.

References

1. Armando, A., Carbone, R., Costa, G., Merlo, A.: Android permissions unleashed. In: Proceedings of the 28th IEEE Computer Security Foundations Symposium, CSF 2015, Italy, Verona (2015)
2. Armando, A., Costa, G., Merlo, A.: Bring your own device, securely. In: Proceedings of the 28th Annual ACM Symposium on Applied Computing, SAC 2013, Coimbra, Portugal, 18–22 March 2013, pp. 1852–1858 (2013)
3. Armando, A., Merlo, A., Migliardi, M., Verderame, L.: Would you mind forking this process? a denial of service attack on android (and some countermeasures). In: Gritzalis, D., Furnell, S., Theoharidou, M. (eds.) SEC 2012. IFIP AICT, vol. 376, pp. 13–24. Springer, Heidelberg (2012)
4. Bartoletti, M., Costa, G., Degano, P., Martinelli, F., Zunino, R.: Securing java with local policies. J. Object Technol. 8(4), 5–32 (2009)
5. Bartoletti, M., Costa, G., Zunino, R.: Jalapa: Securing java with local policies: Tool demonstration. Electr. Notes Theor. Comput. Sci. 253(5), 145–151 (2009)
6. Bartoletti, M., Degano, P., Ferrari, G.L.: Enforcing secure service composition. In: Proceedings of the 18th Computer Security Foundations Workshop (CSFW) (2005)
7. Bartolett, M., Degano, P., Ferrari, G.-L.: History-based access control with local policies. In: Sassone, V. (ed.) FOSSACS 2005. LNCS, vol. 3441, pp. 316–332. Springer, Heidelberg (2005)
8. Bartoletti, M., Degano, P., Ferrari, G.L.: Planning and verifying service composition. J. Comput. Secur. 17(5), 799–837 (2009)
9. Bartoletti, M., Degano, P., Ferrari, G.-L., Zunino, R.: Types and effects for resource usage analysis. In: Seidl, H. (ed.) FOSSACS 2007. LNCS, vol. 4423, pp. 32–47. Springer, Heidelberg (2007)
10. Bartoletti, M., Degano, P., Ferrari, G.L., Zunino, R.: Model checking usage policies. Math. Struct. Comput. Sci. 25(3), 710–763 (2015)
11. Bartoletti, M., Zunino, R.: LocUsT: a tool for checking usage policies. Technical report TR-08-07, Dip. Informatica, Univ. Pisa (2008)
12. Bugiel, S., Davi, L., Dmitrienko, A., Fischer, T., Sadeghi, A.-R.: Xmandroid: a new android evolution to mitigate privilege escalation attacks. Technical report TR-2011-04, Technische Univ. Darmstadt, April 2011
13. Burguera, I., Zurutuza, U., Nadjm-Therani, S.: Crowdroid: behavior-based malware detection system for android. In: Proceedings of the 1st ACM Workshop on Security and Privacy in Smartphones and Mobile Devices (SPSM 2011) (2011)
14. Chaudhuri, A.: Language-based security on android. In: Proceedings of the ACM SIGPLAN Fourth Workshop on Programming Languages and Analysis for Security, PLAS 2009, pp. 1–7. ACM, New York (2009)

15. Costa, G., Martinelli, F., Mori, P., Schaefer, C., Walter, T.: Runtime monitoring for next generation java ME platform. Comput. Secur. **29**(1), 74–87 (2010)
16. Enck, W., Octeau, D., McDaniel, P., Chaudhuri, S.: A study of android application security. In: Proceedings of the 20th USENIX Conference on Security, SEC 2011, p. 21. USENIX Association, Berkeley (2011)
17. Felt, A.P., Chin, E., Hanna, S., Song, D., Wagner, D.: Android permissions demystified. In: Proceedings of the 18th ACM Conference on Computer and Communications Security, CCS 2011, pp. 627–638. ACM, New York (2011)
18. Felt, A.P., Hanna, S., Chin, E., Wang, H.J., Moshchuk, E.: Permission redelegation: attacks and defenses. In: 20th Usenix Security Symposium (2011)
19. Furia, C.A., Mandrioli, D., Morzenti, A., Rossi, M.: Modeling Time in Computing. Monographs in Theoretical Computer Science. An EATCS Series. Springer, Heidelberg (2012)
20. Nauman, M., Khan, S., Zhang, X.: Apex: extending android permission model and enforcement with user-defined runtime constraints. In: Proceedings of the 5th ACM Symposium on Information, Computer and Communications Security, ASIACCS 2010, pp. 328–332. ACM, New York (2010)
21. Necula, G.C.: Proof-carrying code. In: Twenty-Fourth ACM Symposium on Principles of Programming Languages (1997)
22. Ongtang, M., Mclaughlin, S., Enck, W., Mcdaniel, P.: Semantically rich application-centric security in android. In: ACSAC 2009: Annual Computer Security Applications Conference (2009)
23. Schlegel, R., Zhang, K., Zhou, X., Intwala, M., Kapadia, A., Wang, X.: Soundcomber: a stealthy and context-aware sound trojan for smartphones. In: Proceedings of the 18th Annual Network & Distributed System Security Symposium (2011)
24. Shabtai, A., Fledel, Y., Kanonov, U., Elovici, Y., Dolev, S., Glezer, C.: Google android: a comprehensive security assessment. IEEE Secur. Priv. **8**(2), 35–44 (2010)
25. Shin, W., Kiyomoto, S., Fukushima, K., Tanaka, T.: A formal model to analyze the permission authorization and enforcement in the android framework. In: Proceedings of the 2010 IEEE Second International Conference on Social Computing, SOCIALCOM 2010, pp. 944–951. IEEE Computer Society, Washington, DC (2010)
26. Zhou, Y., Zhang, X., Jiang, X., Freeh, V.W.: Taming information-stealing smartphone applications (on android). In: Beres, Y., Balacheff, B., Sadeghi, A.-R., Sasse, A., McCune, J.M., Perrig, A. (eds.) TRUST 2011. LNCS, vol. 6740, pp. 93–107. Springer, Heidelberg (2011)

Global Protocol Implementations via Attribute-Based Communication

Rocco De Nicola$^{(\boxtimes)}$, Claudio Antares Mezzina$^{(\boxtimes)}$, and Hugo Torres Vieira$^{(\boxtimes)}$

IMT Institute for Advanced Studies Lucca, Lucca, Italy
{rocco.denicola,claudio.mezzina,hugotvieira}@imtlucca.it

Abstract. Several type systems have been developed to address the conformance between specifications and implementations, where types are specifications and type-checking ensures the conformance relation. In this paper, we take a different perspective and assume that programming takes place only at the specification level, by using a type language that captures protocols of interaction. Specifications provide the global interaction scheme and lay the basis for an automatic (provably correct) generation of implementations. The latter is obtained by a translation into a rich formalism that relies on attribute-based communication, whose expressiveness permits modeling in a natural way the symmetric link between message recipient and emitter.

1 Introduction

Distribution is becoming a default condition of computing systems such as databases hosted in cloud providers or services that support personal and professional interaction, not to mention the materialization of the internet of things paradigm that will allow our refrigerators to automatically shop on our behalf. To carry out their tasks, such systems crucially rely on *interaction* for the purpose of coordination or to pass information around. Distributed parties must then agree on a common protocol of interaction in order to establish productive collaborations. For unproductive examples, consider that one party is trying to send a message that nobody will ever be willing to receive, or that some other party is waiting for a message that will never arrive.

Reasoning on protocols of interaction is naturally carried out by considering the *global* interaction scheme. Indeed, to understand the functioning of distributed systems it is certainly more adequate to reason on the global interaction scheme rather than considering individually the *local* views of the different components. For example, in the context of business protocols one typically specifies system behavior considering a global view, and only afterwards she/he considers compliance of the actual implementation with the global specification. The implementation is carried out by assembling different components each providing its individual contribution to achieve the prescribed goal. We illustrate the notions of global and local views in Fig. 1, by means of a protocol adapted from [11].

© Springer International Publishing Switzerland 2015
C. Bodei et al. (Eds.): Degano Festschrift, LNCS 9465, pp. 219–237, 2015.
DOI: 10.1007/978-3-319-25527-9_15

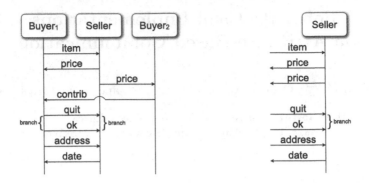

Fig. 1. Global and local protocol views

This problem of relating global specifications with their distributed implementation has been addressed in the context of type systems based on multiparty asynchronous session types by Honda, Yoshida and Carbone in [11]. There, specifications are given in the form of *global types* that are related to local types via a projection mechanism. *Local types* are, in turn, related to site-level implementations via a typing relation. Recent approaches focus on releasing the burden of a typed framework by synthesizing (inferring) the global types out of the implementations [13] and by considering an intermediate specification language somewhat in between global types and implementations [4], the latter being inspired by the global protocol implementation language introduced in [3]. However, such approaches heavily rely on typing to ensure the overall soundness of the framework.

In this paper, inspired by [3,4], we concentrate on specifications: given that global specifications are the natural setting for reasoning on protocol correctness, we consider them also as a natural programming mechanism. Then, in order to transform global specifications in (concrete) implementations, we provide an automatic translation mechanism that permits synthesizing *correct by construction* site-level implementations that guarantee conformance with the interaction protocol prescribed by the global specifications. As target of our transformation function we use a rich formalism called AbC [1,2] that relies on a powerful communication model based on attributes. Communication takes place in a broadcast fashion and communication links among components are dynamically established by taking into account interdependences determined by predicates over attributes. The AbC formalism permits modeling not only related sets of interactions (*sessions*) but also singling out the participants involved at each step of the protocol, even when multiple participants have access to the communication medium.

We view our contribution as a proof of concept of an approach that aims at developing behavior domain specific languages which are related to (more) general purpose programming languages in a rigorous way. Such precise relation supports the transference of properties from one language to the other, so any analysis performed on top of the specification can be directly conveyed to the implementation, eliminating the conformance burden and lifting specification languages to first-class actors in software development.

In the remainder of the document, we first introduce the language for global protocol specification (Sect. 2) and the AbC formalism (Sect. 3). Then we present the encoding of the former into the second (Sect. 4) and discuss its adequacy (Sect. 5). A final section contains some concluding remark and suggestions for future work.

2   Global Protocol Specifications

Our starting point is the language of global types introduced in [11], which we adapt here to serve as language for global protocol specifications that explicitly specifies the interactions between the different components. An interaction between parties A and B, in particular the case where A sends a message to B, is denoted by $A \to B$. We assume that in our model messages are *labelled*, i.e., two parties interact if one is willing to send a message with label ℓ and the other is willing to receive a message with the same label. For the sake of simplicity, we omit communicated values and argue they can be added in a simple, or at least orthogonal, way with respect to the development reported in this document.

We then denote by $A \to B(\ell).G$ a synchronization of A and B on message ℓ, after which the protocol proceeds to the stage specified by G. This basic interaction construct is included (as a particular case) in a richer communication primitive which can be used to specify alternative behaviors. We denote by $A \to B\{\ell_i.G_i\}_{i \in I}$ a synchronization between parties A and B on either one of the ℓ_i messages (where $i \in I$), after which the protocol proceeds to the corresponding G_i, being the choice determined by the emitting party. For example $Buyer \to Seller\{\texttt{accept}.G_1; \texttt{reject}.G_2\}$ represents a synchronization between parties *Buyer* and *Seller* on either an $\texttt{accept}$ or a $\texttt{reject}$ message, and the choice will determine whether to proceed as specified by G_1 and G_2. It is the *Buyer* responsibility to (internally) choose which one, while the *Seller* is ready to synchronize on either of the (externally) chosen ones.

Example 1. Consider the following protocol specification in which a buyer (B_1) wants to buy an item from a seller (S), then the seller sends the price both to the original buyer and to a second buyer (B_2) who is willing to contribute to the purchase. After that, B_2 communicates to B_1 the amount to which he can contribute to the purchase and B_1 communicates to the seller whether the price is fine for him or not; in the former case he also sends his address and sets himself to receive a date for the delivery.

$$G = B_1 \to S(\texttt{item}).S \to B_1(\texttt{price}).S \to B_2(\texttt{price}).B_2 \to B_1(\texttt{contrib}).$$
$$B_1 \to S\{\texttt{ok}.B_1 \to S(\texttt{address}).S \to B_1(\texttt{date}) + \texttt{quit}.\texttt{end}\}$$

Protocols may also be specified using a parallel composition, denoted by $G_1 \parallel G_2$, a terminated protocol $\texttt{end}$, and recursion $\mu X.G$ which, combined with a recursion variable X, supports the specification of infinite behaviors. The complete syntax for global protocols is presented in Fig. 2, where we assume given an infinite set of participant names $\mathcal{N}$, ranged over by A, B, C, an infinite set of labels $\mathcal{L}$, ranged over by ℓ, and an infinite set of recursion variables X, ranged over by X, Y, Z.

$$G ::= A \to B\{\ell_i.G_i\}_{i \in I} \mid G_1 \parallel G_2 \mid \textbf{end} \mid \mu X.G \mid X$$

Fig. 2. Syntax of global protocols

In order to single out the sort of protocols we are interested in, we introduce some auxiliary (syntactic) notions. We denote by $\mathbf{n}(G)$ the set of all participant's names of a global protocol G and by $\mathbf{rn}(G)$ the set of participants names which are ready to output a message. The two sets are inductively defined as follows.

$$\mathbf{n}(G) \triangleq \begin{cases} \{A, B\} \cup \bigcup_{i \in I} \mathbf{n}(G_i) & \text{if } G = A \to B\{\ell_i.G_i\}_{i \in I} \\ \mathbf{n}(G_1) \cup \mathbf{n}(G_2) & \text{if } G = G_1 \parallel G_2 \\ \varnothing & \text{if } G = \textbf{end} \\ \varnothing & \text{if } G = X \\ \mathbf{n}(G') & \text{if } G = \mu X.G' \end{cases}$$

$$\mathbf{rn}(G) \triangleq \begin{cases} \{A\} & \text{if } G = A \to B\{\ell_i.G_i\}_{i \in I} \\ \mathbf{rn}(G_1) \cup \mathbf{rn}(G_2) & \text{if } G = G_1 \parallel G_2 \\ \varnothing & \text{if } G = \textbf{end} \\ \varnothing & \text{if } G = X \\ \mathbf{rn}(G') & \text{if } G = \mu X.G' \end{cases}$$

The set of participants is useful to identify *independent* parts of a protocol, while the set of active emitting parties is used to single out those parties that are willing to emit messages. Both notions are used to capture *well-formed* global protocols, defined next.

Definition 1 (Well-formedness). *A global protocol G is well formed, if $\vdash G$ can be derived using the rules given in Fig. 3.*

$$\vdash \textbf{end} \qquad \vdash X \qquad \frac{\vdash G_1 \qquad \vdash G_2 \qquad \mathbf{n}(G_1) \cap \mathbf{n}(G_2) = \varnothing}{\vdash G_1 \parallel G_2}$$

$$\frac{\forall i \quad \vdash G_i \qquad A \neq B \qquad \mathbf{rn}(G_i) \subseteq \{A, B\}}{\vdash A \to B\{\ell_i.G_i\}_{i \in I}} \qquad \frac{\vdash G\{{}^G/_X\}}{\vdash \mu X.G}$$

Fig. 3. Rules for well-formed global protocols

Our notion of well-formedness is in line with the linearity conditions imposed to global types in [11]. Let us now comment on rules of Fig. 3. The terminated protocol and the recursion variable are well formed. The parallel composition is well formed only if the two branches are well formed and independent. Independence is guaranteed by disjointness of the sets of participants. Notice that communication is captured by the interaction construct $(\cdot \to \cdot)$, so parallel composition is different from the one found in many process algebra.

In $A \to B\{\ell_i.G_i\}$ we also enforce that it is either A or B to initiate synchronizations in any of the G_i branches. The rationale for this choice is message loss in the underlying broadcast-like communication model: if the emitting party is already active to send a message and the receiving party is not yet listening then the message may be lost. We have grounded our presentation on a *synchronous* communication model, which is not to be viewed as an imposition on the implementation, but in our target implementation language message outputs are carried out in a "fire and forget" fashion: if the receiving party is ready then the message is received, otherwise the message is lost. Whenever necessary we may introduce some additional communication steps in our protocol descriptions so as to ensure parties are listening before sending messages.

Finally, the recursive protocol is well formed if the one step unfolding is well formed. The one step unfolding is enough for our purposes as (i) recursive protocols that include parallel compositions are excluded due to the independence condition (ii) participants willing to send a message in the next iteration must be involved in the last interaction of the current iteration. Both conditions will then hold for any number of unfoldings and protocol evolutions. To ensure the unfolding is carried out only once while proving a protocol is well formed we (pragmatically) replace the variable by the recursion body only and not by the entire recursion. We assume recursive protocols are contractive, i.e., all variables are guarded by an interaction construct, and that all variables are bound.

We now define the semantics of our protocol language, to endow the language with a rigorous notion of behavior, which is instrumental for the establishment of an operational correspondence between the specification and the implementation. In particular, the semantics keeps track of the synchronization information in the transition labels, in order to establish the direct correspondence between global protocols and site-level implementations. Transition labels are of the form $A \to B(\ell)$, mentioning the parties involved in the synchronization and the message label. We use α to range over the set of such transition labels, denoted by $\mathcal{I}$ and defined by $\mathcal{I} = \{A \to B(\ell) \mid A, B \in \mathcal{N} \wedge \ell \in \mathcal{L}\}$.

We write $G \xrightarrow{\alpha} G'$ to say that protocol G evolves in one step to protocol G' via synchronization α, if such transition can be derived using the rules in Fig. 4.

Well-formedness is invariant under protocol evolutions, as expressed in the following proposition.

Proposition 1. *If* $\vdash G$ *and* $G \xrightarrow{\alpha} G'$ *then* $\vdash G'$.

Proof. By induction on the derivation of $G \xrightarrow{\alpha} G'$ following expected lines. □

$$\frac{G\{^{\mu X.G}/x\} \xrightarrow{\alpha} G'}{\mu X.G \xrightarrow{\alpha} G'} \qquad \frac{k \in I}{A \to B\{\ell_i.G_i\}_{i \in I} \xrightarrow{A \to B(\ell_k)} G_k} \qquad \frac{G_1 \xrightarrow{\alpha} G_1'}{G_1 \parallel G_2 \xrightarrow{\alpha} G_1' \parallel G_2}$$

$$\frac{G_2 \xrightarrow{\alpha} G_2'}{G_1 \parallel G_2 \xrightarrow{\alpha} G_1 \parallel G_2'}$$

Fig. 4. Protocol operational semantics

A direct corollary of Proposition 1 is that well-formed protocols never reach ill-formed configurations.

3   AbC

Having defined the language for global protocol descriptions we now present the site-level implementation language, AbC [2], a core calculus centered on attribute-based communication. We introduce a simplified version of AbC in the sense that we abstract away from value passing. Systems in AbC are represented as sets of parallel components. Each component is equipped with a set of attributes whose values can be modified by means of internal actions. Communication among components takes place in a broadcast fashion, with the distinctive feature that only components satisfying the predicate specified by the emitting party over specific attributes receive a given message, provided that they are willing to do so and that the emitter also satisfies the predicates specified by the recipients. The semantics for output actions in AbC is non-blocking while input actions are blocking in that they can only take place through synchronization with an available broadcasted message. Since we abstract away from value passing, broadcasts here can be viewed as multiparty synchronization. Hence we say that a process initiates a multiparty synchronization or that it is waiting for one.

Syntax and Semantics. The syntax of AbC is reported in Fig. 5. A system in AbC consists of a number of *components*. A component C can be either the null component $\mathbf{0}$, the *process* P with a set of *attributes* Γ, written $\Gamma : P$, or the

(*Components*)	$C ::= \mathbf{0} \mid \Gamma : P \mid C_1 \parallel C_2$
(*Processes*)	$P ::= \mathbf{0} \mid \Pi.P \mid @\Pi.P \mid [a := v].P \mid P_1 + P_2 \mid \mu X.P \mid X$
(*Predicates*)	$\Pi ::= \mathbf{tt} \mid a = v \mid \Pi_1 \wedge \Pi_2 \mid \neg \Pi$

Fig. 5. AbC syntax

$$\Gamma \models \mathbf{tt} \quad \text{for all } \Gamma \qquad\qquad \Gamma \models a = v \text{ if } \Gamma(a) = v$$
$$\Gamma \models \Pi_1 \wedge \Pi_2 \text{ if } \Gamma \models \Pi_1 \text{ and } \Gamma \models \Pi_2 \qquad \Gamma \models \neg \Pi \text{ if not } \Gamma \models \Pi$$

Fig. 6. Predicate satisfaction

parallel composition $C_1 \parallel C_2$ of two components. In a component $\Gamma : P$ we refer to Γ as the attribute environment. We denote by $\mathcal{C}$ and $\mathcal{P}$ respectively the set of AbC components and AbC processes.

A process P can be either the idle process $\mathbf{0}$, an action prefixed process, a choice $P_1 + P_2$ between two processes, the recursive process $\mu X.P$ or a process variable X. There are three kinds of action prefixes. The attribute-based *input* Π waits for a synchronization from any process whose attributes satisfy the predicate Π; the attribute-based *output* $@\Pi$ initiates a synchronization to all the processes whose attributes satisfy the predicate Π; and the attribute update $[a := v]$ sets to v the value of attribute a.

We let variables a, b and their decorated versions to range over the set $\mathcal{A}$ of all attributes. Moreover we let v and its decorated versions to range over the set $\mathcal{V}$ of all possible attribute values. An environment of attributes Γ is a function $\Gamma : \mathcal{A} \rightarrow \mathcal{V}$; we write $\Gamma(a)$ to indicate the value of the attribute a in the environment Γ. A *predicate* Π can be either tt, or a check on the value of a particular attribute (e.g. $a = v$), or the logic conjunction of two predicates $\Pi_1 \wedge \Pi_2$, or the negation of a predicate $\neg\Pi$. We denote by $\Gamma[a \mapsto v]$ the update of Γ defined as $\Gamma[a \mapsto v](a') = \Gamma(a')$ if $a \neq a'$, v otherwise.

A predicate Π is satisfied by an environment Γ, written $\Gamma \models \Pi$, if $\Gamma \models \Pi$ can be derived by rules in Fig. 6. Predicate tt is satisfied by any environment Γ; predicate $a = v$ is satisfied by Γ only if a belongs to the domain of Γ and its value is equal to v; predicate $\Pi_1 \wedge \Pi_2$ is satisfied by Γ if both Π_1 and Π_2 are satisfied by Γ; predicate $\neg\Pi$ is satisfied by Γ if Γ does not satisfy Π.

(E.PARC) $C_1 \parallel C_2 \equiv C_2 \parallel C_1$ (E.PARA) $C_1 \parallel (C_2 \parallel C_3) \equiv (C_1 \parallel C_2) \parallel C_3$

(E.PARN) $C \parallel \mathbf{0} \equiv C$ (E.GB) $\Gamma : \mathbf{0} \equiv \mathbf{0}$ (E.CHN) $P + \mathbf{0} \equiv P$

(E.CHC) $P_1 + P_2 \equiv P_2 + P_1$ (E.CHA) $P_1 + (P_2 + P_3) \equiv (P_1 + P_2) + P_3$

(E.PR) $\Gamma : P_1 \equiv \Gamma : P_2$ if $P_1 \equiv P_2$ (E.REC) $\mu X.P \equiv P\{\mu X.P/X\}$

Fig. 7. Structural congruence for AbC

We use $\mathcal{U}$ to refer to the set of all possible assignments of the form $[a := v]$, and $\mathcal{S}$ to refer to the set of all possible synchronization predicates of the form $(\Pi, \Pi_{i \in 1..n})$. We let u and its decorated versions to range over $\mathcal{U}$, and s to range over $\mathcal{S}$, while we let β to range over the set $\mathcal{U} \cup \mathcal{S}$. The operational semantics of AbC is defined via a (labelled) reduction relation over components $\rightarrow \subseteq \mathcal{C} \times (\mathcal{U} \cup \mathcal{S}) \times \mathcal{C}$ and a structural congruence relation $\equiv$, which is a binary relation over processes and components $\equiv \subseteq \mathcal{P}^2 \times \mathcal{C}^2$. Relation $\equiv$ is defined as the smallest congruence on processes and components that satisfies the rules in Fig. 7. Rules E.PARC, E.PARA and E.PARN correspond to the classical commutative monoid laws for parallel $\parallel$ (*associativity*, *commutativity* and identity $\mathbf{0}$); while rules E.CHN, E.CHC, and E.CHA model the commutative monoid

$$(\text{EQV}) \; \frac{C \equiv C_1 \quad C_1 \xrightarrow{\beta} C_2 \quad C_2 \equiv C'}{C \xrightarrow{\beta} C'}$$

$$(\text{UPD}) \; \Gamma : [a := v].P + Q \parallel C \xrightarrow{[a:=v]} \Gamma[a \mapsto v] : P \parallel C$$

$$(\text{COM}) \; \frac{\forall i \quad \Gamma \models \Pi_i \quad \Gamma_i \models \Pi \quad \text{notr}(C,\Gamma,\Pi)}{\Gamma : @\Pi.P + Q \parallel \prod_{i=1}^{n} \Gamma_i : \Pi_i.P_i + Q_i \parallel C \xrightarrow{\Pi,\Pi_{i..n}} \Gamma : P \parallel \prod_{i=1}^{n} \Gamma_i : P_i \parallel C}$$

$$\text{notr}(C,\Gamma,\Pi) \text{ if } C \not\equiv \Gamma' : \Pi'.P + Q \parallel C' \text{ with } \Gamma' \models \Pi \text{ and } \Gamma \models \Pi'$$

Fig. 8. Transition rules for AbC

laws for choice $+$ (with identity $\mathbf{0}$). Rule E.GB allows for the garbage collection of a component $\Gamma : \mathbf{0}$ that has finished its computation, rule E.PR supports lifting equivalence from process level to component level, and rule E.REC deals with unfolding/folding of recursive processes.

The relation $\longrightarrow$ is defined as the smallest binary relation on components that satisfies the rules of Fig. 8. Rule EQV states that the reduction relation is closed under structural congruence $\equiv$. Rule UPD allows a process to update its attribute environment. Rule COM regulates the multiparty synchronization: when in the system there is an *emitter* $\Gamma : @\Pi.P$ then all *listener* components $\Gamma_i : \Pi_i.P_i$ of the system that can synchronize evolve accordingly. A listener component $\Gamma_i : \Pi_i.P_i$ is able to synchronize if its environment satisfies the emitter predicate and its predicate is satisfied by the emitter environment, that is $\Gamma \models \Pi_i$ and $\Gamma_i \models \Pi$. Condition $\text{notr}(C,\Gamma,\Pi)$, in the premises of the rule, specifies that there are no other enabled listeners in the system so as to ensure that all the available ones synchronize; said otherwise a listener cannot avoid taking part in a synchronization for which it is enabled. Notation $\prod_{i=1}^{n} C_i$ stands for $C_1 \parallel \ldots \parallel C_n$, where there is no need to indicate how the latter expression is parenthesized because the parallel operator is associative by rule E.PARA. When $n = 0$ we have that $\prod_{i=1}^{n} C_i = \mathbf{0}$.

4   Synthesis of Global Protocols in AbC

We now define the synthesis from global protocol specifications to AbC.

Definition 2 (Synthesis). *The synthesis* $[\![\cdot]\!] : \mathcal{G} \to \mathcal{C}$ *is a partial function from a global protocol specification to an* AbC *component, defined on top of the function* $(\![\cdot]\!) : \mathcal{G} \times \mathcal{N} \to \mathcal{P}$, *which is a partial function from a pair global protocol specification, party name to an* AbC *process. Both functions are given in Fig. 9.*

Before commenting on the synthesis procedure, let us explain the general idea behind it. Each site (or party) of a global specification G is translated into a component $\Gamma : P$ where the attribute environment exhibits two attributes (with their respective values): *id* and *lab*. We assume that names *id* and *lab* are fixed and distinct and are reserved to the synthesis function. As the name suggests *id* is the attribute used to distinguish the identity of the site, and its value is set to the site name (e.g., A), while attribute *lab* is used for branch selection during the communication. These two attributes are sufficient to guarantee that whenever in the global specification there is an interaction $A \to B\{\ell_i.G_I\}_{i \in I}$, between sites A and B, then site A will communicate only with site B, and site B will synchronize on a specific label only with site A, being both conditions ensured by the predicates over the two attributes.

The synthesis $[\![G]\!]$ is defined as the parallel composition of the synthesis of its sites, as shown in Fig. 9. Let us note that each site is endowed with an attribute environment containing the pair (id, A) with $A \in \mathsf{n}(G)$ being the identity of the party. In this way each AbC (local) component generated by the synthesis is univocally identified by its *id* attribute. The synthesis of a global specification G with respect to a site A is given by the function $(\![G]\!)_A$.

The synthesis of a global specification $(\![A \to B\{\ell_i.G_i\}_{i \in I}]\!)_C$, with $A, B, C \in \mathcal{N}$, has three possible behaviors depending on the fact that:

$C = A$: we encode the interaction between A and B by first specifying that A has to choose a particular label ℓ_i among the prescribed set ($i \in I$). This is achieved by composing a sum of processes of the form $[lab := \ell_i].@(id = B).(\![G_i]\!)_A$, leaving the branch selection to be performed via attribute update. Hence first the processes internally chooses a label and then communicates its choice to the party B (which is the only component exhibiting the pair (id, B)).

$C = B$: we encode that B receives from A a particular branch selection via a specific label ℓ_i. This is why the result is a sum of processes of the form $(id = A) \wedge (lab = \ell_i).(\![G_i]\!)$ indicating the fact that each process in the summation is able to synchronize with the component whose identity is A on any particular label ℓ_i, where the summation includes the set of prescribed labels.

$C \neq A$ and $C \neq B$: the party C is not directly involved in the communication, in which case we impose that in all branches the behavior of C has to be the same (as in [11]), hence the translation corresponds to one of the branches.

The synthesis of a parallel composition $G_1 \parallel G_2$ with respect to a site C is defined as the parallel composition of the synthesis of G_1 and G_2. Notice that in a well-formed protocol site C will only be involved in at most one of the parallel branches, so we are only interested in the case when at least one the underlying synthesis (of G_1 or G_2) yields process $\mathbf{0}$. Recursion operator is mapped into the corresponding operator of AbC, where we distinguish between the case where site C has a role in the recursive protocol from the one he has none, so as to avoid degenerate processes (e.g., $\mu X.\mathbf{end}$). Specification recursion variable X is mapped into the same (process) recursion variable X. Terminated protocol specification $\mathbf{end}$ is translated into the idle process $\mathbf{0}$.

$$[\![G]\!] \triangleq \prod_{A \in \mathsf{n}(G)} \{(id, A)\} : (\![G]\!)_A$$

$$(\![A \to B\{\ell_i.G_i\}_{i \in I}]\!)_A \triangleq \sum_{i \in I} [lab := \ell_i].@(id = B).(\![G_i]\!)_A$$

$$(\![A \to B\{\ell_i.G_i\}_{i \in I}]\!)_B \triangleq \sum_{i \in I} (id = A) \wedge (lab = \ell_i).(\![G_i]\!)_B$$

$$(\![A \to B\{\ell_i.G_i\}_{i \in I}]\!)_C \triangleq (\![G_k]\!)_C \ \text{ if } \forall_{i \in I} (\![G_i]\!)_C = (\![G_k]\!)_C \text{ for } k \in I \text{ and } A \neq C \neq B$$

$$(\![G_1 \parallel G_2]\!)_C \triangleq (\![G_1]\!)_C \parallel (\![G_2]\!)_C$$

$$(\![\mu X.G]\!)_C \triangleq \mu X.(\![G]\!)_C \ \text{ if } C \in \mathsf{n}(G)$$

$$(\![\mu X.G]\!)_C \triangleq \mathbf{0} \ \text{ if } C \notin \mathsf{n}(G)$$

$$(\![X]\!)_C \triangleq X$$

$$(\![\mathtt{end}]\!)_C \triangleq \mathbf{0}$$

Fig. 9. Synthesis of global protocol specifications in AbC

To better understand how the synthesis works, let us consider the following example, where we use $\Pi_{\{A,\ell\}}$ to denote the predicate $(id = A) \wedge (lab = \ell)$ that is used in inputs to refer to the id of the message emitter and to the label ℓ of the message, and Π_A to denote the predicate $(id = A)$ used in outputs to refer to the id of the message receiver.

Example 2. Consider the global protocol specification of Example 1:

$$G = B_1 \to S(\mathtt{item}).S \to B_1(\mathtt{price}).S \to B_2(\mathtt{price}).B_2 \to B_1(\mathtt{contrib}).$$
$$B_1 \to S\{\mathtt{ok}.B_1 \to S(\mathtt{address}).S \to B_1(\mathtt{date}) + \mathtt{quit.end}\}$$

Then the synthesis of G in AbC is given in Fig. 10, given $\mathsf{n}(G) = \{B_1, S, B_2\}$.

$$[\![G]\!] \quad = \quad \{(id, B_1)\} : Buyer_1 \parallel \{(id, S)\} : Seller \parallel \{(id, B_2)\} : Buyer_2$$

$$Buyer_1 \quad = \quad [lab := \mathtt{item}].@(id = S).\Pi_{\{S,\mathtt{price}\}}.\Pi_{\{B_2,\mathtt{contrib}\}}.$$
$$([lab := \mathtt{ok}]@(id = S).[lab := \mathtt{address}]@(id = S).\Pi_{\{S,\mathtt{date}\}}.\mathbf{0}$$
$$+ [lab := \mathtt{quit}]@(id = S).\mathbf{0})$$

$$Seller \quad = \quad \Pi_{\{B_1,\mathtt{item}\}}.[lab := \mathtt{price}]@(id = B_1).[lab := \mathtt{price}]@(id = B_2).$$
$$(\Pi_{\{B_1,\mathtt{ok}\}}.\Pi_{\{B_1,\mathtt{address}\}}.[lab := \mathtt{date}]@(id = B_1).\mathbf{0}$$
$$+ \Pi_{\{B_1,\mathtt{quit}\}}.\mathbf{0})$$

$$Buyer_2 \quad = \quad \Pi_{\{S,\mathtt{price}\}}.[lab := \mathtt{contrib}]@(id = B_1).\mathbf{0}$$

Fig. 10. Encoding example

5 Operational Correspondence

In this section we establish a precise operational correspondence between our protocol description language and the site level implementations in AbC generated by the synthesis. The semantics of the languages presented earlier, where transitions record synchronization information, supports the establishment of a precise correspondence between each interaction in the global protocols and a corresponding environment update (mimicking a choice) plus a communication step in AbC. The actual semantics may be viewed as an instrumentation (adding labels to reductions) of an unlabelled reduction relation like the one in, e.g., [2]; such an instrumentation does not add or remove any behavior from the models, it simply decorates the behavioral trees with extra information.

Since the dynamic semantics of the synthesis involves environment updates which are not initially prescribed by the synthesis, our results are parameterized by environment updates. We introduce some auxiliary notation to handle environment updates. We use σ to refer to an environment update based on a partial function from participant names to message labels $\sigma : \mathcal{N} \to \mathcal{L}$. Moreover, given a component C, we denote by $\sigma(C)$ the extension of the local environments in C defined as $\sigma(\mathbf{0}) = \mathbf{0}$, $\sigma(C_1 \parallel C_2) = \sigma(C_1) \parallel \sigma(C_2)$ and $\sigma(\Gamma : P) = (\sigma(\Gamma)) : P$. The environment update is defined as $\sigma(\Gamma) = \Gamma[lab \mapsto \ell]$ if $(id, A) \in \Gamma$ and $\sigma(A) = \ell$ otherwise $\sigma(\Gamma) = \Gamma$, hence the environment is updated accordingly depending on whether σ specifies an update for a specific participant or not.

As a first step, we prove some auxiliary results that focus on single-threaded global protocols, and we establish a normal form characterization of the result of a synthesis. We start by ensuring that in a sequential protocol there is only one party actively willing to emit an output, or, in other words, all parties except one are waiting on a message input.

Lemma 1. *Let G be such that $\vdash G$, $[\![G]\!]$ is defined and either $G = A \to A'\{\ell_i.G_i\}_{i \in I}$ or $G = \mu X.A \to A'\{\ell_i.G_i\}_{i \in I}$. For all B such that $B \neq A$ we have that there exist B', ℓ'_i, G'_i, for i in some I', such that $(\![G]\!)_B \equiv \sum_{i \in I'}(id = B') \wedge (lab = \ell'_i).\,(\![G'_i]\!)_B$.*

Proof. By induction on the definition of $(\![G]\!)_B$. We note that, by well-formedness, all emitting parties must be engaged in the previous interaction, which leaves out only the one emitting in the first interaction (A). The case for recursion amounts to unfolding at the level of the target language. □

From Lemma 1 and considering the definition of synthesis we may now characterize in a precise way the structure of the result of a synthesis.

Proposition 2 (Synthesis Normal Form). *Let G be such that $\vdash G$, $[\![G]\!]$ is defined and either $G = A \to A'\{\ell_i.G_i\}_{i \in I}$ or $G = \mu X.A \to A'\{\ell_i.G_i\}_{i \in I}$. We have that:*

$$\sigma([\![G]\!]) \equiv \sigma(\{(id, A)\}) : \sum_{i \in I}[lab := \ell_i].@(id = A').\,(\![G_i]\!)_A$$
$$\parallel \sigma(\{(id, A')\}) : \sum_{i \in I}(id = A) \wedge (lab = \ell_i).\,(\![G_i]\!)_{A'}$$
$$\parallel \prod_{B \in \mathtt{n}(G) \setminus \{A, A'\}} \sigma(\{(id, B)\}) : (\![G_k]\!)_B$$

for any $k \in I$, *where, for every* $B \in n(G) \setminus \{A, A'\}$ *we have that there exist* B', ℓ'_i, G'_i *for* i *in some* I' *such that* $(\!|G_k|\!)_B \equiv \sum_{i \in I'} (id = B') \wedge (lab = \ell'_i).(\!|G'_i|\!)_B.$

Proof. Immediate by Definition 2 (Synthesis) and by Lemma 1. We remark that the synthesis for parties not involved in the initial interaction is guaranteed, by definition, to be the same for all branches, so we may take any of them.   □

We also introduce the principle required to handle recursive protocols.

Lemma 2. *If* $\vdash \mu X.G$ *and* $[\![G]\!]$ *is defined then* $\sigma([\![\mu X.G]\!]) \equiv \sigma([\![G\{^{\mu X.G}/_X\}]\!])$.

Proof. By induction on the definition of $\sigma([\![\mu X.G]\!])$ following standard lines.   □

In order to establish the wanted results about operational correspondence, we define a function that allows us to rewrite (back and forth) the transition labels of one model in the other, and introduce some auxiliary notation.

Definition 3 (Transition Label Correspondence). *We take* f *as a function* $f : \mathcal{I} \to \mathcal{U} \times \mathcal{S}$ *defined as* $f(A \to B(\ell_i)) = ([lab := \ell_i], (\Pi_B, \Pi_{\{A, \ell_i\}}))$ *and its inverse* $f^{-1} : \mathcal{U} \times \mathcal{S} \to \mathcal{I}.$

In the following, we write $C \xrightarrow{f(\alpha)} C_1$ instead of $C \xrightarrow{u} C' \xrightarrow{s} C_1$, with $f(\alpha) = (u, s)$. Also, we use σ_α defined as $\sigma_\alpha(A) = \ell$ for $\alpha = A \to B(\ell)$ and $\sigma_\alpha \circ \sigma$ to refer to the composition of σ_α and σ. We use σ to capture the environment updates throughout system evolution, so as to match the updates caused by internal choices associated to message outputs. We now establish the strict correspondence between a single-threaded global protocol and its respective synthesis.

Lemma 3. *Let* G *to be such that* $\vdash G$, $[\![G]\!]$ *is defined and either* $G = A \to A'\{\ell_i.G_i\}_{i \in I}$ *or* $G = \mu X.A \to A'\{\ell_i.G_i\}_{i \in I}$. *For any* α, u, s, σ *we have that:*

1. $G \xrightarrow{\alpha} G'$ *then* $\sigma([\![G]\!]) \xrightarrow{f(\alpha)} \sigma_\alpha \circ \sigma([\![G']\!])$;
2. *if* $\sigma([\![G]\!]) \xrightarrow{u} C' \xrightarrow{s} C$ *then* $G \xrightarrow{f^{-1}(u,s)} G'$ *with* $C \equiv \sigma_\alpha \circ \sigma([\![G']\!])$, *where* $f^{-1}(u, s) = \alpha$. *Moreover, if* $\sigma([\![G]\!]) \xrightarrow{\beta} C''$ *then* $\beta = u$ *and* $C'' \equiv C'$, *and also if* $C' \xrightarrow{\beta'} C'''$ *then* $\beta' = s$ *and* $C''' \equiv C$.

Proof.

1. By induction on the derivation of $G \xrightarrow{\alpha} G'$. The case of the recursive protocol follows directly from the induction hypothesis and Lemma 2. Otherwise we have that $G = A \to A'\{\ell_i.G_i\}_{i \in I}$, and also that $G' = G_j$ and $\alpha = A \to A'(\ell_j)$ for some j in I. From $G = A \to A'\{\ell_i.G_i\}_{i \in I}$ and $\vdash G$ we conclude by Proposition 2 that:

$$\sigma([\![G]\!]) \equiv \sigma(\{(id, A)\}) : \sum_{i \in I} [lab := \ell_i].@(id = A').(\!|G_i|\!)_A$$
$$\|\ \sigma(\{(id, A')\}) : \sum_{i \in I} (id = A) \wedge (lab = \ell_i).(\!|G_i|\!)_{A'}$$
$$\|\ \prod_{B \in n(G) \setminus \{A, A'\}} \sigma(\{(id, B)\}) : (\!|G_j|\!)_B$$

since $j \in I$, where, for every $B \in \mathrm{n}(G) \setminus \{A, A'\}$ we have that there exist B', ℓ'_i, G'_i for i in some I', such that $(\!|G_k|\!)_B \equiv \sum_{i \in I'} (id = B') \wedge (lab = \ell'_i) . (\!|G'_i|\!)_B$. By Definition 3 we have that $f(A \to A'(\ell_j)) = ([lab := \ell_j], (\Pi_{A'}, \Pi_{\{A, \ell_j\}}))$. It is immediate to conclude that $\sigma([\![G]\!])$ exhibits transition $[lab := \ell_j]$ after which a $(\Pi_{A'}, \Pi_{\{A, \ell_j\}})$ transition as follows, where $\sigma_\alpha \circ \sigma(\{(id, A)\}) = \{(id, A), (lab, \ell_j)\}$ and $\sigma_\alpha \circ \sigma(\Gamma) = \sigma(\Gamma)$ elsewhere:

$$\sigma([\![G]\!]) \xrightarrow{f(\alpha)} \sigma_\alpha \circ \sigma(\{(id, A)\}) : (\!|G_j|\!)_A \parallel \sigma_\alpha \circ \sigma(\{(id, A')\}) : (\!|G_j|\!)_{A'}$$
$$\parallel \prod_{B \in \mathrm{n}(G) \setminus \{A, A'\}} \sigma_\alpha \circ \sigma(\{(id, B)\}) : (\!|G_j|\!)_B$$

hence, $\sigma([\![G]\!]) \xrightarrow{f(\alpha)} \sigma_\alpha \circ \sigma([\![G_j]\!])$ where $G_j = G'$ thus completing the proof of 1.

2. By induction on the derivation of $\sigma([\![G]\!]) \xrightarrow{u} C'$. The case of the recursive protocol follows from induction hypothesis and Lemma 2. Otherwise we have that $G = A \to A' \{\ell_i . G_i\}_{i \in I}$, which together with $\vdash G$ gives us:

$$\sigma([\![G]\!]) \equiv \sigma(\{(id, A)\}) : \sum_{i \in I} [lab := \ell_i] . @(id = A') . (\!|G_i|\!)_A$$
$$\parallel \sigma(\{(id, A')\}) : \sum_{i \in I} (id = A) \wedge (lab = \ell_i) . (\!|G_i|\!)_{A'}$$
$$\parallel \prod_{B \in \mathrm{n}(G) \setminus \{A, A'\}} \sigma(\{(id, B)\}) : (\!|G_j|\!)_B$$

for any $j \in I$, where, for every $B \in \mathrm{n}(G) \setminus \{A, A'\}$ we have that there exist B', ℓ'_i, G'_i for i in some I' such that $(\!|G_k|\!)_B \equiv \sum_{i \in I'} (id = B') \wedge (lab = \ell'_i) . (\!|G'_i|\!)_B$. We may observe that the only possible transition is $[lab := \ell_k]$ for some $k \in I$ as follows:

$$\sigma([\![G]\!]) \xrightarrow{[lab := \ell_k]} C' \equiv \{(id, A), (lab, \ell_k)\} : @(id = A') . (\!|G_k|\!)_A$$
$$\parallel \sigma(\{(id, A')\}) : \sum_{i \in I} (id = A) \wedge (lab = \ell_i) . (\!|G_i|\!)_{A'}$$
$$\parallel \prod_{B \in \mathrm{n}(G) \setminus \{A, A'\}} \sigma(\{(id, B)\}) : (\!|G_k|\!)_B$$

where we consider G_k instead of G_j since $k \in I$. At this point we may immediately observe that the only possible transition, up to structural congruence, has label $(\Pi_{A'}, \Pi_{\{A, \ell_k\}})$ as captured in the following:

$$C' \xrightarrow{(\Pi_{A'}, \Pi_{\{A, \ell_k\}})} C \equiv \{(id, A), (lab, \ell_k)\} : (\!|G_k|\!)_A$$
$$\parallel \sigma(\{(id, A')\}) : (\!|G_k|\!)_{A'}$$
$$\parallel \prod_{B \in \mathrm{n}(G) \setminus \{A, A'\}} \sigma(\{(id, B)\}) : (\!|G_k|\!)_B$$

We remark that it is the only possible transition since there is only one output, which specifies A' as the receiving party. We also have that $f^{-1}([lab := \ell_k], (\Pi_{A'}, \Pi_{\{A, \ell_k\}})) = \alpha = A \to A'(\ell_k)$ and $A \to A' \{\ell_i . G_i\}_{i \in I} \xrightarrow{\alpha} G_k$ and also that $\{(id, A), (lab, \ell_k)\} = \sigma_\alpha \circ \sigma\{(id, A)\}$ and $\sigma_\alpha \circ \sigma(\{(id, B)\}) = \sigma(\{(id, B)\}$ for $B \neq A$ from which we have $C \equiv \sigma_\alpha \circ \sigma([\![G_k]\!])$. $\qquad \square$

Lemma 3 gives a precise symmetric correspondence between the behaviors of a single-threaded global protocol and those of its synthesis, including an account for the two-step evolution of the synthesis that is the only possible behavioral path. We can now establish some compositionality principles that allow for lifting our reasoning to parallel (well-formed thus independent) global protocols.

Lemma 4. *Let G_1 and G_2 be such that $\vdash G_1 \parallel G_2$ and $C \equiv \sigma(\llbracket G_1 \parallel G_2 \rrbracket)$. We have that $C \equiv \sigma(\llbracket G_1 \rrbracket) \parallel \sigma(\llbracket G_2 \rrbracket)$.*

Proof. By induction on the definition of $\sigma(\llbracket G_1 \parallel G_2 \rrbracket)$ following standard lines. $\square$

Lemma 5. *Let G_1 and G_2 be such that $\vdash G_1 \parallel G_2$ and $C \equiv \sigma(\llbracket G_1 \parallel G_2 \rrbracket)$. If $C \xrightarrow{\beta} C'$ then there is C'' such that $\sigma(\llbracket G_i \rrbracket) \xrightarrow{\beta} C''$ and $C' \equiv C'' \parallel \sigma(\llbracket G_j \rrbracket)$ for i,j such that $\{i,j\} = \{1,2\}$.*

Proof. By induction on the derivation of $\sigma(\llbracket G_i \rrbracket) \xrightarrow{\beta} C''$. Notice that if β is a choice then the result follows trivially. Notice also that if β is a communication then it can be confined to either G_1 or G_2 since, by well-formedness, G_1 and G_2 have disjoint sets of participants and all communications in a result of a synthesis are regulated by participant identifiers. $\square$

Lemmas 4 and 5 ensure we may reason on parallel branches of global protocols separately, as both their synthesis and their behaviors are independent with respect to (global protocol) parallel composition.

Before presenting our main result, we introduce auxiliary notation and a predicate that help in the generalization of the relation between global protocols and their synthesis. We abbreviate $C \xrightarrow{\beta_1} C_1 \xrightarrow{\beta_2} \ldots \xrightarrow{\beta_k} C'$ with $C \xrightarrow{\bar{\beta}} C'$, where $\bar{\beta} = \beta_1, \beta_2, \ldots, \beta_k$, and likewise for $G \xrightarrow{\bar{\alpha}} G'$. In case $\bar{\beta} = \varnothing$ (or $\bar{\alpha} = \varnothing$) we consider that $C = C'$ (or $G = G'$, respectively). Also, $\sigma_{\bar{\alpha}}$ denotes $\sigma_{\alpha_k} \circ \ldots \circ \sigma_{\alpha_2} \circ \sigma_{\alpha_1}$ where $\bar{\alpha} = \alpha_1, \alpha_2, \ldots, \alpha_k$. When $\bar{\alpha} = \varnothing$ we consider $\sigma_{\bar{\alpha}}$ to be the empty (no-effect) environment update. Finally, we introduce a predicate to check that each α action has a corresponding β action given two respective traces. We write $\bar{\alpha} \Leftarrow \bar{\beta}$ if there are two injective mappings, say g and h, that map each α_i to a β_j and to a β_k such that $\alpha_i \in \bar{\alpha}$, $\beta_{g(i)}, \beta_{h(i)} \in \bar{\beta}$, $g(i) < h(i)$ and $\alpha_i = f^{-1}(\beta_j, \beta_k)$.

Theorem 1 (Correspondence). *Let G to be such that $\vdash G$ and $\llbracket G \rrbracket$ is defined. For any $\alpha, \sigma, \bar{\beta}$ we have that:*

1. *if $G \xrightarrow{\alpha} G'$ then $\sigma(\llbracket G \rrbracket) \xrightarrow{f(\alpha)} \sigma_\alpha \circ \sigma(\llbracket G' \rrbracket)$;*
2. *if $\sigma(\llbracket G \rrbracket) \xrightarrow{\bar{\beta}} C'$ then there is $\bar{s}, \bar{\alpha}, G'$ such that $C' \xrightarrow{\bar{s}} C$ and $C \equiv \sigma_{\bar{\alpha}} \circ \sigma(\llbracket G' \rrbracket)$ and $G \xrightarrow{\bar{\alpha}} G'$ and $\bar{\alpha} \Leftarrow \bar{\beta}, \bar{s}$.*

Proof.

1. By induction on the derivation of $G \xrightarrow{\alpha} G'$, following non-surprising lines. Notice that the base case follows directly from Lemma 3 while the case for the parallel composition relies on Lemma 4.
2. By induction on the length of $\bar{\beta}$. Base case when $\bar{\beta}$ has length zero is immediate, and the case when $\bar{\beta}$ has length one follows by induction on the derivation of the transition of $\sigma(\llbracket G \rrbracket)$ considering Lemmas 3 and 5.

We sketch the proof for the case when $\bar{\beta}$ has length n. Using Lemma 5 we can trace the behavior u to the synthesis of a thread of G, say G_1. Considering Lemma 3 we have that $\beta_1 = u$, hence $\sigma(\llbracket G_1 \rrbracket) \xrightarrow{u} C_1$ and we also have that the only possible behavior of C_1 is such that $C_1 \xrightarrow{s} C_1'$ and, taking $\alpha_1 = f^{-1}(u,s)$, $G_1 \xrightarrow{\alpha_1} G_1'$ and $C_1' \equiv \sigma_{\alpha_1} \circ \sigma(\llbracket G_1' \rrbracket)$. We consider two distinct cases: either (1) $s \in \bar{\beta}$ or (2) $s \notin \bar{\beta}$.

(1) Considering the only possible behavior of C_1 is s we have that every transition between u and s in $\bar{\beta}$ does not involve C_1. Hence we may pull up front s in $\bar{\beta}$ yielding $\bar{\beta}'$ such that $\sigma(\llbracket G \rrbracket) \xrightarrow{\bar{\beta}'} C'$ and $\beta_1' = u = \beta_1$ and $\beta_2' = s$, hence $\alpha_1 = f^{-1}(\beta_1', \beta_2')$ while for all other labels the relative position is preserved. From $G_1 \xrightarrow{\alpha_1} G_1'$ we have that there is G' such that $G \xrightarrow{\alpha_1} G'$. Also from $\sigma(\llbracket G_1 \rrbracket) \xrightarrow{u,s} C_1'$ and $C_1' \equiv \sigma_{\alpha_1} \circ \sigma(\llbracket G_1' \rrbracket)$ and from Lemma 4 we have that $\sigma(\llbracket G \rrbracket) \xrightarrow{u,s} C''$ and $C'' \equiv \sigma_{\alpha_1} \circ \sigma(\llbracket G' \rrbracket)$. At this point we observe that $\sigma_{\alpha_1} \circ \sigma(\llbracket G' \rrbracket) \xrightarrow{\beta_3', \dots} C'$ and we are in the condition to apply the induction principle so as to obtain there is $\bar{s}, \bar{\alpha}', G''$ such that $C' \xrightarrow{\bar{s}} C$ and $C \equiv \sigma_{\bar{\alpha}'} \circ \sigma_{\alpha_1} \circ \sigma(\llbracket G'' \rrbracket)$ and $G' \xrightarrow{\bar{\alpha}'} G''$ and $\bar{\alpha}' \Leftarrow \beta_3', \dots, \bar{s}$. The result is immediate by observing that $G \xrightarrow{\alpha_1, \bar{\alpha}'} G''$ and that $\alpha_1, \bar{\alpha}' \Leftarrow \bar{\beta}', \bar{s}$ which implies $\alpha_1, \bar{\alpha}' \Leftarrow \bar{\beta}, \bar{s}$.

(2) Since $s \notin \bar{\beta}$ we have that component C_1 is not involved in any transition in $\beta_2, \dots$. Let us take G_2 such that $G \equiv G_1 \parallel G_2$ hence $\sigma(\llbracket G \rrbracket) \equiv \sigma(\llbracket G_1 \rrbracket) \parallel \sigma(\llbracket G_2 \rrbracket)$ (Lemma 4). We have that $\sigma(\llbracket G_2 \rrbracket) \xrightarrow{\beta_2, \dots} C_2$ and $C' \equiv C_1 \parallel C_2$. At this point we may apply the induction principle so as to obtain there is $\bar{s}, \bar{\alpha}, G'$ such that $C_2 \xrightarrow{\bar{s}} C$ and $C \equiv \sigma_{\bar{\alpha}} \circ \sigma(\llbracket G_2' \rrbracket)$ and $G_2 \xrightarrow{\bar{\alpha}} G_2'$ and $\bar{\alpha} \Leftarrow \beta_2, \dots, \bar{s}$. From $C_2 \xrightarrow{\bar{s}} C$ and $C_1 \xrightarrow{s} C_1'$ and $C' \equiv C_1 \parallel C_2$ we have that $C' \xrightarrow{\bar{s}, s} C_1' \parallel C$. From $C \equiv \sigma_{\bar{\alpha}} \circ \sigma(\llbracket G_2' \rrbracket)$ and $C_1' \equiv \sigma_{\alpha_1} \circ \sigma(\llbracket G_1' \rrbracket)$ we have that $C_1' \parallel C \equiv \sigma_{\alpha_1} \circ \sigma(\llbracket G_1' \rrbracket) \parallel \sigma_{\bar{\alpha}} \circ \sigma(\llbracket G_2' \rrbracket)$ and hence, considering Lemma 4 and noticing that σs have no effect in independent branches, we have that $C_1' \parallel C \equiv \sigma_{\bar{\alpha}} \circ \sigma_{\alpha_1} \circ \sigma(\llbracket G_1' \parallel G_2' \rrbracket)$. From $G_1 \xrightarrow{\alpha_1} G_1'$ and $G_2 \xrightarrow{\bar{\alpha}} G_2'$ and $G \equiv G_1 \parallel G_2$ we have that $G \xrightarrow{\alpha_1, \bar{\alpha}} G_1' \parallel G_2'$. It is immediate to observe that $\alpha_1 \Leftarrow u, s$ which together with $\bar{\alpha} \Leftarrow \beta_2, \dots, \bar{s}$ yields $\alpha_1, \bar{\alpha} \Leftarrow u, \beta_2, \dots, \bar{s}, s$ thus completing the proof for this case. $\square$

Theorem 1 characterizes the correspondence between global protocols and their synthesis in a general way: each action of the global protocol can be mimicked by a pair of actions in the synthesis; all behaviors of the synthesis complemented by some (synchronization) steps can be traced back to behaviors of the global protocols. The latter in particular assures there is no divergence in the synthesis from what the global protocols prescribe. However, we are also interested in a particular case of this correspondence when we consider coupled actions in the synthesis (which are the only possible ones for single-threaded protocols in the light of Lemma 3). In fact, observing that in the result of a synthesis the only possible behavior is a choice (u), and that after a choice there can only be one synchronization (s) we can focus on coupled actions in general.

Corollary 1 (Correspondence Invariance). *Let G to be such that $\vdash G$ and $\llbracket G \rrbracket$ is defined. For any $\alpha_1, \alpha_2, \ldots, \alpha_k$ we have that $G \xrightarrow{\alpha_1} G_1 \xrightarrow{\alpha_2} G_2 \ldots \xrightarrow{\alpha_k} G_k$ iff*

$$\llbracket G \rrbracket \xrightarrow{f(\alpha_1)} \sigma_{\alpha_1}(\llbracket G_1 \rrbracket) \xrightarrow{f(\alpha_2)} \sigma_{\alpha_2} \circ \sigma_{\alpha_1}(\llbracket G_2 \rrbracket) \ldots \xrightarrow{f(\alpha_k)} \sigma_{\alpha_k} \circ \ldots \circ \sigma_{\alpha_2} \circ \sigma_{\alpha_1}(\llbracket G_k \rrbracket)$$

Corollary 1 gives us a precise correspondence between global protocol specifications and distributed site-level implementations, bidirectionally matching all possible behaviors between protocols and implementations. The semantics of the languages, where transitions are labeled with the synchronization information, supports the establishment of the matching of the global protocols and their AbC implementations. We may also observe the local environment changes as a consequence of the evolutions in a precise way. Thanks to the equivalence between protocols and their synthesis, we can concentrate on the specifications and take conformance of the implementations for granted.

6   Conclusion and Related Work

This paper provides a proof of concept of a software development methodology that consists in programming specifications and relying on provably correct translations into more operational models. Taken at this level of generality, we may consider instances of this methodology the development of compilers that date back to the 50's or more recent work on model-driven engineering and domain specific languages, although not all of such instances support provably correct translations. If we consider the specific realm of distributed systems, and that of conformance of implementations with respect to specifications given in the same language, we find several approaches that rely on behavioral relations [9,15]. However, to the best of our knowledge, none of the approach based on behavioral relations aims at the automatic generation of implementations from high level specifications.

One intensively pursued line of research is concerned with type systems that provide a means to verify that implementations conform to the specifications given by means of types. In particular for communication-centered systems, there are several approaches based on session-types, see e.g. [10], which establish, via a typing relation, a correspondence between system behavior and channel usage protocols. Such relation typically involves a verification procedure, and at least for explicitly typed languages, it requires reasoning on both the type and the programming language. Here, we have taken a different approach by considering only the language of specifications (types) and by relying on a provably correct translation mechanism. In this way, we support programming at a higher abstraction level and avoid conformance checking, as the synthesized implementations are correct by construction.

Our global protocol specification language corresponds to global types [11], except that our messages have no contents. The similarities include the close correspondence between our well-formedness conditions and the linearity conditions [11] imposed to protocols. We argue that adding value passing is orthogonal to the present development, potentially raising specific challenges only in the case of channel passing. The approaches described in [3,4] are perhaps the closest to ours. In both approaches global protocol descriptions are session-typed in order to ensure the correspondence with site-level implementations obtained by means of a projection function. In our approach, the programmer does not have to deal with two different specification languages and we entirely avoid type verification. However, we do not deal with multiple sessions, each taking place in a different medium, even if they could be modeled using AbC attributes in a straightforward way. In our opinion, multiple sessions/protocols should not be given in a single specification, we believe that it is necessary to follow fundamental programming languages principles, namely modularity in order to tame complexity. We envision that distinct sessions should be specified via different modules, each of them exposing communication interfaces where actual dependencies between different sessions are specified.

Another closely related approach is reported in [7,8,12]. Indeed the basic idea is the same: generating correct by construction implementations from specifications. Their language of global specifications is similar to ours, and a specialized language is introduced for the purpose of implementations; [7] introduces also value support, which, as mentioned before, we view as an orthogonal issue. The main difference lays in the underlying site-level implementation language. We take as starting point an attribute-based communication model and show that it is general enough to support a directed synthesis procedure for session-like interaction. Other approaches, to model the link between message recipient and emitter either introduce specialized constructs or rely on typing to ensure that messages are exchanged (in particular received) from the parties prescribed by the choreography. Using AbC we specify in a natural way to whom a message is to be sent and from whom a message is supposed to be received, as *identity* is just a specific attribute that can be exposed. We also model *sessions* in a natural way, again by handling them as attributes.

In our approach, the ability to express communicating partners in a natural way helps ensure that AbC processes are complying with the global specification. The communications prescribed by the global specification are guaranteed by the communication attributes in a way somehow similar to the one enforced by runtime monitors (e.g., [5,6]). In this context, we find of particular interest dealing with the issue of adaptation with synthesis used to replace incorrect programs with correct by construction ones.

We believe our approach can be extended to richer protocol specification languages, involving more intricate protocol structures, such as multicast or generic sequential composition. In fact multicast can be directly represented in AbC. Departing from the setting of multiparty session types, we believe it would be interesting to extend the language at the level of the way peers are engaged to participate in protocols. Currently we rely on identifying the participants by name. However, since our underlying communication model is based on attributes, we can naturally accommodate identifying the processes involved in a protocol on a more qualitative basis, e.g., by choosing as interacting partner the best rated one or the less active one.

Our ultimate aim is to find ways to convey our ideas into practice, so as to show that techniques introduced in the formal methods community can have an impact on the expedite development of reliable software, in the spirit of [14].

Acknowledgments. We would like to thank the anonymous reviewers for their feedback and insightful remarks, which helped us to improve the quality of this document. Also, we would like to thank the editors of this volume, Chiara, Corrado and Giangi, for giving us the possibility of contributing to this volume. Most of all, we would like to thank Pierpaolo that with his dedication to research and his quest for scientific rigor has been an example for generations of scholars.

References

1. Alrahman, Y.A., De Nicola, R., Loreti, M.: On expressiveness and behavioural theory of attribute-based communication. Technical Report CSA #10, IMT Institute for Advanced Studies Lucca (2015)
2. Alrahman, Y.A., De Nicola, R., Loreti, M., Tiezzi, F., Vigo, R.: A calculus for attribute-based communication. In: Proceedings of the 30th Annual ACM Symposium on Applied Computing, SAC 2015, pp. 1840–1845. ACM (2015)
3. Carbone, M., Honda, K., Yoshida, N.: Structured communication-centered programming for web services. ACM Trans. Program. Lang. Syst. **34**(2), 8 (2012)
4. Carbone, M., Montesi, F.: Deadlock-freedom-by-design: multiparty asynchronous global programming. In: The 40th Annual ACM SIGPLAN-SIGACT Symposium on Principles of Programming Languages, POPL 2013, pp. 263–274. ACM (2013)
5. Castellani, I., Dezani-Ciancaglini, M., Pérez, J.A.: Self-adaptation and secure information flow in multiparty structured communications: a unified perspective. In: Proceedings Third Workshop on Behavioural Types, BEAT 2014. EPTCS, vol. 162, pp 9–18 (2014)
6. Coppo, M., Dezani-Ciancaglini, M., Venneri, B.: Self-adaptive monitors for multiparty sessions. In: Proceedings of the 22nd Euromicro International Conference on Parallel, Distributed, and Network-Based Processing, PDP 2014, pp. 688–696. IEEE Computer Society (2014)
7. Preda, M.D., Gabbrielli, M., Giallorenzo, S., Lanese, I., Mauro, J.: Dynamic choreographies. In: Holvoet, T., Viroli, M. (eds.) COORDINATION 2015. LNCS, vol. 9037, pp. 67–82. Springer, Heidelberg (2015)
8. Preda, M.D., Giallorenzo, S., Lanese, I., Mauro, J., Gabbrielli, M.: AIOCJ: a choreographic framework for safe adaptive distributed applications. In: Combemale, B., Pearce, D.J., Barais, O., Vinju, J.J. (eds.) SLE 2014. LNCS, vol. 8706, pp. 161–170. Springer, Heidelberg (2014)
9. De Nicola, R.: Extensional equivalences for transition systems. Acta Inf. **24**(2), 211–237 (1987)
10. Honda, K., Vasconcelos, V.T., Kubo, M.: Language primitives and type discipline for structured communication-based programming. In: Hankin, C. (ed.) ESOP 1998. LNCS, vol. 1381, pp. 122–138. Springer, Heidelberg (1998)
11. Honda, K., Yoshida, N., Carbone, M.: Multiparty asynchronous session types. In: Proceedings of the 35th ACM SIGPLAN-SIGACT Symposium on Principles of Programming Languages, POPL 2008, pp. 273–284. ACM (2008)

12. Lanese, I., Guidi, C., Montesi, F., Zavattaro, G.: Bridging the gap between interaction- and process-oriented choreographies. In: Proceedings of the Sixth IEEE International Conference on Software Engineering and Formal Methods, SEFM 2008, pp. 323–332. IEEE Computer Society (2008)
13. Lange, J., Tuosto, E., Yoshida, N.: From communicating machines to graphical choreographies. In: Proceedings of the 42nd Annual ACM SIGPLAN-SIGACT Symposium on Principles of Programming Languages, POPL 2015, pp. 221–232. ACM (2015)
14. Montesi, F.: Kickstarting choreographic programming. CoRR, abs/1502.02519 (2015)
15. van Glabbeek, R.J.: The linear time - branching time spectrum. In: Baeten, J.C.M., Klop, J.W. (eds.) CONCUR '90 Theories of Concurrency: Unification and Extension. LNCS, vol. 458, pp. 278–297. Springer, Heidelberg (1990)

Symbolic Protocol Analysis with Disequality Constraints Modulo Equational Theories

Santiago Escobar[1], Catherine Meadows[2]([⊠]), José Meseguer[3],
and Sonia Santiago[3]

[1] DSIC-ELP, Universitat Politècnica de València, Valencia, Spain
sescobar@dsic.upv.es
[2] Naval Research Laboratory, Washington, D.C., USA
meadows@itd.nrl.navy.mil
[3] University of Illinois at Urbana-Champaign, Champaign, USA
{meseguer,soniasp}@illinois.edu

Abstract. Research in the formal analysis of cryptographic protocols has produced much good work in the solving of equality constraints, developing new methods for unification, matching, and deducibility. However, considerably less attention has been paid to disequality constraints. These also arise quite naturally in cryptographic protocol analysis, in particular for analysis of indistinguishability properties. Thus methods for deciding whether or not they are satisfiable could potentially be quite useful in reducing the size of the search space by protocol analysis tools. In this paper we develop a framework for reasoning about disequality constraints centered around the paradigm of the *most discriminating Dolev-Yao attacker*, who is able to detect a disequality if it is satisfied in some implementation of the crypto-algebra satisfying given equality properties. We develop several strategies for handling disequalities, prove their soundness and completeness, and demonstrate the result of experimental analyses using the various strategies. Finally, we discuss how disequality checking algorithms could be incorporated within symbolic reachability protocol analysis methods.

1 Introduction

The area of formal analysis of cryptographic protocols has been an active one since the mid 1980's. The idea is to verify protocols that use cryptography to guarantee security against an attacker —commonly called the *Dolev-Yao* attacker [9]— who has complete control of the network. One of the most popular approaches to the formal verification of cryptographic protocols is model checking, in which the interaction of the protocol with the attacker is symbolically executed.

Many model checkers rely on logical features to symbolically analyze a protocol, either by carrying constraints, whose solutions determine whether an attack

---

© Springer International Publishing Switzerland 2015 (outside the US)
C. Bodei et al. (Eds.): Degano Festschrift, LNCS 9465, pp. 238–261, 2015.
DOI: 10.1007/978-3-319-25527-9_16

exists, or by including logical variables, whose possible instantiations determine whether an attack exists. In these logical model checkers, several types of constraints need to be solved, or at least be checked for satisfiability. They include equality constraints modulo equational properties (typically solved by equational unification techniques), deducibility constraints, and disequality constraints of the form $t \neq t'$, also modulo some equational axioms.

Such disequality constraints appear quite often in many applications. The simplest come from the symbolic description of attack states, where we may want to specify that two functional expressions, or two principals must be *different*. For example, we might want to specify a state in which Alice accepts a key K as being shared with Bob, and Bob accepts a key K' as being shared with Alice, but $K \neq K'$. Another related use of disequality constraints comes from the analysis of indistinguishability properties, where the intruder needs to distinguish between two protocol executions. In models such as [3,22] this is formulated in terms of equality and disequality constraints that must be satisfied. We illustrate the issues that can arise with the following protocol, which will be used as a running example.

Consider the standard example of Diffie-Hellman without authentication, in which two parties exchange Diffie-Hellman key halves and use them to construct a shared key. This is subject to a man-in-the-middle attack in which the attacker learns the contents of encrypted information sent between two honest principals. The attack is performed by having the man-in-the-middle perform a Diffie-Hellman key exchange with Alice (impersonating Bob) and another Diffie-Hellman key exchange with Bob (impersonating Alice). Thus the attack can also be described as one in which Alice sends an encrypted secret, apparently to Bob, and Bob receives the same encrypted secret, apparently from Alice, but the key used to encrypt the message sent by Alice and the key encrypting the message received by Bob are different.

The equational theory used by the protocol is as follows. There is an operator $*$ which is associative and commutative (AC), a constant g used as a public generator, an operator exp satisfying the equation $exp(exp(g, N_1), N_2) = exp(g, N_1 * N_2)$, and encryption and decryption operators e and d respectively, satisfying the equation $d(K, e(K, X)) = X$. These two equations can be oriented as rewrite rules $exp(exp(g, N_1), N_2) \rightarrow exp(g, N_1 * N_2)$ and $d(K, e(K, X)) \rightarrow X$ that are confluent modulo the AC property of $*$. This makes equality in this theory decidable by simplification to normal form with these two rules modulo AC.

Alice and Bob exchange Diffie-Hellman key pairs $exp(g, N_A)$ and $exp(g, N_B)$. Then they respectively compute $exp(exp(g, N_A), N_B)$ and $exp(exp(g, N_B), N_A)$, which are both equal to $exp(g, N_A * N_B)$ by the equational theory. Alice uses the result as a key to encrypt a fresh secret S_A and sends it to Bob. The protocol is seen differently by Bob and Alice, as shown in the second and third columns, by using a variable X, Y, and Z for terms a participant cannot identify as having been correctly generated.

Alice and Bob	Alice	Bob
$A \rightarrow B : exp(g, N_A)$	$A \rightarrow B : exp(g, N_A)$	$A \rightarrow B : X$
$B \rightarrow A : exp(g, N_B)$	$B \rightarrow A : Z$	$B \rightarrow A : exp(g, N_B)$
$A \rightarrow B : e(exp(g, N_A * N_B), S_A)$	$A \rightarrow B : e(exp(Z, N_A), S_A)$	$A \rightarrow B : e(exp(X, N_B), Y)$

The attack we are looking for is one in which the Alice and Bob agree on the secret but not on the key:

Alice	Bob	Constraints
$A \to B : exp(g, N_A)$	$A \to B : X$	$exp(X, N_B) \neq exp(Z, N_A)$
$B \to A : Z$	$B \to A : exp(g, N_B)$	
$A \to B : e(exp(Z, N_A), S_A)$	$A \to B : e(exp(X, N_B), S_A)$	

An attack that leads to this result is described as follows:
Alice and Bob

1. $A \to I_B : exp(g, N_A)$
2. $I_A \to B : exp(g, N_{I_A})$
3. $B \to I_A : exp(g, N_B)$
4. $I_B \to A : exp(g, N_{I_B})$
5. $A \to I_B : e(exp(g, N_A * N_{I_B}), S_A)$
6. Intruder generates key $exp(exp(g, N_A), N_{I_B})$ and extracts S_A
7. $I_A \to B : e(exp(g, N_B * N_{I_A}), S_A)$
8. Disequality $exp(g, N_A * N_{I_B}) \neq exp(g, N_B * N_{I_A})$ is satisfied

Since the terms $exp(g, N_A * N_{I_B})$ and $exp(g, N_B * N_{I_A})$ are both *irreducible* by the rules and different modulo AC, we have $exp(g, N_A * N_{I_B}) \neq_E exp(g, N_B * N_{I_A})$, where E is the equational theory of exponentation specified by the above two equations and the AC axioms.

However, if we construct the attack by working backwards from the attack states, the disequality constraint contains variables X and Z, and we find ourselves facing a choice:

Do we try to solve the constraint right away, or do we wait for later?

The easiest, but not the most efficient, way of handling the constraint is to ignore it until the initial state is reached. At that point all the terms will be more instantiated than at any earlier point in a backwards path to the intial state, and we will be in a good position to check whether the constraint is solvable. However, this means that it is possible that a number of searches with states where the disequality constraint is in fact unsolvable will be kept alive until the initial state is reached, thus bloating the search space when they could have been discarded much earlier. This suggests trying to address the constraint earlier, in an attempt to determine whether or not a constraint containing variables is satisfiable.

Satisfiability of disequalities between terms with variables is a non-trivial problem, especially since checking for solvability must be performed *modulo* the equational properties of the protocol's cryptographic functions. Furthermore, the problem of solving a set of disequalities for a given equational theory, known as the *disunification* problem [6], is less well understood than the problem of unification. It is very well understood when the theory has no axioms (the so-called free case) and has been studied for various equational theories commonly used in automated deduction following different methods, e.g., [1,4,5]. However, this work has mostly concentrated on algorithms for solvability in the *initial algebra* of the given equational theory, that is, the quotient $T_{\Sigma/E}$ of the algebra of ground terms $\mathcal{T}_{\Sigma}$ modulo the equations E, where Σ is the set of symbols appearing in E. For exclusive-or, for example, the initial algebra $\mathcal{T}_{\Sigma/XOR}$ is the singleton set $\{[0]\}$ consisting of the XOR-equivalence class $[0]$, so in this algebra all terms must be equal and *no* disequalities can be satisfied. However, for cryptographic protocols in the Dolev-Yao model we are generally interested in an infinite class of algebras each consisting of: some finite set of constants, a countable set of nonces, and terms that can be built from constants and nonces using other function symbols, such as those describing decryption or concatenation. We may also ultimately be interested in *computational models*, which include probability distributions over n-length strings of 0's and 1's. This means that restricting disunification problems to initial algebras, though possible, can sometimes be too restrictive for cryptographic protocol verification.

In protocol verification we assume the worse, namely, that the attacker can use knowledge of equalities *and* disequalities modulo the equational theory E satisfied by the cryptographic functions to mount an attack. In particular we assume that the attacker knows the theory E, but may not fully know the details of the implementation, i.e., the algebra used to implement such cryptographic functions. How can such an attacker *maximize* its chances to mount an attack? It does so by using its knowledge about: (i) the messages that it has already learned; (ii) the equational theory E; and (iii) disequalities modulo E, to try to mount an attack in all ways possible. But how can disequalities modulo E be handled by the attacker? In the absence of full knowledge by the attacker about the particular implementation, its best bet, the one maximizing its chances, is to assume that the attack can be mounted in *some* implementation, that is, that there is *some* model of the equations E, i.e., some algebra satisfying the equations E, where the disequalities can be solved, and then try all possible attacks under that assumption. We call such an attacker a *most discriminating Dolev-Yao attacker*, because the set of disequalities satisfiable in a given implementation is always a (not necessarily strict) *subset* of those that hold in some implementation. In the absence of knowledge about the implementation this *increases the attacker's chances*, since the attacker may be able to distinguish some disequalities actually holding in the unknown implementation that it could not have distinguished if it had mistakenly assumed some other implementation.

Two observations may be helpful here:

1. Full knowledge by the attacker of the actual implementation can be used to *reduce* the number of attacks to be tried. However, for a complex implementation a symbolic method to decide solvability of disequalities between terms with variables may not exist at all.
2. The most discriminating attacker will detect all inequalities that hold true for a given implementation, but may also detect some false ones. However, detecting false inequalities does not prevent the attacker from finding any genuine attack that is possible when only the theory E is assumed.[1]

---

[1] It is well-known that protocols proved secure modulo equational axioms E may sometimes be attacked at the computational level. That is why the qualification that an attack is possible "when only the theory E is assumed" is important here.

This suggests the following protocol analysis strategy: (i) in the absence of knowledge about the implementation details, the strongest formal analysis possible modulo E is to assume a most discriminating Dolev-Yao attacker; but (ii) if implementation details can safely be assumed and symbolic satisfiability of disequalities assuming such an implementation is decidable, then this can be used to reduce the state space, since symbolic states with unsatisfiable disequalities in the given implementation will be detected and discarded earlier. In this paper we focus on case (i), and study methods to: (a) decide satisfiability of disequalities without knowledge of the implementation; and (b) reduce as much as possible the state space when searching for an attack.

Let us further expand on these ideas. Suppose that we begin with an equational theory (Σ, E). Since the symbols Σ used in the actual model of interest will be implemented in some (Σ, E)-algebra $\mathcal{A}$, the most discriminating Dolev-Yao attacker possible should be able to settle whether a disequality $u \neq v$ can be satisfied in *some* such (Σ, E)-algebra $\mathcal{A}$. As we show in this work, this will be the case iff $u \neq v$ can be satisfied in the *free* (Σ, E)-algebra $\mathcal{T}_{\Sigma/E}(X)$, where the family of variables X has a countable set of variables for each sort. We furthermore show that $u \neq v$ is satisfiable in $\mathcal{T}_{\Sigma/E}(X)$ iff $u \neq_E v$. Therefore, if the equality relation $=_E$ is decidable, the most-discriminating Dolev-Yao attacker can be automated.

The automation can be made even more efficient if (Σ, E) has the *finite variant property* [7], so that E decomposes as $E = B \cup E_0$ with the equations E_0 (oriented as rules) convergent and coherent modulo the axioms B that have a finitary unification algorithm and so that each term t has a finite set of most general E_0, B-variants. The point is that a disequality $u \neq v$ may arise sometime during the process of model checking symbolically the security of a given protocol; but as the symbolic reachability analysis proceeds, the disequality $u \neq v$, carried as a constraint, will become instantiated as $u\theta \neq v\theta$ by various substitutions θ. Moreover $u\theta \neq v\theta$ *could* become unsatisfiable even though the original $u \neq v$ was satisfiable. As we show in the paper, combining ideas from [7] with ideas from our own work on how to reduce the state space during reachability analysis by using *irreducibility constraints*[10], we can simultaneously achieve two important goals:

1. automate a most discriminating Dolev-Yao attacker for general security attacks, including attacks violating indistinguishability properties; and
2. reduce the space of reachable states, in some cases substantially, by using irreducibility constrains and reducing the $(\Sigma, E_0 \cup B)$-satisfiability of disequalities to the (Σ, B)-satisfiability of their variants using such constrains.

We have implemented this most discriminating Dolev-Yao attacker modulo a theory (Σ, E) having the finite variant property in the Maude-NPA tool [14], and have tested and experimented with several disequality checking strategies to reduce the search space on a suite of benchmarks to obtain a better insight about their effectiveness.

The rest of the paper is organized as follows. In Sect. 2 we provide some background on term rewriting. Section 3 recalls the symbolic reachability framework used in the Maude-NPA tool, which is extended as follows. First, in Sect. 4, we extend the symbolic reachability framework by adding disequalities, and show how the Maude-NPA is adapted to this new framework. Second, in Sect. 5, we further extend the new symbolic reachability analysis containing disequalities to also include variant generation for disequalities and checking their associated irreducibility constraints, and again show how the Maude-NPA can be adapted to this new combined framework. Third, in Sect. 6, we discuss how these refinements for checking disequalities can be used to reduce the search space using various checking strategies and show, using a suite of examples, how this can pay off in practice. We then conclude in Sect. 7.

2   Background on Term Rewriting

We follow the classical notation and terminology from [24] for term rewriting and from [18,19] for rewriting logic and order-sorted notions. We assume an *order-sorted signature* $\Sigma = (S, \leq, \Sigma)$ with a partially ordered set of sorts $(S, \leq)$. We also assume an S-sorted family $\mathcal{X} = \{\mathcal{X}_s\}_{s \in S}$ of disjoint variable sets with each $\mathcal{X}_s$ countably infinite. $\mathcal{T}_\Sigma(\mathcal{X})_s$ is the set of terms of sort s, and $\mathcal{T}_{\Sigma,s}$ is the set of ground terms of sort s. We write $\mathcal{T}_\Sigma(\mathcal{X})$ and $\mathcal{T}_\Sigma$ for the corresponding order-sorted term algebras. We assume throughout that Σ has *non-empty sorts*, that is, that $\mathcal{T}_{\Sigma,s} \neq \emptyset$ for each $s \in S$. We write $Var(t)$ for the set of variables present in a term t. The subterm of t at position p is $t|_p$, and $t[u]_p$ is the result of replacing $t|_p$ by u in t. A *substitution* σ is a sort-preserving mapping from a finite subset of $\mathcal{X}$ to $\mathcal{T}_\Sigma(\mathcal{X})$. The identity substitution is id. Application of substitution σ to a term t is denoted $t\sigma$. The restriction of σ to a set of variables V is $\sigma|_V$. The composition of two substitutions is $X(\sigma \circ \theta) = (X\sigma)\theta$ for $X \in \mathcal{X}$.

A Σ-*equation* is an unoriented pair $t = t'$, where $t, t' \in \mathcal{T}_\Sigma(\mathcal{X})$ have a common typing $t : s$, $t' : s$, $s \in S$. Given a set E of Σ-equations, provable equality in order-sorted equational logic [19] defines a congruence relation $=_E$ on terms $t, t' \in \mathcal{T}_\Sigma(\mathcal{X})$, also denoted $E \vdash t = t'$. The E-*subsumption* order on terms $\mathcal{T}_\Sigma(\mathcal{X})_s$, written $t \sqsupseteq_E t'$ (meaning that t is *more general* modulo E than t'), holds if $\exists\sigma\ t\sigma =_E t'$. For a set E of Σ-equations, a E-*unifier* for a Σ-equation $t = t'$ is a substitution σ s.t. $\sigma(t) =_E \sigma(t')$. For $Var(t) \cup Var(t') \subseteq W$, a set of substitutions $CSU_E^W(t = t')$ is said to be a *complete* set of E-unifiers of an equation $t = t'$ away from W iff: (i) each $\sigma \in CSU_E^W(t = t')$ is an E-unifier of $t = t'$; (ii) for any E-unifier ρ of $t = t'$ there is a $\sigma \in CSU_E^W(t = t')$ such that $\sigma|_W \sqsupseteq_E \rho|_W$ (i.e. $(\exists\tau)\ \forall x \in W\ x\sigma\tau =_E x\rho$); (iii) for all $\sigma \in CSU_E^W(t = t')$, $Dom(\sigma) \subseteq (Var(t) \cup Var(t'))$ and $Ran(\sigma) \cap W = \emptyset$. If the set of variables W is irrelevant or is understood from the context, we write $CSU_E(t = t')$ instead of $CSU_E^W(t = t')$. We say $CSU_E(t = t')$ is *finitary* if it contains a finite number of E-unifiers.

A Σ-*rewrite rule* is an oriented pair $l \rightarrow r$, where $l \notin \mathcal{X}$, $Var(r) \subseteq Var(l)$, and $l, r \in \mathcal{T}_\Sigma(\mathcal{X})$ have a common typing $l : s$, $r : s$, $s \in S$. An *(unconditional) order-sorted rewrite theory* is a triple (Σ, E, R) with Σ an order-sorted signature, E a set of Σ-equations, and R a set of Σ-rewrite rules. The relation $\rightarrow_{R,E}$ on $\mathcal{T}_\Sigma(\mathcal{X})$ is defined as: $t \xrightarrow{p}_{R,E} t'$ (or $\rightarrow_{R,E}$) if p is a position of t, $l \rightarrow r \in R$,

$t|_p =_E l\sigma$, and $t' = t[r\sigma]_p$ for some σ. A term u is in $\rightarrow_{R,E}$-canonical form (or is R, E-irreducible) if there is no v such that $u \rightarrow_{R,E} v$.

A *decomposition* (Σ, B, E_0) of an equational theory E is a rewrite theory that satisfies the following properties: (i) B is regular, sort-preserving and uses top-sort variables, (ii) B has a finitary unification algorithm, and (iii) the rules E_0 are *convergent* modulo B, i.e., sort-decreasing, confluent, terminating, and coherent modulo B. Given a decomposition $E = (\Sigma, B, E_0)$, the E_0, B-canonical form of a term t is denoted by $t\downarrow_{E_0,B}$. Given a decomposition $E = (\Sigma, B, E_0)$, an E_0, B-variant of a term t is a pair (t', θ) such that $t' =_B (t\theta)\downarrow_{E_0,B}$. A decomposition (Σ, B, E_0) has the *finite variant (FV) property* if there is a complete and finite set of most general variants for each term (see [15] for details). If a decomposition (Σ, B, E_0) of an equational theory E has the *finite variant property*, there is an algorithm to compute a finite complete set $CSU_E(t = t')$ of E-unifiers [15].

3   Symbolic Reachability Analysis by Narrowing

In this section we recall basic facts about narrowing modulo equations of [25] using topmost rewriting as a semantic framework for symbolic reachability analysis of protocols under algebraic properties. We first define reachability goals.

Definition 1 *(Reachability goal).* *Given an order-sorted rewrite theory* (Σ, E, R), *a reachability goal is defined as a pair* $t \xrightarrow{?}{}^*_{R,E} t'$, *where* $t, t' \in T_\Sigma(\mathcal{X})_s$ *for some sort* s. *It is abbreviated as* $t \xrightarrow{?}{}^* t'$ *when the theory is clear from the context;* t *is the* source *of the goal and* t' *is the* target. *A substitution* σ *is a* R, E-*solution of the reachability goal (or just a solution for short) iff there is a substitution* σ *for which there is a sequence* $t\sigma \rightarrow_{R,E} u_1 \rightarrow_{R,E} \cdots \rightarrow_{R,E} u_{k-1} \rightarrow_{R,E} t'\sigma$.

A set Γ *of substitutions is said to be a* complete set of solutions *of* $t \xrightarrow{?}{}^*_{R,E} t'$ *iff: (i) every substitution* $\sigma \in \Gamma$ *is a solution of* $t \xrightarrow{?}{}^*_{R,E} t'$, *and (ii) for any solution* ρ *of* $t \xrightarrow{?}{}^*_{R,E} t'$, *there is a substitution* $\sigma \in \Gamma$ *more general than* ρ *modulo* E, *i.e.,* $\sigma|_{Var(t) \cup Var(t')} \sqsupseteq_E \rho|_{Var(t) \cup Var(t')}$.

If in a goal $t \xrightarrow{?}{}^*_{R,E} t'$, terms t and t' are ground, then goal solving becomes a standard rewriting modulo E reachability problem. However, since we allow terms t, t' with variables, we need a mechanism more general than standard rewriting to find solutions of reachability goals. *Narrowing* generalizes rewriting by performing *unification* at non-variable positions instead of the usual matching. Specifically, narrowing instantiates the variables in a term by a E-unifier that enables a rewrite modulo E with a given rule and a term position.

Definition 2 *(Narrowing modulo E).* *Given an order-sorted rewrite theory* (Σ, E, R), *the narrowing relation on* $T_\Sigma(\mathcal{X})$ *modulo* E *is defined as* $t \rightsquigarrow_{\sigma,R,E} t'$ *(or* $\rightsquigarrow_\sigma$ *if* R, E *is understood) iff there is* $p \in Pos_\Sigma(t)$, *a rule* $l \rightarrow r$ *in* R *such that* $Var(t) \cap (Var(l) \cup Var(r)) = \emptyset$, *and* $\sigma \in CSU_E^V(t|_p = l)$ *for a set* V *of variables containing* $Var(t)$, $Var(l)$, *and* $Var(r)$, *such that* $t' = (t[r]_p)\sigma$.

The reflexive and transitive closure of narrowing is defined as $t \stackrel{\sigma}{\leadsto}^*_{R,E} t'$ iff either $t = t'$ and $\sigma = id$, or there are terms $u_1, \ldots, u_n$, $n \geq 1$, and substitutions $\sigma_1, \ldots, \sigma_{n+1}$ s.t. $t \leadsto_{\sigma_1,R,E} u_1 \leadsto_{\sigma_2,R,E} u_2 \cdots u_n \leadsto_{\sigma_{n+1},R,E} t'$ and $\sigma = \sigma_1 \cdots \sigma_{n+1}$.

Soundness and completeness of narrowing for solving reachability goals is proved in [25] for order-sorted *topmost* rewrite theories, i.e., rewrite theories were all the rewrite steps happen at the top of terms.

3.1   Reachability Analysis in Maude-NPA

In this section we give a high-level summary of the general narrowing-based approach implemented in Maude-NPA. For further information, please see [12,14]. Note that our treatment of symbolic reachability analysis modulo equations by narrowing is completely general and *tool-independent*. We only use Maude-NPA for illustration purposes to give examples, and also because its implementation supports the irreducibility conditions discussed in this paper. Multiset rewrite rules, used as a model for protocol analysis [2,20], is another example of topmost rewrite theories where reachability properties are checked.

Given a protocol $\mathcal{P}$, states are modeled as elements of an initial algebra $T_{\Sigma_{\mathcal{P}}/E_{\mathcal{P}}}$, where $\Sigma_{\mathcal{P}}$ is the signature defining the sorts and function symbols (for the cryptographic functions and for all the state constructor symbols) and $E_{\mathcal{P}}$ is a set of equations specifying the *algebraic properties* of the cryptographic functions and the state constructors. Therefore, a concrete state is an $E_{\mathcal{P}}$-equivalence class $[t] \in T_{\Sigma_{\mathcal{P}}/E_{\mathcal{P}}}$ with t a ground $\Sigma_{\mathcal{P}}$-term. However, we explore *symbolic state patterns* $[t(x_1, \ldots, x_n)] \in T_{\Sigma_{\mathcal{P}}/E_{\mathcal{P}}}(\mathcal{X})$ on the free $(\Sigma_{\mathcal{P}}, E_{\mathcal{P}})$-algebra over a set of sorted variables $\mathcal{X}$.

In Maude-NPA [12,14], a *state pattern* in a protocol execution is a term t of sort State, $t \in T_{\Sigma_{\mathcal{P}}/E_{\mathcal{P}}}(X)_{\mathsf{State}}$, which is a term of the form $\{S_1 \& \cdots \& S_n \& \{IK\}\}$ where $\&$ is an associative-commutative union operator with identity symbol $\emptyset$. Each element in the set is either a *strand* S_i (see below) or the *intruder knowledge* $\{IK\}$ (see below) at that state.

The *intruder knowledge* $\{IK\}$ also belongs to the state and is represented as a set of facts. There are two kinds of intruder facts: positive knowledge facts (the intruder knows m, i.e., $m \in \mathcal{I}$), and negative knowledge facts (the intruder *does not yet know* m but *will know it in a future state*, denoted by $m \notin \mathcal{I}$), where m is a message expression.

A *strand* [16] represents the sequence of messages sent and received by a principal executing the protocol and is represented as a sequence of messages $[msg_1^-, msg_2^+, msg_3^-, \ldots, msg_{k-1}^-, msg_k^+]$ such that msg_i is a term of sort Msg, msg^- (also written $-msg$) represents an *input* message, and msg^+ (also written $+msg$) represents an *output* message. Strands are used to represent both the actions of honest principals (with a strand specified for each protocol role) and the actions of an intruder (with a strand specified for each intruder action). In Maude-NPA strands evolve over time; the symbol | is used to divide past and future. Also, we keep track of all the variables of sort

Fresh generated by a concrete strand. That is, all the variables $r_1,\ldots,r_j$ of sort **Fresh** (corresponding to new, unguessable values such as nonces) generated by a strand are made explicit right before the strand, as follows: $::r_1,\ldots,r_j::[\,m_1^\pm,\ \ldots,\ m_i^\pm\mid m_{i+1}^\pm,\ \ldots,\ m_k^\pm\,]$ where $msg_1^\pm,\ldots,msg_i^\pm$ are the past messages, and $msg_{i+1}^\pm,\ldots,msg_k^\pm$ are the future messages ($msg_{i+1}^\pm$ is the immediate future message). The nils are present so that the bar may be placed at the beginning or end of the strand if necessary, but we often remove them, except when there is nothing else between the vertical bar and the beginning or end of a strand. A strand $::r_1,\ldots,r_j::[msg_1^\pm,\ldots,msg_k^\pm]$ is a shorthand for $::r_1,\ldots,r_j::[nil\mid msg_1^\pm,\ldots,msg_k^\pm,nil]$. When it is necessary to identify a strand to distinguish it from other strands, we will do so via a *role name* in parentheses appearing before the strand, e.g. $(Alice)::r_1,\ldots,r_k::[msg_1^\pm,\ldots,msg_n^\pm]$.

Example 1. The strand specification of the Diffe-Hellman protocol described in the Introduction is as follows. Note that we specify a strand for each honest principal, namely Alice and Bob.

$$(Alice)::r,r'::::[+(exp(g,n(A,r))),$$
$$-(X),$$
$$+(e(exp(X,n(A,r)),sec(A,r')))]\ \&$$
$$(Bob)::r''::[-(Y),$$
$$+(exp(g,n(B,r''))),$$
$$-(e(exp(Y,n(B,r'')),Sr))]$$

Intruder strands are also included for each function. For example, the intruder's capability to encrypt a message M with a key K is described by the strand:

$$[-(M),-(K),+(e(K,M))]$$

The protocol analysis methodology of Maude-NPA is then based on *backward reachability analysis*, where we begin with one or more state patterns corresponding to *attack states*, and want to prove or disprove that they are *unreachable* from the set of initial protocol states. In order to perform such a reachability analysis we must describe how states change as a consequence of principals performing protocol steps and of the intruder actions. This can be done by describing such state changes by means of a set $R_\mathcal{P}$ of *rewrite rules*, so that the rewrite theory $(\Sigma_\mathcal{P},E_\mathcal{P},R_\mathcal{P})$ characterizes the behavior of protocol $\mathcal{P}$ modulo the equations $E_\mathcal{P}$.

The following rewrite rules describe the general state transitions, where each state transition implies moving the vertical bar of one strand:

$$\{SS\ \&\ [L\mid M^-,L']\ \&\ \{M{\in}\mathcal{I},IK\}\}\to\{SS\ \&\ [L,M^-\mid L']\ \&\ \{IK\}\}\qquad(1)$$
$$\{SS\ \&\ [L\mid M^+,L']\ \&\ \{IK\}\}\to\{SS\ \&\ [L,M^+\mid L']\ \&\ \{IK\}\}\qquad(2)$$
$$\{SS\ \&\ [L\mid M^+,L']\ \&\ \{M{\notin}\mathcal{I},IK\}\}\to\{SS\ \&\ [L,M^+\mid L']\&\ \{M{\in}\mathcal{I},IK\}\}\quad(3)$$

where variables L,L' denote lists of input and output messages of the form m^+ or m^- within a strand, IK denotes a set of intruder facts ($m{\in}\mathcal{I}$, $m{\notin}\mathcal{I}$), and SS denotes a set of strands. In a *forward execution* of the protocol strands,

Rule (1) synchronizes an input message with a message already learned by the intruder, Rule (2) accepts output messages but the intruder's knowledge is not increased, and Rule (3) accepts output messages and the intruder's knowledge is positively increased. For an unbounded number of sessions, we have extra rewrite rules (one for each positive message in a protocol or intruder strand) that dynamically introduce additional strands into a state.

$$\{ SS \,\&\, [\,l_1 \,|\, u^+, \, l_2\,] \,\&\, \{u{\notin}\mathcal{I}, K\} \rightarrow \{SS \,\&\, \{u{\in}\mathcal{I}, K\}\} \,|\, [\,l_1, \, u^+, \, l_2\,] \in \mathcal{P}\} \quad (4)$$

For example, the intruder capability $[(X)^-, (Y)^-, (X*Y)^+]$ produces the following extra rewrite rule adding a new strand (when the rule is executed backwards) if a message of the form $X*Y$ appears in the intruder knowledge:

$$\{SS \,\&\, [X^-, Y^- \,|\, (X*Y)^+] \,\&\, \{(X*Y){\notin}\mathcal{I}, IK\}\} \rightarrow \{SS \,\&\, \{(X*Y){\in}\mathcal{I}, IK\}\}$$

Therefore, the set of rewrite rules that define the forwards execution of a protocol in Maude-NPA is $R_\mathcal{P} = \{(1), (2), (3)\} \cup (4)$.

The way to analyze *backwards* reachability is then relatively easy, namely, to run the protocol "in reverse". This can be achieved by using the set of rules $R_\mathcal{P}^{-1}$, where $v \longrightarrow u$ is in $R_\mathcal{P}^{-1}$ iff $u \longrightarrow v$ is in $R_\mathcal{P}$.

Example 2. The protocol of Example 1 can be modeled as a rewrite theory $(\Sigma_\mathcal{P}, E_\mathcal{P}, R_\mathcal{P})$ where $R_\mathcal{P}$ is the reversed version of the generic rewrite rules (1)–(3) plus the rewrite rules for introducing new strands. The final pattern used as an input to the backwards symbolic reachability analysis to find the attack described in the Introduction is as follows, including both Alice and Bob at the end of their execution and two generic variables for an unknown set of strands and an unknown set of intruder facts, respectively:

$$\begin{aligned} \{(\text{Alice}) \quad &::r, r'::: [+(exp(g, n(A, r))), \\ &\qquad -(X), \\ &\qquad +(e(exp(X, n(A, r)), sec(A, r'))) \,|\, nil] \,\& \\ (\text{Bob}) \quad &::r''::[-(Y), \\ &\qquad +(exp(g, n(B, r''))), \\ &\qquad -(e(exp(Y, n(B, r'')), sec(A, r'))) \,|\, nil] \,\& \\ &SS \,\&\, \{(exp(X, n(A, r)) \neq exp(Y, n(B, r''))), IK\}\} \end{aligned}$$

This pattern requires the intruder to distinguish the disequality $exp(X, n(A, r)) \neq exp(Y, n(B, r''))$.

4   Distinguishing Disequalities Modulo an Equational Theory

As explained in the Introduction, to increase our confidence in formal protocol verification with an attacker capable to distinguish messages, we want to perform such an analysis with the most discriminating possible attacker model. In this section we make this more precise.

We say that an attacker is able to "distinguish" two messages u and v if it is able to distinguish the disequality $u \neq v$, that is, to detect that the negation $\neg(u = v)$ can be satisfied modulo an equational theory (Σ, E) for the protocol's cryptographic functions.

Assume that the equational theory satisfied by the cryptographic functions of the given protocol is (Σ, E), with Σ an order-sorted signature with non-empty sorts, and E a set of equations. Suppose now that a symbolic attack has been found under the assumption that the attacker can distinguish a disequality $u \neq v$. Since the attack is symbolic, assuming $\overrightarrow{y} = Var(u = v)$, an *actual attack* will exist if the variables $\overrightarrow{y}$ can be instantiated in a model of the equations E such that $u \neq v$ still holds after instantiation.

The existence of an actual attack in *some* implementation can be made precise as follows. First of all, note that an implementation of the cryptographic functions satisfying algebraic properties E is in fact a (Σ, E)-algebra $\mathcal{A}$. However, *the attacker may not fully know the details of such an implementation $\mathcal{A}$.* Therefore, an *attack is possible at all* if:

1. An attack state $\langle St, \Psi \rangle$, with St a state pattern and $\Psi = \bigwedge_{i=1}^{n} u_i \neq_E v_i$, can be reached by symbolic reachability analysis modulo E from an initial state of the protocol.
2. There is an implementation, i.e., a (Σ, E)-algebra $\mathcal{A}$ and an assignment $a \in [\overrightarrow{x} \rightarrow A]$ with $\overrightarrow{x} = Var(\Psi)$ such that $\mathcal{A}, a \models \Psi$.

But condition 2 is precisely the notion of *satisfiability*:

Definition 3. *Given an equational theory (Σ, E), a conjunction of disequalities $\Psi = \bigwedge_{i=1}^{n} u_i \neq_E v_i$ is (Σ, E)-satisfiable iff there is a (Σ, E)-algebra $\mathcal{A}$ and an assignment $a \in [\overrightarrow{x} \rightarrow A]$ with $\overrightarrow{x} = Var(\Psi)$ such that $\mathcal{A}, a \models \Psi$. Equivalently, Ψ is (Σ, E)-satisfiable iff there exists a (Σ, E)-algebra $\mathcal{A}$ such that $\mathcal{A} \models (\exists \overrightarrow{x})\Psi$.*

Stated this way, the search for the most discriminating Dolev-Yao attacker becomes the search for the *most disequality discriminating (Σ, E) algebra*. If we are interested only in satisfiability of the *disequalities*, then we claim that such an algebra is precisely $\mathcal{T}_{\Sigma/E}$, the free (Σ, E)-algebra on the variables $\mathcal{X}$, where for each sort s in Σ, $\mathcal{X}_s$ is a countably infinite set of variables.

Theorem 1. *Let $\mathcal{A}$ be any (Σ, E)-algebra with Σ having non-empty sorts and let $\Psi = \bigwedge_{i=1}^{n} u_i \neq_E v_i$ be a conjunction of disequalities; then if $\mathcal{A} \models \exists \Psi$, we must have $\mathcal{T}_{\Sigma/E}(\mathcal{X}) \models \exists \Psi$. Furthermore, $\mathcal{T}_{\Sigma/E}(\mathcal{X}) \models \exists \Psi$ iff for each $u_i \neq v_i$ in Ψ, $E \vdash u_i \neq v_i$, i.e., $u_i \neq_E v_i$.*

Proof. Let $\overrightarrow{y} = Var(\Psi)$. Without loss of generality we may assume that $\overrightarrow{y} \subseteq \mathcal{X}$. Since $\mathcal{A} \models \exists \Psi$, there is an assignment $a : \overrightarrow{y} \longrightarrow A$ such that $\mathcal{A}, a \models \Psi$. We claim that $\mathcal{T}_{\Sigma/E}(\mathcal{X}) \models \exists \Psi$ with assignment $[id] : \mathcal{X} \ni x \mapsto [x]_E \in \mathcal{T}_{\Sigma/E}(\mathcal{X})$. The proof is by contradiction. Suppose that it does not. This means that $\mathcal{T}_{\Sigma/E}(\mathcal{X}), [id] \not\models \Psi$. Therefore, there must be a j, $1 \leq j \leq n$ such that $\mathcal{T}_{\Sigma/E}(\mathcal{X}), [id] \not\models u_j \neq v_j$. That is, such that $[u_j]_E = [v_j]_E$ and, since Σ is a signature with non-empty sorts, this exactly means that $E \vdash u_j = v_j$. Since $\mathcal{A} \models E$ then, by the Completeness Theorem [19] for order-sorted equational logic, $\mathcal{A} \models u_j = v_j$. But this is a contradiction, since then $\mathcal{A}, a \models u_j = v_j$, and therefore $\mathcal{A}, a \nvDash \bigwedge_{i=1}^{n} u_i \neq v_i$. This proves the first part of the theorem. To see the second part, apply the first part to $\mathcal{A} = \mathcal{T}_{\Sigma/E}(\mathcal{X})$ itself. Then $\mathcal{T}_{\Sigma/E}(\mathcal{X}) \models \exists \Psi$ iff $\mathcal{T}_{\Sigma/E}(\mathcal{X}), [id] \models \Psi$, iff for each $u_i = v_i$, $1 \leq i \leq n$ in Ψ we have $[u_i]_E \neq [v_i]_E$ in $\mathcal{T}_{\Sigma/E}$ i.e., iff $E \vdash u_i = v_i, 1 \leq i \leq n$ as claimed.   □

We can now state more precisely what we mean by a *most discriminating* Dolev-Yao attacker. This is an attacker who can determine whether or not a disequality $u \neq v$ is *satisfiable* in *some* implementation of the cryptographic functions such that the equations E hold, regardless of the choice of such an implementation.

Corollary 1. *A conjunction of disequalities* $\Psi = \bigwedge_{i=1}^{n} u_i \neq v_i$ *is* (Σ, E)- *satisfiable iff* $u_i \neq_E v_i, 1 \leq i \leq n$, *iff* $\mathcal{T}_{\Sigma/E}(\mathcal{X}), [id] \models \Psi$.

If the E equality relation $t =_E t'$ is decidable, this corollary, therefore, gives us a decision procedure that a most-discriminating Dolev-Yao attacker can use to decide whether or not Ψ is satisfiable modulo E in *some* implementation of the cryptographic functions where the equations E hold.

Let us illustrate these ideas with our running example.

Example 3. As explained in the Introduction, our running protocol is subject to an attack where the intruder is finally able to distinguish the disequality $exp(g, N_A * N_{I_B}) \neq exp(g, N_B * N_{I_A})$. That is, the symbolic reachability analysis from the attack pattern described in Example 2 reaches an initial state where the variables of the disequality $exp(X, n(A, r)) \neq exp(Y, n(B, r''))$ have been instantiated in such a way that the intruder can check that it is satisfiable modulo E. More specifically, in such an initial state the disequality $exp(X, n(A, r)) \neq exp(Y, n(B, r''))$ is instantiated as the disequality $exp(g, n(A, r) * n(i, r')) \neq exp(g, n(B, r'') * n(i, r''))$, where $n(i, r')$ and $n(i, r'')$ denote two different nonces generated by the intruder. Since $exp(g, n(A, r) * n(i, r')) \neq_E exp(g, n(B, r'') * n(i, r''))$ holds, because both sides are in canonical form and different modulo AC, this disequality is indeed (Σ, E)-satisfiable.

We use the results proved in this section to define a generic framework to perform symbolic reachability analysis extended with disequality constrains modulo an equational theory (Σ, E) in the next section. That is, given a protocol whose cryptographic functions are modelled by an equational theory (Σ, E), we check whether the intruder can distinguish certain disequalities in the free (Σ, E)- algebra $\mathcal{T}_{\Sigma/E}(\mathcal{X})$.

4.1   Symbolic Reachability Analysis with Disequality Constraints

We present a tool-independent framework for symbolic reachability analysis that extends narrowing modulo an equational theory by considering the satisfiability of disequalities. First, we extend the notion of a protocol state to include, besides the usual information about its various strands and the intruder's knowledge, also the *disequalities* that need to be satisfied at the given stage of protocol analysis. We express this notion by the concept of *constrained state*.

Definition 4 (Constrained State). *Given an order-sorted topmost rewrite theory* $(\Sigma, E, \mathcal{R})$ *a constrained state is a pair* $\langle St, \Psi \rangle$ *consisting of a state expression St and a disequality constraint, i.e., a set* Ψ *of disequalities understood as a conjunction* $\Psi = \bigwedge_{i=1}^{n} u_i \neq_E v_i$ *of disequalities modulo E. Note that* u_i *and* v_i *may not be subterms of St, since disequalities will be accumulated along an execution path.*

Given a protocol $\mathcal{P}$*, a constrained state* $\langle St, \Psi \rangle$ *is satisfiable if the constraint set* $\Psi = \bigwedge_{i=1}^{n} u_i \neq v_i$ *is* (Σ, E)*-satisfiable, i.e. iff* $u_i \neq_E v_i, 1 \leq i \leq n$.

Given a constrained state $\langle St, \Psi \rangle$ with $\Psi = \bigwedge_{i=1}^{n} u_i \neq v_i$ we define its *semantics* $[\![\langle St, \Psi \rangle]\!]$ as the set of all substitution instances of the form:

$$[\![\langle St, \Psi \rangle]\!] = \{St\theta \mid \theta \in [\mathcal{X} \to \mathcal{T}_{\Sigma_{\mathcal{P}}}(\mathcal{X})] \wedge u_i\theta \neq_E v_i\theta, 1 \leq i \leq n\}$$

Then we have the following lemma, that allows us to simplify constrained state.

Lemma 1 (Optimizations). *Let* $(\Sigma, E, \mathcal{R})$ *be an order-sorted topmost rewrite theory, and* $\langle St, \Psi \rangle$ *a constrained state with* $\Psi = \bigwedge_{i=1}^{n} u_i \neq v_i$.

1. *If there is an index* $j, 1 \leq j \leq n$, *such that* $u_j =_E v_j$, *then* $[\![\langle St, \Psi \rangle]\!] = \emptyset$.
2. *If there is an index* $j, 1 \leq j \leq n$, *such that* $CSU_E(u_j = v_j) = \emptyset$, *then* $[\![\langle St, \Psi \rangle]\!] = [\![\langle St, \Psi' \rangle]\!]$ *where* $\Psi' = \bigwedge_{i=1, i \neq j}^{n} u_i \neq v_i$.

Proof. To prove case 1, note that, by Corollary 1, Ψ is then unsatisfiable. To prove case 2, first observe that we always have $[\![\langle St, \Psi \rangle]\!] \subseteq [\![\langle St, \Psi' \rangle]\!]$. We just need to prove the containment $[\![\langle St, \Psi' \rangle]\!] \subseteq [\![\langle St, \Psi \rangle]\!]$. Thus, consider $St\theta \in [\![\langle St, \Psi' \rangle]\!]$, i.e., we have $u_i\theta \neq_E v_i\theta$ for $1 \leq i \leq n, i \neq j$. But since $CSU_E(u_j = v_j) = \emptyset$ we must also have $u_j\theta \neq_E v_j\theta$, and therefore, $St\theta \in [\![\langle St, \Psi \rangle]\!]$, as desired.   □

4.2 Constrained Reachability Analysis in Maude-NPA

In this section we explain in detail how Maude-NPA can be fully adapted to the framework described in Sect. 4.1 in order to perform constrained symbolic reachability analysis for protocols satisfying the FV property.

The behavior of a protocol $\mathcal{P}$ is now modeled by a rewrite theory $(\Sigma_{\mathcal{P}}, E_{\mathcal{P}}, R_{\mathcal{P}})$ whose states are constrained states, represented in Maude-NPA as state expressions, i.e., as terms of sort State, where the disequality constraint Ψ is seen as part of the intruder knowledge. That is, constrained state is of the form:

$$\{s_1 \ \& \ s_2 \ \& \ \cdots \ \& \ s_n \ \& \ \{m_1 \in \mathcal{I}, \ldots, m_k \in \mathcal{I}, m_1' \notin \mathcal{I}, \ldots, m_j' \notin \mathcal{I}, u_1 \neq v_1, \ldots, u_l \neq v_l\}\}$$

where s_1 & s_2 & $\cdots$ & s_n are strands.

The set of rewrite rules $R_{\mathcal{P}}$ describing a protocol's execution can be obtained by adapting the rules in $R_{\mathcal{P}}$ to consider constrained states. Since disequalities are now part of the intruder knowledge, as explained above, Rules (1), (2), (3), and (4) remain the same. Syntactically we can view $\neq$ as a new *constructor symbol* added to the signature $\Sigma_{\mathcal{P}}$, so that we can now add disequality constraints $u \neq v$ as new facts to the intruder knowledge.

A feature of Maude-NPA originally documented in [12, Definition 7] to perform case analysis by splitting a state based on the intruder knowledge, and which has not been included in our latest presentations of Maude-NPA, can now be described easily using disequalities. When there are two E-unifiable terms $t_1 \in \mathcal{I}$ and $t_2 \in \mathcal{I}$ in the intruder knowledge of a state, it is possible that those two terms will become E-equal in the initial state, though they may be different modulo E in the current state. Thus the symbolic search needs to consider both cases: t_1 and t_2 are different, or they are the same. In [12, Definition 7], this was solved by splitting a state with $t_1 \in \mathcal{I}$ and $t_2 \in \mathcal{I}$ in the intruder knowledge into *two* states: one in which $t_1 = t_2$, and another in which the disequality $t_1 \neq t_2$ is added to the state as a constraint.

To model this type of state splitting we just need two more rules that allow Maude-NPA to check whether some facts in the intruder knowledge can be unified and, in such a case, create two versions of the same state, one where both facts unify and another one where they are necessarily different, and, thus, add a new disequality to the constrained state. These two cases are described by the two rules below, respectively.

$$\{SS \ \& \ \{M_1 \in \mathcal{I}, (M_1 = M_2), IK\}\} \rightarrow \{SS \ \& \ \{M_1 \in \mathcal{I}, M_2 \in \mathcal{I}, IK\}\}$$
$$\{SS \ \& \ \{M_1 \in \mathcal{I}, M_2 \in \mathcal{I}, (M_1 \neq M_2), IK\}\} \rightarrow \{SS \ \& \ \{M_1 \in \mathcal{I}, M_2 \in \mathcal{I}, IK\}\}$$

However, Maude-NPA performs backwards narrowing and the equality constraint $M_1 = M_2$ can be simply solved by E-unification, just replacing the first rule by the following rule where one variable M is used instead of the two variables M_1 and M_2. Equational E-unification will provide the desired behavior above, since by having the same variable M in two intruder facts, the equality constraint $M_1 = M_2$ will be tested but also solved, simplifying the search space.

$$\{SS \ \& \ \{M \in \mathcal{I}, IK\}\} \rightarrow \{SS \ \& \ \{M \in \mathcal{I}, M \in \mathcal{I}, IK\}\} \quad (5)$$
$$\{SS \ \& \ \{M_1 \in \mathcal{I}, M_2 \in \mathcal{I}, (M_1 \neq M_2), IK\}\} \rightarrow \{SS \ \& \ \{M_1 \in \mathcal{I}, M_2 \in \mathcal{I}, IK\}\} \quad (6)$$

Therefore, the rewrite rules that define the forwards execution of a protocol in Maude-NPA are now $R_{\mathcal{P}} = \{(1), (2), (3)\} \cup (4) \cup \{ (5) \cup (6)\}$.

In summary, by making explicit a feature already implicit in Maude-NPA, namely that:

1 the intruder knowledge can be of the form $IK = IK' \ \& \ \Psi$ where IK' consist entirely of facts $M \in \mathcal{I}$ and $M' \notin \mathcal{I}$, and Ψ is a conjuction of disequality constraints, and

2 some rewrite rules such as rule (6) when applied backwards can *add* now disequality constraints $M_1 \neq M_2$ to the intruder knowledge,

we can seamlessly extend the semantic framework of Maude-NPA to one where:

(i) states of the form $\{SS \& IK' \& \Psi\}$ do in fact correspond to *constrained states* of the form $\langle\{SS \& IK'\}, \Psi\rangle$,
(ii) the *semantics* of such states is precisely $[\![\langle\{SS \& IK'\}, \Psi\rangle]\!]$, and
(iii) narrowing is seamlessly extended to constrained states, allowing us to model by rules (5) and (6) the case splitting of states that was already performed before, but was formerly treated as a state optimization feature.

Note that, since Maude-NPA searches backwards, checking the unsatisfiability of a state's constraint can be used for state space reduction purposes. More specifically, given a constrained state containing an unsatisfiable disequality, then no initial constrained state can be reached by searching backwards from this constrained state and, thus, it can safely be discarded.

5   Symbolic Reachability with Disequalities Modulo FVP Theories

Lemma 1 above defines two methods to improve the search space: (i) discard a state with a disequality $u \neq v$ whenever $u =_E v$, since both terms are equal modulo the equational theory for *any* possible implementation of the cryptographic functions, and (ii) remove disequalities of the form $u \neq v$ such that $CSU_E(u = v) = \emptyset$, since they are true for any possible implementation of the cryptographic functions. In this section we consider a third method to improve the search space by generating the variants of a disequality $u \neq v$.

When the equational theory (Σ, E) has a decomposition (Σ, B, E_0) satisfying the Finite Variant Property (FVP) (see Sect. 2) and B has a finitely B-unification algorithm, we can have a better satisfiability method for disequalities.

Corollary 2. *Given an decomposition (Σ, B, E_0) of an equational theory (Σ, E), a disequality $\exists \overrightarrow{y}\ u \neq v$, with $\overrightarrow{y} = Var(u \neq v)$, and a E_0, B-normalized substitution $\alpha \in [\overrightarrow{y} \to \mathcal{T}_\Sigma(\mathcal{X})]$, the following statements are equivalent:*

1. $\mathcal{T}_{\Sigma/E}(\mathcal{X}), [\alpha]_E \models u \neq v$
2. $(u\alpha)\!\downarrow_{E_0,B} \neq_B (v\alpha)\!\downarrow_{E_0,B}$
3. *there exists an E_0, B- variant $(u' \neq v', \theta)$ of $u \neq v$ (where, as said above $\neq$ is understood as a constructor symbol), and an E_0, B-irreducible substitution γ such that*
   (a) $(u\alpha)\!\downarrow_{E_0,B} =_B u'\gamma$,
   (b) $(v\alpha)\!\downarrow_{E_0,B} =_B v'\gamma$,
   (c) $u'\gamma \neq_B v'\gamma$, and
   (d) $\alpha =_B \theta\gamma$

Thus, given such an equational theory, we can improve the search space by computing the variants of disequalities in the hope that we can detect an inconsistency earlier in the search space. Note, however, the crucial *irreducibility* requirements that for a disequality $u \neq v$ and one of its variants $(u' \neq v', \theta)$ such that $\alpha =_B \theta\gamma$ we must have $u'\gamma\downarrow_{E_0,B} = u'\gamma$, and $v'\gamma\downarrow_{E_0,B} = v'\gamma$. That is, u' and v' must be kept *irreducible* under the allowed instantiations.

The computation of the variants of disequalities does not happen in a void, but in the context of the constrained term $\langle St, \Psi \rangle$. Therefore, a constrained state $\langle St, \Psi \rangle$ is indeed a term where we can compute *its variants* $(\langle St_1, \Psi_1 \rangle, \theta_1), \dots (\langle St_k, \Psi_k \rangle, \theta_k)$, which will now come with *extra irreducibility conditions* generated from certain subterms in both St_i and Ψ_i. Note that in Maude-NPA a constrained state $\langle \{SS \& \{IK\}\}, \Psi \rangle$ is represented as an extended state of the form $\{SS \& \{IK', \Psi\}\}$.

Example 4. For example, the constrained state shown below, which is obtained after one backwards reachability step from the attack pattern of Example 2:

$$\{(\text{Alice}) \quad ::r, r'::: [+(exp(g, n(A, r))), -(X),$$
$$+(e(exp(X, n(A, r)), sec(A, r'))) \mid nil] \ \&$$
$$(\text{Bob}) \qquad ::r'':: [-(Y), +(exp(g, n(B, r''))) \mid$$
$$-(e(exp(Y, n(B, r'')), sec(A, r')))] \ \&$$
$$SS \ \& \ \{(exp(X, n(A, r)) \neq exp(Y, n(B, r''))), IK\}\}$$

has the following four variants, where the terms $irr(M)$ are the irreducibility requirements on the term M.

1. Applying the *id* substitution:

$$\{(\text{Alice}) ::r, r' : :: [+(exp(g, n(A, r))), -(X),$$
$$+(e(exp(X, n(A, r)), sec(A, r'))) \mid nil] \ \&$$
$$(\text{Bob}) ::r'':: [-(Y), +(exp(g, n(B, r''))) \mid$$
$$-(e(exp(Y, n(B, r'')), sec(A, r')))] \ \&$$
$$SS\& \ \{(exp(X, n(A, r)) \neq exp(Y, n(B, r''))),$$
$$irr(exp(X, n(A, r))), irr(exp(Y, n(B, r''))), IK\}\}$$

2. Applying substitution $\{X \mapsto exp(g, NS)\}$, where NS is a variable of the sort for product of nonces:

$$\{(\text{Alice}) ::r, r'::: [+(exp(g, n(A, r))), -(exp(g, NS)),$$
$$+(e(exp(g, n(A, r) * NS), sec(A, r'))) \mid nil] \ \&$$
$$(\text{Bob}) ::r'':: [-(Y), +(exp(g, n(B, r''))) \mid$$
$$-(e(exp(Y, n(B, r'')), sec(A, r')))] \ \&$$
$$SS \ \& \ \{(exp(g, n(A, r) * NS) \neq exp(Y, n(B, r''))),$$
$$irr(exp(g, n(A, r) * NS)), irr(exp(Y, n(B, r''))), IK\}\}$$

3. Applying substitution $\{Y \mapsto exp(g, NS')\}$, where NS' is a variable of the sort for product of nonces:

$$\{(\text{Alice})::r, r'::::[+(exp(g, n(A, r))), -(X),$$
$$+(e(exp(X, n(A, r)), sec(A, r'))) \mid nil]\&$$
$$(\text{Bob})::r''::[-(exp(g, NS'')), +(exp(g, n(B, r''))) \mid$$
$$-(e(exp(g, n(B, r'') * NS')), sec(A, r')))] \&$$
$$SS \&\{(exp(X, n(A, r)) \neq exp(g, n(B, r'') * NS')),$$
$$irr(exp(X, n(A, r))), irr(exp(g, n(B, r'') * NS')), IK\}\}$$

4. Applying substitution $\{X \mapsto exp(g, NS), Y \mapsto exp(g, NS')\}$, where NS and NS' are variables of the sort for product of nonces:

$$\{(\text{Alice}) \quad ::r, r'::::[+(exp(g, n(A, r))), -(exp(g, NS)),$$
$$+(e(exp(g, n(A, r) * NS), sec(A, r'))) \mid nil] \&$$
$$(\text{Bob}) \quad ::r''::[-(exp(g, NS')), +(exp(g, n(B, r''))) \mid$$
$$-(e(exp(g, n(B, r'') * NS'), sec(A, r')))] \&$$
$$SS \& \{(exp(g, n(A, r) * NS) \neq exp(g, n(B, r'') * NS')),$$
$$irr(exp(g, n(A, r) * NS)), irr(exp(g, n(B, r'') * NS')), IK\}\}$$

5.1 Constrained Symbolic Reachability Analysis Modulo FVP Theories

In the following we explain in detail how both the framework for constrained symbolic reachability analysis with disequalities presented in Sect. 4.1 and the framework for symbolic reachability analysis with irreducibility constraints presented in [10] can be combined. A useful insight from [10] is that irreducibility is *context-sensitive*. For example, in a symbolic state all terms in the intruder knowledge as well as "negative" terms $-M$ in strands corresponding to messages received or to be received must indeed be irreducible; but positive terms $+M$, which typically describe cryptographic operations to be performed by a principal before sending the resulting message M, need not be irreducible. This intuition is captured by the notion of *contextual rewrite theory*.

Definition 5 (Contextual Rewrite Theory). [10] *A contextual rewrite theory is a tuple* $(\Sigma, B, E_0, R, \phi)$ *where* $(\Sigma, B \cup E_0, R)$ *is an order-sorted topmost rewrite theory,* (Σ, B, E_0) *is a decomposition of the equational theory* $(\Sigma, B \cup E_0)$, *and* ϕ, *called the* irreducibility requirements, *is a function mapping each* $f \in \Sigma$ *to a set of its arguments, i.e.,* $\phi(f) \subseteq \{1, \ldots, ar(f)\}$, *where* $ar(f)$ *is the number of arguments of* f. *The set of maximal irreducible positions of a term* t *is denoted by* $\phi(t)$.

A term t *is called* ϕ, E_0, B-*irreducible (or just* ϕ-*irreducible) if for each* $p \in \phi(t)$, $t|_p{\downarrow}_{E_0,B} =_B t|_p$, *and strongly* ϕ-*irreducible if for any* E_0, B-*normalized substitution* σ, $t\sigma$ *is* ϕ-*irreducible.*

We extend the notion of constrained state (Definition 4) to the contextual case.

Definition 6 *(Contextual Constrained State). Given a contextual order-sorted topmost rewrite theory* $(\Sigma, B, E_0, R, \phi)$ *a constrained state is a term of the form* $\langle St, \Pi, \Psi \rangle$. *More specifically,* Π *is a set of* Σ-*terms such that each term* $w \in \Pi$ *must be kept* E_0, B-*irreducible (we say* Π *are the* E_0, B-*irreducibility constraints) and* Ψ *is a conjunction of disequalities modulo* $E_0 \cup B$. *A contextual constrained state is* satisfiable *iff (i) the constraint set* Ψ *is satisfiable; and (ii) each* $w \in \Pi$ *is irreducible.*

Given a contextual constrained state $\langle St, \Pi, \Psi \rangle$ with $\Pi = w_1, \ldots, w_k$ and $\Psi = \bigwedge_{i=1}^n u_i \neq v_i$ we define its *semantics* $[\![\langle St, \Pi, \Psi \rangle]\!]$ in $\mathcal{T}_{\Sigma/E}(\mathcal{X})$ as the set of all substitution instances of the form:

$$[\![\langle St, \Pi, \Psi \rangle]\!] = \{ St\theta \mid \theta \in [\mathcal{X} \to \mathcal{T}_{\Sigma_\mathcal{P}}(\mathcal{X})] \wedge (u_i\theta){\downarrow}_{E_0,B} \neq_B (v_i\theta){\downarrow}_{E_0,B}, 1 \le i \le n,$$
$$\wedge \; w_i\theta = (w_i\theta){\downarrow}_{E_0,B}, 1 \le i \le k \}$$

Essentially, the framework of [10] carries along the irreducibility constraints Π associated to each state and performs some specific tasks:

1. Generate variants of all the subterms in a state St according to mapping ϕ, that is, for subterms of St at positions $\phi(St)$; in Maude-NPA only the symbol $\_\in\mathcal{I}$ for positive intruder facts and the symbol $-(\_)$ for input messages in a strand have their arguments marked as irreducible by the irreducibility function ϕ.
2. For each group of variants of the subterms of St at positions $\phi(St)$, add those terms to Π as irreducibility constraints.
3. Include Π as irreducibility constraints in each equational unification problem associated to backwards narrowing by using the concept of *asymmetric equational unification* (see [10]) so that the computed unifiers never invalidate the irreducibility constraints.

In our extended framework for disequalities, the only added requirements are that we must: (i) generate variants of disequalities Ψ; and (ii) add to Π irreducibility constraints associated to Ψ. But this can be easily done extending Σ to a signature $\Sigma^{\neq}$ by adding the symbol $\_ \neq \_$ and specifying the irreducibility of both arguments using the function ϕ.

5.2   Contextual Constrained Reachability Analysis in Maude-NPA

In this section we explain in detail how Maude-NPA can be fully adapted to the framework described in Sect. 5.1 in order to perform contextual constrained symbolic reachability analysis for protocols with FVP theories.

Given a protocol $\mathcal{P}$ its behavior is now modeled by a contextual constrained rewrite theory $(\Sigma_\mathcal{P}^{\neq}, E_\mathcal{P}, R_\mathcal{P}, \phi)$. Constrained states are represented in Maude-NPA as regular states, that is, as terms of sort State, where the irreducibility information is also part of the intruder knowledge. That is, constrained states $\langle St, \Pi, \Psi \rangle$ are represented as extended states of the form:

$$\{s_1 \, \& \, s_2 \, \& \, \cdots \, \& \, s_n \, \&$$
$$\{m_1 \in \mathcal{I}, \ldots, m_i \in \mathcal{I}, m'_1 \notin \mathcal{I}, \ldots, m'_j \notin \mathcal{I},$$
$$irr(w_1), \ldots, irr(w_l), \; u_1 \neq v_1, \ldots, u_k \neq v_k \}\}$$

The set of rewrite rules $R_{\mathcal{P}}$ describing a protocol's execution is equivalent to these in Sect. 4.2. Therefore, the rewrite rules that define the forwards execution of a protocol in Maude-NPA is the same as in Sect. 4.2. The only difference is how Maude-NPA establishes the positions of the function ϕ but this is simple: $\phi(\_ \in \mathcal{I}) = \{1\}$, $\phi(-(\_)) = \{1\}$, and $\phi(\_ \neq \_) = \{1, 2\}$.

In summary, we reuse an existing framework for irreducibility constraints in Maude-NPA in the following way:

1. the intruder knowledge can be of the form $IK = IK' \, \& \, \Pi \, \& \, \Psi$, where IK' consist entirely of facts $M \in \mathcal{I}$ and $M \notin \mathcal{I}$, Π is a list of terms $w_1, \ldots, w_k$, understood as irreducibility constraints, and Ψ is a conjunction of disequality constraints, and
2. we add irreducibility information for the disequality symbol $\neq$ so that the framework generates variants and adds irreducibility constraints automatically.

We therefore seamlessly extend the semantic framework of Maude-NPA to one where:

(i) states of the form $\{SS \, \& \, \{IK' \, \& \, \Pi \, \& \, \Psi\}\}$ do in fact correspond to *contextual constrained states* of the form $\langle \{SS \, \& \, \{IK'\}\}, \Pi, \Psi \rangle$,

(ii) the *semantics* of such states is precisely $[\![\langle \{SS \, \& \, \{IK'\}\}, \Pi, \Psi \rangle]\!]$, and

(iii) the framework for narrowing with irreducibility constraints of [10] is used.

6   Experiments

We have performed an experimental evaluation to compare the performance of the different approaches, presented in this paper to deal with disequality constraints when performing symbolic protocol analysis modulo equational theories. Table 1 gathers the results of our experiments, which are also available online at http://www.dsic.upv.es/~sescobar/Maude-NPA/disequalities.html. More specifically, we have analyzed several cryptographic protocols in the Maude-NPA tool, considering the following approaches:

– **Strategy** 0: Search for an attack by starting from an attack pattern and going backwards towards an initial state, where any disequality constraint included in the attack pattern or added during the backwards process is *ignored* until the initial state is reached.

- **Strategy** A: We work as in strategy 0, but any disequality constraint included in the attack pattern or added during the backwards process is checked for *equality*. That is, we discard any state containing a disequality $u \neq v$ such that $u =_E v$. In reality, since $E = B \cup E_0$ with E_0 convergent modulo B, we discard any state containing a disequality $u \neq v$ such that $u{\downarrow}_{E_0,B} =_B v{\downarrow}_{E_0,B}$.
- **Strategy** $A + B$: We work as in strategy A, but any disequality constraint included in the attack pattern or added during the backwards process is checked for *unifiability*. That is, given a state containing a disequality $u \neq v$ such that $CSU_{B \cup E_0}(u = v) = \emptyset$, we remove the disequality and keep the rest of the state.
- **Strategy** $A + C$: We work as in strategy A but any disequality constraint included in the attack pattern or added during the backwards process is replaced by its variants and appropriate irreducibility constraints. That is, given a state St containing a disequality $u \neq v$ (this easily generalizes to a set of disequalities), we generate its variants $(u_1 \neq v_1, \theta_1), \ldots, (u_k \neq v_k, \theta_k)$ and obtain the appropriate states $St_1, \ldots, St_k$ by replacing the disequality $u \neq v$ by $u_i \neq v_i$, adding two irreducibility constraints $irr(u_i)$ and $irr(v_i)$, and applying the substitution θ_i to the resulting state. For each of the variant states, we discard it if it contains a disequality $u' \neq v'$ such that $u' =_B v'$.
- **Strategy** $A + B + C$: We put together all three ideas A, B, and C. That is, given a state St containing a disequality $u \neq v$, we generate its variants states $St_1, \ldots, St_k$. Now, for each one of the variant states, we discard it if it contains a disequality $u' \neq v'$ such that $u' =_B v'$. And, furthermore, we remove any disequality $u'' \neq v''$ such that $CSU_B(u'' = v'') = \emptyset$ satisfying the irreducibility constraints, i.e., for every substitution $\rho \in CSU_B(u'' = v'')$ and every irreducibility constraints $irr(w)$ in the state, $w\rho$ is still E_0, B-irreducible.

We have analyzed a suite of protocols already specified in Maude-NPA. Below we describe in detail the experiments we have performed. Note that for some protocols we have performed several analyses searching for different types of attacks, i.e., starting from different attack patterns.

- For the Diffie-Hellman protocol described in the Introduction, we have performed three analyses searching for three different attacks, namely: (i) the attack described in the Introduction, (ii) a secrecy attack, and (iii) an authentication attack. They correspond to labels "DH-diseq", "DH-sec" and "DH-auth" in Table 1, respectively.
- We have analyzed a protocol involving exclusive-or, namely "XOR-esorics" (the running example protocol of [10]).
- For the standard Needham-Schroeder protocol [21] (NSPK) and its fixed version proposed by Lowe in [17] (NSL) we have considered two types of attacks: (i) a secrecy attack in which the intruder can learn a nonce generated by a honest principal, referred as protocols "NSPK-sec" and "NSL-sec", respectively; and (ii) an authentication attack in the style of our running example, which includes a disequality in the attack patter, referred as protocols "NSPK-diseq" and "NSL-diseq", respectively.

– We have also analyzed two versions of the NSL protocol, namely the Needham-
Schroeder-Lowe Modified Protocol with ECB (following the informal specification given in [8]), and a version in which one of the concatenation operators is
replaced by an exclusive-or, presented in [23]. These two protocols are labeled
in Table 1 as "NSL-ECB" and "NSL-XOR", respectively. In both cases we
searched for a secrecy attack.
– Protocol "SecReT06" corresponds to a protocol with an attack using type
confusion and a bounded version of associativity presented in [13], whereas
protocol "SecReT07" is a short version of the Diffie-Hellman protocol that
was presented in [11].
– Finally, protocol "Indist-ENC" corresponds to a protocol involving cancella-
tion of encryption and decryption, presented in [22], for which we analyzed
an indistinghishability property.

Table 1 summarizes all the experiments. For example, the analysis of the
DH-diseq protocol using *Strategy 0* generated 147 states, whereas the analysis
following *Strategy $A + B + C$* generated 105 states. The reader can check that
there is no clear conclusion about which strategy is the best: e.g., $A + B + C$
is the best for DH-auth but C is not good for DH-diseq and B is the key for
NSPK-diseq. For attack states that do not include disequalities (all protocol
analyses with the suffix "sec") the strategies had no affect either way.

On the other hand, even if the search space associated to a protocol is bigger
or smaller depending on the strategy, the same results are always obtained. We
show the detailed execution of two protocols, DH-diseq and NSPK-diseq, for
strategies $A + B$ and $A + B + C$; DH-diseq in Tables 2 and 3 and NSPK-diseq in
Tables 4 and 5. For DH-diseq, the best strategy was $A + B$ and the reader can

Table 1. Total number of states generated for each protocol and each strategy

Protocol	Strat. 0	Strat. A	Strat. $A + B$	Strat. $A + C$	Strat. $A + B + C$
DH-diseq	147	90	90	105	105
DH-sec	113	113	113	113	113
DH-auth	129	129	129	129	115
XOR-esorics	22	22	22	22	22
NSPK-sec	27	27	27	27	27
NSPK-diseq	235	209	203	209	203
NSL-sec	19	19	19	19	19
NSL-diseq	254	225	265	225	265
NSL-ECB	85	85	85	85	85
NSL-XOR	24	24	24	24	24
SecReT06	6	6	6	6	6
SecReT07	9	9	9	9	9
Indist-ENC	5	5	5	5	5

Table 2. States and execution time for DH-diseq protocol with Strategy $A + B$

	1	2	3	4	5	6	7	8	9	10	11	12	Total
States	4	8	8	8	12	12	13	13	6	3	2	1	90
Time (s)	11,2	14,8	35,0	62,1	43,3	80,5	120,9	173,8	74,2	25,6	12,7	3,7	657,6

Table 3. States and execution time for DH-diseq protocol with Strategy $A + B + C$

	1	2	3	4	5	6	7	8	9	10	11	12	Total
States	4	8	10	12	16	15	15	13	6	3	2	1	105
Time (s)	9,8	12,1	28,2	68,5	99,1	138,7	146,8	187,6	113,7	26	14,5	6,3	851,3

Table 4. States and execution time for NSPK-diseq protocol with Strategy A + B

	1	2	3	4	5	6	7	8	9	Total
States	4	9	15	29	46	54	33	11	2	203
Time (s)	2,1	5,5	12,2	29,9	55,7	90,2	95,5	60,8	17,5	369,4

Table 5. States and execution time for NSPK-diseq protocol with Strategy $A + B + C$

	1	2	3	4	5	6	7	8	9	Total
States	4	9	15	29	46	54	33	11	2	203
Time (s)	2,1	5,5	5,5	24,5	56,8	90,0	96,0	60,8	17,6	358,9

check that the number of states for $A+B+C$ is increased already at the beginning
of the backwards search, since the variants of the disequalities are generated at
the very beginning. In this protocol, the backwards search is able to instantiate
the disequalities in the right form and, thus, variant generation becomes useless
because it generates multiple redundant paths leading to the same initial state.
However, those paths are discarded further below in the backwards search and
the two search spaces become the same from depth 8 on. The execution time is
clearly different, since variant generation is expensive. For NSPK-diseq, the best
strategy is to use B, either in $A + B$ or $A + B + C$, thus Tables 4 and 5 show
that generating the variants of the disequalities helps to reduce the execution
time, since the strategy $A + B$ implies a unifiability test using the whole theory
$B \cup E_0$ whereas $A + B + C$ implies a unifiability test using only B.

    We can give several conjectures as to why the performance of strategies B
and C were variable. For the case of C, variant generation can provide more
fine-grained control of disequalities, but the production of variants also generates more states, as shown by the analysis above. For the case of B, it is at first
harder to see why merely removing a disequality from a state, without removing
or adding any states, would have an effect on the number of states. However,
strategy B has an effect on Maude-NPA's subsumption partial order reduction,

in which (essentially) states that are subsumed by other states are discarded as redundant. Removing a disequality constraint could have effects on the subsumption relation either way. The solution here would appear to be integrate strategy B more closely with the subsumption partial order reduction.

7   Conclusions

We have provided a framework for reasoning about disequalities in formal cryptographic protocol analysis that takes into account the idea of a *most discriminating Dolev-Yao intruder* who can detect any inequality that may hold in an implementation. We have used this framework to develop a number of strategies for handling disequalities, whose soundness and completeness we have also proved in this paper. We have also implemented these strategies in Maude-NPA and assessed their performance experimentally.

We do not expect the usefulness of this framework to stop here however. We expect to continue to use it to refine our strategies and develop new ones. In particular, we expect it to be helpful in the development and implementation of disunification algorithms that can be applied to cryptographic protocol analysis, a topic we are currently investigating.

Acknowledgements. This work has been partially supported by NSF grant CNS 13-19109, by the EU (FEDER) and the Spanish MINECO under grant TIN 2013-45732-C4-1-P, and by Spanish Generalitat Valenciana under grant PROMETEOII/2015/013.

References

1. Baader, F., Schulz, K.U.: Combination techniques and decision problems for disunification. Theor. Comput. Sci. **142**(2), 229–255 (1995)
2. Blanchet, B.: Using horn clauses for analyzing security protocols. In: Cortier, V., Kremer, S. (eds.) Formal Models and Techniques for Analyzing Security Protocols. Cryptology and Information Security Series, vol. 5, pp. 86–111. IOS Press, March 2011
3. Blanchet, B., Abadi, M., Fournet, C.: Automated verification of selected equivalences for security protocols. J. Log. Algebr. Program. **75**(1), 3–51 (2008)
4. Comon, H., Lescanne, P.: Equational problems and disunification. J. Symb. Comput. **7**, 371–425 (1989)
5. Comon, H.: Complete axiomatizations of some quotient term algebras. In: Albert, J.L., Monien, B., Artalejo, M.R. (eds.) Automata, Languages and Programming. LNCS, vol. 510, pp. 469–480. Springer, Heidelberg (1991)
6. Comon, H.: Disunification: a survey. In: Computational Logic - Essays in Honor of Alan Robinson, pp. 322–359 (1991)
7. Comon-Lundh, H., Delaune, S.: The finite variant property: how to get rid of some algebraic properties. In: Giesl, J. (ed.) RTA 2005. LNCS, vol. 3467, pp. 294–307. Springer, Heidelberg (2005)
8. Cortier, V., Delaune, S., Lafourcade, P.: A survey of algebraic properties used in cryptographic protocols. J. Comput. Secur. **14**(1), 1–43 (2006)

9. Dolev, D., Yao, A.: On the security of public key protocols. IEEE Trans. Inf. Theory **29**(2), 198–208 (1983)
10. Erbatur, S., et al.: Effective symbolic protocol analysis via equational irreducibility conditions. In: Foresti, S., Yung, M., Martinelli, F. (eds.) ESORICS 2012. LNCS, vol. 7459, pp. 73–90. Springer, Heidelberg (2012)
11. Escobar, S., Hendrix, J., Meadows, C., Meseguer, J.: Diffie-Hellman cryptographic reasoning in the Maude-NRL protocol analyzer. In: Proceedings of the 2nd International Workshop on Security and Rewriting Techniques (SecReT 2007) (2007)
12. Escobar, S., Meadows, C., Meseguer, J.: A rewriting-based inference system for the NRL protocol analyzer and its meta-logical properties. Theor. Comput. Sci. **367**(1–2), 162–202 (2006)
13. Escobar, S., Meadows, C., Meseguer, J.: Equational cryptographic reasoning in the Maude-NRL protocol analyzer. In: Proceedings of the 1st International Workshop on Security and Rewriting Techniques (SecReT 2006). ENTCS, vol. 171, no. 4, pp. 23–36. Elsevier (2007)
14. Escobar, S., Meadows, C., Meseguer, J.: Maude-NPA: cryptographic protocol analysis modulo equational properties. In: Aldini, A., Barthe, G., Gorrieri, R. (eds.) FOSAD 2007/2008/2009. LNCS, vol. 5705, pp. 1–50. Springer, Heidelberg (2009)
15. Escobar, S., Sasse, R., Meseguer, J.: Folding variant narrowing and optimal variant termination. J. Log. Algebr. Program. **81**(7–8), 898–928 (2012)
16. Thayer Fabrega, F.J., Herzog, J., Guttman, J.: Strand spaces: what makes a security protocol correct? J. Comput. Secur. **7**, 191–230 (1999)
17. Lowe, G.: Breaking and fixing the Needham-Schroeder public-key protocol using FDR. In: Margaria, T., Steffen, B. (eds.) TACAS 1996. LNCS, vol. 1055, pp. 147–166. Springer, Heidelberg (1996)
18. Meseguer, J.: Conditional rewriting logic as a unified model of concurrency. Theor. Comput. Sci. **96**(1), 73–155 (1992)
19. Meseguer, J.: Membership algebra as a logical framework for equational specification. In: Presicce, F.P. (ed.) Recent Trends in Algebraic Development Techniques. LNCS, vol. 1376, pp. 18–61. Springer, Heidelberg (1997)
20. Mödersheim, S., Viganò, L., Basin, D.A.: Constraint differentiation: Search-space reduction for the constraint-based analysis of security protocols. J. Comput. Secur. **18**(4), 575–618 (2010)
21. Needham, R.M., Schroeder, M.D.: Using encryption for authentication in large networks of computers. Commun. ACM **21**(12), 993–999 (1978)
22. Santiago, S., Escobar, S., Meadows, C., Meseguer, J.: A formal definition of protocol indistinguishability and its verification using Maude-NPA. In: Mauw, S., Jensen, C.D. (eds.) STM 2014. LNCS, vol. 8743, pp. 162–177. Springer, Heidelberg (2014)
23. Sasse, R., Escobar, S., Meadows, C., Meseguer, J.: Protocol analysis modulo combination of theories: a case study in Maude-NPA. In: Cuellar, J., Lopez, J., Barthe, G., Pretschner, A. (eds.) STM 2010. LNCS, vol. 6710, pp. 163–178. Springer, Heidelberg (2011)
24. TeReSe: Term Rewriting Systems. Cambridge University Press, Cambridge (2003)
25. Thati, P., Meseguer, J.: Symbolic reachability analysis using narrowing and its application verification of cryptographic protocols. J. Higher-Order Symb. Comput. **20**(1–2), 123–160 (2007)

Language Representability of Finite P/T Nets

Roberto Gorrieri[✉]

Dipartimento di Informatica — Scienza e Ingegneria,
Università di Bologna, Mura A. Zamboni, 7, 40127 Bologna, Italy
roberto.gorrieri@unibo.it

Abstract. Finite-net Multi-CCS is a CCS-like calculus which is able to model atomic sequences of actions and, together with parallel composition, also multi-party synchronization. This calculus is equipped with a labeled transition system semantics and also with an unsafe P/T Petri net semantics, which is sound w.r.t. the transition system semantics. For any process p of the calculus, the net associated to p by the semantics has always a finite number of places, but it has a finite number of transitions only for so-called well-formed processes. The main result of the paper is that well-formed finite-net Multi-CCS processes are able to represent all finite, statically reduced, P/T Petri nets.

1 Introduction

Labeled transition systems with finitely many states and transitions can be expressed by the CCS [18] sub-calculus of *finite-state processes*, i.e., the sequential processes generated from the empty process **0**, prefixing $\mu.p$, alternative composition $p_1 + p_2$ and a finite number of process constants C, each one equipped with a defining equation $C \stackrel{def}{=} p$. This famous result of Milner offers a process calculus to express, up to isomorphism, all finite-state labeled transition systems.

This paper addresses the same language expressibility problem for finite labeled Place/Transition Petri nets without capacity bounds on places. We single out a fragment (called *finite-net processes*) of an extension of CCS (called Multi-CCS, fully described in [14]), such that not only all processes of this fragment generate finite P/T nets, but also for any finite (statically reduced) P/T net we can find a term of the calculus that generates it. This solves the open problem of providing a process calculus representing finite P/T Petri nets, and opens interesting possibilities of cross-fertilization between the areas of Petri nets and process calculi. In particular, it is now possible, on the one hand, (*i*) to define any (statically reduced) finite P/T net compositionally and (*ii*) to study algebraic laws for net-based behavioral equivalences (such as net isomorphism) over such a large class of systems; on the other hand, it is now possible (*iii*) to reuse all the techniques and decidability results available for P/T nets [8] also for this fragment of Multi-CCS, as well as (*iv*) define non-interleaving semantics, typical of Petri nets [7], also for finite-net Multi-CCS.

Finite-net Multi-CCS includes the operator $\underline{\alpha}.s$ of *strong prefixing* (in contrast to normal prefixing $\mu.t$), which states that the visible action α is the initial

© Springer International Publishing Switzerland 2015
C. Bodei et al. (Eds.): Degano Festschrift, LNCS 9465, pp. 262–282, 2015.
DOI: 10.1007/978-3-319-25527-9_17

part of an atomic sequence that continues with the sequential process s. So, by strong prefixing, a transition can be labeled with a sequence of visible actions. This operator, introduced in [11,12] with a slightly different semantics, is also at the base of multiparty synchronization, obtained as an atomic sequence of binary CCS-like synchronizations. In finite-net Multi-CCS, parallel composition may occur inside the body of a recursively defined constant C; on the contrary, the restriction operator (νa) is not allowed in the body of C. So, a finite-net process may be represented as $(\nu L)t$, where L is a set of actions (if L is empty, the restriction operator is not present) and t a restriction-free process.

We equip finite-net Multi-CCS with a net semantics that, differently from the approach by Degano et al. [4–6,19], uses *unsafe* P/T nets, as done in [9,10] for a CCS sub-calculus without restriction, and in [1] for the π-calculus, where however inhibitor arcs are used to model restriction. The approach extension to restriction and strong prefixing is not trivial and passes through the introduction of an auxiliary set of *restricted* actions i.e., actions which are only allowed to synchronize. We prove that the net semantics associates a P/T net $Net(p)$ to any finite-net Multi-CCS process p, such that $Net(p)$ has finitely many places; if p is *well-formed*, then $Net(p)$ has also finitely many transitions; intuitively, process p is well-formed if the sequences that p may generate via strong prefixing have never the possibility to synchronize. We also provide a soundness result, i.e., p and $Net(p)$ are bisimilar [18]. Finally, we also prove the *representability theorem*: for any finite, statically reduced, P/T net N, we can find a well-formed, finite-net Multi-CCS process p_N such that $Net(p_N)$ and N are isomorphic.

The paper is organized as follows. Section 2 contains some basic background. Section 3 introduces *finite-net Multi-CCS* and its labeled transition system semantics. Section 4 defines the net semantics for the calculus, presents the finiteness theorem (for any well-formed process p, $Net(p)$ is finite), one example of net construction and the soundness theorem (p and $Net(p)$ are bisimilar). Section 5 proves the language expressibility theorem, i.e., the representability theorem mentioned above. Finally, some conclusions are drawn in Sect. 6. This paper is an extended abstract of [15], where additional detail can be found.

2   Background

2.1   Labeled Transition Systems and Bisimulation

Definition 1. *A labeled transition system (or LTS for short) is a triple $TS = (Q, A, \rightarrow)$ where*

- Q *is the set of states,*
- A *is the set of labels,*
- $\rightarrow \subseteq Q \times A \times Q$ *is the transition relation.*

In the following $q \xrightarrow{a} q'$ denotes $(q, a, q') \in \rightarrow$. A rooted transition system is a pair (TS, q_0) where $TS = (Q, A, \rightarrow)$ is a labeled transition system and $q_0 \in Q$ is the initial state.   □

Definition 2. *Given two LTSs* $TS_1 = (Q_1, A, \rightarrow_1)$ *and* $TS_2 = (Q_2, A, \rightarrow_2)$ *a bisimulation between* TS_1 *and* TS_2 *is a relation* $R \subseteq (Q_1 \times Q_2)$ *such that if* $(q_1, q_2) \in R$ *then for all* $a \in A$

- $\forall q_1'$ *such that* $q_1 \xrightarrow{a}_1 q_1'$, $\exists q_2'$ *such that* $q_2 \xrightarrow{a}_2 q_2'$ *and* $(q_1', q_2') \in R$
- $\forall q_2'$ *such that* $q_2 \xrightarrow{a}_2 q_2'$, $\exists q_1'$ *such that* $q_1 \xrightarrow{a}_1 q_1'$ *and* $(q_1', q_2') \in R$.

If $TS_1 = TS_2$ *we say that* R *is a bisimulation on* TS_1. *Two states* q *and* q' *are bisimilar,* $q \sim q'$, *if there exists a bisimulation* R *such that* $(q, q') \in R$. □

2.2   Place/Transition Petri Nets

We recall some basic notions on P/T Petri nets (see, e.g., [3,20,21] for an introduction). We use here a non-standard notation that better suits our needs.

Definition 3. *Let* $\mathbb{N}$ *be the set of natural numbers. Given a set* S, *a* finite multiset *over* S *is a function* $m : S \rightarrow \mathbb{N}$ *such that the set* $dom(m) = \{s \in S \mid m(s) \neq 0\}$ *is finite. The set of all finite multisets over* S, $\mathcal{M}_{fin}(S)$, *is ranged over by* m. *A multiset* m *such that* $dom(m) = \emptyset$ *is called* empty *and is denoted with* $\emptyset$, *with abuse of notation. We write* $m \subseteq m'$ *if* $m(s) \leq m'(s)$ *for all* $s \in S$. *The operator* $\oplus$ *denotes* multiset union: $(m \oplus m')(s) = m(s) + m'(s)$. *The operator* $\ominus$ *denotes* multiset difference: *if* $m' \subseteq m$, *then* $(m \ominus m')(s) = m(s) - m'(s)$. *The* scalar product *of a number* j *with* m *is* $(j \cdot m)(s) = j \cdot (m(s))$. *A finite multiset* m *over a finite set* $S = \{s_1, \ldots, s_n\}$ *can be represented as* $k_1 \cdot s_1 \oplus k_2 \cdot s_2 \oplus \ldots \oplus k_n \cdot s_n$, *where* $k_j = m(s_j) \geq 0$ *for* $j = 1, \ldots, n$. □

Definition 4. *A labeled P/T Petri net is a tuple* $N = (S, A, T)$, *where*

- S *is the set of* places, *ranged over by* s *(possibly indexed),*
- A *is a set of* labels, *ranged over by* a *(possibly indexed), and*
- $T \subseteq (\mathcal{M}_{fin}(S) \setminus \emptyset) \times A \times \mathcal{M}_{fin}(S)$ *is the set of* transitions, *ranged over by* t *(possibly indexed), such that* $\forall a \in A \; \exists t \in T$ *labeled* a.

A P/T net is finite *if both* S *and* T *are finite. A finite multiset over* S *is called a* marking. *Given a marking* m *and a place* s, *we say that the place* s *contains* $m(s)$ *tokens. Given a transition* $t = (m, a, m')$, *we use the notation* ${}^{\bullet}t$ *to denote its* pre-set m *(which cannot be an empty marking),* $t^{\bullet}$ *for its* post-set m' *and* $l(t)$ *for its* label a. *Hence, transition* t *can be also represented as* ${}^{\bullet}t \xrightarrow{l(t)} t^{\bullet}$.

A P/T system is a tuple $N(m_0) = (S, A, T, m_0)$, *where* (S, A, T) *is a P/T net and* m_0 *is a finite multiset over* S, *called the* initial marking. □

Note that our definition of T as a set of triples ensures that the net is *transition simple*, i.e., for any $t_1, t_2 \in T$, if ${}^{\bullet}t_1 = {}^{\bullet}t_2$ and $t_1^{\bullet} = t_2^{\bullet}$ and $l(t_1) = l(t_2)$, then $t_1 = t_2$. Note also that we are assuming that a transition has a nonempty pre-set. These are the only two constraints we impose over the definition of a P/T net (*cf* [3,20,21]). The additional condition that the set A of labels is covered by T (i.e., for each $a \in A$ there exists $t \in T$ with label a) is just for economy.

Definition 5. *Two P/T nets $N_1 = (S_1, A, T_1)$ and $N_2 = (S_2, A, T_2)$ are isomorphic — denoted by $N_1 \cong N_2$ — if there exists a bijection $f : S_1 \to S_2$, homomorphically extended to markings, such that $(m, a, m') \in T_1$ iff $(f(m), a, f(m')) \in T_2$. Two systems $N_1(m_1)$ and $N_2(m_2)$ are isomorphic if N_1 and N_2 are isomorphic by f, which, additionally, preserves the initial markings: $f(m_1) = m_2$.* □

Definition 6. *Given a P/T net $N = (S, A, T)$, we say that a transition t is enabled at marking m, written as $m[t\rangle$, if $\bullet t \subseteq m$. The execution of t enabled at m produces the marking $m' = (m \ominus \bullet t) \oplus t^\bullet$, denoted by $m[t\rangle m'$. The set of markings reachable from m, denoted by $[m\rangle$, is defined as the least set such that*

- $m \in [m\rangle$ *and*
- *if $m_1 \in [m\rangle$ and, for some transition $t \in T$, $m_1[t\rangle m_2$, then $m_2 \in [m\rangle$.*

Given a P/T system $N(m_0) = (S, A, T, m_0)$, we say that m is reachable if m is reachable from the initial marking m_0. A P/T system $N(m_0) = (S, A, T, m_0)$ is said safe if for all $m \in [m_0\rangle$ and for all $s \in S$ we have that $m(s) \leq 1$. □

Definition 7. *Given a P/T system $N(m_0) = (S, A, T, m_0)$, the interleaving marking graph of $N(m_0)$ is the rooted LTS $IMG(N(m_0)) = ([m_0\rangle, A, \to, m_0)$, where the transition relation $\to \subseteq \mathcal{M}_{fin}(S) \times A \times \mathcal{M}_{fin}(S)$ is defined by $m \xrightarrow{a} m'$ if and only if there exists a transition $t \in T$ such that $m[t\rangle m'$ and $l(t) = a$.* □

Definition 8. *A P/T system $N(m_0) = (S, A, T, m_0)$ is dynamically reduced if*

- $\forall s \in S \; \exists m \in [m_0\rangle$ *such that $m(s) \geq 1$, and*
- $\forall t \in T \; \exists m, m' \in [m_0\rangle$ *such that $m[t\rangle m'$.* □

Definition 9. *Given a finite P/T net $N = (S, A, T)$, we say that a transition t is statically enabled by a set of places $S' \subseteq S$, denoted by $S'[t\rangle$, if $dom(\bullet t) \subseteq S'$.*

Given two sets of places $S_1, S_2 \subseteq S$, we say that S_2 is statically reachable in one step from S_1 if there exists a transition $t \in T$, such that $S_1[t\rangle$, $dom(t^\bullet) \not\subseteq S_1$ and $S_2 = S_1 \cup dom(t^\bullet)$; this is denoted by $S_1 \xRightarrow{t} S_2$. The static reachability relation $\implies^* \subseteq \wp(S)_{fin} \times \wp(S)_{fin}$ is the least relation such that

- $S_1 \implies^* S_1$ *and*
- *if $S_1 \implies^* S_2$ and $S_2 \xRightarrow{t} S_3$, then $S_1 \implies^* S_3$.*

A set of places $S_k \subseteq S$ is the largest set statically reachable from S_1 if $S_1 \implies^* S_k$ and for all $t \in T$ such that $S_k[t\rangle$, we have that $dom(t^\bullet) \subseteq S_k$.

Given a finite P/T system $N(m_0) = (S, A, T, m_0)$, we denote by $[\![dom(m_0)\rangle$ the largest set of places statically reachable from $dom(m_0)$, i.e., the largest S_k such that $dom(m_0) \implies^* S_k$. A finite P/T net system $N(m_0) = (S, A, T, m_0)$ is statically reduced if all the places are statically reachable from the places in the initial marking, i.e., if $[\![dom(m_0)\rangle = S$. □

If a finite P/T system $N(m_0) = (S, A, T, m_0)$ is statically reduced, then all the transitions in T are statically enabled by S. Moreover, if a P/T system $N(m_0)$ is dynamically reduced, then it is also statically reduced. However, there are statically reduced P/T systems that are not dynamically reduced. For instance, the statically reduced P/T net system $N(s_1) = (\{s_1, s_2, s_3\}, \{a, b\}, \{(s_1, a, s_2), (2 \cdot s_1, b, s_3)\}, s_1)$ cannot reach dynamically place s_3.

3 Finite-net Multi-CCS

3.1 Syntax

Let $\mathcal{L}$ be a denumerable set of names (inputs), ranged over by $a, b, \ldots$. Let $\overline{\mathcal{L}}$ be the set of co-names (outputs), ranged over by $\overline{a}, \overline{b}, \ldots$. The set $\mathcal{L} \cup \overline{\mathcal{L}}$, ranged over by $\alpha, \beta, \ldots$, is the set of visible actions. With $\overline{\alpha}$ we mean the complement of α, assuming that $\overline{\overline{\alpha}} = \alpha$. Let $Act = \mathcal{L} \cup \overline{\mathcal{L}} \cup \{\tau\}$, such that $\tau \notin \mathcal{L} \cup \overline{\mathcal{L}}$, be the set of actions, ranged over by μ. Action τ denotes an invisible, internal activity. Let $\mathcal{C}$ be a denumerable set of process constants, disjoint from Act, ranged over by $A, B, C, \ldots$. The process terms are generated by the following abstract syntax

$$
\begin{aligned}
s &::= \mathbf{0} \mid \mu.t \quad\mid \underline{\alpha}.s \mid s + s \\
t &::= s \mid t \mid t \quad\mid C \\
p &::= t \mid (\nu a)p
\end{aligned}
$$

where we are using three syntactic categories: s, to range over sequential processes (i.e., processes that start sequentially), t, to range over restriction-free processes, and, finally p, to range over restricted processes.

As for CCS [18], term $\mathbf{0}$ is the terminated process, $\mu.t$ is a normally prefixed process where action μ is first performed and then t is ready, Note that $s + s'$ is the sequential process obtained by the alternative composition of *sequential* processes s and s'; hence we are restricting the use of $+$ to so-called *guarded sum*. Term $t \mid t'$ is the parallel composition of t and t'. $(\nu a)p$ is process p where the name a is made private by applying the restriction operator over a. Finally, C is a process constant, equipped with a defining equation $C \stackrel{def}{=} t$, i.e., the body of a constant must be a restriction-free process. The only new operator of the calculus is *strong prefixing*: $\underline{\alpha}.s$ is a process, where the *strong prefix* α is the first action of a transaction that continues with the *sequential* process s (provided that s can complete the transaction). We sometimes use the syntactic convention of writing $(\nu a)((\nu b)p))$ as $(\nu a, b)p$. Generalizing this convention, a finite-net Multi-CCS process may be represented as $(\nu L)t$, where L is a set of actions (if L is empty, the restriction operator is not present) and t is a restriction-free process.

The set $\mathcal{P}$ of *processes* contains those terms which uses only *finitely many* constants and are, w.r.t. process constants they use, *closed* (all the constants possess a defining equation) and *guarded* (for any defining equation $C \stackrel{def}{=} t$, any occurrence of a constant in t is within a *normally prefixed* subprocess $\mu.t'$ of t). $\mathcal{P}_{seq}$ is the set of *sequential processes*, i.e., those of syntactic category s. With abuse of notation, $\mathcal{P}$ will be ranged over by $p, q, r, \ldots$ (hence p may denote any kind of process terms, also sequential ones), possibly indexed.

Definition 10. *For any finite-net Multi-CCS process p, we define the set of its sequential subterms $sub(p)$ by means of the auxiliary function (with the same name, with abuse of notation) $sub(p, \emptyset)$, whose second parameter is a set of already known constants, initially empty.*

$$
\begin{aligned}
sub(\mathbf{0}, I) &= \{\mathbf{0}\} & sub(\mu.p, I) &= \{\mu.p\} \cup sub(p, I) \\
sub(\underline{\alpha}.p, I) &= \{\underline{\alpha}.p\} \cup sub(p, I) & sub((\nu a)p, I) &= sub(p, I)
\end{aligned}
$$

$$sub(p_1 + p_2, I) = \{p_1 + p_2\} \cup sub(p_1, I) \cup sub(p_2, I)$$
$$sub(p_1 \mid p_2, I) = sub(p_1, I) \cup sub(p_2, I)$$
$$sub(A, I) = \begin{cases} \emptyset & A \in I, \\ sub(p, I \cup \{A\}) & A \notin I \wedge A \overset{def}{=} p \end{cases}$$

$\square$

Proposition 1. *For any finite-net Multi-CCS process p, the set of its sequential subterms $sub(p)$ is finite.* $\square$

3.2   Operational Semantics with LTSs

The operational semantics for the calculus is given by the LTS $(\mathcal{P}, \mathcal{A}, \longrightarrow)$, where the states are the processes in $\mathcal{P}$, $\mathcal{A} = \{\tau\} \cup (\mathcal{L} \cup \overline{\mathcal{L}})^+$ is the set of labels (ranged over by σ and composed of the invisible action τ and by sequences of *visible* actions), and $\longrightarrow \subseteq \mathcal{P} \times \mathcal{A} \times \mathcal{P}$ is the minimal transition relation generated by the rules listed in Table 1.

Table 1. Operational rules (symmetric rule (Sum₂) omitted)

$$(\text{Pref}) \; \frac{}{\mu.p \overset{\mu}{\longrightarrow} p} \qquad (\text{Cong}) \; \frac{p \equiv p' \overset{\sigma}{\longrightarrow} q' \equiv q}{p \overset{\sigma}{\longrightarrow} q} \qquad (\text{Sum}_1) \; \frac{p \overset{\sigma}{\longrightarrow} p'}{p + q \overset{\sigma}{\longrightarrow} p'}$$

$$(\text{Par}) \; \frac{p \overset{\sigma}{\longrightarrow} p'}{p \mid q \overset{\sigma}{\longrightarrow} p' \mid q} \qquad (\text{S-Pref}) \; \frac{p \overset{\sigma}{\longrightarrow} p'}{\underline{\alpha}.p \overset{\alpha \diamond \sigma}{\longrightarrow} p'} \; \alpha \diamond \sigma = \begin{cases} \alpha & \text{if } \sigma = \tau, \\ \alpha\sigma & \text{otherwise} \end{cases}$$

$$(\text{S-Res}) \; \frac{p \overset{\sigma}{\longrightarrow} p'}{(\nu a)p \overset{\sigma}{\longrightarrow} (\nu a)p'} \; a, \overline{a} \notin n(\sigma)$$

$$(\text{S-Com}) \; \frac{p \overset{\sigma_1}{\longrightarrow} p' \quad q \overset{\sigma_2}{\longrightarrow} q'}{p \mid q \overset{\sigma}{\longrightarrow} p' \mid q'} \; Sync(\sigma_1, \sigma_2, \sigma)$$

Table 2. Synchronization relation *Sync*

	$\sigma \neq \epsilon$	$\sigma \neq \epsilon$
$Sync(\alpha, \overline{\alpha}, \tau)$	$Sync(\alpha\sigma, \overline{\alpha}, \sigma)$	$Sync(\overline{\alpha}, \alpha\sigma, \sigma)$

We briefly comment on the rules that are less standard. Rule (S-pref) allows for the creation of transitions labeled by sequences of actions. In order for $\underline{\alpha}.p$

to make a move, it is necessary that p be able to perform a transition, i.e., the rest of the transaction. Hence, if $p \xrightarrow{\sigma} p'$ then $\underline{\alpha}.p \xrightarrow{\alpha \diamond \sigma} p'$, where $\alpha \diamond \sigma = \alpha$ if $\sigma = \tau$, $\alpha \diamond \sigma = \alpha\sigma$ otherwise. Rule (S-Com) has a side-condition on the possible synchronizability of σ_1 and σ_2. Relation $Sync$ is defined by the axioms of Table 2. $Sync(\sigma_1, \sigma_2, \sigma)$ holds if at least one of the two sequences is a single action, say $\sigma_1 = \overline{\alpha}$, and the other starts with the complementary action α. Note that it is not possible to synchronize two sequences. This means that, usually, a multi-party synchronization can take place only among one *leader*, i.e., the process performing the atomic sequence, and as many other components (the *servants*), as is the length of the atomic sequence, where each servant executes one visible action. This is strictly the case for so-called *well-formed processes*, i.e., processes that do not allow for the synchronization of two sequences, not even indirectly (see Definition 13). Rule (S-Res) is slightly more general than the corresponding one for CCS, as it requires that no action in σ can be a or $\overline{a}$ (with $n(\sigma)$ we denote the set of all actions occurring in σ). There is one further rule, called (Cong), which makes use of the structural congruence $\equiv$, induced by the three axioms in Table 3. Axioms **E1** and **E2** are for associativity and commutativity, respectively, of the parallel operator. Axiom **E3** is for unfolding and explains why we have no explicit operational rule for handling constants in Table 1. Rule (Cong) enlarges the set of transitions derivable from a given process p, as the following example shows. The intuition is that a transition is derivable from p if it is derivable from any p' obtained as a rearrangement in any order (or association) of all of its sequential subprocesses.

Table 3. Axioms generating the structural congruence $\equiv$

E1	$(p \mid q) \mid r = p \mid (q \mid r)$	
E2	$p \mid q = q \mid p$	
E3	$A = q$	if $A \stackrel{def}{=} q$

Table 4. Multi-party synchronization among three processes

$$\cfrac{\cfrac{b.p \xrightarrow{b} p}{\underline{a}.b.p \xrightarrow{ab} p} \qquad \overline{a}.q \xrightarrow{\overline{a}} q}{\cfrac{\underline{a}.b.p \mid \overline{a}.q \xrightarrow{b} p \mid q \qquad \overline{b}.r \xrightarrow{\overline{b}} r}{(\underline{a}.b.p \mid \overline{a}.q) \mid \overline{b}.r \xrightarrow{\tau} (p \mid q) \mid r}}$$

Example 1. Consider process $(\underline{a}.b.p \,|\, \overline{a}.q) \,|\, \overline{b}.r$. The ternary synchronization among them, $(\underline{a}.b.p \,|\, \overline{a}.q) \,|\, \overline{b}.r \xrightarrow{\tau} (p \,|\, q) \,|\, r$, can take place, as proved in Table 4, without using rule (Cong). However, if we consider the very similar process $\underline{a}.b.p \,|\, (\overline{a}.q \,|\, \overline{b}.r)$, then we can see that $\underline{a}.b.p$ is able to synchronize with both $\overline{a}.q$ and $\overline{b}.r$ at the same time, only by means of rule (Cong). If we consider the slightly different variant process $(\underline{a}.b.p \,|\, \overline{b}.r) \,|\, \overline{a}.q$, we see easily that, without rule (Cong), no ternary synchronization is possible, because $Sync(ab, \overline{b}, a)$ does not hold. This example shows that, by using the axioms **E1** and **E2**, it is possible to reorder the servant subcomponents (in this example, subprocesses $\overline{a}.q$ and $\overline{b}.r$) in such a way that the actions they offer are in the expected order by the leader process (in this example, $\underline{a}.b.p$). □

Two finite-net Multi-CCS processes p and q are *bisimilar*, written $p \sim q$, if there exists a bisimulation $R \subseteq \mathcal{P} \times \mathcal{P}$ such that $(p, q) \in R$.

4   Operational Net Semantics

4.1   Places and Markings

The finite-net Multi-CCS processes are built upon the denumerable set $\mathcal{L} \cup \overline{\mathcal{L}}$, ranged over by α, of visible actions. We assume we have also $\mathcal{L}' = \{a' \mid a \in \mathcal{L}\}$ and $\overline{\mathcal{L}'} = \{\overline{a}' \mid \overline{a} \in \overline{\mathcal{L}}\}$, where $\mathcal{L}' \cup \overline{\mathcal{L}'}$, ranged over by α', is the set of auxiliary *restricted* actions; by definition, each restricted action α' corresponds exactly to one visible action α. Set $\mathcal{G} = \mathcal{L} \cup \overline{\mathcal{L}} \cup \mathcal{L}' \cup \overline{\mathcal{L}'}$ is the set of visible or restricted actions, ranged over by γ. The set of all actions $Act_{\gamma} = \mathcal{G} \cup \{\tau\}$, ranged over by μ (with abuse of notation), is used to build the set of *extended*, finite-net Multi-CCS processes $\mathcal{P}^{\gamma}$. The infinite set of places, ranged over by s, is $S_{MCCS} = \mathcal{P}^{\gamma}_{seq}$, i.e., the set of all the sequential processes whose prefixes are in Act_{γ} and whose strong prefixes are in $\mathcal{G}$.

Table 5. Decomposition function

$dec(\mathbf{0}) = \emptyset$	$dec(\mu.p) = \{\mu.p\}$
$dec(\underline{\gamma}.p) = \{\underline{\gamma}.p\}$	$dec(p + p') = \{p + p'\}$
$dec(p \,|\, p') = dec(p) \oplus dec(p')$	$dec(C) = dec(p)$ if $C \overset{def}{=} p$
$dec((\nu a)p) = dec(p)\{a'/a\}$	$a' \in \mathcal{L}'$ is the restricted action corresponding to a

Function $dec : \mathcal{P}^{\gamma} \to \mathcal{M}_{fin}(S_{MCCS})$ (see Table 5) defines the decomposition of extended processes into markings. Process **0** generates no places. The decomposition of a sequential process p produces one place with name p. This is the case of $\mu.p$ (where μ can be any action in Act_{γ}), $\underline{\gamma}.p$ and $p + p'$. Parallel composition is interpreted as multiset union. The decomposition of a restricted process $(\nu a)p$ — where $a \in \mathcal{L}$ — generates the multiset obtained from the decomposition of p, to which the substitution $\{a'/a\}$ is applied; the application of the substitution $\{a'/a\}$ to a multiset is performed elementwise. Finally, a process constant is first unwound once (according to its defining equation) and then decomposed. We assume that, in the decomposition of $(\nu a)p$, the choice of the restricted name is fixed by the rule that associates to a visible action a its *unique* corresponding restricted action a'. Note also that, as a finite-net process is of the form $(\nu L)t$ with $L = \{a_1, a_2, \ldots, a_n\}$, it can be first translated into the restriction-free process $t\{a'_1/a_1\} \ldots \{a'_n/a_n\}$ (shortened as $t\{L'/L\}$, for $L' = \{a'_1, \ldots, a'_n\} \subseteq \mathcal{L}'$), and then decomposed to obtain a multiset. This means that we can restrict our attention to restriction-free processes built over Act_γ, as a restricted process $(\nu L)t$ in $\mathcal{P}$ is mapped via dec to the same marking of the restriction-free process $t\{L'/L\}$ in $\mathcal{P}^\gamma$. Guardedness of constants is essential to prove the following obvious fact.

Proposition 2. *For any $p \in \mathcal{P}^\gamma$, $dec(p)$ is a finite multiset of places.* $\square$

Of course, function dec is not injective, because it considers the parallel operator as commutative, associative, with $\mathbf{0}$ as neutral element. As a matter of fact, $dec((p \mid q) \mid r) = dec(p \mid (q \mid r))$, $dec(p \mid q) = dec(q \mid p)$, $dec(p \mid \mathbf{0}) = \mathbf{dec(p)}$, $dec(A) = dec(p)$ if $A \overset{def}{=} p$, etc. However, one can prove that it is surjective.

4.2   Properties of Places and Markings

Function $sub(-)$ can be extended to a finite set S of places (i.e., of sequential processes) as $sub(S) = \bigcup_{s \in S} sub(s)$. The goal is to prove that the sequential subterms of p are the same sequential subterms of $dom(dec(p))$. This property will be useful in proving (Theorem 1) that each place statically reachable from $dom(dec(p))$ belongs to $sub(p)$ (up to a possible renaming of bound names to the corresponding restricted names), so that, since $sub(p)$ is finite for any p, the set of all the places statically reachable from $dom(dec(p))$ is finite as well.

Proposition 3. *If p is restriction-free, then $sub(p) = sub(dom(dec(p)))$, while if $p = (\nu L)t$, then $sub(p)\{L'/L\} = sub(dom(dec(p)))$.* $\square$

Now we define a notion of *well-behaved* set of places (and *well-formed* process), which will be useful in the next section in proving that any transition statically enabled by a well-behaved set S is such that no synchronization of sequences is possible (Proposition 6). As a matter of fact, the definition of relation $Sync(\sigma_1, \sigma_2, \sigma)$ requires that at least one of σ_1 or σ_2 be a single action; this is not enough to prevent that two sequences may synchronize, even if indirectly. For instance, consider the three processes $p_1 = \underline{a}.b.\mathbf{0}$, $p_2 = \overline{a}.\mathbf{0}$ and $p_3 = \underline{\overline{b}}.c.\mathbf{0}$, which may perform $ab, \overline{a}, \overline{b}c$, respectively; then a ternary synchronization is possible, because first we synchronize p_1 and p_2, by $Sync(ab, \overline{a}, b)$, getting a single action b, which can be then used for a synchronization with p_3, by $Sync(b, \overline{b}c, c)$; in such a way, the two atomic sequences ab and $\overline{b}c$ have been synchronized. So, we would like to mark $\{p_1, p_2, p_3\}$ as not well-behaved and $(p_1 \,|\, p_2) \,|\, p_3$ as not well-formed. Some auxiliary definitions are needed.

Definition 11 (Initials for sequential processes). *For any sequential process p, $In(p) \subseteq \mathcal{A}$ is the set of* initials *of p, defined inductively as*

$$In(\mathbf{0}) = \emptyset \qquad\qquad In(\mu.p) = \{\mu\}$$
$$In(\underline{\alpha}.p) = \alpha \diamond In(p) \qquad In(p_1 + p_2) = In(p_1) \cup In(p_2)$$

where $\alpha \diamond In(p) = \{\alpha \diamond \sigma \mid \sigma \in In(p)\}$. □

Definition 12 (Names in sequences of a sequential process). *Let $ns(p) \subseteq \mathcal{G}$ be the set of (free) names occurring in sequences of length two or more of a sequential process p. Set $ns(p)$ is defined as the least set satisfying the following:*

$$ns(\mathbf{0}) = \emptyset \qquad\qquad ns(\underline{\alpha}.p) = ns(p) \cup \{\alpha\} \cup \bigcup_{\sigma \in In(p) \wedge \sigma \neq \tau} n(\sigma)$$
$$ns(\mu.p) = ns(dec(p)) \qquad ns(p_1 + p_2) = ns(p_1) \cup ns(p_2)$$

where $ns(-)$ is extended over a set S of places as $ns(S) = \bigcup_{s \in S} ns(s)$. □

Definition 13 (Well-formed process and well-behaved set of places). *A set of places S is* well-behaved *if there exist no $\beta \in \mathcal{G}$ such that $\beta \in ns(S)$ and $\overline{\beta} \in ns(S)$. A process p is* well-formed, *denoted $wf(p)$, if $dom(dec(p))$ is well-behaved.* □

Example 2. Let us consider three processes $p_1 = \underline{a}.b.\mathbf{0}$, $p_2 = \overline{a}.\mathbf{0}$ and $p_3 = \underline{b}.c.\mathbf{0}$. Note that $wf(p_i)$ because $\{p_i\}$ is well-behaved for $i = 1, 2, 3$. We also have that $wf(p_1 \,|\, p_2)$, as no action of $ns(p_1) = \{\overline{a}, b\}$ occurs complemented in $ns(p_2) = \emptyset$. However, it is not the case that $wf((p_1 \,|\, p_2) \,|\, p_3)$, because there exists an action, namely b, such that $b \in ns(p_1)$ and $\overline{b} \in ns(p_3)$. □

4.3 Net Transitions

Let $\mathcal{A}^\gamma = \{\tau\} \cup \mathcal{G}^+$, ranged over by σ with abuse of notation, be the set of labels, and let $\rightarrow \subseteq \mathcal{M}_{fin}(S_{MCCS}) \times \mathcal{A}^\gamma \times \mathcal{M}_{fin}(S_{MCCS})$, be the least set of transitions generated by the rules in Table 6, where in a transition $m_1 \xrightarrow{\sigma} m_2$, m_1 is the multiset of tokens to be consumed, σ is the label of the transition and m_2 is the multiset of tokens to be produced.

Let us comment the axiom and rules of Table 6. Axiom (pref) states that if one token is present in the place $\mu.p$ then a μ-labeled transition is derivable from marking $\{\mu.p\}$, producing the marking $dec(p)$. This holds for any μ, i.e., for the invisible action τ, for any visible action α as well as for any restricted action α'. Transitions with labels containing restricted actions should not be taken in the resulting net, as we accept only transitions labeled on $\mathcal{A}$. However, these transitions are useful in producing the required transitions, as two complementary restricted actions can synchronize, producing a τ-labeled transition

Table 6. Rules for net transitions (symmetric rule (sum$_2$) omitted)

(pref) $\dfrac{}{\{\mu.p\} \xrightarrow{\mu} dec(p)}$	(sum$_1$) $\dfrac{\{p\} \xrightarrow{\sigma} m}{\{p + p'\} \xrightarrow{\sigma} m}$
(s-pref) $\dfrac{\{p\} \xrightarrow{\sigma} m}{\{\gamma.p\} \xrightarrow{\gamma \diamond \sigma} m}$	(s-com) $\dfrac{m_1 \xrightarrow{\sigma_1} m_1' \; m_2 \xrightarrow{\sigma_2} m_2'}{m_1 \oplus m_2 \xrightarrow{\sigma} m_1' \oplus m_2'} Sync(\sigma_1, \sigma_2, \sigma)$

or shortening the synchronized sequence. In rule (s-pref), γ ranges over visible actions α and *restricted* ones α'; this rule requires that the premise transition $\{p\} \xrightarrow{\sigma} m$ be derivable by the rules, starting from the sequential process p. Rule (sum$_1$) and its symmetric (sum$_2$) are as expected: the transition from place $p + p'$ are those from places p and p', as both p and p' are sequential. Finally, rule (s-com) explains how synchronization takes place: it is needed that m_1 and m_2 perform synchronizable sequences σ_1 and σ_2, producing σ; here we assume that $Sync$ has been extended also to restricted actions in the obvious way, i.e., a restricted action $\overline{\alpha'}$ can be synchronized only with its complementary restricted action α' or with a sequence beginning with α'. As an example, net transition $\{\underline{a}.b'.p, \overline{a}.q, \overline{b'}.r\} \xrightarrow{\tau} dec(p) \oplus dec(q) \oplus dec(r)$ is derivable as proved in Table 7.

Table 7. The proof of a net transition

(s-com) $\dfrac{\text{(s-pref)} \dfrac{\text{(pref)} \dfrac{}{\{b'.p\} \xrightarrow{b'} dec(p)}}{\{\underline{a}.b'.p\} \xrightarrow{ab'} dec(p)} \quad \text{(pref)} \dfrac{}{\{\overline{a}.q\} \xrightarrow{\overline{a}} dec(q)}}{\{\underline{a}.b'.p, \overline{a}.q\} \xrightarrow{b'} dec(p) \oplus dec(q)}$

(s-com) $\dfrac{\{\underline{a}.b'.p, \overline{a}.q\} \xrightarrow{b'} dec(p) \oplus dec(q) \quad \text{(pref)} \dfrac{}{\{\overline{b'}.r\} \xrightarrow{\overline{b'}} dec(r)}}{\{\underline{a}.b'.p, \overline{a}.q, \overline{b'}.r\} \xrightarrow{\tau} dec(p) \oplus dec(q) \oplus dec(r)}$

Note that the transitions generable by the rules can be labeled also with restricted actions, while we are interested only in transitions that are labeled on $\mathcal{A} = \{\tau\} \cup (\mathcal{L} \cup \overline{\mathcal{L}})^+$. Hence, the P/T Petri net for finite-net Multi-CCS is the triple $N_{MCCS} = (S_{MCCS}, \mathcal{A}, T_{MCCS})$, where the infinite set $T_{MCCS} = \{(m_1, \sigma, m_2) \mid m_1 \xrightarrow{\sigma} m_2$ is derivable by the rules and $\sigma \in \mathcal{A}\}$ is obtained by filtering out those transitions derivable by the rules such that no restricted name α' occurs in σ. For instance, in the example above, the derivable transition $\{b'.p\} \xrightarrow{b'} dec(p)$ is not a transition in T_{MCCS} because its label is not in $\mathcal{A}$, while $\{\underline{a}.b'.p, \overline{a}.q, \overline{b'}.r\} \xrightarrow{\tau} dec(p) \oplus dec(q) \oplus dec(r)$ belongs to T_{MCCS}.

4.4   Properties of Net Transitions

Proposition 4. *Let $t = m_1 \xrightarrow{\sigma} m_2$ be a transition derivable by the rules in Table 6. Then, $sub(dom(m_2)) \subseteq sub(dom(m_1))$.*   □

Proposition 5. *If $t = m_1 \xrightarrow{\sigma} m_2$ is derivable by the rules and $dom(m_1)$ is well-behaved, then $dom(m_2)$ is well-behaved.*   □

Corollary 1. *If S_1 is well behaved and $S_1 \xRightarrow{t} S_2$, then S_2 is well-behaved.*   □

Now we want to prove that when a transition $m \xrightarrow{\sigma} m'$, whose label $\sigma \neq \tau$, involves in its proof some sequence of length greater than one, then the names of σ are all contained in $ns(dom(m))$.

Lemma 1. *If $t = (m, \sigma, m')$ is derivable by the rules of Table 6, and either $|\sigma| \geq 2$ or $\sigma \neq \tau$ and there exists a transition label σ' in its proof tree with $|\sigma'| \geq 2$, then $n(\sigma) \subseteq ns(dom(m))$.*   □

Corollary 2. *If $t = (m, \gamma, m')$ is derivable by the rules of Table 6 by using rule (s-com), then $\gamma \in ns(dom(m))$.*   □

Note that transition $t = (m, \sigma, m')$ is derivable by the rules of Table 6 without using rule (s-com) if and only if m is a singleton, i.e., $|m| = 1$. On the contrary, rule (s-com) is used if and only if m is not a singleton, i.e. $|m| \geq 2$.

Proposition 6. *If $t = (m, \sigma, m')$ is derivable by the rules and $dom(m)$ is well-behaved, then the proof of t never synchronizes two sequences, not even indirectly.*

Proof. By induction on the proof of t. If $|m| = 1$ is, then rule (s-com) is never used, and so no synchronization of sequences is possible. Otherwise, by (s-com) $m = m_1 \oplus m_2$, $m' = m'_1 \oplus m'_2$, $t_1 = (m_1, \sigma_1, m'_1)$ and $t_2 = (m_2, \sigma_2, m'_2)$ are derivable, with $Sync(\sigma_1, \sigma_2, \sigma)$. As $dom(m)$ is well-behaved, so are also $dom(m_1)$ and $dom(m_2)$; hence, by induction, in the proofs of transitions t_1 and t_2 two sequences are never synchronized. So, it remains to prove that the thesis holds for the resulting σ. By definition of Sync, if $\sigma = \tau$, then both σ_1 and σ_2 are complementary actions, say $\sigma_1 = \gamma$ and $\sigma_2 = \overline{\gamma}$. If both t_1 and t_2 are derived by using rule (s-com), then t synchronizes two sequences, even if indirectly; however, this is not possible, because Corollary 2 would ensure that $\gamma \in ns(dom(m_1))$ and $\overline{\gamma} \in ns(dom(m_2))$, contradicting that $dom(m_1 \oplus m_2)$ be well-behaved. Therefore, t_1 or t_2 is derived without using rule (s-com) and so no synchronization of sequences is produced. By definition of Sync, if $\sigma \neq \tau$, then either σ_1 or σ_2 is a sequence of length greater than one; w.l.o.g. assume that $|\sigma_1| \geq 2$ and $\sigma_2 = \overline{\gamma}$. By Lemma 1, $n(\sigma_1) \subseteq ns(dom(m_1))$, in particular, $\gamma \in ns(dom(m_1))$. If t_2 were derived by using rule (s-com), then t synchronizes two sequences, even if indirectly; however, this is not possible, because Corollary 2 would ensure that $\overline{\gamma} \in ns(dom(m_2))$, contradicting that $dom(m_1 \oplus m_2)$ be well-behaved.   □

Remark 1. By the proof of the proposition above, it is clear that any transition $t = m_1 \xrightarrow{\sigma} m_2$ derivable from a *well-behaved* set of places $dom(m_1)$ is such that in the proof tree for t, whenever rule (s-com) is used with premise transitions t_1 and t_2, at least one of the two, say t_1 w.l.o.g., is such that ${}^\bullet t_1$ is a singleton and $l(t_1)$ is a single action in Act^γ. That is, any derivable transition t from a well-behaved set of places $dom(m_1)$ is such that one sequential process $s \in dom(m_1)$ acts as the *leader* of the multi-party synchronization, while the other sequential components contribute each with a single action, acting as *servants*.   □

4.5   The Reachable Subnet $Net(p)$

Given a process $p \in \mathcal{P}^\gamma$, the P/T system associated to p is the subnet of N_{MCCS} statically reachable from the initial marking $dec(p)$. We indicate with $Net(p)$ such a subnet.

Definition 14. *Let p be a process. The P/T system statically associated to p is $Net(p) = (S_p, A_p, T_p, m_0)$, where $m_0 = dec(p)$ and*

$$S_p = [\![dom(m_0))\rangle \quad computed\ in\ N_{MCCS},$$
$$T_p = \{t \in T_{MCCS} \mid S_p[\![t\rangle\}$$
$$A_p = \{\sigma \in \mathcal{A} \mid \exists t \in T_p, \sigma = l(t))\}$$

The following two propositions present facts that are obviously true by construction of the net $Net(p)$ associated to a finite-net Multi-CCS process p.

Proposition 7. *For any $p \in \mathcal{P}$, $Net(p)$ is a statically reduced P/T net.*   □

Proposition 8. *For any restriction-free $t \in \mathcal{P}$, let $Net(t) = (S, A, T, m_0)$. Then, for any $n \geq 1$, $Net(t^n) = (S, A, T, n \cdot m_0)$, where $t^1 = t$ and $t^{n+1} = t \mid t^n$.*
For any $(\nu L)t \in \mathcal{P}$, let $Net((\nu L)t) = (S, A, T, m_0)$. Then, for any $n \geq 1$, $Net((\nu L)(t^n)) = (S, A, T, n \cdot m_0)$.   □

Definition 14 suggests a way of generating $Net(p)$ with an algorithm based on the inductive definition of the static reachability relation (see Definition 9): Start by the initial set of places $dom(dec(p))$, and then apply the rules in Table 6 in order to produce the set of transitions (labeled on $\mathcal{A}$) statically enabled at $dom(dec(p))$, as well as the additionally places statically reachable by means of such transitions. Then repeat this procedure from the set of places statically reached so far. The problems with this algorithm are two:

- the obvious *halting condition* is "until no new places are statically reachable"; of course, the algorithm terminates if we know that the set S_p of places statically reachable from $dom(dec(p))$ is finite; additionally,
- at each step of the algorithm, we have to be sure that the set of transitions derivable from the current set of statically reachable places is finite.

We are going to prove these two facts: (i) S_p is finite for any $p \in \mathcal{P}$, and (ii) for any *well-formed* process p, and for any set of places S, statically reachable from $dom(dec(p))$, the set of transitions statically enabled at S is finite.

Theorem 1. *For any $p \in \mathcal{P}$, let $Net(p) = (S_p, A_p, T_p, m_0)$ be defined as in Definition 14. Then, set S_p is finite.*

Proof (Sketch). Any set of places, statically reachable from $dom(m_0)$, is composed only of (possibly, one-time-renamed) sequential subterms of p; this can be proved by induction on the static reachability relation $\Longrightarrow^*$, using Propositions 3 and 4. As $sub(p)$ is finite, by Proposition 1, the thesis follows. □

We now want to prove that for any *well-formed* finite-net Multi-CCS process p, and for any set of places $S \subseteq S_{MCCS}$, statically reachable from $dom(dec(p))$, the set of transitions statically enabled at S is finite. Some auxiliary definitions and results are necessary. Given a single place $s \in S$, by $s \vdash t$ we mean that transition $t = (\{s\}, \sigma, m)$ is derivable by the rules in Table 6, hence with $\sigma \in \mathcal{A}^\gamma$.

Lemma 2. *Set $T_s = \{t \mid s \vdash t\}$ is finite, for any $s \in S_{MCCS}$.* □

Given a finite set of places $S \subseteq S_{MCCS}$, let T_1 be $\bigcup_{s \in S} T_s$, i.e., the set of all transitions, with a singleton preset in S, derivable by the rules with labeling in $\mathcal{A}^\gamma$. Set T_1 is finite, being the finite union (as S is finite) of finite sets (as T_s is finite for any s). If p is well-formed (i.e., if $dom(dec(p))$ is well-behaved), then any S statically reachable from $dom(dec(p))$ is well-behaved by Corollary 1. Let $k \in \mathbb{N}$ be the length of the longest label of any transition in T_1. Remark 1 explains that if a multi-party transition t is derivable by the rules from the well-behaved set $dom(^\bullet t) \subseteq S$, then its proof contains $k+1$ synchronizations at most, each one between a transition (labeled with a sequence) and a *singleton-preset* transition (labeled with a *single* action). Therefore, the set of all the transitions statically enabled at a well-behaved set S can be defined by means of a sequence of sets T_i of transitions, for $2 \le i \le k+1$, where each transition $t \in T_i$ has a preset $^\bullet t$ composed of i tokens, as follows:

$$T_i = \{(m_1 \oplus m_2, \sigma, m_1' \oplus m_2') \mid$$
$$\exists \sigma_1 \exists \gamma.(m_1, \sigma_1, m_1') \in T_{i-1}, (m_2, \gamma, m_2') \in T_1, Sync(\sigma_1, \gamma, \sigma)\}$$

Note that T_2 is finite, because T_1 is finite; inductively, T_{i+1}, for $2 \le i \le k$ is finite, because T_i and T_1 are finite. The set T_S of all the transitions statically enabled at S is $\{t \mid t \in \bigcup_{i=1}^{k+1} T_i \wedge l(t) \in \mathcal{A}\}$, where only transitions labeled on $\mathcal{A}$ are considered. T_S is finite, being a finite union of finite sets; therefore, we have the following result.

Proposition 9. *If $S \subseteq S_{MCCS}$ is a well-behaved, finite set of places, then set T_S of all the transitions enabled at S is finite.* □

Example 3. Consider the non-well-formed process $p = (\nu a)(a.\mathbf{0} \,|\, (\underline{\overline{a}}.a.\mathbf{0} \,|\, \overline{a}.\mathbf{0}))$. We have that $dec(p) = a'.\mathbf{0} \oplus \underline{\overline{a'}}.a'.\mathbf{0} \oplus \overline{a'}.\mathbf{0}$, which is not well-behaved because $a' \in ns(\underline{\overline{a'}}.a'.\mathbf{0})$ and $\overline{a'} \in ns(\underline{\overline{a'}}.a'.\mathbf{0})$. Transition $t_1 = a'.\mathbf{0} \oplus \underline{\overline{a'}}.a'.\mathbf{0} \oplus \overline{a'}.\mathbf{0} \xrightarrow{\tau} \emptyset$ is derivable, because first we synchronize $\overline{a'}a'$ with a', yielding a', which is then synchronized with $\overline{a'}$, yielding τ. However, the occurrence of a' produced by the first synchronization may be used to synchronize an additional $\overline{a'}a'$, yielding a' again. Therefore, it is not difficult to see that also $t_n = a'.\mathbf{0} \oplus n \cdot \underline{\overline{a'}}.a'.\mathbf{0} \oplus \overline{a'}.\mathbf{0} \xrightarrow{\tau} \emptyset$, is statically enabled at $dom(dec(p))$, for any $n \geq 1$. Hence, the set of transitions statically enabled at $dom(dec(p))$ is infinite. □

Theorem 2. *For any well-formed, finite-net Multi-CCS process p, $Net(p) = (S_p, A_p, T_p, m_0)$ is a finite, statically reduced, P/T net.* □

Example 4 **(1/3 Semi-counter).** For the well-formed process $p = (\nu c)A$, where $A \stackrel{def}{=} inc.(A \,|\, (\underline{c}.\underline{c}.dec.\mathbf{0} + \overline{c}.\mathbf{0}))$, three occurrences of inc are needed to enable one dec. $Net(p)$ is the net (S_p, A_p, T_p, m_0) we are going to construct, where the initial marking m_0 is $dec(p) = dec((\nu c)A) = dec(A)\{c'/c\} = \{inc.(A \,|\, (\underline{c}.\underline{c}.dec.\mathbf{0} + \overline{c}.\mathbf{0}))\}\{c'/c\} = \{s_1\}$; place s_1 is $inc.(A_{\{c'/c\}} \,|\, (\underline{c'}.\underline{c'}.dec.\mathbf{0} + \overline{c'}.\mathbf{0}))$, where the new constant $A_{\{c'/c\}}$ is obtained by applying the substitution $\{c'/c\}$ to the body of A: $A_{\{c'/c\}} \stackrel{def}{=} inc.(A_{\{c'/c\}} \,|\, (\underline{c'}.\underline{c'}.dec.\mathbf{0} + \overline{c'}.\mathbf{0}))$. Now, only transition $t_1 = \{s_1\} \xrightarrow{inc} \{s_1, s_2\}$ is derivable from $dom(m_0) = \{s_1\}$, where $s_2 = \underline{c'}.\underline{c'}.dec.\mathbf{0} + \overline{c'}.\mathbf{0}$ is a new statically reachable place. Note that s_2 can produce two transitions in T_{s_2}, namely $t' = \{s_2\} \xrightarrow{c'c'dec} \emptyset$ and $t'' = \{s_2\} \xrightarrow{\overline{c'}} \emptyset$, but both are not labeled with a sequence in $\mathcal{A}$. However, these transitions can be composed by means of rule (s-com), as shown in Table 8, to produce transition $t_2 = 3 \cdot s_2 \xrightarrow{dec} \emptyset$, which does not add any new reachable place. So, $S_p = \{s_1, s_2\}$ and $T_p = \{t_1, t_2\}$. □

Table 8. The proof of a net transition, where $s_2 = \underline{c'}.\underline{c'}.dec.\mathbf{0} + \overline{c'}.\mathbf{0}$

$$
\dfrac{
  \dfrac{
    \dfrac{
      \dfrac{
        \dfrac{
          \dfrac{}{\{dec.\mathbf{0}\} \xrightarrow{dec} \emptyset}\text{(pref)}
        }{\{\underline{c'}.dec.\mathbf{0}\} \xrightarrow{c'dec} \emptyset}\text{(s-pref)}
      }{\{\underline{c'}.\underline{c'}.dec.\mathbf{0}\} \xrightarrow{c'c'dec} \emptyset}\text{(s-pref)}
    }{\{s_2\} \xrightarrow{c'c'dec} \emptyset}\text{(sum}_1\text{)}
    \quad
    \dfrac{
      \dfrac{}{\{\overline{c'}.\mathbf{0}\} \xrightarrow{\overline{c'}} \emptyset}\text{(pref)}
    }{\{s_2\} \xrightarrow{\overline{c'}} \emptyset}\text{(sum}_2\text{)}
  }{\{s_2, s_2\} \xrightarrow{c'dec} \emptyset}\text{(s-com)}
  \quad
  \dfrac{
    \dfrac{}{\{\overline{c'}.\mathbf{0}\} \xrightarrow{\overline{c'}} \emptyset}\text{(pref)}
  }{\{s_2\} \xrightarrow{\overline{c'}} \emptyset}\text{(sum}_2\text{)}
}{\{s_2, s_2, s_2\} \xrightarrow{dec} \emptyset}\text{(s-com)}
$$

4.6 Soundness

Proposition 10. *For any process $p \in \mathcal{P}$, if $p \overset{\sigma}{\longrightarrow} p'$ then there exist $t \in T_p$ and $p'' \equiv p'$ such that $dec(p)[t\rangle dec(p'')$ with $l(t) = \sigma$.*

Proof. The proof is by induction on the proof of transition $p \overset{\sigma}{\longrightarrow} p'$. $\square$

Proposition 11. *For any process $p \in \mathcal{P}$, if there exists $t \in T_p$ such that $dec(p)[t\rangle dec(p')$ with $l(t) = \sigma$, then $p \overset{\sigma}{\longrightarrow} p'$.*

Proof. By induction on (the definition of) $dec(p)$ and then on the proof of t. $\square$

We are now ready to state the soundness theorem: the interleaving marking graph associated to $Net(p)$ is bisimilar to the LTS rooted in p.

Theorem 3 (Soundness). *For any process $p \in \mathcal{P}$, $p \sim dec(p)$.*

Proof. If $R = \{(p, dec(q)) \mid p, q \in \mathcal{P} \wedge p \equiv q\}$ is a bisimulation, then the thesis follows trivially, as $p \equiv p$. As a matter of fact, on the one hand, if $p \overset{\sigma}{\longrightarrow} p'$, then, by Proposition 10, there exist a transition t, with $l(t) = \sigma$, and a process p'', with $p'' \equiv p'$, such that $dec(p)[t\rangle dec(p'')$, and $(p', dec(p'')) \in R$. On the other hand, if $dec(q)[t\rangle dec(q')$, with $l(t) = \sigma$, then, by Proposition 11, we have $q \overset{\sigma}{\longrightarrow} q'$; as $p \equiv q$, by rule (Cong), $p \overset{\sigma}{\longrightarrow} q'$, and $(q', dec(q')) \in R$, as required. $\square$

5 A Process Term for Any Finite P/T Net

In this section we address the following problem: given a finite, statically reduced, P/T Petri net system $N(m_0)$, labeled on $\mathcal{L} \cup \{\tau\}$, can we single out a finite-net Multi-CCS process $p_{N(m_0)}$ such that $Net(p_{N(m_0)})$ and $N(m_0)$ are isomorphic? The answer to this question is positive.

The translation from nets to processes we are going to present defines a constant C_i in correspondence to each place s_i; the definition of the constant C_i contains a summand composed of a new bound name y_i, which is used in order to distinguish syntactically all the constants bodies, so that no fusion of two constants to the same place is possible when applying the reverse step from the generated process term to its associated net. Moreover, the translation considers a bound name x_i^j for each pair (s_i, t_j), where s_i is a place and t_j is a transition; such bound names are used to synchronize all the components participating in transition t_j. The constant C_i, associated to place s_i, has a summand c_i^j for each transition t_j, which may be $\mathbf{0}$ when s_i is not in the preset of t_j. Among the many places in the preset of t_j, the one with minimal index (as we assume that places are indexed) plays the role of *leader* of the multiparty synchronization (i.e., the process performing the atomic sequence of inputs x_i^j to be synchronized with single outputs $\bar{x}_i^j$ performed by the other *servant* participants).

Definition 15. *Let $N(m_0) = (S, A, T, m_0)$ — with $S = \{s_1, \ldots, s_n\}$, $A \subseteq \mathcal{L} \cup \{\tau\}$, $T = \{t_1, \ldots, t_k\}$, and $l(t_j) = a_j$ — be a finite, statically reduced, P/T net* *system. Function $INet(-)$, from finite, statically reduced, P/T net systems to well-formed, finite-net Multi-CCS processes is defined as*

$$INet(N(m_0)) = (\nu L)(\underbrace{C_1|\cdots|C_1}_{m_0(s_1)}|\cdots|\underbrace{C_n|\cdots|C_n}_{m_0(s_n)})$$

where $L = \{y_1,\dots,y_n\} \cup \{x_1^1,\dots,x_n^1, x_1^2,\dots,x_n^2,\dots,x_1^k,\dots,x_n^k\}$, and each C_i has a defining equation

$$C_i \stackrel{def}{=} c_i^1 + \cdots + c_i^k + y_i.0$$

where each c_i^j, for $j = 1,\dots,k$, is equal to

- **0**, if $s_i \notin {}^\bullet t_j$;
- $a_j.\Pi_j$, if ${}^\bullet t_j = \{s_i\}$;
- $\overline{x}_i^j.0$, if ${}^\bullet t_j(s_i) > 0$ and ${}^\bullet t_j(s_{i'}) > 0$ for some $i' < i$ (i.e., s_i is not the leader for the synchronization on t_j);
- $\underbrace{\underline{x}_{i+1}^j \cdots \underline{x}_{i+1}^j}_{{}^\bullet t_j(s_{i+1})} \cdots \cdots \underbrace{\underline{x}_n^j \cdots \underline{x}_n^j}_{{}^\bullet t_j(s_n)}.a_j.\Pi_j$, if ${}^\bullet t_j(s_i) = 1$ and s_i is the leader of the synchronization (i.e., ${}^\bullet t_j(s_{i'}) > 0$ for no $i' < i$, while ${}^\bullet t_j(s_{i'}) > 0$ for some $i' > i$);
- $\overline{x}_i^j.0 + \underbrace{\underline{x}_i^j \cdots \underline{x}_i^j}_{{}^\bullet t_j(s_i)-1} \cdot \underbrace{\underline{x}_{i+1}^j \cdots \underline{x}_{i+1}^j}_{{}^\bullet t_j(s_{i+1})} \cdots \cdots \underbrace{\underline{x}_n^j \cdots \underline{x}_n^j}_{{}^\bullet t_j(s_n)}.a_j.\Pi_j$, otherwise (i.e., s_i is the leader and ${}^\bullet t_j(s_i) \geq 2$).

Finally, process Π_j is defined as $\Pi_j = \underbrace{C_1|\cdots|C_1}_{t_j^\bullet(s_1)}|\cdots|\underbrace{C_n|\cdots|C_n}_{t_j^\bullet(s_n)}$. □

Note that $INet(N(m_0))$ is a *finite-net Multi-CCS process*: in fact, the restriction operator occurs only at the top level, applied to the parallel composition of a number of constants; each constant has a body that is sequential and restriction-free. Note also that $INet(N(m_0))$ is a *well-formed* process: in fact, each *strong prefix* is an input x_i^j, and any sequence ends with an action $a_j \in A$ which is either an input or τ; hence, no synchronization of sequences is possible.

Example 5. Consider the net $N(m_0)$ of Fig. 1, where transition t_1 is labeled with a, t_2 with b and t_3 with c. Applying the translation above, we obtain the (well-formed) finite-net Multi-CCS process

$$INet(N(m_0)) = (\nu L)(C_1 \,|\, C_1 \,|\, C_1 \,|\, C_2 \,|\, C_2)$$

where $L = \{y_1, y_2, y_3\} \cup \{x_1^1, x_2^1, x_3^1, x_1^2, x_2^2, x_3^2, x_1^3, x_2^3, x_3^3\}$, and

$$C_1 \stackrel{def}{=} (\overline{x}_1^1.0 + \underline{x}_1^1.a.C_1) + (\overline{x}_1^2.0 + \underline{x}_1^2.\underline{x}_2^2.b.0) + \underline{x}_2^3.\underline{x}_3^3.c.C_3 + y_1.0$$
$$C_2 \stackrel{def}{=} 0 + \overline{x}_2^2.0 + \overline{x}_2^3.0 + y_2.0$$
$$C_3 \stackrel{def}{=} 0 + 0 + 0 + y_3.0$$

□

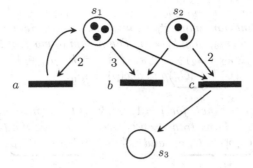

Fig. 1. A simple net.

Now we are ready to state our main result, the so-called *representability theorem.*

Theorem 4 (Representability theorem). *Let $N(m_0) = (S, A, T, m_0)$ be a finite, statically reduced, P/T net system such that $A \subseteq \mathcal{L} \cup \{\tau\}$, and let $p = INet(N(m_0))$. Then, $Net(p)$ is isomorphic to $N(m_0)$.*

Proof (Sketch). Assume that process $p = INet(N(m_0))$ is as in Definition 15. For notational convenience, $(\sum_{j=1}^{k} c_i^j) + y_i.\mathbf{0}$ is denoted by p_i, i.e., $C_i \stackrel{def}{=} p_i$. Let $\rho = \{L'/L\}$ be a substitution that maps each bound name x_i^j (or y_i) to its corresponding restricted name $x_i'^j$ (or y_i') in $\mathcal{L}'$, for $i = 1, \ldots, n$ and $j = 1, \ldots, k$. Let $Net(p) = (S', A', T', m_0')$. Then, $m_0' = dec(p)$ is the multiset

$$dec((\nu L)(\underbrace{C_1 | \cdots | C_1}_{m_0(s_1)} | \cdots | \underbrace{C_n | \cdots | C_n}_{m_0(s_n)})) =$$

$$dec(\underbrace{C_1 | \cdots | C_1}_{m_0(s_1)} | \cdots | \underbrace{C_n | \cdots | C_n}_{m_0(s_n)})\rho = m_0(s_1) \cdot p_1\rho \oplus \cdots \oplus m_0(s_n) \cdot p_n\rho.$$

because $C_i \stackrel{def}{=} p_i$ for $i = 1, \ldots n$ and so $dec(C_i) = \{p_i\}$. Hence, the initial places are all of the form $p_i\rho$, where such a place is present in m_0' only if $m_0(s_i) > 0$. We assume that each place s_i' in S' is of the form $p_i\rho$, that are all distinct because each p_i contains one distinguishing summand $y_i.\mathbf{0}$. Hence, there is a bijection $f : S \to S'$ defined by $f(s_i) = s_i' = p_i\rho$, which is the natural candidate isomorphism function. Then it remains to prove that f is an isomorphism:

1. $f(m_0) = m_0'$,
2. $t = (m, a, m') \in T$ implies $f(t) = (f(m), a, f(m')) \in T'$, and
3. $t' = (m_1', a, m_2') \in T'$ implies there exists $t = (m_1, a, m_2) \in T$ such that $f(t) = t'$, i.e., $f(m_1) = m_1'$ and $f(m_2) = m_2'$.

From items (2) and (3) above, it follows that $A = A'$.

Proof of 1: Let $m_0 = k_1 \cdot s_1 \oplus k_2 \cdot s_2 \oplus \cdots \oplus k_n \cdot s_n$, where $k_i = m_0(s_i) \geq 0$ *for* $i = 1, \ldots, n$; *note that, for simplicity's sake, we have considered all the places: if a place, say* s_h, *is not in* m_0, *then* $k_h = 0$. *The mapping via* f *of the initial marking is* $f(m_0) = k_1 \cdot f(s_1) \oplus k_2 \cdot f(s_2) \oplus \cdots \oplus k_n \cdot f(s_n) = k_1 \cdot p_1 \rho \oplus k_2 \cdot p_2 \rho \oplus \cdots \oplus k_n \cdot p_n \rho$
$= dec(\underbrace{C_1 | \cdots | C_1}_{k_1 \ times} | \cdots | \underbrace{C_n | \cdots | C_n}_{k_n \ times}) \rho = dec(p) = m_0'$.

Proof of 2: we prove that, for $j = 1, \ldots, k$, if $t_j = (m, a, m') \in T$, then $t_j' = (f(m), a, f(m')) \in T'$. *From transition* t_j, *we can derive the two processes* $P_j = (\underbrace{C_1 \rho | \cdots | C_1 \rho}_{\bullet t_j(s_1)} | \cdots | \underbrace{C_n \rho | \cdots | C_n \rho}_{\bullet t_j(s_n)})$ *and* $P_j' = (\underbrace{C_1 \rho | \cdots | C_1 \rho}_{t_j^\bullet(s_1)} | \cdots | \underbrace{C_n \rho | \cdots | C_n \rho}_{t_j^\bullet(s_n)})$
such that $f(\bullet t_j) = dec(P_j)$ *and* $f(t_j^\bullet) = dec(P_j')$.

According to Definition 15, for each $C_i = p_i$, *we have a summand* c_i^j *in* p_i, *such that* $Q_j = (\underbrace{c_1^j \rho | \cdots | c_1^j \rho}_{\bullet t_j(s_1)} | \cdots | \underbrace{c_n^j \rho | \cdots | c_n^j \rho}_{\bullet t_j(s_n)})$. *By inspecting the shape of* t_j *and the definition of the various* c_i^j's, *one can get convinced that* $(dec(Q_j), l(t_j), dec(P_j'))$ *is a derivable transition. Hence, since each* p_i *is a summation containing the summand* c_i^j, *also* $(dec(P_j), l(t_j), dec(P_j'))$ *is derivable and belongs to* T', *as required.*

Proof of 3: The details can be found in [15].   □

6   Conclusion

The class of finite-net Multi-CCS processes represents a language for describing finite, statically reduced, P/T Petri nets. This is not the only language expressing finite P/T nets: the first (and only other) one is Mayr's PRS [17], which however is rather far from a typical process algebra as its basic building blocks are rewrite rules (or net transitions) instead of actions and, for instance, it does not contain any scope operator like restriction.

A bit pretentiously, we claim that finite-net Multi-CCS is *the* language for finite Petri nets. The main argument defending this claim is that the parallel operator $- \parallel -$ of a language able to express Petri nets is to be

- *permissive*: in a process $p \parallel q$, the actions p can perform cannot be prevented by q. This requirement is necessary because P/T Petri nets are permissive as well, meaning that if a transition t is enabled at a marking m, then t is also enabled at a marking $m' \supseteq m$; the parallel operator of Multi-CCS is permissive, while this is not the case for other parallel operators, such as the CSP one $p \parallel_A q$ [16].
- Also, the parallel operator $- \parallel -$ is to be ACI (*associative, commutative, with an identity*); this requirement because the decomposition of a parallel process into a marking has to reflect that a marking is a (finite) *multiset*.
- Moreover, the parallel operator should be able to express multi-party synchronization, because a net transition, which may have a preset of any size, can

be generated by means of a synchronization among many participants, actually as many as are the tokens in its preset. The Multi-CCS parallel operator can model multi-party synchronization, by means of the interplay with the strong prefixing operator. Other process algebras offer parallel operators with multi-party synchronization capabilities, but in Multi-CCS multi-party synchronization is "programmable", meaning that we can prescribe the order in which the various participants are to interact, independently of the syntactic position they occupy within the global term and without resorting to a global synchronization function, as in the case of some ACP dialects [2].

The multi-party synchronization discipline has been chosen as simple as possible: a sequence can synchronize with an action at a time, in the exact order they occur in the sequence: we feel that the choices made in this paper are the minimal ones that allows for the representability of finite P/T nets. Summing up, any other language, if any, able to represent finite P/T Petri nets should possess these necessary features, which, altogether, seem to be exclusive of finite-net Multi-CCS, or that at least are very rare in the panorama of process algebras.

Finally, a few observations about the differences of this paper with respect to its earlier version [13]. First, the definition of finite-net Multi-CCS is a bit simpler now, in order to capture the minimal language capable of representing all finite P/T nets. Second, the net $Net(p)$ associated to a process p is statically reduced: this ensures that $Net(p)$ and $Net(p \mid p)$ are the same unmarked net, but with a different initial marking; on the contrary, in [13] $Net(p)$ was only dynamically reduced. Third, the finiteness theorem was wrongly stated in [13]: in fact, $Net(p)$ is finite not for all finite-net processes, but only for *well-formed* finite-net processes. Fourth, the construction of the finite-net process $p = INet(N(m_0))$ from the net system $N(m_0)$ is inaccurate in [13], as $Net(p)$ may have more transitions than $N(m_0)$.

Acknowledgment. Massimo Morara is thanked for pointing out the inaccuracy in the definition of the process $INet(N(m_0))$ in [13]. The anonymous referees are thanked for their comments, which will be considered for the full version [15].

References

1. Busi, N., Gorrieri, R.: Distributed semantics for the π-calculus based on Petri nets with inhibitor arcs. J. Logic Algebraic Program. **78**(3), 138–162 (2009)
2. Baeten, J.C.M., Basten, T., Reniers, M.A.: Process Algebra: Equational Theories of Communicating Processes. Cambridge Tracts in TCS, vol. 50. Cambridge University Press, Cambridge (2010)
3. Desel, J., Reisig, W.: Place/transition Petri nets. In: [22], pp. 122–173 (1998)
4. Degano, P., De Nicola, R., Montanari, U.: A distributed operational semantics for CCS based on C/E systems. Acta Informatica **26**(1–2), 59–91 (1988)
5. Degano, P., De Nicola, R., Montanari, U.: Partial orderings descriptions and observations of nondeterministic concurrent processes. In: de Roever, W.-P., Rozenberg, G., de Bakker, J.W. (eds.) Linear Time, Branching Time and Partial Order in Logics and Models for Concurrency. LNCS, vol. 354, pp. 438–466. Springer, Heidelberg (1989)

6. Degano, P., Gorrieri, R., Marchetti, S.: An exercise in concurrency: a CSP process as a condition/event system. In: Rozenberg, G. (ed.) APN 1988. LNCS, vol. 340, pp. 85–105. Springer, Heidelberg (1988)
7. Degano, P., Meseguer, J., Montanari, U.: Axiomatizing the algebra of net computations and processes. Acta Informatica **33**(7), 641–667 (1996)
8. Esparza, J.: Decidability and complexity of Petri net problems: an introduction. In: [22], pp. 374–428 (1998)
9. Goltz, U.: On representing CCS programs by finite Petri nets. In: Janiga, L., Chytil, M.P., Koubek, V. (eds.) MFCS 1988. LNCS, vol. 324, pp. 339–350. Springer, Heidelberg (1988)
10. Gorrieri, R., Montanari, U.: SCONE: a simple calculus of nets. In: Klop, J.W., Baeten, J.C.M. (eds.) CONCUR 1990. LNCS, vol. 458, pp. 2–30. Springer, Heidelberg (1990)
11. Gorrieri, R., Montanari, U.: Towards hierarchical specification of systems: a proof system for strong prefixing. Int. J. Found. Comput. Sci. **1**(3), 277–293 (1990)
12. Gorrieri, R., Marchetti, S., Montanari, U.: A^2CCS: atomic actions for CCS. Theor. Comput. Sci. **72**(2–3), 203–223 (1990)
13. Gorrieri, R., Versari, C.: A process calculus for expressing finite place/transition Petri Nets. In: Proceedings of the EXPRESS 2010. EPTCS (2010). doi:10.4204/EPTCS.41.6, arXiv:1011.6433v1
14. Gorrieri, R., Versari, C.: Introduction to Concurrency Theory: Transition Systems and CCS. EATCS Text in Computer Science. Springer (2015)
15. Gorrieri, R.: Language representability of finite place/transition Petri Nets. www.cs.unibo.it/gorrieri/papers.html
16. Hoare, C.A.R.: Communicating Sequential Processes. Prentice-Hall, Englewood Cliffs (1985)
17. Mayr, R.: Process rewrite systems. Inf. Comput. **156**(1–2), 264–286 (2000)
18. Milner, R.: Communication and Concurrency. Prentice-Hall, Englewood Cliffs (1989)
19. Olderog, E.R.: Nets, Terms and Formulas. Cambridge Tracts in TCS, vol. 23. Cambridge University Press, Cambridge (1991)
20. Peterson, J.L.: Petri Net Theory and the Modeling of Systems. Prentice-Hall, Englewood Cliffs (1981)
21. Reisig, W.: Petri Nets: An Introduction. EATCS Monographs on TCS. Springer, Heidelberg (1985)
22. Reisig, W., Rozenberg, G. (eds.): APN 1998. LNCS, vol. 1491. Springer, Heidelberg (1998)

Soulmate Algorithms

Fabrizio Luccio and Linda Pagli$^{(\boxtimes)}$

Dipartimento di Informatica, Università di Pisa, Pisa, Italy
{luccio,pagli}@di.unipi.it

Abstract. Consulting dating on-line sites, or adopting greedy algorithms, exhaustive search, approximation, and random search are some of the strategies that can be used to find a soulmate. We discuss techniques and show true life examples, leaving the choice of selecting the most satisfactory method to the reader interested in such an activity.

Keywords: On-line dating · Mating complexity · Soulmate computability · Algorithms for love

1 Introduction

Books, movies and songs are full of stories of people moving around in search of a soulmate. The strategies are numerous, with different characteristics. Some are fast and others take years; some are based on reasoning and calculations, others on emotions, others are purely random; some make use of the most advanced technologies; others, intuitive and naive, have been employed for centuries. Our purpose is not to show which one is the most successful but only to describe a set of observed strategies in terms of algorithmic techniques.

Dating on line is the last frontier for finding the soulmate. The search, done through specialized Web sites, is the broadest possible because it can reach everybody in the world through the net. Even if the sites do not precisely describe the algorithms used for matching people, it is realistic to assume that the main strategy is to match profiles with requirements. Each person gives a description of her/himself according to a list of characteristics and specifies a list of requirements of the desired person. According to [1] the profiles of people used by a popular site are not exactly those declared because people tend to enhance social desirability for themselves, while a more accurate image can be rebuilt from the Internet. The rationale is that our profile is better expressed by the big quantity of our footsteps recorded in the network than by our own description of ourselves. Data analysts can acquire this knowledge if they can access the right amount of data. One site employs directly Facebook identities declaring that this information is kept strictly confidential (see [2]). Other sites, specializing in mating travelers interested in accidental company more than searching for the true soulmate, connect people on the basis of their geographical locations. Our aim, hopefully having some practical interest, is to show that the most used matching strategies cover only one part of the spectrum and are possibly not the best for finding the soulmate.

© Springer International Publishing Switzerland 2015
C. Bodei et al. (Eds.): Degano Festschrift, LNCS 9465, pp. 283–291, 2015.
DOI: 10.1007/978-3-319-25527-9_18

Nowadays people seek for the soulmate several times because life expectance is longer and relationships do not necessarily last forever as before. So in different periods of their life, and with an incredible optimism, a great number of persons start the quest again hoping to eventually find the *true* soulmate. Since the experience of these authors on real stories is limited, we refer to events taken from cinema, books, and songs framing them into algorithmic structures, and invite people to suggest other stories that can enter in our little collection of examples.

2   Naive Approaches

A common method (and, in the opinion of many, the best method) for mating people is through *arranged marriages*. It is based on a *greedy* algorithm that in each step selects the choice that appears the best. This strategy not always produces the optimal solution, but for many problems provides an acceptable result. We can make whatever choice seems the best at the moment and then solve subproblems that can arise later.

This is the way candidates are selected in arranged marriages, an ancient tradition still maintained in several cultures as for instance in India. Parents (or close relatives) are in charge of selecting the best opportunities for their children, sometimes without even consulting the individuals concerned. This is done through a sequence of choices that refine the set of possible candidates step by step, until a final candidate remains. Similarly, weddings are arranged usually between men from rich countries and women from poorer countries, as shown in a movie where the two main characters are sensational Claudia Cardinale and Alberto Sordi [8].

An important area of application relates to royal families. Royal weddings are traditionally used to strengthen political and economical relationships between nations. According to a greedy strategy first a target nation is selected. Then the set is restricted to candidates with the required degree of nobility. Further selections are then performed on other less relevant parameters to arrive to a very small number of possible candidates. Sometimes, however, the most relevant parameters are surprising. At the end of the nineteenth century the king of a country now member of the European Union was convinced to marry a princess of a small Balkan state for enhancing the phenotype of the royal species, because she was very tall and the king was unusually short.

If the objective function is the enhancement of the diplomatic relations of the two countries, this greedy strategy leeds to the optimal solution; if that function accounts for the happiness of the marriage this strategy is probably quite weak. However, there is evidence of counterexamples: the weddings of *Joan of Castile*, called *Joan the Mad*, and *Philip the Handsome* of Austria (see for example [9]). She was sixteen when she married him and it was lust at the first sight. She was very passionate and felt *madly* in love with her handsome husband for her whole life. They had six children in around six years, that is the time their marriage lasted until the king died at the age of twenty eight. The story says that she was *mad* of jealousy for his unfaithfulness but recent studies show that she became mad after being imprisoned for political reasons. She survived to Philip for half a century in complete loneliness.

If the story of Joan and Philip, though sad, gleams of nobility and love, very bitter is the story of the movie mentioned above where the bride arrives in Australia from Italy with the hope of a better life, to discover a crude reality. In this case the greedy algorithm produces a very poor result because, before the marriage, they exchanged fake information. But even the smartest algorithm fails if the initial data are incorrect.

Greedy algorithms are possibly inaccurate but they are "polynomially" fast. If instead we want to explore all possibilities we must often adopt an *exhaustive strategy* that may require exponential time. So the problem is practically unsolvable if a complete exponential exploration is needed.

Giacomo Casanova, a gentleman from Venice of the eighteenth-century, has become famous for his numerous, complicated and elaborate affairs with women. His name is now synonymous with *womanizer* and his behavior is considered inappropriate. However who knows if he simply wanted to find his soulmate and used for this purpose an exhaustive search? If none of the women encountered appeared to be adequate, he had to continue his search. Maybe if he found the true soulmate he would have stopped his reckless behavior. So we discourage this strategy at least for the long time that it can take. Hopefully better strategies are possible as it will be shown in the following sections.

If one does not desire to have her/his future arranged by others, or to implement a searching strategy personally, can turn to the wealth of specialized services offered by dating on-line sites without getting to know in detail the algorithms used. These sites keep secret their algorithms, however, it seems reasonable that a score function is computed from the profile and requirements of the costumer and those of the available dates. The more appropriate is the function, and the more are the features taken into account, the better will be the possible matching.

Based on the ranking of the score function the customer will be advised on the best possible dates with whom she/he can start a first approach. Although advertisement of the most popular current dating sites promise new and innovative strategies, we can expect that they consist of a refinement of known matching procedures now based on the study of long-lasting relations arising from big Internet data [2]. Other sites are most sophisticated, like for example the one of Pierluigi Crescenzi of Florence specializing in "incontri" (encounters) [3]. At the end dating sites seem to merely use greedy algorithms, but their great success relies on the possibility of reaching virtually everybody in the net.

3   Undecidability

The theory of computability is generally regarded as being highly abstract and far from everyday human activities. A rebuttal, however, comes from the conduct of Martin, the main character of Milan Kundera's novel "The Golden Apple of Eternal Desire" [4] who

... is able to do something I'm incapable of. Stop any woman on any street.

And in fact, aside from his abominable habits, we take Martin as a paradigm of strictly logical behavior.[1]

A great heritage of Alan Turing is the knowledge that, *inter pares* (among Turing Machines, in that specific case), one cannot establish the behavior of another if not simulating her or his actions. So, if in front of a dilemma one goes on forever before taking a decision, no other can predict such a behavior in finite time. Martin has tuned his dating algorithm on the basis of this knowledge.

Martin considers all women as algorithms of which he is the data. And he knows that anyone of them may take infinite time before eventually accepting him as a partner even for a single intimate encounter. Note that he does not necessarily refer to a sexual encounter since

... those who do not go after anything but this last level are wretched, primitive men.

So he proceeds developing different dating actions in parallel that will be presented here in geek style as a sequence of consecutive steps performed in discrete times. These actions are integrated by a concurrent activity called *sighting* aimed at recording names and other contact data of as many women as possible among the ones that have attracted us as possibly desirable partners. In fact

from his vast experience, he has come to the conclusion that it is not as difficult, for someone with high numerical requirements, to seduce a girl as it is to know enough girls one hasn't yet seduced.

He then proceeds with parallel courting steps, each one with a different *sighted* woman, jumping from one adventure to the other until some of them would get to a satisfactory conclusion without wasting too much time with women who are slow in deciding.

The method is inspired by one adopted by Georg Cantor in his studies on infinite sets. Refer to matrix M in Fig. 1 where $M[i, j]$ shows the results of courting phase i on woman j. The results are coded as Y for "yes", N for "no", and W for "wait, can't decide yet". In particular women are labelled as $w_1, w_2, \ldots$ (in fact, although Martin can stop any woman the sighted set remains denumerable) and courting steps are divided into phases $p_1, p_2, \ldots$ associated with the progressive number of encounters with any woman. We do not impose a limit on the number of rows and columns of M because Martin has infinite patience to go through successive steps, and has tremendous sighting possibilities so the set of women grows continuously.

The arrows on M show the order in which Martin travels along his adventures. This is a key point. Each entry of M will be reached in finite (although possibly very long) time, so each woman that will decide for yes at some time

---

[1] The relationship between Martin's conduct and computability theory was pointed out for the first time in [5].

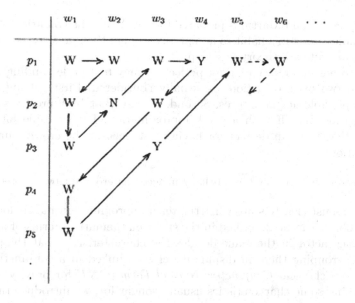

Fig. 1. The matrix M of Martin's courting steps.

will be certainly reached and satisfied. To speed-up the process if a woman w_j decides for yes or no in phase p_i, the entries in column j and rows $> i$ are henceforth disregarded. So, although in the example the first sighted woman w_1 is not willing to take a decision in a short time (and possibly she will never take one), the forth woman w_4 will see her love dream come true in phase 1 in the seventh step of Martin's tour.

Now what about if woman w_1 will never decide? In Martin's strategy she has to be visited at each step, that is forever. A person without a solid mathematical background could be induced to stop dating with w_1 after a certain number of steps, deducing from her past behavior that she will never take a decision. But Martin has learned from Turing that the halting problem is undecidable and continues dating w_1 with a hope of a final positive decision. On the other hand, as the number of steps between the ones spent with w_1 in phases i and $i+1$ is of order $O(i)$ (in fact is upper bounded by the length of a diagonal in M), he will waste less and less time in percent as the process goes on.

4   Complexity and Approximation

Although mathematically intriguing, the conduct of Martin raises a philosophical problem on the very same concept of soulmate. The most prestigious advocate of this concept was Plato that, in his Symposium, stated the *existence and unicity* of the soulmate for any person (independently of the sex of both souls, as it may be expected). The condition of existence confirms that searching for a soulmate is a legitimate activity although the number of steps required maybe exceedingly large (and Martin is prepared for this). But the condition of uniqueness contradicts Martin's habit to accept any woman that says yes, unless a new philosophical soulmate theory is set up.

On the other hand searching for perfection may be too demanding in everyday life, so two ways of action are usually considered. First getting the best among all possible acquaintances. Second, in case that best prefers somebody else, contenting oneself with a good approximation. For example [6] all Italians know that Isaia, in despair for having lost Zazà in the crowd, turns to an approximation:

Se non troverò / lei, ch'è tanto bella, / m'accontenterò / 'e trovà'a sorella...[2]

However we must clearly state what the term approximation means for us.

The problem can be described in the strict mathematical terms of a decision process. Each actor in the game decides the characteristics that the soulmate must have, grouping them in disjunctive clauses linked in a conjunction. This gives rise to a classical *Conjunctive Normal Form* (*CNF* for brevity). So, just for mentioning some characteristics usually sought for, we introduce the logical variables:

a animal-rights activist / b: boring / g: gentle / i: intriguing / k: over 75 kilos / m: at most 29 / r: very rich

The sign $\neg$ will be used for complementing some of the variables, and disjunctive clauses will be formulated in order to make the search not too much demanding. For example the CNF:

$$F = (m \vee r) \wedge (\neg a \vee g) \wedge (\neg a \vee i) \wedge (\neg b) \wedge (g \vee \neg m \vee \neg r) \wedge (a \vee k \vee \neg r)$$

states that the mate must be either at most 29 or very rich - obviously better if both (clause 1); if animal-rights activist, must be at least gentle and intriguing (clauses 2 and 3 combined); absolutely cannot be boring (clause 4); etc. Note that this CNF is satisfiable, for example for $k, r = true$ and $a, b, m = false$, no matter how gentle or intriguing the candidate will be. However adding two simple clauses like $(\neg i)$ and $(a \vee b)$ the form becomes not satisfiable and the mate cannot exist.

Unfortunately the CNF satisfiability problem is **NP**-complete, that is deciding if a chosen set of clauses is satisfiable requires exponential time unless **P** = **NP**. Then a long list of requests has a high probability to be useless and one should content her/himself of a maximum satisfiability solution, that is selecting the maximum number of clauses that can be contemporarily satisfied. But, unfortunately again, maximum satisfiability is **NP**-hard and the claim must be further reconsidered, reducing the request to a number of clauses within a guaranteed approximation ratio of the maximal solution.

---

[2] If I won't find her / who is so beautiful / I will settle for / finding her sister ...

Alas, even this problem is intractable! Satisfiability approximation is in fact **APX**-hard, that is it does not admit a polynomial-time approximation scheme unless **P** = **NP**. The disconsolate mate seeker must abandon the idea of getting a mathematically solid result and proceed heuristically. A squalid solution will be built incrementally arranging the clauses in order of decreasing urgency (a purely personal criterion with no mathematical counterpart) and then choosing them one by one, discarding the clauses that are incompatible with the ones already selected.

The wise says: "The optimality is difficult to obtain, the quasi-optimality is usually good enough". Attaining an approximate solution is the most common outcome of everyday problems, as it happens in the movie *When Harry met Sally* [10]. The two have known each other for years, and are very good friends. Their dating experiences with others continue to highlight their different approaches to relationships and sex. Each one is involved in the search of the perfect partner and each one, in different times, faces heavy defeats. They take a long time to discover, only at the end of the story, that they were bound to each other. In this case they accept the approximate solution of an only apparently friend mate because in reality they find their true soulmate.

5 Randomized Algorithms

As known randomness may help in designing sequence of actions aimed at reaching precise objectives, but there are cases in which relying on unpredictable events helps a great deal. So randomness can be used to design efficient algorithms expressed in rigorous mathematical terms. The family of randomized algorithms called *Monte Carlo* uses random choices to obtain a *probably* correct result in a *certainty* short time. The result can then be wrong but the probability of this event can be made as small as required.

In the novel of Milan Kundera *The unbearable lightness of being* [7] Tereza meets Tomas by chance for the first time and immediately likes him. But how can she know if he is really her true soulmate?

> Tomas appears in the hotel restaurant at the same time as the radio is playing Beethoven. We do not even notice the great majority of such coincidences. If the seat Tomas occupied had been occupied instead by the local butcher, Tereza never would have noticed that the radio was playing Beethoven. But her nascent love inflamed her sense of beauty, and she would never forget that music.

Tereza at every new coincidence becomes more and more aware that the events bring her towards Tomas. The coincidence noticed by Tereza are five:

(1) Tomas appears in the restaurant where she works.
(2) When she notices him, the radio is playing Beethoven which has a particular meaning for her.

(3) Six is the number of the key of his room and this number is also the number of a former Tereza's house. (She also immediately informs him that she will be free from work at six, but this seems more an advance than a coincidence).
(4) When she meets him after work he is sitting in her habitual bench.
(5) He is reading a book, that is, he is doing the same as her favorite activity.

Tereza reads chance events like signs from fate. As we blame her? She unconsciously follows a Monte Carlo strategy. First of all, assume that a negative reaction of Tomas is sufficient to establish that Tomas is not the good one, while a random positive event must be taken with caution. Let us imagine that such an event e happens. Still there is a probability $p << 1$ that the event is not so positive, hence Tomas is not the soulmate. If n independent positive events $e_1, e_2, ..., e_n$ occur, each one with probability p_i of being deceptive, Tomas is not the soulmate with total probability $P = p_1 \times p_2 \times ... \times p_n$. P decreases for increasing values of n, if n is sufficiently large the value P is so small that can be neglected, also because is less than the probability that Tereza e Tomas die in the next hour.

Tereza takes her decision after only five events and she falls in love with Tomas precisely because of the coincidences: for her five events are sufficient. If for example $p_i = 1/10$ for all i, we have $P = 1/10^5$ that is indeed a safe condition. If she were more cautious, she could have waited for further positive events before deciding.

Kundera explains Tereza's method of interpretation saying:

the individual composes his life according to the laws of beauty.

He criticizes those readers who are dismayed at the coincidences in a novel, since:

...it is right to chide man for being blind to such coincidences in his daily life.
For he thereby deprives his life of a dimension of beauty.

So Kundera speaks of beauty and we agree, but we are on the side of Tereza because she followed a randomized algorithm that provably gives a very good result.

6   Concluding Remarks

There is no much more to say, if not that all the algorithmic techniques discussed above are aimed at satisfying the personal requests of single actors without considering a global mating optimization as hopefully should be. This is why we have not even mentioned the classical family of algorithms for finding optimal matchings in bipartite graphs, like for example the ones for the well known *stable marriage* problem solvable in polynomial time [11], and its possible more demanding extensions that become exponentially difficult.

Global happiness is bitterly infringed in the name of selfish satisfaction.

References

1. http://seigradi.corriere.it/2014/01/23/il-matematico-che-ha-scoperto-lalgoritmo-perfetto-per-trovare-una-donna/ (2014)
2. Big Data and Relationships: Is there a secret Algorithm for Love? The Big Data Landscape. http://www.bigdatalandscape.com/blog/big-data-relationships-secret-algorithm-love
3. Crescenzi, P.: Firenze. http://www.editelonline.it/222337-1/incontri-in-corso-agenzia-per-single-di-pierluigi-crescenzi-agenzie-matrimoniali.html
4. Kundera, M.: Laughable Loves. Faber and Faber, London (2000)
5. Luccio, F., Pagli, L.: Algoritmi divinità e gente comune. ETS, Pisa (1999)
6. Cutolo, R., Cioffi, G.: Dove sta Zazà. Ed. Musicali Cioffi, Napoli (1944)
7. Kundera, M.: The Unbearable Lightness of Being. Faber and Faber, London (1984)
8. Zampa, L.: Bello, onesto, emigrato Australia sposerebbe compaesana illibata. CEIAD Columbia (1971)
9. Belli, G.: El pergamino de la seducción. Seix Barral, Barcelona (2005)
10. Reiner, R.: When Harry met Sally. Columbia Pictures (1989) (writer Nora Ephron)
11. Knuth, D.E.: Stable marriage and its relation to other combinatorial problems. In: CRM Proceedings and Lecture Notes, vol. 10. American Mathematical Society (1991)

Active Knowledge, LuNA and Literacy for Oncoming Centuries

Victor Malyshkin[1,2]([✉])

[1] Institute of Computational Mathematics and Mathematical Geophysics Russian
Academy of Sciences, Novosibirsk, Russia
malysh@ssd.sscc.ru
http://ssd.sscc.ru
[2] National Research University of Novosibirsk, Novosibirsk, Russia

Abstract. The concept of active knowledge implementation on the basis
of the theory of structural program synthesis, modern technologies and
their necessary developments are considered. The theory is proposed for
technological description, accumulation, keeping, processing and application of active knowledge. On this basis the notion of literacy for the
future is suggested. The concept was implemented in the frame of the
LuNA project aimed at elimination of parallel programming from the
process of large-scale numerical models development.

Keywords: Active knowledge · Program synthesis · Active knowledge
base · Structural program synthesis · Program automatic construction ·
Literacy · LuNA fragmented programming system

> LITERACY is the capability of a
> human being to describe, to keep,
> to understand and to apply the
> knowledge.

1 Introduction

During last years, the computing technologies have substantially changed our life.
In this simple technological paper we would like to look at new progressive technology – technology of active knowledge – that can be partially implemented right
now basing on the current scientific knowledge, accumulated in scientific computations, theoretical models of parallel computations [1–6], technological results and
current system software that are now in use or under development [7–16].

The approach to a possible pragmatic application of the theory of structural
program synthesis [6] to the development of the active knowledge technology is
discussed. The sum of the current theoretical results provides understanding of
the approaches to the solution of active knowledge problem. It is interesting now

© Springer International Publishing Switzerland 2015
C. Bodei et al. (Eds.): Degano Festschrift, LNCS 9465, pp. 292–303, 2015.
DOI: 10.1007/978-3-319-25527-9_19

to look at how the problem could be solved and technologically[1] implemented. In this technological paper the problem of the current implementability of the active knowledge technology is considered.

2   Active and Passive Knowledge

Principal idea. The problem of active knowledge technology creation was principally solved in the frame of the theories of program synthesis. Below the technologically implementable approach, based on the theory of structural program synthesis, that is ready for implementation right now, is mostly discussed.

2.1   Passive Representation of the Knowledge

There are now four main problems to utilize the knowledge represented in passive form:

1. Currently existing phonetic systems of knowledge description, keeping and processing are actually the systems of *passive* knowledge (texts, movies, etc.) representation, i.e., this knowledge description cannot be applied directly, automatically. Keeping in the hands a book(s) with the complete enough description of the technology of a bridge construction, a desired/specified bridge cannot be constructed automatically even after the magic incantations were pronounced. This is so, because a computer doesn't understand phonetic text and unable to extract the knowledge from it.
2. In order to utilize such passive knowledge, the people should adopt (read, understand and be able correctly to apply) a large body in the literature of the subject. It takes generally about 25 and even more years. Also, the technologies are now permanently under modifications and the process of learning is being permanent.
3. A big volume of passive knowledge is already accumulated. Sometimes the passive knowledge is not in (intensive) use and even can be forgotten and lost.
4. Also application programs, implementing passive knowledge, are usually developed as "black box" and cannot be automatically modified in accordance with a user demands.

2.2   Active Representation of the Knowledge

In order to overcome the above mentioned problems, the knowledge should be represented in *active* form that can be understood by a computer system and applied automatically to solution of a certain specified problem. Active knowledge representation should provide knowledge extraction from its description and the knowledge use for solution of a certain application problem [13].

---

[1] The term *technological* is used in order to denote that a specified object (theory, model, problem, algorithm, program, etc.) can be implemented for practically acceptable time and with necessary properties, with the use of acceptable number of resources.

Mathematical logic describes the way to solve the problem of active knowledge representation, understanding and application in four steps:

- development of complete enough axiomatic theory (AT),
- application problem formulation in terms of the theory,
- derivation of a desirable algorithm for application problem solution (APS),
- generation of a program, implementing derived APS algorithm.

2.3   Logic Program Synthesis

The method is based on the sufficiently complete AT, describing an object domain. Within the frame of this theory the necessary assertions are proved or disproved from the set of axioms.

The fact is, the method is technologically not implementable, at least because of too high complexity of APS algorithms derivation and the absence of a possibility to provide desirable pragmatic properties both derived APS algorithms and implementing programs.

2.4   Technological Requirements to Representation

Technological description of AT should provide:

1. In order to avoid high complexity of APS algorithm derivation, an AT should be described partially [14], only the necessary APS algorithms should be derivable in the frame of the AT. This de facto means, that AT (knowledge base of the partial object domain) description should be generated from a problem formulation.
2. An AT is defined partially not taking care of completeness of the AT. Practically it means, that as a rule, an AT should be defined for solution the only problem or, may be, for solution of few problems.
3. Derived APS algorithms should be represented as a set of recursively countable set of functional terms [17]. Therefore, a language of partial AT description should be a language for description of sets of all operations of functional terms with their input and output variables. This language can be understood by a computer. This is the basis for creation of new writing and literacy. Ability to operate with AT will define soon the literacy of human being.
4. An AT description should be easy extendable, in order to include into the AT the descriptions of the other problems solutions when the need arises. It should be simple technological (not scientific) work.
5. Program, implementing derived algorithm, should be generated automatically and possess by all the desirable properties (arbitrary program is not acceptable), like:
   - to be executed in parallel;
   - to be tunable (statically and dynamically) to all the available resources of a computer system;
   - able to be executed on heterogeneous distributed computer system;

- with dynamic workload balancing;
- to have the demanded level of reliability;
- to be modified on a user demand,

and many other pragmatic properties.

3   Technological Notion of Knowledge

It is necessary to define a technologically implementable method to describe, to accumulate and, what is the most important, correctly to exploit the knowledge, represented in the active form, without knowledge adaptation by a human being in all the thinkable details.

3.1   Structural Program Synthesis (SPS)

For the reason of high complexity of an APS algorithms derivation in the frame of logic programming we are forced to use in practice the methods with lesser possibilities for the knowledge description, but more suitable for computer processing. One of such methods is based on imposing a structure on the knowledge base that reflects the associative dependences between the objects of the object domain. In the process of an algorithm derivation, the explicit representation of these dependences in a computer permits to use the associative search instead of the random search in logic programming. The method of structural program synthesis [6] is based on this idea. Rephrased idea of structural program synthesis is:

- There is no any technological sense to develop the general theory for algorithm derivation from functional specification. A partially defined AT can be successfully used providing an acceptable quality both algorithms and implementing programs.
- A desirable program should be constructed out of accumulated well-developed ready-made modules each of which represents one step $((A, A \supset B) \supset B)$ of APS derivation.

In the method of structural program synthesis (program synthesis on the basis of computational models) the completeness of the theory is not considered at all. In principle, *the description of an object domain includes only that objects which were already implemented in practice with an acceptable[2] quality.* The method is based on a carefully designed partially defined object domain description, on such partial AT, in which only necessary problems are well solved. Often, in such partially defined AT, a solution of the only necessary problem is constructed.

The theory of structural program synthesis [6] satisfies all the above requirements. This method was applied to parallel implementation of different large-scale numerical models [10, 16] and the necessary experience was gained, algorithms and programs were developed.

---

[2] The term *acceptable* is used in order to denote that a specified solution, quality, program, resources allocation, etc., can be used in practice because, for example, better solution doesn't exist or is not known now.

3.2   The Notion of Knowledge

Omitting unnecessary here details, the program module (procedure, subroutine, hardware block) will be considered to be *atomic unit* of an active knowledge. Such module represents one step $((A, A \supset B) \supset B)$ of APS derivation. The execution of this module will result in the *active knowledge application*. The algorithms, used into this module, implement the active knowledge. For instance, the knowledge of arithmetic is now implemented inside the module called *calculator*. From now nobody needs to know algorithms of arithmetic and mental arithmetic in order successfully to utilize the arithmetic.

A set of all the knowledge units of an object domain (library of modules) does not yet constitute the knowledge base, because on this set different relations exist, in particular, the relation of information dependencies or neighborhood relation. These relations should also be described and implemented in a generated program. Also for any module the (input) variables, to which only this module is permitted to be applied for computing another (output) variables should be described. Any module denotes the step of an APS algorithm derivation. Thus, knowledge base is actually a partially defined AT, represented by a set of steps of an APS algorithm derivation. An example is given below.

With this technological definition of the active knowledge, the main objects of knowledge processing will be algorithms and programs. Therefore, the well-known methods of APS algorithms derivation and program synthesis can be applied to the description and processing of the knowledge base [6].

4   Technological Model of Knowledge

Thus, let us consider shortly the computational model [6] as the basis for definition of the knowledge base.

4.1   The General Definition of the Program Synthesis Problem

The knowledge base (actually partially defined AT) in the method of structural program synthesis constitutes a set of ready-made modules (programs, subroutines). For each module the allowable sets of input and output variables are defined. The solution of a specified problem is assembled out of these modules if possible. If this is not possible, the AT is extended by adding new modules to the knowledge base. Also, if the solution of a specified problem does not satisfy the user, then some modules should be replaced by better modules or new modules be added.

The general formulation of the program synthesis problem is:
Given:

− class S of input problem specifications,
− class P of resulting programs,
− equivalence relation $\sim$ on P,
− quality relation $>$ on P, that satisfies the axioms of the partial order.

The algorithm $A : S \to P$ should be found such that:

- program $p = A(s), p \in P$, satisfies the specification $s \in S$,
- p is the best (in the sense $>$) program among $\{p \mid p = A(s)\}$.

In such a way, the algorithm $A : S \to P$ solves a program synthesis problem, that is, for every specification $s \in S$, the algorithm A constructs an element $p = A(s), p \in P$, which is the best program among all the programs solving a specified problem s.

4.2 Computational Model Definition

Given [6]:

- The finite set $\mathbf{X} = \{x, y, \ldots, z\}$ of variables for representation of different computed values;
- The finite set $\mathbf{F} = \{a, b, \ldots, c\}$ of functional symbols (operations, Fig. 1a), $m \geq 0$ is the number of input variables, $n \geq 0$ is the number of output variables;
- $in(a) = (x_1, \ldots, x_m)$ is a set of input variables, $out(a) = (y_1, \ldots, y_n)$ is a set of output variables (Fig. 1), if $i \neq j \to y_i \neq y_j$ & $x_i \neq x_j$.

Model $C = (\mathbf{X}, \mathbf{F})$ is called *simple computational model* (SCM). Operation $a \in \mathbf{F}$ describes the possibility to compute the variables $out(a)$ from the variables $in(a)$, for example, with the use of a certain procedure. The model can be graphically depicted (Fig. 1).

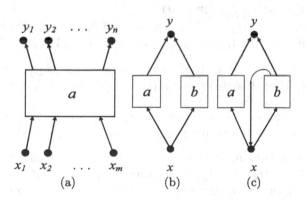

Fig. 1. Examples of operations, variables and model

Let $V \subseteq \mathbf{X}$, $F \subseteq \mathbf{F}$ be given. A set of functional terms $T(V, F)$ is defined as follows:

1. If $x \in V$, then x is a term $t, t \in T(V, F)$; $in(t) = \{x\}$; $out(t) = \{x\}$.

2. Let $\{t^1, \ldots, t^s\} \subseteq T(V, F)$ and $a \in F$, $in(a) = (x_1, \ldots, x_s)$ be given. The term $t = a(t^1, \ldots, t^s)$ is included into $T(V, F)$ if $\forall i(x_i \in out(t^i))$, $in(t) = \bigcup_{i=1}^{s} in(t^i)$, $out(t) = out(a)$. Here $t = a(t^1, \ldots, t^s)$ denotes that t is the term $a(t^1, \ldots, t^s)$.

A term is depicted as a tree that contains both operations and variables of the term.

We say that a term t computes a variable y if $y \in out(t)$. A set of terms $T(V, F)$ defines all the variables of the SCM that can be computed from V variables. A set of terms $T_V^W = \{t \in T(V, F) \mid out(t) \cap W \neq \emptyset\}$ computes all those variables from W that can be computed from V variables.

Any such subset $R \subseteq T_V^W$ that $\forall x \in W \exists t \in R(x \in out(t))$ is called (V, W)-plan. This (V, W)-plan defines an algorithm computing the variables W from the variables V. Here V and W denote the sets of input and output variables of the algorithm, respectively. Everywhere further a recursively countable set of functional terms is considered as a representation of an algorithm.

In order to satisfy all the technological requirements to AT representation, the axioms are not used, they are not formulated. Instead, AT is representation by the set of all possible in AT derivation steps. These steps (functions, modules) actually constitute the computational model.

Interpretation. Let $V \subseteq \mathbf{X}$ be given. *Interpretation* $\mathbf{I}$ in the domain D is a function that assigns:

- to every variable $x \in V$ an entry $d_x = I(x) \in D$, d_x is a value of the variable x in the interpretation $\mathbf{I}$,
- to every operation $a \in F$, $in(a) = \{x_1, x_2, \ldots, x_m\}$, $out(a) = \{y_1, y_2, \ldots, y_n\}$, a computable function $f_a : D^m \to D^n$,
- to every term $t = a(t_1, t_2, \ldots, t_m)$, a superposition of the functions is assigned in accord with the rule $\mathbf{I}(a(t_1, t_2, \ldots, t_m)) = f_a(\mathbf{I}(t_1), \mathbf{I}(t_2), \ldots, \mathbf{I}(t_m))$.

If $t = a(t_1, t_2, \ldots, t_m)$ is an arbitrary term, $in(a) = \{x_1, x_2, \ldots, x_m\}$, $out(a) = \{y_1, y_2, \ldots, y_n\}$, then $\mathbf{I}(out(a)) = val(t) = (d_1, d_2, \ldots, d_n) = f_a(val_{x_1}(t_1), val_{x_2}(t_2), \ldots, val_{x_n}(t_n))$.

Further it is assumed that for every function $f_a = \mathbf{I}(a)$ there exists a module (procedure) mod_a that can be used in a program to compute the function f_a.

Correct Interpretation. If there exist two different terms t_1 and t_2, $y \in out(t_1) \cap out(t_2)$, $in(t_1) \cup in(t_2) \subseteq V$, then $val_y(t_1) = val_y(t_2)$ in the interpretation $\mathbf{I}$, and the interpretation $\mathbf{I}$ is called *correct interpretation*. In the correct interpretation for any variable y, any pair of the terms t_1 and t_2, $y \in out(t_1) \cap out(t_2)$ yields the same value, $val_y(t_1) = val_y(t_2)$.

For definition of mass computations this model should be extended by inclusion of indexed operations and indexed variables (arrays). This technical work can be easily done. Obviously, in this extended model, a mass algorithm is represented by an infinite recursively countable set of functional terms.

A program that implements an algorithm, represented by a set of functional terms, can be constructed with the procedure calls to mod_a in the order not contradicting to the information dependences between the operations imposed by the terms structure. Usually, a run-time system is used to implement all the calls in a proper order.

4.3   An Example of Knowledge Base, i.e. Partially Defined AT

Below (Fig. 3) the example of the description of the application partially defined axiomatic theory TRIANGLE is given. The partially defined axiomatic theory TRIANGLE is the part of an axiomatic theory GEOMETRY. The axiomatic theory TRIANGLE does not describe the whole theory GEOMETRY, but only that its part that provides the solution of the problem, formulated in Fig. 2. Actually, the TRIANGLE is assembled out of the objects of GEOMETRY. The problem formulation defines:

- the sets of input $V = \{x, z, \gamma, \alpha\}$ and output $W = \{s\}$ variables of the problem,
- the necessary partial AT in which only this problem can be solved is assembled out of notions, valid for problem formulation and found in the active knowledge base. An algorithm of the formulated problem solution is derived on the partial AT and represented here as the set of two functional terms t_1 and t_2.

If some another problem is needed to be solved then new suitable modules and variables should be included into the AT for this problem solution.

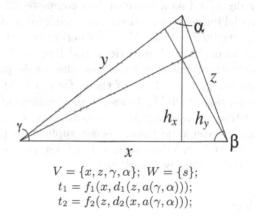

$$V = \{x, z, \gamma, \alpha\}; \; W = \{s\};$$
$$t_1 = f_1(x, d_1(z, a(\gamma, \alpha)));$$
$$t_2 = f_2(z, d_2(x, a(\gamma, \alpha)));$$

Fig. 2. Problem formulation

The capability to create similar knowledge base, to describe and to apply it constitutes the nature of the new literacy for active knowledge description.

Next time it is necessary to draw the attention, that computational model cannot contain unknown solution of a problem. It contains only well-known units of knowledge (ready-made modules). This means, that with the use of the method of structural program synthesis any user will be able to solve a problem with the quality equal to the quality of the best known solution.

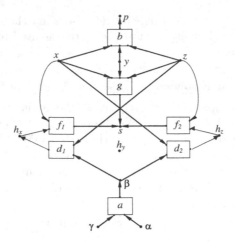

Fig. 3. Partial axiomatic theory TRIANGLE

4.4   Particle-In-Cell Method

Particle-In-Cell method (PIC) is widely used for numerical modeling in physics and chemistry [10,16]. But PIC is applied individually to the solution of an individual problem of numerical modeling. Therefore, now the PIC application cannot be formally described as a more or less complete AT. Fortunately, the methods of PIC parallel implementation are now well known and can be formally described within a partially described AT. This permits to generate a framework for solution of a certain problem of numerical modeling in which a user develops the sequential fragments of the codes whereas the whole parallel program is automatically assembled/generated out of them, for more details see [10,15].

Parallel implementation of PIC includes parallel implementation such sophisticated system algorithms as dynamic resources allocation, processes migration, dynamic load balancing, dynamic tuning of an application program to all the available resources, etc. Clearly, that solution of these problems should be formally described within a partially described AT.

4.5   LuNA Project

The above described approach was implemented within the LuNA project of fragmented programming system [10,11,13,15]. LuNA project is directed to the elimination of parallel programming from the process of large scale numerical models development. In fact LuNA is the system for implementation of AT, described as computational model.

The LuNA fragmented programming system makes:

– accept as input the knowledge description of an object domain (computational model here) and the lists of input and output variables,

- a desired numerical algorithm(s) of a problem solution is derived and represented as recursively countable set of functional terms [6,17],
- the desirable program implementing the derived algorithm is automatically generated. Both algorithm and program possess by all the desired/specified pragmatic properties (to be executed in parallel, dynamic load balancing, dynamic tuning to all the available resources, etc.).

Massivity and regularity of numerical algorithms allow generating parallel programs of acceptable quality. One of the serious problem of LuNA implementation is the replacement of the well-known in sequential programming system algorithms by distributed system algorithms with local interactions (DSALI), especially DSALI for distributed resources allocation, optimization of the generated program execution, dynamic load balancing and many others problems of dynamic optimization. LuNA is under permanent modification.

Now LuNA is able already to generate practical parallel programs implementing different application of PIC methods for large-scale simulation.

4.6   New Literacy

Now the new incipient literacy, based on the capability of a human being to create, to understand and to apply AT is arising. Technically, new writing language (AT writing) may contain the facility for sets of modules and variables description, like this is done in LuNA. New literacy (AT-literacy) includes also the ability to create a proper AT.

Earlier, the human population was divided into the following groups:

- the literate people which were able to read and to write texts,
- the semiliterate people which were able to read but not to write texts,
- the illiterate people which could neither read nor write the texts.

The current human population also begins to become stratified, dividing into the following groups:

- the illiterate people which mostly look at the screens and press the buttons, may be, they know phonetic alphabet and are able to read the text. They are usually not able to write reasonable texts.
- the semiliterate people who are able to read and to write phonetic texts. They know some systems of passive knowledge representation and are able to read and to adopt the knowledge in the passive representation,
- the literate people, who are able to operate with ATs and, certainly, will be able to create, to process, to understand and to utilize the knowledge in the active representation, in AT writing.

The current phonetic writing provides the accumulation of the knowledge in a passive form. As a rule, with the use of this literacy a human being is able to adopt and to apply the knowledge in one object domain, only.

The AT-literacy will practically infinitely extend the abilities of a human being to adaptation of new object domains. This literacy will substantially change the representations of new scientific and industrial technologies. AT writing should provide at least a description of recursively countable sets of modules and variables.

Instead of an object domain adaptation in all its details, only the ability to formulate a problem will be needed. In this manner, for instance, 10 object domains can be adopted.

The ability to formulate the problems will be the basis of education in the future. Only a few people, good mathematicians, also experienced in parallel computing technologies, will be doing by the most interesting work, i.e., the development of the active knowledge bases.

5   Conclusion

Models of parallel computation are now successfully utilized in scientific and industrial modeling. Above consideration demonstrates that these models will be applied for modeling social phenomena too. AT writing will co-exists in parallel with phonetic writing.

It seems, that next 50 or may be 100 years and even more IT community will be doing by the creation of active knowledge bases: transformation of currently accumulated passive knowledge bases into active form and creation new one. This is not single-step process. The sphere of programming systems application will be narrowing and instead the systems, implementing AT (like LuNA), should be developed.

Finally, I would like to remark the following. The human society on its way to more progressive organization meets many problems. Current American movies often frighten us by extraterrestrials, monsters, etc. But new literacy is really far more terrible thing, bad dream, that threaten to the humanity by degradation (human population moronization) in next one or two centuries, because with the use of active knowledge technology human beings do not need to think.

It is clear, that the uncontrolled development of any scientific discipline, including such inoffensive thing as literacy, can lead to humanity self-destruction. Therefore, united nations and states must provide a global control on applications of **any** new scientific result.

Hope, I am not fully right and this prediction will not be proved.

References

1. Zadykhailo, I.B.: Sostavlenie tsiklov po parametricheskim zapisyam spetsialnogo vida. Zhurnal vychislitelnoi mathematiki i mathematicheskoi physiki 3(2), 337–357 (1963). (in Russian)
2. Manna, Z., Waldinger, R.: Synthesis: dreams -> programs. IEEE Trans. SE **SE–5**, 294–398 (1979)
3. Ershov, Y.L., Goncharov, S.S., Sviridenko, D.I.: Semantic programming. Information Processing: Proceedings of IFIP 10th World Computer Congress Series, vol. 10, Amsterdam, pp. 1113–1120 (1986)

4. Giannesini, F., Kanoui, H., Pasero, R., Caneghem, M.: Prolog. International Computer Science Series. Addison-Wesley, Wokingham (1986)
5. Genesereth, M.R., Nilsson, N.J.: Logical Foundation of Artificial Intelligence. Morgan Kaufmann, Los Altos (1987)
6. Valkovskii, V.A., Malyshkin, V.E.: Synthesis of Parallel Programs and Systems on the Basis of Computational Models, Nauka, Novosibirsk, p. 128 (1988). (in Russian, Sintez parallelnykh programm i sistem na vychislitelnykh modelyakh)
7. Andrianov, A.N., Efimkin, K.N., Zadykhailo, I.B.: Nonprocedural language for mathematical physics. Program. Comput. Softw. **17**(2), 10–22 (1992)
8. Andrianov, A.N., Efimkin, K.N., Levashov, V.Y., Shishkova, I.N.: The NORMA language application to solution of strong nonequilibrium transfer processes problem with condensation of mixtures on the multiprocessor system. In: Dongarra, J., Alexandrov, V.N., Tan, C.J.K., Juliano, B.A., Renner, R.S. (eds.) ICCS-ComputSci 2001. LNCS, vol. 2073, pp. 502–510. Springer, Heidelberg (2001)
9. Malyshkin, V.: Assembling of parallel programs for large scale numerical modeling. In: Handbook of Research on Scalable Computing Technologies, Chap. 13, pp. 295–311. IGI Global, USA (2010)
10. Kraeva, M.A., Malyshkin, V.E.: Assembly technology for parallel realization of numerical models on MIMD-multicomputers. Future Gener. Comput. Syst. Elsevier Sci. **17**(6), 755–765 (2001)
11. Kireev, S., Malyshkin, V.: Fragmentation of numerical algorithms for parallel subroutines library. J. Supercomputing **57**(2), 161–171 (2011)
12. Bosilca, G., Bouteiller, A., Danalis, A., Faverge, M., Haidar, A., Herault, T., Kurzak, J., Langou, J., Lemarinier, P., Ltaeif, H., Luszczek, P., YarKhan, A., Dongarra, J.: Flexible development of dense linear algebra algorithms on massively parallel architectures with DPLASMA. In: Proceedings of the Workshops of the 25th IEEE International Symposium on Parallel and Distributed Processing, Anchorage, Alaska, USA, pp. 1432–1441. IEEE (2011)
13. Malyshkin, V.: How to create the magic wand. Currently implementable formulation of the problem. In: The Proceedings of the 5-th SoMeT International Conference on New Trends in Software Methodologies, Tools and Techniques, vol. 147, pp. 127–132. IOS Press, Quebec, 28–30 September 2006
14. Malyshkin, V.: Two approaches to program synthesis or implementation of partially defined theories. In: Proceedings of the 11th International Conference on New Trends in Software Methodologies, Tools and Techniques, vol. 246, pp. 285–291. IOS Press, USA (2012)
15. Malyshkin, V.E., Perepelkin, V.A.: The PIC implementation in LuNA system of fragmented programming. J. Supercomputing **69**(1), 89–97 (2014). Springer
16. Kireev, S.: A parallel 3D code for simulation of self-gravitating gas-dust systems. In: Malyshkin, V. (ed.) PaCT 2009. LNCS, vol. 5698, pp. 406–413. Springer, Heidelberg (2009)
17. Kleene, S.C.: Introduction to Metamathematics. Princeton University Press, Princeton (1952)

There are Two Sides to Every Question
Controller Versus Attacker

Fabio Martinelli[✉], Ilaria Matteucci, and Francesco Santini

Istituto di Informatica e Telematica, IIT-CNR, Pisa, Italy
{Fabio.Martinelli,Ilaria.Matteucci,Francesco.Santini}@iit.cnr.it

Abstract. We investigate security enforcement mechanisms that run in parallel with a system; the aim is to check and modify the run-time behaviour of a possible attacker in order to guarantee that the system satisfies some security policies. We focus on a CSP-like quantitative process-algebra to model such processes. Weights on actions are modelled with semirings, which represent a parametric structure where to cast different metrics. The basic tools are represented by a quantitative logic and a model checking function. First, the behaviour of the system is removed from the parallel computation with respect to some security property to be satisfied. Secondly, what remains is refined in two formulas with respect to the given operator executed by a controller. The result describes what a controller has to do to prevent a given attack.

1 Introduction

Security is frequently in conflict with functional requirements, such as costs, execution times, and rates, as well as performance requirements of a system, making 100 % security an impossible or overly expensive goal to be accomplished. Therefore, the relevant question is not whether a system is secure, but rather how much security it provides under such "soft" constraints.

In addition, we can use security-oriented metrics, as the vulnerability exposure (the sum of known and unpatched vulnerabilities), the worst case loss (the maximum money-value of the damage/loss that could be inflicted), the data transmission exposure (the unencrypted data-transmission volume), or the detection performance (a measure of the effectiveness of the detection mechanisms implemented on the system) [8]. Instead of a plain yes/no answer, quantitative levels of security can express different degrees of protection, and allow a security expert to reason about the trade-off between security and conflicting requirements. Quantitative security analysis [19] has been already applied, *e.g.*, to name a few, for quantifying the side-channel leakage in cryptographic algorithms, for capturing the loss of privacy in statistical data analysis or information flows, and for quantifying security in anonymity networks.

Concurrent languages (*e.g.*, process algebras) are expressive enough to model a system, a controller, and an attacker within the same formalism. As a prototypical example, in this work we choose *Generalised Process Algebra* (*GPA*) [9]

The author is supported by MIUR PRIN 2010XSEMLC "Security Horizons".

© Springer International Publishing Switzerland 2015
C. Bodei et al. (Eds.): Degano Festschrift, LNCS 9465, pp. 304–318, 2015.
DOI: 10.1007/978-3-319-25527-9_20

featuring a CSP-style synchronisation; actions are weighted over a semiring algebraic-structure. In a quantitative process, transitions are labelled with some quantity, denoting a cost or a benefit associated with a step in the behaviour of a system. Indeed, the main actors on stage are the GPA behaviour-descriptions of *(i)* a system S, *(ii)* a controller C, and *(iii)* an attacker A, which all run in parallel and may synchronise on a set of action $L \subseteq Act$. S represents the correct behaviour of a (software) system, while A attempts to divert S from the expected path. A controller is implemented to correct/mitigate a threat against the system (*insertion*), suppress the impact of a threat (*suppression*), or ignore it (*acceptance*), i.e., $C \triangleright^{\mathbb{K}} A$. These actors are required to follow a plot, defined in terms of a formula ϕ in a c-semiring Hennessy-Milner Logic (*c-HM*) [25]. Such formula specifies the requested behaviour, and its evaluation corresponds to a semiring value, i.e., the amount of weight needed to follow that behaviour. Clearly, the overall cost depends on action-weights of S, C, as well as A, and, more in particular, on the action performed by C in order to restrain the behaviour of A (i.e., insertion, suppression, or acceptance).

Our main tool consists of a quantitative partial model-checking function (QPMC) we use to remove S from the scene, since its performance is not significant for our purposes: indeed we want to focus on the other two actors on the stage. Hence, the specification of S is moved from $S\|_L(C \triangleright^{\mathbb{K}} A)$ to ϕ, which becomes ϕ' consequently to the application of the QPMC function to ϕ with respect to S. The next and final step is the application of QPMC to refine ϕ' in a binary c-semiring Hennessy-Milner formula (*c-HM^2*) whose modalities represent the couple of action a_1 and a_2 that respectively represent the reaction of C and A: if A plays a_2, then C plays a_1.

In this way, we are able to identify the requested property ϕ on the shoulders of C and A, knowing exactly what C has to do for a given A. This corresponds to an amount t of weight demanded to satisfy ϕ: if t is the requested level of time-delay on the execution of S, when A introduces a delay then C has to react to A by performing some action with the aim to maintain t. "Does C exist or not exist? That is the question". Therefore, in this paper we find an answer to $\exists C \, \forall A \, S\|_L(C \triangleright^{\mathbb{K}} A) \models_t \phi$.

The main basic ideas behind this work are an advancement of what is proposed in [25], where, among other results, we propose a unidimensional *c-HM* logic and a similar QPMC function. The paper is organised as a five-act drama, following the Freytag's structure-pyramid.[1] Section 2 is our *exposition*: we introduce the necessary preliminary notions at the heart of our approach, i.e., semirings, GPA, and definitions for quantitative control-rules, and the related work. Then, Sect. 3 is the *rising action* part; it builds toward the point of greatest interest, an approach to security of the presented ingredients. Afterwards, we reach the *climax* in Sect. 4: there we show how to apply the QPMC function on control-rules. During the *falling action* (Sect. 5) we provide an example of our approach on the *Chinese Wall* policy, while Sect. 6 presents a *dénouement*, i.e., a resolution of the plot (conclusions and future work).

---

[1] Freytag, Gustav. *Die Technik des Dramas*. Hirzel, 1872.

2   Setting up the Scene

We start this section by introducing the algebraic formalism we adopt to represent quantitative metrics on which we evaluate countermeasures' behaviour in the following of the paper.

2.1   Semiring

Definition 1 (c-semiring [6]). *A c-semiring is a five-tuple* $\mathbb{K} = \langle K, +, \times, \mathbf{0}, \mathbf{1} \rangle$ *such that K is a set,* $\mathbf{1}, \mathbf{0} \in K$, *and* $+, \times : K \times K \to K$ *are binary operators making the triples* $\langle K, +, \mathbf{0} \rangle$ *and* $\langle K, \times, \mathbf{1} \rangle$ *commutative monoids (semigroups with identity), satisfying (i) (distributivity)* $\forall a, b, c \in K.a \times (b+c) = (a \times b) + (a \times c)$, *(ii) (annihilator)* $\forall a \in A.a \times \mathbf{0} = \mathbf{0}$, *and (iii) (top element)* $\forall a \in K.a + \mathbf{1} = \mathbf{1}$.

The idempotency of $+$ leads to the definition of a partial ordering $\leq_K$ over the set K (K is a poset). Such partial order is defined as $a \leq_K b$ if and only if $a + b = b$, and $+$ becomes the *least upper bound* (*lub*) of the lattice $\langle K, \leq_K \rangle$. This intuitively means that b is "better" than a. As a consequence, we can use $+$ as an optimisation operator that always chooses the best available solution. Other properties can be derived on c-semirings [6]: (i) both $+$ and $\times$ are monotone over $\leq_K$, (ii) $\times$ is intensive (i.e., $a \times b \leq_K a$), and (iii) $\langle K, \leq_K \rangle$ is a complete lattice where $\mathbf{0}$ and $\mathbf{1}$ are its bottom and top elements, respectively.

Some examples of semiring instantiation are: *boolean* $\langle \{F, T\}, \vee, \wedge, F, T \rangle$ *fuzzy* $\langle [0, 1], \max, \min, 0, 1 \rangle$, *bottleneck* $\langle \mathbb{R}^+ \cup \{+\infty\}, \max, \min, 0, \infty \rangle$, *probabilistic* $\langle [0, 1], \max, \hat{\times}, 0, 1 \rangle$ (known as the Viterbi semiring), *weighted* $\langle \mathbb{R}^+ \cup \{+\infty\}, \min, \hat{+}, +\infty, 0 \rangle$. Capped operators stand for their arithmetic equivalent.

2.2   Quantitative Controller Operator

A controlling strategy [12] is a run-time execution trace of a controller C that follows the behaviour of a target A. The resulting behaviour is denoted by $C \triangleright^{\mathbb{K}} A$, where $\mathbb{K}$ is the semiring used for specifying quantities on each executed action so that it is possible to quantitatively estimate the contribution of the countermeasures in the system workflow. Indeed, injecting a controller in a possible point of failure may increase, *e.g.*, the cost of the system, especially when it is activated to react to an attack.

Generalized Process Algebra. In this paper we model both a controller and a target as GPA processes [9]. GPA, i.e., *Generalized Process Algebra*, is a quantitative process algebra, whose transitions are labelled by pairs (a, k) where k is a quantity of a semiring associated to an action a.

Definition 2. *The set $\mathcal{L}$ of agents, or processes, in GPA over a countable set of transition labels Act and a semiring $\mathbb{K}$ is defined by the grammar*

$$P ::= 0 \mid (a, k).P \mid P + P \mid P \|_L P \mid X$$

where $a \in Act$, $k \in K$, $L \subseteq Act$, and X belongs to a countable set of process variables, coming from a system of co-recursive equations of the form $X \triangleq P$. We write $GPA_{\mathbb{K}}$ for the set of GPA processes labelled with weights in $\mathbb{K}$.

In order to give the flavour of the meaning of GPA operators, we informally describe their semantics:[2] process 0 describes inaction or termination; $(a, k).P$ performs action a with weight k, and then it evolves into P; $P + P'$ non-deterministically behaves as either P or P'; $P\|_L P'$ describes the process in which P and P' proceed concurrently and independently on all the actions that are not in L. On the other hand, all the actions in L are synchronisation points, meaning that the computation advances if and only if both P and P' perform the same action in L at the same time. $X \triangleq P$ allows to associate the behaviour of a process P (body) with a process variable name X (identifier).

Semantics Definitions for Quantitative Control-Rules. To denote controller and (its) target processes, hereafter we will use C and A respectively. The alphabets of C, A, and of the resulting process $C \triangleright^{\mathbb{K}} A$ are different. C may perform *control* actions of the form a, $\boxminus a$, $\boxplus a.b$ for $a, b \in Act$, denoting respectively the actions of *acceptance*, *suppression*, and *insertion*, which regulate the actions of A. The resulting process $C \triangleright^{\mathbb{K}} A$ may perform internal actions, denoted by τ, as a consequence of suppression. Each action of C, A, and $C \triangleright^{\mathbb{K}} A$ is associated with a value of a semiring $\mathbb{K}$, i.e., (a, k), where $k \in \mathbb{K}$ is a quantity associated with this action a.

Table 1. Semantics definitions for quantitative control-rules.

$$\frac{C \xrightarrow{a,k} C' \quad A \xrightarrow{a,k'} A'}{C \triangleright^{\mathbb{K}} A \xrightarrow{a,k \times k'} C' \triangleright^{\mathbb{K}} A'} \text{ (A)} \quad \frac{C \xrightarrow{\boxminus a,k} C' \quad A \xrightarrow{a,k'} A'}{C \triangleright^{\mathbb{K}} A \xrightarrow{\tau,k \times k'} C' \triangleright^{\mathbb{K}} A'} \text{ (S)} \quad \frac{C \xrightarrow{\boxplus a.b,k} C' \quad A \xrightarrow{a,k'} A'}{C \triangleright^{\mathbb{K}} A \xrightarrow{b,k} C' \triangleright^{\mathbb{K}} A} \text{ (I)}$$

C follows the execution trace of A step by step, and it reacts to each step of the target according to one of the rules in Table 1. Note that, neither the controller nor the target performs τ actions independently.

The *acceptance rule* (A) in Table 1 constrains a controller and a target to perform the same action, in order for it to be observed in the resulting behaviour. In particular, if A performs an action a with a weight k', and the same action is performed by C with a weight k (so it is allowed on the system), then $E \triangleright^{\mathbb{K}} F$ performs a with an observed value that is the $\times$ of those of the controller and target, i.e., $k \times k'$.

The *suppression rule* allows C to hide an action a, but it counts its weight because it has been executed by A anyway. Hence, the suppression rule (S) in Table 1 allows the controller to hide target actions by performing a control action $\boxminus a$ with a measure k. The target wants to perform an action a with a weight k', but the action is not performed by the controlled entity and the observed result

---

[2] The interested reader can find the formal semantics of GPA processes defined in [9].

is a τ action, with the value computed as the product $k \times k'$ of the suppressing and the target actions. Then $C \triangleright^{\mathbb{K}} A$ performs an action τ that *suppresses* action a, i.e., a becomes invisible from external observation.

Finally, the *insertion rule* (I) in Table 1 describes the capability of correcting some undesirable behaviour of a target A: it inserts another action in A's execution trace by performing a control action $\boxplus a$ followed by an action b. The insertion cost corresponds to the value of C only, i.e., k; this accounts for the fact that A does not perform any action, but it rather stays in its current state.

2.3 Related Work

There is a significant bulk of work devoted to the enforcement of security mechanisms, *e.g.*, [18,23,29]. As foremost examples (due to similarities with respect to this work) we recall security automata [29], designed to prevent bad executions, and edit automata [4], which are able to edit their input sequences by suppressing, inserting, or replacing observed actions. One can also use concurrent languages (*e.g.*, process algebras), to model both the target and the control system in the same formalism [17,23,26].

As a prototypical example, we choose GPA process algebra [9], featuring a CSP-style synchronisation with actions weighted over a semiring. We add to it control-operators in the style of edit automata, in order to study enforcement strategies from the quantitative standpoint. Compared to the existing literature, our work identifies an abstract approach to quantitative and multi-dimensional aspects of security. The quest for a unifying formalism is witnessed by the significant amount of inhomogeneous work in quantitative notions of security and enforcement. The problem of finding an optimal control strategy is considered by Easwaran et al. in [16] in the context of software monitoring, taking into account rewards and penalties. In [27], the optimal policy can be derived by solving the optimisation problem of a Markov Decision Process. Bielova and Massacci propose in [5] a notion of *edit distance* among traces, which extends to an ordering over controllers. In [14], a notion of cost similar to the one we propose is used to compare several enforcement mechanisms that are correct (in the boolean sense). In this work, we follow some intuitive leads from [24] to move from qualitative to quantitative enforcement, and generalise that idea by using semirings. In [15] the possibility that the controller allows some policy violations is quantified over traces for non-safety policies, where a controller cannot be both correct and fully transparent. In [10], the authors use a notion of *lazy* controllers, which are able to check the security of a system at some point in time, proposing a probabilistic quantification of the expected risk. In the context of access control, Molloy et al. [28] use a machine-learning approach to predict a decision for a given request, and, at the same time, to balance the risk of error against the cost of contacting the real mechanism to get a decision. Non-binary measures of security have also been considered for access-control systems, *e.g.*, in [11,30].

In [13], Degano et al. propose a formal framework to specify and enforce quantitative security policies. The framework consists of (*i*) a stochastic process calculus to express the measurable space of computations in terms of Continuous Time Markov Chains; *(ii)* a stochastic modal logic (a variant of CSL) to represent the bound constraints on execution speed; *(iii)* potential or actual enforcement mechanisms of quantitative security policies. The potential enforcement computes the probability of policy violations, thus supporting the user to accept/discard a component when the probability of security violation is below/above a suitable chosen threshold. The actual enforcement computes instead the deviation of execution speed from an acceptable rate.

In [7] the authors take advantage of an operational semantics with the aim to predict quantitative measures on systems describing cryptographic protocols. Moreover, they also introduce a possible attacker in the model. The transitions of the system carry enhanced labels: rates are assigned to transitions by only looking at these labels. Finally, transition systems are mapped to Markov chains and an evaluation of system performance is obtained by using standard tools.

In [2] the authors investigate usage automata, a formal model for specifying policies on the usage of resources. Usage automata extend finite state automata with some additional features, parameters and guards, that improve their expressivity. The authors check the decidability if a given computation complies with a usage policy.

3   Quantitative Security Approach

In the literature on qualitative enforcement of secure systems, several approaches have been developed, as we have recalled in Sect. 2.3. A possible approach for the specification, analysis, and synthesis of secure systems is based on the *open system* paradigm [22], where the considered system and a possible malicious agent interacting with it are represented as two processes that work in parallel.

The same approach can be used when we pass from a qualitative to a quantitative analysis of such system S. The unspecified part of S is a component whose behaviour is not known a priori, and we want S to be quantitatively secure, whatever the behaviour of such unspecified components is. A is the possible attacker whose behaviour is a priori unknown; $L \subseteq Act$ is the set of possible synchronisation actions; thus $S\|_L A$ is the overall (partially specified) system, on which we require that:

$$\forall A \quad S\|_L A \models_t \phi.$$

ϕ is a logic formula expressing some behavioural requirements, such as security requirements as well as performance or cost constraints (i.e., non-functional requirements), and t denotes a required level of satisfaction: the evaluation of ϕ with respect to $S\|_L A$ has to be equal to t. Formally,

Definition 3 ($\models_k$). *A process P satisfies a c-HM formula ϕ with a threshold-value t, i.e., $P \models_t \phi$, if and only if the interpretation of ϕ on P is equal to t. Formally: $P \models_t \phi \Leftrightarrow t = [\![\phi]\!]_P$.*

Even if it is not always possible to check all different behaviours of component A, nevertheless it is possible to define distinct countermeasures that follow the rules of the controller operator $\rhd^{\mathbb{K}}$ defined in Table 1. These countermeasures are specified as execution traces of a controller process denoted by C. They guarantee the system to properly work by forcing the desired behaviour of unspecified components, in such a way that the system satisfies ϕ according to a predefined value t. Hence, the question here is if there exists an implementation that, by monitoring the behaviour of an unspecified component A, guarantees S to satisfy the required security property with a certain value t:

$$\exists C \quad \forall A \quad S\|_L(C \rhd^{\mathbb{K}} A) \models_t \phi$$

First of all we apply a QPMC function inspired from the work in [25], with the purpose to evaluate ϕ with respect to the behaviour of S. In this way we obtain a new formula $\phi' = \phi_{//s}$ and we only have to monitor the attacker's behaviour A. ϕ' represents the necessary and sufficient conditions that $C \rhd^{\mathbb{K}} A$ has to satisfy in order to guarantee the security of S. Indeed, the problem we have to solve reduces to the following one:

$$\exists C \quad \forall A \quad (C \rhd^{\mathbb{K}} A) \models_t \phi' \tag{1}$$

It is worth noting that we neither know the behaviour of the controller process C, nor the one of attacker A. The only information we have is the semantics rules of the controller operator $\rhd^{\mathbb{K}}$. Based on that, we have developed a quantitative partial model checking function able to refine the formula $\phi' \in$ c-HM into a binary formula $\phi'' \in$ c-HM^2 able to specify the set of quantitative controller execution traces for any attacker execution trace. The basic idea is that, knowing the possible reaction rules that drive the behaviour of a controller and the quantitative security requirements that S has to satisfy, it is possible to find the necessary and sufficient condition both the controller and the target has to quantitatively satisfy in order to assure the system security. Indeed, we consider both the controller and the target behaviours as unknown.

To this aim, we propose a variant of a quantitative Hennessy-Milner logic, the c-HM logic firstly proposed in [25]; thus, we can specify a property on couples of actions, extending it to c-HM^2 (see Sect. 3.1). Afterwards, we define a different version of the QPMC function [25], allowing us to refine a formula ϕ' with respect to the semantics definition of the controller operator (see Sect. 4). This refinement allows us to write each action of the execution trace of the controlled process as a couple of actions, respectively representing the weight contribution to that action of both the controller and the target.

3.1   Binary C-Semiring Hennessy-Milner Logic (c-HM^2)

We start by assembling the transition system on which c-HM^2 is defined:

Definition 4 (MLTS). *A (finite) Multi-Labelled Transition-System (MLTS) is a five-tuple $MLTS = (S, Act^2, \mathbb{K}, T, s_0)$, where S is the countable (finite) state-space, $s_0 \in S$ is the initial state, Act^2 is a finite set of transition labels, where each label is a couple of labels in Act, i.e., the label $\langle a_1, a_2 \rangle \in Act^2$ and $a_1, a_2 \in L$.*

$\mathbb{K}$ *is a semiring used for the definition of transition weights, and* $T : (S \times Act^2 \times S) \longrightarrow \mathbb{K}$ *is the transition weight-function.*

Definition 5 syntactically defines the correct formulas given over an MLTS.

Definition 5 (Syntax). *Given an MLTS* $M = \langle S, Act^2, \mathbb{K}, T, s_0 \rangle$, *and let* $\tilde{a} \in Act^2$, *the syntax of a formula* $\phi \in \Phi_M$ *is as follows, where* $k \in K$:

$$\phi ::= k \mid \phi_1 = \phi_2 \mid \phi_1 + \phi_2 \mid \phi_1 \times \phi_2 \mid \phi_1 \sqcap \phi_2 \mid \langle \tilde{a} \rangle \phi \mid [\tilde{a}] \phi$$

The semiring operators $+$, $\sqcap$ (the glb), and $\times$ are used in place of classical logic operators $\vee$ and $\wedge$, in order to compose the truth values of two formulas together. Truth values are all the $k \in K$. In particular, while *false* corresponds to $\mathbf{0}$, we can have different degrees of *true*, where "full truth" is $\mathbf{1}$. As a reminder, when the $\times$ operator is idempotent, then $\times$ and $\sqcap$ coincide (Sect. 2.1). Moreover we can use $=$ to compare the evaluation of two formulas: the result is $\mathbf{1}$ if they are both evaluated to the same $k \in K$, $\mathbf{0}$ otherwise (i.e., it corresponds to $\Leftrightarrow$ in boolean logic).[3] Finally, we have the two classical modal operators, i.e., "possibly" ($\langle \cdot \rangle$), and "necessarily" ($[\cdot]$).

Table 2. Semantics of c-HM^2. $\sum(\emptyset) = \mathbf{0}$ and $\sqcap(\emptyset) = \mathbf{1}$.

$$
\begin{aligned}
[\![k]\!](s) &= k \in K \quad \forall s \in S \\
[\![\phi_1 = \phi_2]\!](s) &= \begin{cases} 1 \ if \ [\![\phi_1]\!](s) = [\![\phi_2]\!](s) \\ 0 \ otherwise \end{cases} \\
[\![\phi_1 + \phi_2]\!](s) &= [\![\phi_1]\!](s) + [\![\phi_2]\!](s) \\
[\![\phi_1 \times \phi_2]\!](s) &= [\![\phi_1]\!](s) \times [\![\phi_2]\!](s) \\
[\![\phi_1 \sqcap \phi_2]\!](s) &= [\![\phi_1]\!](s) \sqcap [\![\phi_2]\!](s) \\
[\![\langle a \rangle \phi]\!](s) &= \sum_{(s \xrightarrow{(a,k_a)} s') \in T} (k_a \times [\![\phi]\!](s')) \\
[\![[a]\phi]\!](s) &= \bigsqcap_{(s \xrightarrow{(a,k_a)} s') \in T} (k_a \times [\![\phi]\!](s'))
\end{aligned}
$$

The semantics of a formula ϕ is given on a finite MLTS $M = \langle S, Act^2, \mathbb{K}, T, s_0 \rangle$, where the set of states S corresponds to the set of finite GPA processes. The purpose is to check the specification defined by ϕ over the behaviour of a couple of GPA processes. The semantics of a formula, $[\![\ ]\!]_M : (\Phi_M \times S) \longrightarrow K$ (see Table 2), computes a semiring value associated with a formula in a given state $s \in S$ of an MLTS M.

In Table 2 and in the following (when clear from the context), we omit M from $[\![\ ]\!]_M$ for the sake of readability. It is worth noting that, due to the expressive

---

[3] We can think of further operators between formulas, *e.g.*, $\{=, \geq, \approx_\epsilon\}$.

power of c-HM^2, we deal with *safety properties, e.g.,* properties expressing that, if something goes wrong, then it can be detected in a finite number of steps.

Note that, the notion of satisfiability given in Definition 3 holds also for a c-HM^2 formula ϕ on a binary MLTS $M = \langle S, Act^2, \mathbb{K}, T, s_0 \rangle$. A binary MLTS may also represent a couple of processes composed as an *independent combination* of two processes P_1 and P_2, hereafter denoted as (P_1, P_2).

Definition 6 (Binary Process). *Let P_1 and P_2 be two GPA processes. A binary process $(P_1, P_2) \in GPA \times GPA$ is the juxtaposition of two processes and it is fully characterised by the following rule:*

$$\frac{P_1 \xrightarrow{(a,h)} P_1' \quad P_2 \xrightarrow{(b,s)} P_2'}{(P_1, P_2) \xrightarrow{((a,b),h\times s)} (P_1', P_2')}$$

Note that, the semantic interpretation of a binary process is given through a binary MLTS. In particular, according to the definition of binary transition function, the set of states of a binary process is the union of the two sets of states of both the processes. In this way, either both processes perform an action being in the same state or, they are *asynchronous* processes, i.e., both component P_1 and P_2 contribute in the transition of the combined process (P_1, P_2), even when one of the two performs the 0 action.

4   Quantitative Partial Model Checking for Controller Operator

In order to solve the problem in Eq. 1, we define a QPMC function with the purpose to evaluate $\phi' \in$ c-HM with respect to the application of controller rules, i.e., to controller strategies. As a remainder, ϕ' is obtained from the initial ϕ by removing S from the parallel computation, and "adding" it to ϕ ($\phi' = \phi_{//s}$, see Sect. 3). Our goal in this section is to obtain a refinement of ϕ', i.e., $\phi'' \in$ c-HM^2, which also depends on $\triangleright^{\mathbb{K}}$.

The QPMC function we use to achieve such goal is defined in Table 3. Being the logic closed with respect to the QPMC function, the interpretation of the formulas obtained through the application of the function is straightforward. Theorem 1 proposes a result similar to the one in [1].

Theorem 1. *Let C and A two processes in GPA such that $C \triangleright^{\mathbb{K}} A \in GPA$ and (C, A) is a binary process in GPA $\times$ GPA, $\mathbb{K}$ a totally ordered c-semiring with $k \in K$, as well as ϕ' a c-HM formula and $\phi'' = \mathcal{W}(C \triangleright^{\mathbb{K}} A, \phi)$ a c-HM^2 formula, the following holds:*

$$[\![\phi']\!]_{(C \triangleright^{\mathbb{K}} A)} = [\![\phi'']\!]_{(C,A)}$$

Due to this result, the problem in Eq. 1 can be simplified as follows:

$$\exists C \; \forall A \quad (C, A) \models_t \mathcal{W}(C \triangleright^{\mathbb{K}} A, \phi') \tag{2}$$

where $\mathcal{W}(C \vartriangleright^{\mathbb{K}} A, \phi')$ is a c-HM^2 formula that describes, in a unique way for each action of the process A, that the reaction of a controller C guarantees the quantitative satisfaction of the initial system's requirements. Hence, it is worth observing that a security controller needs to make a *decision* in order to select the *best* reaction (if any). This decision is supported by the quantitative value associated to each reaction. However, in general, the decision for a single action can change according to the actions previously executed by A. For instance, in the Chinese Wall policy (see an example in Sect. 5), a user can *a priori* access to a resource from any company, unless in the past she has accessed to a resource from another company in the same conflict-of-interest class.

Moreover, dealing with quantitative aspects, it is important to distinguish between the decision process, i.e., C, and the actual implementation of the controlled process, i.e., $C \vartriangleright^{\mathbb{K}} A$. Indeed, it is possible to specify the best editing strategy by associating particular costs with actions. For instance, by setting the acceptance cost to a minimum, we showed that it is always the best strategy to accept a correct action. Similarly, by associating an infinite cost with the suppression of a particular action, we can model the concept of *uncontrollable action* [3], that is, an action that has to be accepted, such as the tick of a clock.

Table 3. A QPMC function (i.e., $\mathcal{W}$) for quantitative controller operator $\vartriangleright^{\mathbb{K}}$.

$\mathcal{W}(C \vartriangleright^{\mathbb{K}} A, k) = k$

$\mathcal{W}(C \vartriangleright^{\mathbb{K}} A, \phi_1 = \phi_2) = (\mathcal{W}(C \vartriangleright^{\mathbb{K}} A, \phi_1) = \mathcal{W}(C \vartriangleright^{\mathbb{K}} A, \phi_2))$

$\mathcal{W}(C \vartriangleright^{\mathbb{K}} A, \phi_1 \times \phi_2) = \mathcal{W}(C \vartriangleright^{\mathbb{K}} A, \phi_1) \times \mathcal{W}(C \vartriangleright^{\mathbb{K}} A, \phi_2)$

$\mathcal{W}(C \vartriangleright^{\mathbb{K}} A, \phi_1 + \phi_2) = \mathcal{W}(C \vartriangleright^{\mathbb{K}} A, \phi_1) + \mathcal{W}(C \vartriangleright^{\mathbb{K}} A, \phi_2)$

$\mathcal{W}(C \vartriangleright^{\mathbb{K}} A, \phi_1 \sqcap \phi_2) = \mathcal{W}(C \vartriangleright^{\mathbb{K}} A, \phi_1) \sqcap \mathcal{W}(C \vartriangleright^{\mathbb{K}} A, \phi_2)$

$$\mathcal{W}(C \vartriangleright^{\mathbb{K}} A, [a]\phi) = \bigsqcap_{C \vartriangleright^{\mathbb{K}} A \xrightarrow{(a,k_a)} (C \vartriangleright^{\mathbb{K}} A)'} (k_a^{(a,a)} \times [(a,a)]\mathcal{W}(C' \vartriangleright^{\mathbb{K}} A', \phi)) \sqcap$$

$$\sqcap (k_a^{(\boxplus b.a, b)} \times [(\boxplus b.a, b)]\mathcal{W}(C' \vartriangleright^{\mathbb{K}} A, \phi))$$

$$\mathcal{W}(C \vartriangleright^{\mathbb{K}} A, [\tau]\phi) = \bigsqcap_{C \vartriangleright^{\mathbb{K}} A \xrightarrow{(\tau,k_\tau)} (C \vartriangleright^{\mathbb{K}} A)'} k_\tau^{(\boxminus a, a)} \times ([(\boxminus a, a)]\mathcal{W}(C' \vartriangleright^{\mathbb{K}} A', \phi))$$

$$\mathcal{W}(C \vartriangleright^{\mathbb{K}} A, \langle a \rangle \phi) = \sum_{C \vartriangleright^{\mathbb{K}} A \xrightarrow{(a,k_a)} (C \vartriangleright^{\mathbb{K}} A)'} (k_a^{(a,a)} \times (\langle (a,a) \rangle \mathcal{W}(C' \vartriangleright^{\mathbb{K}} A', \phi)) +$$

$$+ (k_a^{(\boxplus b.a, b)} \times \langle (\boxplus b.a, b) \rangle \mathcal{W}(C' \vartriangleright^{\mathbb{K}} A, \phi))$$

$$\mathcal{W}(C \vartriangleright^{\mathbb{K}} A, \langle \tau \rangle \phi) = \sum_{C \vartriangleright^{\mathbb{K}} A \xrightarrow{(\tau,k_\tau)} (C \vartriangleright^{\mathbb{K}} A)'} (k_\tau^{(\boxminus a, a)} \times \langle (\boxminus a, a) \rangle \mathcal{W}(C' \vartriangleright^{\mathbb{K}} A', \phi))$$

5 A Simple Example

To exemplify our approach, let us consider a very simple example. For sake of simplicity, we omit the system S: the goal is to show how the QPMC function works with respect to controller operations. To do this, let us now consider a well-known access-control policy for distributed systems: the *Chinese Wall* policy.

To evaluate the security level of $C \triangleright^{\mathbb{K}} A$, each action is weighted with a semi-ring value expressing a security-evaluation score for that action. Security, trust, functionality, and performance can be represented by different semirings. In this section, we use weights from $\mathbb{S} = \langle \{\underline{i}, \underline{l}, \underline{m}, \underline{g}, \underline{e}\}, \max, \min, \underline{i}, \underline{e} \rangle$, where the chain $\underline{insecure} \leq \underline{low} \leq \underline{medium} \leq \underline{good} \leq \underline{excellent}$ models a set of security levels. When we compose two levels together we choose the worst, while preference goes to the higher level.

Given two sets of resources (*e.g.*, files or data) V and W, such policy states that one can choose to access either to V or to W, but if an access to V is performed (setting the security level of access to V to $\underline{e}$) then it is no more possible to access to W; consequently, the access to W has security level $\underline{i}$. Clearly, this also holds vice-versa, i.e., if we open an element x of W then we can not access to any element in V. Note that, in this example, the required security level to access to set W, i.e., $\underline{l}$, is less than the required security level to access to V, that is $\underline{e}$. The reason is that V collects more sensitive information. The Chinese Wall policy is expressed by a formula $\phi = \phi_1 + \phi_2$ where

$$\phi_1 = [access\_V]\underline{e} \times [access\_W]\underline{i} \qquad\qquad \phi_2 = [access\_W]\underline{l} \times [access\_V]\underline{i}.$$

In this example, we consider an insertion controller $\triangleright^{\mathbb{S}}$, and we require $C \triangleright^{\mathbb{S}} A$ to satisfy the Chinese Wall policy with a security equal to g.

By using the QPMC function with respect to the controller operator $\triangleright^{\mathbb{S}}$, we have that:

$$C \triangleright^{\mathbb{S}} A \models_g \phi \Leftrightarrow (C, A) \models_g \phi'$$

where $\phi' = \mathcal{W}(C \triangleright^{\mathbb{S}} A, \phi) = \phi_1' + \phi_2'$, and

$$
\begin{aligned}
\phi_1' = \mathcal{W}(C \triangleright^{\mathbb{S}} A, \phi_1) = &(k_{access\_V}^{(access\_V, access\_V)} \times [(access\_V, access\_V)]\underline{e}) \\
&\sqcap (k_{access\_V}^{(\boxplus access\_W.access\_V, access\_W)} \\
&\times [(\boxplus access\_W.access\_V, access\_W)]\underline{e}) \\
&\times (k_{access\_W}^{(access\_W, access\_W)} \times [(access\_W, access\_W)]\underline{i}) \\
&\sqcap (k_{access\_W}^{(\boxplus access\_V.access\_W, access\_V)} \\
&\times [(\boxplus access\_V.access\_W, access\_V)]\underline{i}) \\
\phi_2' = \mathcal{W}(C \triangleright^{\mathbb{S}} A, \phi_2) = &(k_{access\_W}^{(access\_W, access\_W)} \times [(access\_W, access\_W)]\underline{l}) \\
&\sqcap (k_{access\_W}^{(\boxplus access\_V.access\_W, access\_V)} \\
&\times [(\boxplus access\_V.access\_W, access\_V)]\underline{l}) \\
&\times (k_{access\_V}^{(access\_V, access\_V)} \times [(access\_V, access\_V)]\underline{i}) \\
&\sqcap (k_{access\_V}^{(\boxplus access\_W.access\_V, access\_W)} \\
&\times [(\boxplus access\_W.access\_V, access\_W)]\underline{i})
\end{aligned}
$$

According to Theorem 1, to verify if $C \triangleright^S A$ quantitatively satisfies the Chinese Wall policy with a security level g, it is necessary and sufficient to evaluate ϕ' with respect the binary process $(\overline{C}, A)$. A priori we do not know the behaviour of A, however, due to the quantitative nature of the proposed framework, we can infer some constraints on the controller process C, which help the synthesis of the *best* controller, if it exists.

As a remainder, the weight of an accepted action is equal to the product (i.e., $\times$) of the weights of both the actions respectively performed by C and A, while the weight of an inserted action is equal only to the weight associated with the action of C. This leads to the following considerations:

- If the attacker does not perform the correct action, *e.g.*, it tries to access to W after accessing to V (or vice versa), the controller C may insert the correct action *access_V* with an appropriate security level, *e.g.*, better than $\underline{g}$. In this way, the controller assures that the Chinese Wall policy is satisfied with the required security level $\underline{g}$.
- If the attacker performs the correct action, but with a security level worse than the required one, *e.g.*, $\underline{g}$ in the example, the controller, accepting the correct action, does not increase the level of security. Thus, the Chinese Wall policy is not satisfied because the required security level is not respected. This is the case in which both C and A perform a valid sequence of actions, *e.g.*, one *access_V* each, but the level of one of these actions is worse than $\underline{g}$. In this case, the controller guarantees that the Chinese Wall Policy is not violated by not changing the security level of the attacker actions, and accepting the correct action. However, also in this case as well as in the previous one, C can insert the correct action with the correct security level in such a way to not halt the execution and, at the same time, guarantee the satisfaction of ϕ. It is worth noting that, another possible scenario may happen when an agent A try to access to W with a security level l. This does not violate the requirement imposed by ϕ, but it violates the satisfaction requirements, because $\underline{l}$ is worse than $\underline{g}$. Also in this case, C can fix the execution trace by inserting the correct action with a more appropriate security level.

6   Conclusion

We have presented a verification framework to study quantitative properties associated with a formula ϕ, i.e., properties with an associated weight. Such a value is interpreted as how costly the verification of a property is. The conundrum has consisted in investigating controller-agents C accepting, suppressing, or inserting actions in the behaviour of an attacker A, while considering the correct functioning of a system S. The question we have address in this paper is $\exists C \; \forall A \; S \| (C \triangleright^{\mathbb{K}} A) \models_t \phi$. As in Sect. 1, we again come across a triangled structure: the drama triangle[4] is a psychological and social model of human

---

[4] First described by Stephen Karpman, M.D., in his 1968 article *"Fairy Tales and Script Drama Analysis"*.

interaction used in psychology and psychotherapy. At its vertices we find the Victim (S), the Persecutor (A), and the Rescuer (C). With the aid of a QPMC function we remove S from the global parallel computation (moving it into ϕ), and we refine ϕ' investigating the duties of C and A in order to satisfy ϕ: such approach helps us to better understand C and A separately.

In the future we plan to extend this work in several ways. For instance, we plan to have a multidimensional decomposition of properties, instead of a bi-dimensional one as in this paper: we would like to follow the pioneering proposal in [20], thus decomposing quantitative properties satisfied by an n-ary context into n local quantitative constraints, each of them satisfied by a unary (quantitative) context. Each context represents a different component of a distributed system. In such a way, we can improve the approach by taking into account fully-distributed systems with multiple components and attackers. Another direction is the extension of the framework to use more than one measure in order to evaluate a context. Such measures can be combined and ordered, *e.g.*, by using the lexicographical ordering, in such a way that controlling strategies can be selected with respect to the optimisation of the trade-off between some of them. Finally, we would like to manage infinite contexts by extending our logic to deal with fix-points; to achieve this goal, suggestions could come from the work in [21].

References

1. Andersen, H.R.: Partial model checking. In: LICS 1995, p. 398. IEEE Computer Society (1995)
2. Bartoletti, M., Degano, P., Ferrari, G.L., Zunino, R.: Model checking usage policies. Math. Struct. Comput. Sci. **25**(3), 710–763 (2015)
3. Klaedtke, F., Zălinescu, E., Jugé, V., Basin, D.: Enforceable security policies revisited. In: Degano, P., Guttman, J.D. (eds.) Principles of Security and Trust. LNCS, vol. 7215, pp. 309–328. Springer, Heidelberg (2012)
4. Bauer, L., Ligatti, J., Walker, D.: Edit automata: enforcement mechanisms for run-time security policies. Int. J. Inf. Secur. **4**(1–2), 2–16 (2005)
5. Bielova, N., Massacci, F.: Predictability of enforcement. In: Erlingsson, Ú., Zannone, N., Wieringa, R. (eds.) ESSoS 2011. LNCS, vol. 6542, pp. 73–86. Springer, Heidelberg (2011)
6. Bistarelli, S., Montanari, U., Rossi, F.: Semiring-based constraint satisfaction and optimization. J. ACM **44**(2), 201–236 (1997)
7. Bodei, C., Curti, M., Degano, P., Priami, C.: A quantitative study of two attacks. Electr. Notes Theor. Comput. Sci. **121**, 65–85 (2005)
8. McQueen, M., Boyer, W.: Ideal based cyber security technical metrics for control systems. In: Hämmerli, B.M., Lopez, J. (eds.) CRITIS 2007. LNCS, vol. 5141, pp. 246–260. Springer, Heidelberg (2008)
9. Buchholz, P., Kemper, P.: Quantifying the dynamic behavior of process algebras. In: Gilmore, S., de Luca, L. (eds.) PROBMIV 2001, PAPM-PROBMIV 2001, and PAPM 2001. LNCS, vol. 2165, p. 184. Springer, Heidelberg (2001)
10. Caravagna, G., Costa, G., Pardini, G.: Lazy security controllers. In: Samarati, P., Petrocchi, M., Jøsang, A. (eds.) STM 2012. LNCS, vol. 7783, pp. 33–48. Springer, Heidelberg (2013)

11. Cheng, P.C., Rohatgi, P., Keser, C., Karger, P.A., Wagner, G.M., Reninger, A.S.: Fuzzy multi-level security: an experiment on quantified risk-adaptive access control. In: Proceedings of the 2007 IEEE S&P, pp. 222–230. IEEE Computer Society (2007)

12. Ciancia, V., Martinelli, F., Ilaria, M., Morisset, C.: Quantitative evaluation of enforcement strategies (position paper). In: Danger, J.-L., Debbabi, M., Marion, J.-Y., Garcia-Alfaro, J., Heywood, N.Z. (eds.) FPS 2013. LNCS, vol. 8352, pp. 178–186. Springer, Heidelberg (2014)

13. Degano, P., Mezzetti, G., Ferrari, G.-L.: On quantitative security policies. In: Malyshkin, V. (ed.) PaCT 2011. LNCS, vol. 6873, pp. 23–39. Springer, Heidelberg (2011)

14. Drábik, P., Martinelli, F., Morisset, C.: Cost-aware runtime enforcement of security policies. In: Jøsang, A., Samarati, P., Petrocchi, M. (eds.) STM 2012. LNCS, vol. 7783, pp. 1–16. Springer, Heidelberg (2013)

15. Drábik, P., Martinelli, F., Morisset, C.: A quantitative approach for inexact enforcement of security policies. In: Freiling, F.C., Gollmann, D. (eds.) ISC 2012. LNCS, vol. 7483, pp. 306–321. Springer, Heidelberg (2012)

16. Easwaran, A., Kannan, S., Lee, I.: Optimal control of software ensuring safety and functionality. Tech. Rep. MS-CIS-05-20, University of Pennsylvania (2005)

17. Gay, R., Mantel, H., Sprick, B.: Service automata. In: Barthe, G., Datta, A., Etalle, S. (eds.) FAST 2011. LNCS, vol. 7140, pp. 148–163. Springer, Heidelberg (2012)

18. Khoury, R., Tawbi, N.: Which security policies are enforceable by runtime monitors? a survey. Computer Science Review 6(1), 27–45 (2012)

19. Köpf, B., Malacaria, P., Palamidessi, C.: Quantitative security analysis (Dagstuhl seminar 12481). Dagstuhl Reports 2(11), 135–154 (2013)

20. Larsen, K.G., Xinxin, L.: Compositionality through an operational semantics of contexts. J. Logic Comput. 1(6), 761–795 (1991)

21. Lluch-Lafuente, A., Montanari, U.: Quantitative mu-calculus and CTL defined over constraint semirings. TCS 346(1), 135–160 (2005)

22. Martinelli, F.: Analysis of security protocols as open systems. TCS 290(1), 1057–1106 (2003)

23. Martinelli, F., Matteucci, I.: Through modeling to synthesis of security automata. ENTCS 179, 31–46 (2007)

24. Martinelli, F., Matteucci, I., Morisset, C.: From qualitative to quantitative enforcement of security policy. In: Kotenko, I., Skormin, V. (eds.) MMM-ACNS 2012. LNCS, vol. 7531, pp. 22–35. Springer, Heidelberg (2012)

25. Martinelli, F., Matteucci, I., Santini, F.: Quantitative security on distributed systems. In: EPTCS (ed.) Proceedings of the 13th International Workshop on Quantitative Aspects of Programming Languages and Systems (QAPL 2015) (2015) (accepted for publication)

26. Martinelli, F., Matteucci, I.: Partial model checking, process algebra operators and satisfiability procedures for (automatically) enforcing security properties. Tech. rep, IIT-CNR (2005)

27. Martinelli, F., Morisset, C.: Quantitative access control with partially-observable markov decision processes. In: Proceedings of CODASPY 2012, pp. 169–180. ACM (2012)

28. Molloy, I., Dickens, L., Morisset, C., Cheng, P.C., Lobo, J., Russo, A.: Risk-based security decisions under uncertainty. In: Proceedings of the second ACM Conference on Data and Application Security and Privacy, CODASPY 2012, pp. 157–168. ACM (2012)

29. Schneider, F.B.: Enforceable security policies. ACM Trans. Inf. Syst. Secur. **3**(1), 30–50 (2000)
30. Zhang, L., Brodsky, A., Jajodia, S.: Toward Information Sharing: Benefit And Risk Access Control (BARAC). In: Proceedings of POLICY 2006, pp. 45–53 (2006)

From Safety Critical Java Programs to Timed Process Models

Bent Thomsen[1]([⊠]), Kasper Søe Luckow[2], Lone Leth[1], and Thomas Bøgholm[1]

[1] Department of Computer Science, Aalborg University, Aalborg, Denmark
bt@cs.aau.dk
[2] Carnegie Mellon Silicon Valley, NASA Ames, Moffett Field, USA

Abstract. The idea of analysing real programs by process algebraic methods probably goes back to the Occam language using the CSP process algebra [43]. In [16,24] Degano et al. followed in that tradition by analysing Mobile Agent Programs written in the Higher Order Functional, Concurrent and Distributed, programming language Facile [47], by equipping Facile with a process algebraic semantics based on true concurrency. This semantics facilitated analysis of programs revealing subtle bugs that would otherwise be very hard to find. Inspired by the idea of translating real programs into process algebraic frameworks, we have in recent years pursued an agenda of translating hard-real-time embedded safety critical programs written in the Safety Critical Java Profile [33] into networks of timed automata [4] and subjecting those to automated analysis using the UPPAAL model checker [10]. Several tools have been built and the tools have been used to analyse a number of systems for properties such as worst case execution time, schedulability and energy optimization [12–14,19,34,36,38]. In this paper we will elaborate on the theoretical underpinning of the translation from Java programs to timed automata models and briefly summarize some of the results based on this translation. Furthermore, we discuss future work, especially relations to the work in [16,24] as Java recently has adopted first class higher order functions in the form of lambda abstractions.

1 Introduction

There is a growing interest in adopting Java technology in the real-time systems domain as witnessed by the large research community working on several aspects of realizing this goal. Notably, research has focused on devising appropriate real-time systems models for Java to address inherent issues such as lack of real-time tasks, high-precision clocks and a memory model not relying on (time unpredictable) garbage collection. In particular, this has led to the development of the Real-Time Specification for Java (RTSJ) [15] and the Safety Critical Java (SCJ) [33] profile.

Java is usually implemented via a translation to Java Byte Code (JBC), which is then either interpreted by a Java Virtual Machine (JVM) or further translated to native code. To accommodate the real-time execution demands of

© Springer International Publishing Switzerland 2015
C. Bodei et al. (Eds.): Degano Festschrift, LNCS 9465, pp. 319–338, 2015.
DOI: 10.1007/978-3-319-25527-9_21

the RTSJ and SCJ programming models the underlying execution environment, the JVM, must exhibit temporal predictable behavior to allow reasoning about timeliness. One way of achieving time predictable execution of the JVM is to implement it in hardware, e.g. the aJile Systems [3] and the Java Optimized Processor (JOP) project [39]. There are also a number of software implementations of the JVM facilitating time predictable execution on time predictable commodity hardware platforms. The FijiVM [41], Hardware Near Virtual Machine (HVM) [30], JamaicaVM [2] and PicoPERC [40] are examples of this.

To address timing analysis of this environment, we have developed a tool, TETASARTS[1], that allows the real-time system to be developed in a platform independent way. The tool is targeted at schedulability analysis of SCJ tasks taking into account a refined system model that accounts for the exact release patterns of the tasks, their relative releases, interleavings, and resource sharing. In addition, the timing model is rich enough to facilitate analysis of other properties pertaining to the verification of a real-time system including processor utilisation and processor idle time, Worst Case Execution Time (WCET), Worst Case Response Time (WCRT) taking into account pre-emption and task interactions, and Worst Case Blocking Time (WCBT). TETASARTS is the result of merging the ideas from locally developed methods for timing analysis; TetaJ [26], METAMOC [21], SARTS [14] and the TIMES [7] framework for schedulability analysis using UPPAAL [22]. TETASARTS resembles an optimizing compiler translating an SCJ system into a Network of Timed Automata (NTA) amenable to model checking. The model is constructed such that model checking simulates an abstract execution of the real-time tasks, taking into account the exact execution environment and scheduling policy. It is built around a modular architecture that enables platform models to be replaced seamlessly, thereby making it possible to conduct analysis of systems running on software implementations of the JVM as well as hardware implementations of the JVM.

Although Java was not originally equipped with or designed for mathematical foundations, the theoretical underpinnings of Java have by now been explored by many researchers. In this paper we will elaborate on the theoretical underpinning of the translation from Java programs to timed automata models and briefly summarize some of the results.

The paper is organized as follows; Sect. 2 gives an overview of related work. Section 3 gives an overview of the Safety Critical Java programming model. Section 4 gives an overview of to implementations of the JVM supporting the SCJ programming model. Section 5 presents the theoretical model of Timed Automata. Section 6 presents an overview of the TETASARTS tool. Section 7 presents the translation from JBC to Timed Automata and Sect. 8 presents our conjecture that this translation is correct. Section 9 presents various optimizations and Sect. 10 presents evaluation of the TETASARTS tool. Section 11 presents the conclusions and future work, especially relations to the work in [16,24] as Java recently has adopted first class higher order functions in the form of lambda abstractions.

---

[1] TETASARTS can be downloaded at http://people.cs.aau.dk/~luckow/tetasarts/.

2   Related Work

Roscoe et al. were probably the first to analyse real programs written in the Occam language by process algebraic methods using the CSP process algebra [43]. Degano et al. followed in that tradition by analyzing Mobile Agent Programs written in the Higher Order Functional, Concurrent and Distributed, programming language Facile [47], by equipping Facile with a process algebraic semantics based on true concurrency [16,24]. This semantics facilitated analysis of programs revealing subtle bugs that would otherwise be very hard to find. More recently Java programs have been analyzed for correct calling order of methods using the Concurrency Workbench [29].

For analysing timing properties of systems, the traditional methods for schedulability analysis include response time analysis [17]. For each task, the response time is calculated, and the system is schedulable if the response times for the tasks are less than their respective deadlines. Tools and techniques based on the traditional methods tend to be rather conservative.

The TIMES [7] tool presents a model-based, control-flow sensitive technique for schedulability analysis in which a specification for the real-time system is built as a set of tasks modeling their timing properties e.g. cost, dependencies, and deadlines. Supplementary code can be provided. This results in an NTA model which is checked using the UPPAAL [10] model checker. TIMES does not perform timing analysis of the code associated with the tasks, which must be performed using external WCET analysis tools such as aiT [25], METAMOC [21], WCET Analyzer (WCA) [44] or TetaJ [26]. The aiT and METAMOC tools are targeted at timing analysis of C-programs and use respectively a combination of abstract interpretation and integer linear programming, and model checking. For Java, either WCA or TetaJ can be used. WCA makes available two techniques for timing analysis; model checking and Implicit Path Enumeration [32]. WCA, however, is targeted at the JOP [39], a JVM implementation in hardware. For dedicated schedulability analysis of Java programs, SARTS [14] can be used which also employs a model-based technique itself inspired from TIMES.

Bandera [20] is a tool for generating automata descriptions for various model checkers such as PROMELA for the SPIN [28] model checker given the program source of the Java system. Java Pathfinder (JPF) [31] can also be used for software model checking of Java real-time systems. TETASARTS is inspired by the idea of approaching software model checking by considering the translation process from software to finite-state models as an optimising compiler.

3   The SCJ Real-Time Programming Model

Safety critical applications have different complexity levels. To cater for this the SCJ programming model is based on tasks grouped in missions, where a mission encapsulates a specific functionality or phase in the lifetime of the real-time system as a set of schedulable entities. The SCJ specification lets developers tailor the capabilities of the platform to the needs of the application through three compliance levels. Level 0, provides a simple, frame-based cyclic executive model which is single threaded with a single mission. Level 1 extends this model with multi-threading via periodic and aperiodic event handlers, multiple missions, and a fixed-priority preemptive scheduler (FPS). Level 2 lifts restrictions on threads and supports nested missions.

A mission encapsulates a specific functionality or phase in the lifetime of the real-time system as a set of schedulable entities. For instance, a flight-control system may be composed of take-off, cruising, and landing each of which can be assigned a dedicated mission. A schedulable entity handles a specific functionality and has release parameters describing the release pattern and temporal scope e.g. release time and deadline. The release pattern is either periodic or aperiodic.

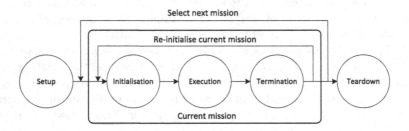

Fig. 1. Overview of the mission concept [36].

The mission concept is depicted in Fig. 1 and contains five phases;

Setup where the mission objects are allocated during start-up of the system. This phase is not considered time-critical.

Initialisation where all object allocations related to the mission or to the entire applications are performed. This phase is time-critical in applications with mode changes consisting of a sequence of missions.

Execution during which all application logic is executed and schedulable entities are set for execution according to a pre-emptive priority scheduler. This phase is time-critical.

Cleanup is entered if the mission terminates and is used for completing the execution of all schedulable entities as well as performing cleanup-related functionality. After this phase, the same mission may be restarted, a new is selected, or the Teardown phase is entered. This phase is time-critical in applications with mode changes consisting of a sequence of missions.

Teardown is the final phase in the lifetime of the application and comprises deallocation of objects and release of locks etc. This phase is not time-critical.

SCJ introduces a memory model based on the concept of *scoped memory* from the RTSJ, which circumvents the use of a garbage collected heap during real-time execution, easing the verification of timing properties of SCJ systems.

4   Real-Time Execution Platforms

The SCJ programming model provides a structuring framework for applications with hard real-time requirements. Next such applications need an execution platform. For applications written in C this is usually a hardware processor. However, Java applications are typically translated into JBC which are then either interpreted or further translated into native code before execution, also called ahead-of-time (AOT) execution, or during, also called just-in-time (JIT) execution. This approach entails a time predictable implementation of each JBC.

The simplest way to ensure a time predictable execution of each Jave Bytecode is to implement the JVM in hardware. This is the approach taken by the JOP [39]. The JOP is implemented on an FPGA (Altera Cyclone EP1C6Q240 or EP1C12Q240). The JOP has its own micro code instruction set with most JBC having a one-to-one mapping. However, some are more complex and are implemented as a sequence of JOP micro codes, some are even implemented in Java. The end result is that for each JBC its execution can be bounded and its WCET be determined. Important for WCET analysis of programs executing on the JOP is that the JOP does not feature data caches, but features a method cache which must be taken into account.

The HVM [30, 45] is a lean JVM implementation intended for use in resource-constrained embedded devices with as low as 256 KB ROM and 20 KB RAM. It features both iterative interpretation, Java-to-C compilation (AOT), and a hybrid of the two. The HVM employs *JVM specialisation*; a JVM is produced specifically for hosting the JBC program of a given application. This is done using the ICECAP-TOOLS Eclipse-plugin, which analyzes the JBC program and produces an executable for the target platform. The analyses and transformations can be extended, and incorporate a number of (static) optimizations for improving performance of the JVM and for reducing its size. This includes receiver-type analysis for potentially devirtualising method calls and intelligent class linking which computes a conservative set of classes and methods that are used in the application. Only this set will be embedded in the final HVM executable. It also conservatively estimates the set of JBC that will actually be used. The HVM is self-contained and does not rely on the presence of an OS or a C standard library. The HVM has been ported to the Atmel AVR ATmega2560 microcontroller, Arduino and Lego EV3 [30].

5   Timed Automata

This section presents an overview of the Timed Automata formalism, based on [5,9,11]. A Timed Automaton is a finite state machine extended with a finite set of non-negative real-valued `clock` variables. Traditionally, vertices in the graph are called `locations`, which are connected by `edges`. The set of clocks is denoted by C. Clocks are distinguished from usual program variables in that their operations are limited to inspection and reset to zero. For traditional Timed Automata, clocks implicitly increase their values with rate one as time progresses, that is, if time elapses by d, all clocks synchronously advance by d. Formally, a **clock valuation** over the set of clocks, C, is a mapping $v : C \to \mathbb{R}_+$, where $\mathbb{R}_+$ denotes the set of non-negative reals. $\mathbb{R}_+^C$ denotes the set of all clock valuations. Then, for a valuation $v \in \mathbb{R}_+^C$ and a time delay, $d \in \mathbb{R}_+$, $v + d$ is the clock valuation that for each $c \in C$ assigns $v(c) + d$. For a set of clocks $X \subseteq C$, $v[Y]$ is the valuation assigning to each $x \in Y$ zero (i.e. it is a reset of x) and $v(x)$ when $x \notin Y$. A Timed Automaton can have conditions on the clock values called **guards** for edges and **invariants** for locations. In general, conditions that depend on clock values are **clock constraints** and $B(C)$ is the set of conjunctions over simple constraints of the form $x \sim c$ (or $x - y \sim c$), where $x, y \in C$, $c \in \mathbb{N}$ and $\sim \in \{<, \leq, =, \geq, >\}$. When a clock constraint on an edge is satisfied, that edge is capable of being fired. Firing of an edge happens instantaneously. In locations, clock constraints are used to constrain the time spent in that location.

Definition 1 (Timed Automaton). *A Timed Automaton is a tuple $\mathcal{A} = \langle L, l_0, \Sigma, C, E, I \rangle$, where L is a set of locations, $l_0 \in L$ is the initial location, C is the set of clocks, Σ is a set of (co-)actions (which are denoted by ! and ?, respectively) and the internal τ-action, $E \subseteq L \times B(C) \times \Sigma \times 2^C \times L$ is the set of edges between locations with a guard, an action, and a set of clocks to be reset. $I : L \to B(C)$ is the map assigning to each location an invariant i.e. a clock constraint.*

In the following, $l \xrightarrow{g,a,r} l'$ denotes $\langle l, g, a, r, l' \rangle \in E$, where $l, l' \in L$, $g \in B(C)$, $a \in \Sigma$, and $r \in 2^C$. Guards and invariants will be considered as sets of clock valuations, and $v \models I(l)$ denotes that the clock valuation v satisfies $I(l)$, i.e. the clock constraints representing the invariant of location l.

The semantics of a Timed Automaton $\mathcal{A} = \langle L, l_0, \Sigma, C, E, I \rangle$ is a timed labelled transition system $\langle S, s_0, \to \rangle$ where states are pairs $(l, v) \in S \subseteq L \times \mathbb{R}_+^C$ with $v \models I(l)$, $s_0 = (l_0, u_0)$ is the initial state, and $\to \subseteq S \times (\mathbb{R}_+ \cup A) \times S$ is the transition relation which can be either

(i) a delay transition $(l, v) \xrightarrow{d} (l, v')$ where $d \in \mathbb{R}_+$ is a delay and $v' = v + d$ if $\forall d'$ s.t. $0 \leq d' \leq d \implies v + d' \models I(l)$; or

(ii) a discrete transition $(l, v) \xrightarrow{a} (l', v')$ if there exists an edge $l \xrightarrow{g,a,Y} l'$ such that $v \models g$, $v' = v[Y]$ and $v' \models I(l')$.

Timed Automata $\mathcal{A}_1, \dots, \mathcal{A}_n$ can be composed into a Network of Timed Automata using the CCS parallel composition operator, i.e., $\mathcal{A}_1 | \cdots | \mathcal{A}_n$. Let $\mathcal{A}^j = \langle L^j, l_0^j, C, A, E^j, I^j \rangle$, with $j = 1, 2, \dots, n$ be a Network of n Timed Automata. The location is now defined as a vector $\bar{l} = (l^1, l^2, \dots, l^n)$. The notation $\bar{l}[l_i'/l_i]$ denotes the update of location vector $\bar{l}$ where the ith element l_i is substituted by l_i'. The invariant functions are composed into a single function over location vectors i.e. $I(\bar{l}) = \wedge_i I_i(l_i)$. Again, the semantics of a Network of Timed Automata can be defined as a timed labelled transition system $\langle S, s_0, \to \rangle$, where states, S, are now defined by the set $S = (L^1 \times L^2 \times \dots \times L^n) \times \mathbb{R}_+^C$, the initial state defined by $s_0 = (\bar{l}_0, v_0) \in S$, and the transition relation, $\to \subseteq S \times (\mathbb{R}_+ \cup A) \times S$, can now either be

(i) a delay transition $(\bar{l}, v) \xrightarrow{d} (\bar{l}, v')$ where $d \in \mathbb{R}_+$ is a delay and $v' = v + d$ if $\forall d'$ s.t. $0 \le d' \le d \implies v + d' \models I(\bar{l})$;

(ii) a discrete transition $(\bar{l}, v) \xrightarrow{a} (\bar{l}[l_i'/l_i], v')$ if there exists an edge $l_i \xrightarrow{g,a,Y} l_i'$ such that $v \models g$, $v' = v[Y]$ and $v' \models I(\bar{l}'[l_i'/l_i])$; or

(iii) a synchronisation transition $(\bar{l}, v) \xrightarrow{\tau} (\bar{l}[l_j'/l_j, l_i'/l_i], v')$ for Timed Automata $\mathcal{A}_i$ and $\mathcal{A}_j$ if there exist edges $l_i \xrightarrow{g_i, c!, Y_i} l_i'$ and $l_j \xrightarrow{g_j, c?, Y_j} l_j'$ such that $v \models g_i \wedge g_j$, $v' = v[Y_i \cup Y_j]$ and $v' \models I(\bar{l}[l_j'/l_j, l_i'/l_i])$.

Note that the above definition follows the standard definition of the CCS parallel composition operator. This will facilitate the simulation result presented later in this paper. The definition given in [11] only allows internal transitions in clause (ii) as the Network of Timed Automata (NTA) verified by the UPPAAL model checker are closed systems and thus the parallel composition operator has an implicit hiding operator.

6 TetaSARTS

TETASARTS is a fully automated tool for conducting timing analysis, such as schedulability analysis, of JBC real-time systems taking into account the particular execution environment consisting of either a software implementation of the JVM on a commodity hardware platform or a hardware implementation of the JVM. TETASARTS employs a model-based technique for making a control-flow sensitive analysis of the JBC real-time system. It keeps a tight correspondence between the actual real-time system application code and the model used for analysis, by generating TA models amenable to model checking using UPPAAL. A further benefit of using model checking is that a counterexample is provided in case the system is non-schedulable.

Two options are available for representing the execution environment: an *explicit representation* or an *inline representation*. The explicit representation incorporates the control-flow of the JBC implementations used by the specific JVM hosting the real-time system. To reflect the behavior of the JBC interpreter of the JVM, this scheme is modelled as well. Simulating the execution of the JVM is achieved by including TA models of the hardware. By using this option TETASARTS is conducting schedulability analysis by simulating an abstract execution of the entire real-time system. This increases the overall complexity of the analysed system, but also provides the potential for more precise analysis since the dynamic behavior of e.g. caching and pipelining is accounted for. For the inline representation TETASARTS inlines the execution times of each of the instructions in the model. These could be provided for various reasons; for JOP, the execution times are fixed, and can be found in the documentation. The inlined instruction execution times may also be available from a WCET analysis tool or from a measurement-based approach by using a stopwatch. The benefit of using an inline representation is simplicity; the dynamic behavior of the execution environment is not incorporated in the simulation, but potentially at the expense of precision, because cache-effects and timing anomalies inherent on many platforms, significantly influence instruction execution times.

TETASARTS supports real-time tasks from SCJ with periodic or sporadic release patterns. However, it assumes that all real-time tasks are created as part of system initialisation, but future extensions will support the missing concepts from SCJ. It also supports synchronisation mechanisms such as synchronised methods in Java. The effect including synchronisation is reported in [14].

In the following sections we look at how an SCJ application is translated into a set of timed automata and how optimizations akin to those found in optimizing compilers can help reduce the model to cope with the inherent state space explosion.

How the set of program automata is combined with timed automata modeling the scheduler, sporadic and periodic task firing, the JVM and the hardware platform, forming a NTA suitable for analysis with the UPPAAL model checker, is reported in [38]. Schedulability analysis can be performed by verifying that a deadlock state is never reachable within the feasibility interval [27]. This can only be the case if one or more of the real-time tasks do not finish within their deadlines. Thus schedulability is expressed by the Timed Computation Tree Logic (TCTL) specification $A\square$!*deadlock*.

7   From Java Byte Code to Timed Automata

To translate an SCJ application to an NTA, the SCJ program is first compiled to JBC with a standard Java compile like `javac`. The resulting JBC forms the starting point for the transformation. The original Java source code is only used in relation to handling loops. TETASARTS constructs an extended control flow graph (CFG) in the Timed Intermediate Representation (TIR) format (see below) for each method used in the system. The TIR is translated to a Timed Automaton for each method. These are then combined into an NTA called the `Program NTA`. The `Program NTA` captures the behavior of the system by simulating a control-flow sensitive execution of each real-time task in the system. As depicted in Fig. 2 generating the `Program NTA` is a process composed of stages akin to those found in an optimising compiler.

Fig. 2. From SCJ to TA

TETASARTS initially identifies the real-time tasks of the system. With the handlers of these as entry points, TETASARTS explores the call-graph and limits the construction of TIR to methods part of the reachable execution path. This reduces the overall translation time remarkably since it avoids CFG reconstruction for all methods but the relevant ones. The TIR is subsequently decorated with loop bound information extracted from the original source code using a comment-based approach where loop bounds are annotated using the format $//@loopbound = \langle loop \rangle$.

The output of different Java compilers including javac, ECJ, Jikes and GCJ, shows that all produced loop constructs are *reducible* [1], that is, they contain a single loop header that is always visited when the loop is executed. Furthermore, a reducible loop contains at least one back edge which returns control from the loop body to the loop header. To identify reducible loops, TETASARTS employs a loop identification analysis based on the algorithm presented in [1]. When loops have been identified, extracting the loop bound from the source code is trivial since the source code line numbers are available from the JBC.

Generating TIR. The first step in the process is, for each method used in the system, to generate the intermediate representation, TIR:

Definition 2 (TIR). TIR *is an extended Control-Flow Graph* $G = \langle B, L, E \rangle$ *composed of basic blocks,* B, *edges,* $E \subseteq B \times L \times B$, *where* $l \in L$ *decorates the CFG with extra information such as loop bounds, JVM instructions and types.*

A basic block is a linear sequence of instructions, $i_1, i_2, \ldots, i_n$, that does not contain jumps nor jump targets, hence having a single entry and a single exit point. An edge, $e = \langle b_1, l, b_2 \rangle$, connecting the two basic blocks, b_1 and b_2, denotes that a control flow path exists between the last instruction of b_1 and the first instruction of b_2. When basic blocks have been connected, the CFG is expanded with nodes/edges for each instruction in a basic block. Thus each edge in TIR is labeled with exactly one instruction.

We also introduce the operation $succ(b) = \{b' \mid b, b' \in B \text{ and } \langle b, l, b' \rangle \in E\}$. Following the idea presented in [6] we introduce a transition system for a CFG by defining: $b \xrightarrow{l} b'$ whenever $\langle b, l, b' \rangle \in E$.

Generating the NTA. We first introduce two sets of JBC instructions; *JBCInst* contains all defined JBC instructions, and

$$CallInst = \{invokevirtual, invokespecial, invokedynamic,$$
$$invokeinterface, invokestatic\}$$

that is, all JBC instructions used for invocation that transfer control to another method. For ease of notation, we also extend the use of *succ* to apply for use with instructions i.e.

$$succ_b(i) = \{i_{nxt} \mid \langle b, l, b' \rangle \in E \text{ and } i \in l \text{ and } \langle b', l', b'' \rangle \in succ(b) \text{ and } i_{nxt} \in l'\}$$

The intuition is that $succ_b(i)$ is the set of instructions immediately following instruction i in the CFG, i.e. the instructions labeling edges with origin in $succ(b)$. We omit the subscript b from $succ_b(i)$ when b is obvious from the context.

Definition 3 (Left Merging TAs). *For convenience, we define the left merging operator of two TAs,* $\lhd : TA \times TA \to TA$:

$$\lhd(\langle L, l_0, \Sigma, C, E, I \rangle, \langle L', l_0', \Sigma', C', E', I' \rangle) = \langle L \cup L', l_0, \Sigma \cup \Sigma', C \cup C', E \cup E', I \cup I' \rangle$$

The left merge operator is easily generalized to take a set of TA as the second argument.

Definition 4 (TIR Translation). *Let CFG be the control-flow graph of method* m, $chan : m \to chanName$ *be the function that provides a unique channel name,* $chanName$, *for the method* m, $l_0(m)$ *be a unique new location for the method* m, l_{first} *be the location generated by* $genTA_{inst}$ *for the first instruction of CFG, and similarly* l_{last} *the location generated by* $genTA_{inst}$ *for the last instruction of CFG. Then*

$$TA_{CFG} = TA_{boil} \underset{\substack{i \in b \\ b \in CFG}}{\lhd} genTA_{inst}(i)$$

where $TA_{boil} = \langle \{l_0, l_{first}, l_{last}\}, l_0, \{chan(m)!, chan(m)?\}, C, E, \emptyset \rangle$,
with $E = \{l_0 \xrightarrow{chan(m)?} l_{first}, l_{last} \xrightarrow{chan(m)!} l_0(m)\}$,
and $C = \begin{cases} \{execTime\} & \text{if Inline representation is used} \\ \emptyset & \text{if Explicit representation is used} \end{cases}$

and where $execTime$ is used for monitoring the inlined instruction execution times.

Generating the TA stubs for JBC instructions is parameterised on the particular type of that instruction such that

$$genTA_{inst}(i) = \begin{cases} genTA_{call}(i) & \text{if } i \in CallInst \\ genTA_{sim}(i) & \text{if } i \in JBCInst \setminus CallInst \end{cases}$$

That is, $genTA_{call}$ generates the TA stub of JBC instructions that invokes methods, whereas $genTA_{sim}$ generates the TA of all other JBCs.

$genTA_{call}$ and $genTA_{sim}$ are further parameterised depending on whether the execution environment is explicitly modelled or inlined in the Program NTA with static instruction execution times and without a JVM NTA and a Hardware NTA.

$$genTA_{sim}(i) = \begin{cases} genTA_{sim_{in}} & \text{if inline representation is used} \\ genTA_{sim_{exp}} & \text{if explicit representation is used} \end{cases}$$

$$genTA_{call}(i) = \begin{cases} genTA_{call_{in}} & \text{if inline representation is used} \\ genTA_{call_{exp}} & \text{if explicit representation is used} \end{cases}$$

We also define the auxiliary function $loc : TA \to Location$ that returns the initial location associated with a TA stub generated for an instruction, $edge : TA \to Edge$ that returns the outgoing edges of the initial location of a generated TA stub for an instruction, $sync : Edge \to chanName$ that returns the channel name for an edge, and $Callees : i \to M$ where $i \in CallInst$ that provides the set of potential receivers of a method call. Translating TIR to a **Program** NTA used along with an explicit representation of the execution environment is performed according to Definition 5.

Definition 5 (Explicit Representation Translation). *For translating simple instructions, we use*

$$genTA_{sim_{exp}} : Instruction \rightarrow TA = \langle L, l_0, \Sigma, C, E, I \rangle$$

which is defined as:

$$genTA_{sim_{exp}}(i) = \langle \{l_i\}, l_i, \{jvm\_exec!\}, \emptyset, E, \emptyset \rangle$$

where

$$E = \bigcup_{\substack{\forall i_{nxt} \in \\ succ(i)}} \left\{ \left\langle l_i \xrightarrow{running[tID], jvm\_exec!, jvm\_inst:=[\![i]\!]} loc(genTA_{instr}(i_{nxt})) \right\rangle \right\}$$

Method calling instructions are translated using

$$genTA_{call_{exp}} : Instruction \rightarrow TA = \langle L, l_0, \Sigma, C, E, I \rangle$$

which is defined as:

$$genTA_{call_{exp}}(i) = \langle \{loc(genTA_{sim_{exp}}(i)), l_{call}, l_{wait}, l_{ret}\}, loc(genTA_{sim_{exp}}(i)),$$
$$\{jvm\_exec!\} \cup \{a!, a?|a \in chan(callees(i))\}, \emptyset, E, I \rangle$$

where

$$E = edge(genTA_{sim_{exp}}(i))$$

$$\bigcup_{\substack{\forall M \in \\ callees(i)}} \left\{ \left\langle l_{call} \xrightarrow{running[tID], chan(M)!} l_{wait} \right\rangle \right\}$$

$$\bigcup_{\substack{\forall M \in \\ callees(i)}} \left\{ \left\langle l_{wait} \xrightarrow{running[tID], chan(M)?} l_{ret} \right\rangle \right\}$$

$$\cup \left\{ \left\langle l_{ret} \xrightarrow{urgent} loc(genTA_{instr}(i_{nxt})) \right\rangle \right\}$$

and

$$I = \{\langle l_{call}, execTime == 0 \rangle, \langle l_{ret}, execTime == 0 \rangle\}$$

In Definition 5, the guard as generated by $genTA_{sim_{exp}}$, ensures that the edge can only be fired if the real-time task with ID tID is set to run as governed by the scheduler. The *urgent* label means that the edge is fired immediately; when being in l_{ret}, time is not allowed to progress and the edge is fired instantaneously. The update statement is used for communicating the instruction, i, to the JVM NTA. Furthermore, to initiate the simulation of i, a synchronisation action is initiated on the jvm_exec channel. Whenever the JVM NTA is capable of processing a new instruction, it receives on jvm_exec. The TA stub generated by $genTA_{call_{exp}}$ makes a non-deterministic choice between all possible receivers of the call by generating an outgoing edge with a synchronisation action to the respective TA simulating the receiver. Afterwards, the process waits in l_{wait} until the simulation of the callee finishes at which point the process synchronises on the same synchronisation channel, transferring control back to the caller.

For generating the Program NTA for use with an inline representation of the execution environment, we add the function $wcet : i \to \mathbb{N}$ that returns the statically defined WCET for instruction i on the particular execution environment. The translation is performed according to Definition 6.

Definition 6 (Inline Representation Translation). *Translating simple instructions is done using*

$$genTA_{sim_{in}} : Instruction \to TA = \langle L, l_0, \Sigma, C, E, I \rangle$$

which is defined as:

$$genTA_{sim_{in}}(i) = \langle \{l_i\}, l_i, \emptyset, \emptyset, E, I \rangle$$

where

$$E = \bigcup_{\substack{\forall i_{nxt} \in \\ succ(i)}} \left\{ \left\langle l_i \xrightarrow{execTime==\llbracket wcet(i) \rrbracket, execTime:=0} loc(genTA_{instr}(i_{nxt})) \right\rangle \right\}$$

and

$$I = \{ \langle l_i, execTime \leq \llbracket wcet(i) \rrbracket \ \&\& \ execTime' == running[tID] \rangle \}$$

Translating method calling instructions is done using

$$genTA_{call_{in}} : Instruction \to TA = \langle L, l_0, \Sigma, C, E, I \rangle$$

which is defined as:

$$genTA_{call_{in}}(i) = \langle \{loc(genTA_{sim_{in}}(i)), l_{wait}\}, loc(genTA_{sim_{in}}(i)),$$
$$\{a!, a? | a \in chan(callees(i))\}, \emptyset, E, I \rangle$$

where

$$E = edge(genTA_{sim_{in}}(i))$$

$$\bigcup_{\substack{\forall M \in \\ callees(i)}} \left\{ \left\langle loc(genTA_{sim_{in}}(i) \xrightarrow{execTime==\llbracket wcet(i) \rrbracket, chan(M)!, execTime:=0} l_{wait} \right\rangle \right\}$$

$$\bigcup_{\substack{\forall M \in \\ callees(i)}} \left\{ \left\langle l_{wait} \xrightarrow{chan(M)?, execTime:=0} loc(genTA_{instr}(succ(i))) \right\rangle \right\}$$

Translation to an inline representation follows the same pattern as that for an explicit representation. The notable difference is the inclusion of the instruction execution times on the edges.

8   Correctness of Translation

In this section we conjecture that the translation of an SCJ application is correct. The correctness is stipulated through a simulation relation between TIR and Program NTA, relying on results from [18] proving the correctness of the translation from Java to JBC and [6] proving simulation between JCB and CFG.

Conjecture 1. For each method m in an SCJ application, the TIR representation of method m is in a simulation relation with the TA generated for m using Definition 4 and the Explicit Representation Translation in Definition 5.

A proof of the above conjecture will follow the lines of [6]. There are two cases:

(1) The CFG of a method m can do a transition $b \xrightarrow{l} b'$ whenever $\langle b, l, b' \rangle \in E$ where $i \in l$ and $i \in sim_{exp}$, then $genTA_{sim_{exp}}(i)$ $\xrightarrow{running[tID],jvm\_exec!,jvm\_inst:=[\![i]\!]} l_{loc}$ where $l_{loc} \in loc(genTA_{instr}(i_{nxt}))$.

(2) The CFG of a method m can do a transition $b \xrightarrow{l} b'$ whenever $\langle b, l, b' \rangle \in E$ where $i \in l$ and $i \in call_{exp}$ then $genTA_{call_{in}}(i)$ $\xrightarrow{running[tID],jvm\_exec!,jvm\_inst:=[\![i]\!]} l_{call} \xrightarrow{running[tID],chan(M)!} l_{wait}$ $\xrightarrow{running[tID],chan(M)?} l_{ret} \xrightarrow{urgent} l_{loc}$ where $l_{loc} \in loc(genTA_{instr}(i_{nxt}))$.

Conjecture 2. For each method m in an SCJ application, the Program TA generated for m using Definition 4 and the Explicit Representation Translation in Definition 5 is in a simulation relation with the Program TA generated for m using Definition 4 and the Implicit Representation Translation in Definition 6.

A proof of the above conjecture will establish a simulation between the Explicit Representation Translation and the Implicit Representation Translation, noting that when $genTA_{sim_{exp}}(i) \xrightarrow{running[tID],jvm\_exec!,jvm\_inst:=[\![i]\!]} l_{loc}$ where $l_{loc} \in loc(genTA_{instr}(i_{nxt}))$ then $genTA_{sim_{in}}(i) \xrightarrow{execTime==[\![wcet(i)]\!],execTime:=0} l'_{loc}$ where $l'_{loc} \in loc(genTA_{instr}(i_{nxt}))$ for $i \in sim_{exp}$, and similarly matching transitions can be found for $i \in call_{exp}$.

9   Analyses and Optimisations

To cope with the inherent problem of state space explosion, our method adopts a variety of analyses, optimisations, and transformations to reduce the size of each state and the state space that needs exploration. All transformations and optimisations are incorporated without affecting the soundness of our method.

Inlining TAs. UPPAAL uses the CCS parallel composition operator for allowing interleaving of actions as well as allowing hand-shake synchronisations. For the parallel composition, $\mathcal{A}_1 \parallel \mathcal{A}_2 \parallel \cdots \parallel \mathcal{A}_n$, the product TA necessarily has to be constructed. This is entirely syntactical, but turns out to be computationally expensive which is the reason why UPPAAL computes the product TA on-the-fly during verification. To lower the verification time even more, TETASARTS inlines TAs wherever possible prior to the verification to reduce the size of the product TAs. Inlining TAs involves a series of steps. First a TA dependency graph is built over how TETASARTS simulates invocation of methods using synchronisation channels. Thus Definition 7 only applies for the modeling approach adopted in TETASARTS.

Definition 7 (TA Dependency Graph). *A TA dependency graph $G = \langle V, E \rangle$ is a DAG where the vertices, V, represent the TAs of the NTA system, and edges, $E \subseteq V \times V$ represent that a dependency exists between two TAs. Let $\mathcal{A}_i$ where $i \in \{1, 2\}$ be two TAs and let $E_{\mathcal{A}_i}$ denote the set of edges in TA $\mathcal{A}_i$. C denotes an arbitrary synchronisation channel. A dependency among $\mathcal{A}_1$ and $\mathcal{A}_2$ is created when there exists two edges, $\{e_{\mathcal{A}_i}, e'_{\mathcal{A}_i}\} \in E_{\mathcal{A}_i}$ where $i \in \{1, 2\}$ if*

$$e_{\mathcal{A}_1} = \langle l_{\mathcal{A}_1} \xrightarrow{g_{\mathcal{A}_1}, C!, u_{\mathcal{A}_1}, r_{\mathcal{A}_1}} l'_{\mathcal{A}_1} \rangle \qquad e'_{\mathcal{A}_1} = \langle l'_{\mathcal{A}_1} \xrightarrow{C?} l''_{\mathcal{A}_1} \rangle$$

$$e_{\mathcal{A}_2} = \langle l_{\mathcal{A}_2} \xrightarrow{g_{\mathcal{A}_2}, C!, u_{\mathcal{A}_2}, r_{\mathcal{A}_2}} l'_{\mathcal{A}_2} \rangle \qquad e'_{\mathcal{A}_2} = \langle l'_{\mathcal{A}_2} \xrightarrow{C?} l''_{\mathcal{A}_2} \rangle$$

where $\{e_{\mathcal{A}_1}, e'_{\mathcal{A}_1}, e_{\mathcal{A}_2}, e'_{\mathcal{A}_2} \mid sync(e) = C \text{ where } e \in E_{\mathcal{A}_1} \cup E_{\mathcal{A}_2}\}$, that is C is a channel only appearing on edges $e_{\mathcal{A}_1}, e'_{\mathcal{A}_1}, e_{\mathcal{A}_2}$ and $e'_{\mathcal{A}_2}$ in $\mathcal{A}_1$ and $\mathcal{A}_2$.

Assume that a dependency exists between the TAs $\mathcal{A}_1$ and $\mathcal{A}_2$ due to the existence of edges $e_{\mathcal{A}_1}, e'_{\mathcal{A}_1}, e_{\mathcal{A}_2}, e'_{\mathcal{A}_2}$ whose structure follows the definitions in Definition 7. A new TA $\mathcal{A}_{in}$ is created such that $\mathcal{A}_{in} = \mathcal{A}_1 \lhd \mathcal{A}_2$ except that $\{e_{\mathcal{A}_1}, e'_{\mathcal{A}_1}, e_{\mathcal{A}_2}, e'_{\mathcal{A}_2}\} \notin E_{\mathcal{A}_{in}}$. In addition, two new edges are added to $E_{\mathcal{A}_{in}}$:

$$e_{init} = \langle l'_{\mathcal{A}_1} \xrightarrow{g_{\mathcal{A}_1}, \tau, u_{\mathcal{A}_1}} l''_{\mathcal{A}_2} \rangle \quad e_{ret} = \langle l'_{\mathcal{A}_2} \xrightarrow{g_{\mathcal{A}_2}, \tau, u_{\mathcal{A}_2}} l''_{\mathcal{A}_1} \rangle$$

If the option of inlining the instruction execution times in the `Program NTA` is enabled, TETASARTS is capable of reducing the state space by aggregating edges that are fired sequentially according to Definition 8.

Definition 8 (Sequentially Executing Instructions). *Let $i_1, i_2, \ldots, i_n$ be the sequence of instructions following an execution path in the program. $i_1, i_2, \ldots, i_n$ are sequentially executing if $\forall i_k$ s.t. $1 \leq k \leq n$ then $\mid succ(i_k) \mid = 1$*

Edge aggregation is now performed according to Definition 9.

Definition 9 (Edge Aggregation). *Let $SeqInst$ be a set of sequentially executing instructions according to Definition 8. The total execution of $SeqInst$ is then $aggWCET = \sum_{i \in SeqInst} wcet(i)$.*

Let $SeqLoc = \{l_i \mid i \in SeqInst\}$ and let $SeqEdges$ denote the set of edges with source location l s.t. $l \in SeqLoc$ and let $\mathcal{A}$ be the TA with locations L s.t. $SeqLoc \subseteq L$ and edges E s.t. $SeqEdges \subseteq E$. $\mathcal{A}$ is updated s.t. $L = L \setminus SeqLoc$ and $E = E \setminus SeqEdges$

Let l and l' denote the first and last location in $SeqLoc$. e_{agg} is a new edge s.t. $e_{agg} = \langle l \xrightarrow{execTime == [\![aggWCET]\!]} l' \rangle$. Furthermore, the invariants of $\mathcal{A}$ are updated s.t. $\langle l, execTime \leq [\![aggWCET]\!] \ \&\& \ execTime' == running[tID] \rangle$

JVM NTA Specialisation. Many embedded systems do not use floating point arithmetic hence leaving out all the JBCs that handle doubles and floats. Moreover, many other JBCs are only rarely used. Due to this, our method employs an analysis that conservatively estimates the set of JBCs the program is actually using. The analysis traverses TIR and visits every instruction i. Whenever an instruction i is visited such that $i \notin JBCInst_{used}$, it is added to $JBCInst_{used}$. All TA_i such that $i \notin JBCInst_{used}$ are removed from the final NTA.

Devirtualisation. From a static viewpoint, the run-time type of an object can be any subclass of that type. Therefore, naively, a virtual method call site is modelled as a nondeterministic choice between all possible callees which, in cases with large class hierarchies, contributes significantly to the size of the state space.

TETASARTS employs static program analyses known from optimising compilers to devirtualise virtual method calls or at least limit the amount of possibilities of dynamically-dispatched methods. The methods are used when invoking the *callees* function previously introduced. TETASARTS makes available different approaches since the precision of devirtualisation comes at the cost of increased NTA generation time:

Class Hierarchy Analysis (CHA) considers the declared type of the callee and combines it with complete information about the class hierarchy. If a virtual method call is made on method m where the declared type of the receiver is denoted C and has subtypes $\{S_1, S_2, \ldots, S_n\}$, then only C and the subtypes that override m will be considered [23].

Rapid Type Analysis (RTA) is an extension to CHA which combines the information about globally instantiated types and intersects it with the class hierarchy information about the callsite as obtained by CHA [8].

Variable Type Analysis (VTA) makes a conservative estimate of the set of types that may possibly reach each variable in methods [46].

10 Evaluation

In this section, we demonstrate the applicability of TETASARTS using representative examples of real-time systems, and evaluate on the effects of the optimisations. All results were obtained by running UPPAAL on a machine with an Intel Xeon X5670 @ 2.93 GHz and 32 GB of memory. The systems are:

Class Hierarchy consists of four classes forming a hierarchy of height four. Each class overrides method `compute()` which performs a resource intensive calculation. Eight real-time tasks call different implementations of `compute()`. It is used for showing the effect of employing receiver type analysis.

Sequential Computation is composed of ten real-time tasks performing calculations using only a few conditional JBCs. This is used for demonstrating the effect of edge aggregation.

Simple RTS consists of nine real-time tasks performing calculations using only a few different JBCs. This system is used for demonstrating the effect of JVM specialisation and inlining TAs.

Minepump is the classic text-book example of a minepump control system that manages the operation of a water pump based on environmental conditions such as water level and methane concentration [12,17,26].

Real-Time Sorting Machine (RTSM) is an example of an embedded real-time system that manages two motors for sorting coloured bricks based on measurements from sensory equipment [14].

MD5SCJ is based on five periodic tasks calculating the MD5 sum of a byte array. The implementation of the MD5 task has been used in oSCJ [42].

For evaluating the effect of the optimisations, we have used an inline representation of the JOP execution environment. The results are shown in Table 1. As shown, all optimisations decrease the analysis time significantly. Especially inlining TAs and JVM specialisation are evidently of high importance. Edge aggregation is also important and should be enabled whenever an inline representation of the execution environment is used. Using VTA for devirtualisation is also recommended. As shown, having an exact representation of the execution environment yields long verification times and high memory demands. This was also anticipated due the number of TAs and their complexity. Further results can be found in [35,37].

Table 2 shows the results of analysing representative examples of real-time systems. The subscript indicates whether an explicit or an inline representation of the execution environment is used.

11   Conclusion

In this paper we have given an overview of the Safety Critical Java Profile and its programming model based on tasks grouped in missions, encapsulating a specific functionality or phase in the lifetime of a hard real-time system as a set of schedulable entities. We have given an overview of two execution platforms for SCJ, the JOP [39] and the HVM [30,45] and we have given an overview of the TETASARTS tool for conducting schedulability analysis of JBC real-time systems which is able to take into account the particular execution environment consisting of either a software implementation of the JVM and commodity

Table 1. The effect of the optimisations.

System	Optimisations	Analysis time	Mem. usage
Class hierarchy	CHA	1 m 44 s	65 MB
Class hierarchy	RTA	1 m 7 s	52 MB
Class hierarchy	VTA	29 s	37 MB
Simple RTS	All	27 s	70 MB
Simple RTS	No TA inlining	3 m 59 s	360 MB
	No JVM special		
Seq. computation	All	35 s	70 MB
Seq. computation	No edge aggr	1 m 2 s	167 MB

Table 2. Results obtained using TetaSARTS.

System	Exec. env	Analysis time	Mem. usage
RTSM	JOP_{in}	11	19 MB
RTSM	JOP_{exp}	17 m 19 s	166 MB
Minepump	JOP_{in}	1 s	12 MB
Minepump	JOP_{exp}	6 m 18 s	62 MB
Minepump	$HVMAVR_{exp}$	15 h 25 m 16 s	17933 MB

embedded hardware or a hardware implementation of the JVM. TETASARTS keeps a tight correspondence between the actual real-time system application code and the model used for analysis. We have briefly summarized some of the results based on this translation.

The main contribution is an elaboration on the theoretical underpinning of the translation from Java programs to timed automata models conjecturing that a simulation relation can be established between CFGs of methods in the system and their representations as TA. We conjecture the overall correctness by transitivity, relying on results from [18] proving the correctness of the translation from Java to JBC and from [6] proving simulation between JCB and CFG.

Our approach of analyzing real programs by process algebraic methods follows in the footsteps of [43] where programs in the Occam language are analyzed using the CSP process algebra and [16,24] where Degano et al. analyzed Mobile Agent Programs written in the Higher Order Functional, Concurrent and Distributed, programming language Facile [47].

Recently the Java language has been enhanced with anonymous higher order functions in the form of lambda abstractions. This makes Java a full-fledged higher order object oriented, functional and concurrent language. Furthermore, even embedded JVM platforms, such as JOP and HVM now have support for multi-core, and thus some level of true code migration incorporated. Thus we expect that the work in [16,24] will become extremely relevant in the analysis of systems for the Internet-of-Things, as Java moves into this territory.

References

1. Aho, A.V., Lam, M.S., Sethi, R., Ullman, J.D.: Compilers: Principles. Techniques and Tools. Pearson Education, London (2006)
2. Aicas: JamaicaVM User Manual: Java Technology for Critical Embedded Systems (2010)
3. aJile Systems: http://www.ajile.com/
4. Alur, R.: Timed automata. In: Halbwachs, N., Peled, D.A. (eds.) CAV 1999. LNCS, vol. 1633, pp. 8–22. Springer, Heidelberg (1999)
5. Alur, R., Dill, D.L.: A theory of timed automata. Theor. Comput. Sci. **126**(2), 183–235 (1994)
6. Amighi, A., de Carvalho Gomes, P., Gurov, D., Huisman, M.: Provably correct control flow graphs from Java bytecode programs with exceptions. Int. J. Softw. Tools Technol. Transfer, 1–32 (2015). http://dx.doi.org/10.1007/s10009-015-0375-0
7. Amnell, T., Fersman, E., Mokrushin, L., Pettersson, P., Yi, W.: TIMES: a tool for schedulability analysis and code generation of real-time systems. In: The 1st International Workshop on Formal Modeling and Analysis of Timed Systems, May 2003
8. Bacon, D.F., Sweeney, P.F.: Fast static analysis of c++ virtual function calls. In: Proceedings of the 11th ACM SIGPLAN Conference on Object-oriented Programming, Systems, Languages, and Applications. OOPSLA 1996, pp. 324–341. ACM, New York (1996)
9. Baier, C., Katoen, J.-P.: Principles of Model Checking, vol. 26202649. The MIT Press, Cambridge (2008)
10. Bengtsson, J., Larsen, K., Larsson, F., Pettersson, P., Yi, W.: Uppaal - a tool suite for automatic verification of real-time systems. In: Alur, R., Henzinger, T.A., Sontag, E.D. (eds.) HS 1995. LNCS, vol. 1066, pp. 232–243. Springer, Heidelberg (1996)
11. Bengtsson, J.E., Yi, W.: Timed automata: semantics, algorithms and tools. In: Desel, J., Reisig, W., Rozenberg, G. (eds.) Lectures on Concurrency and Petri Nets. LNCS, vol. 3098, pp. 87–124. Springer, Heidelberg (2004)
12. Bøgholm, T., Frost, C., Hansen, R., Jensen, C., Luckow, K., Ravn, A., Søndergaard, H., Thomsen, B.: Towards harnessing theories through tool support for hard real-time Java programming. Innovations Syst. Softw. Eng. **9**(1), 17–28 (2013)
13. Bøgholm, T., Hansen, R.R., Ravn, A.P., Thomsen, B., Søndergaard, H.: A predictable Java profile: rationale and implementations. In: Proceedings of the 7th International Workshop on Java Technologies for Real-Time and Embedded Systems. JTRES 2009, pp. 150–159 (2009)
14. Bøgholm, T., Kragh-Hansen, H., Olsen, P., Thomsen, B., Larsen, K.G.: Model-based schedulability analysis of safety critical hard real-time Java programs. In: Proceedings of the 6th International Workshop on Java Technologies for Real-time and Embedded Systems. JTRES 2008, pp. 106–114 (2008)
15. Bollella, G.: The Real-time Specification for Java. Addison-Wesley Java Series. Addison-Wesley, Boston (2000)
16. Borgia, R., Degano, P., Priami, C., Leth, L., Thomsen, B.: Understanding mobile agents via a non-interleaving semantics for facile. In: Schmidt, D.A., Cousot, R. (eds.) SAS 1996. LNCS, vol. 1145, pp. 98–112. Springer, Heidelberg (1996)
17. Burns, A., Wellings, A.: Real-Time Systems and Programming Languages: ADA 95, Real-Time Java, and Real-Time POSIX, 4th edn. Addison-Wesley Educational Publishers Inc., Boston (2009)

18. Börger, E., Schulte, W.: Defining the Java virtual machine as platform for provably correct Java compilation. In: Brim, L., Gruska, L., Zlatuška, J. (eds.) MFCS 1998. LNCS, vol. 1450, pp. 17–35. Springer, Heidelberg (1998)

19. Bøgholm, T., Thomsen, B., Larsen, K.G., Mycroft, A.: Schedulability analysis abstractions for safety critical Java. In: 2012 IEEE 15th International Symposium on Object/Component/Service-Oriented Real-Time Distributed Computing (ISORC), pp. 71–78, April 2012

20. Corbett, J.C., Dwyer, M.B., Hatcliff, J., Laubach, S., Robby, C.S.P., Zheng, H.: Bandera: extracting finite-state models from Java source code. In: Proceedings of the 2000 International Conference on Software Engineering, pp. 439–448 (2000)

21. Dalsgaard, A.E., Olesen, M.C., Toft, M., Hansen, R.R., Larsen, K.G.: META-MOC: modular execution time analysis using model checking. In: 10th International Workshop on Worst-Case Execution Time Analysis (2010)

22. David, A., Illum, J., Larsen, K., Skou, A.: Model-Based Framework for Schedulability Analysis Using UPPAAL 4.1, pp. 93–119. CRC Press, Boca Raton (2009)

23. Dean, J., Grove, D., Chambers, C.: Optimization of object-oriented programs using static class hierarchy analysis. In: Tokoro, M., Pareschi, R. (eds.) ECOOP 1995. LNCS, vol. 952, pp. 77–101. Springer, Heidelberg (1995)

24. Degano, P., Priami, C., Leth, L., Thomsen, B.: Causality for debugging mobile agents. Acta Informatica 36(5), 335–374 (1999)

25. Ferdinand, C.: Worst case execution time prediction by static program analysis. In: 2004 Proceedings, 18th International Symposium on Parallel and Distributed Processing, p. 125. IEEE (2004)

26. Frost, C., Jensen, C.S., Luckow, K.S., Thomsen, B.: WCET analysis of Java bytecode featuring common execution environments. In: 9th International Workshop on Java Technologies for Real-Time and Embedded Systems (2011)

27. Goossens, J., Devillers, R.: The non-optimality of the monotonic priority assignments for hard real-time offset free systems. Real-Time Syst. 13, 107–126 (1997)

28. Holzmann, G.J.: The model checker spin. IEEE Trans. Softw. Eng. 23(5), 279–295 (1997)

29. Huisman, M., Gurov, D.: CVPP: a tool set for compositional verification of control-flow safety properties. In: Beckert, B., Marché, C. (eds.) FoVeOOS 2010. LNCS, vol. 6528, pp. 107–121. Springer, Heidelberg (2011)

30. HVM (Hardware near Virtual Machine): http://www.icelab.dk/

31. JPF: Java PathFinder Tool-set (2014). http://babelfish.arc.nasa.gov/trac/jpf

32. Li, S.: Y.-T., Malik, S.: Performance analysis of embedded software using implicit path enumeration. In: Proceedings of the 32nd Annual ACM/IEEE Design Automation Conference. DAC 1995, pp. 456–461. ACM, New York (1995)

33. Locke, D., Scott Andersen, B., Brosgol, B., Fulton, M., Henties, T., Hunt, J.H., Nielsen, J.O., Nilsen, K., Schoeberl, M., Tokar, J., Vitek, J., Wellings, A: Safety-Critical Java Technology Specification, Public draft (2013)

34. Luckow, K.S., Bøgholm, T., Thomsen, B.: Supporting development of energy-optimised Java real-time systems using TetaSARTS. In: WiP Proceedings of the 19th Real-Time and Embedded Technology and Application Symposium, pp. 41–44 (2013)

35. Luckow, K.S., Bøgholm, T., Thomsen, B., Larsen, K.G.: TetaSARTS: modular timing and performance analysis of safety critical Java systems. Practice and Experience, Concurrency and Computation (2014)

36. Luckow, K.S., Thomsen, B., Korsholm, S.E.: HVM-TP: a time predictable and portable Java virtual machine for hard real-time embedded systems. In: 12th International Workshop on Java Technologies for Real-Time and Embedded Systems (2014)
37. Luckow, K.S.: Platforms and model-based analyses for real-time Java. Ph.D. thesis, Department of Computer Science, Aalborg University (2014). http://people.cs.aau.dk/luckow/thesis.pdf
38. Luckow, K.S., Bøgholm, T., Thomsen, B., Larsen, K.G.: TetaSARTS: a tool for modular timing analysis of safety critical Java systems. In: Proceedings of the 11th International Workshop on Java Technologies for Real-Time and Embedded Systems. JTRES 2013, pp. 11–20 (2013)
39. Schoeberl, M.: JOP: a Java optimized processor for embedded real-time systems. Number ISBN 978-3-8364-8086-4. VDM Verlag Dr. Müller (2008)
40. Nilsen, K.: Differentiating features of the PERC virtual machine. Technical report, CTO, Atego (2009). http://www.aonix.com/pdf/percwhitepaper_e.pdf
41. Pizlo, F., Ziarek, L., Vitek, J.: Real time Java on resource-constrained platforms with Fiji VM. In: Proceedings of the 7th International Workshop on Java Technologies for Real-Time and Embedded Systems. JTRES 2009, pp. 110–119. ACM, New York (2009)
42. Plsek, A., Zhao, L., Sahin, V.H., Tang, D., Kalibera, T., Vitek, J.: Developing safety critical Java applications with oscj/l0. In: Proceedings of the 8th International Workshop on Java Technologies for Real-Time and Embedded Systems. JTRES 2010, pp. 95–101. ACM, New York (2010)
43. Roscoe, A.W., Richard Hoare, C.A.: The laws of Occam programming. Theor. Comput. Sci. **60**(2), 177–229 (1988)
44. Schoeberl, M., Puffitsch, W., Pedersen, R.U., Huber, B.: Worst-case execution time analysis for a Java processor. Softw. Pract. Experience **40**(6), 507–542 (2010)
45. Søndergaard, H., Korsholm, S.E., Ravn, A.P.: Safety-critical Java for low-end embedded platforms. In: Proceedings of the 10th International Workshop on Java Technologies for Real-Time and Embedded Systems. JTRES 2012, pp. 44–53. ACM, New York (2012)
46. Sundaresan, V., Hendren, L., Razafimahefa, C., Vallée-Rai, R., Lam, P., Gagnon, E., Godin, C.: Practical virtual method call resolution for Java. SIGPLAN Not. **35**(10), 264–280 (2000)
47. Thomsen, B., Leth, L., Kuo, T.-M.: A facile tutorial. In: Montanari, U., Sassone, V. (eds.) CONCUR 1996. LNCS, vol. 1119, pp. 278–298. Springer, Heidelberg (1996)

When to Move to Transfer Nets
On the Limits of Petri Nets as Models for Process Calculi

Gianluigi Zavattaro[⊠]

Department of Computer Science and Engineering, Focus Team,
University of Bologna and INRIA, Mura A. Zamboni 7, 40127 Bologna, Italy
gianluigi.zavattaro@unibo.it

Abstract. Pierpaolo Degano has been an influential pioneer in the investigation of Petri nets as models for concurrent process calculi (see e.g. the well-known seminal work by Degano–De Nicola–Montanari also known as DDM88). In this paper, we address the limits of classical Petri nets by discussing when it is necessary to move to the so-called Transfer nets, in which transitions can also move to a target place all the tokens currently present in a source place. More precisely, we consider a simple calculus of processes that interact by generating/consuming messages into/from a shared repository. For this calculus classical Petri nets can faithfully model the process behavior. Then we present a simple extension with a primitive allowing processes to atomically rename all the data of a given kind. We show that with the addition of such primitive it is necessary to move to Transfer nets to obtain a faithful modeling.

1 Introduction

The study of the relationship between two relevant computational models like process calculi and Petri nets has attracted a lot of attention within the concurrency theory community since the second half of the 80s. One of the initial motivations for associating to process calculi a Petri net semantics was to enrich the formers with a truly concurrent semantics, instead of the interleaving semantics usually given in terms of a labeled transition system. In particular, one of the most influential work along this line of research is the seminal work by Degano, De Nicola, and Montanari [7] which was inspired by the observation that in Milner's CCS [15], under the classical interleaving semantics, *"causal dependencies remain non-recoverable (for instance the behavior of $\alpha|\beta + \alpha.\beta$ and that of $\alpha|\beta$ cannot be differentiated)"*. Another motivation for equipping process calculi with Petri net semantics is to resort to analysis or decidability results well-known for Petri nets. For instance, in [4] Petri nets were used to prove the decidability of termination in a CCS-like process calculus with asynchronous communication via a shared repository of data. In fact, Petri nets represent one of the most interesting models for infinite state systems in which properties like reachability, coverability, boundedness, as well as many others, are still decidable (see [10] for a nicely written and comprehensive survey about decidability results for Petri nets).

© Springer International Publishing Switzerland 2015
C. Bodei et al. (Eds.): Degano Festschrift, LNCS 9465, pp. 339–353, 2015.
DOI: 10.1007/978-3-319-25527-9_22

In this paper we focus on a specific research problem that we have encountered in several papers dedicated to the study of the decidability of properties, like *termination* and *divergence*, in several classes of process calculi. By termination in this paper we mean the existence of a completed finite computation, while by divergence we mean the existence of an infinite computation. The proof technique that we frequently adopted is based on translations from the process calculi of interest to Petri nets, in order to resort to already known decidability results for Petri nets.

In the already mentioned paper [4] we considered a calculus of processes communicating via a common data repository by means of output, input, read, and test for absence primitives. We first proved that, if data are guaranteed to be in the data space immediately after the execution of an output operation, the calculus is Turing complete (hence termination is undecidable). On the contrary, if output operations are asynchronous, in the sense that emitted data become available only after an unpredictable delay, the calculus is no longer Turing powerful because termination turns out to be decidable. The proof exploited a non-trivial Petri net semantics for the asynchronous version of the calculus.

In other papers we had to consider extended versions of Petri nets. For instance, in [5] we considered a similar calculus with processes communicating via a common data space, but with a *notify* primitive instead of the test for absence. The notify operation allows processes to register their interest in the emission of a given kind of datum; when such a datum is produced, all the registered processes receive a corresponding notification. For this calculus, we considered Petri nets with Transfer arcs, that are arcs able to move all the tokens present in a source place to a corresponding target place. On the contrary, in [6] we considered Petri nets with Reset arcs, which are used to remove all the tokens currently available in a place. In that paper, we considered a timed version of shared data space communication, in which data have an associated time out and must be cancelled when they expire. More recently, in [8] we considered again Transfer Petri nets, but in the rather different context of BioAmbients, a calculus where processes are placed inside nested locations and can execute operations for entering, exiting or merging ambients.

Intuitively, in that papers we had to move to extended versions of Petri nets due to the difficulty in the definition of appropriate encodings of the considered calculi into classical Petri nets. The increased expressive power of Transfer or Reset nets w.r.t. classical Petri nets has been investigated in [9]. In particular, we have that properties like reachability and termination are decidable for classical Petri nets while this is not the case for Transfer and Reset nets; properties like boundedness is decidable for classical and Transfer nets while this is not the case for Reset nets; and finally properties like divergence or coverability are decidable for all of these classes of nets.[1]

---

[1] In [9] a slightly different terminology is used: termination refers to the guarantee that all the computations completes, thus corresponding to the negation of the property that we call divergence in this paper.

From a formal point of view, there are cases that strictly require to move from classical to extended Petri nets to equip a process calculus with a faithful Petri net semantics. To clarify this specific point, in this paper we fully formalize in a simplified setting one of these cases. More precisely, we identify a basic calculus of processes performing input and output operations on a shared data space, extended with a primitive for renaming all the data of a given kind. We first show that for the basic version of the calculus without renaming, it is possible to define a faithful encoding by using classical Petri nets. By faithful encoding, here we mean that there exists a one-to-one correspondence between process reductions in the calculus and transition firings in the Petri net. Then we move to the version of the calculus with the renaming primitive, and we show that termination is undecidable for this version of the calculus. This undecidability result shows that there exists no recursive encoding from the calculus to classical Petri nets that preserves and reflects at least termination. Then we consider Transfer Petri nets, and we show that with this extended version of Petri nets it is again possible to define a faithful encoding. This also proves that divergence, as well as boundedness and coverability, are decidable for the calculus with the renaming primitive.

Structure of the Paper. In Sect. 2 we define the DS calculus, the initial version of our language for processes communicating via input and output operations on a common repository, and we present a faithful modeling of the DS calculus into classical Petri nets. In Sect. 3, inspired by the *copy-collect* primitive proposed in [17], we define the RenDS calculus that includes a new primitive $ren(a, b)$ that renames to b all the instances of a in the data space. For this calculus we prove the undecidability of termination (hence also the impossibility to equip RenDS with a termination preserving classical Petri net semantics) and then we show a faithful modeling in terms of Transfer Petri nets. Section 4 draws some concluding remarks.

2 The DS Calculus

In this section we present the syntax and the semantics of a simple calculus of processes communicating by introducing and consuming data into/from a shared repository.

Definition 1 (Processes). *Let Name, ranged over by a, b, ..., be a denumerable set of names. Processes are defined by the following grammar:*

$$\alpha ::= in(a) \quad | \quad out(a)$$
$$P ::= \sum_{i \in I} \alpha_i.P_i \quad | \quad !\alpha.P \quad | \quad P|P$$

The basic process actions are $in(a)$ and $out(a)$ denoting the consumption/emission of one instance of datum a from/into the shared data space. The term $\sum_{i \in I} \alpha_i.P_i$ denotes a process ready to perform any of the action α_i, and then proceed by executing the corresponding continuation P_i. We use $\mathbf{0}$ to denote such process in case $I = \emptyset$, and we will usually omit trailing **0**. The replicated process $!\alpha.P$ performs an initial action α and then spawns the continuation P by keeping $!\alpha.P$ in parallel. Two parallel processes P and Q are denoted with $P|Q$.

Example 1. As an example, we consider a simple producer-consumer system:

$$!in(prod).out(job).in(done).(\ out(prod) + out(end)\ )\ |$$
$$!in(cons).(\ in(job).out(done).out(cons) + in(end)\ )$$

The producer process is triggered by a *prod* datum; it produces a *job* request, waits for the corresponding *done* message, and then nondeterministically decides whether to continue with another job production phase or complete by emitting the message *end*. The consumer process is triggered by a *cons* datum; it consumes a *job* request, produces the corresponding *done* messages, and repeats until an *end* message is received instead of a *job* request.

A system includes also a shared data space where data are stored and consumed.

Definition 2 (Systems). *A system is a pair $\langle P, S \rangle$ where P is a process and S is a multiset over Name.*

In the following, $\uplus$ stands for multiset union and with $S(a)$ we denote the number of instances of a in the multiset S.

Example 2. Let P be the process defined in Example 1. The system

$$\langle P, \{prod, cons\} \rangle$$

represents the initial state of the produced-consumer system where the data space contains the two *prod* and *cons* data necessary to initially trigger the producer and consumer processes, respectively.

In order to define the operational semantics of systems we first define a labeled transition system on processes which indicates the possible input and output actions, and then we define a transition relation on systems which defines the effect of the execution of process actions on the shared data space.

Definition 3 (Process semantics). *The semantics of processes is defined by a labeled transition system on processes with two kinds of labels: $in(a)$ and $out(a)$. The transition system is the least one satisfying the axioms and rules reported in Table 1.*

The PRE rule simply allows a sum process to execute one of its initial action and then continue with the corresponding continuation. REPL allows $!\alpha.P$ to execute α, spawn an instance of the continuation P, and keep $!\alpha.P$ in parallel. Finally, PAR allows a parallel process to execute an action.

We can now complete the definition of the operational semantics taking into account systems.

Table 1. The transition system for processes (symmetric rule of PAR omitted).

$$\text{PRE}: \quad \cfrac{j \in I}{\sum_{i \in I} \alpha_i.P_i \xrightarrow{\alpha_j} P_j} \qquad\qquad \text{REPL}: \; !\alpha.P \xrightarrow{\alpha} !\alpha.P \mid P \qquad \text{PAR}: \; \cfrac{P \xrightarrow{\alpha} P'}{P|Q \xrightarrow{\alpha} P'|Q}$$

Table 2. The reduction relation for systems (brackets in singletons are omitted).

$$\cfrac{P \xrightarrow{in(a)} P'}{\langle P, \mathcal{S} \uplus a \rangle \to \langle P', \mathcal{S} \rangle} \qquad\qquad \cfrac{P \xrightarrow{out(a)} P'}{\langle P, \mathcal{S} \rangle \to \langle P', \mathcal{S} \uplus a \rangle}$$

Definition 4 (System semantics). *The semantics of systems is defined by the minimal transition system satisfying the rules in Table 2.*

The transitions for systems simply allows processes to consume and introduce data from/to the shared data space.

Example 3. Let $\langle P, \{prod, cons\} \rangle$ be the producer-consumer system defined in Example 2. According to the transition system in Definition 4, such system can generate sequences of emissions and consumptions of *prod* and *cons* messages, combined with the emissions and consumptions of *job* and *done* data. Such sequences of actions could be either infinite, or –in case they are maximal, i.e., they cannot be extended– terminating with the production and consumption of an *end* datum. In this last case, the data space is guaranteed to be finally empty because all the *job* requests are consumed, as well as all the corresponding *done* acknowledgement, and also the final *end* message is removed.

We now consider a Petri net semantics for this simple calculus. We first recall the classical definition of Petri nets, then we discuss how to use them to model the behavior of systems of our DS calculus.

Definition 5 (Petri nets). *A Petri net is a tuple $N = (S, T, m_0)$, where S and T are finite sets of* places *and* transitions, *respectively. A finite multiset over the set S of places is called a* marking, *and m_0 is the* initial marking. *Given a marking m and a place p, we say that the place p contains a number of tokens equal to the number of instances of p in m (written $m(p)$). A transition $t \in T$ is a pair of markings denoted with ${}^\bullet t$ and $t^\bullet$ (the* preset *and* postset *of the transition, respectively). A transition t (also denoted with ${}^\bullet t \rightarrowtail t^\bullet$) can fire in the marking m if ${}^\bullet t \subseteq m$ (where $\subseteq$ is multiset inclusion); upon transition firing the new marking of the net becomes $n = (m \setminus {}^\bullet t) \uplus t^\bullet$ (where $\setminus$ and $\uplus$ are the difference and union operators for multisets, respectively). This is written as $m \mapsto n$.*

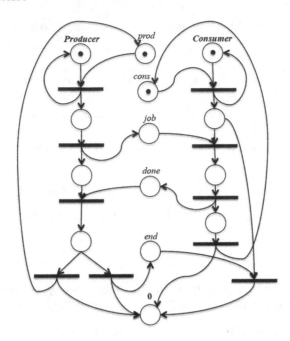

Fig. 1. Petri net for the producer-consumer example

Petri nets are graphically depicted by representing places with circles and transitions with rectangles. Edges connect circles to rectangles: an edge from a circle to a rectangle indicates a place in the preset of a transition, while an edge from a rectangle to a circle indicates a place in the postset of a transition. Dots inside circles represent tokens inside places.

Example 4. In Fig. 1 we depict a Petri net representing the behavior of the producer-consumer system defined in Example 3. The behavior of the producer process is reported on the left, while the consumer is on the right. Places in the middle of the figure represent the possible data in the data space (*prod, cons, job, done* and *end*) and the trailing empty **0** process.

We now discuss how to translate systems of the DS calculus into Petri nets. The idea is to represent sequential processes and data by means of tokens inside corresponding places. Sequential processes are of two possible kinds: $\sum_{i \in I} \alpha_i.P_i$ and $!\alpha.P$. Parallel processes will be represented by a multiset of tokens, one for

Table 3. Process decomposition function

$$dec(\textstyle\sum_{i \in I} \alpha_i.P_i) = \{\textstyle\sum_{i \in I} \alpha_i.P_i\} \quad dec(!\alpha.P) = \{!\alpha.P\} \quad dec(P|Q) = dec(P) \uplus dec(Q)$$

Table 4. Petri net transitions

$$\texttt{IN}: \quad \{\textstyle\sum_{i \in I} \alpha_i.P_i, a\} \rightarrowtail dec(P_j) \quad j \in I, \alpha_j = in(a)$$

$$\texttt{OUT}: \quad \{\textstyle\sum_{i \in I} \alpha_i.P_i\} \rightarrowtail dec(P_j) \uplus \{a\} \quad j \in I, \alpha_j = out(a)$$

$$\texttt{REPIN}: \quad \{!in(a).P, a\} \rightarrowtail dec(P) \uplus \{!in(a).P\}$$

$$\texttt{REPOUT}: \quad \{!out(a).P\} \rightarrowtail dec(P) \uplus \{a\} \uplus \{!out(a).P\}$$

each sequential process composed in parallel. Formally, let P be a process, with $dec(P)$ we denote the multiset defined in Table 3. The possible Petri net transitions, denoted with $\mathcal{T}$, are defined in Table 4. The execution of an $in(a)$ action consumes a token from place a, while an $out(a)$ action produces such a token. After execution of the action, tokens are produced in the places corresponding to the process continuation. Notice that the transitions involving the replicated processes $!in(a).P$ or $!out(a).P$ consume and then reproduce the corresponding tokens; in this way the tokens remain available for future transitions involving those replicated processes.

Definition 6. *Let* $\langle P, \mathcal{S} \rangle$ *be a system. We define the Petri net* $Net(P, \mathcal{S}) = (P, T, \boldsymbol{m_0})$ *as follows:*

- $S = \{Q \mid Q \text{ is a sequential process in } P\} \cup \{a \mid a \text{ occurs in } \mathcal{S} \text{ or in } P\}$
- $T = \{c \rightarrowtail p \in \mathcal{T} \mid dom(o) \subseteq S\}$
- $\boldsymbol{m_0} = dec(P) \uplus \mathcal{S}$

Example 5. It is easy to see that the Petri net in Fig. 1 corresponds to $Net(P, \{prod, cons\})$ where $\langle P, \{prod, cons\} \rangle$ is the system in Example 2.

The strict correspondence between the process calculus and the Petri net semantics is formalized as follows. We omit the proof of this correspondence result because standard.

Proposition 1. *Let* $\langle P, \mathcal{S} \rangle$ *be a system, and* $Net(P, \mathcal{S}) = (P, T, \boldsymbol{m_0})$ *be the corresponding Petri net. Let Q be a process composed of sequential processes occurring in P, and $\mathcal{V}$ be a multiset of data occurring in P or in $\mathcal{S}$. We have that* $\langle Q, \mathcal{V} \rangle \to \langle Q', \mathcal{V}' \rangle$ *if and only if* $dec(Q) \uplus \mathcal{V} \mapsto dec(Q') \uplus \mathcal{V}'$ *in* $Net(P, \mathcal{S})$.

3   The RenDS Calculus: Shared Data Space with Renaming

We now consider an extension of the DS calculus with a primitive for renaming all the data of a given kind. This renaming mechanism is inspired by the *copy-collect* primitive proposed in [17]. In that paper, a language with multiple data spaces is considered, and the *copy-collect* primitive is used to move all the data

matching a given pattern from a source space to a target space. As in DS we
have only one data space, we adapt this primitive by considering an operation
$ren(a, b)$ which changes to b all the instances of datum a in the data space. We
call RenDS this extended calculus.

The syntax of processes is the same as in Definition 1 with the addition of a
new action:

$$\alpha ::= \quad \cdots \quad | \quad ren(a, b)$$

Example 6. We now consider an alternative version of the producer-consumer
example in which the producer can repeatedly produce job requests without
waiting for the indication that the previous job request has been accomplished.
When the consumer starts, only the job requests already issued will be served
while subsequent requests will remain pending.

$$!in(prod).out(job).(\ in(done)\ |\ out(prod)\ )\ |$$
$$in(cons).ren(job, todo).(\ !in(todo).out(done)\ |\ in(prod)\ )$$

The producer process is triggered by a *prod* datum; it produces a *job* request
and then waits for the *done* message, but in parallel reproduces the *prod* datum
to repeatedly issue an arbitrary number of requests. The consumer process is
triggered by a *cons* datum; as a first action renames all the *job* requests in
todo, and then it serves the *todo* activities. Subsequent *job* requests will remain
pending. The consumer has also the ability to stop the producer by consuming
the *prod* datum.

The semantics for processes is defined as in Table 1 with the addition of the
label $ren(a, b)$, while the semantics of systems is defined by the two rules in
Table 2 with the addition of the following one for the renaming primitive:

$$\frac{P \xrightarrow{ren(a,b)} P' \quad S'(a) = 0 \quad S'(b) = S(a) + S(b) \quad \forall c \notin \{a, b\}.S'(c) = S(c)}{\langle P, S \rangle \to \langle P', S' \rangle}$$

Example 7. Let P be the process defined in Example 6. The initial system is
$\langle P, \{prod, cons\} \rangle$ with *prod* and *cons* in the data space, to trigger the producer
and the consumer, respectively. It is worth to note that this system can either
have an infinite computation in which infinitely many *job* requests are issued, or
it terminates in such a way that the final system will contain the same number of
instances of the $in(done)$ process and of the *job* datum, representing the pending
requests issued after the consumer transforms the current *job* requests into *todo*
data.

We now consider the problem of modeling with Petri nets the processes of the
new calculus RenDS. Intuitively, this translation is not easy to be defined due to
the impossibility to perform in the Petri net "global" actions that act atomically
on all the tokens currently present in a place. In fact, in classical nets, transitions
always consume the same amount of tokens. On the contrary, an operation like

$ren(a, b)$ has an effect which is dependent on the current system state, because all the a data must atomically be renamed into b.

In order to formalize this negative result, i.e., classical Petri nets are not sufficiently expressive to model the new calculus with renaming, we proceed as follows. We start from the observation that the existence of a terminating computation is decidable for Petri nets [13], then we prove that termination is undecidable in RenDS. Hence we can conclude that there exists no computable termination preserving encoding of RenDS into classical Petri nets. It is worth to observe that for the DS calculus in Sect. 2, the presented encoding into Petri nets obviously preserves termination (trivial corollary of Proposition 1), hence termination is decidable in DS.

We prove the undecidability of termination in RenDS by reduction from the halting problem in Random Access Machines (RAMs). A RAM [18], denoted in the following with R, is a computational model composed of a finite set of registers $r_1, \ldots, r_n$, that can hold arbitrary large natural numbers, and by a program composed by indexed instructions $(1 : I_1), \ldots, (m : I_m)$, that is a sequence of simple numbered instructions, like arithmetical operations (on the contents of registers) or conditional jumps. An internal state of a RAM is given by $(i, c_1, \ldots, c_n)$ where i is the program counter indicating the next instruction to be executed, and $c_1, \ldots, c_n$ are the current contents of the registers $r_1, \ldots, r_n$, respectively.

Without loss of generality, we assume that the registers contain the value 0 at the beginning and at the end of the computation, and that the execution of the program begins with the first instruction $(1 : I_1)$. The assumption on the initially empty registers is justified by the possibility to add to programs a prologue that introduces the desired values in the registers, while the assumption on the finally empty registers is justified by the possibility to add to programs a conclusion that decrements all the registers to 0 before halting. In other words, the initial configuration is $(1, 0, \ldots, 0)$. The computation continues by executing the other instructions in sequence, unless a jump instruction is encountered. The execution stops when the instruction $Halt$ is reached. More formally, we indicate by $(i, c_1, \ldots, c_n) \to_R (i', c_1', \ldots, c_n')$ the fact that the configuration of the RAM R changes from $(i, c_1, \ldots, c_n)$ to $(i', c_1', \ldots, c_n')$ after the execution of the i-th instruction.

In [16] it is shown that the following two instructions are sufficient to model every recursive function:

- $(i : Succ(r_j))$: adds 1 to the content of register r_j;
- $(i : DecJump(r_j, s))$: if the contents of register r_j is not zero then decreases it by 1 and go to the next instruction, otherwise jumps to instruction s.

We start by presenting how to encode RAM instructions into processes of the RenDS calculus:

$$\begin{aligned}
[\![(i : Succ(r_j))]\!] \quad &: \ !in(p_i).out(r_j).out(p_{i+1}) \\
[\![(i : DecJump(r_j, s))]\!] &: \ !in(p_i).(\ in(r_j).out(p_{i+1}) \ + \ ren(r_j, loop).out(p_s) \ ) \\
[\![(i : Halt)]\!] \quad &: \ in(p_i).!in(loop).out(loop)
\end{aligned}$$

The idea is to represent the content of the register r_j with a corresponding number of instances of the datum r_j in the data space. The program counter is modeled by a datum p_i indicating that the i-th instruction is the next one to be executed. The modeling of the i-th instruction always starts with the consumption of the p_i datum. An increment instruction on r_j simply produces one datum r_j, while a decrement consumes such a datum. A faithful modeling of a test for zero on r_j should be able to detect the absence of data r_j. As there are no primitives for performing such a test, we consider a nondeterministic modeling according to which a test for zero on r_j could be successful even if the data space contains some r_j instances. But if this occurs, we use the renaming primitive to atomically rename all the currently present r_j data into *loop* data. The presence of *loop* data forbids the possibility for the RAM modeling to terminate: in fact, the encoding of a *Halt* instruction enters in an infinite loop in case there is at least one datum *loop* in the data space.

We now present the full definition of our encoding. Let R be a RAM with m instructions, and let $(i, c_1, \ldots, c_n)$ be one of its configurations. With

$$[\![(i, c_1, \ldots, c_n)]\!]_R = \langle \prod_{1 \leq i \leq m} [\![(i : I_i)]\!], \{p_i, \underbrace{r_1, \cdots, r_1}_{c_1 \ times}, \cdots, \underbrace{r_n, \cdots, r_n}_{c_n \ times}\} \rangle$$

we denote the system representing the configuration $(i, c_1, \ldots, c_n)$.

We now prove that our encoding is termination preserving, from which we conclude the undecidability of termination for the RenDS process calculus.

Theorem 1. *Let R be a RAM. We have that R terminates if and only if $[\![(1, 0, \ldots, 0)]\!]_R$ terminates.*

Proof. We start with the *only if* part. Assume R terminates. We have that $[\![(1, 0, \ldots, 0)]\!]_R$ can faithfully reproduce the terminating computation of R without producing any *loop* data. This computation of $[\![(1, 0, \ldots, 0)]\!]_R$ terminates because the encoding of the *Halt* instruction definitely consumes the program counter datum, and remains blocked trying to consume a *loop* datum.

We now consider the *if* part. Assume that $[\![(1, 0, \ldots, 0)]\!]_R$ terminates. Every terminating computation completes by reaching the encoding of a *Halt* instruction (all the other instructions are replicated and reproduce the program counter datum before terminating) and never produce any *loop* datum (otherwise the encoding of the *Halt* instruction perform an infinite loop). The RAM R can execute an equivalent computation reaching a *Halt* instruction because the increment and decrement instructions can be obviously mimicked, as well as the test for zero actions. In fact, such actions are surely executed when the tested register is empty, otherwise a *loop* datum would have been produced. □

As a trivial corollary, from the undecidability of the halting problem for RAMs we can conclude the undecidability of termination for the RenDS calculus.

The undecidability of termination implies the impossibility to define a termination preserving encoding of the RenDS calculus into Petri nets. We can however obtain a correspondence result if we move to Petri nets with Transfer arcs [12], allowing for the atomic movement of all the tokens currently present in a source place to a target place. Transfer nets represent an interesting extension of Petri nets; in [9] it has been proven that they are more expressive than classical Petri nets because reachability (as well as termination) is no longer decidable, while other properties like divergence, boundedness or coverability are still decidable.

Definition 7 (Petri nets with Transfer arcs). *A Petri net with Transfer arcs is defined as a Petri net $N = (S, T, \boldsymbol{m_0})$ with the difference that the transitions t in T are now triples, containing besides the preset $\bullet t$ and the postset $t \bullet$ also a partial function t_f from places to places (transitions are now denoted with $\bullet t \xrightarrow{t_f} t\bullet$). Given a transition $\bullet t \xrightarrow{t_f} t\bullet$ we assume that $dom(t_f) \cap t\bullet = \emptyset$, i.e. the places in the preset of a transition t, cannot be source places for transfer arcs of t. As for Petri nets, a transition t can fire in the marking $\boldsymbol{m}$ if $\bullet t \subseteq \boldsymbol{m}$; upon transition firing the new marking becomes $\boldsymbol{n}$ where*

$$\boldsymbol{n}(p) = \begin{cases} \boldsymbol{m}(p) - \bullet t(p) + t\bullet(p) + \sum_{p'.t_f(p')=p} \boldsymbol{m}(p') & \text{if } p \notin dom(t_f) \\ t\bullet(p) + \sum_{p'.t_f(p')=p} \boldsymbol{m}(p') & \text{if } p \in dom(t_f) \end{cases}$$

Intuitively, for places that are not sources of transfer arcs, besides the usual preset and postset modifications, there is also the possibility to add tokens transferred from corresponding source places of transfer arcs. For places which are sources of transfer arcs, only the new introduced tokens must be taken into account because the previously present tokens are consumed by the corresponding transfer arc. Also in this case, the effect of the firing of a transition is written $\boldsymbol{m} \mapsto \boldsymbol{n}$.

Typically, transfer arcs are depicted as arcs from places to places, connected to the corresponding transition by a line.

Example 8. In Fig. 2 we depict a Petri net representing the behavior of the producer-consumer system defined in Example 7. The behavior of the producer process is reported on the left, while the consumer is on the right. Places in the middle of the figure represent the possible data in the data space (*prod, cons, job, todo, done* and *end*) and the trailing empty **0** process. Notice the transfer arc from the *job* to the *todo* place, used by the consumer to take under consideration all and only those job requests that have been already issued when the consumer starts.

We now discuss how to translate systems of the RenDS calculus into Petri nets with Transfer arcs. This translation is obtained as simple extension of the one in Definition 6. Sequential processes and the decomposition function is defined exactly as for the previous DS calculus. The unique difference is at the level of transitions: we simply add transitions to model the renaming of data from a to b, with a transfer arc from the place a to the place b. All other actions are modeled as already done for the DS calculus. The new set of transitions, denoted with $\mathcal{T}_{ren}$, is defined in Table 4 plus the new rules in Table 5.

Definition 8. *Let $\langle P, S \rangle$ be a system of the RenDS calculus. We define the Petri net with Transfer arcs $Net_{ren}(P, S) = (P, T, \boldsymbol{m_0})$ as follows:*

Table 5. Petri net transitions for renaming

$$\{\textstyle\sum_{i\in I}\alpha_i.P_i\} \overset{\{a\mapsto b\}}{\rightarrowtail} dec(P_j) \quad j\in I, \alpha_j = ren(a,b)$$

$$\{!ren(a,b).P\} \overset{\{a\mapsto b\}}{\rightarrowtail} dec(P) \uplus \{!ren(a,b).P\}$$

- $S = \{Q \mid Q$ is a sequential process in $P\} \cup \{a \mid a$ occurs in S or in $P\}$
- $T = \{c \overset{t}{\rightarrowtail} p \in \mathcal{T}_{ren} \mid dom(c) \subseteq S\}$
- $m_0 = dec(P) \uplus S$

Example 9. It is easy to see that the Transfer Petri net depicted in Fig. 1 corresponds to $Net_{ren}(P, \{prod, cons\})$ where $\langle P, \{prod, cons\}\rangle$ is the system in Example 7.

We conclude by formalizing the correspondence between the operational semantics of the RenDS calculus and the corresponding Petri net with Transfer arcs. Also in this case we omit the proof of this correspondence result because standard.

Proposition 2. *Let* $\langle P, S\rangle$ *be a system of the* RenDS *calculus, and* $Net_{ren}(P, S) = (P, T, m_0)$ *be the corresponding Petri net with Transfer arcs.*

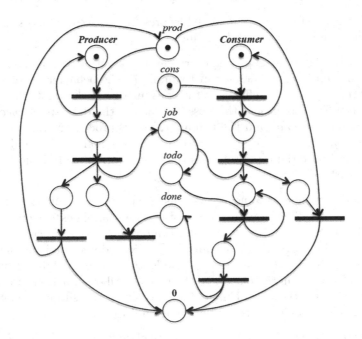

Fig. 2. Petri net for the producer-consumer example with renaming

Let Q be a process composed of sequential processes occurring in P, and $\mathcal{V}$ be a multiset of data occurring in P or in $\mathcal{S}$. We have that $\langle Q, \mathcal{V} \rangle \rightarrow \langle Q', \mathcal{V}' \rangle$ if and only if $dec(Q) \uplus \mathcal{V} \mapsto dec(Q') \uplus \mathcal{V}'$ in $Net_{ren}(P, \mathcal{S})$.

4 Conclusion

The relationship between traditional concurrency models like process calculi and Petri nets has been one of those research topics, within the concurrency theory community, to which Pierpaolo Degano gave a fundamental initial contribution (see the seminal work [7]). A detailed description of the extremely vast literature concerning the relationship between process calculi and Petri nets is out of the scope of this paper. Here, we simply recall few relatively recent relevant papers.

In [1] a Petri net semantics is used to prove the decidability of termination (called convergence in that paper) in a version of CCS with replication instead of recursion, in which name restriction –usually called also name generation– cannot occur inside replication. This syntactic limitation guarantees that only boundedly many distinct names can be generated. In [14] a precise relationship between name passing calculi –in particular the π-calculus– and classical Petri nets has been established, by showing which are the precise restrictions to be imposed to name-generation and name-passing mechanisms in order to resort to a Petri net semantics. Open nets are instead used in [2] to equip with a net semantics an asynchronous version of CCS with replication and a limited form of restriction that cannot occur under the scope of a replication. Open nets are classical Petri nets including open places and the possibility for distinct nets to interact on open places. The advantage of Open nets is that they allow for a compositional definition of the net encoding. Moreover, they naturally support the modeling of restriction: free names (i.e. non restricted names) are modeled with open places while bound names (i.e. restricted names) are modeled with private places.

In this paper, we have focused on those cases in which in order to faithfully model a process calculus it is necessary to consider extended versions of Petri nets. This happens, for instance, when the process calculus includes global synchronization mechanisms. Classical Petri net transitions, in fact, always consume a predefined amount of tokens from the input places, thus the number of consumed tokens is independent from the current token distribution. Global synchronization mechanisms, on the contrary, are defined as functions depending on the current (global) state of the system.

In particular, we have formalized a simple data-centric calculus for which it is possible to define a faithful classical Petri net semantics, and then we extend it with a simple primitive that globally renames all the data of a given kind that are currently available. We prove that the addition of this global primitive strictly requires to move to an extended class of Petri nets (in this case we consider Transfer Petri nets) in order to define a faithful net modeling. Formally speaking, the encodings that we define between a process calculus and a Petri net have a one-to-one correspondence between reductions in the process calculus and transition firings in the Petri net. The impossibility to define an encoding, on the contrary, consider also weaker encodings in which only termination is preserved (i.e. a process terminates if and only if its encoding in the Petri net has a terminating computation).

Translating process calculi into Petri nets is useful because it allows for the application of Petri net analysis techniques, or decidability results, back to the initial process calculi. It is interesting to observe that there are cases in which also extended versions of Petri nets fail, like for instance in [3]. In that paper, a process calculus with replication and name generation is defined, for which it is possible to produce unboundedly many different active processes due to the dynamic generation of new names. The presence of unboundedly many different processes forbids the application of Petri nets; in fact, Petri nets only has a predefined finite amount of possible(and transitions). In that paper, the decidability of divergence was proved by resorting to Well Structured Transition Systems (WSTS) [11], a meta model which is more general than Petri nets (and their usual extensions) and for which a rich set of interesting properties like divergence, coverability, or those expressible by means of simple temporal logic, are proved to be decidable.

References

1. Aranda, J., Valencia, F.D., Versari, C.: On the expressive power of restriction and priorities in CCS with replication. In: de Alfaro, L. (ed.) FOSSACS 2009. LNCS, vol. 5504, pp. 242–256. Springer, Heidelberg (2009)
2. Baldan, P., Bonchi, F., Gadducci, F., Monreale, G.V.: Modular encoding of synchronous and asynchronous interactions using open petri nets. Sci. Comput. Program. **109**, 96–124 (2015)
3. Busi, N., Gabbrielli, M., Zavattaro, G.: On the expressive power of recursion, replication and iteration in process calculi. Math. Struct. Comput. Sci. **19**(6), 1191–1222 (2009)
4. Busi, N., Gorrieri, R., Zavattaro, G.: On the expressiveness of linda coordination primitives. Inf. Comput. **156**(1–2), 90–121 (2000)
5. Busi, N., Zavattaro, G.: On the expressiveness of event notification in data-driven coordination languages. In: Smolka, G. (ed.) ESOP 2000. LNCS, vol. 1782, p. 41. Springer, Heidelberg (2000)
6. Busi, N., Zavattaro, G.: Expired data collection in shared dataspaces. Theor. Comput. Sci. **3**(298), 529–556 (2003)
7. Degano, P., De Nicola, R., Montanari, U.: A distributed operational semantics for CCS based on condition/event systems. Acta Inf. **26**(1/2), 59–91 (1988)
8. Delzanno, G., Zavattaro, G.: Reachability problems in bioambients. Theor. Comput. Sci. **431**, 56–74 (2012)
9. Dufourd, C., Finkel, A., Schnoebelen, P.: Reset nets between decidability and undecidability. In: Larsen, K.G., Skyum, S., Winskel, G. (eds.) ICALP 1998. LNCS, vol. 1443, p. 103. Springer, Heidelberg (1998)
10. Esparza, J., Nielsen, M.: Decidability issues for petri nets - a survey. Bull. EATCS **52**, 244–262 (1994)
11. Finkel, A., Raskin, J., Samuelides, M., Begin, L.V.: Monotonic extensions of petri nets: Forward and backward search revisited. Electr. Notes Theor. Comput. Sci. **68**(6), 85–106 (2002)

12. Ciardo, G.: Petri nets with marking-dependent arc cardinality: Properties and analysis. In: Valette, R. (ed.) ICATPN 1994. LNCS, vol. 815, pp. 179–198. Springer, Heidelberg (1994)

13. Mayr, E.W.: An algorithm for the general petri net reachability problem. In: Proceedings of the 13th Annual ACM Symposium on Theory of Computing, 11–13 May 1981, Milwaukee, Wisconsin, USA, pp. 238–246. ACM (1981)

14. Meyer, R., Gorrieri, R.: On the relationship between π-calculus and finite place/transition Petri nets. In: Bravetti, M., Zavattaro, G. (eds.) CONCUR 2009. LNCS, vol. 5710, pp. 463–480. Springer, Heidelberg (2009)

15. Milner, R.: Communication and Concurrency. PHI Series in Computer Science. Prentice Hall, Upper Saddle River (1989)

16. Minsky, M.L.: Computation: Finite and Infinite Machines. Prentice-Hall, Englewood Cliffs (1967)

17. Rowstron, A.I.T., Wood, A.: Solving the linda multiple rd problem using the copy-collect primitive. Sci. Comput. Program. **31**(2–3), 335–358 (1998)

18. Shepherdson, J.C., Sturgis, J.E.: Computability of recursive functions. J. ACM **10**, 217–255 (1963)

ℓ: An Imperative DSL to Stochastically Simulate Biological Systems

Roberto Zunino[1,2]([✉]), Đurica Nikolić[2,4], Corrado Priami[1,2],
Ozan Kahramanoğulları[1,2], and Tommaso Schiavinotto[2,3]

[1] Università degli Studi di Trento, Trento, Italy
[2] The Microsoft Research - University of Trento Centre for Computational
and Systems Biology, Rovereto, TN, Italy
roberto.zunino@unitn.it
[3] U-Hopper, Trento, Italy
[4] Chair of Software Engineering, ETH Zurich, Zurich, Switzerland

Abstract. Language-based modelling of biological systems is a growing field of research. Many proofs of concept have been published in the last decade. We propose a domain specific language, imperative in style, to step ahead of proof of concepts. Our DSL is compiled into C# and exploits the benefits of C# optimising compilers to gain in time performance of simulations. We report benchmarks of its implementation relying on a mass-action model of the MAPK cascade and a Michaelis-Menten model of the one-carbon metabolism.

1 Introduction

Systems biology is a growing field in which lab experiments and computational activities are increasingly integrated [20,22,23,30]. Modelling and simulation is used to better understand the dynamics of regulatory, signalling and metabolic networks. Simulation techniques roughly span along two axis: deterministic/stochastic and qualitative/quantitative techniques. In this paper we fix our context in stochastic, quantitative approaches.

There are many formalisms that can be adopted to represent biological systems. Petri nets with their stochastic variants are surely the first formalism adopted for simulating interacting systems [25,27] and have been then applied to biological systems as well [19]. The graphical formalism of Petri nets is appealing and easy to visualize, but it makes it difficult to exploit compositionality of nets to build models incrementally. Another modelling technique is based on the chemical reaction formalism that lists all the reactions that a system can perform, i.e. on reaction networks (see [2] for an introduction). This formalism is easy to read, but it suffers the combinatorial explosion problem that also classical ODE systems have (a species/a variable is needed for any state a component of the system can pass through and this number is exponential with respect to the binding/unbinding interactions) [9]. Among the main formalisms of this class we mention P-systems [32]. Starting with the stochastic π-calculus [29], stochastic process algebras emerged as a language-based modelling formalism

© Springer International Publishing Switzerland 2015
C. Bodei et al. (Eds.): Degano Festschrift, LNCS 9465, pp. 354–374, 2015.
DOI: 10.1007/978-3-319-25527-9_23

for biology [1,3,5,28,31]. Kappa [7,8] has a special role, because it contributed to the rule-based modelling approach mainly represented by BNG [13]. Similarly, we mention beta-binders [31] and BlenX [10,12], because they are evolutions of the stochastic π-calculus and have inspired our DSL. We further refine our reference context, considering language-based modelling formalisms for stochastic, quantitative simulation of biological systems.

We propose a new language (ℓ), specifically designed to model and simulate biological systems. ℓ is a DSL with an imperative core, which allows the modeler to equip the representations of biological elements with local states that can be updated when the elements react. ℓ includes rule-based constructs to conveniently specify the most common state updates (e.g., protein association). Other kinds of state updates can still be expressed by providing an imperative subroutine to run whenever a given reaction occurs. The computational model of ℓ is reaction based to improve performance and readability in comparison to process algebras. Indeed, using an imperative core allowed us to efficiently implement ℓ by compiling to C#, thereby avoiding the overhead of interpretation. At the same time, modelers are often more familiar with imperative programming than process algebras.

The underlying computational model of ℓ is based on biological complexes represented as unordered lists of their components with their multiplicity – i.e., as multisets. From the point of view of expressiveness, this poses ℓ in the middle of the spectrum: it is more expressive than formalisms representing only atomic biochemical species, such as Petri nets, while being rougher than languages modeling the full graph of the biochemical bonds in complexes, such as Kappa.

When using biochemical reaction networks, the modeler has to create a unique species for each complex which might be created during the system evolution, and do so ahead of time. This can also require the modeler to manually specify a large amount of reactions, even if many of them are very similar. For instance, to model the fact that a molecule in a complex may have two states (e.g. because one of its sites can become phosphorylated) the modeler has to duplicate the number of species for that complex. In ℓ, the modeler does not have to precompute the species ahead of time, and the redundancies in reactions can often be captured using ℓ rules.

When compared with graph-based languages which use a more detailed representation for complexes, ℓ loses some expressiveness. Still, in practice this is often not a problem since the biological knowledge of the exact binding links between components of a complex is not available most of the time. In such cases, the modeler can be more comfortable to work in a language which does not require to provide more information than what is actually known.

Finally, it is becoming fundamental to trace the location of species within cells when studying the behaviour of their internal networks [21]. We therefore equip our DSL with a simple notion of space and primitives to manage it and to represent the movement of species.

Monte Carlo simulation is a keystone in our reference context and a special role in simulation of biological systems is played by the Gillespie's stochastic simulation algorithm (SSA) [15]. Under some assumptions, Gillespie proved this algorithm to be exact with respect to the chemical master equation when simulating (bio-)chemical reactions. Many variants of this algorithm have been proposed to improve its time performance, e.g. [14,16], sometimes resulting in approximate results [4,17]. In our ℓ implementation, we exploited the exact stochastic simulation algorithm RSSA [35–37], which uses a probabilistic rejection mechanism to speed up simulation. Roughly, RSSA performs a first approximate-but-fast simulation step, and then validates its outcome. With high probability, the step can be accepted as it is; instead, in the remaining cases, it is refined further so that the outcome is exact.

The original contribution of this paper is twofold. First, we present our new DSL for modelling biological systems, and describe its implementation. Second, we benchmark our ℓ implementation against several other tools for biological system modeling and simulation.

2 ℓ Design and Intuition

Building on the extensive experience we gained in the use of stochastic π-calculus and *BlenX* for modelling biological systems, we stepped ahead with five main design goals in mind:

1. *Performance.* The use of modelling and simulation techniques for real biological systems is calling for better performances in comparison to the state of the art of process algebras derived formalisms.
2. *Local states.* Process algebra derived languages and agent-based systems usually manage the change of state of a component of the system by exploiting message passing and differentiation of processes. This mechanism is most of the time too complex to express a change of state from inactive to active of an element for which just a boolean flag would work fine.
3. *Reactions vs. Processes.* Chemical reactions are a well-known formalism to represent biochemical pathways and allows the modeller to discuss models with biologists in an easy way. Process-based representations are not so intuitive when the size of the system grows. This is because of the synchronisation issues and message passing between components that make it difficult to involve biologists in the modelling activities.
4. *Standard programming techniques.* Process algebras is an advanced topic even for computer scientists and their programming technique is not within the background of most of the programmers and modellers. We opted for an imperative style of programming which is familiar to most people having a science background.
5. *Space.* It is becoming increasingly evident that cell compartments cannot be ignored to precisely account for the mechanistic details of biological processes. We opted for primitive notions of space and translocation in ℓ.

The main performance bottleneck of process algebra based formalisms is the need to check structural congruence of processes to count the number of elements of a given type in the system. Since this number is used in computing the transition rates of the system, an optimisation in this step would account for a substantial time saving in simulation. In particular, a main challenge is identifying whether complexes (usually represented as graphs) represent the same species. This amounts to deciding graph isomorphism, because we need to distinguish complexes made of the same elements when they are bound together differently. For instance the complex ABC in which A is bound to B and to C is usually distinct from the one in which B is bound to A and to C even if both complexes are made of A, B and C.

In practice, biologists do not really know how the proteins in a complex are bound together most of the time. If we keep the graph representation of complexes we are forced to do assumptions on the structure of complexes that are not supported by experimental evidence. Therefore, we decided to represent complexes as multisets (a complex may contain more copies of the same element) of boxes (biological components). We lose the expressivity of representing the binding structure of complexes, but we gain in performance.

The advantage of process-based and agent-based systems over chemical reactions is that an interaction can be associated with operations that modify the state of the system depending on the context, possibly modifying agents/components not involved in the firing reaction. Our choice is then representing components as boxes with an internal state that can be manipulated by reaction rules equipped with pieces of imperative code that are run as side conditions of the reaction. We extend the computational model of reactions with the ability of implementing modifications to the system as a consequence of the reaction selected.

Finally, ℓ is designed to be an imperative language so to be familiar to most potential users which are familiar with imperative programming. An additional value of this choice is that we can easily run blocks of ℓ code by compiling them into C# and exploit the optimising compilers as well as the tools developed for C#.

We refer to Fig. 1 to describe the modelling intuition of ℓ and its dynamics. A system is a multiset of complexes (Fig. 1a) - the blue layouts with green ellipsis). A standalone box in the system is represented as a complex of just one element (*e.g.*, the complexes $C4$ and $C5$ in the figure). The type of boxes in Fig. 1(a) are

```
A{x:int,y:real}; B{z:int}; G{}
```

and the complexes are

```
C1[A{x=0,y=.1}, A{x=5,y=.3}, B{z=1}, G{}, G{}],
C2[A{x=3,y=.1}, G{}],
C3[B{z=2}, B{z=2}], C4[G{}], C5[G{}]
```

To simplify the writing of reaction rules we adopt patterns so that we define families of rules that apply to complexes with similar characteristics like *all the complexes that contain at least an A* - this is what the pattern $[A, *]$ in the assoc rule expresses) in the figure to either (b) or (c). In this way, a modeler can write

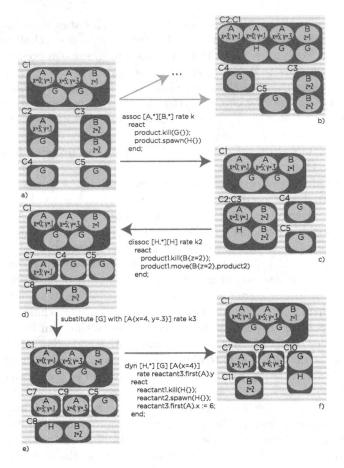

Fig. 1. ℓ intuition. (a) A system is a multiset of complexes ($C1$–$C5$). Boxes may have local variables. Reaction rules are defined on patterns that identify complexes to which they can be applied and have code associated with to modify the system when the reaction is fired. Special variables (product and reactant) are pre-defined to access the elements of the complexes identified by the patterns. More than a complex can satisfy a pattern: (b) and (c) are two possible target states of the first **assoc** rule. The main types of rules are **assoc** to form complexes, **dissoc** to split complexes (from (c) to (d)), **substitute** to replace an element with another one (from (d) to (e)) and **dyn** for general rules (from (e) to (f)). Note that the syntax used in this picture is a simplification just to convey the intuition of the language. The actual model is provided online [6].

a rule such as **assoc** $[A, *]$ $[B, *]$ to express that the presence of A and B in two complexes can cause their association, e.g. because A and B have interaction sites that can cause a bond between them. In such cases, the association rate might simply be a constant (as in Fig. 1) or a more complex formula, which can also depend on the whole complex, including the part matched by the wildcards $*$. In the latter case, the modeler can write their own code to compute the wanted rate.

In some models, the actual condition under which association is possible is more involved that the mere presence of A and B in the complexes. In such cases ℓ allows to restrict association using when followed by the wanted condition, which can be programmed by the modeler.

A complex matches a pattern if there is a bijection between the boxes in the pattern and in the complex. If the pattern contains the special character $*$ that matches any box, it is enough to find an injection from the boxes in the pattern into the ones of the complex. For instance the patterns on the left columns in Fig. 2 are matched by the complexes on the right columns.

| [A,*] | C1, C2 |
| [B,*] | C1, C3 |

| [B] | (no match) |
| [A,G] | C2 |

| [A,G,*] | C1, C2 |
| [A{x=3},*] | C2 |

Fig. 2. Pattern matching in the complexes in Fig. 1(a). The patterns on the left match with the complexes on the right.

The dynamics of systems is defined by reaction rules with code associated that modifies the system after the reaction is performed. There are four reaction rules: assoc (that merges two distinct complexes that match the patterns in the rule); dissoc (removes from a complex that matches the first pattern a sub-complex that matches the second pattern); substitute (replaces a complex that matches the first pattern with a complex that matches the second one); dyn (applies the code in the reaction to the complexes that match the patterns). The reactions have stochastic rates that can be either constants or user-defined functions. The code associated with a reaction can access the reactants and the products through predefined variables $reactant_1, .., reactant_n$ and $product_1, .., product_m$; the index of each reactant/product follows the order in which they appear in the rule. The actions that can be performed are deletion of a box from a complex, spawning of some new boxes within a complex, movement of a box from one complex to another, and update of the fields of boxes.

Consider the rule assoc leading from (a) to either (b) or (c) in Fig. 1. The first computational step is the identification of all the complexes in (a) that match the patterns in the rule. The first pattern is matched by $C1$ and $C2$ and the second pattern is matched by $C1$ and $C3$ (see Fig. 2). $C1$ matches both patterns, but its multiplicity in the system is one, so we cannot associate a $C1$ molecule with another one of the same species. Therefore, the possible complexes resulting from the assoc rule are $C1 : C3$ (not depicted in the figure), $C2 : C1$ (depicted in (b)) and $C2 : C3$ (depicted in (c)).

The complex $C2 : C1$ is obtained by merging $C2$ and $C1$ and then applying the code between the syntactic brackets react and end. The complex obtained by the merge can be accessed by the variable *product* and the associated actions are performed on the product. Hence a copy of the box G is removed and one copy of H is added. Similarly, the complex $C2 : C3$ is generated. For the sake of completeness, note that the kill(G{}) command affects a complex which might not have any G box inside – all we know is that it matches with the pattern $[A, *]$. In such case, no G would be removed. Note that the modeler can also check whether a G is present using an if conditional. Further, it is possible to refine the pattern as $[A, G, *]$ and prevent association when G is not present.

The stochastic rate and the concentrations of the complexes matching the patterns determine which reaction to fire among the enabled ones through a race condition.

Consider the rule dissoc leading from (c) to (d) in Fig. 1. We have to identify the complexes matching the first pattern (and there is only $C2 : C3$) and remove from the selected one the sub-complex made of exactly one H boxe (to avoid ambiguities no $*$ is allowed in the second pattern of a dissoc). The application of the rule generates a complex containing one A and two B and a complex containing one H. We now run the code associated with the rule. We remove a B from the first product complex and we move the remaining B from the first product to the second one, resulting in the complexes $C7$ and $C8$.

Consider the rule substitute leading from (d) to (e) in Fig. 1. The complexes that match the first pattern are $C4$ and $C5$. Assume that the stochastic simulation algorithm selects $C4$. We then replace $C4$ with the complex specified in the second position of the rule and we run the associated code to update the x field to 4, yielding $C9$.

Consider the rule dyn leading from (e) to (f) in Fig. 1. $C8$ matches the first pattern, $C5$ matches the second pattern and $C9$ matches the last pattern. The rule dyn just runs its associated code. Therefore, we remove an H from $C8$ yielding $C11$, we add an H to $C5$ yielding $C10$ and we set x to 6 in $C9$.

We end this section by considering space. We included in ℓ the primitive type location to assign boxes to compartments and the reaction rule move to let boxes move from one compartment to another one. An example is in Fig. 3. Each compartment is associated with a name that acts as a location in the move rule that translocates a complex matching the pattern in the rule accordingly. The first rule in the figure translocates A from the extracellular space into the cytosol. The second move rule shows that also the movement actions can have code associated with them; in fact, the complex containing F is moved from the cytosol to the nucleus and the x field of its D component is updated to 3. The last move in the figure translocates the complex containing C from the organelle to the cytosol. After the three move in Fig. 3 the system on the left is mapped into the system on the right.

It is possible to write rules which affect only one compartment. For instance, the rule assoc $[A][B]$ in *cytosol* rate k allows $[A]$ and $[B]$ to associate only in the cytosol compartment. Concretely, $[A]$@*cytosol* and $[A]$@*extracellular space* are handled as two distinct biochemical species. By comparison, writing assoc $[A][B]$ rate k would allow association to be performed in any compartment. More specifically, if a copy of $[A]$ and a copy of $[B]$ are found in the *same* compartment, they can associate with rate k. Association across compartments is still prevented.

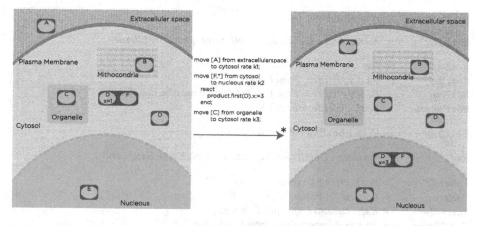

Fig. 3. ℓ space and movement: the basic type location is used to denote cell compartments and the move reaction (that can also have a react part) is used to implement the translocation of complexes from one compartment to another. The star on the arrow denotes more than one step (three in this case).

3 ℓ Syntax

Figure 4 reports the syntax of ℓ in BNF form. Note that optional items are not denoted as usual within square brackets because square brackets are tokens of ℓ. Therefore, we let $\langle A \rangle^*$, $\langle A \rangle^+$, and $\langle A \rangle^?$ denote at least zero, at least one, and at most one occurrence of A, respectively.

BasicType stands for a primitive type used in ℓ: bool, int, real and location, whereas *BasicLiteral* ranges over their values. The meaning of bool, int and real is the usual one, whereas location represents the set of compartment names.

BoxDecl is the declaration of a *box*: it specifies a name for the box (Ide - interpreted as the type of the box, hence *BoxType*) together with a possibly empty sequence Ide : *BasicType* that are its *fields* and their types. The name of the fields is unique inside the box. *BoxExp* represents a box having all its declared fields instantiated. For example, $A\{x : \text{int}; y : \text{real}\}$ is a declaration of a box type A containing fields x and y of type int and real respectively, and it can be instantiated as $A\{x = 3; y = 1.0\}$. We use Box to denote the set of all possible box instantiations. A *BoxPattern* shares the same syntax of a *BoxExp*, however it may not provide a value for all fields; this will be used for counting and searching for boxes.

For any set S, we write mset S for the set of multisets over S, which we sometimes identify with the set of functions $S \to \mathbb{N}$. *CplxExp* represents complexes as multisets of boxes, *i.e.*, it is a non-empty sequence of the form $Exp : BoxExp$, where Exp is an integer expression that denotes the number of instances of $BoxExp$ in the complex. When $Exp = 1$, we can omit it. For instance, $[2 : A\{x = 3; y = 1.0\}, B\{\}]$ is a complex. We use Cplx = location $\times$ mset Box to denote the set of all possible complexes.

BasicType	::= bool | int | real | location
BasicLiteral	::= *BoolLiteral* | *IntLiteral* | *RealLiteral* | *LocationLiteral*
BoxType	::= *Ide*
BoxDecl	::= *BoxType*{⟨*Ide* : *BasicType*; ⟩*}
BoxExp	::= *BoxType*{⟨*Ide* = *Exp*; ⟩*} (each field must be initialized)
BoxPattern	::= *BoxType*{⟨*Ide* = *Exp*; ⟩*}
CplxExp	::= [*Exp* : *BoxExp* ⟨, *Exp* : *BoxExp*⟩*]
Run	::= run *Exp* : *CplxExp*@*Exp* ⟨; *Exp* : *CplxExp*@*Exp*⟩* end
Pattern^{no*}	::= *BoxPattern* | *BoxPattern*, *Pattern^{no*}*
Pattern	::= *Pattern^{no*}* | *Pattern^{no*}*, *
RateValue	::= *Exp* | custom *Exp* | mm *Exp* : *Exp*
RateClause	::= ⟨in *Exp*⟩$^?$ ⟨when *Exp*⟩$^?$ rate *RateValue*
Exp	::= *BasicLiteral* | *Ide* | (*Type*) null | *Exp* && *Exp* | ¬*Exp* | *Exp* = *Exp*
	| *Exp* < *Exp* | *Exp* + *Exp* | *Exp* − *Exp* | *Exp* * *Exp* | *Ide*(⟨*Exp*⟨, *Exp*⟩*⟩$^?$)
	| *BoxOps* | *CplxOps*
BoxOps	::= *Exp*.*Ide* | *Exp*.first(*BoxPattern*) | *Exp*.count(*BoxPattern*)
	| *Exp*.spawn(*BoxExp*)
CplxOps	::= spawn(*CplxExp*@*Exp*) | count(*Pattern*@*Exp*)
AssocDecl	::= assoc [*Pattern*] [*Pattern*] *RateClause* react *Block*
DissocDecl	::= dissoc [*Pattern*] [*Pattern^{no*}*] *RateClause* react *Block*
DynDecl	::= dyn ⟨[*Pattern*]⟩* *RateClause* react *Block*
SubstituteDecl	::= substitute ⟨[*Pattern*]⟩* with ⟨*CplxExp*⟩* *RateClause* react *Block*
MoveDecl	::= move [*Pattern*] from *Exp* to *Exp* rate *RateValue* react *Block*
Block	::= var *Ide* := *Exp*; *Block* | *Cmd* ; *Block* | end
Cmd	::= skip | *Ide* := *Exp* | if *Exp* then *Block* else *Block*
	| while *Exp* do *Block* | *Ide*(⟨*Exp*⟨, *Exp*⟩*⟩$^?$) | return *Exp* | *BoxCmd*
BoxCmd	::= *Exp*.*Ide* := *Exp* | *Exp*.kill() | *Exp*.kill(*BoxPattern*) | *Exp*.assoc(*Exp*)
	| *Exp*.move(*BoxPattern*, *Exp*) | foreach *Ide* : *BoxType* in *Exp Block*
Type	::= *BasicType* | *BoxType* | cplx | void
FunDecl	::= *Type Ide*(⟨*Type Ide* ⟨, *Type Ide*⟩*⟩$^?$) *Block*
LetDecl	::= let *Ide* := *Exp*
Decl	::= *AssocDecl* | *DissocDecl* | *DynDecl* | *MoveDecl* | *SubstituteDecl* |
	BoxDecl | *FunDecl* | *LetDecl*
SpaceDecl	::= location ⟨*LocationLiteral*⟩*
Model	::= ⟨*SpaceDecl*; ⟩$^?$⟨*Decl*; ⟩* *Run*

Fig. 4. Syntax of ℓ.

The whole initial system state is defined by the *Run* clause. It specifies a list of complexes of the form Exp_1 : $CplxExp$@Exp_2, where Exp_1 is the initial population of the complex in the system which is being modeled, and Exp_2 is the compartment the complex belongs to. Note that isolated boxes in a system are actually represented by a singleton complex, made of just that box.

The dynamics of the system is specified by multiset rewriting rules, which continuously modify the system at hand (if no rule applies, the system does not evolve further). Rules are based on complex patterns. A *Pattern* is a sequence of *BoxPattern*, possibly followed by a wildcard ∗. A pattern without ∗ matches with complexes having exactly the specified boxes, whereas the wildcard allows the pattern to match with complexes including other boxes as well. The order in which boxes appear in patterns is irrelevant: patterns are handled up to associativity and commutativity. A *BoxPattern* of the form $B_1\{f_1 = v_1, \ldots, f_n = v_n\}$ matches with a box $B_2\{g_1 = h_1, \ldots, g_m = h_m\}$ if $B_1 = B_2$, $n \leq m$ and for each $i \in [1..n]$ there exists $j \in [1..m]$ such that $f_i = g_j$ and $v_i = h_j$. Then, we say that a complex $c \in \mathsf{Cplx}$ matches with a pattern p, denoted with $p \vdash c$, if one of the following conditions holds:

- p does not end with ∗, and there is a *bijective* mapping θ between box patterns in p and boxes in c, where correspondent elements match;
- p does end with ∗, and there is an *injective* mapping θ between box patterns in p and boxes in c, where correspondent elements match.

The following example illustrates pattern matching.

Example 1. Consider complexes $c_1 = [A\{x = 1\}]$, $c_2 = [B\{\}]$, $c_3 = [A\{x = 0\}, A\{x = 1\}]$, $c_4 = [A\{x = 1\}, B\{\}]$ and $c_5 = [A\{x = 1, y = 4\}]$ and patterns $p_1 = [A]$, $p_2 = [A, A]$, $p_3 = [A, *]$, $p_4 = [B]$, $p_5 = [B, *]$ and $p_6 = [A\{x = 1\}]$. Then, only the following relations hold: $p_1 \vdash c_1$, $p_1 \vdash c_5$, $p_2 \vdash c_3$, $p_3 \vdash c_1$, $p_3 \vdash c_3$, $p_3 \vdash c_4$, $p_3 \vdash c_5$, $p_4 \vdash c_2$, $p_5 \vdash c_2$, $p_5 \vdash c_4$, $p_6 \vdash c_1$, $p_6 \vdash c_5$.   ∎

The rewriting rules specify stochastic rates rate *Exp* in their *RateClause* to be applied stochastically. The rate expression can inspect the boxes in the reactants via special variables $\mathsf{reactant}_i$, where i ranges from 1 to the number of reactants. For instance,

$$\mathsf{assoc}\ [A]\ [B, *]\ \mathsf{rate}\ 5.2 * \mathsf{reactant}_1.\mathsf{first}(A\{\}).\mathsf{mass}$$

states that the rule firing rate is proportional to the mass of (the box A of) the first reactant. By default, rate expressions follow the *mass action kinetics* law, and are implicitly multiplied by the abundance of each reactant. For instance, in a system having 10 complexes $[A]$ and 20 complexes $[B, C]$, the rate mentioned above is implicitly multiplied by $10 \cdot 20$. Another common kinetics law is Michaelis-Menten and it is expressed by *RateValue* mm. All the other kinetic laws (*e.g.*, Hill kinetics) can be defined by *RateValue* custom.

Expressions *Exp* of ℓ are built from constants (*BasicLiteral*, Ide, *null*) through logical operators, relational operators and arithmetic operators. It is also possible to call functions. The expressions more peculiar to ℓ are *BoxOps* to access fields of boxes (*Exp*.Ide), to search for boxes within a complex (first), to count boxes matching a pattern (count) or to spawn a new box (spawn). There are also expressions acting on complexes (*CplxOps*) to spawn new complexes or count existing ones.

For instance, the expression spawn($[2 : B\{x = 3, y = 4\}, 1 : A]$) will spawn a new complex comprising two B boxes and one A box, and evaluate to a reference for such complex. After that, the expression count($[A, *]$) will evaluate to the number of all the complexes in the current system having at least one A box, including the one which has just been created. Furthermore, if c is a variable referring to the complex we just spawned, c.first(B).y will evaluate to 4, while c.count($B\{x = 3\}$) will evaluate to 2, since two such boxes were created.

Finally, note that operators in expressions expect their arguments to be of a compatible type, e.g. we can not sum non-numeric values such as complexes. Further, most rules involving an Exp expect it to evaluate to a value of the correct type (e.g. in rate Exp we expect a real number as the result of Exp. In ℓ this is checked statically through a simple, standard type system.

3.1   Rewriting Rules

We now discuss the rewriting rules, which control the evolution of a system. ℓ has five kinds of such rules, namely assoc, dissoc, dyn, move and substitute. A rule

$$\text{assoc } p_1 \ p_2 \ RateClause \text{ react } Block$$

allows pairs of reacting complexes matching with p_1 and p_2 to associate. When that happens, the two reactant complexes merge their boxes and form a new larger complex, mimicking the association of two macromolecules. The $RateClause$ specifies the conditions and speed under which association happens. Its general form is

$$\text{in } Exp_1 \text{ when } Exp_2 \text{ rate } Exp_3$$

requiring that (1) reactants have to be located in the compartment Exp_1, (2) the boolean condition Exp_2 must be true, and (3) the reaction is performed with stochastic rate Exp_3 (according to mass action law, or the other laws discussed earlier). The part "in Exp_1" is optional: when missing, the association is performed in every possible compartment. Similarly, the absence of "when Exp_2" causes the association to be always performed. The optional constraints "in Exp_1 when Exp_2" can also be applied to ℓ rules other than assoc, with analogous semantics.

When an assoc rule is fired, after the complexes are associated the code block specified in the react part is run. This can access the newly formed product (via a special product variable) and modify it further, e.g., by changing box fields, or adding/removing boxes, or spawning entirely new complexes. For instance, a rule

$$\text{assoc } [A\{x = 3\}, *] \ [B] \text{ rate } 1.0 \text{ react product.first}(A\{x = 3\}).x := 4; \text{end}$$

will generate complexes of the form $[A\{x = 4\}, B, *]$, since the react block changes the value of x.

A rule

$$\text{dissoc } p_1 \ p_2 \ RateClause \text{ react } Block$$

specifies the dual operation to assoc, i.e. the dissociation of a complex into two subcomplexes. Here, p_1 specifies the complex to break up, whereas p_2 matches with a subcomplex to separate. No wildcard $*$ is allowed in p_2, since that would cause an arbitrary random subcomplex to be detached. This restriction is represented in Fig. 4 by $Pattern^{no*}$. In the case p_2 has multiple matches inside the reactant, we let all of them define an equally probable dissociation, hence effectively dividing the rate among all the possible splits. In other words, the rate in the rule is the cumulative rate of all the possible dissociations, and when the rule is selected to fire a random match of p_2 is chosen to be split from the rest of the complex. After that, the react code block is run, and can access the new complexes using the two special variables $product_1$ and $product_2$.

A rule

$$\text{dyn } p_1 \ldots p_n \, RateClause \text{ react } Block$$

is used to define a generic molecular dynamics. Its semantics is similar to the one of assoc, except that no complex merge is performed, and the react code block still has access to the unmerged complexes $reactant_1, \ldots, reactant_n$. This rule effectively subsumes assoc and (most forms of) dissoc, in that association/dissociation can be programmed manually in the react code block, exploiting the commands $c1.assoc(c2)$ and $c1.move(B\{\ldots\}, c2)$. While dyn is a very general-purpose mechanism, associations and dissociations are so common to deserve their own constructs in the language. The modeler has to use dyn only for, $e.g.$, monomolecular reactions or reactions involving more than two reactants.

A rule

$$\text{substitute } p_1 \ldots p_n \text{ with } CplxExp_1 \ldots CplxExp_m \, RateClause \text{ react } Block$$

is used when we want to substitute the complexes satisfying the patterns $p_1, \ldots, p_n$ with the concrete complexes corresponding to $CplxExp_1, \ldots, CplxExp_m$. After that, the code $Block$ is run, possibly accessing the new complexes via $product_i$. Note that using substitute one can easily import standard reaction networks. Indeed a chemical reaction $A + B \rightarrow C$ with rate k can simply be expressed by substitute $[A][B]$ with $[C]$ rate k with no react block.

A rule

$$\text{move } p \text{ from } Exp_1 \text{ to } Exp_2 \text{ rate } RateValue \text{ react } Block$$

is used for moving the complexes satisfying a given pattern p from the compartment identified by Exp_1 to the one identified by Exp_2. The code $Block$ is then run, possibly altering the moved complexes via the special variables $product_i$. It is worth noting that both move and substitute can be modeled using the dyn rule. Despite such rules being theoretically redundant, they represent common situations in biochemical reactions, hence they deserve their own construct.

The code blocks in rules are written in a simple statically-typed imperative language. Variable types ($Type$) include all the basic ones ($BasicType$), boxes (each $BoxDecl$ declares a new type), and complexes (cplx). The value of a variable having a box or complex type is a reference to those. A set of primitives allows one to freely access and modify boxes and complexes. For instance, adding boxes in a complex is done via the expression *Exp*.spawn(*BoxExp*), which creates a box *BoxExp* inside complex *Exp* and evaluates to a reference to the new box. Removing a box instead is done with the command *Exp*.kill(*BoxPattern*), which searches for a box matching the pattern within complex *Exp* and deletes it. Similar operations can be done at the complex level. New complexes are created by the expression spawn(*CplxExp@Exp*) which creates a complex *CplxExp* in compartment *Exp*, evaluating to a reference to the new complex. Existing complexes are removed via *Exp*.kill(), where *Exp* evaluates to a reference to the complex. It is also possible to merge two complexes, as it happens for association (assoc). More generally, one can loop over all the boxes of a given type in a complex using the command foreach *b* : *BoxType* in *complex*. Also, the expression *Exp*.first(*BoxPattern*) returns a box matching *BoxPattern* among those in complex *Exp*. Finally, ℓ includes many common imperative constructs such as assignment, conditional, while loops, and function calls, whose meaning is standard.

Example 2. As a simple example, we provide an ℓ model for the enzymatic reaction shown below:

$$E + S \underset{k_{-1}}{\overset{k_1}{\rightleftharpoons}} ES \overset{k_2}{\longrightarrow} EI \overset{k_3}{\longrightarrow} E + P$$

The first double arrow models an enzyme molecule (E) associating to and dissociating from a substrate molecule (S). When associated, the complex ES can react (second arrow): the enzyme changes the substrate into some intermediate molecule (I). This reaction is not reversible. Then, the intermediate molecule can dissociate from the enzyme, which releases a product (P) in the system (third arrow). In ℓ, we can model this behavior as follows. Below, the react blocks are used to change S into I, and then I into P. Note that K_1, K_{-1}, K_2, K_3 are the stochastic constants corresponding to k_1, k_{-1}, k_2, k_3, respectively (for a definition of the translation from deterministic to stochastic rate constants see *e.g.*, [38]).

```
E{}    S{}    I{}    P{}
assoc [E] [S] rate K₁
dissoc [E, S] [S] rate K₋₁
substitute [E, S] with [E{}, I{}] rate K₂
dissoc [E, I] [I] rate K₃ react
      product₂.kill(I{});
      product₂.spawn(P{});
end;
run 100 : [E];  100 : [S]; end
```

Example 3. We want to model a macromolecule *A* which can be tagged using some *marker*. The marker may be present in different quantities in different molecules. Further, two molecules can interact, making the marker diffuse from one molecule to the other one, proportionally to the difference of marker amounts the molecules have.

To model the scenario above, we use a box A with a real field *marker* for storing the amount of marker. Coding the diffusion of the marker is then simple, as shown below.

```
A{marker : real}
dyn [A] [A] rate K react
    var a1 := reactant₁.first(A{});
    var a2 := reactant₂.first(A{});
    var delta := 0.50 * (a1.marker − a2.marker);
    a1.marker := a1.marker − delta;
    a2.marker := a2.marker + delta;
end;
run 100 : [A{marker = 100.0}]; 100 : [A{marker = 0.0}]; end          ■
```

4   Performance Benchmark of ℓ

In this section we first discuss some of the implementation choices we made. Then we introduce the benchmark models we selected and discuss the performance of ℓ on those.

4.1   Implementation Choices

We developed an ℓ implementation focusing on the expected performance. A main choice we faced was whether ℓ should be interpreted or compiled. While an interpreter looked easier to build, a compiler could translate ℓ to low level code which is faster to execute. Eventually, we settled on building a compiler which, given a ℓ model, is able to generate C# code. This provides several benefits. First, using an expressive imperative target language makes it easy to generate code for ℓ, which is also imperative. Second, we can leverage the existing compilers from our target language to machine code and exploit the low level code optimizations they perform. Third, using a typed target language provides more confidence on the correctness of the translation, in the spirit of using a typed assembly language [26]. For instance, we can map each ℓ box type to its own target type, preventing confusion. Lastly, by choosing C# we can integrate ℓ with the .NET platform thus allowing the modeler to call .NET functions written in different languages, should this be needed.

When designing the data structures to store the ℓ state, we faced more choices. Our simulator does not precompute the reaction network before starting the actual simulation, but generates new species (complexes) whenever they appear in the simulated model. Whenever a new species appears, we match it with all the patterns occurring in the rules at hand, and save the result of the match for later usage. If a model uses p patterns and during its evolution creates s species, we only need to perform $p \cdot s$ matches, independently of the length of the simulation. Note that the number of species can be infinite, either because larger and larger complexes are formed by the model, or because boxes are instantiated with infinitely make distinct field values. In such cases, we incur a performance penalty only when a species is firstly created, and patterns are matched against it. We do not pay any cost for species which do not occur in the simulation run. This is unlike the approaches based on network precomputation, which have to enumerate each species which might occur during the simulation, and potentially generate a large network.

Once patterns and species are matched, we can simulate the CTMC determined by the ℓ rules. Our implementation can either use the standard Gillespie SSA (Direct Method) or the more efficient RSSA. In both cases, rate expressions are evaluated to compute propensities whenever we need to update them. This happens frequently for SSA and infrequently for RSSA.

Whenever a rule carrying a react code block is fired, our simulator runs the block and compares how the state changed saving the differences in a cache, together with the species that triggered the rule. Therefore, if the rule is triggered again in the future, we can entirely skip the execution of the block and access the cached result. This relies on the result of the block being determined completely by the reactants. This property is ensured by the ℓ semantics, with the only exception of the count expression. Indeed, using count the ℓ code can refer to the current population of a species which does not appear as a reactant in the rule at hand. We rule out this corner case with a simple static syntactic check. When this check fails, we disable the caching of results for the rule at hand.

4.2 Performance

We compare ℓ performance (both with direct method - SSA [15] - and with the RSSA algorithm [36]) with Dizzy (both direct method and next reaction method) and BNG (which, to the best of our knowledge, is based on a variant of the direct method). We also compared ℓ with BetaWorkbench [11], KaSim [24] and SPiM [28]. These latter comparisons are not reported in the plots because ℓ turned out to be at least 10 times faster than all of these tools.

The selected models for benchmarks are a classical MAPK cascade model and a new model of the one-carbon metabolism recently published in [34]. Both models are made available [6]. The one-carbon metabolism model is made of 13 reactions with Michaelis-Menten rates. The model describes the folate cycle and its connection to DNA methylation activity.

The reason for the choice of the MAPK and one-carbon metabolism models is to compare the performance both with mass-action kinetics and Michaelis-Menten kinetics. We start discussing the results of the MAPK model simulation (see Fig. 5). We used $10^2, 10^3, 10^4, 10^5$ as scaling factors for the number of molecules in the systems. ℓ is performing better than all the other tools and we observe an increasing gain in performance of ℓ as the scaling factor grows. We also observe an almost linear growth of the simulation time with the scaling factor. As expected, ℓ with RSSA is always performing better than ℓ with the Direct Method.

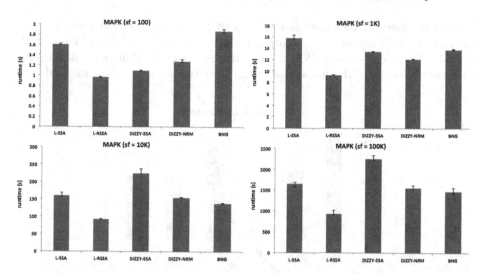

Fig. 5. Performance of ℓ with direct method (SSA) and RSSA, Dizzy with direct method (DM) and next reaction method (NRM), BNG running the MAPK model with scaling factors (sf) $10^2, 10^3, 10^4, 10^5$. The running times are averages of several runs.

We used the MAPK model to study the overhead that ℓ implementation is introducing with respect to the RSSA algorithm used in isolation (see Fig. 6). Also in this case we used the same scaling factors as before for the MAPK model to see whether the overhead of the implementation depends on the number of molecules in the system. We observe that the overhead is almost constant, independent of the number of molecules and less than 5%.

To test ℓ implementation of custom rate functions and the specific implementation for Michaelis-Menten (MM) dynamics, we used the one-carbon metabolism model. The performance results are in Fig. 7. Custom rates introduce a high overhead in the implementation and decrease considerably the performance of ℓ. The optimization for Michaelis-Menten dynamics is recovering

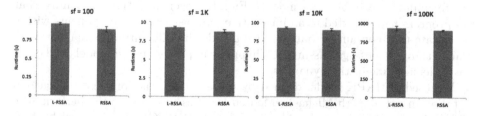

Fig. 6. Overhead introduced by the implementation of ℓ on the RSSA algorithm, comparing ℓ with RSSA and our standalone implementation of RSSA. Tests used the MAPK model with different scaling factors (sf). The scale for the y axis is in seconds. The running times are averages of several runs

most of the performance lost. Indeed, ℓ with the Direct Method and the optimization for MM dynamics is performing almost as good as BNG and Dizzy with the Next Reaction Method. When ℓ uses RSSA with MM dynamics, it becomes the best performer with almost half of the time of the second best method.

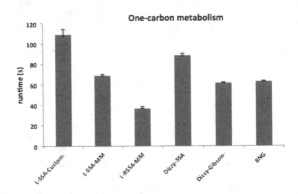

Fig. 7. Performance of ℓ with direct method and custom rates, direct method and Michaelis-Menten rates (MM), RSSA with Michaelis-Menten rates, Dizzy with direct method (DM), next reaction method (NRM), and BNG running the one-carbon metabolism model. The running times are averages of several runs.

5   Conclusions

We presented a new DSL (ℓ) for modelling and simulating biological systems. The motivation underlying the design of ℓ was to improve performance with respect to available solutions in order to be able to address real case studies by maintaining the compositionality features of process algebra based languages. To improve performance we represented complexes as multisets of components rather than graphs, thus avoiding the bottleneck due to checking graph isomorphism. We lose structural information on complexes that however is rarely available in practice. We also moved from a process-based computational model to a reaction-based one to improve readability of models. Finally, to enlarge the community that can program ℓ we resorted to an imperative DSL associating components with a local state that contains variables. This avoids the difficulty of managing state change through message passing as it happens in process based models and eases the understanding of the dynamics.

We used a MAPK model defined by mass action reactions and one-carbon metabolism model with Michaelis-Menten kinetics to compare the performance of ℓ with other widely used tools like Dizzy and BNG, as well as with other language-based simulators of biological systems like BetaWorkbench, SPiM and KappaSim. ℓ performed largely better than all the considered tools both in the case of mass action and Michaelis-Menten dynamics. We also checked the overhead introduced by the ℓ implementation with respect to a standalone RSSA implementation and we showed that it is limited (at most 5 %) and independent of the number of molecules in the system. Of course, there are many other tools against which we could compare our implementation: among these, StochKit2 [33] appears to be one of the better optimized ones.

Finally, the simple structure of ℓ allows us to easily map reaction-based models into ℓ models, including the ones that are represented by graphical formalisms such as Style [18]. Indeed, a tool for importing reaction networks has been developed [6].

Acknowledgments. The authors would like to thank the whole COSBI team for fruitful discussions and extensive testing of the language implementation. This work has been supported by a grant of the Provincia Autonoma di Trento.

A ℓ Semantics

The semantics of an ℓ model is given by assigning it a Continuous Time Markov Chain (CTMC). The CTMC describes how the initial system, which is a multiset of complexes, evolves over time. Obtaining a formal definition for this CTMC poses no significant challenge, and can be done exploiting standard techniques. We intuitively summarize its key ideas in this section, focusing only on the rules of the form

> dyn $p_1 \ldots p_n$ rate custom $rateExp$ react $block$
>
> dissoc p_1 p_2 rate custom $rateExp$ react $block$

Indeed, all the other rules can be desugared into the above small kernel.

The set of complexes is defined as the set of all multisets over boxes at a location from location, $i.e.$, Cplx $=$ location $\times$ mset Box, and we use $[box_1, \ldots, box_n]@loc$ to denote a generic element of Cplx. We define a $system$ $\mu \in$ Sys $=$ mset Cplx as a multiset of complexes. In our formalization we store boxes and complexes at specific $addresses$ of the heap. The set of all these addresses is denoted by Address, and we use α to range over it. We define Environment $=$ Ide $\to$ Address, the set of $environments$ ρ, $i.e.$, maps assigning addresses to variables, and Store $=$ Address $\to$ Value, the set of $stores$ σ, $i.e.$, maps assigning values to addresses. The set Value comprises basic type values, locations, box values (represented as maps from fields to values), and complex values. Complex values are represented as multisets of addresses pointing to the contained boxes, the whole multiset being tagged with its location.

The formal CTMC definition for rules has to carefully count the number of matches between the pattern tuple $p_1 \ldots p_n$ and the complexes in a system. Since patterns can overlap (e.g. each of $p_1 = [A, *], p_2 = [B, *]$ matches with both complexes $C_1 = [A, B, X]$, $C_2 = [A, B, Y]$), we resort to $canonic$ matches to avoid counting the same combination many times ($p_1, p_2 \vdash C_1, C_2$ should be the same as $p_1, p_2 \vdash C_2, C_1$).

Definition 1. The $simple\ matches$ of a tuple of patterns $\boldsymbol{p} = \langle p_1, \ldots, p_n \rangle$ in a system $\mu \in$ Sys is given by

$$simple(\boldsymbol{p}, \mu) = \{C \in \mathsf{Cplx}^n \mid \{C_1, \ldots, C_n\} \subseteq \mu \ \wedge \ \boldsymbol{p} \vdash C \ \wedge \ \forall i, j. \ C_i.\mathsf{loc} = C_j.\mathsf{loc}\}$$

Let $<$ stand for any total strict ordering relation over Cplx. This induces the lexicographic ordering on n-tuples of Cplx, which we shall also denote with $<$. Further, let the relation $\sim$ hold between two complex tuples differing only by the order of their components, *i.e.*, when the first tuple is a permutation of the second.

Definition 2. The *canonic matches* of a tuple of patterns $\boldsymbol{p} = \langle p_1, \ldots, p_n \rangle$ in a system $\mu \in$ Sys is given by

$$canonic(\boldsymbol{p}, \mu) = \{\boldsymbol{C} \in simple(\boldsymbol{p}, \mu) \mid \nexists \boldsymbol{C}' \in simple(\boldsymbol{p}, \mu). \ \boldsymbol{C}' \sim \boldsymbol{C} \wedge \boldsymbol{C}' < \boldsymbol{C}\}$$

We can now build the set of stochastic transitions associated to a dyn rule. We generate a transition between states μ and μ' for each canonic match in μ, which makes the react code block to change μ into μ'.

Definition 3. Given a rule of the form dyn $\boldsymbol{p}$ rate $rateExp$ react $Block$ and two systems μ, μ', we generate the (decorated) set of rates of transitions as follows.

$$rates(\mu\,\mu' \text{ dyn } \boldsymbol{p} \text{ rate } rateExp \text{ react } Block) =$$
$$\left\{ \langle \boldsymbol{C}, a \rangle \,\middle|\, \begin{array}{l} \boldsymbol{C} = \langle C_1, \ldots, C_n \rangle \in canonic(\boldsymbol{p}, \mu) \ \wedge \ \hat{\mu} = \mu \setminus \boldsymbol{C} \ \wedge \\ \langle \hat{\rho}, \hat{\sigma} \rangle = \text{alloc}(\text{reactant}_1 = C_1, \ldots, \text{reactant}_n = C_n) \ \wedge \\ a = \text{value}(\mathcal{E}(rateExp)\langle \hat{\mu}, \hat{\rho}, \hat{\sigma} \rangle) \ \wedge \\ \mu' = \hat{\mu} \cup \text{extractCplx}(\mathcal{C}(Block)\langle \hat{\mu}, \hat{\rho}, \hat{\sigma} \rangle) \end{array} \right\}$$

Above, we exploited some auxiliary operators, which we discuss now. Given a multiset of complexes $\{C_1, \ldots C_n\}$, we denote with $\text{alloc}(x_1 = C_1, \ldots, x_n = C_n)$ the environment and store obtained by allocating the multiset in store and making variables $x_1, \ldots, x_n$ refer to them. The operation extractCplx performs the inverse operation, retrieving the multiset of complexes (*i.e.*, an element of Sys) which are in a store σ. Further, we assumed a (standard) semantics for expressions and commands. (For the sake of simplicity, we neglect non terminating programs.)

$$\mathcal{E} : Exp \times \text{Sys} \times \text{Environment} \times \text{Store} \rightarrow \text{Value} \times \text{Store},$$
$$\mathcal{C} : (Block \cup Cmd) \times \text{Sys} \times \text{Environment} \times \text{Store} \rightarrow \text{Store}.$$

Handling dissoc is done similarly.

Definition 4. Given a rule of the form dissoc $p_1\ p_2$ rate $rateExp$ react $Block$, and two systems μ, μ', we generate the set of (decorated) rates of transitions as follows.

$$rates(\mu, \ \mu', \text{ dissoc } p_1 p_2 \text{ rate } rateExp \text{ react } Block) =$$
$$\left\{ \langle \langle C_1, \theta \rangle, a \rangle \,\middle|\, \begin{array}{l} \langle C_1 \rangle \in canonic(p_1, \mu) \wedge p_2, * \vdash_\theta C_1 \wedge C_2 = \theta(p_2) \wedge \\ \hat{\mu} = \mu \setminus \{C_1\} \ \wedge \ \langle \hat{\rho}, \hat{\sigma} \rangle = \text{alloc}(\text{reactant}_1 = C_1) \wedge \\ a = \text{value}(\mathcal{E}(rateExp)\langle \hat{\mu}, \hat{\rho}, \hat{\sigma} \rangle)/|\{\theta \mid p_2, * \vdash_\theta C_1\}| \ \wedge \\ \langle \hat{\rho}', \hat{\sigma}' \rangle = \text{alloc}(\text{product}_1 = C_1 \setminus C_2, \text{product}_n = C_n) \wedge \\ \mu' = \hat{\mu} \cup \text{extractCplx}(\mathcal{C}(Block)\langle \hat{\mu}, \hat{\rho}', \hat{\sigma}' \rangle) \end{array} \right\}$$

Defining the final CTMC only requires summing over rules. A CTMC here is formalized as a function mapping two states (in Sys) to its transition rate.

Definition 5. Let R be a set of rules. We define $\mathsf{CTMC}(R) : \mathsf{Sys} \times \mathsf{Sys} \to \mathbb{R}$ as follows:

$$\mathsf{CTMC}(R) = \lambda\mu, \mu'. \sum_{r \in R} \mathsf{CTMC}(r)(\mu)(\mu')$$
$$\mathsf{CTMC}(r) = \lambda\mu, \mu'. \sum_{\langle -, a\rangle \in rates(\mu, \mu', r)} a$$

References

1. Bracciali, A., Brunelli, M., Cataldo, E., Degano, P.: Stochastic models for the in silico simulation of synaptic processes. BMC Bioinform. **9**(4), S7 (2008)
2. Brijder, R., Ehrenfeucht, A., Main, M.G., Rozenberg, G.: A tour of reaction systems. Int. J. Fond. Comput. Sci. **22**(7), 1499–1517 (2011)
3. Brodo, L., Degano, P., Priami, C.: A stochastic semantics for bioambients. In: Malyshkin, V.E. (ed.) PaCT 2007. LNCS, vol. 4671, pp. 22–34. Springer, Heidelberg (2007)
4. Cao, Y., Gillespie, D.T., Petzold, L.R.: Efficient step size selection for the tau-leaping simulation method. J. Chem. Phys. **124**(4), 044109 (2006)
5. Ciocchetta, F., Hillston, J.: Bio-pepa: a framework for the modelling and analysis of biological systems. Theor. Comput. Sci. **410**(33–34), 3065–3084 (2009)
6. COSBI: Lsim, the ℓ simulator. http://www.cosbi.eu/research/prototypes/L
7. Danos, V., Feret, J., Fontana, W., Harmer, R., Krivine, J.: Rule-based modelling of cellular signalling. In: Caires, L., Vasconcelos, V.T. (eds.) CONCUR 2007. LNCS, vol. 4703, pp. 17–41. Springer, Heidelberg (2007)
8. Danos, V., Feret, J., Fontana, W., Krivine, J.: Scalable simulation of cellular signaling networks. In: Shao, Z. (ed.) APLAS 2007. LNCS, vol. 4807, pp. 139–157. Springer, Heidelberg (2007)
9. Deeds, E.J., Krivine, J., Feret, J., Danos, V., Fontana, W.: Combinatorial complexity and compositional drift in protein interaction networks. PLoS ONE **7**(3), e32032–e32032 (2012)
10. Dematté, L., Larcher, R., Palmisano, A., Priami, C., Romanel, A.: Programming biology in BlenX. In: Choi, S. (ed.) Systems Biology for Signaling Networks, pp. 777–820. Springer, New York (2010)
11. Dematté, L., Priami, C., Romanel, A.: The beta workbench: a computational tool to study the dynamics of biological systems. Briefings Bioinform. **9**(5), 437–449 (2008)
12. Dematté, L., Priami, C., Romanel, A.: The BlenX language: a tutorial. In: Degano, P., Zavattaro, G., Bernardo, M. (eds.) SFM 2008. LNCS, vol. 5016, pp. 313–365. Springer, Heidelberg (2008)
13. Faeder, J.R., Blinov, M.L., Hlavacek, W.S.: Rule-based modeling of biochemical systems with bionetgen. In: Maly, I.V. (ed.) Systems Biology. Methods in Molecular Biology, pp. 113–167. Humana Press, New York (2009)
14. Gibson, M., Bruck, J.: Efficient exact stochastic simulation of chemical systems with many species and many channels. J. Phys. Chem. A **104**(9), 1876–1889 (2000)
15. Gillespie, D.T.: A general method for numerically simulating the stochastic time evolution of coupled chemical reactions. J. Comp. Phys. **22**(4), 403–434 (1976)
16. Gillespie, D.T.: Exact stochastic simulation of coupled chemical reactions. J. Phys. Chem. **81**(25), 2340–2361 (1977)

17. Gillespie, D.T.: Approximate accelerated stochastic simulation of chemically reacting systems. J. Chem. Phys. **115**(4), 1716–1733 (2001)
18. Gostner, R., Baldacci, B., Morine, M.J., Priami, C.: Graphical modeling tools for systems biology. ACM Computing Surveys, to appear (2014)
19. Heiner, M., Gilbert, D., Donaldson, R.: Petri nets for systems and synthetic biology. In: Degano, P., Bernardo, M., Zavattaro, G. (eds.) SFM 2008. LNCS, vol. 5016, pp. 215–264. Springer, Heidelberg (2008)
20. Hood, L., Galas, D.: The digital code of DNA. Nature **421**(6921), 444–448 (2003)
21. Hung, M.C., Link, W.: Protein localization in disease and therapy. J. Cell Sci. **124**(20), 3381–3392 (2011)
22. Kitano, H.: Computational systems biology. Nature **420**(6912), 206–210 (2002)
23. Kitano, H.: Systems biology: a brief overview. Science **295**, 1662–1664 (2002)
24. Krivine, J., Feret, J.: Kasim, the kappa simulator. http://www.kappalanguage.org
25. Molloy, M.K.: On the integration of delay and throughput measures in distributed processing models. Ph.D. thesis, UCLA, Los Angeles, CA (1981)
26. Morrisett, G., Walker, D., Crary, K., Glew, N.: From system f to typed assembly language. ACM Trans. Program. Lang. Syst. **21**(3), 527–568 (1999)
27. Natkin, S.: Les Reseaux de Petri Stochastiques et leur Application a l'Evaluation des Systèmes Informatiques. Ph.D. thesis, CNAM, Paris, France (1980), thèse de Docteur Ingegneur
28. Phillips, A., Cardelli, L.: Efficient, correct simulation of biological processes in the stochastic Pi-calculus. In: Gilmore, S., Calder, M. (eds.) CMSB 2007. LNCS (LNBI), vol. 4695, pp. 184–199. Springer, Heidelberg (2007)
29. Priami, C.: Stochastic pi-calculus. Comput. J. **38**(7), 578–589 (1995)
30. Priami, C.: Algorithmic systems biology. CACM **52**(5), 80–88 (2009)
31. Priami, C., Quaglia, P.: Operational patterns in beta-binders. In: Priami, C. (ed.) Transactions on Computational Systems Biology I. LNCS (LNBI), vol. 3380, pp. 50–65. Springer, Heidelberg (2005)
32. Păun, G.: Computing with membranes. J. Comput. Syst. Sci. **61**(1), 108–143 (2000)
33. Sanft, K.R., Wu, S., Roh, M.K., Fu, J., Lim, R.K., Petzold, L.R.: StochKit2: software for discrete stochastic simulation of biochemical systems with events. Bioinformatics **27**(17), 2457–2458 (2011)
34. Scotti, M., Stella, L., Shearer, E.J., Stover, P.J.: Modeling cellular compartmentation in one-carbon metabolism. WIREs Syst. Biol. Med. **5**, 343–365 (2013)
35. Thanh, V.H.: On efficient algorithms for stochastic simulation of biochemical reaction systems. Ph.D. thesis, University of Trento, Italy (2013). http://eprints-phd.biblio.unitn.it/1070/
36. Thanh, V.H., Priami, C., Zunino, R.: Efficient rejection-based simulation of biochemical reactions with stochastic noise and delays. J. Chem. Phys. **141**(13), 134116 (2014)
37. Thanh, V.H., Zunino, R., Priami, C.: On the rejection-based algorithm for simulation and analysis of large-scale reaction networks. J. Chem. Phys. **142**(24), 244106 (2015)
38. Wu, J., Vidakovic, B., Voit, E.O.: Constructing stochastic models from deterministic process equations by propensity adjustment. BMC Syst. Biol. **5**(1), 187 (2011)

Author Index

Printed in the United States
By Bookmasters